ROTHMANS RUGBY LEAGUE YEARBOOK 1986-87

Raymond Fletcher and David Howes

ROTHMANS

Queen Anne Press

A *Queen Anne Press* PRESS BOOK

© **Rothmans Publications Ltd 1986**

First published in Great Britain in 1986 by
Queen Anne Press, a division of
Macdonald & Co (Publishers) Ltd
Greater London House
Hampstead Road
London NW1 7QX

A BPCC plc Company

Front Cover:
Great Britain centre Garry Schofield en route to one of his record breaking four tries against New Zealand in the second 1985 Whitbread Trophy Bitter Test.

Back Cover:
Wigan winger Henderson Gill, who was recalled for Great Britain against France in 1986.

ACKNOWLEDGEMENTS
The compilers would like to acknowledge the assistance of the Rugby League Record Keepers' Club, club secretaries and individuals in providing material as a further source of reference for accuracy.

PHOTOGRAPHS
Modern day domestic photographs in this *Rothmans Rugby League Yearbook* are from the files of the *Rugby Leaguer,* the only weekly newspaper dedicated solely to the 13-a-side code. The compilers acknowledge the co-operation of Chief Photographer Gerald Webster and his staff.
The colour photographs on the front and back covers are by freelance photographer Andrew Varley.

Rothmans Rugby League Yearbook — 1986-87
  1. Rugby football — Great Britain —
  Periodicals
  796.33.3.0941 GV945.9.G7

ISBN 0 356 12416 9 (cased)
      0 356 12417 7 (limp)

Photoset by New Rush Filmsetters, London

Reproduced, printed and bound in Great Britain by Hazell Watson & Viney Ltd., Aylesbury, Bucks.
Member of the BPCC Group,

Rothmans Rugby League Yearbook 1986-87

CONTENTS

EDITORIAL PREFACE

Now into its sixth edition, *Rothmans Rugby League Yearbook* has developed a well defined — and apparently much appreciated — role in the game's fast-growing library.

With the visit of the 1986 Kangaroos generating great interest, we decided to lift our policy of recording only British data, and have included extensive Australian international records. It was an editorial policy which was to boost the profits of Anglo-Aussie telephone and postal services!

From the reviews of the media and readers, it has been confirmed that Rothmans provides useful reference material to major events within the current campaign. To amplify that service, a policy of 20-year reviews of relevant statistics has been adopted following initial, more comprehensive, details. New readers will be pleased to know that limited stocks of the five back numbers are available from Rugby League Headquarters.

Despite the introduction of official match-by-match statistical report forms, the compilation of facts and figures from the club scene does not get any easier and thanks are due again to the band of record keepers willing to share their research for the sake of common accuracy.

We are, as ever, delighted to pay tribute to the greatest game of all by recording the feats of the 13-a-side code, continually inspired by the constructive reviews of our colleagues in the media and the Rugby League public's support in maintaining the Yearbook's position as the sport's best seller. Heartfelt thanks to the most professional and caring of house editors, Celia Kent, and to our better halves for their endless patience and support.

● Facts and figures in this Yearbook as at 1st June 1986.

RAYMOND FLETCHER, of the *Yorkshire Post*
DAVID HOWES, Rugby League Public Relations Officer

FOREWORD

For the sixth time we are delighted to launch an edition of the *Rothmans Rugby League Yearbook*.

In the years that we have been involved with Rugby League we have come to admire the strength of administration and the efficiency and enthusiasm of all involved in the game.

Few sports are as well served by the people running the game as Rugby League. This book is also fortunate in being produced by two of the most knowledgeable and caring of Rugby League writers.

At times when many British sports have reached new lows both on and off the field of play, it is impressive to see that Rugby League continues to flourish.

Our fervent hope is that this publication continues to be as strong as the sport which it records.

Holmes joins Bradford Northern for £80,000

MEMORIES

INVICTA & BRIDGEND RULED OUT

RECORD BID FOR ELLERY

£100,000 for Lydon

Super League demand by ten leading clubs

Britain emerge from the wilderness

MEMORIES

1985-86 HEADLINES

Behind the facts and figures of the 1985-86 season were a selection of stories which made big headlines:

TERRY HOLMES SIGNS

Bradford Northern pulled off one of the greatest Rugby Union signings of all time when they captured Wales and British Lions scrum half Terry Holmes. The fee of £80,000 is a record for a Rugby Union player. Northern had pursued the Wales captain for a long time and he finally made a much publicised signing in the Yorkshire TV studios at Leeds on 3rd December. Although the Cardiff star gained many honours as an RU player some felt he had left it too late to make an impact in Rugby League, at almost 29. Others questioned his record of injuries, especially to his shoulders. He answered: 'I am quite happy about my fitness . . .'

HOLMES' DEBUT DISASTER

Terry Holmes dislocated his left shoulder after only 13 minutes of his debut for Bradford Northern at Swinton on 8th December. Northern officials hustled the Rugby Union star away to a private clinic as the national media were kept at bay. It was a big disappointment for the crowd of 5,247 — treble Swinton's average. To add to Bradford's gloom they lost a dour relegation battle 8-0.

Disaster struck again when Holmes attempted a comeback in a Slalom Lager Alliance match against Batley at Odsal on 21st January. This time he played for 42 minutes before the same shoulder was dislocated again. The injury ruled him out for the rest of the season but after a special strengthening operation Holmes vowed he would be back for the new campaign.

RECORD TRANSFER DEALS

Two record transfer deals rocked the Rugby League world. Wigan signed Ellery Hanley from Bradford Northern in a cash-plus-players deal worth £150,000 and later signed Joe Lydon from Widnes for £100,000 cash. Hanley signed for Wigan after the Test back had refused to play for Bradford following a pay dispute. He signed on 16th September with Phil Ford and Steve Donlan going to Bradford plus £85,000. The cash part beat the £72,500 Wigan received from Hull K.R. for Test full back George Fairbairn in June 1981. The deal doubled that of £75,000 when Andy Gregory moved from Widnes to Warrington for cash plus John Fieldhouse in January 1985.

The first £100,000 straight cash deal came with Wigan's signing of Test back Lydon on 20th January. Eric Hughes added to the sensation by quitting as Widnes's coach because he was not consulted about the transfer.

Ellery Hanley, subject of a record £150,000 transfer deal between Bradford Northern and Wigan.

THE STEVE FORD AFFAIR

The New Year opened with the Welsh Rugby Union banning Cardiff winger Steve Ford for life for having trials with Leeds although he claimed he had not received any money or signed professional forms. Ford (20) played three matches for Leeds including a pre-season friendly as an unnamed trialist before the Loiners announced his capture after playing against York on 6th October. Although Ford agreed to join them he did not sign professional forms and returned home. Soon after playing for Cardiff RU again, the Welsh RU was informed of his matches for Leeds and they banned him for life. The Rugby League Council then took action. Having previously left the RU discrimination row in the hands of the British Amateur RL Association, they decided to launch a protest campaign which attracted national publicity. In May it was announced that the RU International Board was to be asked by the home countries to allow RU and amateur RL players to play each code without being discriminated against. It was the 'free gangway' for which BARLA had campaigned many years. Meanwhile, Ford remained banned and he played several trial matches with Salford.

SUPER LEAGUE THREAT

Threats of a Super League breakaway followed a secret meeting of 10 top clubs. A statement on 18th March said the leading clubs required more direct influence and control of the game, plus a bigger share of the financial rewards. The 10 clubs represented at the Headingley, Leeds, meeting were Wigan, Leeds, Hull, Hull K.R., Halifax, Warrington, Widnes, Bradford Northern, Salford and St. Helens. Two other clubs, Leigh and Oldham, later joined the group. Fears of a breakaway were allayed when a meeting of the RL Council on 7th May agreed to put a series of resolutions to the June AGM designed to appease the group's demands, including the reduction of Division One to 14 clubs and the cutting of the levy paid by the top clubs from 15 to eight per cent. The Council used its powers immediately to allocate successful clubs a larger share of sponsorship prizes.

NEW CLUBS

Only four days before the opening of the season, the Rugby League Council confirmed the suspension of Bridgend and Southend Invicta from the Second Division. The Welsh club — formerly Cardiff City — was taken out of the fixtures for not being able to secure a ground, while the Essex outfit — formed as Kent Invicta — was considered not to have prepared a team for the new campaign. Their omission meant that the published Second Division fixtures, designed to provide each club with 28 games, were scrapped and the remaining 18 clubs decided to adopt a formula of playing each other home and away, a total of 34 matches. Southend Invicta went into liquidation shortly afterwards, Bridgend deciding not to seek reinstatement for the 1986-87 season. At a special meeting of clubs on 1st May, a three-man consortium applied for the entry into the Second Division of a club based at Stockport County's soccer ground. Of the 28 clubs present, only four voted in favour after studying the club's proposed structure and finances.

AUSTRALIAN IMPORTS DOMINANT

The continued influence of the Australian imports swept the British club scene with three of the six major Greenalls Man of Steel awards going Down Under. The 1986 Greenalls Man of Steel title and a cheque for £1,500 went to Hull K.R.'s Gavin Miller, the former Cronulla skipper also collecting the First Division Player of the Year award. Ex-Kangaroo Chris Anderson, captain of new champions Halifax, was chosen as Coach of the Year. It was the first time that any of the prestigious Man of Steel awards had gone overseas. The season marked the introduction of a quota system of five graded overseas players per club and among the many Australian stars to make an impact were top try scorer Steve Halliwell, Noel Cleal, Les Boyd, Steve Ella, Greg Dowling and David Liddiard.

SPRINGBOKS BOUND INTO BRITAIN
Big spending Wigan pulled off a transfer coup which made international headlines with a reported £75,000 double deal for South African Rugby Union internationals Ray Mordt and Rob Louw. The Springbok duo signed before television cameras on 14th December after a series of negotiations with a number of clubs including Hull and St. Helens. Mordt played on the wing in the 1986 John Player Special Trophy final before being ruled out for the season with knee trouble, while back row forward Louw struggled to make an impact at first team level. St. Helens made an offer to Springbok centre Danie Gerber, while Warrington approached team-mate Nass Botha.

Springbok recruits Ray Mordt (left) and Rob Louw being greeted at Central Park by joint coach Colin Clarke.

GAME MOURNS CLIVE SULLIVAN

More than 1,000 Rugby League personalities and followers packed Hull's Holy Trinity Church for a memorial service for former Great Britain captain Clive Sullivan MBE who died from cancer at the age of 42 on 8th October. The Great Britain Test squad, preparing to face New Zealand, gained his widow's permission to name their new lion mascot 'Sully' in his memory. Sullivan was the only player to score more than 100 tries for both Hull and Hull K.R.

TROPHY DRAW FIASCO

The mystery of an extra ball in the bag reduced the John Player Special Trophy third round draw to a farce. The draw, shown live on BBC-TV's Breakfast Time on 3rd December, had to be made again 40 minutes later. Eight numbered balls representing the third round teams should have been in the bag but an extra one was found.

The first ball drawn out was Wigan's, followed by number one Barrow, who had been knocked out in the second round. After officials had exchanged quick, puzzled glances Barrow's ball was ignored and the draw continued.

York were the last to be called out but that still left one ball in the bag, logically Hull's, and Secretary-General David Oxley quickly announced York v. Hull. The rest of the draw was Wigan v. Leigh, Widnes v. St. Helens and Warrington v. Hull K.R. The re-draw rebounded on York who had to visit Trophy holders Hull K.R. St. Helens' luck changed with a home draw against Hull, but Wigan had a tougher task at Warrington, while Widnes met Leigh. Joe Seddon, the RL chairman, picked out the numbered balls along with Don Whiting, Special Events Manager for the sponsors. It was explained later that the offending ball had stuck in the lining of the padded bag from the previous round.

JUNE

Hull list prop Trevor Skerrett at £75,000 .... Wakefield Trinity offer Harold Box and Malcolm Swann at £5,000 each and Gary Cocks at £3,000 .... Scrum half Kevin Harkin returns to Wakefield Trinity on loan from Hull, who seek a £10,000 fee .... St. Helens suffer a third successive defeat on their tour of New Zealand, going down 26-10 to Manukau .... Salford chase Australian Test veteran Ray Price .... Wigan Test winger Henderson Gill joins South Sydney on a summer contract .... Great Britain centre Vince Gribbin seeks a move from Whitehaven .... Warrington recruit controversial Australian star Les Boyd on a 12-month contract .... Clubs hit by a 500 per cent increase in insurance premiums following the Bradford City fire tragedy .... After consideration, Allan Agar decides to continue as coach of Featherstone Rovers .... Welshman Paul Prendiville listed by Hull for the second time, the fee being £10,000 .... St. Helens Test duo Neil Holding and Andy Platt join Brisbane Wests for the rest of the summer after the club's New Zealand tour .... Hull, St. Helens, Wigan and Bradford Northern lead the chase as Leigh prepare to sell John Woods .... Hull K.R. coach Roger Millward travels Down Under to tempt Australian Test prop Greg Dowling to Craven Park .... Whitehaven offer Vince Gribbin at £75,000 .... Elland Road chosen as a Test venue for the first time, the first two Tests with New Zealand being staged at Headingley and Wigan .... Oldham sign full back David Liddiard from Sydney club Parramatta .... Malcolm Reilly ends speculation by agreeing to coach Castleford for an 11th successive season .... The League A.G.M. votes by the narrowest of margins to reduce promotion and relegation to three-up, three-down .... Brewers John Smiths take over sponsorship of the Yorkshire Cup .... Phil Kitchin returns as coach of Whitehaven, three years after being sacked .... Warrington list Moroccan wingman Hussein M'Barki at £10,000 .... St. Helens director Joe Seddon appointed chairman of the League .... Fulham move to new headquarters at the Central Polytechnic Ground at Chiswick .... Rochdale Hornets call an extraordinary general meeting to decide the future of the club .... Widnes reject Salford offer of Stewart Williams for Keiron O'Loughlin .... Former Test forward Jim Mills elected as a Widnes committee member .... St. Helens bid £45,000 for Leigh's John Woods as Hull emerge as favourites for his signature .... Relegated Leigh appoint former senior referee Stan Wall as assistant to coach Alex Murphy .... Widnes formally end Vince Karalius's overseer role and leave coach Eric Hughes in sole control .... Promoted Swinton agree to hire Bolton Wanderers ground for four major matches, with an option on a further two .... Wigan list Colin Whitfield at £35,000 at his own request .... League appoint four new senior referees, Mike Loftus, Paul Houghton, Ray Tennant and Barry Simpson .... Warrington recruit Test forward Alan Rathbone from Bradford Northern for around £40,000.

JULY

Australian Test star Steve Rogers joins Widnes .... Salford snap up Australian duo Neil Baker, from South Sydney, and Canterbury Bankstown's Brian Battese .... Leigh reject bids for John Woods of £50,000 from Hull and £55,000 from St. Helens .... Injury forces Barrow's Eddie Szymala to quit .... Oldham end 14-week chase by signing Australian forward Mal Graham, formerly with Hunslet .... Kangaroo Test forward Greg Dowling agrees to join Wigan .... The Professional Players Association approves a League plan to introduce a quota system for overseas players .... Australian Test back Steve Ella turns down Hull and Oldham offers and signs for Wigan .... Warrington continue their spending spree by recruiting high scoring Manly back Phil Blake ....

Bradford Northern clinch the John Woods deal by agreeing a £65,000 fee with Leigh .... Hull obtain the services of Australian prop forward Geoff Gerard .... Home Secretary Leon Brittan brings Rugby League into line with the Safety in Sport Act .... Clubs face an estimated bill of £750,000 for ground improvements .... Australian signings flood in with Canterbury prop Peter Johnston to Hull K.R., North Sydney back Cliff Lyons to Leeds, Canterbury Bankstown packman Geoff Robinson to Halifax and Leigh recruiting young trio Steve Halliwell, Trevor Cogger and Peter Mayoh .... Wigan offer £50,000 for Oldham's £100,000-rated Andy Goodway .... Widnes stand off Tony Myler returns to the Great Britain training squad .... Workington Town list skipper Paul Grimes at £6,000 .... After two years on offer at £40,000, with loan spells at Leigh and Hunslet, Bradford Northern prop Gary Van Bellen asks to come off the list .... Wakefield Trinity sign experienced duo John Millington, from Hull K.R., and Carlisle's Graham Evans .... Hull's famous threepenny stand closed by the local authority under the new safety regulations .... Forward Mick Scott rejoins Halifax in £10,000 move from Wigan .... Halifax also snap up Leigh scrum half Gary Stephens for £5,000 .... Wigan break the record fee for a forward by signing Oldham's Andy Goodway for £65,000 .... Oldham complete their Australian recruitment with capture of utility back Gary Warnecke from Western Suburbs .... Halifax land Queenslanders Joe Kilroy and Cavill Heugh .... Warrington businessman Fred Woods leads successful takeover bid at Rochdale Hornets.

AUGUST

Hard up Doncaster put Colts international full back Kevin Harcombe on offer to pay an increased fire insurance premium .... Whitehaven reduce Vince Gribbin's fee by £20,000 to £55,000 .... Back row forward Alan Platt, rated at £35,000 by Oldham, stages a one-man strike.... Batley agree deal with Barrow for the permanent transfer of forward Kevin James.... Rochdale Hornets go on a spending spree with the recruitment of Andy Timson (Castleford), Kevin Harcombe (Doncaster), David Wood and Brian Dunn (Wigan), Eric Fitzsimons (Hunslet), Ian Duane (Warrington) and Kiwi Mike Kuiti .... Sheffield Eagles sign Steve Lane from French club Roanne.... After internal problems, Leigh's John Woods finally signs on the dotted line for Bradford Northern .... Great Britain stage a first-ever training week at Lilleshall.... Widnes prop Kevin Tamati joins Warrington on a three-year contract .... St. Helens offer terms to Australian Test skipper Wally Lewis.... Bridgend search for a new ground after being told to leave Coychurch Road and having a move to Maesteg turned down.... Leeds join Wigan and Widnes in the chase for Australian Test centre Gene Miles.... Mark Graham named as captain of the Kiwi touring party to visit Europe .... St. Helens sign Balmain goalkicking winger Ross Conlon .... Wigan winger Dennis Ramsdale forced to retire after suffering concussion for the sixth time in 18 months .... Ellery Hanley registers a hat-trick as Great Britain beat Hull K.R. 28-8 in the first of three warm-up matches.... Hull-bound Geoff Gerard and British-based Kiwi players threaten legal action over the League's import quota system .... A-team football boosted by Slalom Lager's £15,000 three-year sponsorship of the Alliance.... Leigh recruit their fourth Australian, centre Steve Brockwell.... Great Britain record 32-4 success in Oldham practice game.... Castleford prop Gary Connell advised to quit because of neck injury.... Sydney club Penrith chase Wigan's Shaun Edwards.... Two month ban imposed in Sydney rules Kiwi centre Dean Bell out of the opening fixtures of the New Zealanders' British tour.... Great Britain held to a 16-16 draw by Cumbria at Workington in the final warm-up match.... Challenge Cup winners Wigan hammer League champions Hull K.R. 34-6 in the Okells Charity Shield encounter on the Isle of Man.... John Holmes retires after 17 years with Leeds.... Rugby League Council suspend Southend Invicta and Bridgend .... Hull, Hull K.R., Warrington and Wigan get Council's permission for an extra overseas import, having signed Kiwi talent before the lifting of the Australian transfer ban .... Yorkshire RU winger Andrew Staniland joins Leeds.

SEPTEMBER

Bradford Northern dealt opening day of the season blow by Ellery Hanley's 11th hour withdrawal at Warrington because of money dispute.... Wigan's Test winger Henderson Gill breaks a leg in the first league match at home to Castleford .... Ellery Hanley's transfer request turned down by Bradford Northern .... Australian Test centre Gene Miles rules out British club duty because of lack of fitness.... Oldham sign Warrington winger Hussein M'Barki.... Castleford import Australian full back Jamie Sandy from Brisbane Easts.... Hull K.R. prop forward Roy Holdstock retires at 29 .... Bradford Northern claim that Ellery Hanley has asked for £100,000 a year, including £700 a week .... Hull K.R. bring over Eastern Suburbs prop Lindsey Johnston .... Rugby League Council rules that all First Division clubs must field an A-team from 1986-87 .... Wigan winger Brian Juliff joins Halifax for £6,000 .... Pay rebel Ellery Hanley ruled out of the Yorkshire side in the Rodstock War of the Roses clash and puts his Test spot at risk .... Rochdale Hornets tempt Steve Nash out of retirement .... Wigan line up £150,000 Hanley deal with £85,000 cash and Test players Phil Ford and Steve Donlan going to Bradford Northern .... New Zealand Olympic sprinter Gary Henley-Smith signs for Wigan.... After a six-day wait, Wigan clinch the Ellery Hanley transfer package .... Whitbread Trophy Bitter pump £170,000 into sponsorship of Great Britain over two years, plus £230,000 on promotional back-up .... Harry Pinner named as Great Britain captain .... Britain's 19-man squad for the first Kiwi Test includes 21-year-old Leeds prop Brendan Hill .... Hull turn down a transfer request from 20-year-old Test prop Andy Dannatt .... Hunslet sign New Zealand trio of Glen Barlow, Kuku Benioni and Steve Kemble, brother of Hull's Test star Gary .... Widnes's Australian Test star Steve Rogers breaks a leg after only 15 minutes of British club football .... In the same league match at Wigan, forward Steve O'Neill breaks a leg a minute after half-time .... Salford centre Keiron O'Loughlin appeals against a four-match ban imposed after 'trial by television' .... Barrow forward Steve Kirkby appeals against a 10-match ban and is given a new sentence of 15 games.

OCTOBER

New Zealand land in Britain for their 11th tour .... Swinton prop Alan Hodkinson retires after 18 years as a professional .... Having had a *sine die* ban lifted after serving two years, amateur star Dick Fairbank signs for Halifax .... Batley re-sign scrum half Neil Pickerill .... Great Britain coach Maurice Bamford is appointed Leeds City Council Rugby League development officer .... Hull and Hull K.R. demand a start-of-season deadline for the return of British players on Australian clubs .... Kiwis open the tour with a 14-8 defeat by Wigan .... South African RU stars Danie Gerber, Ray Mordt and Rob Louw express interest in joining British Rugby League clubs .... Former Great Britain captain Clive Sullivan dies of cancer at 42 .... Salford take Whitehaven centre Vince Gribbin on loan .... Top comedian Bobby Ball joins the Rochdale Hornets' board .... Widnes recruit Australian forward Noel Cleal from Sydney club Manly-Warringah ....

New Zealand beat Great Britain Under-21s 16-12 at Bradford .... Hull K.R. Test packman Chris Burton ruled out of first Test by two-match ban .... Champions Hull K.R. go down 10-20 to New Zealand .... Wigan collect the Lancashire Cup for the 17th time with a record 34-8 victory over Warrington .... Badly bruised shoulder rules Shaun Wane out of first Test selection .... Warrington prop Bob Eccles out for the rest of the year with a broken hand .... Widnes second row man John Fieldhouse receives shock Test call up as a prop .... Kiwis run out 32-6 victors of Cumbria at Whitehaven .... Mansfield Marksman axe coach Mick Blacker following record 76-6 defeat by Leigh .... Kiwi centre Gary Prohm announces decision to return Down Under at the end of the season .... Dewsbury protest about the handling of their League game with Widnes by New Zealand guest referee Dennis Hales .... Halifax sign John Crossley from Bradford Northern, swap Alan Shillito and £5,000 for Castleford's Neil James and take Oldham hooker Alan McCurrie on loan .... New Zealand win the first Test 24-22 with a converted try three minutes from the end .... Salford recruit Barrow prop Steve Herbert in exchange for centre Stewart Williams .... Andy Goodway threatens to quit Test football .... Hull K.R. turn down a Chris Rudd transfer request for the second time in 18 months .... Second tour defeat for New Zealand with Yorkshire recording an 18-8 victory at Bradford .... Hull K.R. and Leeds chase Bradford Northern's Jeff Grayshon .... Blackpool Borough's £20,000-rated prop Hugh Waddell watched by Swinton, Widnes and St. Helens .... Hull K.R. lift the John Smiths Yorkshire Cup by defeating Castleford 22-18 at Headingley .... New Zealand run up record score against St. Helens with a 46-8 hammering .... Wigan packman Graeme West called up by Kiwis for the tour match at Leeds .... Allan Agar resigns as coach of Featherstone Rovers after 62-0 defeat at Wigan .... Great Britain

Under-21s captain Paul Groves breaks a leg
.... Salford chase Welsh Rugby Union
winger Glen Webbe .... New Zealand record
a 16-10 victory in a torrid affair at Leeds ....
The Kiwis recall Graeme West for the second
Test .... Leeds sign veteran prop Jeff
Grayshon.

NOVEMBER

Record breaker Garry Schofield grabs four
tries and 16 points in Great Britain's 25-8
second Test victory over New Zealand ....
Kiwis bounce back to record 32-12 success
at Widnes .... New Zealand axe four forwards and give Test debuts to Darrell
Williams and Wayne Wallace in third Test
shake-up .... Wigan list scrum half Keith
Holden at £25,000 .... Paul Daley quits as
coach of Hunslet .... Salford recruit Warrington reserve hooker Steve Moylan to replace
broken leg victim Paul Groves .... Salford
decide not to sign on-loan centre Vince Gribbin .... Featherstone Rovers scrum half
Deryck Fox signs summer contract for
Sydney club Western Suburbs .... Rugby
League Council invite two amateur teams into
the Silk Cut Challenge Cup .... Hunslet appoint Peter Jarvis as coach .... Tense 6-6
third Test marred by two police officers
breaking up an on-going brawl .... Rugby
League Council decree that British players
should return from Australian club duty a
week before the domestic season opens ....
Widnes referee Ron Campbell chosen to take
charge of France-Kiwi Tests .... Batley coach
George Pieniazek takes over at Featherstone
.... Deryck Fox puts in a transfer request at
Featherstone .... Rugby League Council
rules that clubs must provide video facilities
for the visiting club .... Bath RU coaches
visit Hull K.R. to study coaching techniques
... International Board Secretary and former
Rugby League Secretary Bill Fallowfield dies
.... Players in the third Test brawl are repri-
manded by the League .... Featherstone
Rovers offer John Gilbert at £35,000 .... But

the Colliers turn down Deryck Fox's request
for a move .... Oldham list half back Ian
Birkby at £12,000 .... Frost causes postpone-
ment of the Lancashire-Kiwi clash at Oldham
.... Swinton forward Les Holliday fined £100
and given suspended three-month ban for
pushing a Slalom Lager Alliance referee ....
Easingwold referee Gerry Kershaw sends off
five players in finale of the Kiwi tour at Hull
.... St. Helens axe coach Billy Benyon and
poach Leigh's Alex Murphy .... Skipper
David Watkinson asks for a move from Hull
K.R. .... Leigh act quickly in appointing
Tommy Dickens as coach .... Rochdale
Hornets transfer list hooker Kevin Lowe at
£10,000 .... Wakefield Trinity send S.O.S.
to the local council as debts pass £300,000 ....
Wigan hooker Paul O'Neill given £12,000
price tag .... £5,000 fee put on Oldham full
back Alan Taylor .... League send Bamford
to watch French Test side under the control
of Australian Tas Baitieri .... Oldham run
into cash flow problems after only two games
out of 10 at home .... Bradford Northern
chase Wales RU captain Terry Holmes ....
Great Britain threequarter Carl Gibson asks
for a move from Batley .... Hunslet offer
loose forward Terry Hudson at £5,000 and re-
sign Castleford forward Jimmy Crampton ....
Brian Lockwood is appointed coach of Batley
.... Mansfield Marksman take on Bill
Kirkbride as coach .... Halifax's Australian
centre Tony Anderson signed on a summer
contract by Sydney club Canterbury
Bankstown .... Bradford Northern's chase
for Terry Holmes hots up .... Hunslet pay
£4,000 for Oldham hooker Alan McCurrie
.... Springboks Ray Mordt and Rob Louw
fly to Britain for contract talks with interested
clubs.

DECEMBER

More than a million BBC Breakfast Time
viewers witness a hasty re-draw after a ninth
ball disrupts the quarter-final draw of the
John Player Special Trophy .... Wales RU

captain Terry Holmes joins Bradford Northern in an £80,000 deal .... Paul Lyman has transfer request turned down by Featherstone Rovers .... Barrow referee Bernie Walker demoted .... York place £100,000 rating on stand off Graham Steadman .... Wakefield Trinity's long-term future secured by deal with the local council .... Australian Test star Steve Rogers returns home after specialist rules him out until March .... Sydney club Canterbury Bankstown chase Hull K.R. winger Garry Clark .... England forward Andy Kelly walks out on Hull K.R. after being dropped into the A-team .... Hunslet and Mansfield Marksman given suspended £250 fines after a brawl .... Terry Holmes taken off with a dislocated shoulder after only 13 minutes of Bradford Northern debut at Swinton .... Hull lead the chase for Springbok duo Ray Mordt and Rob Louw .... Dewsbury list loose forward Neil Kelly at £10,000 .... Four top Sydney clubs bid to tempt Ellery Hanley for a summer spell of club duty .... Hull make an offer to Ray Mordt as St. Helens enter the negotiations .... South African Test player Naas Botha turns down Warrington offer .... Bradford Northern scrum half Dean Carroll seeks a move .... Wigan sign Ray Mordt and Rob Louw in reputed £75,000 double deal .... Warrington list veteran prop Glyn Shaw at £5,000 .... Wigan decide to offload New Zealanders Gary Henley-Smith and Danny Campbell to make way for quota players Mordt and Louw .... St. Helens make written offer to Springbok Danie Gerber .... Leigh resist St. Helens move for Sydney-based centre Steve Halliwell .... Bradford Northern accept Carlisle offer of £20,000 for Dean Carroll .... Loose forward Mark Fleming priced at £20,000 by Bradford Northern .... Hunslet's Graham Idle joins Rochdale Hornets on a free transfer .... Fulham snap up Wigan's Gary Henley-Smith .... Bramley second row man Karl Harrison joins Featherstone Rovers for £20,000 .... Batley

ask £100,000 for Carl Gibson .... Rochdale Hornets' new board make 20th signing in Warrington winger Paul Fellows for £5,000 .... Coach Arthur Bunting asked to resign after eight trophy-filled years at Hull .... South African Danie Gerber turns down St. Helens' offer .... Sent off Les Boyd, having just returned from 12-month and 15-month suspensions, is found not guilty by the League's Disciplinary Committee .... Record receipts of £52,000 recorded by Wigan as 21,000-plus watch the Boxing Day derby with St. Helens .... Hull offer promotion to assistant coach Kenny Foulkes .... Wigan lose attractive home clash with Hull because of failure of new £80,000 undersoil heating system.

JANUARY

Springboks Ray Mordt and Rob Louw arrive in Britain for duty with Wigan .... Broken arm victim Trevor Clark ruled out for the rest of his stay with Leeds .... Wales RU impose a life ban on winger Steve Ford for having trials with Leeds .... St. Helens coach Alex Murphy ordered into the stand by referee Derek Fox for verbal abuse .... Kenny Foulkes accepts coaching post at Hull .... York reduce the asking price on stand off Graham Steadman from £100,000 to £80,000 .... Five local council delegates on Wakefield Trinity's new nine-man committee .... Rugby League Council decide to fight the Welsh Rugby Union's life sentence and seek legal advice on the grounds of discrimination .... St. Helens list prop Tony Burke at £40,000 .... Widnes threequarter Joe Lydon agrees to join Australian club Illawara for the summer .... Coach Maurice Bamford names four new faces in a 26-man squad to meet France — Steve Hampson, Tony Marchant, Graham King and Neil James .... Wakefield Trinity recruit Hull K.R. forward duo Roy Holdstock and David Hall .... Oldham offer Tom Nadiola at £4,000 and free Australian Colin Penola .... Warrington sign St. Helens schoolboy star Neil Harman in the face of stiff competition .... Kenny Foulkes appoints Kiwi Fred Ah Kuoi as his assistant coach at Hull .... Batley snap up veteran Eddie Cunningham .... Test star John Fieldhouse signs a summer contract with Sydney club Western Suburbs .... Wigan lift the John Player Special Trophy, beating Hull K.R. 11-8 at Elland Road .... Barrow chase York's Graham Steadman .... Warrington's Alan Rathbone threatens to quit after being sent off for the second time in four games .... Blackpool Borough reject Carlisle's £10,000 offer for England prop Hugh Waddell .... St. Helens place a national newspaper advertisement for Rugby Union forward converts .... Workington Town coach Jackie Davidson quits after 32-5 hammering at Doncaster .... Hull offer three-year £100,000 contract to Kangaroo scrum half Peter Sterling .... Halifax sign Wigan utility back Colin Whitfield for a club record £25,000 .... Bradford Northern forward Dick Jasiewicz asks to come off the transfer list .... Wantaway St. Helens prop Tony Burke decides to stay after Saints accept a £30,000 bid from Featherstone Rovers .... Sydney referee Kevin Roberts appointed to take charge of the Whitbread Trophy Bitter Tests between Great Britain and France .... Free transfer Danny Campbell moves from Wigan to neighbours Leigh .... Bramley offer wingers Steve Lund and David Dyas, and forward pair Steve Pitchford and Tony Garforth in Challenge Cup deadline sale .... Oldham stand off David Topliss seriously injured in two-car accident .... Great Britain Under-21s crash 19-6 in France .... Challenge Cup deadline world record £100,000 swoop by Wigan for Joe Lydon, Widnes coach Eric Hughes quitting in protest at not being consulted on the transfer .... Leeds pay out club record £50,000 for Batley threequarter Carl Gibson .... Carlisle sign Barrow forward Steve Kirkby for £15,000 .... Doug Laughton accepts Widnes's invitation to return to the coaching post at Naughton

Park .... Yorkshire County clinch three-year £45,000 cup deal with brewers John Smiths .... Terry Holmes dislocates his shoulder again after 42 minutes of a reserve team comeback .... St. Helens supremo Alex Murphy severely reprimanded for verbal abuse of a referee .... Oldham put £65,000 price tag on Test forward Mick Worrall .... After six years of sponsoring the Championship and Premiership, Slalom Lager decide not to renew the contract .... North of England RU winger Maurice Cotter turns down professional terms with Widnes .... Runcorn Highfield list goalkicker Peter Wood and scrum half Kevin Blythin .... Packman Andy Timson sends Rochdale Hornets a retirement letter after only seven games .... St. Helens make a third offer to Springbok centre Danie Gerber .... Australian Gavin Miller signs a new two-year contract with Hull K.R. .... St. Helens place £15,000 asking price on goalkicking winger Sean Day .... Shaun Wane ruled out of Under-21 captaincy by a two-match ban .... Wigan prop Greg Dowling temporarily blinded by lime markings on the Widnes pitch.

FEBRUARY
Sports Council Chairman John Smith pledges to resolve the Union-League wrangle .... Widnes agree transfer deal with Featherstone Rovers for centre John Gilbert, who refuses to move .... The League decide to admit four amateur clubs into the Challenge cup from 1987 .... Halifax step up the chase for Springbok star centre Danie Gerber .... Great Britain axe Chris Arkwright for non-attendance at training and call up Wigan centre David Stephenson .... Veteran Eric Hughes joins St. Helens .... Banned Welsh RU winger Steve Ford joins Salford for trials .... Hull K.R. sign Kiwi half back Gordon Smith for a fifth season .... Widnes clinch John Gilbert signing for £27,000 .... Featherstone Rovers pay York £50,000 for stand off Graham Steadman .... Huddersfield snap up

Mark Campbell from Sheffield Eagles for £2,500 .... Former Test forward Don Furner named as coach of Australia .... Clubs battle against snow and frost to stage 12 of the 16 first round Silk Cut Challenge Cup ties .... Wigan prop Neil Courtney forced to quit with a freak shoulder injury .... Ex-Test winger John Atkinson resigns as coach of Carlisle .... Halifax hand over £13,000 for Widnes winger Wilf George .... Blow for Hull as scrum half Peter Sterling signs a new contract with Sydney club Parramatta .... Harry Pinner in club-or-country row as Great Britain Test clashes with a twice postponed Cup match.... The League rule that Harry Pinner captains Britain in the World Cup in Avignon .... Prop Harold Henney moves from Fulham to Runcorn Highfield .... Australian club Illawara chases Wigan Test prop Shaun Wane .... Great Britain struggle to gain a World Cup point in disappointing 10-10 draw against France .... Great Britain management duo Maurice Bamford and Les Bettinson to visit Australia during the summer on a spying mission .... Bradford Northern agree to switch first round Challenge Cup tie with Wakefield Trinity from snowbound Odsal to underground-heated Headingley .... The League allow Dewsbury two more attempts to stage their much postponed tie with St. Helens at Crown Flatt, then insist on switch to Headingley .... Welsh RU decide to lobby the International Board for a change in laws regarding amateurism .... Widnes launch a £500,000 ground improvement plan featuring 3,000 seats, bars, gyms, indoor bowling and sauna .... Bradford Northern's Terry Holmes returns to Wales after a shoulder operation .... Doncaster accept £2,500 offer to switch Challenge Cup tie from Tatters Field to Headingley .... Dewsbury stage Challenge Cup tie at Headingley under protest and go down fighting to St. Helens 22-19 .... The League put six outstanding second round ties back a fortnight to retain the stature of the Challenge Cup and the return

Test against France .... Wigan lose appeal against TV cameras covering derby Challenge Cup tie with St. Helens .... Paul Rose quits at Hull .... Injury withdrawal by Harry Pinner, Jeff Grayshon, Mick Burke and Ellery Hanley introduces Great Britain Test debutants David Laws, Neil James, Tony Marchant and Kevin Rayne .... The League decide to take the Charity Shield from the Isle of Man to the mainland.

MARCH
Great Britain's preparations for the return Test with France rocked by 11th hour withdrawal of injured Ellery Hanley, adding to fitness test failures Harry Pinner, Mick Burke and Jeff Grayshon .... Wakefield Trinity take Swinton's £8,000-rated Ken Jones on loan .... Debutant Neil James takes the Man of the Match award in Britain's 24-10 success over France at Wigan .... Salford and Widnes plan a trial match on Luton Town's artificial surface .... Great Britain management introduce psychoanalysis into Test preparation programme .... Wigan Springbok Ray Mordt undergoes a knee operation .... First Division season extended by 48 hours .... Wigan lose appeal against their Silk Cut Challenge Cup tie with St. Helens being televised .... Australian prop Greg Dowling indicates willingness to return for another season at Wigan .... Hull list Kiwi James Leuluai at £50,000 .... Packman Neil Clawson offered at £10,000 by Featherstone Rovers .... Blackpool Borough talk to soccer club Preston North End about possibility of staging an end of season game .... Reg Bowden resigns as coach of Warrington .... Dual Welsh international Tommy David agrees to join Widnes on a match-by-match basis .... Fulham cease to trade and announce plans to wind up on 1st April .... Leigh axe Test winger Des Drummond from Challenge Cup side at Hull K.R. for non-attendance at training .... Assistant coach Tony Barrow appointed to a caretaker

role at Warrington .... Des Drummond put on transfer list at world record £120,000 .... Meeting of representatives from 10 clubs threaten breakaway movement .... Des Drummond returns to Leigh .... The League calls a special Council meeting to discuss development plans .... Extra sponsorship boosts the staging of the Okells Charity Shield on the Isle of Man for a further year .... New Zealand Test centre Mark Ella agrees to join St. Helens for the coming season .... Castleford reach Wembley for the first time since 1970, defeating an Oldham side still waiting to visit the twin towers .... Peter Fox and Alex Murphy reappointed as coaches of Yorkshire and Lancashire respectively for the 1986 Rodstock War of the Roses clash to be staged at Headingley, Leeds .... Skipper Lee Crooks signs a new five-year contract to end speculation of his pending departure from Hull .... Great Britain and St. Helens captain Harry Pinner listed at £95,000 .... Des Drummond suspended for two weeks by Leigh after verbal clash with club officials .... Hull K.R. and Leeds in epic Silk Cut Challenge Cup semi-final clash.

APRIL

Fulham saved from liquidation at the 11th hour by takeover group headed by former Kent Invicta chairman Paul Faires .... Mick Morgan retires at 37 after dispute with Oldham .... Warrington list Andy Gregory at £120,000 .... Doncaster plan liquidation move .... Hull K.R. beat Leeds 17-0 in Elland Road replay to reach Wembley .... Whitehaven, backed by sponsors BNFL, sign Welsh RU international centre Bob Ackerman on £40,000 contract .... Leigh and Des Drummond settle their differences .... Brewers Bass to sponsor the Championship and Premiership in new three-year £400,000 deal .... Hull K.R. main victims of end of season fixture congestion with nine games in 17 days .... Rugby League Council decide to discuss major policy changes at meeting on

7th May .... Challenge Cup finalists Castleford make arrangements to fly Brisbane-based Ian French and Jamie Sandy back for Wembley .... Great Britain coach Maurice Bamford recalls George Fairbairn, Trevor Skerrett, Mike Smith, Dave Heron, Andy Gregory and Brian Noble in 29-man summer preparation squad .... Oldham skipper Mal Graham threatens to quit Watersheddings after failing to agree new terms .... Oldham stalwart supporter Eddie Elson (81) named Traveleads Top Fan 1986 .... Rugby League Management Committee recommends that artificial playing surfaces be banned .... Thirteen-all draw at Thrum Hall gives Halifax the Slalom Lager Championship title and saves Featherstone Rovers from relegation amid controversial claims that the match finished nearly three minutes early .... The 1986 Australian itinerary announced with 13-match programme featuring a first-ever Test at Manchester United's Old Trafford ground .... Great Britain and Widnes stand off Tony Myler joins Sydney club Balmain for the summer .... Stockport County consortium apply for League membership .... Salford and Bradford Northern move in for Oldham's want-away Australian Mal Graham .... Halifax fail to land French RU centre Philippe Sella .... Phil Hogan breaks his arm less than a week away from Hull K.R.'s Wembley bid .... Rochdale Hornets chase Warrington's Ken Kelly as player-coach .... Full back Kevin Harcombe listed at £55,000 by Rochdale Hornets .... Doncaster sign Rochdale Hornets second row man Andy Timson.

MAY

Underdogs Castleford beat Hull K.R. 15-14 to lift the Silk Cut Challenge Cup at Wembley .... Castleford scrum half Bob Beardmore awarded the Lance Todd Trophy .... Sydney club Eastern Suburbs renew chase for Wigan's Ellery Hanley .... Widnes referee Robin Whitfield appointed for the summer three-match Test series between Australia and New Zealand .... Coach Jim Crellin resigns at Swinton .... Rugby League Council supports the top clubs by sending a series of proposals to the AGM, including a reduction of the First Division from 16 to 14 clubs and the levy coming down from 15 to eight per cent .... Hull K.R. utility back John Lydiat joins Australian club Ipswich for the summer .... Leeds release Australian back row forward Terry Webb from his contract with one year to run .... Former Kangaroo full back Graham Eadie considers a comeback with Halifax .... Oldham hand over £5,000 for Featherstone Rovers forward Neil Clawson, son of ex-Testman Terry .... Hull K.R. loose forward Gavin Miller is named Greenalls Man of Steel and First Division Player of the Year, fellow Australian Chris Anderson collecting the Coach of the Year award .... Hull K.R. beat off Wigan challenge to re-sign Kiwi prop Mark Broadhurst after a year's return to New Zealand .... Rochdale Hornets reject Widnes offer of utility man John Myler in exchange for Australian Phil McKenzie and cash .... Bradford Northern beat Salford to the signature of Australian forward Mal Graham, previously with Oldham and Hunslet ....

Warrington break two records to lift the Slalom Lager Premiership Trophy, trouncing Halifax 38-10 at Elland Road, Leeds .... Assistant coach Les Boyd collects two tries and the Harry Sunderland Trophy .... Caretaker coach Tony Barrow offered full-time contract by Warrington .... Alan Rhodes quits as coach of Sheffield Eagles .... Castleford winger Steve Gill named as first-ever Slalom Lager Alliance Player of the Year .... Wigan announce the appointment of an overseas coach while still retaining joint bosses Colin Clarke and Alan McInnes, but do not reveal his identity .... Rochdale Hornets make unsuccessful move for New Zealand national coach Graham Lowe .... A three-man consortium bid to launch Rugby League at Stockport County's ground attracts only four pro-votes from 28 clubs at special meeting .... Winger Phil Fox wants away from Second Division champions Leigh .... Widnes sign Australian hooker Phil McKenzie from Rochdale Hornets .... Maurice Bamford withdraws Trevor Skerrett from the Great Britain preparation squad and adds Wigan's Shaun Wane, Shaun Edwards and Lance Todd Trophy winner, Bob Beardmore.

Bradford Northern's Terry Holmes, ex-Wales Rugby Union skipper.

Leeds centre David Creasser en route to a Silk Cut Challenge Cup semi-final touchdown despite the last ditch tackle of Hull K.R. full back George Fairbairn.

CLUBS

The following is a focus on the 34 professional Rugby League clubs, the section providing each club with a profile and an analysis of their 1985-86 campaign on a match by match basis with a summary for each first team player.

KEY
In the individual club profiles the following headings are featured:
First season refers to when the club gained senior league status. In some instances clubs have disbanded and re-formed, sometimes under different titles. For record purposes these changes are ignored except where there has been a break of more than one full season.
Honours. Until they were scrapped in 1970, the Yorkshire and Lancashire Leagues were one of the honours in the professional game. Before 1903 they operated under the title of the Yorkshire and Lancashire Senior Competitions. Winners of these senior competitions are listed under Yorkshire and Lancashire League Champions. The pre-1903 Yorkshire Senior Competition should not be confused with the league operating for A-teams in Yorkshire which had the same title.
Coaches. Changes in the appointment of a club's coach during 1985-86 are shown in brackets.
Attendances. Crowds in brackets are at neutral venue.
Appearances. Players' totals are based on official teamsheets submitted to the League after each first team match. + indicates playing substitute appearance.

In the match by match review for each club the following abbreviations are used:

YC	— Yorkshire Cup	A	—	Away
LC	— Lancashire Cup	W	—	Won
SLC	— Slalom Lager Championship	L	—	Lost
SD	— Second Division	D	—	Drawn
JPS	— John Player Special Trophy	dg	—	Drop goal
CC	— Challenge Cup	Fr	—	France
PT	— Premiership Trophy	Aus	—	Australia
P	— Preliminary Round	NZ	—	New Zealand
H	— Home	Pr	—	Probationer

BARROW

Ground:	Craven Park
Colours:	Royal blue jerseys, blue shorts
First Season:	1900-01
Nickname:	Shipbuilders
Chairman:	Bob Brady
Secretary:	Wilf Livingstone
Coach:	Ivor Kelland (May 1985-)
Honours:	**Challenge Cup** Winners, 1954-55 Beaten finalists, 1937-38, 1950-51, 1956-57, 1966-67 **John Player Trophy** Beaten finalists 1980-81 **Lancashire Cup** Winners, 1954-55, 1983-84 Beaten finalists, 1937-38 **Division Two** Champions, 1975-76, 1983-84
Records:	Attendance: 21,651 v. Salford (League) 15 Apr, 1938 **Season** Goals: 135 by J. Ball, 1956-57 Tries: 50 by J. Lewthwaite, 1956-57 Points: 305 by I. Ball, 1979-80 **Match** Goals: 12 by F. French v. Maryport, 19 Feb, 1938; W. Horne v. Cardiff, 8 Sep, 1951; S. Tickle v. Kent Invicta, 8 Apr, 1984 Tries: 6 by V. Cumberbatch v. Batley, 21 Nov, 1936; J. Thornburrow v. Maryport, 19 Feb, 1938; F. Castle v. York, 29 Sep, 1951 Points: 28 by K. Jarrett v. Doncaster, 25 Aug, 1970; S. Tickle v. Kent Invicta,

8 Apr 1984
Highest score: 83-3 v. Maryport, 1937-38
Highest against: 71-15 v. St. Helens, 1958-59

1985-86 PLAYERS' SUMMARY

	App	Tries	Goals	Dr	Pts
Blacker, Brian	10	7	—	—	28
Brown, Dave	18	10	—	—	40
Cairns, David	39	8	—	—	32
Carter, Dane	5	1	—	—	4
Clough, Dave	2 + 3	—	—	—	—
Dwyer, Tim	16	12	29	—	106
Elliott, David	6	3	—	—	12
Elliott, Tony	27 + 2	7	—	—	28
Fairhurst, Jimmy	2 + 2	—	—	—	—
Fitzgerald, Mark	7 + 1	5	—	—	20
Flynn, Malcolm	3	1	—	—	4
Gleaves, Mark	4	—	—	—	—
Hadley, Derek	3 + 3	—	—	—	—
Heselwood, David	10 + 6	4	—	—	16
Hudson, Gary	1	—	—	—	—
James, Mick	21 + 1	7	—	—	28
Kay, Tony	6 + 4	7	—	—	28
Kendall, David	14 + 4	1	—	—	4
Kendall, Gary	25 + 7	10	—	—	40
Kirkby, Steve	1 + 1	—	—	—	—
Lightfoot, John	18 + 1	2	—	—	8
Livesey, Dave	2 + 1	1	—	—	4
McConnell, Ralph	8 + 5	5	—	—	20
McNichol, Anthony	7 + 1	4	—	—	16
Miles, Steve	2	—	—	—	—
Moore, Terry	16 + 1	14	—	—	56
Morrison, Steve	1	—	—	—	—
Moses, Graham	0 + 2	—	—	—	—
Mossop, Steve	23 + 4	2	—	—	8
Quirk, Les	22	17	—	—	68
Rea, Steve	4 + 3	3	—	1	13
Richardson, Dave	6	—	—	—	—
Smith, Greg	23	4	—	—	16
Sykes, Andy	3 + 3	1	—	—	4
Tickle, Steve	37	13	77	1	207
Turley, Norman	31 + 2	7	28	1	85
Van Bellen, Gary	10	2	—	—	8
Walker, Russ	21 + 4	4	—	—	16
Whittle, Andy	11 + 9	11	—	—	44
Wilkinson, Stuart	6	—	—	—	—
Williams, Stewart	35 + 1	27	—	—	108
TOTALS:					
41 players		200	134	3	1,071

1985-86 MATCH ANALYSIS

Date	Com-petition	H/A	Opponent	Rlt	Score	Tries	Goals	Atten-dance	Referee
30.8.85	SD	H	Blackpool B.	L	16-18	Tickle (2), Moore	Tickle (2)	1553	Houghton
8.9.85	SD	A	Whitehaven	L	10-34	McConnell, Flynn	Tickle	—	—
15.9.85	LC(1)	H	Whitehaven	L	8-12	Fitzgerald, Moore	—	2011	Loftus
18.9.85	SD	H	Doncaster	W	30-8	Quirk (2), Whittle (2), Moore, D. Elliott	Tickle (3)	965	Tickle
22.9.85	SD	H	Leigh	W	14-2	Williams, Whittle	Tickle (3)	2070	Beaumont
29.9.85	SD	A	Huddersfield B.	W	44-20	D. Elliott (2), Fitzgerald (2), Williams, Livesey, Whittle	Tickle (8)	—	—
6.10.85	SD	H	Bramley	W	20-0	Mossop, Williams, Turley, Tickle, Dwyer, Sykes	Tickle, Dwyer	2710	Berry *(continued)*

MATCH ANALYSIS (continued)

13.10.85	SD	H	Keighley	W	74-2	Brown (2), Smith (2), Moore (2), Walker (2), Williams (2), Fitzgerald (2), Dwyer	Dwyer (9), Tickle (2)	2164	Croft
20.10.85	SD	A	Batley	W	26-9	Dwyer, Brown, Moore, Mossop	Dwyer (5)	—	—
27.10.85	SD	H	Fulham	W	40-8	Heselwood (2), Moore (2), Tickle, G. Kendall, Whittle	Tickle (6)	2339	Kershaw
3.11.85	SD	A	Carlisle	W	36-13	Whittle (3), Quirk, Brown, G. Kendall, Moore	Dwyer (4)	—	—
10.11.85	SD	H	Mansfield M.	W	40-0	Williams (3), Cairns, Moore, Whittle, A. Elliott	Dwyer (6)	1875	Tennant
17.11.85	SD	A	Wakefield T.	W	15-12	Dwyer (2)	Tickle (3), Turley (dg)	—	—
24.11.85	JPS(1)	H	Leeds	W	5-2	Whittle	Tickle (dg)	4886	Lindop
1.12.85	JPS(2)	A	Warrington	L	14-34	Williams, James, Cairns	Tickle	—	—
8.12.85	SD	H	Huddersfield B.	W	34-10	James (2), Tickle, Quirk, Williams, Brown, Cairns	Tickle (3)	2115	Tickle
15.12.85	SD	A	Mansfield M.	W	40-0	Turley (2), Quirk, James, Whittle, Tickle, Brown	Tickle (5), Dwyer	—	—
22.12.85	SD	H	Batley	W	32-10	Brown (2), Heselwood (2), G. Kendall, Cairns, Quirk	Tickle (2)	2335	Whitfield
5.1.86	SD	H	Wakefield T.	W	20-6	Quirk (2), Dwyer, Lightfoot	Dwyer (2)	2425	Spencer
12.1.86	SD	A	Hunslet	L	18-20	Dwyer (2), Williams, Tickle	Tickle	—	
19.1.86	SD	H	Carlisle	W	20-8	Dwyer (2), Turley, Williams	Tickle, Turley	1811	Simpson
22.1.86	SD	H	Workington T.	W	48-18	Williams (3), Tickle (3), Moore (2), Dwyer (2)	Tickle (4)	1724	Carter
2.2.86	SD	H	Hunslet	W	48-8	G. Kendall, Moore (2), Williams (2), Tickle, Turley, Dwyer	Tickle (3), Dwyer	1801	Mean
26.2.86	CC(1)	A (at Wigan)	Fulham	W	26-14	Brown (2), Quirk (2), Williams	Turley (3)	—	—
2.3.86	SD	H	Runcorn H.	W	48-10	McConnell (2), Williams, Quirk, Tickle, G. Kendall, A. Elliott, Smith	Turley (8)	1584	Beaumont
9.3.86	CC(2)	H	Castleford	L	6-30	Smith	Turley	3613	Kershaw
16.3.86	SD	H	Whitehaven	W	34-7	D. Kendall, G. Kendall, Turley, McConnell, A. Elliott, James	Turley (5)	2142	Campbell
23.3.86	SD	A	Bramley	W	22-14	Blacker (2), McConnell, A. Elliott	Turley (3)	—	—
28.3.86	SD	A	Blackpool B.	L	20-24	Walker, Blacker, Lightfoot, Williams	Tickle (2)	—	—
31.3.86	SD	A	Workington T.	L	16-36	Quirk (2), Van Bellen	Turley, Tickle	—	—
6.4.86	SD	A	Runcorn H.	W	14-11	Quirk (2), G. Kendall	Tickle	—	—
9.4.86	SD	A	Doncaster	L	10-18	Quirk (2)	Tickle	—	—
13.4.86	SD	H	Rochdale H.	W	30-7	Blacker (3), Williams (2)	Tickle (5)	1609	Holdsworth
20.4.86	SD	A	Leigh	L	18-26	Blacker, Cairns, Williams, Kay	Tickle	—	—
23.4.86	SD	A	Rochdale H.	W	14-8	Tickle, Cairns	Tickle (3)	—	—
27.4.86	SD	A	Keighley	W	58-4	Kay (4), Rea (2), McNichol, Williams, Turley, Walker, Carter	Tickle (7)	—	—
30.4.86	SD	H	Sheffield E.	W	32-8	Williams (3), McNichol (2), Tickle, Kay	Tickle (2)	1520	Fox
5.5.86	SD	A	Fulham	W	50-18	A. Elliott (3), James (2), McNichol, Kay, Van Bellen, G. Kendall	Tickle (5), Turley (2)	—	—
7.5.86	SD	A	Sheffield E.	W	21-1	Cairns (2), Rea	Turley (4), Rea (dg)	—	—

BATTLEY

Ground:	Mount Pleasant
Colours:	Cerise and fawn jerseys, cerise shorts
First Season:	1895-96
Nickname:	Gallant Youths
Chairman:	Michael Lumb
Secretary:	Les Hardy
Coach:	George Pieniazek (Nov 1984-Nov 1985)
	Brian Lockwood (Nov 1985-)
Honours:	**Championship** Winners, 1923-24
	Challenge Cup Winners, 1896-97, 1897-98, 1900-01
	Yorkshire League Winners, 1898-99, 1923-24
	Yorkshire Cup Winners, 1912-13
	Beaten finalists, 1909-10, 1922-23, 1924-25, 1952-53
Records:	Attendance: 23,989 v. Leeds (RL Cup) 14 Mar, 1925
	Season
	Goals: 120 by S. Thompson, 1958-59
	Tries: 29 by J. Tindall, 1912-13
	Points: 281 by J. Perry, 1950-51
	Match
	Goals: 9 by W. Davies v. Widnes, 27 Mar, 1909; S. Thompson v. Keighley, 20 Sep, 1958
	Tries: 5 by J. Oakland v. Bramley, 19 Dec, 1908; Brannan v. Swinton, 17 Jan, 1920; J. Wale v. Bramley, 4 Dec, 1926 and v. Cottingham, 12 Feb, 1927
	Points: 26 by J. Perry v. Liverpool C., 16 Sep, 1951
	Highest score: 52-0 v. Widnes, 1908-09
	Highest against: 78-9 v. Wakefield T., 1967-68

1985-86 PLAYERS' SUMMARY

	App	Tries	Goals	Dr	Pts
Arnold, Derek	27 + 9	1	—	—	4
Bartle, Phil	4	1	—	—	4
Carroll, John	19 + 6	4	—	3	19
Cousins, Kevin	9 + 3	—	—	—	—
Cowan, Murray	7	2	—	—	8
Cummins, Bernard	0 + 2	1	—	—	4
Cunningham, Eddie	15	3	—	—	12
Davies, Tommy	6 + 2	—	—	—	—
Douglas, Ian	27 + 3	2	—	—	8
Durham, Stephen	13 + 5	4	—	—	16
Ferres, Steve	15 + 1	2	1	3	13
Gibson, Carl	18	13	—	—	52
Harrington, Martin	8	—	—	—	—
Hemingway, Neil	30 + 4	2	—	—	8
Illingworth, Neil	14	—	—	—	—
James, Kevin	26 + 3	7	—	—	28
Jones, John	8	3	23	—	58
Madden, Sean	0 + 7	—	—	—	—
McLeary, Jack	12 + 3	—	1	—	2
Oulton, Henry	11	1	20	—	44
Pickerill, Neil	32	9	1	1	39
Presley, Stephen	1 + 2	—	—	—	—
Ratcliffe, Paul	15 + 5	1	7	—	18
Reed, Steve	23	7	—	—	28
Render, Ian	10 + 2	1	—	—	4
Scott, Mark	2 + 1	1	—	—	4
Sowden, Russ	34	5	—	—	20
Speight, Mark	2 + 1	—	—	—	—
Storey, Paul	35	7	—	—	28
West, Brian	15	1	—	—	4
Williams, Andrew	25 + 2	15	—	1	61
Wilson, Michael	0 + 1	—	—	—	—
Wilson, Simon	16	6	37	1	99
Wray, David	2	—	—	—	—

TOTALS:
34 players		99	90	9	585

Ex-Welsh international Eddie Cunningham.

1985-86 MATCH ANALYSIS

Date	Com-petition	H/A	Opponent	Rlt	Score	Tries	Goals	Atten-dance	Referee
30.8.85	SD	A	Bramley	L	13-14	Gibson, James	Oulton (2), Carroll (dg)	—	—
4.9.85	SD	H	Huddersfield B.	W	20-14	Reed, Ferres, Storey, Gibson	Oulton, Ferres	794	Tennant
8.9.85	SD	A	Leigh	L	17-26	James, Carroll	Ratcliffe (4), Carroll (dg)	—	—
15.9.85	YC(1)	H	Dewsbury	L	10-14	Reed, Gibson	Ratcliffe	2148	Kendrew
22.9.85	SD	A	Fulham	W	41-22	Gibson (3), Arnold, Reed, James, Jones	Jones (6), Ferres (dg)	—	—
6.10.85	SD	H	Wakefield T.	W	8-4	Pickerill	Ratcliffe (2)	1865	Croft
13.10.85	SD	A	Huddersfield B.	W	34-8	Jones, Storey, Gibson, Ferres, Pickerill, Cummins	Jones (5)	—	—
20.10.85	SD	H	Barrow	L	9-26	—	Jones (4), Ferres (dg)	1340	Allatt
27.10.85	SD	A	Rochdale H.	L	0-28	—	—	—	—
3.11.85	SD	A	Workington T.	L	14-24	Jones, Williams	Jones (3)	—	—
10.11.85	SD	H	Leigh	L	8-28	Pickerill	Jones (2)	1487	Simpson
17.11.85	SD	A	Carlisle	W	16-8	Gibson, Williams, Pickerill	Jones (2)	—	—
24.11.85	JPS(1)	H	Leigh	L	2-70	—	Jones	1543	Carter
8.12.85	SD	H	Workington T.	W	20-6	Williams (2), Gibson (2), Sowden	—	775	Spencer
15.12.85	SD	H	Keighley	W	15-12	Gibson, Williams	Oulton (3), Pickerill (dg)	896	McDonald
22.12.85	SD	A	Barrow	L	10-32	West, Ratcliffe	Oulton	—	—
26.12.85	SD	A	Hunslet	L	8-26	Scott	Oulton (2)	—	—
1.1.86	SD	H	Hunslet	W	22-0	Gibson (2), Pickerill, Williams	Oulton (3)	1114	Campbell
12.1.86	SD	H	Rochdale H.	W	11-8	Sowden	Oulton (3), Ferres (dg)	1256	Tickle
19.1.86	SD	A	Whitehaven	L	2-6	—	Oulton	—	—
2.2.86	SD	A	Keighley	L	14-16	Douglas, Pickerill	Oulton (2), Pickerill	—	—
16.2.86	CC(1)	A	Bramley	L	6-8	Williams	Wilson	—	—
9.3.86	SD	A	Runcorn H.	D	13-13	Storey, Durham	Wilson (2), Carroll (dg)	—	—
16.3.86	SD	H	Bramley	W	19-0	Durham, Wilson, Douglas	Wilson (3), Williams (dg)	776	Smith
23.3.86	SD	A	Wakefield T.	W	24-6	Williams (2), Cowan, Oulton, Hemingway	Oulton (2)	—	—
28.3.86	SD	H	Doncaster	D	16-16	Cowan, Sowden, Cunningham	Wilson (2)	1055	Tennant
31.3.86	SD	A	Doncaster	W	16-14	James, Storey, Williams	Wilson (2)	—	—
6.4.86	SD	H	Mansfield M.	W	26-6	James, Storey, Durham, Sowden	Wilson (5)	740	Kendrew
13.4.86	SD	A	Sheffield E.	L	6-8	Carroll	Wilson	—	—
17.4.86	SD	H	Carlisle	D	8-8	Williams, Bartle	Wilson	420	Croft
20.4.86	SD	H	Blackpool B.	L	10-20	Reed, Williams	Wilson	607	Fox
27.4.86	SD	H	Whitehaven	W	7-2	Reed	Wilson (1, 1 dg)	751	Carter
30.4.86	SD	H	Runcorn H.	W	42-4	Williams (3), Wilson (2), Reed (2), Pickerill	Wilson (5)	509	Hodgson
2.5.86	SD	H	Sheffield E.	W	38-4	Wilson (2), Storey, James, Cunningham, Durham	Wilson (7)	708	Holdsworth
5.5.86	SD	A	Mansfield M.	W	30-14	Carroll (2), Pickerill, Render, Hemingway, Storey	Wilson (2), McCleary	—	—
8.5.86	SD	A	Blackpool B.	L	2-14	—	Wilson	—	—
11.5.86	SD	H	Fulham	W	28-13	Cunningham, Wilson, James, Sowden, Pickerill	Wilson (4)	725	Fishwick (Pr)

BLACKPOOL BOROUGH

Ground:	Borough Park
Colours:	Tangerine jerseys with black and white broad bands, white shorts
First Season:	1954-55
Nickname:	Seasiders
Chairman:	Jack Hart
Secretary:	Deryk Brown
Coach:	Tommy Dickens (Mar 1982-Nov 1985) Stan Gittins (Nov 1985-)
Honours:	**John Player Trophy** Beaten finalists, 1976-77
Records:	Attendance: 7,614 v. Castleford (RL Cup) 14 Mar, 1964. There was an attendance of 21,000 in an RL Cup-tie against Leigh on Blackpool FC ground on 9 Mar, 1957.

Season
Goals: 89 by J. Maughan, 1958-59
Tries: 30 by T. Frodsham, 1985-86
Points: 201 by P. Fearis, 1957-58

Match
Goals: 11 by N. Turley v. Carlisle, 26 Apr, 1984;
Tries: 4 by T. Wilkshire v. Bradford N, 14 Jan, 1961;
J. Stockley v. Doncaster, 1 Apr, 1984
T. Frodsham v. Bridgend, 14 Apr, 1985

Points: 27 by N. Turley v. Carlisle, 26 Apr, 1984
Highest score: 54-0 v. Carlisle, 1985-86
Highest against: 77-8 v. Wigan, 1963-64

1985-86 PLAYERS' SUMMARY

	App	Tries	Goals	Dr	Pts
Bacon, David	28	8	—	—	32
Bailey, Andrew	14	3	—	—	12
Brennan, Steve	20 + 3	8	—	—	32
Briscoe, Carl	32 + 4	9	—	—	36
Coyle, Bernard	5 + 1	—	—	1	1
Frodsham, Tommy	34	30	—	—	120
Gamble, Paul	11 + 7	—	—	—	—
Green, Jimmy	20 + 3	1	—	—	4
Greenall, Alan	2	1	—	—	4
Grundy, Tracy	23 + 8	2	—	—	8
Hindley, Alan	17 + 2	—	—	—	—
Howarth, Roy	10 + 2	2	26	—	60
Lee, David	3 + 3	1	—	—	4
McLoughlin, Brendan	1 + 2	1	—	—	4
Melling, Steve	27 + 1	14	8	—	72
Moore, Brent	23	11	—	—	44
Nanyn, Mick	27 + 7	13	—	—	52
Platt, Billy	1	—	—	—	—
Price, Billy	35 + 2	5	—	8	28
Roberts, Paul	31	15	6	—	72
Sanderson, Mark.............	14 + 7	3	—	—	12
Subritzky, Peter..............	27 + 1	13	61	1	175
Swann, Malcolm	3 + 2	—	—	—	—
Waddell, Hugh...............	37 + 1	6	5	—	34
Waller, Tony	37	5	—	—	20
Wills, Steve	12 + 13	2	—	—	8
Yates, Mal....................	1 + 2	—	—	—	—
TOTALS:					
27 players......................		153	106	10	834

1985-86 MATCH ANALYSIS

Date	Competition	H/A	Opponent	Rlt	Score	Tries	Goals	Attendance	Referee
30.8.85	SD	A	Barrow	W	18-16	Bacon, Frodsham, Roberts	Subritzky (3)	—	—
1.9.85	SD	A	Fulham	L	2-6	—	Subritzky	—	—
8.9.85	SD	H	Workington T.	L	16-20	Roberts, Lea, McLoughlin	Roberts (2)	580	Croft
15.9.85	LC(1)	A	Warrington	L	3-30	—	Roberts, Coyle (dg)	—	—
22.9.85	SD	A	Hunslet	L	32-38	Frodsham (3), Price, Waddell, Briscoe	Waddell (4)	—	—
29.9.85	SD	A	Runcorn H.	L	20-23	Brennan (3), Wills, Roberts	—	—	—

(continued)

MATCH ANALYSIS (continued)

6.10.85	SD	H	Keighley	W	16-8	Brennan, Roberts	Subritzky (3), Roberts	322	Simpson
13.10.85	SD	A	Doncaster	W	30-20	Frodsham (2), Subritzky, Price, Briscoe	Subritzky (5)	—	—
20.10.85	SD	H	Whitehaven	L	11-20	Roberts, Brennan	Waddell, Price (dg)	638	Spencer
27.10.85	SD	A	Carlisle	W	33-32	Frodsham (2), Subritzky, Bailey, Melling	Subritzky (6, 1dg)	—	—
3.11.85	SD	H	Runcorn H.	W	30-8	Roberts (2), Greenall, Waller, Melling, Frodsham	Melling (3)	306	Allatt
10.11.85	SD	A	Workington T.	L	15-18	Moore, Grundy	Melling (2), Price (3dg)	—	—
17.11.85	SD	H	Doncaster	W	30-13	Frodsham (2), Bacon (2), Waller, Waddell	Melling (2), Roberts	287	Lindop
24.11.85	JPS(1)	H	Wakefield T.	L	22-24	Waller, Waddell, Bailey, Brennan, Melling	Roberts	683	Carter
8.12.85	SD	A	Rochdale H.	L	20-26	Roberts (2), Price, Nanyn	Subritzky (2)	—	—
15.12.85	SD	H	Bramley	W	24-16	Subritzky (2), Brennan, Frodsham, Melling	Subritzky (2)	570	Tickle
22.12.85	SD	A	Whitehaven	W	20-10	Melling, Nanyn, Moore	Subritzky (4)	—	—
26.12.85	SD	H	Carlisle	W	54-0	Nanyn (2), Frodsham (2), Roberts, Waller, Moore, Subritzky, Sanderson, Melling	Subritzky (7)	600	McDonald
1.1.86	SD	A	Leigh	L	8-34	Waddell	Subritzky (2)	—	—
5.1.86	SD	H	Mansfield M.	W	42-10	Nanyn (2), Briscoe (2), Grundy, Price, Subritzky, Bailey	Subritzky (4), Melling	350	Berry
19.1.86	SD	A	Keighley	L	6-12	Moore	Subritzky	—	—
2.2.86	SD	H	Sheffield E.	W	25-12	Moore (2), Melling, Roberts	Subritzky (4), Price (dg)	400	Volante
9.2.86	CC(1)	H	Runcorn H.	W	30-10	Melling (2), Price, Roberts, Moore, Frodsham	Subritzky (2), Price (2dg)	422	Tickle
2.3.86	SD	H	Fulham	L	12-22	Briscoe (2)	Subritzky (2)	410	Loftus
9.3.86	CC(2)	A	Leigh	L	10-31	Subritzky, Waller	Subritzky	—	—
16.3.86	SD	A	Sheffield E.	L	14-21	Nanyn (2), Frodsham	Subritzky	—	—
19.3.86	SD	A	Wakefield T.	L	20-32	Nanyn, Moore, Bacon, Roberts	Howarth (2)	—	—
28.3.86	SD	H	Barrow	W	24-20	Wills, Nanyn, Green, Briscoe	Howarth (4)	703	Hodgson
31.3.86	SD	H	Leigh	L	8-15	Frodsham (2)	—	1505	Croft
6.4.86	SD	A	Huddersfield B.	W	30-10	Frodsham (2), Nanyn, Moore, Briscoe	Howarth (5)	—	—
9.4.86	SD	A	Bramley	L	15-20	Subritzky, Frodsham	Subritzky (3), Price (dg)	—	—
13.4.86	SD	H	Hunslet	W	38-14	Bacon (2), Frodsham (2), Subritzky, Roberts, Melling	Howarth (5)	455	Haigh
17.4.86	SD	H	Rochdale H.	W	22-6	Subritzky, Frodsham, Roberts, Melling, Sanderson	Subritzky	473	Spencer
20.4.86	SD	A	Batley	W	20-10	Moore, Bacon, Frodsham, Briscoe	Howarth (2)	—	—
24.4.86	SD	H	Wakefield T.	W	22-18	Sanderson, Subritzky, Nanyn, Bacon	Howarth (3)	461	Smith
27.4.86	SD	A	Mansfield M.	W	34-26	Howarth (2), Frodsham (2), Melling, Nanyn, Waddell	Howarth (3)	—	—
8.5.86	SD	H	Batley	W	14-2	Moore, Melling	Howarth (2), Subritzky	466	Bowman (Pr)
11.5.86	SD	H	Huddersfield B.	W	44-12	Frodsham (3), Subritzky (2), Waddell, Brennan, Melling	Subritzky (6)	503	Holgate (Pr)

BRADFORD NORTHERN

Ground: Odsal Stadium
Colours: White jerseys with red, amber and black hoops, white shorts
First Season: 1895-96 as "Bradford". Disbanded and became Bradford Northern in 1907-08. Disbanded during 1963-64 and re-formed for start of 1964-65
Nickname: Northern
Chairman: Jack Bates
Secretary: Rita Winter
Coach: Barry Seabourne (May 1985-)
Honours: **Challenge Cup** Winners, 1905-06, 1943-44, 1946-47, 1948-49
Beaten finalists, 1897-98, 1944-45, 1947-48, 1972-73
Championship Beaten finalists, 1947-48, 1951-52
Division One Champions, 1903-04, 1979-80, 1980-81
Division Two Champions, 1973-74
War-time Emergency League Championship winners, 1939-40, 1940-41, 1944-45
Beaten finalists, 1941-42
Yorkshire League Winners, 1899-1900, 1900-01, 1939-40, 1940-41, 1947-48
Yorkshire Cup Winners, 1906-07, 1940-41, 1941-42, 1943-44, 1945-46, 1948-49, 1949-50, 1953-54, 1965-66, 1978-79
Beaten finalists, 1913-14, 1981-82, 1982-83
Premiership Winners, 1977-78
Beaten finalists, 1978-79, 1979-80
John Player Trophy Winners, 1974-75, 1979-80
Records: Attendance: 102,569 Warrington v. Halifax (RL Cup Final replay) 5 May, 1954
Home: 69,429 v. Huddersfield (RL Cup) 14 March, 1953
Season
Goals: 173 by E. Tees, 1971-72
Tries: 63 by J. McLean, 1951-52
Points: 364 by E. Tees, 1971-72

Match
Goals: 14 by J. Phillips v. Batley, 6 Sep, 1952
Tries: 7 by J. Dechan v. Bramley, 13 Oct, 1906
Points: 36 by J. Woods v. Swinton, 13 Oct, 1985
Highest score: 72-9 v. Doncaster, 1973-74; 72-12 v. Hunslet, 1984-85
Highest against: 75-18 v. Leeds, 1931-32

1985-86 PLAYERS' SUMMARY

	App	Tries	Goals	Dr	Pts
Carroll, Dean	15	9	11	3	61
Clawson, Martin	0 + 1	—	—	—	—
Crawford, Adrian	0 + 1	—	—	—	—
Crossley, John	7 + 2	—	—	—	—
Davies, Richard	4	—	—	—	—
Donlan, Steve	33	8	—	—	32
Fennell, Dale	5 + 1	—	—	—	—
Fleming, Mark	17 + 1	3	—	—	12
Ford, Phil	33	14	3	—	62
Francis, Richard	9	—	—	—	—
Godfrey, Heath	18	5	—	—	20
Grayshon, Jeff	3 + 1	—	—	—	—
Hamer, Jon	0 + 1	—	—	—	—
Heron, Wayne	8 + 1	—	—	—	—
Holmes, Terry	1	—	—	—	—
Jackson, Robert	8 + 1	2	—	—	8
Jasiewicz, Dick	24 + 3	2	—	—	8
Kellaway, Bob	19	2	—	—	8
Lumby, Ashley	16 + 2	4	—	—	16
Mallinder, Paul	18 + 2	5	—	—	20
McGowan, Steve	8 + 2	—	—	—	—
Moulden, Darren	13 + 12	1	—	—	4
Mumby, Keith	31	1	—	—	4
Noble, Brian	29	4	—	—	16
Parrish, Steve	15 + 3	2	2	—	12
Parrott, Chris	0 + 3	—	—	—	—
Potts, Martin	6 + 1	—	—	—	—
Preece, Chris	5 + 1	3	—	—	12
Ramsey, Neville	3	1	—	—	4
Redfearn, David	23 + 3	6	—	—	24
Sheldon, Ian	15 + 1	—	—	—	—
Sherratt, Ian	14 + 9	2	—	—	8
Sidebottom, Gary	12 + 6	2	—	—	8
Simpson, Roger	22	6	—	—	24
Stones, Chris	2	—	—	—	—
Sykes, Andy	3 + 1	—	—	—	—
Tuffs, Simon	1 + 1	—	—	—	—
Van Bellen, Gary	12 + 7	—	—	—	—
White, Brendan	22 + 2	—	—	1	1
Woods, John	33	13	97	1	247

TOTALS:
40 players		95	113	5	611

1985-86 MATCH ANALYSIS

Date	Com-petition	H/A	Opponent	Rlt	Score	Tries	Goals	Atten-dance	Referee
1.9.85	SLC	A	Warrington	L	7-32	Fleming	Woods, Carroll (dg)	—	—
4.9.85	SLC	A	Featherstone R.	L	8-15	Carroll	Woods (2)	—	—
8.9.85	SLC	H	Wigan	W	21-16	Woods (2), Noble	Woods (4), Carroll (dg)	7447	Fox
15.9.85	YC(1)	H	Wakefield T.	W	40-15	Simpson (3), Noble (2), Kellaway, Sidebottom, Carroll	Woods (4)	3180	Beaumont
22.9.85	SLC	H	Hull K.R.	L	12-17	Carroll, Sherratt	Woods (2)	5102	Berry
25.9.85	YC(2)	A	Featherstone R.	W	22-11	Carroll (2), Fleming, Woods	Woods (2), Carroll	—	—
29.9.85	SLC	A	Widnes	L	26-28	Moulden, Carroll, Ford, Sidebottom	Woods (5)	—	—
2.10.85	YC(SF)	A	Hull K.R.	L	5-11	—	Woods (2, 1dg)	—	—
6.10.85	SLC	H	Dewsbury	L	8-10	Simpson	Woods (2)	3152	Walker
13.10.85	SLC	H	Swinton	W	48-20	Woods (5), Carroll (2), Ramsey	Woods (8)	3500	Houghton
27.10.85	SLC	A	Hull	L	16-28	Kellaway, Ford, Lumby	Carroll (2)	—	—
3.11.85	SLC	H	Oldham	L	6-24	Ford	Carroll	5091	Campbell
10.11.85	SLC	A	Hull K.R.	L	4-30	Parrish	—	—	—
17.11.85	SLC	H	St. Helens	L	9-18	Ford	Carroll (2, 1dg)	3250	Holdsworth
24.11.85	JPS(1)	A	Sheffield E.	W	24-16	Carroll, Donlan, Sherratt, Parrish	Carroll (4)	—	—
30.11.85	JPS(2)	A	Widnes	L	6-30	Ford	Carroll	—	—
8.12.85	SLC	A	Swinton	L	0-8	—	—	—	—
15.12.85	SLC	H	York	L	12-17	Donlan	Woods (4)	3114	Tennant
22.12.85	SLC	A	Dewsbury	W	26-8	Ford (2), Woods, Redfearn	Woods (5)	—	—
26.12.85	SLC	H	Halifax	L	12-22	Mallinder (2)	Woods (2)	6984	Lindop
1.1.86	SLC	H	Castleford	W	26-18	Mallinder (2), Jasiewicz, Ford	Woods (5)	3568	Spencer
12.1.86	SLC	H	Hull	W	18-8	Lumby, Godfrey	Woods (5)	3568	Hodgson
15.1.86	SLC	A	Salford	L	8-9	Jackson	Woods (2)	—	—
19.1.86	SLC	A	St. Helens	W	18-8	Jackson, Redfearn	Ford (3), Parrish (2)	—	—
2.2.86	SLC	A	York	L	8-9	Donlan	Woods (2)	—	—
22.2.86	CC(1)	H (at Leeds)	Wakefield T.	W	10-8	Lumby, Godfrey	Woods	2649	Holdsworth
9.3.86	CC(2)	H	Bramley	D	20-20	Woods, Donlan, Godfrey, Mallinder	Woods (2)	3037	Spencer
12.3.86	CC(2) Replay	A	Bramley	W	36-2	Ford (2), Simpson (2), Godfrey, Donlan, Woods, Noble	Woods (2)	—	—
16.3.86	CC(3)	A	Oldham	L	1-6	—	White (dg)	—	—
23.3.86	SLC	H	Widnes	W	40-8	Preece (2), Fleming, Lumby, Jasiewicz, Redfearn	Woods (8)	3029	Mean
26.3.86	SLC	H	Warrington	W	16-2	Mumby, Donlan	Woods (4)	2855	Carter
30.3.86	SLC	A	Leeds	W	28-8	Donlan (2), Ford, Woods, Godfrey	Woods (4)	—	—
6.4.86	SLC	A	Oldham	W	16-6	Redfearn (2)	Woods (4)	—	—
9.4.86	SLC	A	Castleford	L	10-28	Ford	Woods (3)	—	—
11.4.86	SLC	H	Leeds	D	10-10	Redfearn	Woods (3)	3612	Haigh
13.4.86	SLC	H	Featherstone R.	L	4-8	—	Woods (2)	3273	Berry
16.4.86	SLC	A	Halifax	L	2-8	—	Woods	—	—
18.4.86	SLC	A	Wigan	L	10-42	Woods, Preece	Woods	—	—
22.4.86	SLC	H	Salford	W	18-8	Ford (2)	Woods (5)	2221	Haigh

BRAMLEY

Ground:	McLaren Field
Colours:	Amber jerseys with black collar, cuffs and V, black shorts
First Season:	1896-97
Nickname:	Villagers
Chairman:	Ron Teeman
Secretary:	Linda Thomas
Coach:	Ken Loxton (Apr-Dec 1985) Allan Agar (Dec 1985-)
Honours:	**BBC2 Floodlit Trophy** Winners, 1973-74
Records:	Attendance: 12,600 v. Leeds (League) 7 May, 1947 **Season** Goals: 130 by J. Wilson, 1961-62 Tries: 34 by P. Lister, 1985-86 Points: 276 by G. Langfield, 1956-57 **Match** Goals: 11 by B. Ward v. Doncaster, 1 Sep, 1974 Tries: 7 by J. Sedgewick v. Normanton, 16 Apr, 1906 Points: 28 by B. Ward v. Doncaster, 1 Sep, 1974 Highest score; 52-17 v. Doncaster, 1974-75 Highest against: 92-7 v. Australia, 1921-22

1985-86 PLAYERS' SUMMARY

	App	Tries	Goals	Dr	Pts
Agar, Allan	2 + 2	—	—	—	—
Bamford, Mick	1 + 1	—	—	—	—
Barraclough, Glen	7 + 3	1	—	—	4
Beale, Graham	23 + 5	2	—	—	8
Bibb, Trevor	31	7	—	—	28
Bowman, Chris	22	13	—	—	52
Box, Harold	8	1	—	1	5
Bullough, Dave	5 + 2	—	—	—	—
Burgess, Mark	7	—	—	—	—
Carroll, Steve	34 + 3	6	—	—	24
Clarkson, Allan	29 + 1	—	—	—	—
Clayton, Peter	11 + 2	—	—	—	—
Coen, Darren	9	1	—	—	4
Cooke, Simon	1 + 3	—	—	—	—
Coventry, Paul	3 + 4	1	—	—	4
Downs, David	5 + 2	—	—	—	—
Dyas, Dave	2 + 1	—	—	—	—
Edmondson, Stephen	8 + 4	—	—	—	—
Fletcher, Paul	23 + 2	6	—	—	24
Garforth, Tony	12 + 1	—	—	—	—
Gascoigne, Andy	1	—	—	—	—
Green, Karl	20 + 7	1	—	—	4
Hankins, Steve	20	—	—	—	—
Harrison, Karl	14	2	—	—	8
Heads, Mick	2	—	—	—	—
Hobbs, Gary	1	—	—	—	—
Kelly, Haydn	28 + 1	9	—	—	36
Kilner, Shaun	40	3	110	—	232
Lister, Peter	35 + 2	34	1	3	141
Longden, Ray	2 + 1	—	—	—	—
Lund, Steve	22	1	—	—	4
Mason, Andy	31	16	—	—	64
Micklethwaite, Karl	2	—	—	—	—
Mitchell, Paul	0 + 1	—	—	—	—
Pitchford, Steve	3	—	—	—	—
Porter, Craig	0 + 2	1	—	—	4
Pudsey, Adrian	1 + 1	—	—	—	—
Raybould, Steve	0 + 1	—	—	—	—
Robinson, Graeme	12 + 1	3	—	—	12
Shipley, Jon	19 + 3	—	—	—	—
Tansley, Ian	1	—	—	—	—
Tennant, Jeff	10 + 2	4	—	—	16
Walton, Gary	2	—	—	—	—
Whittaker, Steve	10 + 4	—	—	—	—
Trialists (3)	1 + 2	—	—	—	—
TOTALS:					
47 players		112	111	4	674

Andy Mason touching down for Yorkshire.

1985-86 MATCH ANALYSIS

Date	Competition	H/A	Opponent	Rlt	Score	Tries	Goals	Attendance	Referee
30.8.85	SD	H	Batley	W	14-13	Mason, Lister	Kilner (3)	1000	Beaumont
1.9.85	SD	A	Mansfield M.	L	18-20	Mason, Green, Harrison	Kilner (3)	—	—
4.9.85	SD	A	Doncaster	W	16-14	Lister (2), Mason	Kilner (2)	—	—
8.9.85	SD	A	Keighley	W	30-12	Kelly (2), Lister, Kilner, Bibb	Kilner (5)	—	—
15.9.85	YC(1)	H	Doncaster	W	22-10	Lister (2), Mason, Bibb	Kilner (3)	582	Fox
22.9.85	SD	A	Workington T.	L	12-34	Lister, Fletcher	Kilner, Lister	—	—
25.9.85	YC(2)	A	Hull K.R.	L	6-30	Lister	Kilner	—	—
29.9.85	SD	H	Fulham	L	24-42	Lister (2), Lund, Mason	Kilner (4)	1050	Houghton
6.10.85	SD.	A	Barrow	L	0-20	—	—	—	—
13.10.85	SD	H	Sheffield E.	W	13-10	Lister, Kelly	Kilner (2), Box (dg)	1050	Simpson
20.10.85	SD	H	Hunslet	L	14-22	Carroll, Kelly	Kilner (3)	1635	Lindop
27.10.85	SD	A	Runcorn H.	W	31-29	Kelly (2), Lister (2) Mason	Kilner (5), Lister (dg)	—	—
3.11.85	SD	H	Rochdale H.	L	10-28	Carroll, Kelly	Kilner	1356	Tennant
10.11.85	SD	A	Fulham	W	20-18	Harrison, Mason, Box	Kilner (4)	—	—
17.11.85	SD	A	Leigh	L	8-54	Bowman	Kilner (2)	—	—
24.11.85	JPS(1)	H	Oldham	L	8-46	Bibb	Kilner (2)	2738	Spencer
8.12.85	SD	H	Carlisle	W	24-10	Bowman, Carroll, Kilner, Beale	Kilner (4)	681	Loftus
15.12.85	SD	A	Blackpool B.	L	16-24	Lister, Coen, Kelly	Kilner (2)	—	—
22.12.85	SD	H	Huddersfield B.	W	16-7	Lister, Mason, Bowman	Kilner (2)	703	Mean
26.12.85	SD	H	Wakefield T.	L	6-19	Mason	Kilner	1644	Volante
1.1.86	SD	A	Wakefield T.	L	6-18	Kelly	Kilner	—	—
12.1.86	SD	A	Sheffield E.	W	14-2	Mason, Fletcher, Coventry	Kilner	—	—
19.1.86	SD	H	Rochdale H.	L	6-12	Lister	Kilner	—	—
16.2.86	CC(1)	H	Batley	W	8-6	Lister	Kilner (2)	1050	Tennant
2.3.86	SD	A	Whitehaven	W	38-14	Lister (2), Mason (2), Bowman, Carroll	Kilner (6), Lister (2dg)	—	—
9.3.86	CC(2)	A	Bradford N.	D	20-20	Bowman, Bibb, Fletcher	Kilner (4)	—	—
12.3.86	CC(2) Replay	H	Bradford N.	L	2-36	—	Kilner	3014	Spencer
16.3.86	SD	A	Batley	L	0-19	—	—	—	—
23.3.86	SD	H	Barrow	L	14-22	Lister (2), Tennant	Kilner (7)	510	Berry
31.3.86	SD	H	Keighley	W	46-10	Lister (2), Mason (2), Bibb (2), Robinson, Bowman	Kilner (7)	653	Holdsworth
6.4.86	SD	A	Hunslet	D	20-20	Fletcher, Lister	Kilner (6)	—	—
9.4.86	SD	H	Blackpool B.	W	20-15	Mason (2), Tennant	Kilner (4)	360	Simpson
13.4.86	SD	H	Doncaster	W	14-10	Lister (2), Robinson	Kilner	630	Spencer
18.4.86	SD	H	Mansfield M.	W	46-20	Bowman (3), Carroll (2), Lister (2), Fletcher	Kilner (7)	357	Beaumont
23.4.86	SD	H	Runcorn H.	W	36-22	Lister (3), Bowman (2), Tennant	Kilner (6)	373	Campbell
27.4.86	SD	H	Workington T.	W	32-22	Lister (2), Bibb, Bowman, Tennant	Kilner (6)	675	Kendrew
30.4.86	SD	A	Huddersfield B.	L	12-38	Bowman, Robinson	Kilner (2)	—	—
5.5.86	SD	A	Carlisle	L	10-14	Beale, Porter	Kilner	—	—
7.5.86	SD	H	Leigh	L	8-21	Fletcher	Kilner (2)	850	Kershaw
11.5.86	SD	H	Whitehaven	W	14-8	Kilner, Lister, Barraclough	Kilner	560	Houghton

CARLISLE

Ground: Brunton Park
Colours: Blue jerseys with red and white band, white shorts
First Season: 1981-82. A Carlisle City team entered the League in 1928-29 but withdrew after 10 matches, winning one
Chairman: Don McDowell
Coach: John Atkinson (Feb 1983-Feb 1986)
Alan Kellett (Feb-May 1986)
Records: Attendance: 5,903 v. Workington T. (Div. 2) 6 Sep, 1981
Season
Goals: 113 by S. Ferres, 1981-82
Tries: 25 by M. Morgan, 1981-82; G. Peacham, 1984-85
Points: 242 by S. Ferres, 1981-82
Match
Goals: 9 by D. Carroll v. Mansfield M., 16 Mar, 1986
Tries: No player has scored more than 3
Points: 21 by D. Carroll v. Mansfield M., 16 Mar, 1986 and v. Fulham, 2 May, 1986
Highest score: 47-18 v Fulham, 1984-85.
Highest against: 72-8 v. St. Helens, 1985-86

1985-86 PLAYERS' SUMMARY

	App	Tries	Goals	Dr	Pts
Armstrong, Colin	17 + 3	—	2	1	5
Binder, Tony	27 + 2	1	—	—	4
Bishop, Gary	4	—	—	1	1
Bond, Gary	6	—	—	—	—
Bowness, Chris	13	5	—	—	20
Carroll, Dean	22	8	61	8	162
Crowther, Ian	4	—	—	—	—
Doyle, Mark	24	7	—	—	28
Elliott, David	11 + 2	1	1	—	6
Graham, John	2 + 3	—	—	—	—
Huddart, Milton	15	3	—	2	14
Kirkby, Steve	15 + 1	4	—	—	16
Langton, Steve	28 + 1	10	—	—	40
Lithgow, Paul	5 + 2	—	—	—	—
Loynes, Dean	18 + 1	2	—	—	8
Lucas, Maurice	8 + 3	2	—	—	8
McAvoy, Brian	10	2	—	—	8
McMullen, Alan	9 + 11	3	—	—	12
Miller, Craig	4	1	—	—	4
Moll, David	0 + 1	—	—	—	—
O'Byrne, Mick	5	—	—	—	—
Pape, Kevin	38	20	—	—	80
Peacham, Gary	29 + 1	20	—	—	80
Peacham, Tony	17 + 2	2	—	—	8
Phillips, Graeme	2 + 4	—	—	—	—
Portz, Karl	35	—	—	—	—
Robinson, Graeme	13 + 3	—	8	—	16
Robinson, Kevin	32	2	—	—	8
Sanderson, Carl	3	—	—	—	—
Scott, Tony	8 + 2	2	—	—	8
Skillen, Mark	2	—	—	—	—
Smith, David	5	2	—	—	8
Stockley, John	18	2	—	—	8
Sutton, Mick	13 + 4	—	—	1	1
Thomas, Mick	7	1	—	—	4
Thomason, Malcolm	16	5	—	—	20
Tunstall, Brian	9 + 1	2	22	—	52
TOTALS: 37 players		107	94	13	629

Carlisle's top goals and points scorer Dean Carroll receives the Slalom Lager — Daily Star Second Division Starman award from Slalom Lager director Miles Eastwood.

1985-86 MATCH ANALYSIS

Date	Com-petition	H/A	Opponent	Rlt	Score	Tries	Goals	Atten-dance	Referee
1.9.85	SD	A	Workington T.	L	11-32	G. Peacham, Langton	Armstrong (1, 1dg)	—	—
4.9.85	SD	A	Keighley	D	20-20	Pape, Huddart, Langton	G. Robinson (4)	—	—
8.9.85	SD	H	Rochdale H.	L	10-16	Huddart, McMullen	Armstrong	730	McDonald
15.9.85	LC(1)	A	St. Helens	L	8-72	Langton, Pape	—	—	—
29.9.85	SD	A	Whitehaven	L	10-17	Doyle, Thomason	Tunstall	—	—
2.10.85	SD	H	Runcorn H.	W	12-2	Thomason, A. Peacham	Tunstall (2)	482	Kendrew
6.10.85	SD	H	Leigh	L	9-20	G. Peacham	Tunstall (2), Huddart (dg)	928	Hodgson
13.10.85	SD	A	Wakefield T.	L	10-36	G. Peacham	Tunstall (3)	—	—
27.10.85	SD	H	Blackpool B.	L	32-33	Tunstall, Langton, Thomason, Lucas, G. Peacham	Tunstall (6)	628	Whitfield
3.11.85	SD	H	Barrow	L	13-36	Pape, Thomas	Tunstall (2), Huddart (dg)	915	Holdsworth
10.11.85	JPS(P)	H	Rochdale H.	L	6-24	Scott	Tunstall	752	Walker
13.11.85	SD	A	Hunslet	W	24-14	G. Peacham (3), Tunstall	Tunstall (4)	—	—
17.11.85	SD	H	Batley	L	8-16	Huddart	Tunstall, G. Robinson	734	Croft
8.12.85	SD	A	Bramley	L	10-24	Pape, Doyle	G. Robinson	—	—
15.12.85	SD	H	Fulham	L	13-14	Pape, Lucas	G. Robinson (2), Bishop (dg)	591	Berry
22.12.85	SD	A	Leigh	L	12-58	McMullen, K. Robinson	Carroll (2)	—	—
26.12.85	SD	A	Blackpool B.	L	0-54	—	—	—	—
12.1.86	SD	A	Huddersfield B.	W	16-8	G. Peacham, Pape, Doyle	Carroll (2)	—	—
19.1.86	SD	A	Barrow	L	8-20	Binder	Carroll (2)	—	—
31.1.86	CC(P)	H	Mansfield M.	W	20-14	G. Peacham, Elliott, Langton, Doyle	Carroll (2)	482	Kershaw
2.2.86	SD	A	Doncaster	L	4-16	Pape	—	—	—
9.2.86	CC(1)	A	Oldham (at Oldham FC)	L	10-56	G. Peacham, Pape	Elliott	—	—
12.3.86	SD	H	Workington T.	W	32-20	G. Peacham (3), Langton (2), Pape	Carroll (4)	600	Smith
16.3.86	SD	H	Mansfield M.	W	45-13	Smith (2), Doyle (2), Kirkby, Carroll, Pape	Carroll (8, 1dg)	516	Houghton
19.3.86	SD	H	Sheffield E.	W	15-9	Carroll, Loynes	Carroll (3, 1dg)	530	Croft
23.3.86	SD	H	Keighley	W	17-2	Carroll, Doyle	Carroll (3, 2dg), Sutton (dg)	675	Fox
27.3.86	SD	A	Runcorn H.	L	10-18	Carroll, G. Peacham	Carroll	—	—
6.4.86	SD	A	Rochdale H.	L	20-24	Thomason (2), Pape	Carroll (4)	—	—
11.4.86	SD	A	Mansfield M.	W	26-14	G. Peacham (3), Pape, McMullen	Carroll (3)	—	—
15.4.86	SD	H	Whitehaven	W	7-0	Scott	Carroll (1, 1dg)	1161	Tickle
17.4.86	SD	A	Batley	D	8-8	Bowness	Carroll (2)	—	—
23.4.86	SD	H	Doncaster	W	32-26	Pape (3), G. Peacham (2), K. Robinson	Carroll (4)	336	Haigh
27.4.86	SD	A	Sheffield	W	23-12	McAvoy (2), Pape, Langton	Carroll (3, 1dg)	—	—
2.5.86	SD	A	Fulham	W	41-22	Carroll (2), Stockley (2), Pape, A. Peacham, Bowness	Carroll (6, 1dg)	—	—
5.5.86	SD	H	Bramley	W	14-10	Langton, G. Peacham, Pape	Carroll	459	McDonald
7.5.86	SD	H	Wakefield T.	L	14-44	Bowness (2), Kirkby	Carroll	450	McDonald
9.5.86	SD	H	Huddersfield B.	W	31-16	Kirkby (2), Bowness, Carroll, Loynes	Carroll (5, 1dg)	400	Barrett (Pr)
11.5.86	SD	H	Hunslet	W	28-8	Pape (2), Langton, Miller, Carroll	Carroll (4)	372	Whitfield

CASTLEFORD

Ground:	Wheldon Road
Colours:	Yellow jerseys with black collar panels, black shorts
First Season:	1926-27. There was also a Castleford team from 1896-97 to 1905-06, inclusive
Nickname:	Glassblowers
Chairman:	David Poulter
Secretary:	Denise Cackett
Coach:	Mal Reilly (Dec 1974-)
Honours:	**Championship** Beaten finalists, 1938-39, 1968-69
	Challenge Cup Winners, 1934-35, 1968-69, 1969-70, 1985-86
	Yorkshire League Winners, 1932-33, 1938-39, 1964-65
	Yorkshire Cup Winners, 1977-78, 1981-82
	Beaten finalists, 1948-49, 1950-51, 1968-69, 1971-72, 1983-84, 1985-86
	Eastern Division Championship Beaten finalists, 1963-64
	BBC2 Floodlit Trophy Winners, 1965-66, 1966-67, 1967-68, 1976-77
	John Player Trophy Winners, 1976-77
	Premiership Beaten finalists, 1983-84
Records:	Attendance: 25,449 v. Hunslet (RL Cup) 3 Mar, 1935
	Season
	Goals: 158 by S. Lloyd, 1976-77
	Tries: 36 by K. Howe, 1963-64
	Points: 334 by R. Beardmore, 1983-84
	Match
	Goals: 17 by S. Lloyd v. Millom, 16 Sep, 1973

Tries: 5 by D. Foster v. Hunslet, 10 Nov, 1972; J. Joyner v. Millom, 16 Sep, 1973; S. Fenton v. Dewsbury, 27 Jan, 1978; I. French v. Hunslet, 9 Feb, 1986
Points: 43 by S. Lloyd v. Millom, 16 Sep, 1973
Highest score: 88-5 v. Millom, 1973-74
Highest against: 62-12 v. St. Helens, 1985-86

1985-86 PLAYERS' SUMMARY

	App	Tries	Goals	Dr	Pts
Beardmore, Bob	38	13	64	1	181
Beardmore, Kevin	15 + 1	9	—	—	36
Chapman, Chris	13 + 1	6	—	—	24
Diamond, Steve	13 + 3	1	6	1	17
England, Keith	33	5	—	—	20
Fenton, Steve	1	—	—	—	—
Fletcher, Ian	2 + 13	—	—	—	—
French, Ian	20	11	—	—	44
Gill, Steve	1	—	—	—	—
Greatbatch, Neil	22 + 2	6	—	—	24
Hartley, Ian	2	—	—	—	—
Higgins, Barry	3	—	—	—	—
Horton, Stuart	28 + 1	6	—	—	24
Hyde, Gary	25 + 1	9	1	—	38
Johnson, Barry	33 + 2	3	—	—	12
Jones, Keith	2 + 1	—	2	—	4
Joyner, John	29 + 2	6	—	—	24
Kear, John	3 + 1	1	—	—	4
Ketteridge, Martin	37 + 3	2	61	—	130
Lord, Gary	14 + 7	1	—	—	4
Marchant, Tony	37	21	—	—	84
Mountain, Dean	11 + 13	3	—	—	12
Orum, Ian	2	—	—	—	—
Payne, Phil	15	3	—	—	12
Plange, David	35 + 1	17	—	—	68
Reilly, Malcolm	1	—	—	—	—
Roockley, David	29 + 5	13	1	—	54
Sandy, Jamie	17 + 1	4	—	—	16
Shillito, Alan	13 + 2	1	—	—	4
Southernwood, Roy	3 + 5	—	—	—	—
Spears, Tony	15 + 6	6	—	—	24
Ward, Kevin	34	3	—	—	12
TOTALS:					
32 players		150	135	2	872

1985-86 MATCH ANALYSIS

Date	Competition	H/A	Opponent	Rlt	Score	Tries	Goals	Attendance	Referee
1.9.85	SLC	A	Wigan	W	12-10	Plange (2), Roockley	—	—	—
4.9.85	YC(P)	H	Sheffield E.	W	38-6	Plange (2), Marchant (2), Joyner, Hyde, R. Beardmore	R. Beardmore (5)	1748	Volante
8.9.85	SLC	H	Hull	W	22-14	Diamond, Joyner, Marchant, Horton	R. Beardmore (3)	4841	Campbell

(continued)

MATCH ANALYSIS (continued)

15.9.85	YC(1)	H	Hunslet	W	60-2	Marchant (4), Chapman (4), Horton, Hyde, Plange	R. Beardmore (4), Diamond (4)	2708	Haigh
18.9.85	SLC	H	York	W	34-6	Hyde (2), Horton, Johnson, Joyner, Roockley	R. Beardmore (5)	2758	Fox
22.9.85	SLC	A	Warrington	L	16-24	R. Beardmore, Plange	R. Beardmore (4)	—	—
25.9.85	YC(2)	A	Halifax	W	24-4	Hyde, Marchant, Spears, Roockley	R. Beardmore (4)	—	—
29.9.85	SLC	H	Swinton	W	28-16	Roockley (2), Marchant, Chapman, K. Beardmore	R. Beardmore (4)	3026	Lindop
2.10.85	YC(SF)	A	Leeds	W	14-10	Spears (2), Plange	R. Beardmore	—	—
6.10.85	SLC	A	Halifax	L	8-14	Ward	R. Beardmore (2)	—	—
13.10.85	SLC	H	St. Helens	W	32-18	K. Beardmore (2), R. Beardmore, French	R. Beardmore (8)	4512	Smith
20.10.85	SLC	A	Oldham	L	22-46	Sandy (2), Hyde	R. Beardmore (5)	—	—
27.10.85	YC(F)	Leeds	Hull K.R.	L	18-22	Marchant (2), R. Beardmore	R. Beardmore (2), Diamond	(12686)	Campbell
3.11.85	SLC	A	Dewsbury	W	30-12	K. Beardmore, Marchant, Spears, Sandy, Lord	R. Beardmore (5)	—	—
10.11.85	JPS(P)	A	West Hull	W	24-10	K. Beardmore, French, Marchant, Hyde	R. Beardmore (4)	—	—
14.11.85	SLC	H	Warrington	L	20-26	Greatbatch, Spears, French, Horton	R. Beardmore (2)	2661	Lindop
24.11.85	JPS(1)	A	York	L	10-12	Spears	R. Beardmore (2), Diamond	—	—
11.12.85	SLC	H	Dewsbury	W	16-12	Ward, Marchant, England	R. Beardmore (2)	2058	Kershaw
15.12.85	SLC	A	Salford	L	8-9	England	Ketteridge (2)	—	—
22.12.85	SLC	H	Leeds	L	18-26	Plange (2)	Ketteridge (5)	4005	Allatt
1.1.86	SLC	A	Bradford N.	L	18-26	Plange, Ward, Roockley	Ketteridge (3)	—	—
12.1.86	SLC	A	Swinton	L	10-12	French, Marchant	Ketteridge	—	—
19.1.86	SLC	H	Oldham	W	28-4	French, Roockley, Marchant, R. Beardmore	Ketteridge (6)	3806	Whitfield
26.1.86	SLC	A	Widnes	L	5-9	Kear	Diamond (dg)	—	—
29.1.86	SLC	A	York	L	14-18	Mountain, Plange, R. Beardmore	R. Beardmore	—	—
2.2.86	SLC	A	Hull	L	12-34	Roockley, England	Ketteridge (2)	—	—
9.2.86	CC(1)	A	Hunslet	W	60-6	French (5), Greatbach (2), Plange, Marchant, England, R. Beardmore	Ketteridge (8)	—	—
5.3.86	SLC	A	Featherstone R.	L	6-21	Greatbatch	Ketteridge	—	—
9.3.86	CC(2)	A	Barrow	W	30-6	Payne (2), Marchant, French, R. Beardmore	Ketteridge (5)	—	—
16.3.86	CC(3)	A	Wigan	W	10-2	Joyner, Roockley	Ketteridge	—	—
22.3.86	CC(SF)	Wigan	Oldham	W	18-7	R. Beardmore (2), Marchant	Ketteridge (3)	(12430)	Campbell
24.3.86	SLC	A	Leeds	L	12-18	Johnson, Roockley	Ketteridge, R. Beardmore	—	—
28.3.86	SLC	H	Halifax	L	14-36	Hyde, Roockley, Payne	Jones	5965	Tickle
31.3.86	SLC	H	Featherstone R.	W	24-16	Joyner (2), Mountain, R. Beardmore	Ketteridge (4)	4659	Whitfield
6.4.86	SLC	A	Hull K.R.	L	8-22	Greatbatch, Plange	—	—	—
9.4.86	SLC	H	Bradford N.	W	28-10	Mountain, Horton, Roockley, Plange	Ketteridge (6)	3011	Allatt
11.4.86	SLC	H	Hull K.R.	W	36-18	K. Beardmore (2), Ketteridge (2), Shillito, Roockley, Marchant	Ketteridge (4)	3389	Campbell
13.4.86	SLC	H	Wigan	L	12-14	K. Beardmore, Chapman	Hyde, Jones	5422	Kershaw
10.4.86	SLC	A	St. Helens	L	12-62	Plange (2)	Ketteridge, Roockley	—	—
20.4.86	SLC	H	Salford	W	30-16	England, R. Beardmore, K. Beardmore, Hyde, Plange	Ketteridge (5)	2947	Hodgson
22.4.86	SLC	H	Widnes	D	16-16	Johnson, Greatbatch, Horton	Ketteridge (2)	2468	Volante
3.5.86	CC(F)	Wembley	Hull K.R.	W	15-14	Marchant, R. Beardmore, Sandy	Ketteridge, R. Beardmore (dg)	(82134)	Whitfield

39

DEWSBURY

Ground: Crown Flatt
Colours: Red, amber and black jerseys, white shorts
First Season: 1901-02
Chairman: Roy Harter
Secretary: Geoff Parrish
Coach: Jack Addy (Feb 1984-)
Honours: **Championship** Winners, 1972-73
Beaten finalists, 1946-47
Division Two Champions, 1904-05
Challenge Cup Winners, 1911-12, 1942-43
Beaten finalists, 1928-29
Yorkshire League Winners, 1946-47
Yorkshire Cup Winners, 1925-26, 1927-28, 1942-43
Beaten finalists, 1918-19, 1921-22, 1940-41, 1972-73
BBC2 Floodlit Trophy Beaten finalists, 1975-76
War League Championship Winners, 1941-42. (1942-43 won final but championship declared null and void because Dewsbury played an ineligible player). Beaten finalists, 1943-44
Records: Attendance: 26,584 v. Halifax (Yorkshire Cup) 30 Oct, 1920
Season
Goals: 145 by N. Stephenson, 1972-73
Tries: 40 by D. Thomas, 1906-07
Points: 368 by N. Stephenson, 1972-73
Match
Goals: 10 by J. Ledgard v. Yorkshire Amateurs, 13 Sep, 1947; N. Stephenson v. Blackpool B, 28 Aug, 1972
Tries: 8 by D. Thomas v. Liverpool C, 13 Apr, 1907
Points: 29 by J. Lyman v. Hull, 22 Apr, 1919
Highest score: 72-0 v. Doncaster, 1984-85
Highest against: 62-5 v. Hull, 1957-58; 62-2 v. Halifax, 1957-58

1985-86 PLAYERS' SUMMARY

	App	Tries	Goals	Dr	Pts
Bailey, Dennis	5	—	—	—	—
Broxholme, Paul	19 + 4	—	—	—	—
Busfield, David	9 + 3	—	—	—	—
Clarke, Phil	1	—	—	—	—
Collins, Mick	23 + 3	5	—	—	20
Cooper, Andy	10 + 3	—	—	—	—
Diskin, Tony	22 + 4	1	—	—	4
Dunford, Shaun	19	1	11	—	26
Garner, Peter	13 + 1	—	—	—	—
Haynes, Les	3 + 4	1	—	—	4
Howells, Steve	10 + 4	—	—	—	—
Howley, Patrick	4	—	3	—	6
Jennings, Paul	26 + 3	4	—	—	16
Kelly, Neil	10 + 1	2	—	—	8
Keyworth, Mark	29 + 1	4	—	4	20
Leary, Geoff	12 + 4	—	—	—	—
Madden, Paul	1	—	—	—	—
Marsden, Graham	13	—	—	—	—
Mason, Keith	26 + 1	1	—	—	4
Mita, Chris	17 + 1	6	—	—	24
Moore, John	16	9	—	—	36
Ramsden, Andy	26 + 1	6	—	—	24
Richardson, Don	21 + 3	1	—	—	4
Sefuiva, David	9 + 2	4	—	—	16
Sharp, Greg	13 + 3	—	—	—	—
Shuttleworth, Paul	19 + 1	2	9	—	26
Squires, Chris	14 + 4	3	—	—	12
Stephenson, Nigel	22 + 7	4	—	—	16
Toole, Timothy	1	—	—	—	—
Vasey, Chris	21 + 1	4	36	—	88
Womersley, Shaun	8 + 2	—	—	—	—
TOTALS:					
31 players		58	59	4	354

Veteran Nigel Stephenson, four tries in 29 appearances.

1985-86 MATCH ANALYSIS

Date	Competition	H/A	Opponent	Rlt	Score	Tries	Goals	Attendance	Referee
1.9.85	SLC	H	Leeds	L	13-22	Collins, Stephenson	Shuttleworth (2), Keyworth (dg)	3986	Smith
4.9.85	SLC	A	Hull K.R.	L	0-42	—	—	—	—
8.9.85	SLC	H	Swinton	W	20-12	Mason, Ramsden, Jennings	Shuttleworth (4)	1472	Beaumont
15.9.85	YC(1)	A	Batley	W	14-10	Kelly (2), Jennings	Shuttleworth	—	—
18.9.85	SLC	A	Hull	L	6-48	Jennings	Shuttleworth	—	—
22.9.85	SLC	A	Halifax	W	16-12	Ramsden (2), Keyworth	Shuttleworth, Dunford	—	—
25.9.85	YC(2)	H	Leeds	L	2-48	—	Dunford	3700	Kershaw
29.9.85	SLC	H	Featherstone R.	L	20-23	Collins (2), Keyworth, Stephenson	Dunford (2)	1750	McDonald
2.10.85	SLC	A	Bradford N.	W.	10-8	Squires, Vasey	Vasey	—	—
13.10.85	SLC	H	Widnes	L	15-18	Collins, Mita	Vasey (3), Keyworth (dg)	1713	Hale (NZ)
20.10.85	SLC	A	Wigan	L	8-58	Mita	Vasey (2)	—	—
3.11.85	SLC	H	Castleford	L	12-30	Mita, Ramsden	Vasey (2)	1990	Whitfield
10.11.85	SLC	A	St. Helens	L	6-24	Dunford	Vasey	—	—
17.11.85	SLC	H	Oldham	L	6-37	Stephenson	Dunford	2496	Houghton
24.11.85	JPS(1)	A	St. Helens	L	6-42	Ramsden	Vasey	—	—
11.12.85	SLC	A	Castleford	L	12-16	Keyworth (2)	Vasey (2)	—	—
15.12.85	SLC	A	Oldham	L	14-48	Sefuiva, Haynes	Vasey (3)	—	—
22.12.85	SLC	H	Bradford N.	L	8-26	Jennings	Vasey (2)	2329	Loftus
26.12.85	SLC	A	Leeds	L	8-28	Mita	Vasey (2)	—	—
1.1.86	SLC	H	Salford	W	12-10	Moore, Sefuiva	Vasey (2)	1006	Tennant
12.1.86	SLC	H	Halifax	L	10-32	Sefuiva (2)	Vasey	3597	Carter
19.1.86	SLC	H	Warrington	L	12-16	Moore, Collins	Vasey (2)	1100	Kershaw
24.2.86	CC(1)	H	St. Helens (at Leeds)	L	19-22	Moore (2), Vasey	Vasey (3), Keyworth (dg)	1948	Mean
9.3.86	SLC	H	Hull	L	12-30	Moore, Vasey	Vasey (2)	1411	Fox
12.3.86	SLC	A	Featherstone R.	L	1-24	—	Keyworth (dg)	—	—
18.3.86	SLC	H	Wigan	L	4-42	Mita	—	1288	Hodgson
23.3.86	SLC	H	St. Helens	L	12-18	Mita, Squires	Vasey (2)	1066	Fox
28.3.86	SLC	A	Salford	L	8-36	Shuttleworth	Vasey (2)	—	—
31.3.86	SLC	H	Hull K.R.	L	14-18	Vasey, Squires	Vasey (3)	1070	Lindop
6.4.86	SLC	A	Warrington	L	0-52	—	—	—	—
13.4.86	SLC	A	York	L	18-39	Stephenson, Shuttleworth, Richardson	Dunford (2), Howley	—	—
16.4.86	SLC	A	Widnes	L	2-24	—	Howley	—	—
20.4.86	SLC	H	York	W	18-15	Moore (3)	Dunford (2), Howley	1011	Whitfield
22.4.86	SLC	A	Swinton	L	16-39	Moore, Diskin, Ramsden	Dunford (2)	—	—

41

DONCASTER

Ground:	Tatters Field
Colours:	Red jerseys, white shorts
First Season:	1951-52
Nickname:	Dons
Chairman:	John Desmond
Coach:	John Sheridan (June 1984-)
Records:	Attendance: 4,793 v. Wakefield T. (League) 7 Apr, 1962. There was an attendance of 10,000 for a Challenge Cup tie against Bradford N. at York Road Stadium on 16 Feb, 1952

Season

Goals: 118 by D. Noble, 1985-86
Tries: 20 by N. Turner, 1985-86
Points: 242 by D. Noble, 1985-86

Match

Goals: 9 by D. Towle v. York, 9 Sep, 1967
Tries: 4 by V. Grace v. Rochdale H, 4 Oct, 1952; B. Tasker v. Leeds, 26 Oct, 1963; J. Buckton v. Rochdale H., 30 Aug, 1981
Points: 18 by D. Towle v. York, 9 Sep, 1967; I. Fortis v. Blackpool B., 5 Sep, 1970
Highest score: 43-5 v. Batley, 1964-65
Highest against: 75-3 v. Leigh, 1975-76

1985-86 PLAYERS' SUMMARY

	App	Tries	Goals	Dr	Pts
Barratt, Dale	5 + 2	—	—	—	—
Burch, Brian	3 + 2	1	—	—	4
Capless, Graham	10	1	—	—	4
Carr, Alan	39	4	—	—	16
Ellis, David	1 + 1	—	—	—	—
Ford, Brian	2	—	—	—	—
Foster, Ben	6 + 4	—	—	—	—
Freeman, Laurence	18	2	—	—	8
Gibbon, Mark	25 + 3	6	—	—	24
Green, John	24	2	—	—	8
Hale, Gary	4	—	—	—	—
Hardy, Alan	6 + 2	1	—	—	4
Harrison, Peter	23 + 4	2	—	—	8
Hutchinson, Alan	31 + 3	11	2	—	48
Jones, Kevin	29 + 1	16	4	—	72
Jowett, Brian	1 + 2	—	—	—	—
Moore, Gary	19 + 7	2	—	—	8
Morris, Dean	5 + 1	1	—	—	4
Morris, Geoff	34	8	—	2	34
Newton, Derek	1 + 2	—	—	—	—
Noble, David	37 + 2	3	112	6	242
O'Toole, Tony	4 + 4	1	—	—	4
Parkhouse, Kevin	38	19	—	—	76
Pennant, Audley	36	5	—	—	20
Pflaster, George	0 + 2	—	—	—	—
Pickett, John	16 + 7	—	—	—	—
Roache, Mark	29 + 1	3	—	—	12
Robinson, Kevin	6 + 7	—	—	—	—
Timson, Andy	4	2	—	—	8
Turner, Neil	35	20	—	—	80
Turner, Paul	4	—	—	—	—
Turner, Richard	2	—	—	3	—
Waite, Kevin	9	3	—	3	15
Walker, Mark	8 + 2	—	—	—	—
Welburn, Chris	2	—	—	—	—
Wilson, Ray	1	—	—	—	—
Trialist	3	2	—	—	8
TOTALS:					
37 players		115	118	11	707

1985-86 MATCH ANALYSIS

Date	Competition	H/A	Opponent	Rlt	Score	Tries	Goals	Attendance	Referee
1.9.85	SD	A	Sheffield E.	W	20-16	Noble, G. Morris, Pennant	Noble (3, 1dg), Waite (dg)	—	—
4.9.85	SD	H	Bramley	L	14-16	Parkhouse (2), Waite	Noble	199	Holdsworth
8.9.85	SD	H	Fulham	L	11-14	Parkhouse, Moore	Noble, Waite (dg)	282	Smith
15.9.85	YC(1)	A	Bramley	L	10-22	Burch	Noble (3)	—	—
18.9.85	SD	A	Barrow	L	8-30	Pennant	Noble (2)	—	—
22.9.85	SD	A	Rochdale H.	L	13-52	Capless, Waite	Hutchinson (2), Waite (dg)	—	—
29.9.85	SD	H	Mansfield M.	W	21-6	Parkhouse, Hutchinson, D. Morris	Noble (4, 1dg)	376	Kershaw
6.10.85	SD	A	Hunslet	L	16-40	G. Morris, Turner	Noble (4)	—	—
13.10.85	SD	H	Blackpool B.	L	20-30	Gibbon (2), Roache	Noble (4)	340	Tennant
27.10.85	SD	H	Keighley	L	17-24	Waite, Freeman, Turner	Noble (2, 1dg)	297	Beaumont
3.11.85	SD	A	Wakefield T.	L	18-28	Parkhouse, Turner, Harrison	Noble (3)	—	—
10.11.85	SD	H	Huddersfield B.	W	24-16	Turner (2), G. Morris, Hutchinson	Noble (4)	379	Loftus
17.11.85	SD	A	Blackpool B.	L	13-30	Pennant, Turner	Noble (2, 1dg)	—	—
24.11.85	JPS(1)	H	Runcorn H.	W	22-20	Gibbon (2), Parkhouse, Harrison	Noble (2, 1dg), G. Morris (dg)	375	McDonald
1.12.85	JPS(2)	A	St. Helens	L	20-36	Parkhouse, Hutchinson, Gibbon	Noble (4)	—	—
8.12.85	SD	H	Runcorn H.		16-10	Turner, Carr, Freeman	Noble (2)	334	Volante
					(abandoned 65 min)				
15.12.85	SD	A	Huddersfield B.	W	12-4	Parkhouse, Jones	Noble (2)	—	—
22.12.85	SD	H	Wakefield T.	L	8-10	Parkhouse	Noble (2)	1054	Tickle
1.1.86	SD	A	Mansfield M.	W	21-20	Hutchinson, Pennant, Gibbon	Noble (4), G. Morris (dg)	—	—
12.1.86	SD	H	Workington T.	W	32-5	Jones (2), Green, Noble, Carr, Hutchinson	Noble (4)	288	Fox
19.1.86	SD	A	Runcorn H.	L	8-12	Jones	Noble (2)	—	—
2.2.86	SD	H	Carlisle	W	16-4	Jones (2), Turner	Jones (2)	308	Irwin (NZ)
9.2.86	CC(1)	H	Salford	W	18-12	Parkhouse (2), Turner	Noble (3)	842	Kendrew
23.2.86	CC(2)	H	Leeds	L	10-28	Jones, Parkhouse	Noble	7636	Fox
			(at Leeds)						
2.3.86	SD	A	Keighley	W	18-12	Noble, Hutchinson	Noble (5)	—	—
9.3.86	SD	H	Rochdale H.	W	14-12	Jones, O'Toole	Noble (3)	926	Haigh
16.3.86	SD	A	Workington T.	W	26-22	Turner (2), Jones, Moore	Noble (5)	—	—
23.3.86	SD	H	Sheffield E.	L	18-28	Parkhouse, Turner, Carr	Noble (3)	1419	Carter
28.3.86	SD	A	Batley	D	16-16	Jones, Green, G. Morris	Noble (2)	—	—
31.3.86	SD	H	Batley	L	14-16	Carr	Noble (5)	1111	Mean
6.4.86	SD	A	Fulham	W	14-12	Turner, G. Morris	Noble (3)	—	—
9.4.86	SD	H	Barrow	W	18-10	Jones, G. Morris, Parkhouse	Noble (3)	570	Houghton
13.4.86	SD	A	Bramley	L	10-14	Turner, Jones	Noble	—	—
20.4.86	SD	H	Whitehaven	W	14-13	Parkhouse (2), G. Morris	Noble	864	Croft
23.4.86	SD	A	Carlisle	L	26-32	Timson, Hutchinson, Turner, Hardy	Noble (5)	—	—
27.4.86	SD	H	Leigh	L	12-20	Parkhouse, Jones	Noble (2)	1715	Lindop
30.4.86	SD	A	Whitehaven	W	27-22	Turner (3), Hutchinson, Pennant	Noble (3, 1dg)	—	—
6.5.86	SD	H	Hunslet	W	42-10	Hutchinson (3), Parkhouse (2), Jones (2)	Noble (7)	735	Allatt
9.5.86	SD	H	Runcorn H.	W	26-10	Roache (2), Timson, Jones, Turner	Jones (2), Noble	837	Mosley
11.5.86	SD	A	Leigh	L	24-46	Trialist (2), Turner, G. Morris	Noble (4)	—	—

FEATHERSTONE ROVERS

Ground:	Post Office Road
Colours:	Blue and white hooped jerseys, blue shorts
First Season:	1921-22
Nickname:	Colliers
Chairman:	Bob Ashby
Secretary:	Terry Jones
Coach:	Allan Agar (Dec 1982-Oct 1985) George Pieniazek (Nov 1985-)
Honours:	**Challenge Cup** Winners, 1966-67, 1972-73, 1982-83 Runners-up, 1951-52, 1973-74 **Championship** Beaten finalists, 1927-28 **Division One** Champions, 1976-77 **Division Two** Champions, 1979-80 **Yorkshire Cup** Winners, 1939-40, 1959-60 Beaten finalists, 1928-29, 1963-64, 1966-67, 1969-70, 1970-71, 1976-77, 1977-78 **Captain Morgan Trophy** Beaten finalists, 1973-74
Records:	Attendance: 17,531 v. St. Helens (RL Cup) 21 Mar, 1959 **Season** Goals: 163 by S. Quinn, 1979-80 Tries: 31 by C. Woolford, 1958-59 Points: 375 by S. Quinn, 1979-80 **Match** Goals: 12 by D. Fox v. Stanningley, 8 Feb, 1964 Tries: 6 by M. Smith v. Doncaster, 13 Apr, 1968 Points: 29 by S. Quinn v. Doncaster, 4 Nov, 1979 Highest score: 65-5 v. Whitehaven, 1970-71 Highest against: 70-2 v. Halifax, 1940-41

1985-86 PLAYERS' SUMMARY

	App	Tries	Goals	Dr	Pts
Banks, Alan	34	6	—	—	24
Barker, Alan	3 + 2	—	—	—	—
Barker, Nigel	31 + 3	5	—	—	20
Bell, Keith	23	2	—	12	20
Bibb, Christopher	0 + 2	—	—	—	—
Burgoyne, Patrick	8	—	—	—	—
Campbell, Mark	7 + 2	—	—	—	—
Chappell, Christopher	6	—	—	—	—
Clarkson, Peter	11 + 9	2	—	—	8
Clawson, Neil	21 + 7	4	—	—	16
Dakin, Alan	1	—	—	—	—
Dorrough, Scott	0 + 2	—	—	—	—
Downs, Craig	0 + 1	—	—	—	—
Fox, Deryck	31	11	13	3	73
Gibbins, Mick	23 + 1	—	—	—	—
Gilbert, John	14	3	—	—	12
Hale, Christopher	1	—	—	—	—
Harrison, Karl	16	2	—	—	8
Heselwood, David	15	2	—	—	8
Hird, Adrian	1	—	—	—	—
Hopkins, Calvin	23 + 1	6	—	—	24
Hunter, John	0 + 1	—	—	—	—
Kellett, Brian	2 + 1	—	—	—	—
Kelly, Neil	1 + 5	—	—	—	—
Langton, Terry	2	—	—	—	—
Lyman, Paul	28	18	—	—	72
Mackintosh, Andy	6 + 3	—	—	—	—
Marsh, Richard	8 + 2	—	—	—	—
Massa, Mark	3	—	—	—	—
Nicholson, Tony	2 + 1	—	—	—	4
Pethybridge, Rod	7	1	—	—	4
Quinn, Steve	24	2	54	1	117
Roiall, Mark	3 + 4	1	—	—	4
Siddall, Gary	6 + 2	1	—	—	4
Slater, Ian	2 + 1	—	—	—	—
Slatter, Tim	2 + 1	—	—	—	—
Smith, Peter	10	1	—	—	4
Spurr, Bob	30 + 3	1	—	—	4
Staniforth, Tony	1	—	—	—	—
Steadman, Graham	11	5	17	—	54
Waites, Brian	11	1	—	—	4
Woolford, Neil	13 + 1	—	—	—	—
Wragg, Simon	1 + 3	—	—	—	—
TOTALS: 43 players		74	84	16	480

1985-86 MATCH ANALYSIS

Date	Competition	H/A	Opponent	Rlt	Score	Tries	Goals	Attendance	Referee
1.9.85	SLC	H	Hull K.R.	L	14-27	Bell, Clawson	Quinn (3)	2884	Campbell
4.9.85	SLC	H	Bradford N.	W	15-8	Barker, Lyman	Quinn (3), Bell (dg)	1817	Lindop
8.9.85	SLC	A	Widnes	L	16-30	Barker, Lyman	Quinn (2), Fox (2)	—	—
15.9.85	YC(1)	A	York	W	26-18	Hopkins (2), Lyman, Waites	Fox (4), Bell (2dg)	—	—
22.9.85	SLC	H	Salford	L	12-16	Hopkins	Fox (4)	1897	Kershaw
25.9.85	YC(2)	H	Bradford N.	L	11-22	Fox, Banks	Quinn, Fox (dg)	2185	Holdsworth
29.9.85	SLC	A	Dewsbury	W	23-20	Hopkins, Siddall, Fox	Quinn (5), Bell (dg)	—	—
6.10.85	SLC	H	Oldham	D	14-14	Lyman, Pethybridge	Quinn (2, 1dg), Bell (dg)	2201	Smith
13.10.85	SLC	A	York	L	12-25	Clarkson, Barker	Quinn (2)	—	—
20.10.85	SLC	H	Halifax	L	10-20	Fox, Roiall	Quinn	3415	Carter
27.10.85	SLC	A	Wigan	L	0-62	—	—	—	—
3.11.85	SLC	H	St. Helens	L	12-38	Lyman	Quinn (4)	2002	Berry
10.11.85	JPS(P)	H	Warrington	L	10-14	Gilbert	Quinn (3)	1803	Beaumont
17.11.85	SLC	H	Wigan	L	12-26	Banks	Quinn (3), Fox	3421	Campbell
24.11.85	SLC	A	Swinton	L	7-14	Clawson	Quinn, Fox (dg)	—	—
22.12.85	SLC	H	Warrington	W	27-14	Gilbert, Quinn, Lyman, Hopkins	Quinn (5), Fox (dg)	1850	Holdsworth
26.12.85	SLC	A	Hull	L	12-18	Lyman, Fox	Quinn (2)	—	—
1.1.86	SLC	H	Hull	D	10-10	Lyman	Quinn (3)	2171	Volante
12.1.86	SLC	H	Leeds	L	18-20	Fox, Harrison, Gilbert	Quinn (3)	3114	Kershaw
19.1.86	SLC	A	Salford	L	12-26	Fox, Quinn	Quinn (2)	—	—
29.1.86	SLC	A	Hull K.R.	L	0-20	—	—	—	—
2.2.86	SLC	A	St. Helens	L	14-44	Spurr, Heselwood, Banks	Fox	—	—
9.2.86	CC(1)	A	Widnes	L	14-18	Lyman (3)	Fox	2378	Loftus
16.2.86	SLC	A	Leeds	L	6-44	Steadman	Steadman	—	—
5.3.86	SLC	H	Castleford	W	21-6	Banks (2), Harrison	Steadman (4), Bell (dg)	2648	Lindop
12.3.86	SLC	H	Dewsbury	W	24-1	Fox (2), Lyman, Clarkson	Steadman (3), Bell (2dg)	1553	Carter
16.3.86	SLC	H	Swinton	W	14-12	Lyman, Heselwood, Hopkins	Steadman	1864	Allatt
23.3.86	SLC	H	York	W	40-10	Lyman (2), Steadman, Barker, Banks, Smith, Clawson	Steadman (6)	2042	Campbell
31.3.86	SLC	A	Castleford	L	16-24	Lyman (2), Barker	Steadman (2)	—	—
6.4.86	SLC	H	Widnes	L	15-16	Fox (2)	Quinn (3), Bell (dg)	1933	Smith
9.4.86	SLC	A	Oldham	W	16-4	Clawson, Steadman, Fox	Quinn (2)	—	—
13.4.86	SLC	A	Bradford N.	W	8-4	Steadman	Quinn, Bell (2dg)	—	—
20.4.86	SLC	A	Halifax	D	13-13	Lyman, Steadman	Quinn (2), Bell (dg)	—	—
22.4.86	SLC	A	Warrington	L	6-30	Bell	Quinn	—	—

FULHAM

Ground:	Polytechnic of Central London Stadium, Chiswick
Colours:	Black jerseys with red and white chevron, black shorts
First Season:	1980-81
Nickname:	Bears
Chairman:	Paul Faires
Secretary:	Tim Lamb
Coach:	Roy Lester (June 1984-Apr 1986) Bill Goodwin (Apr 1986-)
Honours:	**Division Two** Champions, 1982-83
Records:	Attendance: 15,013 v. Wakefield T. (RL Cup) 15 Feb, 1981 at Fulham F.C.

Season

Goals: 136 by S. Diamond, 1982-83
Tries: 27 by J. Crossley, 1982-83
Points: 308 by S. Diamond, 1982-83

Match

Goals: 8 by I. MacCorquodale v. Huddersfield, 12 Oct, 1980
Tries: No player has scored more than 3
Points: 18 by I. MacCorquodale v. Huddersfield, 12 Oct, 1980;
P. Rochford v. York, 4 Nov, 1984
Highest score: 50-5 v. Huyton, 1982-83
Highest against: 58-32 v. Warrington, 1983-84

1985-86 PLAYERS' SUMMARY

	App	Tries	Goals	Dr	Pts
Barrow, Norman	28 + 3	6	7	—	38
Briscoe, Phil	11	1	—	—	4
Bullough, David	16 + 1	9	—	—	36
Cambriani, Adrian	26	10	—	—	40
Cooper, Tony	2 + 1	—	—	—	—
Davis, Mike	21 + 1	8	—	1	33
Dearden, Alan	7	—	—	—	—
Driver, David	4 + 1	2	—	—	8
Duffy, Dan	31	7	—	—	28
Feighnan, Frank	9 + 3	3	—	—	12
Flashman, Brian	1	1	—	—	4
Garner, Steve	14 + 1	3	—	—	12
Gibson, Russ	7 + 1	4	—	2	18
Glover, Mick	24	2	—	—	8
Green, John	1	—	—	—	—
Green, Ken	9 + 7	—	—	—	—
Henley-Smith, Gary	18	8	—	—	32
Henney, Harold	19	6	—	1	25
Herdman, Martin	0 + 1	—	—	—	—
Hoare, Shaun	14 + 1	2	—	—	8
Hodson, Roger	2 + 6	—	—	—	—
Hunter, Brian	6	2	—	—	8
Johnson, Nick	0 + 1	—	—	—	—
Jones, Charlie	25 + 7	5	—	—	20
Kete, Ivan	0 + 2	—	—	—	—
Key, Andy	6 + 3	2	—	—	8
Kinsey, Tony	31 + 1	4	—	—	16
Looker, Tony	9	3	—	—	12
Matthews, Frank	8 + 4	3	—	—	12
Meachin, Colin	0 + 1	—	—	—	—
Millington, Wayne	7	—	—	—	—
Mills, Steve	27	11	—	—	44
Mordell, Bob	5 + 3	—	—	—	—
Nissen, Glen	18 + 2	4	—	—	16
Noel, Tony	1	—	—	—	—
O'Reilly, Tony	1 + 2	2	—	—	8
Platt, Alan	28	5	27	4	78
Platt, Billy	2	—	—	—	—
Rexson, Ian	5 + 2	1	—	—	4
Tinsley, Eddie	5 + 3	—	—	—	—
Townsend, Glen	2 + 2	—	—	—	—
Wilkinson, Chris	31 + 2	10	72	3	187
Worgan, Graham	0 + 1	—	—	—	—
Yates, Mal	0 + 1	—	—	—	—
TOTALS:					
44 players		124	106	11	719

1985-86 MATCH ANALYSIS

Date	Competition	H/A	Opponent	Rlt	Score	Tries	Goals	Attendance	Referee
1.9.85	SD	H	Blackpool B.	W	6-2	Wilkinson	Wilkinson	1008	Tickle
8.9.85	SD	A	Doncaster	W	14-11	Cambriani, Wilkinson, Driver	Wilkinson	—	—
15.9.85	LC(1)	A	Wigan	L	13-24	Cambriani, Garner	Wilkinson (2), Davis (dg)	—	—
18.9.85	SD	A	Wakefield T.	L	10-18	Wilkinson	Wilkinson (3)	—	—
22.9.85	SD	H	Batley	L	22-41	Henney, Platt, Wilkinson, O'Reilly	Wilkinson (3)	1036	Holdsworth
29.9.85	SD	A	Bramley	W	42-24	Kinsey (2), Barrow, Driver, Davis, Henney, Nissen	Wilkinson (7)	—	—
6.10.85	SD	H	Whitehaven	W	21-17	Mills, Duffy, Davis, O'Reilly	Wilkinson (2, 1dg)	992	Smith
13.10.85	SD	A	Rochdale H.	L	6-12	Mills	Wilkinson	—	—
20.10.85	SD	H	Wakefield T.	L	4-18	—	Wilkinson (2)	1233	Loftus
27.10.85	SD	A	Barrow	L	8-40	Key	Wilkinson (2)	—	—
3.11.85	SD	A	Leigh	L	13-42	Jones, Key	Wilkinson (2), Henney (dg)	—	—
10.11.85	SD	H	Bramley	L	18-20	Mills, Henney, Wilkinson	Wilkinson (3)	831	Haigh
17.11.85	SD	A	Workington T.	W	28-24	Henney (2), Kinsey, Davis	Wilkinson (6)	—	—
24.11.85	JPS(1)	H	Warrington	L	13-20	Mills, Duffy	Wilkinson (2, 1dg)	1493	Holdsworth
8.12.85	SD	H	Sheffield E.	W	28-21	Matthews, Bullough, Feighan, Mills	Wilkinson (6)	801	Lindop
15.12.85	SD	A	Carlisle	W	14-13	Bullough, Davis	Barrow (2), Wilkinson	—	—
22.12.85	SD	H	Runcorn H.	W	44-2	Bullough (2), Nissen (2), Cambriani, Barrow, Davis, Matthews, Henney	Barrow (3), Platt	751	Houghton
5.1.86	SD	H	Leigh	L	18-22	Duffy, Hoare, Barrow, Cambriani	Barrow	1001	Simpson
12.1.86	SD	A	Keighley	L	6-18	Cambriani	Barrow	—	—
19.1.86	SD	H	Workington T.	W	36-8	Mills (2), Platt, Davis, Cambriani, Duffy, Jones	Wilkinson (4)	815	Tennant
26.1.86	SD	H	Rochdale H.	W	26-12	Davis (2), Nissen, Garner, Cambriani	Wilkinson (3)	910	Fox
26.2.86	CC(1)	H (at Wigan)	Barrow	L	14-26	Henley-Smith, Duffy	Wilkinson (3)	1220	Smith
2.3.86	SD	A	Blackpool B.	W	22-12	Hoare, Cambriani, Matthews, Garner	Wilkinson (3)	—	—
9.3.86	SD	A	Whitehaven	L	8-18	Platt, Cambriani	—	—	—
16.3.86	SD	A	Huddersfield B.	L	8-14	Feighan	Wilkinson (2)	—	—
6.4.86	SD	H	Doncaster	L	12-14	Jones (2), Cambriani	—	902	Hodgson
16.4.86	SD	A	Runcorn H.	L	8-26	Looker, Rexson	—	—	—
20.4.86	SD	A	Sheffield E.	L	12-23	Looker, Henley-Smith	Platt (2)	—	—
23.4.86	SD	A	Hunslet	W	20-14	Gibson (2), Jones	Platt (3, 1dg), Gibson (dg)	—	—
27.4.86	SD	H	Huddersfield B.	D	26-26	Hunter, Gibson, Bullough, Duffy	Platt (4, 2dg)	803	Campbell
2.5.86	SD	H	Carlisle	L	22-41	Wilkinson, Barrow, Feighan, Henley-Smith	Wilkinson (3)	875	Beaumont
5.5.86	SD	H	Barrow	L	18-50	Kinsey, Bullough, Wilkinson	Wilkinson (3)	586	Campbell
8.5.86	SD	A	Mansfield M.	W	42-16	Glover (2), Wilkinson, Barrow, Henley-Smith, Mills, Bullough	Wilkinson (7)	—	—
10.5.86	SD	H	Mansfield M.	W	43-20	Platt (2), Duffy, Briscoe, Henley-Smith, Gibson, Mills	Platt (7), Gibson (dg)	370	Volante
11.5.86	SD	A	Batley	L	13-28	Wilkinson, Hunter	Platt (2, 1dg)	—	—
16.5.86	SD	H	Hunslet	W	34-28	Henley-Smith (3), Looker, Wilkinson, Barrow	Platt (5)	472	Kershaw
18.5.86	SD	H	Keighley	W	27-14	Mills (2), Bullough (2), Flashman	Platt (3), Wilkinson (dg)	505	Tennant

HALIFAX

Ground:	Thrum Hall
Colours:	Blue and white hooped jerseys, white shorts
First Season:	1895-96
Nickname:	Thrum Hallers
Chairman:	Stan Ackroyd
General Manager:	Tony Beevers
Coach:	Chris Anderson (Nov 1984-)
Honours:	**Championship** Winners, 1906-07, 1964-65
	Beaten finalists, 1952-53, 1953-54, 1955-56, 1965-66
	Division One Champions, 1902-03, 1985-86
	War League Beaten finalists, 1942-43, 1944-45
	Challenge Cup Winners, 1902-03, 1903-04, 1930-31, 1938-39
	Beaten finalists, 1920-21, 1940-41, 1941-42, 1948-49, 1953-54, 1955-56
	Yorkshire League Winners, 1908-09, 1920-21, 1952-53, 1953-54, 1955-56, 1957-58
	Eastern Division Championship Winners, 1963-64
	Yorkshire Cup Winners, 1908-09, 1944-45, 1954-55, 1955-56, 1963-64
	Beaten finalists, 1905-06, 1907-08, 1941-42, 1979-80
	John Player Trophy Winners, 1971-72
	Premiership Trophy Beaten finalists, 1985-86
Records:	Attendance: 29,153 v. Wigan (RL Cup) 21 Mar, 1959
	Season
	Goals: 147 by T. Griffiths, 1955-56
	Tries: 48 by J. Freeman, 1956-57
	Points: 297 by T. Griffiths, 1955-56

Match

Goals: 14 by B. Burton v. Hunslet, 27 Aug, 1972
Tries: 8 by K. Williams v. Dewsbury, 9 Nov, 1957
Points: 31 by B. Burton v. Hunslet, 27 Aug, 1972
Highest score: 76-8 v. Hunslet, 1972-73
Highest against: 64-0 v. Wigan, 1922-23

1985-86 PLAYERS' SUMMARY

	App	Tries	Goals	Dr	Pts
Agar, Malcolm	1	—	—	—	—
Anderson, Chris	35	12	—	—	48
Anderson, Tony	34	11	—	—	44
Beevers, Graham	8 + 2	—	—	—	—
Bond, Steve	10 + 12	—	—	—	—
Cerchione, Mario	3	—	4	—	8
Crossley, John	6 + 11	2	—	—	8
Dixon, Paul	37	13	—	—	52
Fairbank, Dick	1 + 1	—	—	—	—
Garrod, Graham	12	4	—	—	16
George, Wilf	10	2	—	—	8
Heugh, Cavill	29	8	18	—	68
James, Neil	30 + 4	4	—	—	16
Juliff, Brian	22 + 1	4	—	—	16
Kilroy, Joe	25 + 1	7	—	—	28
McCallion, Seamus	36 + 1	9	—	—	36
McCurrie, Alan	0 + 1	—	—	—	—
Riddlesden, Eddie	10 + 4	2	—	—	8
Robinson, Geoff	29 + 1	8	—	—	32
St. Hillaire, Darren	6	1	—	—	4
Scott, Mick	32	2	—	—	8
Smith, Steve	15 + 8	6	29	—	82
Stephens, Gary	37	8	—	7	39
White, Brendan	5	—	—	—	—
Whitfield, Colin	16	3	33	—	78
Wilson, Scott	32 + 1	5	—	—	20
TOTALS:					
26 players		111	84	7	619

1985-86 MATCH ANALYSIS

Date	Competition	H/A	Opponent	Rlt	Score	Tries	Goals	Attendance	Referee
1.9.85	SLC	H	Oldham	D	12-12	Dixon	Cerchione (4)	3967	Volante
4.9.85	SLC	A	Widnes	L	9-12	Dixon, Garrod	Stephens (dg)	—	—
8.9.85	SLC	A	Salford	L	6-22	Stephens	Heugh	—	—
15.9.85	YC(1)	H	Huddersfield B.	W	52-14	Scott (2), Dixon (2), Heugh, C. Anderson, Stephens, St. Hilaire, Riddlesden, McCallion	Heugh (6)	2516	Berry
22.9.85	SLC	H	Dewsbury	L	12-16	C. Anderson, Stephens	Heugh (2)	3145	Lindop
25.9.85	YC (2)	H	Castleford	L	4-24	C. Anderson	—	4012	Lindop
29.9.85	SLC	A	York	W	34-17	T. Anderson (2), Garrod (2), Stephens, Heugh, Juliff	Heugh (3)	—	—
6.10.85	SLC	H	Castleford	W	14-8	T. Anderson, Dixon, Heugh	Heugh	3117	Kershaw
13.10.85	SLC	H	Hull	W	21-8	Wilson (2), Garrod, Smith	Heugh (2), Stephens (dg)	5321	Hodgson
20.10.85	SLC	A	Featherstone R.	W	20-10	Wilson, Kilroy, Dixon, Heugh	Smith (2)	—	—
27.10.85	SLC	H	Salford	W	23-12	Robinson, Juliff, Kilroy, Heugh	Heugh (3), Stephens (dg)	4013	Gomersall (Aus)
10.11.85	SLC	H	Leeds	D	18-8	Wilson, Juliff, Heugh, Kilroy	Smith	5684	Campbell
17.11.85	SLC	A	Warrington	W	14-12	T. Anderson, Kilroy	Smith (3)	—	—
23.11.85	JPS (1)	H	Hull K. R.	L	2-11	—	Smith	4147	Fox
15.12.85	SLC	A	Leeds	W	22-20	C. Anderson (2), Stephens, Smith	Smith (3)	—	—
22.12.85	SLC	H	Wigan	D	12-12	Wilson, James	Smith (2)	8013	Spencer
26.12.85	SLC	A	Bradford N.	W	22-12	Robinson, McCallion, Kilroy, T. Anderson	Smith (3)	—	—
1.1.86	SLC	A	Swinton	W	16-10	Heugh, Dixon	Smith (4)	—	—
5.1.86	SLC	H (at Leeds)	St. Helens	W	27-18	Stephens, T. Anderson, Kilroy, Robinson	Smith (5), Stephens (dg)	4803	Fox
12.1.86	SLC	A	Dewsbury	W	32-10	Smith (2), McCallion (2), Crossley, Dixon, Heugh	Smith (2)	—	—
19.1.86	SLC	A	Hull	W	8-4	Smith (2)		—	—
22.1.86	SLC	H (at Halifax T. FC)	Widnes	L	8-15	Dixon	Smith, Whitfield	6368	Holdsworth
2.2.86	SLC	H	Hull K.R.	D	10-10	Crossley, James	Smith	3904	Kershaw
9.2.86	CC(1)	H	Leeds	L	4-24	Whitfield	—	7422	Lindop
16.2.86	SLC	A (at Oldham FC)	Oldham	W	19-14	T. Anderson, Stephens, Robinson, Juliff	Whitfield, Stephens (dg)	—	—
23.2.86	SLC	A	Wigan	D	6-6	Dixon	Whitfield	—	—
2.3.86	SLC	A	St. Helens	L	10-22	Robinson, Stephens	Whitfield	—	—
9.3.86	SLC	H	Swinton	W	16-14	Robinson, C. Anderson, Dixon	Whitfield (2)	3584	Kendrew
19.3.86	SLC	A	Hull K.R.	W	23-10	McCallion (2), C. Anderson	Whitfield (5), Stephens (dg)	—	—
28.3.86	SLC	A	Castleford	W	36-14	McCallion (2), Robinson, George, Kilroy, James	Whitfield (6)	—	—
31.3.86	SLC	H	Warrington	W	18-6	Robinson, Whitfield, Dixon	Whitfield (3)	5263	Beaumont
9.4.86	SLC	H	York	W	10-6	C. Anderson (2)	Whitfield	3425	Berry
16.4.86	SLC	H	Bradford N.	W	8-2	Whitfield, T. Anderson	—	5092	Croft
20.4.86	SLC	H	Featherstone R.	D	13-13	George, Dixon	Whitfield (2), Stephens (dg)	7465	Volante
26.4.86	PT(1)	H	Hull	W	32-20	C. Anderson (2), James, T. Anderson, Riddlesden	Whitfield (5), Smith	3931	Campbell
11.4.86	PT(SF)	H	Leeds	W	16-13	T. Anderson (2), McCallion	Whitfield (2)	8288	McDonald
18.4.86	PT(F)		Elland Warrington Rd, Leeds	L	10-38	C. Anderson	Whitfield (3)	(13683)	Lindop

HUDDERSFIELD BARRACUDAS

Ground: Arena 84
Colours: Claret and gold jerseys, white shorts
First Season: 1895-96; Added Barracudas to title 1984-85
Nickname: Barracudas
Chairman: John Bailey
Secretary: Louise Hamer
Coach: Chris Forster (Feb 1985-)
Honours: **Championship** Winners, 1911-12, 1912-13, 1914-15, 1928-29, 1929-30, 1948-49, 1961-62
Beaten finalists, 1913-14, 1919-20, 1922-23, 1931-32, 1945-46, 1949-50
Division Two Champions, 1974-75
Challenge Cup Winners, 1912-13, 1914-15, 1919-20, 1932-33, 1944-45, 1952-53
Beaten finalists, 1934-35, 1961-62
Yorkshire League Winners, 1911-12, 1912-13, 1913-14, 1914-15, 1919-20, 1921-22, 1928-29, 1929-30, 1948-49, 1949-50, 1951-52
Eastern Division Beaten finalists, 1962-63
Yorkshire Cup Winners, 1909-10, 1911-12, 1913-14, 1914-15, 1918-19, 1919-20, 1926-27, 1931-32, 1938-39, 1950-51, 1952-53, 1957-58
Beaten finalists, 1910-11, 1923-24, 1925-26, 1930-31, 1937-38, 1942-43, 1949-50, 1960-61
Records: Attendance: 35,136 Leeds v. Wakefield T. (RL Cup SF) 19 April 1947. Home: 32,912 v. Wigan (League) 4 Mar, 1950
Season
Goals: 147 by B. Gronow, 1919-20
Tries: 80 by A. Rosenfeld, 1913-14
Points: 330 by B. Gronow, 1919-20
Match
Goals: 18 by M. Holland v. Swinton Park, 28 Feb, 1914
Tries: 10 by L. Cooper v. Keighley, 17 Nov, 1951
Points: 39 by M. Holland v. Swinton Park, 28 Feb, 1914
Highest score: 119-2 v. Swinton Park, 1913-14
Highest against: 64-17 v. Leeds, 1958-59

1985-86 PLAYERS' SUMMARY

	App	Tries	Goals	Dr	Pts
Benioni, Kuku	1	—	—	—	—
Blacker, Brian	20	7	—	—	28
Boothroyd, Alan	14 + 1	1	—	—	4
Bostock, Mick	33	2	—	—	8
Brooke, Kevin	2 + 2	—	—	—	—
Campbell, Mark	17	7	—	—	28
Charlton, Mark	6 + 4	2	—	—	8
Cockerham, Paul	18 + 3	3	—	—	12
Cook, Billy	8 + 1	6	—	—	24
Cramp, Peter	5	2	—	—	8
Davies, Tom	0 + 2	—	—	—	—
Doughty, Greg	1 + 1	—	—	—	—
Edwards, Tony	8 + 3	1	—	—	4
Farrell, Tony	0 + 1	—	—	—	—
Fitzpatrick, Dennis	18	—	—	—	—
Gillespie, Steve	1	—	—	—	—
Harris, Colin	5 + 3	2	—	—	8
Hirst, Bob	7 + 2	1	13	—	30
Hooper, Trevor	4	1	—	—	4
Humphreys, Les	2	—	—	—	—
Johnson, David	0 + 5	—	—	—	—
Johnson, Jimmy	26 + 1	4	—	—	16
Johnson, Phil	36 + 1	6	2	—	28
Kenworthy, Simon	11 + 2	1	1	—	6
Knight, Glen	7 + 4	1	—	—	4
Leathley, Trevor	35 + 2	10	—	—	40
Lee, Brian	1	—	—	—	—
Marsh, Richard	4	—	—	—	—
Marshall, Nigel	13 + 3	4	—	—	16
McGovern, Terry	21 + 2	5	—	—	20
McHugh, Stan	8 + 6	—	—	—	—
Meehan, Gary	8 + 1	—	—	—	—
Munro, Geoff	5	1	—	—	4
Nelson, David	9 + 9	2	—	—	8
Paterson, Johnny	1 + 5	—	—	—	—
Pickerill, Neil	3 + 1	—	—	1	1
Platt, Billy	28	2	59	7	133
Pollard, Gordon	6 + 1	—	—	—	—
Punter, Mick	0 + 1	1	—	—	4
Rose, Tony	2	—	—	—	—
Schofield, David	2	—	—	—	—
Senior, Gary	34	19	4	—	84
Simpson, Frank	3 + 2	—	—	—	—
Thomas, Ian	21	10	—	—	40
Wright, Craig	13	—	—	—	—
Wroe, Derek	13 + 2	1	—	—	4
Trialist (2)	1 + 3	—	—	—	—

TOTALS:
	App	Tries	Goals	Dr	Pts
48 players		101	79	8	570

1985-86 MATCH ANALYSIS

Date	Com-petition	H/A	Opponent	Rlt	Score	Tries	Goals	Atten-dance	Referee
1.9.85	SD	H	Wakefield T.	D	16-16	Thomas (2), P. Johnson	Hirst (2)	1337	Simpson
4.9.85	SD	A	Batley	L	14-20	P. Johnson, Senior	Hirst (3)	—	—
8.9.85	SD	H	Runcorn H.	W	26-23	J. Johnson, Hooper, Blacker, Hirst, Charlton	Hirst (3)	561	Carter
15.9.85	YC(1)	A	Halifax	L	14-52	Thomas, Charlton	Senior (2), Kenworthy	—	—
18.9.85	SD	A	Runcorn H.	W	17-15	Blacker (2), Leathley	Hirst (2), Pickerill (dg)	—	—
22.9.85	SD	H	Whitehaven	L	14-31	Senior (2), Thomas	Hirst	627	Whitfield
29.9.85	SD	H	Barrow	L	20-44	J. Johnson (2), Kenworthy, Senior	Hirst (2)	715	Volante
6.10.85	SD	A	Workington T.	L	8-32	Thomas, P. Johnson	—	—	—
13.10.85	SD	H	Batley	L	8-34	Leathley, Senior	—	1105	Gomersall (Aus)
20.10.85	SD	H	Leigh	L	2-54	—	Platt	1335	Croft
27.10.85	SD	A	Mansfield M.	W	34-6	Senior (2), Wroe, J. Johnson, McGovern, Thomas	Platt (5)	—	—
3.11.85	SD	H	Hunslet	W	16-10	Cockerham, Senior	Platt (3, 2dg)	907	Kershaw
10.11.85	SD	A	Doncaster	L	16-24	P. Johnson, Leathley, Cockerham	Platt (2)	—	—
17.11.85	SD	H	Rochdale H.	L	12-24	Blacker, Leathley	Platt (2)	1423	Smith
24.11.85	JPS(1)	A	Keighley	L	10-20	Thomas	Platt (3)	—	—
8.12.85	SD	A	Barrow	L	10-34	Blacker, Senior	Platt	—	—
15.12.85	SD	H	Doncaster	L	4-12	Thomas	—	466	Kendrew
22.12.85	SD	A	Bramley	L	7-16	Nelson	Platt (1, 1dg)	—	—
12.1.86	SD	H	Carlisle	L	8-16	Nelson	Platt (2)	420	Tennant
19.1.86	SD	A	Hunslet	D	20-20	Blacker, Senior, McGovern, Campbell	Platt (2)	—	—
2.2.86	SD	H	Workington T.	W	20-10	Blacker, Campbell, Senior	Platt (3), Senior	343	Lindop
9.2.86	CC(1)	H	Rochdale H.	L	4-10	Senior	—	913	Houghton
9.3.86	SD	H	Sheffield E.	L	22-32	Leathley, Marshall, McGovern, Senior	Platt (2), Senior	503	Mean
16.3.86	SD	H	Fulham	W	14-8	Marshall, Senior, Cramp	Platt	406	Tickle
23.3.86	SD	A	Leigh	L	12-22	Platt, Campbell	Platt (2)	—	—
26.3.86	SD	A	Keighley	L	10-21	Thomas (2)	Platt	—	—
30.3.86	SD	A	Sheffield E.	L	6-36	Leathley	Platt	—	—
6.4.86	SD	H	Blackpool B.	L	10-30	Cockerham	Platt (3)	382	Carter
13.4.86	SD	A	Whitehaven	L	12-38	Marshall (2)	P. Johnson (2)	—	—
17.4.86	SD	H	Keighley	D	32-32	Leathley, Campbell, Cook, Bostock, P. Johnson, Boothroyd	Platt (4)	303	Holdsworth
20.4.86	SD	A	Wakefield T.	L	14-22	Campbell (2), Leathley	Platt	—	—
25.4.86	SD	H	Mansfield M.	W	30-14	Knight, Cook, Leathley, Bostock, Senior, Edwards	Platt (3)	334	Allatt
27.4.86	SD	A	Fulham	D	26-26	P. Johnson, Cook, McGovern, Senior	Platt (4, 2dg)	—	—
30.4.86	SD	H	Bramley	W	38-12	Harris, Leathley, Campbell, Senior, McGovern, Cook	Platt (6, 2dg)	353	Volante
7.5.86	SD	A	Rochdale H.	L	16-32	Munro, Cook, Senior	Platt (2)	—	—
9.5.86	SD	A	Carlisle	L	16-31	Platt, Harris, Senior	Platt (2)	—	—
11.5.86	SD	A	Blackpool B.	L	12-44	Punter, Cook	Platt (2)	—	—

HULL

Ground:	The Boulevard
Colours:	Irregular black and white hooped jerseys, white shorts
First Season:	1895-96
Nickname:	Airlie Birds
Chairman:	Peter Darley
Secretary:	Geoff Lythe
Manager:	Arthur Bunting (Jan 1978-Dec 1985)
	Kenny Foulkes (Dec 1985-May 1986)
Honours:	**Championship** Winners, 1919-20, 1920-21, 1935-36, 1955-56, 1957-58 Beaten finalists, 1956-57
	Division One Champions, 1982-83
	Division Two Champions, 1976-77, 1978-79
	Challenge Cup Winners, 1913-14, 1981-82 Beaten finalists, 1907-08, 1908-09, 1909-10, 1921-22, 1922-23, 1958-59, 1959-60, 1979-80, 1982-83, 1984-85
	Yorkshire League Winners, 1918-19, 1922-23, 1926-27, 1935-36
	Yorkshire Cup Winners, 1923-24, 1969-70, 1982-83, 1983-84, 1984-85 Beaten finalists, 1912-13, 1914-15, 1920-21, 1927-28, 1938-39, 1946-47, 1953-54, 1954-55, 1955-56, 1959-60, 1967-68
	John Player Trophy Winners 1981-82 Beaten finalists, 1975-76, 1984-85
	BBC2 Floodlit Trophy Winners, 1979-80
	Premiership Beaten finalists, 1980-81, 1981-82, 1982-83
Records:	Attendance: 28,798 v. Leeds (RL Cup) 7 Mar, 1936
	Season Goals: 170 by S. Lloyd, 1978-79 Tries: 52 by J. Harrison, 1914-15 Points: 369 by S. Lloyd, 1978-79

Match

Goals: 14 by J. Kennedy v. Rochdale H., 7 Apr, 1921; S. Lloyd v. Oldham, 10 Sep, 1978
Tries: 7 by C. Sullivan v. Doncaster, 15 Apr, 1968
Points: 36 by J. Kennedy v. Keighley, 29 Jan, 1921
Highest score: 86-0 v. Elland, 1898-99
Highest against: 57-14 v. St. Helens, 1985-86

1985-86 PLAYERS' SUMMARY

	App	Tries	Goals	Dr	Pts
Ah Kuoi, Fred	31 + 1	8	—	—	32
Arnett, Carl	6 + 2	1	—	—	—
Brand, Michael	6	2	—	—	8
Crooks, Lee	30	9	52	1	141
Dannatt, Andy	3 + 5	2	—	—	8
Divorty, Gary	23 + 7	5	1	—	22
Eastwood, Paul	24 + 3	11	1	—	46
Edmonds, Phil	8 + 3	1	—	—	4
Evans, Steve	16 + 3	3	4	—	20
Gascoigne, Andy	24 + 3	7	—	—	28
Gerard, Geoff	22 + 2	6	—	—	24
Hick, Steve	5 + 3	2	1	—	10
Jackson, Lee	2	1	—	—	4
James, Kevin	9	2	—	—	8
Kemble, Gary	29	4	—	—	16
Leuluai, James	27 + 1	13	—	—	52
Mallinson, Billy	6	2	—	—	8
McCoid, Carl	1	—	—	—	—
Muggleton, John	12 + 1	9	—	—	36
Norton, Steve	21 + 1	1	—	—	4
O'Hara, Andy	34	19	—	—	76
Patrick, Shaun	29	—	—	—	—
Portz, Jimmy	7 + 3	3	—	—	12
Prendiville, Paul	13 + 5	5	13	—	46
Proctor, Wayne	14 + 2	2	—	—	8
Puckering, Neil	22 + 3	3	—	—	12
Rose, Paul	3 + 1	—	—	—	—
Schofield, Garry	23	15	35	1	131
Sharp, Jon	2 + 1	—	—	—	—
Skerrett, Trevor	20 + 1	1	—	—	4
Tomlinson, Alan	1 + 1	1	—	—	4
Vass, Stuart	9 + 4	4	—	—	16
Welham, Paul	4 + 8	1	—	—	4
Windley, Phil	8 + 2	1	—	—	4
TOTALS:					
34 players		143	107	2	788

1985-86 MATCH ANALYSIS

Date	Com-petition	H/A	Opponent	Rlt	Score	Tries	Goals	Atten-dance	Referee
1.9.85	SLC	H	Widnes	L	10-33	Vass, Ah Kuoi	Prendiville	7027	Fox
4.9.85	SLC	A	York	W	22-8	James (2), Prendiville, Gascoigne, Proctor	Prendiville	—	—
8.9.85	SLC	A	Castleford	L	14-22	Puckering, Portz	Crooks (2), Prendiville	—	—
15.9.85	YC(1)	A	Hull K.R.	L	10-12	O'Hara, Crooks	Divorty	—	—
18.9.85	SLC	H	Dewsbury	W	48-6	Ah Kuoi (2), O'Hara (2), Eastwood (2), Puckering, Prendiville, Portz, Skerrett	Prendiville (4)	4991	Croft
22.9.85	SLC	H	Oldham	W	54-12	Gascoigne (2), Ah Kuoi (2), Leuluai (2), Eastwood, Portz, Vass, Crooks	Crooks (7)	7094	Haigh
29.9.85	SLC	A	St. Helens	W	35-22	O'Hara (2), Leuluai (2), Schofield, Eastwood	Crooks (5, 1dg)	—	—
6.10.85	SLC	H	Hull K.R.	W	28-6	Schofield (2), O'Hara, Vass, Gascoigne	Crooks (2), Schofield (2)	12941	Allatt
13.10.85	SLC	A	Halifax	L	8-21	Leuluai	Crooks (2)	—	—
27.10.85	SLC	H	Bradford N	W	28-16	Muggleton, Eastwood, Gerard, Mallinson, Divorty	Crooks (3), Schofield	7442	Kendrew
3.11.85	SLC	H	Swinton	W	16-10	Muggleton (2), Divorty	Schofield, Eastwood	5924	Lindop
17.11.85	Tour	H	New Zealand	L	10-33	Schofield	Crooks, Schofield, Hick	8406	Kershaw
27.11.85	JPS(1)	H	Swinton	W	44-0	Muggleton (3), Leuluai (2), Puckering, Kemble, Eastwood	Crooks (6)	3797	Volante
1.12.85	JPS(2)	H	Salford	W	30-10	Gascoigne (2), Leuluai, Vass, Prendiville	Crooks (5)	5659	Whitfield
11.12.85	JPS(3)	A	St. Helens	L	14-57	Muggleton, Dannatt (2)	Crooks	—	—
15.12.85	SLC	H	St. Helens	D	20-20	Gerard, O'Hara, Evans	Crooks (4)	5668	Carter
22.12.85	SLC	A	Swinton	L	8-16	Eastwood	Crooks, Prendiville	—	—
26.12.85	SLC	H	Featherstone R.	W	18-12	Crooks, Muggleton, Gerard	Crooks (2), Prendiville	4752	Fox
1.1.86	SLC	A	Featherstone R.	D	10-10	Muggleton, Divorty	Prendiville	—	—
12.1.86	SLC	A	Bradford N.	L	8-18	Gerard	Prendiville (2)	—	—
19.1.86	SLC	H	Halifax	L	4-8	Eastwood	—	7726	Allatt
29.1.86	CC(P)	H	Dudley Hill	W	38-10	Schofield (2), O'Hara (2), Evans, Gerard, Crooks	Schofield (4), Evans	2590	Croft
2.2.86	SLC	H	Castleford	W	34-12	Eastwood (2), Kemble, Prendiville, Crooks, Leuluai, Norton	Evans (3)	4137	Berry
8.2.86	CC(1)	A	Hull K.R.	L	6-22	O'Hara	Crooks	—	—
2.3.86	SLC	A	Wigan	L	6-44	Evans	Schofield	—	—
5.3.86	SLC	A	Salford	L	12-15	Gerard, Schofield	Schofield (2)	—	—
9.3.86	SLC	A	Dewsbury	W	30-12	Schofield (2), O'Hara (2), Eastwood, Edmonds	Schofield (3)	—	—
12.3.86	SLC	H	Wigan	L	10-26	Prendiville, Windley	Schofield	6921	Beaumont
19.3.86	SLC	A	Warrington	L	16-43	Crooks (2), Leuluai	Crooks, Prendiville	—	—
23.3.86	SLC	H	Salford	W	34-16	Hick (2), Ah Kuoi, O'Hara, Gascoigne, Crooks	Crooks (5)	4985	McDonald
31.3.86	SLC	H	York	W	16-12	Crooks, Welham, Kemble	Crooks, Schofield	4990	Kendrew
6.4.86	SLC	A	Leeds	W	35-18	O'Hara (2), Schofield (2), Divorty, Kemble	Crooks (3), Schofield (2, 1dg)	—	—
9.4.86	SLC	H	Leeds	W	10-4	Schofield, O'Hara	Schofield	4395	Beaumont
13.4.86	SLC	A	Widnes	L	20-26	O'Hara, Brand, Proctor	Schofield (4)	—	—
16.4.86	SLC	A	Oldham	L	14-15	Schofield, Jackson	Schofield (3)	—	—
20.4.86	SLC	H	Warrington	L	20-33	Leuluai (2), Ah Kuoi	Schofield (4)	4689	Tennant
22.4.86	SLC	W	Hull K.R.	W	28-2	Brand, Tomlinson, Schofield, Ah Kuoi, Divorty, Leuluai	Schofield (2)	—	—
26.4.86	PT(1)	A	Halifax	L	20-32	O'Hara (2), Mallinson, Schofield	Schofield (2)	—	—

53

HULL KINGSTON ROVERS

Ground:	Craven Park
Colours:	White jerseys with red yoke, white shorts
First Season:	1899-1900
Nickname:	Robins
Chairman:	Colin Hutton
Secretary:	Ron Turner
Coach:	Roger Millward MBE (Mar 1977-)
Honours:	**Championship** Winners, 1922-23, 1924-25
	Beaten finalists, 1920-21, 1967-68
	First Division Champions, 1978-79, 1983-84, 1984-85
	Challenge Cup Winners, 1979-80
	Beaten finalists, 1904-05, 1924-25, 1963-64, 1980-81, 1985-86
	John Player Trophy Winners, 1984-85, Beaten finalists, 1981-82, 1985-86
	Premiership Winners, 1980-81, 1983-84, Beaten finalists, 1984-85
	Yorkshire League Winners, 1924-25, 1925-26
	Yorkshire Cup Winners, 1920-21, 1929-30, 1966-67, 1967-68, 1971-72, 1974-75, 1985-86
	Beaten finalists, 1906-07, 1911-12, 1933-34, 1962-63, 1975-76, 1980-81, 1984-85
	BBC2 Floodlit Trophy Winners, 1977-78
	Beaten finalists, 1979-80
	Eastern Division Championship Winners, 1962-63
	Charity Shield Beaten finalists, 1985-86
Records:	Attendance: 22,282 v. Hull, 7 October, 1922. There was a crowd of 27,670 for a League match v. Hull at Hull City FC's Boothferry Park on 3 April, 1953

Season
Goals: 166 by G. Fairbairn, 1981-82
Tries: 45 by G. Prohm, 1984-85
Points: 366 by S. Hubbard, 1979-80
Match
Goals: 14 by A. Carmichael v.
Merthyr Tydfil, 8 Oct, 1910
Tries: 11 by G. West v. Brookland
R., 4 Mar, 1905
Points: 53 by G. West v. Brookland
R., 4 Mar, 1905
Highest score: 73-5 v. Brookland
R., 1904-05
Highest against: 68-0 v. Halifax,
1955-56

1985-86 PLAYERS' SUMMARY

	App	Tries	Goals	Dr	Pts
Beall, Malcolm	3 + 2	—	—	—	—
Burton, Chris	27	1	—	—	4
Cator, Mike	0 + 1	—	—	—	—
Clark, Garry	29	11	—	—	44
Dorahy, John	37	8	99	2	232
Ema, Asuquo	45	4	—	—	16
Fairbairn, George	34	4	27	1	71
Farr, Stuart	3	1	—	—	4
Fletcher, Mike	3 + 7	1	4	—	12
Harkin, Paul	35 + 1	7	—	5	33
Harrison, Chris	1 + 1	—	—	—	—
Harrison, Des	26 + 3	3	—	—	12
Hogan, Phil	30	9	—	—	36
Hutchinson, Carl	2 + 1	—	—	—	—
Johnston, Lindsey	7 + 4	—	—	—	—
Johnston, Peter	23	1	—	—	4
Kelly, Andy	22 + 15	7	—	1	29
Laws, David	45	16	—	—	64
Lydiat, John	21 + 13	10	1	—	42
Marchant, Billy	3	1	—	—	4
Miller, Gavin	40	13	—	—	52
Noble, Rob	2	—	—	—	—
Olsen, Steve	3	—	—	—	—
Parker, Frank	1 + 2	—	—	—	—
Parker, Wayne	2 + 1	—	—	—	—
Prohm, Gary	37	17	—	—	68
Robinson, Ian	12 + 6	1	—	—	4
Rudd, Chris	9 + 10	1	—	—	4
Sims, Gary	5	1	—	—	4
Sissons, Tony	3	—	—	—	—
Smith, Gordon	27 + 13	3	—	—	12
Smith, Mike	31 + 1	• 11	—	—	44
Smith, Steve	7	2	—	—	8
Speckman, Paul	5 + 1	—	—	—	—
Stead, Ray	7	1	—	—	4
Tosney, Andy	2	—	—	—	—
Watkinson, David	35	—	—	—	—

TOTALS:
37 players   134   131   9   807

1985-86 MATCH ANALYSIS

Date	Competition	H/A	Opponent	Rlt	Score	Tries	Goals	Attendance	Referee
25.8.85	Charity Shield	Isle of Man	Wigan	L	6-34	Clark	Lydiat	(4066)	Campbell
1.9.85	SLC	A	Featherstone R.	W	27-14	M. Smith, Ema, Fairbairn, Harkin, Prohm, Kelly	Fairbairn, Harkin (dg)	—	—

(continued)

MATCH ANALYSIS (continued)

4.9.85	SLC	H	Dewsbury	W	42-0	Laws (3), Hogan (2), Burton, Miller, Prohm, Clark	Fairbairn (3)	4478	Kershaw
8.9.85	SLC	H	Warrington	W	12-8	Hogan, Clark	Dorahy (2)	6315	Holdsworth
15.9.85	YC(1)	H	Hull	W	12-10	Hogan (2)	Dorahy (2)	10115	Lindop
22.9.85	SLC	A	Bradford N.	W	17-12	Prohm, Harrison, Harkin	Dorahy (2), Harkin (dg)	–	–
25.9.85	YC(2)	H	Bramley	W	30-6	Prohm (2), Lydiat, Dorahy, Miller	Dorahy (5)	3959	Smith
29.9.85	SLC	H	Wigan	W	19-18	Harrison, Kelly, Prohm	Dorahy (3), Kelly (dg)	9456	Hodgson
2.10.85	YC(SF)	H	Bradford N.	W	11-5	Prohm	Dorahy (3, 1dg)	6008	Fox
6.10.85	SLC	A	Hull	L	6-28	Robinson	Dorahy	–	–
13.10.85	Tour	H	New Zealand	L	10-20	S. Smith	Dorahy (3)	6585	McDonald
20.10.85	SLC	A	St. Helens	L	22-39	Laws (2), Dorahy	Dorahy (5)	–	–
27.10.85	YC(F)	Leeds	Castleford	W	22-18	Miller (2), Clark	Dorahy (5)	(12686)	Campbell
3.11.85	SLC	A	Salford	L	24-27	G. Smith, Ema, Hogan, Dorahy	Dorahy (4)	–	–
10.11.85	SLC	H	Bradford N.	W	30-4	Clark (3), Harkin, M. Smith	Dorahy (5)	5101	Volante
17.11.85	SLC	A	Leeds	W	16-12	Prohm, Clark, Laws	Dorahy (2)	–	–
23.11.85	JPS(1)	A	Halifax	W	11-2	Prohm, Clark	Dorahy, Fairbairn (dg)	–	–
1.12.85	JPS(2)	H	Oldham	W	8-7	Miller	Dorahy, Fairbairn	7069	Campbell
8.12.85	JPS(3)	H	York	W	24-16	Dorahy, Hogan, Miller	Dorahy (6)	6228	Whitfield
15.12.85	SLC	A	Widnes	W	15-8	Lydiat, Dorahy	Dorahy (3), Harkin (dg)	–	–
21.12.85	JPS(SF)	Leeds	St. Helens	W	22-4	Miller, Clark, Hogan, M. Smith	Dorahy (3)	(3856)	Campbell
26.12.85	SLC	A	York	W	22-8	Laws, M. Smith, Dorahy	Dorahy (5)	–	–
1.1.86	SLC	H	York	W	12-6	Laws, G. Smith	Dorahy (2)	5159	Kendrew
11.1.86	JPS(F)	Elland Rd, Leeds	Wigan	L	8-11	Lydiat, Laws	–	(17573)	Holdsworth
15.1.86	SLC	H	Widnes	L	12-24	Prohm	Dorahy (4)	5164	Kendrew
19.1.86	SLC	A	Wigan	L	8-12	Prohm	Dorahy (2)	–	–
29.1.86	SLC	H	Featherstone R.	W	20-0	M. Smith, Fairbairn, Laws, Dorahy	Dorahy (2)	3557	Whitfield
2.2.86	SLC	A	Halifax	D	10-10	Harkin, Laws	Dorahy	–	–
8.2.86	CC(1)	H	Hull	W	22-6	Miller, Kelly, M. Smith	Dorahy (5)	8770	Whitfield
2.3.86	SLC	A	Oldham (at Oldham FC)	W	20-16	Harkin, G. Smith, Miller	Dorahy (4)	–	–
9.3.86	CC(2)	A	York	W	34-6	Kelly (2), Prohm, M. Smith, Lydiat, Hogan	Dorahy (4), Fairbairn	–	–
16.3.86	CC(3)	H	Leigh	W	25-10	Fairbairn, Laws, Prohm, Harkin	Dorahy (4, 1dg)	7928	McDonald
19.3.86	SLC	H	Halifax	L	10-23	Lydiat (2)	Dorahy	6185	McDonald
23.3.86	SLC	A	Warrington	L	16-31	Lydiat, Prohm, Miller	Dorahy (2)	–	–
29.3.86	CC(SF)	Elland Rd, Leeds	Leeds	D	24-24	M. Smith (2), Laws (2)	Dorahy (4)	(23866)	Whitfield
31.3.86	SLC	A	Dewsbury	W	18-14	Simms, Kelly, S. Smith	Fairbairn (3)	–	–
3.4.86	CC(SF)	Elland Rd, Leeds	Leeds	W	17-0	P. Johnston, Lydiat, Kelly	Dorahy (2), Harkin (dg)	(32485)	Whitfield
6.4.86	SLC	H	Castleford	W	22-8	M. Smith, Ema, Miller	Fairbairn (5)	5553	Fox
9.4.86	SLC	H	St. Helens	L	13-22	M. Smith, Rudd	Fairbairn (2), Harkin (dg)	4215	Holdsworth
11.4.86	SLC	A	Castleford	L	18-36	Miller, Fletcher, Marchant	Fairbairn (3)	–	–
13.4.86	SLC	A	Swinton	L	4-10	Fairbairn	–	–	–
15.4.86	SLC	H	Leeds	W	28-12	Clark, Dorahy, Lydiat, Laws, Miller	Fairbairn (4)	3213	Carter
16.4.86	SLC	H	Salford	L	4-28	–	Fletcher (2)	2880	Houghton
18.4.86	SLC	H	Oldham	L	10-22	Stead, Farr	Fletcher	2579	Lindop
20.4.86	SLC	H	Swinton	W	28-20	Prohm, Harrison, Ema, Laws, Harkin	Fairbairn (4)	3291	Simpson
22.4.86	SLC	H	Hull	L	2-28	–	Fletcher	5685	Campbell
27.4.86	PT(1)	L	Wigan	L	0-47	–	–	–	–
3.5.86	CC(F)	Wembley	Castleford	L	14-15	Prohm (2), Lydiat	Dorahy	(82134)	Whitfield

HUNSLET

Ground:	Elland Road
Colours:	Myrtle, flame and white jerseys, white shorts
First Season:	1895-96. Disbanded at end of 1972-73. Re-formed as New Hunslet in 1973-74. Retitled Hunslet from start of 1979-80
Chairman:	Jerry Mason
Secretary:	John Moses
Coach:	Paul Daley (Apr 1981-Nov 1985) Peter Jarvis (Nov 1985-)
Honours:	**Challenge Cup** Winners, 1907-08, 1933-34
	Beaten finalists, 1898-99, 1964-65
	Championship Winners, 1907-08, 1937-38
	Beaten finalists, 1958-59
	Division Two Champions, 1962-63
	Yorkshire Cup Winners, 1905-06, 1907-08, 1962-63
	Beaten finalists, 1908-09, 1929-30, 1931-32, 1944-45, 1956-57, 1965-66
	Yorkshire League Winners, 1897-98, 1907-08, 1931-32
Records:	Attendance: 54,112 v. Leeds (Championship final), 30 Apr, 1938
	Season
	Goals: 181 by W. Langton, 1958-59
	Tries: 34 by A. Snowden, 1956-57
	Points: 380 by W. Langton, 1958-59
	Match
	Goals: 12 by W. Langton v. Keighley, 18 Aug, 1959
	Tries: 7 by G. Dennis v. Bradford N., 20 Jan, 1934
	Points: 27 by W. Langton v. Keighley, 18 Aug, 1959
	Highest score: 75-5 v. Broughton Rec., 1896-97
	Highest against: 76-8 v. Halifax, 1972-73

1985-86 PLAYERS' SUMMARY

	App	Tries	Goals	Dr	Pts
Allan, Mick	1	—	—	—	—
Appleyard, Mick	2	—	—	—	—
Barlow, Glen	8 + 2	2	—	—	8
Bateman, Andy	14 + 6	3	—	—	12
Benioni, Kuku	0 + 1	—	—	—	—
Birkby, Ian	5	—	—	—	—
Bowden, Chris	18 + 5	3	—	—	12
Cawood, Gary	4	—	—	—	—
Crampton, Jimmy	12 + 1	—	—	—	—
Davis, Alex	1 + 1	—	—	—	—
Duane, Dean	1	—	—	—	—
Dufton, Steve	2 + 1	—	—	—	—
Foley, Billy	1	—	—	—	—
Goodyear, George	3	—	5	—	10
Gough, Ian	1	—	—	—	—
Gray, Neil	24	7	—	—	28
Haley, Wayne	3	1	—	—	4
Hirst, John	9 + 2	—	1	—	2
Holmes, Ernest	1	1	—	—	4
Hudson, Terry	9	—	—	—	—
Hullock, Steve	4 + 2	1	—	—	4
Hunt, Ian	2 + 1	—	—	—	—
Idle, Graham	13	1	—	—	4
Irvine, Jimmy	12	1	—	—	4
Kay, Andrew	34	9	20	—	76
Kemble, Steve	13 + 2	3	—	—	12
King, Graham	26	22	—	—	88
Lean, Neil	2	—	—	—	—
Magyar, John	1	—	—	—	—
Marson, Andrew	8 + 5	—	—	—	—
McCurrie, Alan	12 + 1	—	—	—	—
Milton, Roy	10 + 1	5	—	—	20
Mitchell, Keith	12 + 8	3	—	—	12
Moran, Kevin	1	—	—	—	—
Morgan, Paul	6 + 4	—	—	—	—
Murrell, Bryan	33 + 2	7	—	1	29
Newsome, Mark	3 + 5	1	—	—	4
Nicholson, Steve	27	8	—	—	32
Nickle, Steve	1	—	—	—	—
O'Dwyer, Jim	7 + 1	—	—	—	—
Olbison, Kevin	4 + 1	—	—	—	—
Oldroyd, Matthew	2 + 1	—	—	—	—
Penola, Colin	13 + 2	—	—	—	—
Rayner, Neil	6 + 4	—	—	1	1
Reeder, Terry	0 + 1	—	—	—	—
Rowse, Gary	23	4	77	—	170
Rudd, Neil	1 + 2	1	—	—	4
Sampson, Ian	1 + 1	—	—	—	—
Sampson, Roy	9 + 2	1	—	—	4
Saunders, Lee	1 + 1	1	—	—	4
Skerrett, Kelvin	21	12	—	—	48
Tate, Phil	4	1	—	—	4
Waites, Keith	3	1	—	—	4
Warrener, Stan	14 + 4	1	—	—	4
Webb, Darren	1 + 2	—	—	—	—
Wilson, Warren	24	7	—	—	28
Wolford, John	1 + 2	—	—	—	—
Wood, Mark	33 + 1	3	—	—	12
TOTALS:					
58 players		110	103	2	648

1985-86 MATCH ANALYSIS

Date	Competition	H/A	Opponent	Rlt	Score	Tries	Goals	Attendance	Referee
1.9.85	SD	A	Keighley	W	38-10	King (3), Kay, Waites, Mitchell	Rowse (7)	—	—
4.9.85	SD	H	Mansfield M.	W	24-6	Kay, Murrell, Bateman	Rowse (6)	1013	Loftus
8.9.85	SD	H	Sheffield E.	L	10-22	Tate	Rowse (3)	902	Berry
15.9.85	YC(1)	A	Castleford	L	2-60	—	Rowse	—	—
22.9.85	SD	H	Blackpool B.	W	38-32	Barlow, Rowse, Bowden, King, Gray, Rudd, Kay	Rowse (5)	903	Tennant
29.9.85	SD	A	Leigh	L	16-30	King, Idle, Skerrett	Rowse (2)	—	—
6.10.85	SD	H	Doncaster	W	40-16	Skerrett (3), Rowse, Kay, Wilson, Wood	Rowse (6)	821	Houghton
13.10.85	SD	A	Whitehaven	L	6-28	Bowden	Rowse	—	—
20.10.85	SD	A	Bramley	W	22-14	King, Gray, Skerrett	Rowse (5)	—	—
25.10.85	SD	H	Workington T.	W	32-30	King (3), Murrell	Rowse (8)	663	Simpson
3.11.85	SD	A	Huddersfield B.	L	10-16	Wilson	Rowse (3)	—	—
13.11.85	SD	H	Carlisle	L	14-24	R. Sampson, Wilson, Gray	Rowse	493	Spencer
17.11.85	SD	A	Mansfield M.	W	38-6	King (3), Mitchell, Murrell, Wood	Rowse (7)	—	—
24.11.85	JPS(1)	H	Workington T.	W	20-12	Skerrett, King, Nicholson, Kemble	Rowse (2)	726	Tennant
1.12.85	JPS(2)	A	Leigh	L	6-48	Hullock	Rowse	—	—
15.12.85	SD	A	Sheffield E.	L	16-26	Nicholson, Skerrett, Kemble, Murrell	—	—	—
22.12.85	SD	H	Rochdale H.	L	18-37	King (2), Kay	Rowse (3)	1140	Haigh
26.12.85	SD	H	Batley	W	26-8	King (2), Barlow, Skerrett	Rowse (5)	1021	Smith
1.1.86	SD	A	Batley	L	0-22	—	—	—	—
12.1.86	SD	H	Barrow	W	20-18	Rowse (2), Skerrett, King	Rowse (2)	684	Kendrew
19.1.86	SD	H	Huddersfield B.	D	20-20	King (2), Nicholson	Rowse (4)	752	Volante
26.1.86	CC(P)	H	Kells	W	20-8	Kay, Bowden, Nicholson	Rowse (4)	1200	Carter
2.2.86	SD	A	Barrow	L	8-48	Kemble, Bateman	—	—	—
9.2.86	CC(1)	H	Castleford	L	6-60	Kay	Rowse	2358	McDonald
16.2.86	SD	H	Whitehaven	L	16-29	King (2), Mitchell	Kay (2)	449	Berry
9.3.86	SD	H	Keighley	W	24-4	Murrell, Wilson, Wood	Kay (6)	536	Loftus
16.3.86	SD	H	Runcorn H.	D	14-14	Murrell, Gray, Wilson, Kay	—	377	Tennant
30.3.86	SD	A	Wakefield T.	L	4-26	—	Kay (2)	—	—
3.4.86	SD	A	Rochdale H.	L	5-28	Skerrett	Rayner (dg)	—	—
6.4.86	SD	H	Bramley	D	20-20	Milton (2), Skerrett, Gray	Kay (2)	671	Lindop
3.4.86	SD	A	Blackpool B.	L	14-38	Kay, Skerrett, Wilson	Kay	—	—
16.4.86	SD	H	Leigh	L	12-24	Gray (2)	Kay (2)	617	Kendrew
20.4.86	SD	A	Workington T.	W	19-14	Milton (2), Murrell	Kay (3), Murrell (dg)	—	—
23.4.86	SD	H	Fulham	L	14-20	Bateman, Nicholson, Milton	Hirst	283	Mean
27.4.86	SD	A	Runcorn H.	L	2-37	—	Goodyear	—	—
30.4.86	SD	H	Wakefield T.	L	8-24	Nicholson, Irvine	—	950	Houghton
6.5.86	SD	A	Doncaster	L	10-42	Kay, Haley,	Kay	—	—
11.5.86	SD	A	Carlisle	L	8-28	Nicholson, Saunders	—	—	—
16.5.86	SD	A	Fulham	L	28-34	Nicholson, Warrener, Holmes, Wilson, Newson	Goodyear (4)	—	—

KEIGHLEY

Ground:	Lawkholme Lane
Colours:	White jerseys with scarlet and emerald green V, white shorts
First Season:	1901-02
Nickname:	Lawkholmers
Chairman:	Colin Farrar
Secretary:	Betty Spencer
Coach:	Geoff Peggs (Nov 1983-Sep 1985) Peter Roe (Sep 1985-)
Honours:	**Division Two** Champions, 1902-03 **Challenge Cup** Beaten finalists, 1936-37 **Yorkshire Cup** Beaten finalists, 1943-44, 1951-52
Records:	Attendance: 14,500 v. Halifax (RL Cup) 3 Mar, 1951 **Season** Goals: 155 by B. Jefferson, 1973-74 Tries: 30 by J. Sherburn, 1934-35 Points: 331 by B. Jefferson, 1973-74 **Match** Goals: 11 by R. Walker v. Castleford, 13 Jan, 1906; H. Cook v. Hull K.R., 31 Oct, 1953 Tries: 5 by I. Jagger v. Castleford, 13 Jan, 1906; S. Stacey v. Liverpool C., 9 Mar, 1907 Points: 24 by J. Phillips v. Halifax, 5 Oct, 1957 Highest score: 67-0 v. Castleford, 1905-06 Highest against: 92-2 v. Leigh, 1985-86

1985-86 PLAYERS' SUMMARY

	App	Tries	Goals	Dr	Pts
Allen, Mick	4	—	—	—	—
Aspey, Steve	3	—	—	—	—
Atkinson, Colin	6 + 1	—	—	—	—
Bardgett, Joe	22 + 1	2	—	—	8
Bragger, Ian	34 + 1	10	—	—	40
Buckton, John	1 + 1	—	—	—	—
Butterfield, Jeff	35 + 1	7	—	—	28
Dews, Campbell	12 + 1	1	—	—	4
Dixon, Keith	6 + 1	1	1	—	6
Dwyer, Mark	14 + 2	3	—	—	12
Ellis, Dave	3	—	—	—	—
Ellis, Kevin	7 + 6	2	—	—	8
Fairhurst, Ian	22 + 5	1	45	—	94
Farmer, Nick	1	—	—	—	—
Fisher, Adam	11 + 1	1	—	—	4
Goodyear, Frank	10 + 5	—	—	—	—
Green, John	16 + 1	1	7	—	18
Hawksworth, Mick	20 + 4	11	—	—	44
Higgins, Andy	2	—	—	—	—
Hughes, Brian	1	—	—	—	—
Hunt, Ian	2	—	—	—	—
Hurst, John	7 + 1	—	—	—	—
Illingworth, Sam	0 + 1	—	—	—	—
Jackson, Mark	1	—	—	—	—
Johnson, Will	3 + 1	—	—	—	—
Lord, Mark	2	—	—	—	—
Marshall, Nigel	4 + 1	1	—	—	4
Mason, Max	6 + 1	2	—	—	8
Mather, Steve	17	7	—	—	28
McDermott, Paul	2	1	—	—	4
Meakin, Andy	1	—	—	—	—
Moll, David	14 + 1	7	—	—	28
Moses, Paul	20 + 1	7	8	6	50
Newton, Howard	1 + 1	—	—	—	—
Nixon, David	1 + 1	—	—	—	—
Page, Steve	11	—	5	—	10
Pitts, John	11 + 6	2	—	—	8
Priestley, Ray	4 + 1	—	—	—	—
Proctor, Rob	32	1	—	—	4
Race, Wayne	13 + 1	3	—	—	12
Ragan, Mark	7 + 9	—	1	—	2
Roe, Peter	30 + 1	4	—	—	16
Stockhill, Ian	2 + 3	—	—	—	—
Townend, Jeff	2 + 1	—	—	—	—
Turner, Fred	34 + 1	1	—	—	4
Waites, Keith	12	2	—	—	8
Walsh, Tim	7 + 2	—	—	—	—
Winterbottom, Rick	27 + 2	5	1	1	23
Trialists (4)	4 + 2	—	—	—	—
TOTALS:					
52 players		83	68	7	475

1985-86 MATCH ANALYSIS

Date	Competition	H/A	Opponent	Rlt	Score	Tries	Goals	Attendance	Referee
1.9.85	SD	H	Hunslet	L	10-38	Moll	Fairhurst (3)	1024	Hodgson
4.9.85	SD	H	Carlisle	D	20-20	Moll (2), K. Ellis	Fairhurst (4)	467	Haigh
8.9.85	SD	H	Bramley	L	12-30	Moll, Bragger	Fairhurst (2)	796	Kershaw
15.9.85	YC(1)	A	Leeds	L	12-60	Turner, Mather	Green, Winterbottom	—	—
18.9.85	SD	A	Whitehaven	L	0-32	—	—	—	—
22.9.85	SD	A	Mansfield M.	L	18-20	Mather, Marshall, Bardgett	Fairhurst (3)	—	—
29.9.85	SD	H	Rochdale H.	L	16-25	Butterfield, Fairhurst, Moll	Green (2)	1162	Loftus
6.10.85	SD	A	Blackpool B.	L	8-16	Bragger	Fairhurst (2)	—	—
13.10.85	SD	A	Barrow	L	2-74	—	Fairhurst	—	—
20.10.85	SD	H	Runcorn H.	W	15-3	Bragger, Winterbottom, Hawksworth	Green, Winterbottom (dg)	619	Houghton
27.10.85	SD	A	Doncaster	W	24-17	Mather (2), Roe, Hawksworth	Green (3), Ragan	—	—
3.11.85	SD	A	Sheffield E.	L	9-22	Bardgett	Fairhurst (2), Moses (dg)	—	—
10.11.85	JPS(P)	H	Jubilee	W	24-6	Mather (2), Fisher, Hawksworth	Fairhurst (4)	1007	Kendrew
17.11.85	SD	A	Runcorn H.	W	32-19	Butterfield (2), Hawksworth, Bragger, Pitts, Winterbottom	Fairhurst (4)	—	—
24.11.85	JPS(1)	H	Huddersfield B.	W	20-10	Hawksworth, Bragger, K. Ellis	Fairhurst (4)	1264	Berry
1.12.85	JPS(2)	A	York	L	16-21	Hawksworth (2), Bragger	Fairhurst (2)	—	—
15.12.85	SD	A	Batley	L	12-15	McDermott, Dwyer	Fairhurst (2)	—	—
22.12.85	SD	H	Mansfield M.	W	20-10	Hawksworth, Moll, Winterbottom	Fairhusrt (4)	691	Volante
12.1.86	SD	H	Fulham	W	18-6	Moll, Bragger, Green	Fairhurst (3)	645	Campbell
19.1.86	SD	H	Blackpool B.	W	12-6	Mason (2), Dews	—	773	Croft
2.2.86	SD	H	Batley	W	16-14	Butterfield, Bragger, Mather	Fairhurst (2)	921	Allatt
9.2.86	CC(1)	H	Leigh	L	2-24	—	Fairhurst	1968	Hodgson
2.3.86	SD	H	Doncaster	L	12-18	Dwyer, Roe	Fairhurst (2)	710	Tickle
9.3.86	SD	A	Hunslet	L	4-24	Roe	—	—	—
23.3.86	SD	A	Carlisle	L	2-17	—	Page	—	—
26.3.86	SD	H	Huddersfield B.	W	21-10	Moses, Proctor, Dwyer, Race	Page, Moses (3dg)	576	Smith
31.3.86	SD	A	Bramley	L	10-46	Moses, Hawksworth	Page	—	—
6.4.86	SD	H	Sheffield E.	L	9-24	Waites, Moses	Moses (dg)	581	Beaumont
10.4.86	SD	H	Wakefield T.	L	4-54	Race	—	537	Tennant
13.4.86	SD	A	Wakefield T.	L	10-12	Moses (2)	Moses	—	—
17.4.86	SD	A	Huddersfield B.	D	32-32	Winterbottom, Butterfield, Moses, Bragger, Roe, Waites	Moses (4)	—	—
20.4.86	SD	A	Rochdale H.	W	19-18	Hawksworth (2), Moses	Moses (3, 1dg)	—	—
23.4.86	SD	H	Workington T.	L	8-29	Race, Winterbottom	—	386	Kershaw
27.4.86	SD	H	Barrow	L	4-58	Dixon	—	746	Whitfield
30.4.86	SD	A	Leigh	L	2-92	—	Page	—	—
7.5.86	SD	H	Whitehaven	L	0-16	—	—	355	Spencer
9.5.86	SD	H	Leigh	L	4-38	Pitts	—	670	Mean
11.5.86	SD	A	Workington T.	L	2-36	—	Dixon	—	—
18.5.86	SD	A	Fulham	L	14-27	Butterfield (2), Bragger	Page	—	—

LEEDS

Ground: Headingley
Colours: Blue and amber jerseys, white shorts
First Season: 1895-96
Nickname: Loiners
Chairman: Harry Jepson
General
Manager: Joe Warham
Coach: Peter Fox (May 1985-)
Honours: **Championship** Winners, 1960-61, 1968-69, 1971-72
Beaten finalists, 1914-15, 1928-29, 1929-30, 1930-31, 1937-38, 1969-70, 1972-73
League Leaders Trophy Winners, 1966-67, 1967-68, 1968-69, 1969-70, 1971-72
Challenge Cup Winners, 1909-10, 1922-23, 1931-32, 1935-36, 1940-41, 1941-42, 1956-57, 1967-68, 1976-77, 1977-78
Beaten finalists, 1942-43, 1946-47, 1970-71, 1971-72
Yorkshire League Winners, 1901-02, 1927-28, 1930-31, 1933-34, 1934-35, 1936-37, 1937-38, 1950-51, 1954-55, 1956-57, 1960-61, 1966-67, 1967-68, 1968-69, 1969-70
Yorkshire Cup Winners, 1921-22, 1928-29, 1930-31, 1932-33, 1934-35, 1935-36, 1937-38, 1958-59, 1968-69, 1970-71, 1972-73, 1973-74, 1975-76, 1976-77, 1979-80, 1980-81
Beaten finalists, 1919-20, 1947-48, 1961-62, 1964-65
BBC2 Floodlit Trophy Winners, 1970-71
John Player Trophy Winners, 1972-73, 1983-84
Beaten finalists, 1982-83
Premiership Winners, 1974-75, 1978-79
Records: Attendance: 40,175 v. Bradford N. (League) 21 May, 1947

Season
Goals: 166 by B.L. Jones, 1956-57
Tries: 63 by E. Harris, 1935-36
Points: 431 by B.L. Jones, 1956-57
Match
Goals: 13 by B.L. Jones v. Blackpool B., 19 Aug, 1957
Tries: 8 by F. Webster v. Coventry, 12 Apr, 1913; E. Harris v. Bradford N., 14 Sep, 1931
Points: 31 by B.L. Jones v. Bradford N., 22 Aug, 1956
Highest score: 102-0 v. Coventry, 1912-13
Highest against: 71-0 v. Wakefield T., 1945-46

1985-86 PLAYERS' SUMMARY

	App	Tries	Goals	Dr	Pts
Clark, Trevor	8 + 3	2	—	—	8
Conway, Mark	20 + 7	8	20	—	72
Cooper, Colin	1	—	—	—	—
Creasser. David	37	12	84	—	216
Currie, Tony	31 + 1	16	—	—	64
Dick, Kevin	16 + 3	5	7	—	34
Dickinson, Roy	6 + 4	1	—	—	4
Ford, Steve	2	1	—	—	4
Francis, Norman	15	5	—	—	20
Gibson, Carl	19	9	—	—	36
Gill, Paul	8 + 1	2	18	—	44
Grayshon, Jeff	23 + 2	1	—	—	4
Gunn, Richard	1 + 6	—	—	—	—
Hague, Neil	34 + 1	3	2	1	17
Healy, David	5	—	—	—	—
Heron, David	33 + 2	6	—	—	24
Hill, Brendan	21 + 4	4	—	—	16
Ingham, Gareth	1	—	—	—	—
Johnson, Errol	2	—	—	—	—
Lyons, Cliff	27 + 2	16	—	4	68
Maskill, Colin	12 + 7	—	—	—	—
Medley, Paul	16 + 7	8	—	—	32
Mitchell, Pat	1	—	—	—	—
Moorby, Gary	12 + 5	7	—	—	28
Owen, Phil	7 + 3	1	—	—	4
Powell, Roy	29 + 2	5	—	—	20
Pratt, Richard	1	—	—	—	—
Rayne, Keith	23 + 7	3	—	—	12
Rayne, Kevin	30 + 4	7	—	—	28
Sharp, Henry	3	—	—	—	—
Smith, Andy	36	12	—	—	48
Staniland, Andrew	7	2	—	—	8
Turner, Phil	2	—	—	—	—
Ward, David	25 + 1	2	—	—	8
Webb, Terry	19 + 5	3	—	1	13
Wilkinson, Ian	32 + 1	2	—	—	8
Wilson, Mark	7 + 4	4	—	—	16

TOTALS:
37 players .... | | 147 | 131 | 6 | 856

1985-86 MATCH ANALYSIS

Date	Competition	H/A	Opponent	Rlt	Score	Tries	Goals	Attendance	Referee
1.9.85	SLC	A	Dewsbury	W	22-13	Moorby, Dick, Smith	Conway (3), Dick (2)	—	—
8.9.85	SLC	A	Oldham	W	30-14	Wilkinson, Smith, Moorby, Wilson, Hill	Dick (4), Hague	—	—

(continued)

MATCH ANALYSIS (continued)

Date	Comp	H/A	Opponent	Res	Score	Tries	Goals	Att	Referee
15.9.85	YC(1)	H	Keighley	W	60-12	Lyons (3), Smith (2), Moorby (2), Gill, Kevin Rayne, Keith Rayne, Ford	Gill (8)	4775	Tennant
22.9.85	SLC	H	St. Helens	W	21-8	Creasser, Conway, Moorby	Creasser (4), Lyons (dg)	8844	McDonald
25.9.85	YC(2)	A	Dewsbury	W	48-2	Powell (2), Conway (2), Lyons, Smith, Creasser, Wilson, Francis	Conway (4), Creasser (2)	—	—
29.9.85	SLC	A	Salford	W	22-16	Lyons, Wilson, Currie, Heron	Conway (3)	—	—
2.10.85	YC(SF)	H	Castleford	L	10-14	Wilson, Smith	Creasser	10281	Smith
6.10.85	SLC	H	York	L	10-18	Dickinson, Currie	Creasser	5589	Volante
20.10.85	SLC	A	Swinton	W	26-14	Lyons, Smith, Powell, Francis, Keith Rayne	Creasser (3)	—	—
24.10.85	SLC	H	Wigan	L	6-28	Hill	Creasser	9537	Kershaw
29.10.85	Tour	H	New Zealand	L	10-16	Lyons	Creasser (3)	4713	Smith
3.11.85	SLC	A	Warrington	L	18-32	Wilkinson, Medley, Francis	Creasser (2), Conway	—	—
10.11.85	SLC	A	Halifax	D	18-18	Moorby, Hill, Currie, Kevin Rayne	Conway	—	—
17.11.85	SLC	H	Hull K.R.	L	12-16	Francis, Lyons	Creasser (2)	7962	Allatt
24.11.85	JPS(1)	A	Barrow	L	2-5	—	Creasser	—	—
8.12.85	SLC	A	St. Helens	D	12-12	Creasser, Clark	Creasser (2)	—	—
15.12.85	SLC	H	Halifax	L	20-22	Lyons (2), Currie	Creasser (4)	8132	Whitfield
22.12.85	SLC	A	Castleford	W	26-18	Powell, Ward, Moorby, Clark	Creasser (3), Dick, Hague	—	—
26.12.85	SLC	H	Dewsbury	W	28-8	Dick (2), Currie, Smith	Creasser (6)	6266	Kendrew
1.1.86	SLC	H	Oldham	W	22-6	Currie, Lyons, Medley	Gill (5)	9056	Hodgson
12.1.86	SLC	A	Featherstone R.	W	20-18	Lyons, Hague, Currie, Kevin Rayne	Gill (2)	—	—
30.1.86	CC(P)	A	Swinton	W	30-8	Creasser, Kevin Rayne, Smith, Hague, Lyons, Gill	Creasser (2), Gill	—	—
2.2.86	SLC	H	Swinton	W	20-8	Webb (2), Gibson, Currie	Gill (2)	4780	Campbell
9.2.86	CC(1)	A	Halifax	W	24-4	Creasser (2), Gibson (2), Currie	Creasser (2)	—	—
16.2.86	SLC	H	Featherstone R.	W	44-6	Currie (2), Hill, Webb, Dick, Conway, Smith, Gibson	Creasser (3), Conway (3)	6694	Whitfield
23.2.86	CC(2)	A (at Leeds)	Doncaster	W	28-10	Creasser (2), Smith, Keith Rayne, Lyons	Creasser (4)	—	—
27.2.86	SLC	H	Salford	W	34-12	Heron (2), Currie (2), Creasser, Ward	Creasser (5)	4701	Roberts (Aus)
2.3.86	SLC	A	Widnes	L	18-20	Currie, Lyons, Heron	Creasser (3)	—	—
9.3.86	SLC	H	Widnes	W	29-12	Gibson (3), Medley, Lyons	Creasser (4), Lyons (dg)	7229	Berry
16.3.86	CC(3)	A	Widnes	D	10-10	Medley (2)	Creasser	—	—
19.3.86	CC(3) Replay	H	Widnes	W	5-0	—	Creasser (2), Lyons (dg)	(15710)	Kershaw
24.3.86	SLC	H	Castleford	W	18-12	Powell, Heron, Kevin Rayne	Creasser (3)	7085	Beaumont
29.3.86	CC(SF)	Elland Rd, Leeds	Hull K.R.	D	24-24	Currie (2), Creasser, Medley	Creasser (3), Lyons (dg), Webb (dg)	(23866)	Whitfield
30.3.86	SLC	H	Bradford N.	L	8-25	Staniland	Creasser, Conway	6728	Fox
3.4.86	CC(SF)	Elland Rd, Leeds	Hull K.R.	L	0-17	—	—	(32485)	Whitfield
6.4.86	SLC	H	Hull	L	18-35	Grayshon, Dick, Heron	Creasser (3)	6015	Kershaw
9.4.86	SLC	A	Hull	L	4-10	Kevin Rayne	—	—	—
11.4.86	SLC	A	Bradford N.	D	10-10	Staniland, Conway	Creasser	—	—
13.4.86	SLC	H	Warrington	L	6-35	Conway	Creasser	5315	Lindop
15.4.86	SLC	A	Hull K.R.	L	12-28	Creasser, Conway	Conway (2)	—	—
20.4.86	SLC	A	Wigan	L	6-29	Medley	Conway	—	—
22.4.86	SLC	A	York	W	14-12	Hague, Smith	Creasser (3)	—	—
27.4.86	PT(1)	A	St. Helens	W	38-22	Gibson (2), Kevin Rayne, Owen, Medley, Conway	Creasser (7)	—	—
11.5.86	PT(SF)	A	Halifax	L	13-16	Francis, Creasser	Conway, Creasser, Hague (dg)	—	—

61

LEIGH

Ground:	Hilton Park
Colours:	Cherry and white jerseys, white shorts
First Season:	1895-96
Chairman:	Brian Sharples
Secretary:	John Stringer
Coach:	Alex Murphy (Feb-Nov 1985)
	Tommy Dickens (Nov 1985-)

Honours: **Championship** Winners, 1905-06
Division One Champions, 1981-82
Division Two Champions, 1977-78, 1985-86
Challenge Cup Winners, 1920-21, 1970-71
Lancashire Cup Winners, 1952-53, 1955-56, 1970-71, 1981-82
Beaten finalists, 1905-06, 1909-10, 1920-21, 1922-23, 1949-50, 1951-52, 1963-64, 1969-70
BBC2 Trophy Winners, 1969-70, 1972-73
Beaten finalists, 1967-68, 1976-77

Records: Attendance: 31,324 v. St. Helens (RL Cup) 14 Mar, 1953
Season
Goals: 173 by C. Johnson, 1985-86
Tries: 49 by S. Halliwell, 1985-86
Points: 400 by C. Johnson, 1985-86
Match
Goals: 15 by M. Stacey v. Doncaster, 28 Mar, 1976
Tries: 6 by J. Wood v. York, 4 Oct, 1947
Points: 38 by J. Woods v. Blackpool B., 11 Sep, 1977
Highest score: 92-2 v. Keighley, 1985-86
Highest against: 60-8 v. Salford, 1940

1985-86 PLAYERS' SUMMARY

	App	Tries	Goals	Dr	Pts
Ainsworth, Gary	9 + 3	4	—	—	16
Atherton, Wayne	15 + 3	5	—	—	20
Beazant, Darren	3 + 1	1	—	—	4
Brockwell, Simon	8 + 3	4	—	—	16
Campbell, Danny	9 + 1	1	—	—	4
Clarke, Jeff	30 + 2	8	—	—	32
Cogger, Trevor	26 + 1	10	—	—	40
Collier, Andy	1 + 2	—	—	—	—
Cottrell, Tony	26 + 10	5	—	—	20
Davis, Mike	8 + 5	5	—	—	20
Drummond, Des	29	21	2	—	88
Fox, Phil	42	29	—	—	116
Gelling, Bryan	27 + 3	7	—	—	28
Halliwell, Steve	37 + 1	49	—	—	196
Hardman, Paul	3 + 3	—	—	—	—
Henderson, John	34	31	—	—	124
Henson, Robert	5	—	—	—	—
Howarth, Roy	0 + 1	—	—	—	—
Hughes, Gary	12 + 3	3	—	—	12
Johnson, Chris	42	14	171	2	400
Johnson, Phil	36 + 2	8	26	4	88
Kerr, John	19 + 16	16	—	—	64
Manfredi, Tony	0 + 3	—	—	—	—
Mayoh, Peter	16 + 3	8	—	—	32
Mellor, Sean	13	—	—	—	—
O'Toole, David	0 + 1	—	—	—	—
Pyke, Derek	38	10	—	—	40
Ramsdale, Daren	6	—	—	—	—
Riding, Colin	1	—	—	—	—
Tabern, Ray	31 + 9	11	—	—	44
Taylor, David	1	—	—	—	—
Thomas, Mark	5	—	—	—	—
Walkden, Gary	0 + 2	—	—	—	—
Westhead, John	27	8	—	—	32

TOTALS:

	App	Tries	Goals	Dr	Pts
34 players		258	199	6	1,436

Great Britain Under-21 loose forward John Westhead.

1985-86 MATCH ANALYSIS

Date	Com-petition	H/A	Opponent	Rlt	Score	Tries	Goals	Atten-dance	Referee
1.9.85	SD	A	Runcorn H.	W	38-12	Halliwell (2), Gelling, Pyke, Ainsworth, Atherton, Tabern	P. Johnson (5)	—	—
8.9.85	SD	H	Batley	W	26-17	Pyke (2), Halliwell, C. Johnson, Westhead	P. Johnson (3)	2251	Walker
15.9.85	LC(1)	H	Oldham	W	40-12	Henderson (2), Ainsworth, Cogger, Gelling, C. Johnson, Fox	P. Johnson (6)	3500	Campbell
18.9.85	SD	H	Sheffield E.	W	32-18	Henderson (3), Halliwell, Westhead, Fox	P. Johnson (4)	2395	Whitfield
22.9.85	SD	A	Barrow	L	2-14	—	P. Johnson	—	—
25.9.85	LC(2)	H	Widnes	L	14-18	Fox, Kerr	P. Johnson (3)	4000	Spencer
29.9.85	SD	H	Hunslet	W	30-16	Kerr (2), Mayoh (2), Henderson	C. Johnson (5)	2577	Tickle
6.10.85	SD	A	Carlisle	W	20-9	Mayoh, Halliwell, Cogger	C. Johnson (4)	—	—
13.10.85	SD	H	Mansfield M.	W	76-6	Halliwell (4), Drummond (3), Henderson (3), Pyke, Fox, Cogger, Ainsworth	C. Johnson (8), Drummond (2)	2649	Volante
20.10.85	SD	A	Huddersfield B.	W	54-2	Brockwell (2), Clarke, P. Johnson, Tabern, Fox, Halliwell, Cogger, Drummond	C. Johnson (9)	—	—
27.10.85	SD	A	Whitehaven	W	34-11	Halliwell, Mayoh, Westhead, Gelling, Drummond, Kerr	C. Johnson (5)	—	—
3.11.85	SD	H	Fulham	W	42-13	Tabern, Clarke, C. Johnson, Pyke, Mayoh, Fox, Cogger, Westhead	C. Johnson (5)	3072	McDonald
10.11.85	SD	A	Batley	W	28-8	Westhead (2), Mayoh, Kerr, Clarke	C. Johnson (4)	—	—
17.11.85	SD	H	Bramley	W	54-8	Halliwell (2), Fox (2), P. Johnson (2), Henderson, Tabern, Gelling	C. Johnson (9)	2931	Beaumont
24.11.85	JPS(1)	A	Batley	W	70-2	Fox (5), Henderson (3), Kerr, Cottrell, Cogger (2), P. Johnson, Drummond	C. Johnson (7)	—	—
1.12.85	JPS(2)	H	Hunslet	W	48-6	Henderson (3), Clarke, Drummond, Fox, Westhead, Cottrell, Kerr	C. Johnson (6)	3267	Hodgson
8.12.85	JPS(3)	A	Widnes	W	35-31	Drummond (3), Gelling, Pyke, Fox	C. Johnson (5), P. Johnson (dg)	—	—
14.12.85	JPS(SF)	St. Helens	Wigan	L	8-36	P. Johnson, Fox	—	(10509)	Lindop
22.12.85	SD	H	Carlisle	W	58-12	Halliwell (3), Kerr (2), Fox (2), Henderson (2), Mayoh, Drummond	C. Johnson (4), P. Johnson (3)	2903	Campbell
26.12.85	SD	A	Rochdale H.	W	26-8	Cogger, Tabern, Henderson, C. Johnson	C. Johnson (5)	—	—
1.1.86	SD	H	Blackpool B.	W	34-8	Henderson (2), Cottrell, Halliwell, Drummond, Mayoh	C. Johnson (5)	2974	Holdsworth
5.1.86	SD	A	Fulham	W	22-18	Henderson, Halliwell, Kerr, P. Johnson	C. Johnson (3)	—	—
12.1.86	SD	H	Runcorn H.	W	36-18	Drummond (3), Westhead, Henderson, Ainsworth, P. Johnson	C. Johnson (4)	2449	Volante
19.1.86	SD	A	Sheffield E.	W	16-2	Halliwell (2), Fox	C. Johnson (2)	—	—

(continued on page 95)

63

MANSFIELD MARKSMAN

Ground: Alfreton Sports Stadium
Colours: Light and dark blue jerseys, blue shorts
First Season: 1984-85
Chairman: Paul Tomlinson
General
  Manager: David Parker
Coach: Mick Blacker (May 1984-Oct 1985)
  Bill Kirkbride (Nov 1985-Mar 1986)
  Steve Dennison (Apr 1986-)
Records: Attendance: 2,291 v. Wakefield T. (Div. 2) 9 Sep, 1984

Season
Goals: 63 by C. Sanderson, 1984-85
Tries: 13 by S. Nicholson, K. Whiteman, 1984-85
Points: 136 by C. Sanderson, 1984-85

Match
Goals: 7 by B. Holden v. Keighley, 10 Mar, 1985
Tries: 4 by K. Whiteman v. Doncaster, 4 Nov, 1984
Points: 18 by B. Holden v. Keighley, 10 Mar, 1985
Highest score: 54-10 v. Doncaster, 1984-85
Highest against: 76-6 v. Leigh, 1985-86

1985-86 PLAYERS' SUMMARY

	App	Tries	Goals	Dr	Pts
Blackmore, Peter	20 + 4	3	—	—	12
Brannan, Alistair	7	—	—	—	—
Buckton, John	22 + 3	4	18	—	52
Cochrane, Tony	17 + 5	5	—	—	20
Cook, Mark	2 + 2	—	—	—	—
Cummins, Brendan	1	—	—	—	—
Dennison, Steve	19 + 4	1	3	—	10
Duffy, Andy	14	2	—	—	8
Edginton, David	26	2	—	—	8
Fletcher, Andrew	10	4	—	—	16
Fox, Desmond	6	—	—	—	—
Gillespie, Steve	12	—	—	—	—
Goodall, Adrian	5	—	—	—	—
Hardy, Alan	9 + 1	—	3	3	9
Hiley, Greg	13 + 1	1	—	—	4
Hitchen, Gary	6	1	—	—	4
Holden, Barry	22 + 8	1	2	—	8
Hooper, Mick	23 + 2	5	—	—	20
Hornsey, Paul	0 + 1	—	—	—	—
Howarth, Mick	1	1	2	—	8
Hughes, Brian	6 + 1	—	2	—	4
Humphreys, Lee	7	1	—	—	4
Kellett, Neil	20 + 1	6	—	—	24
Knapp, Conrad	2	1	—	—	4
Labross, Mick	4	—	—	—	—
Langton, Terry	15 + 6	2	—	—	8
Lazenby, Rick	1	—	—	—	—
Loynes, Dean	6 + 3	—	—	—	—
Maguire, John	3 + 1	—	—	—	—
McFaul, John	5	—	—	—	—
McSherry, Martin	3 + 1	—	—	—	—
Morgan, Kevin	2	—	—	—	—
Murphy, Martin	1 + 3	—	2	—	4
Nicholson, Grant	14	1	1	—	6
Nicholson, Steve	4	1	—	—	4
Noble, Robert	6 + 2	2	—	—	8
Oates, David	2	—	4	—	8
O'Byrne, Mick	6	2	—	—	8
O'Rourke, Clifton	19 + 3	4	—	—	16
Page, Steve	13 + 2	5	15	—	50
Rose, Graham	0 + 1	—	—	—	—
Rose, Tony	4	—	—	—	—
Sanderson, Carl	8 + 3	—	10	2	22
Scanlon, Andrew	10	—	—	—	—
Sharp, Greg	3	—	—	—	—
Simpkin, Kevin	3	1	—	—	4
Spedding, Paul	8	—	—	—	—
Stevens, Darren	1	—	—	—	—
Stokes, Kevin	7 + 6	—	—	—	—
Waites, Keith	7	1	—	—	4
Walton, Dave	2	—	—	—	—
Welsh, Paul	7 + 2	2	—	—	8
Whitehead, Craig	1	—	—	—	—
Whiteman, Keith	2	—	—	—	—
Willis, Chris	22 + 1	6	—	—	24
Wilson, Andy	6	2	—	—	8
Trialist	3	—	—	—	—
TOTALS:					
57 players		67	62	5	397

1985-86 MATCH ANALYSIS

Date	Com-petition	H/A	Opponent	Rlt	Score	Tries	Goals	Atten-dance	Referee
1.9.85	SD	H	Bramley	W	20-18	S. Nicholson, Wilson, Page, Holden	Page (2)	535	Haigh
4.9.85	SD	A	Hunslet	L	6-24	Page	Page	—	—
8.9.85	SD	A	Wakefield T.	L	10-22	Page, Langton	Page	—	—
15.9.85	SD	A	Sheffield E.	L	12-34	Page (2), Wilson	—	—	—
22.9.85	SD	H	Keighley	W	20-18	Willis, Buckton	Page (4), Sanderson (1, 2dg)	831	Allatt
29.9.85	SD	A	Doncaster	L	6-21	Willis	Page	—	—
6.10.85	SD	H	Rochdale H.	L	0-8	—	—	762	McDonald
13.10.85	SD	A	Leigh	L	6-76	Hitchen	Page	—	—
20.10.85	SD	A	Workington T.	L	14-36	Edginton	Sanderson (5)	—	—
27.10.85	SD	H	Huddersfield B.	L	6-34	Buckton	Dennison	627	Holdsworth
3.11.85	SD	H	Whitehaven	L	12-24	Kellett, Blackmore	Sanderson (2)	464	Croft
10.11.85	SD	A	Barrow	L	0-40	—	—	—	—
17.11.85	SD	H	Hunslet	L	6-38	Buckton	Sanderson	512	Simpson
24.11.85	JPS (1)	A	Wigan	L	0-26	—	—	—	—
1.12.85	SD	H	Sheffield E.	D	14-14	Willis, Waites, O'Byrne	Hughes	517	Croft
8.12.85	SD	A	Whitehaven	L	0-28	—	—	—	—
15.12.85	SD	H	Barrow	L	0-40	—	—	463	Mean
22.12.85	SD	A	Keighley	L	10-20	O'Byrne	Page (3)	—	—
1.1.86	SD	H	Doncaster	L	20-21	G. Nicholson, Hiley, O'Rourke, Langton	Page (2)	407	Whitfield
5.1.86	SD	A	Blackpool B.	L	10-42	Cochrane	G. Nicholson, Hughes, Holden	—	—
19.1.86	SD	H	Wakefield T.	L	8-30	Howarth	Howarth (2)	811	McDonald
31.1.86	CC(P)	A	Carlisle	L	14-20	Edgington, Simpkin, Dennison	Sanderson	—	—
2.2.86	SD	H	Leigh	L	2-32	—	Holden	482	Fox
23.2.86	SD	A	Runcorn H.	L	2-24	—	Hardy (2dg)	—	—
16.3.86	SD	A	Carlisle	L	13-45	Hooper, Fletcher	Dennison (2), Hardy (dg)	—	—
23.3.96	SD	H*	Workington T.	L	18-42	Blackmore (2), Humphreys	Hardy (3)	290	Spencer
6.4.86	SD	A	Batley	L	6-26	Fletcher	Oates	—	—
11.4.86	SD	H	Carlisle	L	14-26	Fletcher, Buckton	Oates (3)	321	Mean
18.4.86	SD	A	Bramley	L	20-46	Kellett, Hooper, Duffy	Buckton (4)	—	—
20.4.86	SD	H	Runcorn H.	L	22-36	Kellett, O'Rourke, Willis, Cochrane	Buckton (3)	258	Holdsworth
25.4.86	SD	A	Huddersfield B.	L	14-30	Cochrane (2)	Buckton (3)	—	—
27.4.86	SD	H	Blackpool B.	L	26-34	Willis, Welsh, Noble, O'Rourke, Cochrane	Buckton (3)	337	Berry
30.4.86	SD	A	Rochdale H.	L	16-36	Hooper, Welsh, O'Rourke	Buckton (2)	—	—
5.5.86	SD	H	Batley	L	14-30	Noble, Hooper, Knapp	Buckton	422	Simpson
8.5.86	SD	H	Fulham	L	16-42	Hooper, Kellett, Fletcher	Buckton (2)	243	Cross (Pr)
10.5.86	SD	A	Fulham	L	20-43	Kellett (2), Duffy, Cochrane	Murphy (2)	—	—

*Home venue switched to Alfreton Sports Stadium and thereafter

OLDHAM

Ground: Watersheddings
Colours: Red and white hooped jerseys, red sleeves, white shorts
First Season: 1895-96
Nickname: Roughyeds
Chairman: Harvey Ashworth
General
  Manager: Frank Myler
Coach: Frank Myler (June 1984-)
Honours: **Championship** Winners, 1909-10, 1910-11,1956-57
Beaten finalists, 1906-07, 1907-08, 1908-09, 1921-22, 1954-55
Division One Champions, 1904-05
Division Two Champions, 1963-64, 1981-82
Challenge Cup Winners, 1898-99, 1924-25, 1926-27
Beaten finalists, 1906-07, 1911-12, 1923-24, 1925-26
Lancashire League Winners, 1897-98, 1900-01, 1907-08, 1909-10, 1921-22, 1956-57, 1957-58
Lancashire Cup Winners, 1907-08, 1910-11, 1913-14, 1919-20, 1924-25, 1933-34, 1956-57, 1957-58, 1958-59
Beaten finalists, 1908-09, 1911-12, 1918-19, 1921-22, 1954-55, 1966-67, 1968-69
Records: Attendance: 28,000 v. Huddersfield (League) 24 Feb, 1912
Season
Goals: 200 by B. Ganley, 1957-58
Tries: 49 by R. Farrar, 1921-22
Points: 412 by B. Ganley, 1957-58
Match
Goals: 14 by B. Ganley v. Liverpool C, 4 Apr, 1959
Tries: 7 by Miller v. Barry, 31 Oct, 1908
Points: 30 by A. Johnson v. Widnes, 9 Apr, 1928
Highest score: 67-6 v. Liverpool C., 1958-59
Highest against: 67-11 v. Hull K.R., 1978-79

1985-86 PLAYERS' SUMMARY

	App	Tries	Goals	Dr	Pts
Ashton, Ray	24 + 7	6	4	4	36
Atkinson, Keith	6 + 1	1	1	—	6
Birkby, Ian	2 + 1	1	—	—	4
Caffery, Brian	2	—	3	—	6
Casey, Leo	3	—	—	—	—
Chisnall, Chris	1 + 1	—	—	—	—
Cook, Les	0 + 1	—	—	—	—
Edwards, Jeff	9 + 2	1	—	—	4
Finch, David	0 + 3	—	—	—	—
Flanagan, Terry	28	2	—	—	8
Foy, Des	26	10	—	—	40
Graham, Mal	27	21	—	—	84
Hawkyard, Colin	6 + 3	—	—	—	—
Hobbs, David	30	4	61	3	141
Jones, Wally	28	—	—	—	—
Kirwan, Paddy	22 + 9	6	—	—	24
Liddiard, David	14 + 1	12	—	—	48
Liddiard, Glen	20 + 1	4	—	—	16
Lowndes, Paul	13 + 7	1	—	—	4
Marsden, Robert	1 + 1	—	—	—	—
M'Barki, Hussein	34	7	—	—	28
Morgan, Mick	21 + 3	2	—	—	8
Morrison, Tony	5 + 1	—	—	—	—
Munro, Geoff	1	—	—	—	—
Nadiole, Tom	5 + 4	—	—	—	—
Ogburn, John	2 + 4	—	—	—	—
Ogden, Tony	1	—	—	—	—
Parrish, Mick	19 + 6	3	22	—	56
Sanderson, Ian	29	4	—	—	16
Sherman, Paul	4	2	—	—	8
Taylor, Alan	3	—	—	—	—
Taylor, Mick	30	6	—	—	24
Topliss, David	15	3	—	—	12
Warnecke, Gary	32	14	—	—	56
Worrall, Mick	18 + 3	3	15	—	42
TOTALS: 35 players		113	106	7	671

David Hobbs, top scorer with 141 points in his first full season at Watersheddings.

1985-86 MATCH ANALYSIS

Date	Com-petition	H/A	Opponent	Rlt	Score	Tries	Goals	Atten-dance	Referee
1.9.85	SLC	A	Halifax	D	12-12	Parrish, Birkby	Parrish (2)	—	—
4.9.85	SLC	H	Swinton	L	12-16	Lowndes, Ashton	Parrish (2)	3047	McDonald
8.9.85	SLC	H	Leeds	L	14-30	Topliss, Edwards, Foy	Parrish	3979	Lindop
15.9.85	LC(1)	A	Leigh	L	12-40	Sherman (2)	Caffrey, Hobbs	—	—
22.9.85	SLC	A	Hull	L	12-54	Sanderson, M. Taylor	Caffrey (2)	—	—
29.9.85	SLC	H	Warrington	W	26-20	Morgan, Ashton, Kirwan, Sanderson	Ashton (2, 1dg), Hobbs (2, 1dg)	3780	Whitfield
6.10.85	SLC	A	Featherstone R.	D	14-14	Graham (2), M'Barki	Hobbs	—	—
13.10.85	SLC	A	Salford	W	34-20	M. Taylor, Foy, D. Liddiard, Hobbs, M'Barki	Hobbs (7)	—	—
20.10.85	SLC	H	Castleford	W	46-22	M'Barki (2), Hobbs, M. Taylor, Foy, Sanderson, D. Liddiard, Warnecke	Parrish (7)	4210	Hodgson
27.10.85	SLC	A	Widnes	D	10-10	Warnecke	Parrish (3)	—	—
3.11.85	SLC	A	Bradford N.	W	24-6	Warnecke (3), D. Liddiard, Parrish	Parrish (2)	—	—
10.11.85	SLC	A	York	W	8-2	Foy, Kirwan	—	—	—
17.11.85	SLC	A	Dewsbury	W	37-6	M. Taylor (2), Graham (2), Morgan, Warnecke, D. Liddiard	Hobbs (4, 1dg)	—	—
24.11.85	JPS(1)	A	Bramley	W	46-8	D. Liddiard (2), Graham (2), Flanagan, M'Barki, Parrish, Warnecke	Hobbs (7)	—	—
1.12.85	JPS(2)	A	Hull K.R.	L	7-8	M'Barki	Hobbs (1, 1dg)	—	—
8.12.85	SLC	H	Salford	W	32-10	D. Liddiard, Ashton, Graham, Warnecke, Hobbs	Hobbs (6)	4859	Smith
15.12.85	SLC	H	Dewsbury	W	48-14	Graham (3), Foy (2), Ashton, Flanagan, G. Liddiard	Hobbs (3), Worrall (3), Ashton (2)	3858	Holdsworth
26.12.85	SLC	H	Widnes	D	10-10	Warnecke	Hobbs (3)	6811	Beaumont
1.1.86	SLC	A	Leeds	L	6-22	Graham	Parrish	—	—
12.1.86	SLC	H	York	W	24-16	Topliss (2), Graham, M'Barki	Hobbs (4)	3581	McDonald
19.1.86	SLC	A	Castleford	L	4-28	G. Liddiard	—	—	—
2.2.86	SLC	A	Warrington	L	4-8	—	Parrish (2)	—	—
9.2.86	CC(1)	H	Carlisle (at Oldham FC)	W	56-10	D. Liddiard (4), Graham (2), Kirwan (2), Sanderson, Taylor, Foy	Hobbs (6)	2785	Spencer
16.2.86	SLC	H	Halifax (at Oldham FC)	L	14-19	Warnecke, Graham	Hobbs (3)	5813	Haigh
2.3.86	SLC	H	Hull K.R. (at Oldham FC)	L	16-20	Ashton, Foy	Hobbs (4)	4011	Allatt
9.3.86	CC(2)	H	Warrington	W	13-6	Worrall, Foy	Worrall (2), Ashton (dg)	6526	Beaumont
16.3.86	CC(3)	H	Bradford N.	W	6-1	D. Liddiard	Hobbs	6962	Whitfield
22.3.86	CC(SF)	Wigan	Castleford	L	7-18	G. Liddiard	Hobbs, Ashton (dg)	(12430)	Campbell
28.3.86	SLC	A	Swinton	W	16-6	Warnecke, Kirwan, Graham	Hobbs (2)	—	—
31.3.86	SLC	A	Wigan	W	26-18	Warnecke, Kirwan, Foy, Hobbs	Hobbs (4), Worrall	—	—
2.4.86	SLC	H	St. Helens	L	12-38	Ashton, Graham	Parrish (2)	4609	Lindop
6.4.86	SLC	H	Bradford N.	L	6-16	Worrall	Hobbs	3739	Volante
9.4.86	SLC	H	Featherstone R.	L	4-16	Worrall	—	2155	Mean
16.4.86	SLC	H	Hull	W	15-14	Warnecke, Atkinson	Worrall (3), Ashton (dg)	2155	Haigh
18.4.86	SLC	A	Hull K.R.	W	22-10	Graham (2), Warnecke	Worrall (5)	—	—
20.4.86	SLC	A	St. Helens	L	12-44	Graham (2)	Worrall, Atkinson	—	—
22.4.86	SLC	H	Wigan	L	4-28	G. Liddiard	—	4833	Croft

ROCHDALE HORNETS

Ground:	Athletic Ground
Colours:	White jerseys with blue and red band, white shorts
First season:	1895-96
Nickname:	Hornets
Chairman:	Fred Wood
Secretary:	Paul Reynolds
Coach:	Charlie Birdsall (Sep 1984-Apr 1986)
Honours:	**Challenge Cup** Winners, 1921-22
	Lancashire League Winners, 1918-19
	Lancashire Cup Winners, 1911-12, 1914-15, 1918-19
	Beaten finalists, 1912-13, 1919-20, 1965-66
	John Player Trophy Beaten finalists 1973-74
	BBC2 Floodlit Trophy Beaten finalists 1971-72
Records:	Attendance: 41,831 Wigan v. Oldham (RL Cup Final) 12 Apr 1924
	Home: 26,664 v. Oldham (RL Cup) 25 Mar, 1922
	Season
	Goals: 115 by K. Harcombe, 1985-86
	Tries: 30 by J. Williams, 1934-35
	Points: 235 by G. Starkey, 1966-67
	Match
	Goals: 10 by H. Lees v. Glasshoughton, 19 Feb, 1938
	Tries: 5 by J. Corsi v. Barrow, 31 Dec, 1921 and v. Broughton Moor, 25 Feb, 1922; J. Williams v. St. Helens, 4 Apr, 1933; N. Brelsford v. Whitehaven, 3 Sep, 1972

Points: 27 by F. Blincow v. Normanton, 17 Oct, 1903
Highest score: 75-15 v. Broughton M., 1914-15
Highest against: 79-2 v. Hull, 1920-21

1985-86 PLAYERS' SUMMARY

	App	Tries	Goals	Dr	Pts
Austin, Greg	20 + 2	12	—	—	48
Austin, Tony	24 + 4	11	—	2	46
Bancroft, Phil	17 + 2	4	13	—	42
Birdsall, Charlie	7 + 3	—	—	—	—
Brown, Dave	4 + 1	—	—	—	—
Burgess, Mark	6 + 6	—	—	—	—
Cartwright, Phil	39	13	—	—	52
Causey, Mark	4	2	—	—	8
Deakin, Chris	21 + 2	—	—	—	—
Dobson, Mark	5	3	—	—	12
Duane, Ian	27	10	—	—	40
Dunn, Brian	37	19	—	—	76
Edge, Phil	22 + 1	8	4	—	40
Evans, David	19 + 12	2	—	—	8
Fairhurst, Alan	25 + 3	4	—	4	20
Fellows, Paul	12 + 1	5	—	—	20
Fitzsimons, Eric	0 + 2	—	—	—	—
Harcombe, Kevin	34 + 1	—	114	1	229
Hardy, Alan	4 + 3	1	—	2	6
Hitchin, Gary	1 + 1	—	—	—	—
Idle, Graham	21	—	—	—	—
Kuiti, Mike	18	6	—	—	24
Lowe, Kevin	6	—	—	—	—
McGiffen, Steve	6 + 1	1	—	—	4
McKenzie, Phil	32 + 1	19	—	—	76
Meachin, Colin	6	1	—	—	4
Mellor, Ian	6	1	—	—	4
Nash, Steve	12 + 10	—	—	—	—
Sanderson, Mark	2	—	—	—	—
Schaefer, Derek	1 + 2	1	—	—	4
Shaw, Glyn	8 + 3	1	—	—	4
Stapleton, John	4 + 3	4	—	—	16
Timson, Andy	11 + 2	2	—	—	8
Whitehead, Craig	0 + 2	—	—	—	—
Willis, Chris	3 + 2	—	—	—	—
Wiltshire, Roy	1	—	—	—	—
Wood, David	37	9	4	—	44
Trialists (7)	5 + 4	—	—	—	—

TOTALS:
44 players .... | | 139 | 135 | 9 | 835

1985-86 MATCH ANALYSIS

Date	Competition	H/A	Opponent	Rlt	Score	Tries	Goals	Attendance	Referee
1.9.85	SD	H	Whitehaven	L	5-10	—	Harcombe (2, 1 dg)	805	Whitfield
8.9.85	SD	A	Carlisle	W	16-10	Timson, Wood, Edge	Harcombe (2)	—	—
15.9.85	LC(1)	H	Widnes	L	6-17	Dunn	Harcombe	1269	Tickle
22.9.85	SD	H	Doncaster	W	52-13	Edge (4), Dunn (2), Wood (2), Fairhurst, Duane	Harcombe (6)	878	Simpson
29.9.85	SD	A	Keighley	W	25-16	G. Austin, Cartwright, Hardy	Harcombe (5), Fairhurst (2 dg), Hardy (dg)	—	—

(continued)

MATCH ANALYSIS (continued)

Date	Comp	H/A	Opponent	W/L	Score	Tries	Goals	Att	
6.10.85	SD	A	Mansfield M.	W	8-0	Fairhurst, Cartwright	—	—	—
13.10.85	SD	H	Fulham	W	12-6	McKenzie	Harcombe (3), Hardy (dg), Fairhurst (dg)	1464	Spencer
20.10.85	SD	A	Sheffield E.	W	40-12	Dunn, Schaefer, T. Austin, Fairhurst, Wood, Edge	Harcombe (8)	—	—
27.10.85	SD	H	Batley	W	28-0	G. Austin (2), Dunn, T. Austin, McKenzie	Edge (4)	1846	Tickle
3.11.85	SD	A	Bramley	W	28-10	G. Austin, T. Austin, Dunn, McKenzie, Kuiti, Cartwright	Harcombe (2)	—	—
10.11.85	JPS(P)	A	Carlisle	W	24-6	McKenzie (2), Duane, Dunn	Harcombe (4)	—	—
17.11.85	SD	A	Huddersfield B.	W	24-12	McKenzie (3), Timson	Harcombe (4)	—	—
24.11.85	JPS(1)	A	Salford	L	12-18	G. Austin	Harcombe (4)	—	—
1.12.85	SD	H	Workington T.	W	36-6	Cartwright (2), Edge, G. Austin, McKenzie	Harcombe (8)	1580	Kendrew
8.12.85	SD	H	Blackpool B.	W	26-20	G. Austin, Kuiti, Bancroft, Cartwright	Harcombe (3), Bancroft (2)	1923	Hodgson
15.12.85	SD	A	Workington T.	L	26-28	Duane (2), Kuiti, G. Austin	Bancroft (5)	—	—
22.12.85	SD	A	Hunslet	W	37-18	Dunn (2), T. Austin, Duane, Cartwright, Fairhurst	Harcombe (6), Fairhurst (dg)	—	—
26.12.85	SD	H	Leigh	L	8-26	—	Harcombe (4)	4050	Tennant
1.1.86	SD	A	Runcorn H.	W	34-10	Fellows (2), G. Austin, T. Austin, McKenzie, Bancroft, Cartwright	Harcombe (3)	—	—
12.1.86	SD	A	Batley	L	8-11	T. Austin	Harcombe (2)	—	—
19.1.86	SD	H	Bramley	W	12-6	G. Austin	Harcombe (4)	1392	Mean
22.1.86	SD	H	Sheffield E.	W	24-4	T. Austin, Bancroft, Kuiti, Dunn	Harcombe (4)	950	Loftus
26.1.86	SD	A	Fulham	L	12-26	McKenzie, Edge	Harcombe (2)	—	—
9.2.86	CC(1)	A	Huddersfield B.	W	10-4	Bancroft, Mellor	Harcombe	—	—
23.2.86	CC(2)	A	Widnes	L	20-36	Cartwright, Kuiti, Wood, Evans	Harcombe (2)	—	—
9.3.86	SD	A	Doncaster	L	12-14	Kuiti, Duane, G. Austin	—	—	—
16.3.86	SD	H	Wakefield T.	W	32-4	Dunn (2), Wood, Duane, McKenzie	Bancroft (6)	1550	Hodgson
23.3.86	SD	A	Whitehaven	L	16-20	Dunn, G. Austin	Harcombe (4)	—	—
28.3.86	SD	A	Leigh	L	23-29	McKenzie, T. Austin, Cartwright, Wood	Harcombe (3), T. Austin (dg)	—	—
31.3.86	SD	H	Runcorn H.	W	32-0	Stapleton (2), Dunn, McKenzie, Shaw, Cartwright	Harcombe (4)	743	Simpson
3.4.86	SD	H	Hunslet	W	28-5	T. Austin, McKenzie, Wood, Meachin	Harcombe (6)	820	Beaumont
6.4.86	SD	H	Carlisle	W	24-20	McKenzie (2), Duane, Fellows, Cartwright	Harcombe (2)	1117	Loftus
13.4.86	SD	A	Barrow	L	7-30	Fellows	Harcombe, T. Austin (dg)	—	—
17.4.86	SD	A	Blackpool B.	L	6-22	Cartwright	Harcombe	—	—
20.4.86	SD	H	Keighley	L	18-19	Dobson, Stapleton, Wood	Harcombe (3)	821	Carter
23.4.86	SD	H	Barrow	L	8-14	Duane (2)	—	597	Lindop
27.4.86	SD	A	Wakefield T.	L	28-32	Fellows, Dobson, Stapleton, Causey, T. Austin	Wood (4)	—	—
30.4.86	SD	H	Mansfield M.	W	36-16	Dunn (2), McKenzie, T. Austin, Dobson, Evans	Harcombe (6)	601	McDonald
7.5.86	SD	H	Huddersfield B.	W	32-16	Dunn (3), McKenzie, McGiffen, Causey	Harcombe (4)	604	Mean

RUNCORN HIGHFIELD

Ground: Canal Street
Colours: Black jerseys with white collar, white shorts
First Season: 1922-23 as Wigan Highfield. Became London Highfield in 1933-34. Became Liverpool Stanley in 1934-35 and changed to Liverpool City in 1951-52. Became Huyton in 1968-69 and changed to Runcorn Highfield in 1984-85. There was also a Liverpool City in 1906-07
Chairman: Terry Hughes
Secretary: Tony Almond
Coach: Geoff Fletcher (Aug 1977-)
Honours: **Lancashire League** Winners, 1935-36
Records: Attendance: 14,000 v. Widnes (Championship semi-final) 2 May, 1936 at Prescott Road
Season
Goals: 126 by P. Wood, 1984-85
Tries: 28 by J. Maloney, 1930-31
Points: 240 by P. Wood, 1984-85
Match
Goals: 11 by P. Wood v. Batley, 21 Oct, 1984
Tries: 5 by J. Maloney v. Bramley, 25 Apr, 1931
Points: 20 by Barnes v. Featherstone Jnrs, 7 Feb, 1931; S. Oakley v. Bramley, 4 May, 1934; P. Twiss v. Warrington, 20 Aug, 1958
Highest score: 59-11 v. Bramley, 1933-34
Highest against: 73-0 v. Warrington, 1950-51

1985-86 PLAYERS' SUMMARY

	App	Tries	Goals	Dr	Pts
Ashcroft, Keith	30 + 2	1	—	—	4
Ball, Jim	25	4	—	—	16
Blackburn, Ian	2 + 1	—	—	—	—
Blackwood, Bob	5 + 4	—	—	—	—
Blythin, Kevin	9	6	—	—	24
Cooper, Terry	1	—	—	—	—
Corwell, Chris	0 + 1	—	—	—	—
Cottam, Nick	2 + 1	—	—	—	—
Cowan, Murray	1	—	—	—	—
Crehan, Glen	21 + 2	7	4	—	36
Crompton, Dave	24 + 3	4	—	—	16
Dainty, Gary	2	—	—	—	—
Daley, Arthur	29 + 1	—	—	—	—
Dooley, Jim	11 + 3	—	—	—	—
Durnin, Paul	14	2	—	—	8
Egan, Martin	13 + 6	1	—	—	4
Fitzpatrick, Paul	23 + 3	8	—	—	32
Fletcher, Geoff	0 + 3	—	—	—	—
Garrity, Brian	34 + 1	24	—	—	96
Garrity, Tony	0 + 1	—	—	—	—
Gauchwin, Steve	3	—	—	—	—
Glover, Peter	2 + 2	—	—	—	—
Grady, Mike	2	—	—	—	—
Grundy, Daryl	2	—	—	—	—
Henney, Harold	13	1	—	—	4
Horne, John	1	—	—	—	—
Hunter, Clive	5 + 2	3	—	—	12
Jackson, Mark	7	—	—	—	—
Jackson, Tony	17 + 2	4	4	—	24
McCabe, John	18 + 2	1	—	—	4
McConnell, Kevin	0 + 1	—	—	—	—
Mitchell, Pat	1	—	—	—	—
Peters, Tony	13 + 2	—	—	—	—
Platt, Billy	1	—	—	—	—
Prescott, Eric	33	6	—	—	24
Rawlinson, Tom	32	5	—	—	20
Roughley, Mike	1	1	—	—	4
Shaw, Mark	8	1	12	—	28
Simm, Steve	10 + 2	3	—	—	12
Smith, Ian	24	4	—	1	17
Tabern, John	6 + 7	—	—	—	—
Tinsley, Eddie	3	—	—	—	—
Tipene, Kevin	2	—	—	—	—
Turley, Norman	3 + 1	1	—	—	4
Walsh, John	0 + 1	—	—	—	—
Wood, Peter	20	—	51	12	114
Woods, Paul	20 + 1	3	14	2	42
Wragg, Chris	1	—	—	—	—
TOTALS:					
48 players		90	85	15	545

1985-86 MATCH ANALYSIS

Date	Com-petition	H/A	Opponent	Rlt	Score	Tries	Goals	Atten-dance	Referee
1.9.85	SD	H	Leigh	L	12-38	Jackson, Rawlinson	Wood (2)	739	Allatt
4.9.85	SD	A	Wakefield T.	L	7-14	Prescott	Wood (1, 1dg)	–	–
8.9.85	SD	A	Huddersfield B.	L	23-26	Fitzpatrick, Ball, Turley	Wood (5, 1dg)	–	–
15.9.85	LC(1)	H	Workington T.	L	16-38	Crehan (2), Roughley	Wood (2)	1000	Spencer
18.9.85	SD	H	Huddersfield B.	L	15-17	Blythin, Ashcroft	Wood (2, 3dg)	430	Smith
29.9.85	SD	H	Blackpool B.	W	23-20	Crompton, Jackson, Fitzpatrick	Wood (5, 1dg)	342	Fox
2.10.85	SD	A	Carlisle	L	2-12	–	Wood	–	–
6.10.85	SD	A	Sheffield E.	L	10-21	Garrity, Simm	Wood	–	–
13.10.85	SD	H	Workington T.	W	28-20	Garrity, Simm, Crehan, Crompton	Wood (5, 2dg)	400	Loftus
20.10.85	SD	A	Keighley	L	3-15	–	Wood (1, 1dg)	–	–
27.10.85	SD	H	Bramley	L	29-31	Rawlinson, Garrity, Crompton, Fitzpatrick	Wood (6, 1dg)	280	Hale (NZ)
3.11.85	SD	A	Blackpool B.	L	8-30	Garrity	Wood (2)	–	–
10.11.85	SD	H	Sheffield E.	W	15-10	Crehan, Rawlinson	Wood (3, 1dg)	401	Berry
17.11.85	SD	H	Keighley	L	19-32	Garrity (2), Ball	Wood (3, 1dg)	280	Hodgson
24.11.85	JPS(1)	A	Doncaster	L	20-22	Woods, Smith, Fitzpatrick	Wood (4)	–	–
8.12.85	SD	A	Doncaster	Aban-doned	10-16	Garrity, Prescott	Wood	–	–
15.12.85	SD	H	Whitehaven	L	14-22	Garrity (2), Fitzpatrick	Wood	350	Simpson
22.12.85	SD	A	Fulham	L	2-44	–	Woods	–	–
1.1.86	SD	H	Rochdale H.	L	10-34	Garrity, Crehan	Woods	540	Carter
5.1.86	SD	A	Whitehaven	L	2-34	–	Crehan	–	–
12.1.86	SD	A	Leigh	L	18-36	Rawlinson, Fitzpatrick, Durnin	Crehan (3)	–	–
19.1.86	SD	H	Doncaster	W	12-8	Fitzpatrick, Rawlinson	Woods (2)	306	Haigh
2.2.86	SD	H	Wakefield T.	L	12-29	Garrity, Crehan	Shaw, Woods	350	Croft
9.2.86	CC(1)	A	Blackpool B.	L	10-30	Garrity, Smith	Wood	–	–
23.2.86	SD	H	Mansfield M.	W	24-2	Garrity (2), Egan, Prescott	Wood (4)	151	Croft
2.3.86	SD	A	Barrow	L	10-48	Woods, Crehan	Wood	–	–
9.3.86	SD	H	Batley	D	13-13	Smith, Prescott	Woods (2, 1dg)	360	Allatt
16.3.86	SD	A	Hunslet	D	14-14	Garrity, Crompton	Jackson (3)	–	–
27.3.86	SD	H	Carlisle	W	18-10	Henney, Jackson, Blythin, Smith	Jackson	350	Berry
31.3.86	SD	A	Rochdale H.	L	0-32	–	–	–	–
6.4.86	SD	H	Barrow	L	11-14	Garrity (2)	Smith (dg), Shaw	300	Houghton
16.4.86	SD	H	Fulham	W	26-8	Ball (2), Jackson, Blythin	Shaw (5)	300	Mean
20.4.86	SD	A	Mansfield M.	W	36-22	Garrity (3), Prescott, Fitzpatrick, Hunter, Shaw	Shaw (4)	–	–
23.4.86	SD	A	Bramley	L	22-36	McCabe, Woods, Durnin, Garrity	Woods (2), Shaw	–	–
27.4.86	SD	H	Hunslet	W	37-2	Blythin (3), Hunter (2), Garrity (2)	Woods (4, 1dg)	350	Tickle
30.4.86	SD	A	Batley	L	4-42	Garrity	–	–	–
7.5.86	SD	A	Workington T.	L	0-28	–	–	–	–
9.5.86	SD	A	Doncaster	L	10-26	Prescott, Simm	Woods	–	–

ST. HELENS

Ground:	Knowsley Road
Colours:	Red and white jerseys, white shorts
First Season:	1895-96
Nickname:	Saints
Chairman:	Lawrie Prescott
Secretary:	Geoff Sutcliffe
Coach:	Billy Benyon (May 1982-Nov 1985)
	Alex Murphy (Nov 1985-)

Honours: **Championship** Winners, 1931-32, 1952-53, 1958-59, 1965-66, 1969-70, 1970-71
Beaten finalists, 1964-65, 1966-67, 1971-72
Division One Champions, 1974-75
League Leaders Trophy Winners, 1964-65, 1965-66
Club Championship (Merit Table) Beaten finalists, 1973-74
Challenge Cup Winners, 1955-56, 1960-61, 1965-66, 1971-72, 1975-76
Beaten finalists, 1896-97, 1914-15, 1929-30, 1952-53, 1977-78
Lancashire Cup Winners, 1926-27, 1953-54, 1960-61, 1961-62, 1962-63, 1963-64, 1964-65, 1967-68, 1968-69, 1984-85
Beaten finalists, 1932-33, 1952-53, 1956-57, 1958-59, 1959-60, 1970-71, 1982-83
Lancashire League Winners, 1929-30, 1931-32, 1952-53, 1959-60, 1964-65, 1965-66, 1966-67, 1968-69
Premiership Winners, 1975-76, 1976-77, 1984-85
Beaten finalists, 1974-75
Western Division Championship Winners, 1963-64
BBC2 Trophy Winners, 1971-72, 1975-76
Beaten finalists, 1965-66, 1968-69, 1970-71, 1977-78, 1978-79

Records: Attendance: 35,695 v. Wigan (League) 26 Dec, 1949
Season
Goals: 214 by K. Coslett, 1971-72
Tries: 62 by T. Van Vollenhoven, 1958-59
Points: 452 by K. Coslett, 1971-72

Match
Goals: 13 by G. Lewis v. Wardley, 16 Feb, 1924; P. Fearis v. Barrow, 14 Feb, 1959; G. Pimblett v. Bramley, 5 Mar, 1978
Tries: 6 by A. Ellaby v. Barrow, 5 Mar, 1932; S. Llewellyn v. Castleford, 3 Mar, 1956 and v. Liverpool C., 20 Aug, 1956; T. Vollenhoven v. Wakefield T., 21 Dec, 1957 and v. Blackpool B., 23 Apr, 1962; F. Myler v. Maryport, 1 Sep, 1969
Points: 29 by P. Fearis v. Barrow, 14 Feb, 1959
Highest score: 73-0 v. Wardley, 1923-24
Highest against: 78-3 v. Warrington, 1908-09

1985-86 PLAYERS' SUMMARY

	App	Tries	Goals	Dr	Pts
Allen, Shaun	20 + 12	5	—	—	20
Arkwright, Chris	35 + 3	5	—	—	20
Bailey, Mark	4 + 9	2	—	—	8
Bottell, Gary	1 + 1	1	—	—	4
Burke, Tony	29	3	—	—	12
Conlon, Ross	16	9	65	—	166
Day, Sean	11	2	34	—	76
Doherty, Paul	0 + 1	1	—	—	4
Dwyer, Bernard	5 + 4	1	6	—	16
Elia, Mark	13	15	1	—	62
Fairclough, David	1 + 1	—	—	—	—
Forber, Paul	15 + 10	2	—	—	8
French, Brett	24	14	—	—	56
Gorley, Peter	23 + 1	—	—	—	—
Grienke, Gary	7 + 5	1	—	—	4
Haggerty, Roy	33	21	—	—	84
Harrison, David	12	2	—	—	8
Holding, Neil	33 + 1	18	—	1	73
Hughes, Eric	13	1	—	—	4
Jones, Paul	0 + 2	—	—	—	—
Ledger, Barry	37	17	9	—	86
Liptrot, Graham	25	2	—	—	8
Litherland, Dennis	9 + 3	4	—	—	16
Loughlin, Paul	24 + 3	4	43	—	102
McCormack, Kevin	6 + 1	3	—	—	12
McIntyre, Colin	1 + 1	—	—	—	—
Meadows, Kevin	16 + 1	9	—	—	36
Parkes, Brian	2 + 1	1	—	—	4
Peters, Steve	15 + 1	3	—	—	12
Pinner, Harry	19 + 1	3	—	—	12
Platt, Andy	26 + 3	10	—	—	40
Round, Paul	24 + 5	13	—	—	52
Seabrook, Derek	2	2	—	—	8
Souto, Peter	2	—	—	—	—
Veivers, Phil	30 + 1	5	—	1	21
Wellens, Kevin	0 + 1	—	—	—	—

TOTALS:
36 players		179	158	2	1,034

1985-86 MATCH ANALYSIS

Date	Competition	H/A	Opponent	Rlt	Score	Tries	Goals	Attendance	Referee
30.8.85	SLC	A	Swinton (at Bolton W. FC)	W	32-14	Round (2), Meadows, Seabrook, Pinner	Day (6)	—	—
4.9.85	SLC	H	Warrington	W	12-6	Ledger, Pinner	Day (2)	6839	Campbell
8.9.85	SLC	H	York	W	30-8	Holding (3), Harrison, Haggerty	Day (5)	4456	Allatt
15.9.85	LC(1)	H	Carlisle	W	72-8	Haggerty (2), Round (2), Holding (2), Litherland, Day, Peters, Burke, Ledger, Dwyer, Bottell	Dwyer (6), Day (4)	3630	Houghton
22.9.85	SLC	A	Leeds	L	8-21	Round	Day (2)	—	—
25.9.85	LC(2)	H	Whitehaven	W	26-8	Litherland (2), Day, Parkes	Day (5)	3853	Whitfield
29.9.85	SLC	H	Hull	L	22-35	Litherland, Platt, Seabrook	Day (5)	5984	Walker
2.10.85	LC(SF)	A	Wigan	L	2-30	—	Day	—	—
13.10.85	SLC	A	Castleford	L	18-32	Peters, French	Conlon (5)	—	—
20.10.85	SLC	H	Hull K.R.	W	39-22	Loughlin, Meadows, Arkwright, Forber, Platt, French	Conlon (7), Veivers (dg)	6201	Whitfield
27.10.85	Tour	H	New Zealand	L	8-46	Haggerty	Conlon (2)	7897	Lindop
3.11.85	SLC	A	Featherstone R.	W	38-12	French (2), Haggerty (2), Meadows, Ledger, Allen	Conlon (5)	—	—
10.11.85	SLC	H	Dewsbury	W	24-6	Haggerty, Ledger, Conlon, French	Conlon (4)	4080	Fox
17.11.85	SLC	A	Bradford N.	W	18-9	Peters, Platt, French, Meadows	Loughlin	—	—
24.11.85	JPS(1)	H	Dewsbury	W	42-6	Ledger (2), Meadows (2), French (2), Holding, Liptrot	Ledger (5)	5364	Allatt
1.12.85	JPS(2)	H	Doncaster	W	36-20	Holding (2), Platt, Meadows, Bailey, Conlon, Ledger	Conlon (4)	4092	Kershaw
8.12.85	SLC	H	Leeds	D	12-12	Veivers	Conlon (4)	6280	Berry
11.12.85	JPS(3)	H	Hull	W	57-14	Arkwright (3), Holding (2), Conlon (2), Ledger (2), Meadows	Conlon (8), Holding (dg)	7536	McDonald
15.12.85	SLC	A	Hull	D	20-20	French, Conlon, Haggerty	Conlon (4)	—	—
21.12.85	JPS(SF)	Leeds	Hull K.R.	L	4-22	—	Conlon (2)	(3856)	Campbell
26.12.85	SLC	A	Wigan	L	14-38	Grienke, Meadows	Conlon (3)	—	—
1.1.86	SLC	H	Widnes	L	16-30	French, Round	Conlon (4)	7526	Kershaw
5.1.86	SLC	A	Halifax (at Leeds)	L	18-27	Forber, Conlon	Conlon (5)	—	—
12.1.86	SLC	A	Warrington	L	16-26	Conlon (2), Elia	Conlon (2)	—	—
19.1.86	SLC	H	Bradford N.	L	8-18	French	Conlon (2)	4486	Loftus
2.2.86	SLC	H	Featherstone R.	W	44-14	Ledger (2), Elia (2), Haggerty (2), French, Conlon, Allen	Conlon (4)	3971	McDonald
24.2.86	CC(1)	A	Dewsbury (at Leeds)	W	22-19	Haggerty (2), Ledger, Holding	Ledger (2), Loughlin	—	—
2.3.86	SLC	H	Halifax	W	22-10	Haggerty, Elia, Holding, Veivers	Day (3)	7406	Campbell
8.3.86	CC(2)	A	Wigan	L	14-24	French, Elia, Allen	Day	—	—
16.3.86	SLC	A	York	W	18-11	Ledger, Elia, French, Haggerty	Loughlin	—	—
19.3.86	SLC	H	Salford	W	28-10	Elia (2), Platt (2), Burke (2)	Ledger (2)	4500	Beaumont
23.3.86	SLC	A	Dewsbury	W	18-12	Haggerty, Pinner, Harrison, Holding	Elia	—	—
28.3.86	SLC	H	Wigan	W	18-13	Elia (2), Haggerty	Loughlin (3)	15587	Allatt
31.3.86	SLC	A	Widnes	W	16-6	Elia, Veivers, McCormack	Loughlin (2)	—	—

(continued on page 95)

73

SALFORD

Ground:	The Willows
Colours:	Red jerseys, white shorts
First Season:	1896-97
Nickname:	Red Devils
Chairman:	John Wilkinson
Secretary:	Graham McCarty
Coach:	Kevin Ashcroft (May 1984-)
Honours:	**Championship** Winners, 1913-14, 1932-33, 1936-37, 1938-39
	Beaten finalists, 1933-34
	Division One Champions, 1973-74, 1975-76
	Challenge Cup Winners, 1937-38
	Beaten finalists, 1899-1900, 1901-02, 1902-03, 1905-06, 1938-39, 1968-69
	Lancashire League Winners, 1932-33, 1933-34, 1934-35, 1936-37, 1938-39
	Lancashire Cup Winners, 1931-32, 1934-35, 1935-36, 1936-37, 1972-73
	Beaten finalists, 1929-30, 1938-39, 1973-74, 1974-75, 1975-76
	Premiership Beaten finalists, 1975-76
	John Player Trophy Beaten finalists 1972-73
	BBC2 Trophy Winners, 1974-75
Records:	Attendance: 26,470 v. Warrington (RL Cup) 13 Feb, 1937
	Season
	Goals: 221 by D. Watkins, 1972-73
	Tries: 46 by K. Fielding, 1973-74
	Points: 493 by D. Watkins, 1972-73
	Match
	Goals: 13 by A. Risman v. Bramley, 5 Apr, 1933 and v. Broughton R., 18 May, 1940; D. Watkins v. Keighley, 7 Jan, 1972; S. Rule v. Doncaster, 4 Sep, 1981
	Tries: 6 by F. Miles v. Lees, 5 Mar, 1898; E. Bone v. Goole, 29 Mar, 1902; J. Hilton v. Leigh, 7 Oct, 1939
	Points: 39 by J. Lomas v. Liverpool C., 2 Feb, 1907
	Highest score: 78-0 v. Liverpool C., 1906-07
	Highest against: 63-5 v. Wigan, 1924-25

1985-86 PLAYERS' SUMMARY

	App	Tries	Goals	Dr	Pts
Baker, Neil	19	11	11	7	73
Battese, Brian	16 + 1	4	—	—	16
Beckett, Adrian	0 + 1	—	—	—	—
Blease, Ian	12 + 2	4	—	—	16
Bloor, Darren	33	14	—	1	57
Byrne, Ged	23	6	—	—	24
Dickens, Steve	11 + 2	2	—	—	8
Disley, Gary	18 + 2	—	—	—	—
Fazackerley, John	1 + 2	—	—	—	—
Fletcher, Paul	33	8	—	—	32
Ford, Steve	9	1	—	—	4
Glynn, Peter	29 + 2	7	—	1	29
Gribbin, Vince	4	3	—	—	12
Griffiths, Clive	15 + 1	2	39	—	86
Griffiths, Steve	2 + 6	1	—	—	4
Groves, Paul	11	2	—	—	8
Herbert, Steve	31	3	—	—	12
Jamieson, Ged	1 + 2	—	—	—	—
Lamb, Nigel	7 + 1	—	—	—	—
Marsh, Ian	18	3	—	—	12
Major, David	18 + 7	4	—	—	16
McTigue, Mike	29 + 2	3	—	—	12
Moylan, Stephen	19	1	—	—	4
Muller, Roby	3	—	—	—	—
O'Loughlin, Keiron	31	9	—	—	36
Pendlebury, John	33	5	34	1	89
Pobjie, Mike	8 + 1	1	—	—	4
Ruddy, David	5 + 5	1	—	—	4
Smith, Ron	1 + 8	—	—	—	—
Taylor, John	1 + 1	—	—	—	—
Wiltshire, Roy	14	7	—	—	28
TOTALS:					
31 players		102	84	10	586

The legendary Gus Risman, holder of the Salford record for most goals in a match.

1985-86 MATCH ANALYSIS

Date	Competition	H/A	Opponent	Rlt	Score	Tries	Goals	Attendance	Referee
1.9.85	SLC	A	York	L	12-14	Fletcher, Groves	C. Griffiths (2)	—	—
4.9.85	SLC	H	Wigan	W	12-8	O'Loughlin, Bloor	C. Griffiths (2)	4404	Walker
8.9.85	SLC	H	Halifax	W	22-6	Fletcher, C. Griffiths, Groves, Bloor	C. Griffiths (2), Baker (2dg)	3266	Kendrew
15.9.85	LC (1)	H	Swinton	W	18-14	Bloor, Pendlebury, O'Loughlin	C. Griffiths (2), Baker (dg), Bloor (dg)	3482	Allatt
22.9.85	SLC	A	Featherstone R.	W	16-12	O'Loughlin, Baker, Bloor	C. Griffiths (2)	—	—
25.9.85	LC (2)	A	Wigan	L	20-22	Baker, Bloor, Marsh	C. Griffiths (4)	—	—
29.9.85	SLC	H	Leeds	L	16-22	Baker (2)	C. Griffiths (4)	3721	Campbell
6.10.85	SLC	A	Warrington	L	19-41	Major (2), Battese	C Griffiths (3), Baker (dg)	—	—
13.10.85	SLC	H	Oldham	L	20-34	Ruddy, C. Griffiths, Baker	C. Griffiths (4)	3563	Carter
23.10.85	SLC	A	Widnes	L	12-27	Gribbin, Bloor	C. Griffiths (2)	—	—
27.10.85	SLC	A	Halifax	L	12-23	Battese, Glynn	Pendlebury (2)	—	—
3.11.85	SLC	H	Hull K.R.	W	27-24	Gribbin (2), Bloor (2), O'Loughlin	Baker (3, 1dg)	2359	Spencer
10.11.85	SLC	A	Wigan	L	8-20	Bloor	Baker (2)	—	—
15.11.85	SLC	H	York	W	22-18	Baker, Moylan, Pobjie, Major	C. Griffiths (3)	1730	Haigh
24.11.85	JPS (1)	H	Rochdale H.	W	18-12	Marsh, Baker, Bloor	C. Griffiths (3)	2844	Loftus
1.12.85	JPS (2)	A	Hull	L	10-30	Fletcher	C. Griffiths (3)	—	—
8.12.85	SLC	A	Oldham	L	10-32	Baker, Blease	Baker	—	—
15.12.85	SLC	H	Castleford	W	9-8	Fletcher, Baker	Baker (dg)	1888	Fox
26.12.85	SLC	H	Swinton	W	21-17	Battese (2), Baker, Glynn	Baker (2), Glynn (dg)	3374	Berry
1.1.86	SLC	A	Dewsbury	L	10-12	Glynn	C. Griffiths (3)	—	—
15.1.86	SLC	H	Bradford N.	W	9-8	Glynn, Wiltshire	Baker (dg)	1709	McDonald
19.1.86	SLC	H	Featherstone R.	W	26-12	Herbert (2), O'Loughlin, Baker, Byrne	Baker (3)	1674	Hodgson
2.2.86	SLC	H	Widnes	W	22-6	Glynn (2), Fletcher, Wiltshire	Pendlebury (3)	2289	Tennant
9.2.86	CC(1)	A	Doncaster	L	12-18	Marsh, Bloor	Pendlebury (2)	—	—
27.2.86	SLC	A	Leeds	L	12-34	Ford, Pendlebury	Pendlebury (2)	—	—
5.3.86	SLC	H	Hull	W	15-12	Wiltshire, O'Loughlin	Pendlebury (3, 1dg)	1281	Holdsworth
16.3.86	SLC	H	Warrington	L	10-19	Byrne, Wiltshire	Pendlebury	2356	Fox
19.3.86	SLC	A	St. Helens	L	10-28	O'Loughlin, Bloor	Pendlebury	—	—
23.3.86	SLC	A	Hull	L	16-34	Blease, Glynn, Byrne	Pendlebury (2)	—	—
28.3.86	SLC	H	Dewsbury	W	36-8	Dickens (2), Blease (2), Byrne, O'Loughlin, McTigue	Pendlebury (4)	1404	Simpson
31.3.86	SLC	A	Swinton	W	24-0	Byrne, Wiltshire, Pendlebury, Herbert, Fletcher	Pendlebury (2)	—	—
13.4.86	SLC	H	St. Helens	L	28-30	Fletcher (2), Bloor (2), Pendlebury	Pendlebury (4)	2790	Whitfield
16.4.86	SLC	A	Hull K.R.	W	28-4	McTigue (2), Wiltshire, Pendlebury, O'Loughlin	Pendlebury (4)	—	—
20.4.86	SLC	A	Castleford	L	16-30	Byrne, Major, Wiltshire	Pendlebury (2)	—	—
22.4.86	SLC	A	Bradford N.	L	8-18	S. Griffiths	Pendlebury (2)	—	—

SHEFFIELD EAGLES

Ground:	Owlerton Stadium
Colours:	White, claret and gold jerseys, white shorts
First Season:	1984-85
Nickname:	Eagles
Chairman:	Geoffrey Dilley
General Manager:	Gary Hetherington
Coach:	Alan Rhodes (May 1984-May 1986)
Records:	Attendance: 1,425 v. Rochdale H.(Div.2) 2 Sept, 1984

Season
Goals: 79 by R. Rafferty, 1985-86
Tries: 16 by P. McDermott, 1984-85
Points: 186 by R. Rafferty, 1985-86

Match
Goals: No player has scored more than 6
Tries: No player has scored more than 3
Points: 16 by D. Cholmondeley v. Huddersfield B., 9 Mar, 1986
Highest score: 36-6 v. Huddersfield B., 1985-86
Highest against: 62-11 v. Warrington, 1985-86

1985-86 PLAYERS' SUMMARY

	App	Tries	Goals	Dr	Pts
Aitchison, Dean	1 + 2	—	—	—	—
Aston, Mark	7	—	—	—	—
Atherton, Mick	1	—	—	—	—
Box, Harold	1 + 1	—	—	—	—
Brennan, Dave	1 + 1	—	—	—	—
Bridgeman, Derek	32 + 3	7	—	—	28
Burgoyne, Paddy	11	4	—	—	16
Campbell, Mark	12 + 3	1	—	—	4
Cholmondeley, Dave	29 + 4	4	9	3	37
Collear, Mick	6 + 2	—	—	—	—
Dickinson, Andy	28	10	—	—	40
Dilley, Julian	1 + 1	—	—	—	—
Donnelly, John	0 + 1	—	—	—	—
Farrell, Kevin	27 + 6	5	—	—	20
Ferres, Steve	4 + 1	—	—	—	—
Gamson, Mark	20 + 2	3	—	—	12
Glancy, John	29	7	—	—	28
Harris, Billy	21 + 1	—	—	—	—
Herdman, Martin	1	—	—	—	—
Hetherington, Gary	20 + 8	1	—	—	4
Hooper, Trevor	1	—	—	—	—
Kuhanaman, Paul	19 + 5	2	1	—	10
Lake, Ernie	6	—	—	—	—
Lane, Steve	31	5	—	—	20
McDermott, Paul	12	5	—	—	20
Pollard, Mervin	1	—	—	—	—
Powell, Darryl	31	9	—	2	38
Pritchard, Gordon	1	—	—	—	—
Rafferty, Roy	36	7	79	—	186
Redfern, Steve	0 + 2	—	—	—	—
Robinson, Steve	1	—	—	—	—
Roiall, Mark	4	2	—	—	8
Schaumkell, Kevin	13 + 1	6	—	—	24
Sherwood, Mitchell	11 + 4	3	—	—	12
Smith, Gary	17	2	—	2	10
Timmins, Stan	0 + 1	—	—	—	—
Walton, Dave	1	—	—	—	—
Welsh, Paul	12 + 6	3	—	—	12
Wilders, Peter	9 + 10	4	—	—	16
Wileman, Vic	4	—	—	—	—
Wright, Scott	17 + 1	1	—	—	4
Trialist	2 + 1	—	—	—	—
TOTALS:					
42 players		91	89	7	549

1985-86 MATCH ANALYSIS

Date	Com-petition	H/A	Opponent	Rlt	Score	Tries	Goals	Atten-dance	Referee
1.9.85	SD	H	Doncaster	L	16-20	Rafferty, Powell, McDermott	Rafferty (2)	504	Lindop
4.9.85	YC(P)	A	Castleford	L	6-38	Wilders	Rafferty	—	—
8.9.85	SD	A	Hunslet	W	22-10	Dickinson (2), McDermott, Powell, Lane	Cholmondley	—	—
15.9.85	SD	H	Mansfield M.	W	34-12	Powell, McDermott, Gamson, Dickinson, Lane, Wilders	Rafferty (5)	609	Smith
18.9.85	SD	A	Leigh	L	18-32	McDermott (2), Dickinson	Rafferty (3)	—	—
22.9.85	SD	H	Wakefield T.	L	6-28	Rafferty	Rafferty	1242	Campbell
6.10.85	SD	H	Runcorn H.	W	21-10	Farrell, Dickinson, Bridgeman	Rafferty (4), Cholmondeley (dg)	496	Beaumont
13.10.85	SD	A	Bramley	L	10-13	Farrell	Rafferty (3)	—	—
20.10.85	SD	H	Rochdale H.	L	12-40	Glancy, Gamson	Rafferty (2)	1658	Tennant
27.10.85	SD	A	Wakefield T.	L	6-8	—	Rafferty (3)	—	—
3.11.85	SD	H	Keighley	W	22-9	Bridgeman, Rafferty, Glancy, Welsh	Rafferty (3)	514	Carter
10.11.85	SD	A	Runcorn	L	10-15	Lane	Rafferty (3)	—	—
17.11.85	SD	H	Whitehaven	L	8-9	Campbell	Rafferty (2)	714	Volante
24.11.85	JPS(1)	H	Bradford N.	L	16-24	Wright, Powell, Hetherington	Rafferty (2)	1342	Simpson
1.12.85	SD	A	Mansfield M.	D	14-14	Cholmondeley, Bridgeman	Rafferty (3)	—	—
8.12.85	SD	A	Fulham	L	21-28	Welsh (2), Schaumkell	Rafferty (4), Powell (dg)	—	—
15.12.85	SD	H	Hunslet	W	26-16	Powell (2), Cholmondeley, Roiall	Rafferty (5)	645	Houghton
22.12.85	SD	A	Workington T.	W	26-8	Bridgeman, Burgoyne, Farrell, Roiall	Rafferty (5)	—	—
12.1.86	SD	H	Bramley	L	2-14	—	Rafferty	400	Lindop
19.1.86	SD	H	Leigh	L	2-16	—	Rafferty	1000	Smith
23.1.86	SD	A	Rochdale H.	L	4-24	Schaumkell	—	—	—
2.2.86	SD	A	Blackpool B.	L	12-25	Schaumkell, Rafferty	Rafferty (2)	—	—
9.2.86	CC(1)	A	Warrington	L	11-62	Burgoyne	Rafferty (3), Smith (dg)	—	—
9.3.86	SD	A	Huddersfield B.	W	32-22	Cholmondeley (2), Khunnaman (2), Powell, Rafferty	Cholmondeley (4)	—	—
16.3.86	SD	H	Blackpool B.	W	21-14	Schaumkell, Glancy, Dickinson, Powell	Rafferty (2), Cholmondeley (dg)	400	Kendrew
19.3.86	SD	A	Carlisle	L	9-15	Farrell (2)	Cholmondeley (dg)	—	—
23.3.86	SD	A	Doncaster	W	26-18	Burgoyne (2), Dickinson, Smith	Cholmondeley (4), Khunnaman (dg)	—	—
30.3.86	SD	H	Huddersfield B.	W	36-6	Glancy (2), Schaumkell (2), Gamson, Bridgeman	Rafferty (6)	650	Spencer
6.4.86	SD	A	Keighley	W	24-9	Wilders, Powell, Lane, Smith	Rafferty (4)	—	—
13.4.86	SD	H	Batley	W	8-6	Dickinson	Rafferty (2)	600	Tickle
20.4.86	SD	H	Fulham	W	23-12	Bridgeman (2), Lane, Sherwood	Rafferty (3), Smith (dg)	700	Houghton
23.4.86	SD	A	Whitehaven	L	4-36	Sherwood	—	—	—
27.4.86	SD	H	Carlisle	L	12-23	Rafferty, Wilders	Rafferty (2)	650	Holdsworth
30.4.86	SD	A	Barrow	L	8-32	Rafferty, Glancy	—	—	—
2.5.86	SD	A	Batley	L	4-38	Sherwood	—	—	—
5.5.86	SD	H	Workington T. (at Doncaster)	W	16-14	Dickinson (2), Glancy	Rafferty (2)	500	Tennant
7.5.86	SD	H	Barrow	L	1-21	—	Powell (dg)	600	Haigh

SWINTON

Ground:	Station Road
Colours:	Blue jerseys with white V, white shorts
First Season:	1896-97
Nickname:	Lions
Chairman:	Ian Clift
Secretary:	Steve Moyes
Coach:	Jim Crellin (Nov 1983-May 1986)
Honours:	**Championship** Winners, 1926-27, 1927-28, 1930-31, 1934-35
	Beaten finalists, 1924-25, 1932-33
	War League Beaten finalists, 1939-40
	Division One Champions, 1962-63, 1963-64
	Division Two Champions, 1984-85
	Challenge Cup Winners, 1899-1900, 1925-26, 1927-28
	Beaten finalists, 1926-27, 1931-32
	Lancashire League Winners, 1924-25, 1927-28, 1928-29, 1930-31, 1960-61
	Lancashire War League Winners, 1939-40
	Lancashire Cup Winners, 1925-26, 1927-28, 1939-40, 1969-70
	Beaten finalists, 1910-11, 1923-24, 1931-32, 1960-61, 1961-62, 1962-63, 1964-65, 1972-73
	BBC Trophy Beaten finalists, 1966-67
	Western Division Championship Beaten finalists, 1963-64
Records:	Attendance: 44,621 Wigan v. Warrington (RL Cup SF) 7 Apr, 1951
	Season
	Goals: 128 by A. Blan, 1960-61
	Tries: 42 by J. Stopford, 1963-64
	Points: 283 by A. Blan, 1960-61
	Match
	Goals: 12 by K. Gowers v. Liverpool C., 3 Oct, 1959
	Tries: 5 by T. Bevan v. Morecambe, 10 Sep, 1898; W.

Wallwork v. Widnes, 15 Dec, 1900; J. Evans v. Bradford N., 30 Sep, 1922; H. Halsall v. St. Helens, 24 Jan, 1925; R. Cracknell v. Whitehaven Rec., 11 Feb, 1928; R. Lewis v. Keighley, 12 Jan, 1946; J. Stopford v. Bramley, 22 Dec, 1962; A. Buckley v. Salford, Apr 8, 1964
Points: 29 by B. McMahon v. Dewsbury, 15 Aug, 1959
Highest score: 76-4 v. Pontefract, 1906-07
Highest against: 76-3 v. Huddersfield, 1945-46

1985-86 PLAYERS' SUMMARY

	App	Tries	Goals	Dr	Pts
Ainsworth, Gary	6	3	—	—	12
Allen, John	13 + 5	3	—	—	12
Arrowsmith, Gary	10 + 2	—	—	—	—
Bate, Derek	26	9	—	—	36
Brown, Jeff	1	—	—	—	—
Cassidy, Frank	11 + 1	1	—	—	4
Connor, Sean	6 + 1	—	—	—	—
Derbyshire, Alan	14	2	—	—	8
Evans, Tex	10	3	—	—	12
Grima, Joe	11 + 1	—	—	—	—
Hewitt, Tony	24 + 1	9	—	—	36
Higgins, Brian	8	2	—	—	8
Hodkinson, Alan	5	—	—	—	—
Holliday, Les	25	2	—	—	8
Holliday, Mike	7 + 4	1	—	—	4
Horrocks, John	9 + 3	—	—	—	—
Hudson, Mark	0 + 1	—	—	—	—
Hunter, Clive	5	—	—	—	—
Jones, Ken	12 + 2	6	10	—	44
Lee, Martin	9	2	—	—	8
Lomax, Bill	10 + 1	—	—	—	—
Maloney, Dave	2	—	—	—	—
Melling, Alex	16	—	—	—	—
Mellor, Paul	0 + 1	—	—	—	—
Mooney, Frank	10	—	—	—	—
Muller, Roby	9 + 1	2	—	—	8
Ratcliffe, Alan	24 + 3	3	—	—	12
Rippon, Andy	0 + 8	—	—	—	—
Rowbottom, Mark	11 + 3	1	—	—	4
Scott, Terry	21 + 1	6	—	—	24
Sheals, Mark	6 + 4	—	—	—	—
Snape, Steve	10	1	—	—	4
Stapleton, John	0 + 2	—	—	—	—
Swann, Malcolm	1	—	—	—	—
Topping, Paul	25 + 2	—	46	2	94
Tuimavave, Paddy	15 + 3	3	—	—	12
Viller, Mark	23 + 4	2	12	—	32
Walsh, Steve	12 + 1	—	—	—	—
Wilson, Danny	17	2	—	3	11
Whittle, Steve	0 + 1	—	—	—	—
Wright, Terry	4 + 1	—	—	—	—
Trialist	1	—	—	—	—
TOTALS:					
42 players		63	68	5	393

1985-86 MATCH ANALYSIS

Date	Com-petition	H/A	Opponent	Rlt	Score	Tries	Goals	Atten-dance	Referee
30.8.85	SLC	H	St. Helens (at Bolton W. FC)	L	14-32	L. Holliday (2)	Topping (3)	3142	Kendrew
4.9.85	SLC	A	Oldham	W	16-12	Allen, Ratcliffe, Jones	Topping, Viller	—	—
8.9.85	SLC	A	Dewsbury	L	12-20	M. Holliday, Higgins	Topping (2)	—	—
15.9.85	LC(1)	A	Salford	L	14-18	Jones, Derbyshire	Topping (3)	—	—
22.9.85	SLC	H	York	L	16-30	Wilson, Allen, Ratcliffe	Topping (2)	1312	Hodgson
29.9.85	SLC	A	Castleford	L	16-28	Bate (2), Higgins	Topping (2)	—	—
6.10.85	SLC	H	Widnes	W	17-6	Viller	Topping (5), Wilson (3dg)	1454	Haigh
13.10.85	SLC	A	Bradford N.	L	20-48	Hewitt (2), Derbyshire, Viller	Topping (2)	—	—
20.10.85	SLC	H	Leeds	L	14-26	Scott, Hewitt	Jones (2), Viller	2448	Fox
27.10.85	SLC	H	Warrington	L	12-28	Scott	Topping (4)	2319	Volante
3.11.85	SLC	A	Hull	L	10-16	Hewitt	Viller (3)	—	—
17.11.85	SLC	A	Widnes	L	16-30	Hewitt, Tuimavave	Viller (4)	—	—
24.11.85	SLC	H	Featherstone R.	W	14-7	Hewitt, Cassidy, Scott	Topping	1336	Kershaw
27.11.85	JPS(1)	A	Hull	L	0-44	—	—	—	—
8.12.85	SLC	H	Bradford N.	W	8-0	Jones	Jones (2)	5247	Carter
15.12.85	SLC	A	Warrington	L	0-42	—	—	—	—
22.12.85	SLC	H	Hull	W	16-8	Jones (2), Snape	Viller (2)	2233	McDonald
26.12.85	SLC	A	Salford	L	17-21	Scott, Jones	Jones (4), Topping (dg)	—	—
1.1.86	SLC	H	Halifax	L	10-16	Tuimavave, Hewitt	Topping	3526	Mean
5.1.86	SLC	A	Wigan	L	0-42	—	—	—	—
12.1.86	SLC	H	Castleford	W	12-10	Bate, Hewitt	Jones (2)	1456	Haigh
19.1.86	SLC	A	York	L	2-36	—	Topping	—	—
30.1.86	CC(P)	H	Leeds	L	8-30	Hewitt	Topping (2)	1348	Houghton
2.2.86	SLC	A	Leeds	L	8-20	Bate, Evans	—	—	—
9.3.86	SLC	A	Halifax	L	14-16	Bate, Scott, Muller	Topping	—	—
16.3.86	SLC	A	Featherstone R.	L	12-14	Ratcliffe, Bate	Topping (2)	—	—
23.3.86	SLC	H	Wigan (at Bolton W. FC)	L	6-28	Rowbottom	Topping	8615	Tickle
28.3.86	SLC	H	Oldham	L	6-16	Tuimavave	Topping	2515	Holdsworth
31.3.86	SLC	H	Salford	L	0-24	—	—	2631	Campbell
6.4.86	SLC	A	St. Helens	L	14-24	Evans, Bate	Topping (3)	—	—
13.4.86	SLC	H	Hull K.R.	W	10-4	Allen	Topping (3)	1472	Loftus
20.4.86	SLC	A	Hull K.R.	L	20-28	Scott, Evans, Wilson, Muller	Topping, Viller	—	—
22.4.86	SLC	H	Dewsbury	W	39-16	Ainsworth (3), Bate (2), Lee (2)	Topping (5, 1dg)	886	Spencer

WAKEFIELD TRINITY

Ground: Belle Vue
Colours: White jerseys with red and blue hoops, white shorts
First Season: 1895-96
Nickname: Dreadnoughts
Chairman: Rodney Walker
Secretary: Alan Pearman
Coach: Len Casey (Apr 1985-)
Honours: **Championship** Winners, 1966-67, 1967-68
Beaten finalists, 1959-60, 1961-62
Division Two Champions, 1903-04
Challenge Cup Winners, 1908-09, 1945-46, 1959-60, 1961-62, 1962-63
Beaten finalists, 1913-14, 1967-68, 1978-79
Yorkshire League Winners, 1909-10, 1910-11, 1945-46, 1958-59, 1959-60, 1961-62, 1965-66
Yorkshire Cup Winners, 1910-11, 1924-25, 1946-47, 1947-48, 1951-52, 1956-57, 1960-61, 1961-62, 1964-65
Beaten finalists, 1926-27, 1932-33, 1934-35, 1936-37, 1939-40, 1945-46, 1958-59, 1973-74, 1974-75
John Player Trophy Beaten finalists, 1971-72
Records: Attendance: 37,906 Leeds v. Huddersfield (RL Cup SF) 21 March, 1936.
Home: 28,254 v. Wigan (RL Cup) 24 Mar, 1962
Season
Goals: 163 by N. Fox, 1961-62
Tries: 38 by F. Smith, 1959-60, D. Smith, 1973-74
Points: 407 by N. Fox, 1961-62
Match
Goals: 12 by N. Fox v. Workington T., 19 Sep, 1970 and v. Batley, 26 Aug, 1967; B. Ward v. Hunslet, 6 Feb, 1971

Tries: 7 by F. Smith v. Keighley, 25 Apr, 1959; K. Slater v. Hunslet, 6 Feb, 1971
Points: 33 by N. Fox v. Batley, 26 Aug, 1967
Highest score: 78-9 v. Batley, 1967-68
Highest against: 69-11 v. Hull, 1920-21; 69-17 v. St. Helens, 1952-53

1985-86 PLAYERS' SUMMARY

	App	Tries	Goals	Dr	Pts
Bell, Nigel	16 + 4	5	—	—	20
Casey, Len	7	—	—	—	—
Cocks, Gary	31 + 6	8	—	—	32
Conway, Billy	3 + 1	—	—	—	—
Davies, Tom	0 + 2	—	—	—	—
Eden, Phil	32 + 1	16	—	—	64
Evans, Graham	4	—	—	—	—
Fletcher, Andrew	3	1	—	—	4
Gearey, Paul	0 + 1	—	—	—	—
Gerard, Graham	13	7	—	1	29
Green, Jimmy	2	—	—	—	—
Green, Steve	7 + 1	2	—	—	8
Hall, David	1 + 2	—	—	—	—
Harkin, Kevin	15 + 2	1	—	—	4
Hendry, Paul	2	—	—	—	—
Hewland, Richard	1	1	—	—	4
Hickman, Kevin	20 + 2	4	—	2	18
Holdstock, Roy	8 + 1	—	—	—	—
Hopkinson, Ian	22 + 9	5	—	—	20
Hughes, Ian	10 + 5	1	—	—	4
Jones, David	10	1	—	—	4
Jones, Ken	5	—	13	—	26
Jowitt, Ian	9	2	—	—	8
Lazenby, Tracey	26 + 1	4	30	3	79
Lyons, John	20 + 3	15	—	6	66
Millington, John	15	—	—	—	—
Parkes, Brian	6 + 1	1	—	—	4
Potts, Steve	0 + 7	—	—	—	—
Ramsey, Neville	0 + 1	—	—	—	—
Robinson, Kevin	8	1	—	—	4
Rotherforth, Lindsay	22	6	—	—	24
Sharp, Greg	1	2	—	—	8
Shaw, Alan	35	1	—	—	4
Smith, Stuart	28 + 4	10	—	—	40
Spencer, Gary	9	5	—	—	20
Swanston, Don	15 + 1	2	—	—	8
Sygrove, Andrew	26	4	49	—	114
Thompson, John	14 + 8	4	—	—	16
Tosney, Andrew	9 + 1	2	—	—	8
Wainman, Stuart	9 + 1	9	19	—	74
Wandless, David	3	—	1	—	2
Whiteman, Keith	23	8	—	—	32
Youngman, Wally	4	—	—	—	—
Trialist	0 + 1	—	—	—	—
TOTALS:					
44 players		128	112	12	748

1985-86 MATCH ANALYSIS

Date	Competition	H/A	Opponent	Rlt	Score	Tries	Goals	Attendance	Referee
1.9.85	SD	A	Huddersfield B.D		16-16	Wainman (2), Jowitt	Wainman (2)	—	—
4.9.85	SD	H	Runcorn H.	W	14-7	Eden, Wainman, Rotherforth	Wainman	1109	Kendrew

(continued)

MATCH ANALYSIS (continued)

8.9.85	SD	H	Mansfield M.	W	22-10	Sygrove, Hopkinson, Lyons, Tosney	Sygrove (3)	1586	Whitfield
15.9.85	YC(1)	A	Bradford N.	L	15-40	Tosney, Lyons	Sygrove (2), Wandless, Lyons (dg)	—	—
18.9.85	SD	H	Fulham	W	18-10	Lyons, Cocks	Sygrove (4), Lyons (2dg)	1449	Volante
22.9.85	SD	A	Sheffield E.	W	28-6	Shaw, Cocks, Eden, Lyons	Sygrove (6)	—	—
29.9.85	SD	H	Workington T.	W	25-4	Lyons (2), Harkin, Thompson	Sygrove (4), Lyons (dg)	2117	Tennant
6.10.85	SD	A	Batley	L	4-8	Wainman	—	—	—
13.10.85	SD	H	Carlisle	W	36-10	Wainman (2), Whiteman, Hopkinson, Thompson, Sygrove	Wainman (6)	2002	Berry
20.10.85	SD	A	Fulham	W	18-4	Smith, Cocks, Sygrove	Wainman (2), Lyons (dg), Gerard (dg)	—	—
27.10.85	SD	H	Sheffield E.	W	8-6	Gerard, Wainman	—	1840	Walker
3.11.85	SD	H	Doncaster	W	28-18	Smith (2), Wainman, Whiteman, Lyons	Wainman (4)	1753	Hodgson
10.11.85	SD	A	Whitehaven	L	16-29	Lazenby, Jones, Wainman	Wainman (2)	—	—
17.11.85	SD	H	Barrow	L	12-15	Eden, Smith	Wainman (2)	1753	McDonald
24.11.85	JPS(1)	A	Blackpool B.	W	24-22	Rotherforth, Lyons, Smith, Cocks	Sygrove (4)	—	—
1.12.85	JPS(2)	H	Wigan	L	21-30	Eden, Lyons, Bell, Rotherforth	Sygrove (2), Lazenby (dg)	7360	Holdsworth
22.12.85	SD	A	Doncaster	W	10-8	Gerard, Smith	Sygrove	—	—
26.12.85	SD	A	Bramley	W	19-6	Fletcher, Lyons, Hopkinson, Gerard	Sygrove, Lyons (dg)	—	—
1.1.86	SD	H	Bramley	W	18-6	Swanston, Gerard, Rotherforth	Sygrove (3)	1224	Smith
5.1.86	SD	A	Barrow	L	6-20	Lyons	Sygrove	—	—
12.1.86	SD	H	Whitehaven	W	19-2	Hickman, Cocks, Eden	Sygrove (3), Hickman (dg)	1785	Whitfield
19.1.86	SD	A	Mansfield M.	W	30-8	Lyons, Bell, Gerard, Eden, Whiteman, Sygrove	Sygrove (3)	—	—
2.2.86	SD	A	Runcorn H.	W	29-12	Sharpe (2), Eden, Thompson, Swanston	Sygrove (4), Lazenby (dg)	—	—
22.2.86	CC(1)	A	Bradford N. (at Leeds)	L	8-10	Whiteman	Sygrove (2)	—	—
2.3.86	SD	A	Leigh	L	6-22	Hewland	Jones	—	—
9.3.86	SD	A	Workington T.	W	22-16	Gerard, Parkes, Smith	Jones (5)	—	—
16.3.86	SD	A	Rochdale H.	L	4-32	—	Jones (2)	—	—
19.3.86	SD	H	Blackpool B.	W	32-20	Cocks (2), Eden (2), Hopkinson, Thompson	Jones (4)	1224	Allatt
23.3.86	SD	H	Batley	L	6-24	Gerard	Jones	1816	Whitfield
30.3.86	SD	H	Hunslet	W	26-4	Eden, Cocks, Robinson, Smith	Sygrove (5)	1600	McDonald
6.4.86	SD	H	Leigh	L	2-12	—	Sygrove	2225	Spencer
10.4.86	SD	A	Keighley	W	54-4	Eden (2), Spencer (2), Lazenby, Bell, Green, Whiteman, Lyons (2)	Lazenby (7)	—	—
13.4.86	SD	H	Keighley	W	12-10	Bell	Lazenby (4)	1429	Simpson
20.4.86	SD	H	Huddersfield B.	W	22-14	Eden (2), Hopkinson, Whiteman	Lazenby (3)	1389	Kendrew
24.4.86	SD	A	Blackpool B.	L	18-22	Rotherforth, Hughes, Lyons	Lazenby (3)	—	—
27.4.86	SD	H	Rochdale H.	W	32-28	Smith (2), Spencer, Hickman, Rotherforth	Lazenby (5, 1dg), Hickman (dg)	1900	Loftus
30.4.86	SD	A	Hunslet	W	24-8	Spencer, Hickman, Whiteman, Bell, Lazenby	Lazenby (2)	—	—
7.5.86	SD	A	Carlisle	W	44-14	Eden (2), Hickman, Green, Lazenby, Jowitt, Spencer, Whiteman	Lazenby (6)	—	—

WARRINGTON

Ground: Wilderspool
Colours: White jerseys with primrose and blue hoop, white shorts
First Season: 1895-96
Nickname: Wire
Chairman: Peter Higham
General Manager: Colin Brown
Coach: Reg Bowden (June 1984-Mar 1986) Tony Barrow (Mar 1986-)
Honours: **Championship** Winners, 1947-48, 1953-54, 1954-55
Beaten finalists, 1925-26, 1934-35, 1936-37, 1948-49, 1950-51, 1960-61
League Leaders Trophy Winners, 1972-73
Club Championship (Merit Table) Winners, 1973-74
Premiership Beaten finalists, 1976-77
Challenge Cup Winners, 1904-05, 1906-07, 1949-50, 1953-54, 1973-74
Beaten finalists, 1900-01, 1903-04, 1912-13, 1927-28, 1932-33, 1935-36, 1974-75
Lancashire League Winners, 1937-38, 1947-48, 1948-49, 1950-51, 1953-54, 1954-55, 1955-56, 1967-68
Lancashire Cup Winners, 1921-22, 1929-30, 1932-33, 1937-38, 1959-60, 1965-66, 1980-81, 1982-83
Beaten finalists, 1906-07, 1948-49, 1950-51, 1967-68, 1985-86
John Player Trophy Winners, 1973-74, 1977-78, 1980-81
Beaten finalists, 1978-79
Premiership Trophy Winners, 1985-86
Beaten finalists 1976-77
Captain Morgan Trophy Winners, 1973-74
BBC2 Trophy Beaten finalists, 1974-75
Records: Attendance: 35,000 Wigan v. Leigh (Lancs. Cup Final) 29 Oct, 1949.
Home: 34,304 v. Wigan (League) 22 Jan, 1949

Season
Goals: 170 by S. Hesford, 1978-79
Tries: 66 by B. Bevan, 1952-53
Points: 363 by H. Bath, 1952-53
Match
Goals: 14 by H. Palin v. Liverpool C., 13 Sep, 1950
Tries: 7 by B. Bevan v. Leigh, 29 Mar, 1948 and v. Bramley, 22 Apr, 1953
Points: 33 by G. Thomas v. St. Helens, 12 Apr, 1909
Highest score: 78-3 v. St. Helens, 1908-09
Highest against: 68-14 v. Hunslet, 1927-28

1985-86 PLAYERS' SUMMARY

	App	Tries	Goals	Dr	Pts
Allen, Dave	9 + 7	·	—	—	—
Bevan, John	2	—	—	—	—
Bishop, Paul	21 + 3	13	63	13	191
Blake, Phil	19	22	—	1	89
Boyd, Les	33	13	—	—	52
Campbell, Roy	0 + 2	1	—	—	4
Carbert, Brian	35 + 1	14	64	—	184
Cullen, Paul	32 + 1	4	—	—	16
Duane, Ronnie	14 + 1	6	—	—	24
Eccles, Bob	11	6	—	—	24
Ford, Paul	14 + 2	—	5	2	12
Forster, Mark	34 + 6	14	—	—	56
Gittins, Tommy	17 + 9	2	—	—	8
Gregory, Andy	32 + 1	8	—	1	33
Gregory, Mike	19 + 2	6	—	—	24
Hesford, Steve	2	—	6	—	12
Hodson, Tony	12 + 4	2	—	—	8
Jackson, Bob	39	6	—	—	24
Johnson, Brian	27 + 2	13	—	—	52
Kelly, Ken	23 + 1	5	—	—	20
Knight, Mark	1 + 1	—	—	—	—
McGinty, Billy	15 +. 7	4	—	—	16
Meadows, Kevin	3 + 2	3	—	—	12
Morris, Steve	0 + 1	—	—	—	—
Peters, Barry	9 + 3	1	—	—	4
Peters, Steve	3 + 1	—	—	—	—
Rathbone, Alan	17 + 2	—	—	—	—
Roberts, Mark	21 + 6	5	—	—	20
Sanderson, Gary	8	2	—	—	8
Shaw, Glyn	3 + 5	1	—	—	4
Tamati, Kevin	36 + 2	2	—	—	8
Thackray, Rick	28 + 1	16	—	—	64
Webb, Carl	18 + 1	3	—	—	12
Worrall, Tony	2 + 1	—	—	—	—
TOTALS:					
34 players		172	138	17	981

1985-86 MATCH ANALYSIS

Date	Competition	H/A	Opponent	Rlt	Score	Tries	Goals	Attendance	Referee
1.9.85	SLC	H	Bradford N.	W	32-7	Thackray (2), Eccles (2), A. Gregory, Carbert, Roberts	Ford (2)	3845	McDonald
4.9.85	SLC	A	St. Helens	L	6-12	Duane	Ford	—	—
8.9.85	SLC	A	Hull K.R.	L	8-12	Eccles	Carbert (2)	—	—
15.9.85	LC(1)	H	Blackpool B.	W	30-3	Kelly, Jackson, Webb, Forster, Carbert	Hesford (5)	2234	Whitfield
22.9.85	SLC	H	Castleford	W	24-16	M. Gregory (2), Kelly, Tamati	Carbert (3), Ford	3066	Carter
25.9.85	LC(2)	H	Workington T.	W	38-4	Blake (2), Eccles (2), Forster, Carbert, Thackray	Carbert (5)	2518	McDonald
29.9.85	SLC	A	Oldham	L	20-26	Kelly, A. Gregory, Eccles	Carbert (4)	—	—
2.10.85	LC(SF)	H	Widnes	W	11-4	Blake, A. Gregory	Hesford, A. Gregory (dg)	5633	McDonald
6.10.85	SLC	H	Salford	W	41-19	Blake (4), Jackson, Thackray	Carbert (8), Blake (dg)	3199	Lindop
13.10.85	LC(F)	St. Helens	Wigan	L	8-34	Johnson	Carbert (2)	(19202)	Holdsworth
20.10.85	SLC	H	York	W	14-12	Kelly, Carbert, Shaw	Carbert	2503	Walker
27.10.85	SLC	A	Swinton	W	28-12	Thackray, McGinty, Kelly, Johnson, Webb, Carbert	Carbert (2)	—	—
3.11.85	SLC	H	Leeds	W	32-18	Johnson (2), Boyd, Bishop, Blake, A. Gregory	Carbert (2), Bishop (2)	3512	Smith
10.11.85	JPS(P)	A	Featherstone R.	W	14-10	Blake (2), Carbert	Carbert	—	—
14.11.85	SLC	A	Castleford	W	26-20	Johnson (2), Blake (2), Cullen	Carbert (3)	—	—
17.11.85	SLC	H	Halifax	L	12-14	Carbert	Bishop (4)	4103	Tickle
24.11.85	JPS(2)	A	Fulham	W	20-13	Forster (2), Webb	Carbert (3), Bishop	—	—
1.12.85	JPS(2)	H	Barrow	W	34-14	Forster (4), Blake, Boyd, Campbell	Bishop (3)	3705	Berry
7.12.85	JPS(3)	H	Wigan	L	22-26	Bishop, Blake, Thackray	Bishop (5)	6737	Holdsworth
15.12.85	SLC	H	Swinton	W	42-0	Blake (3), McGinty (2), Thackray, Boyd, Johnson	Bishop (5)	2814	Hodgson
22.12.85	SLC	A	Featherstone R.	L	14-27	Bishop, Jackson	Bishop (3)	—	—
1.1.86	SLC	H	Wigan	L	10-12	Johnson	Carbert (3)	8148	Lindop
12.1.86	SLC	H	St. Helens	W	26-16	Blake, Roberts, Thackray, Hodson	Carbert (5)	4514	Allatt
19.1.86	SLC	A	Dewsbury	W	16-12	Blake (2), Thackray	Bishop (2)	—	—
2.2.86	SLC	H	Oldham	W	8-4	Boyd, Cullen	—	3405	Carter
9.2.86	CC(1)	H	Sheffield E.	W	62-11	Blake (2), Cullen (2), Jackson, Hodson, M. Gregory, Thackray, McGinty, Peters, Carbert	Carbert (9)	2347	Berry
9.3.86	CC(2)	A	Oldham	L	6-13	Boyd	Carbert	—	—
16.3.86	SLC	A	Salford	W	19-10	Johnston, Carbert, Boyd	Carbert (3), Bishop (dg)	—	—
19.3.86	SLC	H	Hull	W	43-16	Thackray (4), Bishop, Boyd, M. Gregory, Johnson	Carbert (5), Bishop (dg)	2537	Campbell
23.3.86	SLC	H	Hull K.R.	W	31-16	Bishop (2), Carbert, Johnson, M. Gregory	Bishop (5, 1dg)	3305	Hodgson
26.3.86	SLC	A	Bradford N.	L	2-16	—	Bishop	—	—
28.3.86	SLC	H	Widnes	L	13-24	Duane, M. Gregory	Bishop (2, 1dg)	4290	Kershaw
31.3.86	SLC	A	Halifax	L	6-18	Bishop	Bishop	—	—
3.4.86	SLC	A	Wigan	D	10-10	Johnson, Carbert	Bishop	—	—
6.4.86	SLC	H	Dewsbury	W	52-0	Boyd (3), Thackray (2), Duane (2), Forster (2), Jackson, Bishop	Bishop (4)	2485	Tickle
9.4.86	SLC	A	Widnes	W	8-6	Meadows	Carbert, Ford (2dg)	—	—
13.4.86	SLC	A	Leeds	W	35-6	Meadows (2), Carbert, Duane, Forster, A. Gregory, Bishop	Bishop (3, 1dg)	—	—

(continued on page 96)

WHITEHAVEN

Ground:	Recreation Ground
Colours:	Chocolate, blue and gold jerseys, white shorts
First Season:	1948-49
Nickname:	Haven
Chairman:	David Wigham
Secretary:	George Nixon
Coach:	Phil Kitchin (June 1985-)
Records:	Attendance: 18,500 v. Wakefield T. (RL Cup) 19 Mar, 1960

Season

Goals: 141 by J. McKeown, 1956-57
Tries: 29 by W. Smith, 1956-57
Points: 291 by J. McKeown, 1956-57

Match

Goals: 11 by W. Holliday v. Hunslet, 31 Mar, 1962
Tries: 6 by V. Gribbin v. Doncaster, 18 Nov, 1984
Points: 25 by W. Holliday v. Hunslet, 31 Mar, 1962
Highest score: 64-0 v. Doncaster, 1984-85
Highest against: 68-14 v. Leigh, 1983-84

1985-86 PLAYERS' SUMMARY

	App	Tries	Goals	Dr	Pts
Ackerman, Rob	8 + 1	4	—	—	16
Banks, Alan	29	2	—	—	8
Barnes, David	4 + 3	—	—	—	—
Beckwith, Mark	28 + 1	12	—	—	48
Blythin, Kevin	0 + 1	—	—	—	—
Bottell, Gary	13	1	—	—	4
Burney, Steve	20 + 1	5	—	—	20
Cameron, Graham	19 + 3	5	31	1	83
Coles, Kevin	6 + 4	—	—	—	—
Dalton, Jimmy	28	7	—	—	28
Dinsdale, Edwin	3 + 2	1	8	—	20
Ditchburn, Tom	1 + 1	—	—	—	—
D'Leny, Tony	12 + 4	1	—	—	4
Doran, John	1	1	—	—	4
Fearon, Neil	9 + 4	3	—	—	12
Fisher, Billy	15 + 2	4	—	—	16
Flynn, Mal	5	—	—	—	—
Frazer, Neil	2 + 9	1	—	—	4
Gorley, Les	29 + 1	6	—	—	24
Gorley, Peter	1	—	—	—	—
Gribbin, Vince	4	1	—	—	4
Hall, Colin	34 + 3	6	1	1	27
Hetherington, Gary	20 + 1	3	—	—	12
Howse, Steve	36 + 1	3	—	—	12
Hunter, Clive	5	—	—	—	—
Johnston, Frank	9 + 3	3	—	1	13
Lightfoot, David	26	4	57	3	133
Lofthouse, Norman	1	—	—	—	—
McCartney, Duncan	3 + 4	—	—	—	—
McDermott, Paul	11	4	—	—	16
Preston, Gary	1 + 2	2	—	—	8
Radcliffe, Norman	0 + 2	—	—	—	—
Rose, Tony	6 + 2	1	—	—	4
Simpson, Jeff	23	9	—	—	36
Solarie, Tony	36	16	—	—	64
Stoddart, Peter	29 + 1	4	—	4	20
Thompson, Ian	11 + 1	3	—	—	12
Todd, Colin	3 + 2	—	—	—	—
Tomlinson, Brian	3	—	—	—	—

TOTALS:
39 players		112	97	10	652

Great Britain Under-21 winger Jimmy Dalton.

Veteran Cumbrian packman Les Gorley.

1985-86 MATCH ANALYSIS

Date	Com-petition	H/A	Opponent	Rlt	Score	Tries	Goals	Atten-dance	Referee
1.9.85	SD	A	Rochdale H.	W	10-5	Howse, Lightfoot	Lightfoot	—	—
8.9.85	SD	H	Barrow	W	34-10	Beckwith (2), Hall, Solarie, Fisher	Lightfoot (7)	1890	Simpson
15.9.85	LC(1)	A	Barrow	W	12-8	Hetherington, Dalton	Lightfoot (2)	—	—
18.9.85	SD	H	Keighley	W	32-0	Simpson (2), Solarie, Fisher, Hetherington, Dalton	Lightfoot (4)	1297	Spencer
22.9.85	SD	A	Huddersfield B.	W	31-14	Stoddart (2), Burney, D'Leny, Hall	Lightfoot (5), Stoddart (dg)	—	—
25.9.85	LC(2)	A	St. Helens	L	8-26	Fisher	Lightfoot (2)	—	—
29.9.85	SD	H	Carlisle	W	17-10	Solarie, Simpson	Lightfoot (4, 1dg)	2483	Carter
6.10.85	SD	A	Fulham	L	17-21	Burney, Hetherington, Dalton	Lightfoot (2, 1dg)	—	—
13.10.85	SD	H	Hunslet	W	28-6	Solarie (2), Burney, Dalton, Simpson, Banks	Lightfoot (2)	1988	Campbell
20.10.85	SD	A	Blackpool B.	W	20-11	Solarie (3), Fisher	Lightfoot (2)	—	—
27.10.85	SD	H	Leigh	L	11-34	Gorley, Simpson	Lightfoot (1, 1dg)	2879	Loftus
3.11.85	SD	A	Mansfield M.	W	24-12	Frazer, Beckwith, Gorley	Dinsdale (6)	—	—
10.11.85	SD	H	Wakefield T.	W	29-16	Gorley (2), Stoddart, Gribbin, Howse, Solarie	Lightfoot (2), Stoddart (dg)	2106	Kershaw
17.11.85	SD	A	Sheffield E.	W	9-8	Hall	Lightfoot (2), Stoddart (dg)	—	—
24.11.85	JPS(1)	H	Widnes	L	7-12	Beckwith	Lightfoot, Stoddart (dg)	3097	Beaumont
8.12.85	SD	H	Mansfield M.	W	28-0	Simpson (2), Gorley, Lightfoot, Johnston	Lightfoot (4)	1757	Fox
15.12.85	SD	A	Runcorn H.	W	22-14	Solarie, Simpson, Stoddart, Burney	Lightfoot (3)	—	—
22.12.85	SD	H	Blackpool B.	L	10-20	Johnston, Hall	Lightfoot	1926	Carter
26.12.85	SD	H	Workington T.	W	8-4	Lightfoot	Lightfoot, Cameron	3011	Allatt
5.1.86	SD	H	Runcorn H.	W	34-2	Fearon, Simpson, Burney, Solarie, Doran, Dalton, Dinsdale	Lightfoot (3)	1520	Lindop
12.1.86	SD	A	Wakefield T.	L	2-19	—	Lightfoot	—	—
19.1.86	SD	H	Batley	W	6-2	Solarie	Lightfoot	1722	Spencer
9.2.86	CC(1)	A	York	L	6-18	Hall	Lightfoot	—	—
16.2.86	SD	A	Hunslet	W	29-16	Beckwith (2), Cameron, Solarie, McDermott	Lightfoot (4), Johnston (dg)	—	—
2.3.86	SD	H	Bramley	L	14-38	Dalton, Howse, Cameron	Lightfoot	1540	Houghton
9.3.86	SD	H	Fulham	W	18-8	Beckwith (2), Solarie	Cameron (3)	1130	Tennant
16.3.86	SD	A	Barrow	L	7-34	Beckwith	Cameron, Hall (dg)	—	—
23.3.86	SD	H	Rochdale H.	W	20-16	Beckwith (2), Lightfoot	Cameron (4)	1693	Volante
28.3.86	SD	A	Workington T.	W	12-10	Beckwith	Cameron (4)	—	—
13.4.86	SD	H	Huddersfield B.	W	38-12	Ackerman (2), Cameron, McDermott, Thompson, Johnston, Solarie	Cameron (5)	2084	McDonald
15.4.86	SD	A	Carlisle	L	0-7	—	—	—	—
20.4.86	SD	A	Doncaster	L	13-14	McDermott, Banks	Cameron (2, 1dg)	—	—
23.4.86	SD	H	Sheffield E.	W	36-4	Thompson (2), Dalton, Ackerman, Fearon, Gorley, Cameron	Cameron (3), Hall	1395	Simpson
27.4.86	SD	A	Batley	L	2-7	—	Cameron	—	—
30.4.86	SD	H	Doncaster	L	22-27	Solarie, Hall, Ackerman, McDermott	Cameron (3)	1507	Allatt
5.5.86	SD	A	Leigh	L	12-64	Fearon, Preston	Cameron (2)	—	—
7.5.86	SD	A	Keighley	W	16-0	Cameron, Rose, Preston	Cameron (2)	—	—
11.5.86	SD	A	Bramley	L	8-14	Bottell	Dinsdale (2)	—	—

WIDNES

Ground: Naughton Park
Colours: White jerseys, black shorts
First Season: 1895-96
Nickname: Chemics
Chairman: Tom Smith
Secretary: Ron Close
Coach: Eric Hughes (June 1984-Jan 1986)
Doug Laughton (Jan 1986-)
Honours: **Division One** Champions, 1977-78
Championship Beaten finalists, 1935-36
Challenge Cup Winners, 1929-30, 1936-37, 1963-64, 1974-75, 1978-79, 1980-81, 1983-84
Beaten finalists, 1933-34, 1949-50, 1975-76, 1976-77, 1981-82
Lancashire League Winners, 1919-20
Lancashire Cup Winners, 1945-46, 1974-75, 1975-76, 1976-77, 1978-79, 1979-80
Beaten finalists, 1928-29, 1939-40, 1955-56, 1971-72, 1981-82, 1983-84
John Player Trophy Winners, 1975-76, 1978-79
Beaten finalists, 1974-75, 1977-78, 1979-80, 1983-84
Premiership Winners, 1979-80, 1981-82, 1982-83
Beaten finalists, 1977-78
BBC2 Floodlit Trophy Winners, 1978-79
Beaten finalists, 1972-73, 1973-74
Western Division Championship Beaten finalists, 1962-63
Records: Attendance: 24,205 v. St. Helens (RL Cup) 16 Feb, 1961
Season
Goals: 140 by M. Burke, 1978-79
Tries: 34 by F. Myler, 1958-59
Points: 316 by M. Burke, 1978-79

Match
Goals: 11 by R. Whitfield v. Oldham, 28 Oct, 1965
Tries: 5 by E. Cunningham v. Doncaster, 15 Feb, 1981; J. Basnett v. Hunslet, 17 Oct, 1981
Points: 27 by H. Dawson v. Liverpool C., 22 Apr, 1957
Highest score: 59-0 v. Bramley, 1952-53
Highest against: 60-5 v. Oldham, 1927-28

1985-86 PLAYERS' SUMMARY

	App	Tries	Goals	Dr	Pts
Barrow, Scott	10 + 1	2	—	—	8
Basnett, John	38	14	—	—	56
Bayliss, Steve	1	1	—	—	4
Burke, Mick	32	4	47	—	110
Cleal, Noel	16	8	—	—	32
Currier, Andy	9 + 3	2	2	—	12
Dowd, Barry	18 + 4	7	13	—	54
Elwell, Keith	18	1	—	1	5
Eyres, Andrew	0 + 1	—	—	—	—
Eyres, Richard	31 + 3	8	—	1	33
Fieldhouse, John	31 + 1	3	—	—	12
George, Wilf	22	6	—	—	24
Gilbert, John	6	—	—	—	—
Gormley, Ian	16 + 6	5	—	—	20
Haughton, Paul	3 + 1	1	—	—	4
Hulme, David	36 + 1	12	—	—	48
Hulme, Paul	24 + 6	7	—	—	28
Lamb, David	5	1	—	—	4
Linton, Ralph	18 + 2	3	—	—	12
Lydon, Joe	15 + 1	7	12	1	53
Lyon, David	4 + 4	—	—	—	—
Myler, John	34 + 1	1	34	3	75
Myler, Tony	30	11	—	—	44
Newton, Keith	3 + 6	—	—	—	—
O'Neill, Mike	34 + 2	3	—	—	12
O'Neill, Steve	5	—	—	2	2
Platt, Duncan	2 + 3	—	4	—	8
Rogers, Steve	1	—	—	—	—
Ruane, Andy	19 + 2	3	—	—	12
Sephton, Geoff	5 + 1	1	—	—	4
Sorensen, Kurt	18	1	—	—	4
Souto, Peter	1	—	—	—	—
Stockley, Trevor	3 + 1	1	—	—	4
Whitfield, Fred	5 + 1	2	—	—	8
Wright, Darren	23 + 2	5	—	—	20
Wright, Stuart	10	1	—	—	4
TOTALS:					
36 players		121	112	8	716

1985-86 MATCH ANALYSIS

Date	Competition	H/A	Opponent	Rlt	Score	Tries	Goals	Attendance	Referee
1.9.85	SLC	A	Hull	W	33-10	Lydon (2), A. Myler (2), Gormley	Burke (6), S. O'Neill (dg)	—	—
4.9.85	SLC	H	Halifax	W	12-9	D. Hulme	Burke (4)	3016	Spencer
8.9.85	SLC	H	Featherstone R.	W	30-16	Fieldhouse (2), Lydon (2), George	Burke (4), Lydon	3003	Hodgson

(continued)

MATCH ANALYSIS (continued)

15.9.85	LC(1)	A	Rochdale H.	W	17-6	George, Basnett	Burke (4), S. O'Neill (dg)	—	—
22.9.85	SLC	A	Wigan	L	10-32	Currier, Lydon	Burke	—	—
25.9.85	LC(2)	A	Leigh	W	18-14	A. Myler, Lamb, D. Hulme	Lydon (2), J. Myler	—	—
29.9.85	SLC	H	Bradford N.	W	28-26	D. Hulme (2), Haughton, A. Myler	Burke (5), J. Myler (dg), Lydon (dg)	3470	Allatt
2.10.85	LC(SF)	A	Warrington	L	4-11	Stockley	—	—	—
6.10.85	SLC	A	Swinton	L	6-17	Linton	Dowd	—	—
13.10.85	SLC	A	Dewsbury	W	18-15	Linton (2), D. Hulme	Burke (3)	—	—
23.10.85	SLC	H	Salford	W	27-12	Basnett (2), Elwell, George, Barrow	Lydon (3), Elwell (dg)	3629	McDonald
27.10.85	SLC	H	Oldham	D	10-10	George	Lydon (3)	4926	Berry
4.11.85	Tour	H	New Zealand	L	12-32	Eyres, George	J. Myler, Dowd	5181	Kendrew
17.11.85	SLC	H	Swinton	W	30-16	Currier, Eyres, D. Hulme, Lydon, Barrow, George	Lydon (3)	3133	Walker
24.11.85	JPS(1)	A	Whitehaven	W	12-7	Basnett, Cleal	Dowd (2)	—	—
30.11.85	JPS(2)	H	Bradford N.	W	30-6	Cleal (2), Lydon, D. Hulme, Gormley	Burke (5)	2222	Lindop
8.12.85	JPS(3)	H	Leigh	L	31-35	Dowd (2), A. Myler, Cleal, Burke	Burke (5), J. Myler (dg)	6153	Allatt
12.12.85	SLC	H	York	W	14-12	A. Myler, Basnett, Dowd	Burke	1666	Fox
15.12.85	SLC	H	Hull K.R.	L	8-15	A. Myler	Burke, J. Myler	4004	Smith
22.12.85	SLC	A	York	W	26-8	Cleal, P. Hulme, Ruane, Dowd, Basnett	Dowd (3)	—	—
26.12.85	SLC	A	Oldham	D	10-10	Burke, Basnett	Burke	—	—
1.1.86	SLC	A	St. Helens	W	30-16	Basnett (2), Eyres (2), Dowd, A. Myler	Currier (2), Burke	—	—
15.1.86	SLC	A	Hull K.R.	W	24-12	Eyres (2), Cleal, A. Myler, P. Hulme	Dowd (2)	—	—
22.1.86	SLC	A	Halifax (at Halifax T. FC)	L	15-8	Basnett, D. Wright, Dowd	J. Myler (1, 1dg)	—	—
26.1.86	SLC	H	Castleford	W	9-5	P. Hulme	J. Myler (2), Eyres (dg)	4088	Spencer
29.1.86	SLC	H	Wigan	W	16-6	P. Hulme, M. O'Neill, D. Wright	J. Myler (2)	9440	Berry
2.2.86	SLC	A	Salford	L	6-22	D. Wright	J. Myler	—	—
9.2.86	CC(1)	A	Featherstone R.	W	18-14	Cleal, A. Myler, Burke	J. Myler (3)	—	—
23.2.86	CC(2)	H	Rochdale H.	W	36-20	D. Hulme (2), P. Hulme, Ruane, Fieldhouse, Cleal	J. Myler (6)	3706	Holdsworth
2.3.86	SLC	H	Leeds	W	20-18	Whitfield, D. Hulme, Basnett	Dowd (4)	4451	McDonald
9.3.86	SLC	A	Leeds	L	12-29	Bayliss, Whitfield	J. Myler (2)	—	—
16.3.86	CC(3)	H	Leeds	D	10-10	D. Wright	J. Myler (2), Burke	8141	Kershaw
19.3.86	CC(3) Replay	A	Leeds	L	0-5	—	—	—	—
23.3.86	SLC	A	Bradford N.	L	8-40	Dowd	J. Myler (2)	—	—
28.3.86	SLC	A	Warrington	W	24-13	Basnett (2), Eyres, D. Hulme	Platt (4)	—	—
31.3.86	SLC	H	St. Helens	L	6-16	Sephton	Burke	6709	Hodgson
6.4.86	SLC	A	Featherstone R.	W	16-15	Gormley, Basnett, P. Hulme	J. Myler (2)	—	—
9.4.86	SLC	H	Warrington	L	6-8	M. O'Neill	J. Myler	4028	Haigh
13.4.86	SLC	H	Hull	W	26-20	Gormley, P. Hulme, Burke, Ruane, S. Wright	Burke (3)	3016	Allatt
16.4.86	SLC	H	Dewsbury	W	24-2	Eyres, Gormley, D. Wright, D. Hulme	J. Myler (3), Burke	1855	Tickle
22.4.86	SLC	A	Castleford	D	16-16	J. Myler, A. Myler, M. O'Neill	J. Myler (2)	—	—
27.4.86	PT(1)	A	Warrington	L	8-10	Sorensen	J. Myler (2)	—	—

WIGAN

Ground:	Central Park
Colours:	Cherry and white hooped jerseys, white shorts
First Season:	1895-96
Nickname:	Riversiders
Chairman:	Jack Hilton
Coach:	Colin Clarke and Alan McInnes (Aug 1984-May 1986)

Honours: **Championship** Winners, 1908-09, 1921-22, 1925-26, 1933-34, 1945-46, 1946-47, 1949-50, 1951-52, 1959-60 Beaten finalists, 1909-10, 1910-11, 1911-12, 1912-13, 1923-24, 1970-71 **League Leaders Trophy** Winners, 1970-71 **Challenge Cup** Winners, 1923-24, 1928-29, 1947-48, 1950-51, 1957-58, 1958-59, 1964-65, 1984-85 Beaten finalists, 1910-11, 1919-20, 1943-44, 1945-46, 1960-61, 1962-63, 1965-66, 1969-70, 1983-84 **Lancashire League** Winners, 1901-02, 1908-09, 1910-11, 1911-12, 1912-13, 1913-14, 1914-15, 1920-21, 1922-23, 1923-24, 1925-26, 1945-46, 1946-47, 1949-50, 1951-52, 1958-59, 1961-62, 1969-70 **Lancashire War League** Winners, 1940-41 **Lancashire Cup** Winners, 1905-06, 1908-09, 1909-10, 1912-13, 1922-23, 1928-29, 1938-39, 1946-47, 1947-48, 1948-49, 1949-50, 1950-51, 1951-52, 1966-67, 1971-72, 1973-74, 1985-86 Beaten finalists, 1913-14, 1914-15, 1925-26, 1927-28, 1930-31, 1934-35, 1935-36, 1936-37, 1945-46, 1953-54, 1957-58, 1977-78, 1980-81, 1984-85 **John Player Trophy** Winners, 1982-83, 1985-86 **BBC2 Floodlit Trophy** Winners, 1968-69 Beaten finalists, 1969-70 **Charity Shield** Winners, 1985-86 **War League Championship** Winners, 1943-44 Beaten finalists, 1940-41

Records: Attendance: 47,747 v. St. Helens (League) 27 Mar, 1959

Season
Goals: 176 by F. Griffiths, 1958-59
Tries: 62 by J. Ring, 1925-26
Points: 394 by F. Griffiths, 1958-59
Match
Goals: 22 by J. Sullivan v. Flimby & Fothergill, 14 Feb, 1925
Tries: 7 by J. Ring v. Flimby & Fothergill, 14 Feb, 1925; v. Salford, 13 Apr, 1925 and v. Pemberton R., 12 Feb, 1927; W. Boston v. Dewsbury, 20 Aug, 1955 and v. Salford, 30 Apr. 1962; G. Vigo v. St. Helens, 21 Aug, 1976
Points: 44 by J. Sullivan v. Flimby & Fothergill, 14 Feb, 1925
Highest score: 116-0 v. Flimby & Fothergill, 1924-25
Highest against: 58-3 v. Leeds, 1972-73

1985-86 PLAYERS' SUMMARY

	App	Tries	Goals	Dr	Pts
Berry, Cliff	2 + 2	—	—	—	—
Braithwaite, Ron	6 + 2	1	—	—	4
Campbell, Danny	5 + 3	—	—	—	—
Case, Brian	21 + 4	2	—	—	8
Clare, Jeff	2	—	1	—	2
Courtney, Neil	5 + 2	—	—	—	—
Dermott, Martin	3 + 1	—	—	—	—
Donlan, Steve	5	2	—	—	8
Dowling, Greg	25	5	—	1	21
Du Toit, Nick	32 + 10	10	1	—	42
Edwards, Shaun	33 + 3	14	—	—	56
Ella, Steve	23 + 1	21	—	—	84
Fairhurst, Jimmy	3 + 4	2	—	—	8
Ford, Mike	31 + 4	14	—	—	56
Ford, Phil	5	3	—	—	12
Fraser, Paul	1 + 2	—	—	—	—
Gill, Henderson	28	15	3	—	66
Goodway, Andy	36 + 2	8	—	—	32
Hampson, Steve	41 + 2	9	3	—	42
Hanley, Ellery	40	35	8	—	156
Henley-Smith, Gary	7	2	—	—	8
Holden, Keith	0 + 4	1	—	—	4
Kiss, Nicky	39	8	—	—	32
Louw, Rob	1 + 7	2	—	—	8
Lucas, Ian	10 + 2	2	—	—	8
Lydon, Joe	9	2	13	1	35
Mayo, John	0 + 1	—	—	—	—
Mordt, Ray	5	2	—	—	8
O'Neill, Paul	4	—	—	—	—
Potter, Ian	42 + 1	3	—	—	12
Russell, Richard	13 + 3	3	2	—	16
Stephenson, David	41	18	126	2	326
Stott, Phil	7 + 3	6	—	—	24
Wane, Shaun	24 + 4	3	—	—	12
West, Graeme	31 + 5	10	—	—	40
Whitfield, Colin	16 + 1	11	9	—	62
Trialist	2	—	6	—	12

TOTALS:
37 players		214	172	4	1,204

1985-86 MATCH ANALYSIS

Date	Competition	H/A	Opponent	Rlt	Score	Tries	Goals	Attendance	Referee
25.8.85	Charity Shield	Isle of Man	Hull K.R.	W	34-6	Donlan (2), Gill (2), M. Ford	Stephenson (7)	(4066)	Campbell
1.9.85	SLC	H	Castleford	L	10-12	Edwards, Hampson	Stephenson	(10922)	Holdsworth
4.9.85	SLC	A	Salford	L	8-12	P. Ford	Whitfield, Clare	—	—
8.9.85	SLC	A	Bradford N.	L	16-21	P. Ford, Stephenson, Du Toit	Stephenson (2)	—	—
15.9.85	LC(1)	H	Fulham	W	24-13	Henley-Smith, Du Toit, M. Ford, P. Ford, Stephenson	Stephenson (2)	8943	Carter
22.9.85	SLC	H	Widnes	W	32-10	Whitfield (2), Goodway, Hampson, M. Ford, Fairhurst	Whitfield (3), Stephenson	(15050)	Smith
25.9.85	LC(2)	H	Salford	W	22-20	Goodway, Hanley, Hampson, Henley-Smith	Trialist (3)	(11188)	Hodgson
29.9.85	SLC	A	Hull K.R.	L	18-19	Fairhurst, M. Ford, Case	Trialist (3)	—	—
2.10.85	LC(SF)	H	St. Helens	W	30-2	Edwards (2), Wane, Dowling, Ella	Stephenson (5)	(18544)	Campbell
6.10.85	Tour	H	New Zealand	W	14-8	Edwards, Goodway	Stephenson (3)	(12856)	Campbell
13.10.85	LC(F)	St. Helens	Warrington	W	34-8	Ella (2), Kiss, Hanley, Edwards	Stephenson (7)	(19202)	Holdsworth
20.10.85	SLC	H	Dewsbury	W	58-8	Ella (4), Goodway, Whitfield, Dowling, Stephenson, Edwards, Du Toit, Hampson	Stephenson (7)	(10536)	Tickle
24.10.85	SLC	A	Leeds	W	28-6	Ella, M. Ford, Stephenson, Whitfield	Stephenson (6)	—	—
27.10.85	SLC	H	Featherstone R.	W	62-0	Whitfield (3), Hanley (2), Ella (2), Du Toit, Edwards, Case, M. Ford	Stephenson (9)	(11399)	Haigh
3.11.85	SLC	A	York	W	34-12	Whitfield (2), M. Ford, Edwards, Ella, Du Toit	Stephenson (5)	—	—
10.11.85	SLC	H	Salford	W	20-8	M. Ford (2), Ella, Whitfield	Stephenson (2)	(12588)	Holdsworth
17.11.85	SLC	A	Featherstone R.	W	26-12	Stephenson, Stott, Ella, Hanley	Stephenson (5)	—	—
24.11.85	JPS(1)	H	Mansfield M.	W	26-0	Ella, Du Toit, Stott, West	Hampson (3), Stephenson (2)	10040	Kendrew
1.12.85	JPS(2)	A	Wakefield T.	W	30-21	Hanley (2), Ella, Gill, Stott, Goodway	Stephenson (3)	—	—
7.12.85	JPS(3)	A	Warrington	W	26-22	Gill (2), Hanley, Potter, Ella	Stephenson (3)	—	—
14.12.85	JPS(SF)	St. Helens	Leigh	W	36-8	Dowling (3), Ella, Kiss, Hanley	Stephenson (6)	(10509)	Lindop
22.12.85	SLC	A	Halifax	D	12-12	Hanley (2)	Stephenson (2)	—	—
26.12.85	SLC	H	St. Helens	W	38-14	Gill (2), M. Ford, Stephenson, Hanley, Whitfield, Ella	Whitfield (5)	21813	Hodgson
1.1.86	SLC	A	Warrington	W	12-10	Edwards, Gill	Stephenson (2)	—	—
5.1.86	SLC	H	Swinton	W	42-0	M. Ford (2), Stephenson, West, Hanley, Kiss, Du Toit, Gill	Stephenson (4), Gill	12627	Kershaw
11.1.86	JPS(F)	Elland Rd, Leeds,	Hull K.R.	W	11-8	Wane, M. Ford	Stephenson, Dowling (dg)	(17573)	Holdsworth
19.1.86	SLC	H	Hull K.R.	W	12-8	Hanley, West, Goodway	—	14179	Fox
29.1.86	SLC	A	Widnes	L	6-16	West	Stephenson	—	—
9.2.86	CC(1)	A	Workington T. (at Workington FC)	W	56-12	Gill (2), Stott (2), Du Toit (2), West (2), Hanley, Edwards, Lucas, Ella	Stephenson (2), Gill, Du Toit	—	—
23.2.86	SLC	H	Halifax	D	6-6	—	Stephenson (3)	18450	Berry

(continued on page 96)

89

WORKINGTON TOWN

Ground:	Derwent Park
Colours:	White jerseys with blue band, white shorts
First Season:	1945-46
Nickname:	Town
Chairman:	George Graham
Secretary:	John Bell
Coach:	Jackie Davidson (Apr 1985-Jan 1986) Keith Davies (Feb 1986-)
Honours:	**Championship** Winners, 1950-51 Beaten finalists, 1957-58 **Challenge Cup** Winners, 1951-52 Beaten finalists, 1954-55, 1957-58 **Lancashire Cup** Winners, 1977-78 Beaten finalists, 1976-77, 1978-79, 1979-80 **Western Division Championship** Winners, 1962-63
Records:	Attendance: 17,741 v. Wigan (RL Cup) 3 Mar, 1965. There was a crowd of 20,403 at Borough Park for a RL Cup-tie v. St. Helens on 8 Mar, 1952 **Season** Goals: 186 by L. Hopkins, 1981-82 Tries: 49 by J. Lawrenson, 1951-52 Points: 438 by L. Hopkins, 1981-82 **Match** Goals: 11 by I. MacCorquodale v. Blackpool B., 6 Jan, 1973 Tries: 7 by I. Southward v. Blackpool B., 17 Sep, 1955 Points: 33 by I. Southward v. Blackpool B., 17 Sep, 1955 Highest score: 62-15 v. Hunslet, 1963-64 Highest against: 64-4 v. Castleford, 1984-85; 64-18 v. Hull, 1984-85

1985-86 PLAYERS' SUMMARY

	App	Tries	Goals	Dr	Pts
Bailey, Sam	5 + 4	—	—	—	—
Banks, John	13 + 1	5	—	—	20
Beattie, John	27 + 1	12	—	—	48
Beck, David	36	23	—	—	92
Beverley, Harry	25	—	—	—	—
Bower, Ian	24	9	—	—	36
Burgess, Glen	8 + 1	2	—	—	8
Burns, Howard	29 + 1	13	—	1	53
Coles, Colin	3	2	—	—	8
Cottier, Gordon	9	2	—	—	8
Courty, Dave	9 + 3	1	—	—	4
Cowan, Murray	6	1	—	—	4
Denny, Ian	2	1	—	—	4
Falcon, Colin	26 + 2	9	—	—	36
Fraser, Neil	7 + 2	1	—	—	4
Gartland, Kevin	4 + 1	1	—	—	4
Hartley, Ian	16 + 6	—	—	—	—
Hogg, Graham	6 + 5	2	5	—	18
Jones, John	19 + 2	10	—	—	40
Key, Andrew	1	—	—	—	—
Litt, Ian	13 + 5	3	—	—	12
Lowden, David	12 + 2	2	8	—	24
Maguire, Steve	24 + 2	4	4	—	24
Maughan, Kevin	1	—	—	—	—
Moran, Dave	4	1	—	—	4
Murdoch, Paul	0 + 1	—	—	—	—
Nixon, Gary	32 + 4	10	—	—	40
Pattinson, Bill	26	7	—	—	28
Rea, Geoff	27 + 3	3	—	—	12
Riley, David	0 + 1	—	—	—	—
Roper, Tony	4	2	—	—	8
Smith, Gary	35	7	79	1	187
Stafford, Peter	12 + 4	4	—	—	16
Sullivan, Joe	10 + 6	—	—	—	—
Todd, Colin	7	—	—	—	—
Tubman, Keith	12 + 3	2	—	—	8
TOTALS: 36 players		139	96	2	750

1985-86 MATCH ANALYSIS

Date	Com-petition	H/A	Opponent	Rlt	Score	Tries	Goals	Atten-dance	Referee
1.9.85	SD	H	Carlisle	W	32-11	Jones (3), Pattinson (2), Nixon, Bower	Hogg (2)	1446	Spencer
8.9.85	SD	A	Blackpool B.	W	20-16	Smith, Burns, Beattie	Smith (4)	—	—
15.9.85	LC(1)	A	Runcorn H.	W	38-16	Jones (2), Beattie (2), Beck (2), Banks, Pattinson	Hogg (3)	—	—
22.9.85	SD	H	Bramley	W	34-12	Beck (2), Bower (2), Maguire, Banks, Rea	Smith (3)	807	Walker
25.9.85	LC(2)	A	Warrington	L	4-38	—	Smith (2)	—	—
29.9.85	SD	A	Wakefield T.	L	4-25	Hogg	—	—	—
6.10.85	SD	H	Huddersfield B.	W	32-8	Beck (2), Jones (2), Bower, Burns	Smith (4)	647	Tickle
13.10.85	SD	A	Runcorn H.	L	20-28	Burns, Banks, Jones	Smith (4)	—	—
20.10.85	SD	H	Mansfield M.	W	36-14	Beck (2), Beattie, Coles, Smith, Bower, Pattinson	Smith (4)	501	Tickle
25.10.85	SD	A	Hunslet	L	30-32	Falcon, Coles, Smith, Burns, Gartland	Smith (5)	—	—
							Smith (4)	577	Houghton
3.11.85	SD	H	Batley	W	24-14	Bower (2), Nixon, Burgess			
10.11.85	SD	H	Blackpool B.	W	18-15	Smith, Cowan, Rea	Smith (3)	539	Smith
17.11.85	SD	H	Fulham	L	24-28	Falcon (3), Tubman, Nixon	Smith (2)	574	Carter
24.11.85	JPS(1)	A	Hunslet	L	12-20	Rea, Stafford	Smith (2)	—	—
1.12.85	SD	A	Rochdale H.	L	6-36	Beattie	Smith	—	—
8.12.85	SD	A	Batley	L	6-20	Beck	Smith	—	—
15.12.85	SD	H	Rochdale H.	W	28-26	Litt (2), Nixon, Beattie, Stafford	Smith (4)	599	Croft
22.12.85	SD	H	Sheffield E.	L	8-26	Nixon, Denny	—	476	Kershaw
26.12.85	SD	A	Whitehaven	L	4-8	—	Smith (2)	—	—
12.1.86	SD	A	Doncaster	L	5-32	Tubman	Smith (dg)	—	—
19.1.86	SD	A	Fulham	L	8-36	Sullivan, Moran	—	—	—
23.1.86	SD	A	Barrow	L	18-48	Cottier, Beattie, Stafford	Maguire (3)	—	—
2.2.86	SD	A	Huddersfield B.	L	10-20	Burns, Frazer	Smith	—	—
9.2.86	CC(1)	H	Wigan (at Workington FC)	L	12-56	Beattie, Courty	Smith (2)	6346	Campbell
9.3.86	SD	H	Wakefield T.	L	16-22	Beck, Beattie, Falcon	Smith (2)	670	Simpson
12.3.86	SD	A	Carlisle	L	20-32	Beck, Burns, Falcon, Cottier	Smith (2)	—	—
16.3.86	SD	H	Doncaster	L	22-26	Pattinson, Roper, Nixon, Beck	Smith (3)	408	Loftus
23.3.86	SD	A	Mansfield M.	W	42-18	Nixon (2), Beck (2), Beattie, Burgess, Litt, Roper	Smith (5)	—	—
28.3.86	SD	H	Whitehaven	L	10-12	Nixon, Burns	Smith	1966	Lindop
31.3.86	SD	H	Barrow	W	36-16	Beck (3), Smith, Jones, Lowden, Burns	Smith (4)	1025	Carter
10.4.86	SD	H	Leigh	L	20-29	Falcon, Nixon, Burns, Beck	Smith (2)	624	Tickle
13.4.86	SD	A	Leigh	L	8-36	Beck (2)	—	—	—
20.4.86	SD	H	Hunslet	L	14-19	Jones, Falcon, Maguire	Maguire	480	Loftus
23.4.86	SD	A	Keighley	W	29-8	Burns (2), Beattie, Smith, Pattinson	Lowden (4), Burns (dg)	—	—
27.4.86	SD	A	Bramley	L	22-32	Falcon, Lowden, Bower, Stafford	Lowden (3)	—	—
5.5.86	SD	A	Sheffield E. (at Doncaster)	L	14-16	Banks, Beattie, Bower	Lowden	—	—
7.5.86	SD	H	Runcorn H.	W	28-0	Beck, Pattinson, Burns, Hogg	Smith (6)	252	Whitfield
11.5.86	SD	H	Keighley	W	36-2	Beck (2), Smith, Banks, Burns, Maguire	Smith (6)	344	Campbell

YORK

Ground:	Wigginton Road
Colours:	Amber and black jerseys, black shorts
First Season:	1901-02
Nickname:	Wasps
Chairman:	Charles Magson
Secretary:	Ian Clough
Coach:	Phil Lowe (Mar 1983-)
Honours:	**Division Two** Champions, 1980-81
	Challenge Cup Beaten finalists, 1930-31
	Yorkshire Cup Winners, 1922-23, 1933-34, 1936-37
	Beaten finalists, 1935-36, 1957-58, 1978-79
Records:	Attendance: 14,689 v. Swinton (RL Cup) 10 Feb, 1934
	Season
	Goals: 146 by V. Yorke, 1957-58
	Tries: 35 by J. Crossley, 1980-81
	Points: 318 by G. Steadman, 1984-85
	Match
	Goals: 11 by V. Yorke v. Whitehaven, 6 Sep, 1958; C. Gibson v. Dewsbury, 28 Sep, 1980
	Tries: 6 by R. Hardgrave v. Bramley, 5 Jan, 1935
	Points: 26 by G. Steadman v. Batley, 25 Nov, 1984
	Highest score: 60-0 v. Barrow, 1971-72
	Highest against: 75-3 v. Warrington 1950-51

1985-86 PLAYERS' SUMMARY

	App	Tries	Goals	Dr	Pts
Birkby, Ian	6	2	13	—	34
Blackburn, Steve	11 + 3	2	7	1	23
Bowman, Chris	4 + 1	—	—	—	—
Carter, Matt	16	12	—	—	48
Colley, Mick	13 + 8	2	—	—	8
Crooks, Steve	20 + 2	—	—	—	—
Dobson, Steve	33	6	—	8	32
Dreier, Col	7	1	—	—	4
Hagan, Mick	7 + 2	1	—	—	4
Harrison, Chris	36	8	—	—	32
Hughes, Mick	15 + 5	1	—	—	4
Marketo, Mick	17	3	—	—	12
Martin, Peter	20	3	—	—	12
Mercer, Andy	10	1	—	—	4
Midgley, Trevor	29 + 4	—	—	—	—
Morgan, Terry	1	1	1	—	6
Morrell, Wayne	36	11	—	—	44
Pethybridge, Rod	10	3	4	—	20
Phillippo, Peter	26 + 3	1	—	—	4
Price, Gary	32	6	—	—	24
Proctor, Paul	12 + 2	2	—	—	8
Pryce, Geoff	8	1	—	—	4
Rhodes, Chris	8 + 4	—	—	—	—
Rhodes, Darren	0 + 1	—	—	—	—
Smith, Gary	10 + 2	—	—	—	—
Stead, Ray	8	2	—	—	8
Steadman, Graham	19	8	50	1	133
Sullivan, Graham	1	—	—	—	—
Sykes, Andy	5 + 4	—	—	—	—
Tansley, Ian	14 + 4	1	—	—	4
Willey, Sean	27	7	1	—	30
Windshuttle, Ross	5	—	—	—	—
Trialists (4)	2 + 4	—	1	—	2

TOTALS:

36 players		85	77	10	504

York captain Steve Crooks.

1985-86 MATCH ANALYSIS

Date	Com- petition	H/A	Opponent	Rlt	Score	Tries	Goals	Atten- dance	Referee
1.9.85	SLC	H	Salford	W	14-12	Hagan	Steadman (4, 1dg), Blackburn (dg)	1815	Berry
4.9.85	SLC	H	Hull	L	8-22	Steadman, Stead	—	2674	Smith
8.9.85	SLC	A	St. Helens	L	8-30	Stead	Steadman (2)	—	—
15.9.85	YC(1)	H	Featherstone R.	L	18-26	Steadman (2)	Steadman (5)	2283	Croft
18.9.85	SLC	A	Castleford	L	6-34	Harrison	Steadman	—	—
22.9.85	SLC	A	Swinton	W	30-16	Morrell (2), Colley, Steadman, Harrison	Steadman (5)	—	—
29.9.85	SLC	H	Halifax	L	17-34	Colley, Tansley, Harrison	Steadman (2), Dobson (dg)	2837	Holdsworth
6.10.85	SLC	A	Leeds	W	18-10	Steadman, Marketo	Steadman (5)	—	—
13.10.85	SLC	H	Featherstone R.	W	25-12	Harrison, Marketo, Morrell, Willey	Steadman (4), Dobson (dg)	3347	Beaumont
20.10.85	SLC	A	Warrington	L	12-14	Dobson, Morrell	Steadman (2)	—	—
3.11.85	SLC	H	Wigan	L	12-34	Proctor, Carter	Steadman (2)	6197	Hale (NZ)
10.11.85	SLC	H	Oldham	L	2-8	—	Steadman	3306	Whitfield
15.11.85	SLC	A	Salford	L	18-22	Willey, Steadman, Carter	Steadman (3)	—	—
24.11.85	JPS(1)	H	Castleford	W	12-10	Carter	Steadman (4)	3765	Tickle
1.12.85	JPS(2)	H	Keighley	W	21-16	Martin, Proctor, Morrell	Steadman (3), Willey, Dobson (dg)	2511	Smith
7.12.85	JPS(3)	A	Hull K.R.	L	16-24	Phillippo, Carter, Mercer	Pethybridge (2)	—	—
12.12.85	SLC	A	Widnes	L	12-14	Carter (2), Harrison	—	—	—
15.12.85	SLC	A	Bradford N.	W	17-12	Price, Martin, Carter	Pethybridge (2), Dobson (dg)	—	—
22.12.85	SLC	H	Widnes	L	8-26	Willey, Pethybridge	—	2989	Simpson
26.12.85	SLC	H	Hull K.R.	L	8-22	Carter (2)	—	4380	Haigh
1.1.86	SLC	A	Hull K.R.	L	6-12	Martin	Blackburn	—	—
12.1.86	SLC	A	Oldham	L	16-24	Blackburn, Dobson, Carter	Blackburn (2)	—	—
19.1.86	SLC	H	Swinton	W	36-2	Morrell (2), Steadman (2), Carter, Marketo	Steadman (6)	2440	Holdsworth
29.1.86	SLC	H	Castleford	W	18-14	Dobson, Pethybridge, Harrison, Carter	Steadman	2162	Houghton
2.2.86	SLC	H	Bradford N.	W	9-8	Price, Morrell	Dobson (dg)	3021	Smith
9.2.86	CC(1)	H	Whitehaven	W	18-6	Willey (2), Pethybridge, Harrison	Trialist	2339	Fox
9.3.86	CC(2)	H	Hull K.R.	L	6-34	Morrell	Blackburn	5694	Lindop
16.3.86	SLC	H	St. Helens	L	11-18	Morgan, Price	Morgan, Dobson (dg)	1922	Volante
23.3.86	SLC	A	Featherstone R.	L	10-40	Price (2)	Blackburn	—	—
31.3.86	SLC	A	Hull	L	12-16	Dobson, Hughes	Birkby (2)	—	—
6.4.86	SLC	A	Wigan	L	2-42	—	Birkby	—	—
9.4.86	SLC	A	Halifax	L	6-10	Morrell	Birkby	—	—
13.4.86	SLC	H	Dewsbury	W	39-18	Birkby (2), Morrell, Price, Harrison, Willey, Pryce	Birkby (5), Dobson (dg)	2241	Croft
16.4.86	SLC	H	Warrington	L	6-34	Willey	Birkby	1981	Campbell
20.4.86	SLC	A	Dewsbury	L	15-18	Dreier, Dobson	Birkby (3), Dobson (dg)	—	—
22.4.86	SLC	H	Leeds	L	12-14	Dobson, Blackburn	Blackburn (2)	1367	Smith

Dewsbury's Paul Jennings, who touched down four times in 29 appearances.

York back row forward Chris Harrison, scorer of eight tries in 36 matches.

LEIGH MATCH ANALYSIS (continued)

Date	Com-petition	H/A	Opponent	Rlt	Score	Tries	Goals	Atten-dance	Referee
2.2.86	SD	A	Mansfield M.	W	32-2	Henderson, Cogger, P. Johnson, Halliwell, Gelling, C. Johnson	C. Johnson (4)	—	—
9.2.86	CC(1)	A	Keighley	W	24-2	Fox (2), Halliwell, C. Johnson, Henderson	C. Johnson (2)	—	—
2.3.86	SD	H	Wakefield T.	W	22-6	Brockwell, Fox, Halliwell	C. Johnson (5)	2966	Mean
9.3.86	CC(2)	H	Blackpool B.	W	31-10	Henderson (2), Brockwell, Kerr, Tabern, Cogger	C. Johnson (3), P. Johnson (dg)	3241	Campbell
16.3.86	CC(3)	A	Hull K.R.	L	10-25	C. Johnson, Fox	C. Johnson	—	—
23.3.86	SD	H	Huddersfield B.	W	22-12	Campbell, Fox, Halliwell, Tabern	C. Johnson (3)	2499	Simpson
28.3.86	SD	H	Rochdale H.	W	29-23	Halliwell (2), Henderson, Kerr, Tabern	C. Johnson (4, 1dg)	2566	Whitfield
31.3.86	SD	A	Blackpool B.	W	15-8	Fox, Halliwell	C. Johnson (3), P. Johnson (dg)	—	—
6.4.86	SD	A	Wakefield T.	W	12-2	Pyke, C. Johnson	C. Johnson (2)	—	—
10.4.86	SD	A	Workington T.	W	29-20	C. Johnson (2), Hughes, Halliwell, Clarke	C. Johnson (4), P. Johnson (dg)	—	—
13.4.86	SD	H	Workington T.	W	36-8	Drummond (2), Pyke, Kerr, Atherton, Cottrell	C. Johnson (6)	2310	Campbell
16.4.86	SD	A	Hunslet	W	24-12	Halliwell (2), C. Johnson, Davis, Drummond	C. Johnson (2)	—	—
20.4.86	SD	H	Barrow	W	26-18	C. Johnson, Atherton, Henderson, Drummond, Halliwell	C. Johnson (3)	3176	Spencer
27.4.86	SD	A	Doncaster	W	20-12	Halliwell (2), Drummond, Fox	C. Johnson (2)	—	—
30.4.86	SD	H	Keighley	W	92-2	Halliwell (5), Tabern (2), Fox (2), Henderson (2), Pyke (2), C. Johnson, Kerr, Davis	C. Johnson (14)	2224	Tennant
5.5.86	SD	H	Whitehaven	W	64-12	Halliwell (4), Clarke, Gelling, Fox, Cottrell, C. Johnson, Drummond, Davis, Kerr	C. Johnson (8)	2813	Loftus
7.5.86	SD	A	Bramley	W	21-8	Halliwell, Tabern, Kerr	C. Johnson (4, 1dg)	—	—
9.5.86	SD	A	Keighley	W	38-4	Halliwell (2), Hughes (2), Clarke (2), Davis	C. Johnson (5)	—	—
11.5.86	SD	H	Doncaster	W	46-24	Halliwell (4), Atherton (2), Davis, Beazant	C. Johnson (6), P. Johnson	3330	Tidball (Pr)

ST. HELENS MATCH ANALYSIS (continued)

Date	Com-petition	H/A	Opponent	Rlt	Score	Tries	Goals	Atten-dance	Referee
2.4.86	SLC	A	Oldham	W	38-12	Ledger (2), McCormack (2), Holding, Platt	Loughlin (7)	—	—
6.4.86	SLC	H	Swinton	W	24-14	Elia, Loughlin, Ledger, Haggerty	Loughlin (4)	2921	Mean
9.4.86	SLC	A	Hull K.R.	W	22-13	Elia (3), Arkwright	Loughlin (3)	—	—
13.4.86	SLC	A	Salford	W	30-28	Round (2), Haggerty (2), Holding	Loughlin (5)	—	—
16.4.86	SLC	H	Castleford	W	62-12	Round (3), Holding (2), Veivers (2), Haggerty, Bailey, Liptrot, Doherty, Platt	Loughlin (7)	4347	Carter
20.4.86	SLC	H	Oldham	W	44-12	Round (2), Platt (2), Holding, Loughlin, Haggerty, Ledger, Allen	Loughlin (4)	5746	Smith
27.4.86	PT(1)	H	Leeds	L	22-38	Allen, Loughlin, Hughes	Loughlin (5)	6415	Smith

95

WARRINGTON MATCH ANALYSIS (continued)

Date	Competition	H/A	Opponent	Rlt	Score	Tries	Goals	Attendance	Referee
16.4.86	SLC	A	York	W	34-6	Carbert (2), Sanderson, Bishop, A. Gregory, Gittins	Bishop (4), Carbert	—	—
20.4.86	SLC	A	Hull	W	23-20	Roberts, Boyd, Forster, A. Gregory	Bishop (3, 1dg)	—	—
22.4.86	SLC	H	Featherstone R.	W	30-6	Sanderson, Bishop, Roberts, Forster, Gittins	Bishop (4), Ford	2556	Allatt
27.4.86	PT(1)	H	Widnes	W	10-8	Duane	Bishop (2, 2dg)	4890	McDonald
11.5.86	PT(SF)	A	Wigan	W	23-12	Bishop, Roberts, A. Gregory	Bishop (3, 5dg)	—	—
18.5.86	PT(F)	Elland Halifax Rd, Leeds		W	38-10	Boyd (2), Bishop, Tamati, Jackson, Forster, Johnson	Bishop (5)	(13683)	Lindop

WIGAN MATCH ANALYSIS (continued)

Date	Competition	H/A	Opponent	Rlt	Score	Tries	Goals	Attendance	Referee
2.3.86	SLC	H	Hull	W	44-6	West (2), Mordt (2), Goodway, Stephenson, Kiss, Lydon	Stephenson (6)	12476	Haigh
18.3.86	CC(2)	H	St. Helens	W	24-14	Stephenson (2), Ella, Hampson, Hanley	Stephenson (2)	18553	Whitfield
12.3.86	SLC	A	Hull	W	26-10	Ella, Stephenson, Kiss, Hampson	Stephenson (5)	—	—
16.3.86	CC(3)	H	Castleford	L	2-10	—	Lydon	18503	Lindop
18.3.86	SLC	A	Dewsbury	W	42-4	Stephenson, Stott, Wane, Edwards, Potter, Hanley, M. Ford	Stephenson (7)	—	—
23.3.86	SLC	A	Swinton	W	28-6	Goodway, Russell, Hanley, Du Toit, West	Stephenson (4)	—	—
28.3.86	SLC	A	St. Helens	L	13-18	Hampson, Hanley	Stephenson (2, 1dg)	—	—
31.3.86	SLC	H	Oldham	L	18-26	Hanley, Holden, Stephenson	Stephenson (3)	11932	Houghton
3.4.86	SLC	H	Warrington	D	10-10	Hanley, Stephenson	Stephenson	9359	Smith
6.4.86	SLC	H	York	W	42-2	Hanley (2), Russell, Kiss, Edwards, Stephenson, Gill, Lydon	Stephenson (3), Lydon (2)	8321	Tennant
13.4.86	SLC	A	Castleford	W	14-12	Louw (2), Russell	Lydon	—	—
18.4.86	SLC	H	Bradford N.	W	42-10	Hanley (3), Kiss, West, Stephenson, Hampson, Edwards	Stephenson (2), Russell (2), Gill	8198	Whitfield
20.4.86	SLC	H	Leeds	W	29-6	Hanley (2), Edwards, Gill, Stephenson	Hanley (4), Stephenson (dg)	9878	Campbell
22.4.86	SLC	A	Oldham	W	28-4	Hanley (2), Kiss, Hampson, Stephenson	Hanley (4)	—	—
27.4.86	PT(1)	H	Hull K.R.	W	47-0	Hanley (4), Gill (2), Lucas, Braithwaite	Lydon (7, 1dg)	11408	Fox
11.5.86	PT(SF)	H	Warrington	L	12-23	Potter, Hanley	Lydon (2)	16249	Holdsworth

Gary Prohm bid farewell to the British club scene by setting a new tryscoring sequence record.

RECORDS

LEADING SCORERS FOR 1985-86

TOP TEN TRIES

1. Steve Halliwell (Leigh)	49
2. Ellery Hanley (Wigan)	38
3. Peter Lister (Bramley)	34
4. John Henderson (Leigh)	31
5. Tommy Frodsham (Blackpool B.)	30
6. Phil Fox (Leigh)	29
7. Stewart Williams (Barrow)	27
8. Brian Garrity (Runcorn H.)	24
9. Carl Gibson (Leeds)	23
David Beck (Workington T.)	23

● Others with 20 or more: Phil Blake (Warrington), Des Drummond (Leigh), Graham King (Hunslet) 22; Steve Ella (Wigan), Mal Graham (Oldham), Roy Haggerty (St. Helens), Tony Marchant (Castleford) 21; Dane O'Hara (Hull), Garry Schofield (Hull), Neil Turner (Doncaster), Gary Peacham and Kevin Pape (Carlisle) 20.

TOP TEN GOALS
(Including drop goals)

1. Chris Johnson (Leigh)	173
2. David Stephenson (Wigan)	128
3. David Noble (Doncaster)	118
4. Kevin Harcombe (Rochdale H.)	115
5. Shaun Kilner (Bramley)	110
6. John Dorahy (Hull K.R.)	101
7. John Woods (Bradford N.)	98
8. David Creasser (Leeds)	84
9. Dean Carroll (Carlisle)	83
Gary Smith (Workington T.)	83

TOP FIVE DROP GOALS

1. Paul Bishop (Warrington)	13
2. Keith Bell (Featherstone R.)	12
Peter Wood (Runcorn H.)	12
4. Dean Carroll (Carlisle)	11
5. Steve Dobson (York)	8
Billy Price (Blackpool B.)	8

TOP FIVE POINTS

	T	G	DG	Pts
1. Chris Johnson (Leigh)	14	171	2	400
2. David Stephenson (Wigan)	18	126	2	326
3. John Woods (Bradford N.)	13	97	1	247
4. David Noble (Doncaster)	3	112	6	242
5. John Dorahy (Hull K.R.)	8	99	2	232
Shaun Kilner (Bramley)	3	110	0	232

OUTSTANDING SCORING FEATS IN 1985-86

INDIVIDUAL

Most tries in a match:
5 by John Woods (Bradford N.) v. Swinton .... SLC
Phil Fox (Leigh) at Batley .... JPS (1)
Ian French (Castleford) at Hunslet .... CC (1)
Steve Halliwell (Leigh) v. Keighley .... SD

Most goals in a match:
14 by Chris Johnson (Leigh) v. Keighley .... SD

Most points in a match:
36 by John Woods (Bradford N.) v. Swinton ...... SLC
32 by Chris Johnson (Leigh) v. Keighley .... SD

Most drop goals in a match:
5 by Paul Bishop (Warrington) v. Wigan .... PT (1)

TEAM

Highest score:
Leigh 92 v. Keighley 2 .... SD
(Also widest margin)

● There was a total of 26 matches in which one team scored 50 points or more compared with 34 in the previous season. The other 60-plus scores were:

Home:
Leigh 76 v. Mansfield M. 6 .... SD
Barrow 74 v. Keighley 2 .... SD
St. Helens 72 v. Carlisle 8 .... LC (1)
Leigh 64 v. Whitehaven 12 .... SD
Wigan 62 v. Featherstone R. 0 .... SLC
Warrington 62 v. Sheffield E. 11 .... CC (1)
St. Helens 62 v. Castleford 12 .... SLC
Castleford 60 v. Hunslet 2 ....YC (1)
Leeds 60 v. Keighley 12 ....YC (1)

Away:
Batley 2 v. Leigh 70 .... JPS (1)
Hunslet 6 v. Castleford 60 .... CC (1)

Highest score by losing team:
Hunslet 38 v. Blackpool B. 32 .... SD
Carlisle 32 v. Blackpool B. 33 .... SD

● There was a total of 61 matches in which a team scored 20 points or more and lost compared with 47 in the previous season.

High-scoring draws:
Huddersfield B. 32 v. Keighley 32 .... SD
Fulham 26 v. Huddersfield B. 26....................... SD
Hull K.R. 24 v. Leeds 24 .... CC (SF)
Hull 20 v. St. Helens 20 .... SLC
Hunslet 20 v. Huddersfield B. 20 .... SD
Hunslet 20 v. Bramley 20................................ SD
Bradford N. 20 v. Bramley 20 .... CC (1)
Keighley 20 v. Carlisle 20................................ SD

- From the start of the 1983-84 season, the value of a try was raised from three points to four points. It was officially decided that records for most points in a match, season or career would subsequently include the four-point try and no attempt would be made to adjust existing records featuring the three-point try.
- Substitute appearances do not count towards players' full appearance records.

RECORD-BREAKING FEATS IN 1985-86

NEW RECORDS AT A GLANCE . . .

STEVE HALLIWELL scored a club record 49 tries in the season for Leigh which included the most by any centre. All but one of the tries were scored in league matches to give him the Division Two record.

NEIL TURNER finished with a club best of 20 tries in a season for Doncaster after the club record had been held briefly by KEVIN PARKHOUSE.

TOMMY FRODSHAM scored a club record 30 tries in a season for Blackpool Borough.

PETER LISTER scored a club record 34 tries in a season for Bramley.

CHRIS JOHNSON broke two Leigh records with 173 goals and 400 points in the season.

DAVID NOBLE broke two Doncaster records with a season's 118 goals and 242 points.

ROY RAFFERTY broke two Sheffield Eagles records with 79 goals and 186 points in the campaign.

KEVIN HARCOMBE scored a club record 115 goals in the season for Rochdale Hornets.

JOHN WOODS achieved three records with five tries, eight goals and 36 points in one match for Bradford Northern. The five tries equalled a Division One record while the 36 points broke the Bradford and Division One match records.

IAN FRENCH scored a club record-equalling five tries in a match for Castleford.

ELLERY HANLEY of Wigan scored a record-equalling four tries in a Premiership Trophy tie.

GARRY SCHOFIELD achieved two records with four tries and 16 points in a match for Great Britain.

PAUL BISHOP of Warrington kicked a record-equalling five drop goals in a match.

HARRY PINNER of St. Helens reached a career record of 79 one-point drop goals.

DAVID STEPHENSON of Wigan equalled the Lancashire Cup final record of seven goals.

JOHN DORAHY of Hull K.R. equalled the Yorkshire Cup final record of five goals.

DEAN CARROLL scored a club record nine goals and 21 points in a match for Carlisle. BRIAN TUNSTALL held the points record briefly with 16.

DAVID CHOLMONDELEY scored a club record 16 points in a match for Sheffield Eagles.

GARY PROHM took his tryscoring sequence to a Division One record 11 successive matches.

LEIGH achieved a host of records during the season. Division Two records were ... most successive wins of 30 matches; most points in a match with 92; and most points in a season, tallying 1,156. Club records were ... most successive wins of 14 matches, the points in a match feat beaten twice; plus biggest away win. A Rugby League record was ... 1,436 points in all matches.

BLACKPOOL BOROUGH scored their highest total of points in a match with a 54-0 win.

SHEFFIELD EAGLES scored a club record 36-6 victory but went down to a record 62-11 defeat.

HULL suffered a club record 57-14 defeat.

KEIGHLEY crashed to a club record 92-2 defeat.

CARLISLE went down to a club record 72-8 defeat.

CASTLEFORD had a club record 62-12 defeat.

MANSFIELD MARKSMAN crashed to a club record 76-6 defeat.

HUDDERSFIELD BARRACUDAS and KEIGHLEY produced a Division Two record high draw of 32-32.

BLACKPOOL BOROUGH and CARLISLE scored a Division Two record of 32 points by a losing side.

ST. HELENS finished with a Division One record-equalling run of 13 wins.

WIGAN scored a record Lancashire Cup final win of 34-8.

WARRINGTON scored a record Premiership final win of 38-10.

A DIVISION ONE record crowd of 21,813 watched Wigan v. St. Helens.

NEW RECORDS IN DETAIL...

STEVE HALLIWELL scored a club record 49 tries in his first season with Leigh after having made little impact as a player in Australia. His total included a Division Two record of 48 tries and the most by any centre in one season.

The Leigh record had been set by winger Bill Kindon with 36 in 1956-57. Halliwell passed that figure with the fourth of his five tries in a club record 92-2 home defeat of Keighley on 30th April. His five tries also took him past the Division Two record of 34 tries by stand off John Crossley for York in 1980-81.

Halliwell scored one try as a stand off and the remaining 48 was a record season's total by a centre. Tommy Gleeson set the previous record with 45 for Huddersfield in 1913-14, equalled by Hull K.R.'s Gary Prohm in 1984-85.

Halliwell picked up £1,225 from the Greenall Whitley-Sunday People award scheme which offered £25-a-try to the end of the season leader. Twenty-one of his tries came when he touched down in all of Leigh's last eight matches, causing some protests that the total was boosted by simple walk-in tries set up by his colleagues.

The son of former Wigan player Frank Halliwell, Steve was born in England but emigrated to Australia while still an infant.

Halliwell played in all but five of Leigh's 43 matches, his total of 38 matches including one substitute appearance. His record-breaking season was as follows:

	Tries	
Runcorn Highfield ....(A)	2	
Batley ....(H)	1	
Oldham (Lancs. Cup) ....(H)	0	
Sheffield Eagles ....(H)	1	
Barrow ....(A)	0	
Widnes (Lancs. Cup) ....(H)	0	
Hunslet...................................(H)	0	Sub app.
Carlisle...................................(A)	1	
Mansfield Marksman ....(H)	4	
Huddersfield Barracudas ....(A)	1	
Whitehaven.............................(A)	1	
Fulham ....(H)	Did not play	
Batley ....(A)	Did not play	
Bramley ....(H)	2	
Batley (John Player)..................(A)	0	
Hunslet (John Player) ....(H)	0	
Widnes (John Player) ....(A)	Did not play	
Wigan (John Player) ....semi-final	Did not play	
Carlisle ....(H)	3	
Rochdale Hornets.....................(A)	0	
Blackpool Borough ....(H)	1	
Fulham ....(A)	1	
Runcorn Highfield ....(H)	Did not play	
Sheffield Eagles........................(A)	2	
Mansfield Marksman.................(A)	1	
Keighley (RL Cup)....................(A)	1	
Wakefield Trinity.....................(H)	1	
Blackpool Borough (RL Cup) .....(H)	0	
Hull K.R. (RL Cup)..................(A)	0	
Huddersfield Barracudas............(H)	1	
Rochdale Hornets.....................(H)	2	
Blackpool Borough ....(A)	1	
Wakefield Trinity.....................(A)	0	
Workington Town ....(A)	1	
Workington Town....................(H)	0	
Hunslet ....(A)	2	
Barrow ....(H)	1	
Doncaster ....(A)	2	
Keighley ....(H)	5	
Whitehaven.............................(H)	4	
Bramley..................................(A)	1	
Keighley.................................(A)	2	
Doncaster...............................(H)	4	

Totals	Division Two..................	48
	RL Cup........................	1
GRAND TOTAL		**49**

Leigh's Steve Halliwell, record breaking top try scorer.

TOMMY FRODSHAM scored a club record 30 tries in his first full season with Blackpool Borough. The previous record of 22 tries was scored by winger Jimmy Johnson in 1970-71. Frodsham broke the record with the second of his two tries in a 38-14 home defeat of Hunslet on 13th April.

The stand off played in 34 of Blackpool's 38 matches including one at centre and scored two hat-tricks. His record-breaking season was as follows:

		Tries
Barrow	(A)	1
Fulham	(A)	0
Workington Town	(H)	0
Warrington (Lancs. Cup)	(A)	Did not play
Hunslet	(A)	3
Runcorn Highfield	(A)	0
Keighley	(H)	0
Doncaster	(A)	2
Whitehaven	(H)	0
Carlisle	(A)	2
Runcorn Highfield	(H)	1
Workington Town	(A)	Did not play
Doncaster	(H)	2
Wakefield T. (John Player)	(H)	0
Rochdale Hornets	(A)	0
Bramley	(H)	1
Whitehaven	(A)	0
Carlisle	(H)	2
Leigh	(A)	Did not play
Mansfield Marksman	(H)	0
Keighley	(A)	Did not play
Sheffield Eagles	(H)	0
Runcorn H. (RL Cup)	(H)	1
Fulham	(H)	Did not play
Leigh (RL Cup)	(A)	0
Sheffield Eagles	(A)	1
Wakefield Trinity	(A)	0
Barrow	(H)	0
Leigh	(H)	2
Huddersfield Barracudas	(A)	2
Bramley	(A)	1
Hunslet	(H)	2
Rochdale Hornets	(H)	1
Batley	(A)	1
Wakefield Trinity	(H)	0
Mansfield Marksman	(A)	2
Batley	(H)	0
Huddersfield Barracudas	(H)	3
Totals Division Two		29
RL Cup		1
GRAND TOTAL		**30**

NEIL TURNER finished with a Doncaster best of 20 tries in a season after KEVIN PARKHOUSE had briefly held the record with 19 tries.

John Buckton set the old record when the stand off scored 18 tries in 1981-82 and 1982-83. Turner reached that figure with a hat-trick in a 27-22 win at Whitehaven on 30th April and the following week Parkhouse set a new record when the prop's two tries in a 42-10 home defeat of Hunslet on 6th May took his total to 19.

Turner equalled that three days later with a try in a 26-10 home defeat of Runcorn Highfield and finished with the new record of 20 when he scored in the last match of the season, a 46-24 defeat at Leigh on 11th May.

A former Wheatley Hills RU player, Turner made his debut as an unnamed trialist winger when Doncaster lost 14-11 at home to Fulham on 8th September. In his first season he played in 35 of Doncaster's 41 matches including one abandoned game in which he scored one try.

He played 30 matches on the wing and five at centre. His record-breaking total was produced as follows:

		Tries
Sheffield Eagles	(A)	Did not play
Bramley	(H)	Did not play
Fulham	(H)	0
Bramley (Yorks Cup)	(A)	0
Barrow	(A)	Did not play
Rochdale Hornets	(A)	Did not play
Mansfield Marksman	(H)	Did not play
Hunslet	(A)	1
Blackpool Borough	(H)	0
Keighley	(H)	1
Wakefield Trinity	(A)	1
Huddersfield Barracudas	(H)	2
Blackpool Borough	(A)	1
Runcorn H. (John Player)	(H)	0
St. Helens (John Player)	(A)	0
Runcorn H. (abandoned)	(H)	1
Huddersfield Barracudas	(A)	0
Wakefield Trinity	(H)	0
Mansfield Marksman	(A)	0
Workington Town	(H)	0
Runcorn Highfield	(A)	0
Carlisle	(H)	1
Salford (RL Cup)	(H)	1
Leeds (RL Cup)	(A)	0
Keighley	(A)	0
Rochdale Hornets	(H)	0
Workington Town	(A)	2
Sheffield Eagles	(H)	1
Batley	(A)	0
Batley	(H)	0
Fulham	(A)	1
Barrow	(H)	0
Bramley	(A)	1
Whitehaven	(A)	0
Carlisle	(A)	1

Leigh ....(H)	0	
Whitehaven.....................(A)	3	
Hunslet........................(H)	0	
Runcorn Highfield ....(H)	1	
Leigh ....(A)	1	
Totals Division Two...............	18	
Abandoned (Div Two)......	1	
RL Cup........................	1	
GRAND TOTAL	**20**	

PETER LISTER scored a club record 34 tries for Bramley. The previous record of 20 tries had been shared by centre or stand off Willis Rushton (1958-59) and Australian centre Alan Smith (1972-73).

Lister broke the record with the second of his two tries in a 22-14 defeat at home to Barrow on 23rd March.

He began the season as a substitute but scored a try within a few minutes of going on in the first match. He made one other substitute appearance and missed only three of Bramley's 40 matches, playing 31 in the centre and four at stand off. He also kicked four goals, including three drops.

His match-by-match try record of touchdowns was as follows:

	Tries	
Batley.........................(H)	1 Sub app.	
Mansfield Marksman.................(A)	0	
Doncaster ....(A)	2	
Keighley.......................(A)	1	
Doncaster (Yorks. Cup)............(H)	2	
Workington Town ....(A)	1	
Hull K.R. (Yorks. Cup) ....(A)	1	
Fulham.........................(H)	2	
Barrow.........................(A)	0	
Sheffield Eagles ....(H)	1	
Hunslet........................(H)	0	
Runcorn Highfield.................(A)	2	
Rochdale Hornets...................(H)	0	
Fulham ....(A)	Did not play	
Leigh ....(A)	Did not play	
Oldham (John Player) ....(H)	Did not play	
Carlisle ....(H)	Sub app.	
Blackpool Borough ....(A)	1	
Huddersfield Barracudas...........(H)	1	
Wakefield Trinity..................(H)	0	
Wakefield Trinity..................(A)	0	
Sheffield Eagles.................(A)	0	
Rochdale Hornets...................(A)	1	
Batley (RL Cup) ....(H)	1	
Whitehaven........................(A)	2	
Bradford N. (RL Cup) ....(A)	0	
Bradford N. (RL Cup)............(H)	0	
Batley ....(A)	0	
Barrow.........................(H)	2	
Keighley ....(H)	2	

Hunslet..........................(A)	1	
Blackpool Borough ....(H)	0	
Doncaster........................(H)	2	
Mansfield Marksman ....(H)	2	
Runcorn Highfield ....(H)	3	
Workington Town...................(H)	2	
Huddersfield Barracudas...........(A)	0	
Carlisle..........................(A)	0	
Leigh ....(H)	0	
Whitehaven.......................(H)	1	
Totals Division Two.................	30	
Yorkshire Cup	3	
RL Cup......................	1	
GRAND TOTAL	**34**	

CHRIS JOHNSON broke two Leigh records with 173 goals and 400 points in a season. The old records were set by winger or full back Stuart Ferguson with 166 goals and 356 points in 1970-71.

Ferguson's total included eight tries, while Johnson touched down 14 times and included two drop goals in his total.

Johnson did not take over goal kicking until Leigh's seventh match when he kicked five against Hunslet in a 30-16 defeat of Hunslet on 29th September. The full back then totalled his record 173 goals in 37 matches.

He broke Leigh's points record of 356 when he scored 20 at home to Whitehaven in a 64-12 victory on 5th May. The goals record went with the last of Johnson's five in a 38-4 win at Keighley on 9th May.

Johnson's total of 173 goals earned him £865 from the Greenall Whitley-Sunday People award scheme which offered £5-a-goal to the end of season leader.

His match-by-match record is as follows:

	T	G	DG	Pts
Runcorn Highfield..............(A)	0	0	0	0
Batley.........................(H)	1	0	0	4
Oldham (Lancs. Cup)..........(H)	1	0	0	4
Sheffield Eagles ....(H)	0	0	0	0
Barrow.........................(A)	0	0	0	0
Widnes (Lancs. Cup)...........(H)	Did not play			
Hunslet........................(H)	0	5	0	10
Carlisle.........................(A)	0	4	0	8
Mansfield Marksman ....(H)	0	8	0	16
Huddersfield Barracudas.......(A)	0	9	0	18
Whitehaven......................(A)	0	5	0	10
Fulham.........................(H)	1	5	0	14
Batley ....(A)	1	4	0	12
Bramley........................(H)	0	9	0	18
Batley (John Player)............(A)	0	7	0	14
Hunslet (John Player) ....(H)	0	6	0	12
Widnes (John Player)...........(A)	0	5	0	10
Wigan (John Player).............SF	0	0	0	0
Carlisle ....(H)	0	4	0	8
Rochdale Hornets...............(A)	1	5	0	14

Blackpool Borough ....(H)	0	5	0	10
Fulham ....(A)	0	3	0	6
Runcorn Highfield ....(H)	0	4	0	8
Sheffield Eagles ....(A)	0	2	0	4
Mansfield Marksman............(A)	1	4	0	12
Keighley (RL Cup)..............(A)	1	2	0	8
Wakefield Trinity ....(H)	0	5	0	10
Blackpool B. (RL Cup) ....(H)	0	3	0	6
Hull K.R. (RL Cup)............(A)	1	1	0	6
Huddersfield Barracudas.......(H)	0	3	0	6
Rochdale Hornets ....(H)	0	4	1	9
Blackpool Borough ....(A)	0	3	0	6
Wakefield Trinity................(A)	1	2	0	8
Workington Town ....(A)	2	4	0	16
Workington Town...............(H)	0	6	0	12
Hunslet.............................(A)	1	2	0	8
Barrow ....(H)	1	3	0	10
Doncaster...........................(A)	0	2	0	4
Keighley ....(H)	1	14	0	32
Whitehaven ....(H)	1	8	0	20
Bramley ....(A)	0	4	1	9
Keighley...........................(A)	0	5	0	10
Doncaster...........................(H)	0	6	0	12

Totals

Division Two	11	147	2	340
Lancashire Cup.......................	1	0	0	4
John Player...........................	0	18	0	36
RL Cup	2	6	0	20
GRAND TOTALS	**14**	**171**	**2**	**400**

DAVID NOBLE broke two Doncaster records — both of which he already held — with 118 goals and 242 points in the season.

He set the previous goals record with 91, including 12 drop goals, in 1981-82 when he played mostly in the centre and the following season scored a then record 188 points after switching to loose forward midway through the campaign.

Noble broke both records with three goals in the 18-10 home defeat of Barrow on 9th April. His points total

Doncaster back row forward David Noble.

included three tries and six drop goals compared with the 90 goals, including 10 drops, and six tries in 1982-83.

Noble played in all but one of Doncaster's 40 matches last season, including an abandoned match when he kicked two goals. He made two substitute appearances and his 37 full appearances were all at loose forward or second row.

His match-by-match record was as follows:

	T	G	DG	Pts	
Sheffield Eagles.................(A)	1	3	1	11	
Bramley ....(H)	0	1	0	2	
Fulham ....(H)	0	1	0	2	
Bramley (Yorks. Cup)........(A)	0	3	0	6	
Barrow ....(A)	0	2	0	4	
Rochdale Hornets ....(A)	Did not play				
Mansfield Marksman.........(H)	0	4	1	9	
Hunslet ....(A)	0	4	0	8	
Blackpool Borough ....(H)	0	4	0	8	
Keighley...........................(H)	0	2	1	5	
Wakefield Trinity ....(A)	0	3	0	6	
Huddersfield Barracudas ....(H)	0	4	0	8	
Blackpool Borough............(A)	0	2	1	5	
Runcorn H. (John Player)..(H)	0	2	1	5	
St. Helens (John Player) ....(A)	0	4	0	8	
Runcorn H. (Abandoned)...(H)	0	2	0	4	
Huddersfield Barracudas ....(A)	0	2	0	4	
Wakefield Trinity.............(H)	0	2	0	4	
Mansfield Marksman.........(A)	0	4	0	8	
Workington Town ....(H)	1	4	0	12	
Runcorn Highfield ....(A)	0	2	0	4	
Carlisle.............................(H)	0	0	0	0	Sub app.
Salford (RL Cup) ....(H)	0	3	0	6	
Leeds (RL Cup)................(A)	0	1	0	2	
Keighley...........................(A)	1	5	0	14	
Rochdale Hornets ....(H)	0	3	0	6	
Workington Town ....(A)	0	5	0	10	
Sheffield Eagles................(H)	0	3	0	6	
Batley ....(A)	0	2	0	4	
Batley ....(H)	0	5	0	10	
Fulham ....(A)	0	3	0	6	
Barrow ....(H)	0	3	0	6	
Bramley...........................(A)	0	1	0	2	
Whitehaven ....(H)	0	1	0	2	
Carlisle.............................(A)	0	5	0	10	
Leigh...............................(H)	0	2	0	4	
Whitehaven ....(A)	0	3	1	7	
Hunslet ....(H)	0	7	0	14	
Runcorn Highfield.............(H)	0	1	0	2	Sub app.
Leigh ....(A)	0	4	0	8	

Totals

	T	G	DG	Pts
Division Two.......................	3	97	5	211
Abandoned (Div. Two)..........	0	2	0	4
Yorkshire Cup......................	0	3	0	6
John Player	0	6	1	13
RL Cup..............................	0	4	0	8
GRAND TOTALS...............	**3**	**112**	**6**	**242**

ROY RAFFERTY broke two Sheffield Eagles records with 79 goals and 186 points, which included seven tries.

Full back Arnold Hema set the records with 33 goals, including one drop goal, and 77 points in Sheffield's inaugural season of 1984-85. He also scored three tries.

Rafferty broke both records with two goals in Sheffield's 24-16 home defeat against Bradford Northern in a John Player Special Trophy first round match on 24th November.

He missed only one of Sheffield's 37 matches, playing five in the centre and the rest on the wing. His match-by-match record was as follows:

	T	G	DG	Pts
Doncaster..........................(H)	1	2	0	8
Castleford (Yorks. Cup)........(A)	0	1	0	2
Hunslet..............................(A)	0	0	0	0
Mansfield Marksman ....(H)	0	5	0	10
Leigh.................................(A)	0	3	0	6
Wakefield Trinity ....(H)	1	1	0	6
Runcorn Highfield ....(H)	0	4	0	8
Bramley ....(A)	0	3	0	6
Rochdale Hornets ....(H)	0	2	0	4
Wakefield Trinity................(A)	0	3	0	6
Keighley ....(H)	1	3	0	10
Runcorn Highfield...............(A)	0	3	0	6
Whitehaven ....(H)	0	2	0	4
Bradford N. (John Player) ....(H)	0	2	0	4
Mansfield Marksman............(A)	0	3	0	6
Fulham ....(A)	0	4	0	8
Hunslet..............................(H)	0	5	0	10
Wakefield Trinity................(A)	0	5	0	10
Bramley ....(H)	0	1	0	2
Leigh ....(H)	0	1	0	2
Rochdale Hornets................(A)	0	0	0	0
Blackpool Borough ....(A)	1	2	0	8
Warrington (RL Cup) ....(A)	0	3	0	6
Huddersfield Barracudas.......(A)	1	0	0	4
Blackpool Borough ....(H)	0	2	0	4
Carlisle..............................(A)	0	0	0	0
Doncaster ....(A)		Did not play		
Huddersfield Barracudas.......(H)	0	6	0	12
Keighley............................(A)	0	4	0	8
Batley ....(A)	0	2	0	4
Fulham ....(H)	0	3	0	6
Whitehaven........................(A)	0	0	0	0
Carlisle ....(H)	1	2	0	8
Barrow..............................(A)	1	0	0	4
Batley ....(A)	0	0	0	0
Workington Town................(H)	0	2	0	4
Barrow ....(H)	0	0	0	0

Totals

	T	G	DG	Pts
Division Two	7	73	0	174
Yorkshire Cup	0	1	0	2
John Player	0	2	0	4
RL Cup	0	3	0	6
GRAND TOTALS	**7**	**79**	**0**	**186**

KEVIN HARCOMBE kicked a club record 115 goals in his first season with Rochdale Hornets. The previous record was held by former Test forward Bill Holliday with 107 in 1973-74. Harcombe, a close season signing from Doncaster, broke the record with the third of six goals in a 36-16 home defeat of Mansfield Marksman on 30th April.

Harcombe played in 35 of Rochdale's 39 matches, including one substitute appearance. His match-by-match record of marksmanship was as follows:

	Goals
Whitehaven..........................(H)	3 (1)
Carlisle................................(A)	2
Widnes (Lancs. Cup)..............(H)	1
Doncaster.............................(H)	6
Keighley..............................(A)	5
Mansfield Marksman...............(A)	0
Fulham ....(H)	3
Sheffield Eagles.....................(A)	8
Batley ....(H)	Did not play
Bramley..............................(A)	2
Carlisle (John Player) ....(A)	4
Huddersfield Barracudas...........(A)	4
Salford (John Player)...............(A)	4
Workington Town...................(H)	8
Blackpool Borough ....(H)	3
Workington Town ....(A)	Did not play
Hunslet ....(A)	6
Leigh ....(H)	4
Runcorn Highfield...................(A)	3
Batley ....(A)	2
Bramley..............................(H)	4
Sheffield Eagles ....(H)	4
Fulham ....(A)	2
Huddersfield B. (RL Cup) ....(A)	1
Widnes (RL Cup)....................(H)	2
Doncaster ....(A)	0
Wakefield Trinity....................(H)	0 Sub app.
Whitehaven...........................(A)	4
Leigh ....(A)	3
Runcorn Highfield...................(H)	4
Hunslet...............................(H)	6
Carlisle ....(H)	2
Barrow...............................(A)	1
Blackpool Borough ....(A)	1
Keighley ....(H)	3
Barrow...............................(H)	Did not play
Wakefield Trinity....................(A)	Did not play
Mansfield Marksman ....(H)	6
Huddersfield Barracudas...........(H)	4

Totals

		Goals
Division Two...................	103 (1)
Lancashire Cup..............	1
John Player	8
RL Cup........................	3
GRAND TOTAL	**115 (1)**

(1) includes drop goal in total

JOHN WOODS achieved three records with five tries, eight goals and 36 points in Bradford Northern's 48-20 home defeat of Swinton on 13th October. The stand off's five tries equalled the Division One record since the reintroduction of two divisions in 1973. The 36 points broke the Bradford and Division One match records.

Others to have scored five tries in a Division One match are: Roy Mathias (St. Helens winger) v. Rochdale Hornets on 17th February 1974 and v. Workington Town on 23rd December 1979; Parry Gordon (Warrington scrum half) v. Dewsbury on 3rd March 1974; Peter Glynn (St. Helens winger) v. Hull on 16th October 1977; Steve Fenton (Castleford winger) v. Dewsbury on 27th January 1978; Steve Hartley (Hull K.R. centre) v. Huddersfield on 13th April 1979; Kevin Meadows (Oldham winger) at Salford on 20th April 1984.

Bradford's previous points record had been held by Ernest Ward with 34 in a 67-0 home defeat of Liverpool Stanley on 20th October 1945. The centre's total was made up of 11 goals and four tries.

Woods broke the Division One points record of Castleford scrum half Bob Beardmore who scored 34 with 11 goals and three tries in a 54-4 home defeat of Leeds on 2nd October 1983. Woods still holds the Division Two record of 38 points in a match with 13 goals and four tries for Leigh in a 62-15 home defeat of Blackpool Borough on 11th September 1977.

IAN FRENCH scored a Castleford club record-equalling five tries in the 60-6 Silk Cut Challenge Cup first round win at Hunslet on 9th February. The Australian loose forward equalled the feats of wingers Derek Foster v. Hunslet on 10th November 1972; John Joyner v. Millom on 16th September 1973; Steve Fenton v. Dewsbury on 27th January 1978.

ELLERY HANLEY scored a record-equalling four tries in a Premiership Trophy match when Wigan beat Hull K.R. 47-0 in a first round home tie on 27th April.

The stand off equalled the feats of Phil Ford (Wigan winger) v. Hull in 1985 and David Hall (Hull K.R. centre) v. Castleford in 1983, both being first round matches.

GARRY SCHOFIELD achieved two international records with four tries and 16 points in Great Britain's 25-8 second Whitbread Trophy Bitter Test victory over New Zealand at Wigan on 2nd November.

The Hull centre's four tries equalled the most by a Great Britain player in a Test match. Others who have scored four tries are: Jim Leytham (Wigan winger) in the second Test v. Australia at Brisbane on 2nd June 1910; Billy Boston (Wigan winger) in first Test v. New Zealand at Auckland on 24th July 1954; Alex Murphy (St. Helens scrum half) v. France at Leeds on 14th March 1959.

Schofield's 16 points were the most by a British player in a Test against New Zealand, beating the 15 points from six goals and a try by centre Jim Lomas in the Test at Auckland on 30th July 1910.

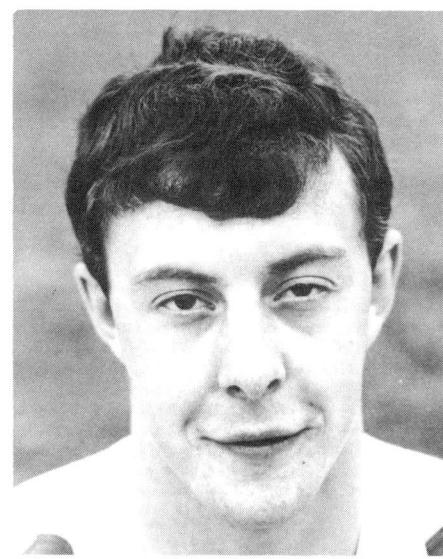

Twin international record breaker Garry Schofield.

In a World Cup match against New Zealand at Pau, France, Leeds stand off John Holmes scored 26 points from 10 goals and two tries on 4th November 1972.

PAUL BISHOP kicked a record equalling five one-point drop goals in Warrington's 23-12 Slalom Lager Premiership semi-final win at Wigan on 11th May. The stand off equalled the five drop goals by Danny Wilson (Swinton stand off) v. Hunslet on 6th November 1983 and Peter Wood (Runcorn Highfield full back) v. Batley on 21st October 1984.

HARRY PINNER kicked only one drop goal during the season but it put the St. Helens loose forward clear as the most prolific scorer of one-pointers with a career total of 79. The record-breaking drop goal came in Great Britain's 25-8 second Whitbread Trophy Bitter Test win over New Zealand on 2nd November.

Pinner had begun the season sharing the lead with Dewsbury's Nigel Stephenson who did not add to his total of 78.

The record refers to the period since the start of 1974-75 when the drop goal was halved to one point in Britain. Stephenson had kicked a drop goal for Dewsbury against Australia in 1973 which was worth one point under international rules but does not count towards the record.

Pinner made his first senior appearance for St. Helens halfway through the second season of one-point drop goals and his record total is made up as follows:

1975-76............... 1
1976-77............... 2 + 1 GB Under-24
1977-78............... 6
1978-79............... 10
1979-80............... 9 + 2 Lancashire, 2 England
1980-81............... 6
1981-82............... 4
1982-83............... 13
1983-84............... 14
1984-85............... 8
1985-86............... 0 + 1 Great Britain
Totals ....73 + 6

DAVID STEPHENSON of Wigan equalled the Lancashire Cup final record of seven goals in the 34-8 defeat of Warrington at St. Helens on 13th October. The centre equalled the feats of Jim Ledgard (Leigh full back) v. Widnes in 1955 and Steve Hesford (Warrington winger) v. Wigan in 1980.

JOHN DORAHY of Hull Kingston Rovers equalled the Yorkshire Cup final record of five goals in the 22-18 defeat of Castleford at Leeds on 27th October. The Australian centre was the 11th player to perform the feat.

DEAN CARROLL scored a Carlisle record nine goals in a match and twice notched up a best of 21 points after BRIAN TUNSTALL held the record briefly with 16 points.

Yorkshire Cup goals record equaller John Dorahy.

Carroll broke two records with nine goals, including a drop, and 21 points in the 45-13 home defeat of Mansfield Marksman on 16th March. He also scored a try. The scrum half equalled the points record with two tries and seven goals, including a drop, in the 41-22 win at Fulham on 2nd May.

Tunstall had become the first Carlisle player to score more than 15 points in a match when the full back got 16 from six goals and a try in the 33-32 home defeat against Blackpool Borough on 27th October.

Carroll already held the goals record, having kicked seven in a 42-8 win at Doncaster on 23rd December 1984 while on an extended loan from Bradford Northern.

After returning to Bradford he was eventually signed by Carlisle in December, 1985.

DAVID CHOLMONDELEY scored a club record 16 points with four goals and two tries in the 32-22 win at Huddersfield Barracudas on 9th March. The hooker was the first to score more than 15 points in a match for Sheffield.

GARY PROHM of Hull Kingston Rovers extended the Division One record tryscoring sequence to 11 successive matches. The New Zealand Test centre broke the record the previous season when he touched down in nine successive league matches for Rovers and continued the run by scoring a try in the first two matches of 1985-86.

The run stretched from 3rd April to 4th September 1985 and brought Prohm a total of 13 tries.

The previous Division One record of eight successive tryscoring matches had been shared by David Smith (Wakefield Trinity winger, 1973-74), Les Jones (St. Helens winger, 1973-74 to 1974-75) and Mal Meninga (St. Helens centre, 1984-85).

LEIGH finished as Division Two champions with an impressive collection of records as follows:

Division Two
Most successive wins — 30. Previous best — Hull won all 26 in 1978-79.
Highest score — 92-2 v. Keighley on 30th April. Also widest margin. Previous best — Barrow 80-8 at Kent Invicta on 8th April 1984; Leigh 75-3 v. Doncaster on 28th March 1976; Dewsbury 72-0 v. Doncaster on 25th November 1984.
Most points in a season: 1,156 in 34 matches .... a record for any league campaign including a Division Two record 205 tries, plus 170 goals including four drop goals. Previous best — 1,126 (196 tries and 177 goals including 12 drops) in 34 matches by Barrow in 1983-84.
All matches
Most points in a season: 1,436 (258 tries and 205 goals including 6 drops) in 43 Cup and League matches. Previous best — 1,267 (215 tries and 212 goals including 17 drops) by St. Helens in 42 Cup and Division One matches in 1984-85.

Club

Most successive wins — 14 matches, all in Division Two. Equalled 12 Division One plus two RL Challenge Cup wins in 1981-82.

Highest score and widest margin: 92-2 v. Keighley on 30th April after 76-6 v. Mansfield Marksman on 13th October. Previous best — 75-3 v. Doncaster on March 28th 1976.

Biggest away score: 70-2 at Batley in John Player Special Trophy first round on 24th November. Previous best — 68-17 at Carlisle in John Player Special Trophy second round on 20th November 1983.

BLACKPOOL BOROUGH scored their highest total of points in a match with a 54-0 home defeat of Carlisle on 26th December. Borough scored 10 tries as they did when running up their previous highest score of 48-8 at home to Thames Board Mills amateurs in the second round of the Challenge Cup on 29th February 1964.

SHEFFIELD EAGLES scored their highest total of points in a match with a 36-6 home win over Huddersfield Barracudas on 30th March. Earlier in the season they had won 34-12 at home to Mansfield Marksman on 15th September to equal the 34-15 home defeat of Keighley on 17th April 1985. Sheffield scored six tries on all three occasions.

SHEFFIELD EAGLES suffered a club record 62-11 defeat in a Silk Cut Challenge Cup first round tie at Warrington on 9th February. The previous highest score of 54-19 was also by Warrington in the first round of the Silk Cut Challenge Cup at Sheffield on 17th February 1985.

HULL went down to a club record 57-14 defeat at St. Helens in a John Player Special Trophy third round tie on 11th December. They had conceded 56 points twice.

The Airlie Birds lost 56-0 at Dewsbury in a Yorkshire League match on 22nd April 1919 and were beaten 56-8 by Wigan on 12th October 1957. Dewsbury and Wigan each scored 14 tries compared with 10 by St. Helens.

KEIGHLEY crashed to a club record 92-2 defeat at Leigh on 30th April. Their previous heaviest defeat was 80-7 at Hull on 29th January 1921 when they conceded 18 tries compared with 16 against Leigh.

CARLISLE went down to a club record 72-8 defeat at St. Helens in a Burtonwood Brewery Lancashire Cup first round tie on 15th September when they conceded 13 tries. Leigh inflicted the previous heaviest defeat with a 12-try 68-17 win at Carlisle in a John Player Special Trophy second round tie on 20th November 1983.

CASTLEFORD conceded a club record 62-12 defeat at St. Helens on 16th April when the Saints ran in 12 tries. The previous highest score against them was 58-8 at Workington Town on 22nd August 1953 with Town scoring 14 tries.

MANSFIELD MARKSMAN crashed to a club record 76-6 defeat at Leigh on 13th October, conceding 14 tries. It beat the 34-12 defeat at Sheffield Eagles on 15th September, which equalled the 34-10 home defeat against Hunslet in the first round of the Silk Cut Challenge Cup on 24th February 1985, conceding six tries each time.

HUDDERSFIELD BARRACUDAS and KEIGHLEY were involved in a Division Two record high-scoring draw of 32-32 on 17th April, each scoring six tries. Ironically, the scoring feat was watched by Huddersfield's lowest-ever home crowd of 303.

The previous highest scoring draw was 30-30 between Doncaster and Rochdale Hornets on 6th April 1980 when both teams also scored six tries each.

BLACKPOOL BOROUGH and CARLISLE were both on the receiving end when scoring a record 32 points by a losing team in a Division Two match.

Borough lost 38-32 at Hunslet on 22nd September and were then the victors when Carlisle lost 33-32 at home on 27th October.

ST. HELENS finished the season with a Division One record-equalling run of 13 successive wins. The record since the reintroduction of two divisions in 1973 was set by Widnes with 13 consecutive wins from the start of the 1981-82 season. Widnes were then held to a 10-10 draw at Hull K.R. and lost 6-3 at home to Bradford Northern.

WIGAN scored a Lancashire Cup final record win of 34-8 against Warrington at St. Helens on 13th October. It beat St. Helens' 30-2 defeat of Oldham at Wigan in 1968. The Saints' win remains the widest margin and was achieved with six tries. Wigan's total included five tries.

WARRINGTON scored a record Premiership win of 38-10 against Halifax at Elland Road, Leeds, on 18th May. It beat the highest score of 36-16 in St. Helens' defeat of Hull K.R. in 1985 and the previous widest margin when Leeds beat Bradford Northern 24-2 in 1979.

WIGAN'S Central Park housed a Division One record crowd of 21,813 for the visit of St. Helens on Boxing Day. The previous best of 20,569 was at the Boulevard for the Hull v. Hull Kingston Rovers Friday night clash on 7th April 1983. The record refers to the period since the reintroduction of two divisions in 1973.

MILESTONES...

BOB BEARDMORE scored the 1,000th point of his Castleford career when he touched down in the 18-14 defeat at York on 29th January. The scrum half finished the season with a total of 1,033 points from 389 goals, including five drop goals, plus 76 tries.

Beardmore made his debut for Castleford on 18th November 1979 when they lost 10-8 at Workington Town.

He holds the club record for points in a season with 334 from 13 tries and 142 goals, including two drop goals, in 1983-84. His goals tally gave him joint leadership of the season's goals chart with Warrington's Steve Hesford.

His best points total in a match is 34 (11 goals, 3 tries) at home to Leeds on 2nd October 1983 which was a Division One record until broken by Bradford Northern's John Woods two years later.

Beardmore's season-by-season totals are as follows:

	T	G	DG	Pts
1979-80	0	0	0	0
1980-81	17	9	1	70
1981-82	13	11	1	62
1982-83	14	117	0	276
1983-84	13	140	2	334
1984-85	6	43	0	110
1985-86	13	64	1	181
Totals	76	384	5	1,033

GRAHAM KING scored the 100th try of his career when he touched down in Hunslet's 20-12 home defeat of Workington Town in the John Player Special Trophy first round win on 24th November.

All the scrum half's 109 tries have been scored for Hunslet. He made his debut as a substitute at Keighley on 13th May 1979 when Hunslet won 20-15. His first full appearance was at Bradford Northern on 16th April 1980 when he scored a try in Hunslet's 41-16 defeat.

King's most prolific season was 1983-84 when he finished second in the try chart with 28, the most by a Hunslet player since the club was re-formed in 1973.

He has scored five hat-tricks including a four-try feat at home to Bramley on 18th April 1984.

King's season-by-season try total is as follows:

1978-79	0
1979-80	2
1980-81	15
1981-82	12
1982-83	15
1983-84	28
1984-85	15
1985-86	22
Total	109

GARY PROHM scored his 100th try for Hull Kingston Rovers in the 25-10 home defeat of Leigh in the third round of the Silk Cut Challenge Cup on 16th March.

A 1980 Kiwi tourist, the New Zealander made his debut for Rovers at home to Hull, whom they beat 16-12 on 22nd September 1982. His first game was at loose forward but he went on to become one of the most prolific tryscoring centres of all time.

Prohm's 45 tries in 1984-85 broke the Hull K.R. record and also equalled the then record for a centre set by Huddersfield's Tommy Gleeson in 1913-14, beaten by Steve Halliwell of Leigh last season.

Another record to fall to Prohm was the Division One sequence of tryscoring matches. From 3rd April to 4th September 1985 he scored at least one try in 11 successive Slalom Lager Championship matches.

Prohm has scored four tries in a match on three occasions for Rovers, plus three hat-tricks.

The New Zealand Test star ended his Hull K.R. career with two tries in the 15-14 defeat against Castleford at Wembley on 3rd May 1986. They took his total for the club to 104 as follows:

1982-83	17
1983-84	25
1984-85	45
1985-86	17
Total	**104**

Ton-up scrum half Neil Holding.

NEIL HOLDING finished the season with more than a century of career tries for St. Helens and representative teams.

The Test scrum half scored his 100th try in all matches with the second of his two touchdowns for Saints in the 72-8 home defeat of Carlisle in the Burtonwood Brewery Lancashire Cup first round on 15th September.

Holding reached his club century with a try in St. Helens' 22-19 Silk Cut Challenge Cup first round away win over Dewsbury, which had been switched to Headingley, on 24th February.

He made his debut for St. Helens as a 17-year-old, touching down in a John Player Trophy first round 28-11 win at Swinton on 23rd October 1977.

Holding's total of 113 tries includes three hat-tricks and is made up as follows:

St. Helens

1977-78	3	
1978-79	7	+ 1 GB Under-24s
1979-80	11	
1980-81	12	+ 1 GB Under-24s
		+ 1 Lancashire
1981-82	8	
1982-83	12	
1983-84	19	
1984-85	17	
1985-86	18	

Great Britain tour

1984	3

Totals

St. Helens	107
GB Under-24s	2
Lancashire	1
Tour	3

GRAND TOTAL.......113

PAUL PRENDIVILLE scored the 100th try of his career when he touched down in Hull's 22-8 win at York on 4th September. It was only his second try in 18 months.

Hull signed Prendiville from Wales RU club Bynea in August 1978 after an impressive trial at full back in a pre-season friendly match against Hull K.R. He made his competitive debut at home to Batley on 1st October that year when he scored a try and two goals in a 42-9 victory.

Although Prendiville made his debut at full back he has played most of his professional rugby on the wing where he gained international honours with Wales.

Prendiville's first season was his most prolific as he finished with 25 tries and was third in the tryscoring list, the only time he has finished in the top ten.

In the latter half of 1983-84 he went on loan to Leeds, scoring five tries. He also scored one try for Wales in 1981-82.

Welshman Paul Prendiville who ended an 18-month wait for his 100th career try.

Prendiville's total of 104 tries includes seven hat-tricks and is made up as follows:

Hull

1978-79	25	
1979-80	16	
1980-81	15	
1981-82	18	+ 1 Wales
1982-83	16	
1983-84	2	
1984-85	1	
1985-86	5	

Leeds

1983-84	5

Totals

Hull	98
Leeds	5
Wales	1

GRAND TOTAL.......104

JOHN WOODS became the 12th player to score a century of Division One tries since the reintroduction of two divisions in 1973 when he scored the first of his five tries in Bradford Northern's 48-20 home defeat of Swinton on 13th October.

The five tries equalled the Division One match record and followed his close season club record £65,000 signing from Leigh, who had just been relegated.

Woods turned professional with Leigh in December 1975 and made a tryscoring debut on the left wing in a home Division One match on 5th September 1976 against Barrow, who were beaten 18-8.

Leigh were relegated the following year but gained immediate promotion and he has played nine seasons of Division One rugby.

In addition to his five-try feat the Great Britain Test centre or stand off has scored five other hat-tricks including four tries in a match once. His most prolific Division One season was 1983-84 when he scored 23 tries for Leigh.

Woods scored 97 Division One tries for Leigh before making his debut for Bradford Northern on 1st September 1985 at Warrington.

Woods' total of 107 tries is made up as follows:

Leigh
1976-77	5
1977-78	In Division Two
1978-79	7
1979-80	18
1980-81	10
1981-82	14
1982-83	10
1983-84	23
1984-85	10

Bradford Northern
1985-86	10

Totals
Leigh	97
Bradford N.	10

GRAND TOTAL.......107

GEORGE FAIRBAIRN scored his 1,000th career point for Hull Kingston Rovers when he kicked a goal in the 27-14 win in the opening league match of the season at Featherstone Rovers on 1st September. The Great Britain Test full back finished the season with a total of 1,070 points from 482 goals, including 19 drop goals, plus 37 tries.

Rovers signed the Scot from Wigan in June 1981 for a then world record £72,500 and he made an eight-goal debut in a 34-7 Yorkshire Cup first round home defeat of Huddersfield on 14th August 1981. He finished that first season with a club record 166 goals.

His best match tally for Rovers is 24 points from nine goals and two tries in a 45-3 home defeat of Whitehaven on 18th April 1982.

Fairbairn's season-by-season totals for Hull K.R. are as follows:

	T	G	DG	Pts
1981-82	13	160	6	365
1982-83	10	83	5	201
1983-84	0	58	1	117
1984-85	10	135	6	316
1985-86	4	27	1	71
Totals	**37**	**463**	**19**	**1,070**

Scotsman George Fairbairn opened the season with his 1,000th career point and closed the 1985-86 campaign with a Wembley debut.

LEADING SCORERS 1895-1970

	TRIES	GOALS	POINTS
1895-96	Hurst (Oldham)..............28	Lorimer (Manningham) 35	Cooper (Bradford)..........106
			Lorimer (Manningham)...106
1896-97	Hannah (Hunslet)............19	Goldthorpe (Hunslet).......26	Rigg (Halifax)...............112
		Sharpe (Liversedge).........26	
1897-98	Hoskins (Salford) 30	Goldthorpe (Hunslet).......66	Goldthorpe (Hunslet)......135
1898-99	Williams (Oldham) 39	Goldthorpe (Hunslet).......67	Jaques (Hull) 169
1899-00	Williams (Oldham) 36	Cooper (Bradford)...........39	Williams (Oldham).........108
1900-01	Williams (Oldham) 47	Goldthorpe (Hunslet).......44	Williams (Oldham).........141
1901-02	Wilson (Broughton R.).....38	James (Broughton R.) 75	Lomas (Salford).............172
1902-03	Evans (Leeds)................27	Goldthorpe (Hunslet).......48	Davies (Batley)..............136
1903-04	Hogg (Broughton R.).......34	Lomas (Salford) 66	Lomas (Salford).............222
1904-05	Dechan (Bradford)..........31	Ferguson (Oldham)..........50	Lomas (Salford).............146
1905-06	Leytham (Wigan) 40	Ferguson (Oldham).........49	Leytham (Wigan)...........160
1906-07	Eccles (Halifax)...............41	Lomas (Salford) 86	Lomas (Salford).............280
1907-08	Leytham (Wigan) 44	Goldthorpe (Hunslet)......101	Goldthorpe (Hunslet)......217
1908-09	Miller (Wigan)................49	Lomas (Salford) 88	Lomas (Salford).............272
	Williams (Halifax) 49		
1909-10	Leytham (Wigan) 48	Carmichael (Hull K.R.)....78	Leytham (Wigan)...........232
1910-11	Kitchen (Huddersfield).....40	Carmichael (Hull K.R.)...129	Carmichael (Hull K.R.)...261
	Rosenfeld (Huddersfield) ..40		
	Miller (Wigan)................40		
1911-12	Rosenfeld (Huddersfield) ..78	Carmichael (Hull K.R.)...127	Carmichael (Hull K.R.)...254
1912-13	Rosenfeld (Huddersfield) ..56	Carmichael (Hull K.R.) 93	Thomas (Wigan)............198
1913-14	Rosenfeld (Huddersfield) ..80	Holland (Huddersfield) ...131	Holland (Huddersfield) ...268
1914-15	Rosenfeld (Huddersfield) ..56	Gronow (Huddersfield) ...136	Gronow (Huddersfield) ...284
	Competitive matches suspended during war years		
1918-19	Francis (Hull)................25	Kennedy (Hull) 54	Kennedy (Hull) 135
1919-20	Moorhouse (Huddersfield).39	Gronow (Huddersfield) ...148	Gronow (Huddersfield) ...332
1920-21	Stone (Hull) 41	Kennedy (Hull) 108	Kennedy (Hull) 264
1921-22	Farrar (Oldham) 49	Sullivan (Wigan)............100	Farrar (Oldham) 213
1922-23	Ring (Wigan) 44	Sullivan (Wigan)............161	Sullivan (Wigan)............349
1923-24	Ring (Wigan) 49	Sullivan (Wigan)............158	Sullivan (Wigan)............319
1924-25	Ring (Wigan) 54	Sullivan (Wigan)............138	Sullivan (Wigan)............282
1925-26	Ring (Wigan) 63	Sullivan (Wigan)............131	Sullivan (Wigan)............274
1926-27	Ellaby (St. Helens)..........55	Sullivan (Wigan)............149	Sullivan (Wigan)............322
1927-28	Ellaby (St. Helens) 37	Thompson (Leeds).........106	Thompson (Leeds).........233
1928-29	Brown (Wigan) 44	Sullivan (Wigan)............107	Sullivan (Wigan)............226
	Mills (Huddersfield).........44		
1929-30	Ellaby (St. Helens) 39	Thompson (Leeds).........111	Thompson (Leeds).........243
1930-31	Harris, E. (Leeds)...........58	Sullivan (Wigan)...........133	Sullivan (Wigan)............278
1931-32	Mills (Huddersfield).........50	Sullivan (Wigan)...........117	Sullivan (Wigan)............249
1932-33	Harris, E. (Leeds)...........57	Sullivan (Wigan)............146	Sullivan (Wigan)............307
1933-34	Brown (Salford) 45	Sullivan (Wigan)............193	Sullivan (Wigan)............404

	TRIES	GOALS	POINTS
1934-35	Harris, E. (Leeds) 47	Sullivan (Wigan) 165	Sullivan (Wigan) 348
1935-36	Harris, E. (Leeds) 63	Sullivan (Wigan) 117	Sullivan (Wigan) 246
1936-37	Harris, E. (Leeds) 40	Sullivan (Wigan) 117	Winnard (Bradford N.) ...257
1937-38	Harris, E. (Leeds) 45	Sullivan (Wigan) 128	Sullivan (Wigan) 271
1938-39	Markham (Huddersfield)...39	Sullivan (Wigan) 124	Risman (Salford)............267
●	For the next six seasons emergency war-time competitions resulted in a reduction of matches and players were allowed to 'guest' for other clubs		
1939-40	Batten (Hunslet) 34	Hodgson (Swinton) 96	Hodgson (Swinton) 207
1940-41	Walters (Bradford N.) 32	Lockwood (Halifax) 70	Belshaw (Warrington) 174
1941-42	Francis (Barrow) 29	Lockwood (Halifax) 91	Lockwood (Halifax)........185
1942-43	Batten (Hunslet) 24	Lockwood (Halifax) 65	Lockwood (Halifax)........136
1943-44	Lawrenson (Wigan) 21	Horne (Barrow) 57	Horne (Barrow)..............144
1944-45	Batten (Bradford N.)........41	Stott (Wakefield T.).........51	Stott (Wakefield T.) 129
●	Normal peace-time rugby resumed		
1945-46	Batten (Bradford N.)........35	Ledgard (Dewsbury)........88	Bawden (Huddersfield) ...239
1946-47	Bevan (Warrington) 48	Miller (Hull)..................103	Bawden (Huddersfield) ...243
1947-48	Bevan (Warrington) 57	Ward (Wigan) 139	Ward (Wigan) 302
1948-49	Cooper (Huddersfield) 60	Ward (Wigan) 155	Ward (Wigan) 361
1949-50	Nordgren (Wigan) 57	Gee (Wigan) 133	Palin (Warrington) 290
		Palin (Warrington) 133	
1950-51	Bevan (Warrington) 68	Cook (Leeds) 155	Cook (Leeds) 332
1951-52	Cooper (Huddersfield) 71	Ledgard (Leigh) 142	Horne (Barrow) 313
1952-53	Bevan (Warrington) 72	Bath (Warrington)..........170	Bath (Warrington)..........379
1953-54	Bevan (Warrington) 67	Metcalfe (St. Helens)......153	Metcalfe (St. Helens)......369
		Bath (Warrington)..........153	
1954-55	Cooper (Huddersfield) 66	Ledgard (Leigh) 178	Ledgard (Leigh) 374
1955-56	McLean (Bradford N.) 61	Ledgard (Leigh) 155	Bath (Warrington)..........344
1956-57	Boston (Wigan)...............60	Jones (Leeds)................194	Jones (Leeds)................496
1957-58	Sullivan (Wigan) 50	Ganley (Oldham) 219	Ganley (Oldham) 453
1958-59	Vollenhoven (St. Helens) ..62	Ganley (Oldham) 190	Griffiths (Wigan) 394
1959-60	Vollenhoven (St. Helens) ..54	Rhodes (St. Helens) 171	Fox (Wakefield T.) 453
		Fox (Wakefield T.) 171	
1960-61	Vollenhoven (St. Helens) ..59	Rhodes (St. Helens) 145	Rhodes (St. Helens) 338
1961-62	Boston (Wigan)...............51	Fox (Wakefield T.) 183	Fox (Wakefield T.) 456
1962-63	Glastonbury (Work'ton T.)41	Coslett (St. Helens)........156	Coslett (St. Helens)........321
1963-64	Stopford (Swinton) 45	Coslett (St. Helens)........138	Fox (Wakefield T.) 313
1964-65	Lake (Wigan) 40	Kellett (Hull K.R.) 150	Killeen (St. Helens)........360
1965-66	Killeen (St. Helens) 32	Killeen (St. Helens)........120	Killeen (St. Helens)........336
	Lake (Wigan) 32		
1966-67	Young (Hull K.R.)...........34	Risman (Leeds) 163	Killeen (St. Helens)........353
	Howe (Castleford) 34		
1967-68	Millward (Hull K.R.).......38	Risman (Leeds) 154	Risman (Leeds) 332
1968-69	Francis (Wigan) 40	Risman (Leeds) 165	Risman (Leeds) 345
1969-70	Atkinson (Leeds)..............38	Tyrer (Wigan)................167	Tyrer (Wigan)................385

LEADING SCORERS 1970-85

TRIES

1970-71
Haigh (Leeds)..40
Jones (St. Helens)..38
Atkinson (Leeds)..36
Sullivan (Hull)...33
Slater (Wakefield T.)......................................33
Wright (Wigan)..33
Wilson (St. Helens)..27
Hynes (Leeds)...25
A. Smith (Leeds)...23
Topliss (Wakefield T.).....................................23
Richards (Salford)...23
Benyon (St. Helens)..23

1971-72
Atkinson (Leeds)..36
Lamb (Bradford N.)...36
Richards (Salford)...35
D. Redfearn (Bradford N.)..................................35
Sullivan (Hull)..33
Watkins (Salford)..29
Hardisty (Leeds)...27
Brown (Widnes)...27
O'Neill (Widnes)...25
Topliss (Wakefield T.).....................................24

1972-73
Atkinson (Leeds)..39
Richards (Salford)...38
Charlton (Salford)...33
Topliss (Wakefield T.).....................................30
Lowe (Hull K.R.)...29
Hardisty (Leeds)...28
A. Smith (Leeds)...28
Dunn (Hull K.R.)...27
D. Redfearn (Bradford N.)..................................27
N. Stephenson (Dewsbury)...................................26
Mathias (St. Helens).......................................26

1973-74
Fielding (Salford)...49
Mathias (St. Helens).......................................40
D. Smith (Wakefield T.)....................................38
Eckersley (St. Helens).....................................26
Fleay (Swinton)..26
Jones (St. Helens)...25
Wilson (St. Helens)..25
Watkins (Salford)..24
Atkinson (Leeds)...23
Lamb (Bradford N.)...22
A. Smith (Leeds)...22
Bevan (Warrington)...22
Ayres (Wigan)..22

1974-75
Dunn (Hull K.R.)...42
Fielding (Salford)...35
Bevan (Warrington)...31
A. Smith (Leeds)...30
Millward (Hull K.R.).......................................30
Atkinson (Leeds)...29
Richards (Salford)...28
Sullivan (Hull K.R.).......................................28
Mathias (St. Helens).......................................27
Dyl (Leeds)..26

1975-76
Richards (Salford)...37
Fielding (Salford)...33
Jones (St. Helens)...31
Briggs (Leigh)...27
D. Smith (Wakefield T.)....................................26
Burton (Castleford)..25
Clark (Hull)...23
Wright (Workington T.).....................................22
Barends (York)...21
Boxall (Hull)..21
Holmes (Leeds)...21
Mathias (St. Helens).......................................21
Butler (Salford)...21

1976-77
Wright (Widnes)..31
Burton (Castleford)..29
D. Smith (Leeds)...28
Fielding (Salford)...27
Dunn (Hull K.R.)...26
Cunningham (St. Helens)....................................26
Topliss (Wakefield T.).....................................24
Richards (Salford)...23
Mathias (St. Helens).......................................23
Barends (York)...22

1977-78
Wright (Widnes)..33
Fielding (Salford)...31
Cunningham (St. Helens)....................................30
Bevan (Warrington)...30
Fenton (Castleford)..30
Vigo (Wigan)...29
Glynn (St. Helens)...28
D. Smith (Leeds)...28
T. Morgan (York)...27
Burton (Castleford)..27

1978-79

Hartley (Hull K.R.)..35
Wright (Widnes)...28
Barends (Bradford N.).......................................25
Lowe (Hull K.R.)...25
Prendiville (Hull)..25
Fielding (Salford)..24
D. Redfearn (Bradford N.)..................................23
Mathias (St. Helens)...22
Bray (Hull)..21
O'Loughlin (Wigan)...21
Sullivan (Hull K.R.)...21

1979-80

Fielding (Salford)..30
Hubbard (Hull K.R.)...30
Munro (Oldham)...29
Ball (Barrow)...27
Bentley (Widnes)...27
Glynn (St. Helens)...27
Mathias (St. Helens)...27
Bevan (Warrington)..26
D. Redfearn (Bradford N.)..................................26
D. Smith (Leeds)...24

1980-81

Crossley (York)...35
Richardson (Castleford)......................................28
Hubbard (Hull K.R.)...25
Hartley (Hull K.R.)..23
McDermott (York)...23
Slater (Huddersfield)...23
Drummond (Leigh)...20
Ball (Barrow)...19
Bevan (Warrington)..19
Cramp (Huddersfield)..19
Hyde (Castleford)..19
Ramsdale (Wigan)...19

1981-82

Jones (Workington T.).......................................31
Drummond (Leigh)...26
Basnett (Widnes)...26
Ashton (Oldham)...26
Morgan (Carlisle)...25
Hartley (Hull K.R.)..23
Hopkins (Workington T.)....................................23
Day (Hull)..23
Evans (Hull)..22
D. Hobbs (Featherstone R.)..................................21
Moll (Keighley)...21

1982-83

Eccles (Warrington)..37
Evans (Hull)..28
Crossley (Fulham)..27
David (Cardiff C.)...26
Topliss (Hull)..24
M'Barki (Fulham)..23
Hyde (Castleford)..22
McDermott (York)...22
Leuluai (Hull)..21
Phil Ford (Warrington)......................................20
Clark (Hull K. R.)...20

1983-84

Schofield (Hull)..38
Lydon (Widnes)..28
King (Hunslet)...28
Woods (Leigh)...27
Basnett (Widnes)...26
Gibson (Batley)..26
Herbert (Barrow)...25
Steadman (York)...25
Prohm (Hull K.R.)...25
Clark (Hull K.R.)..24

1984-85

Hanley (Bradford N.)..55
Prohm (Hull K.R.)...45
Gill (Wigan)...34
Ledger (St. Helens)..30
Meninga (St. Helens)..28
Gibbin (Whitehaven)...27
Gibson (Batley)..26
G. Peacham (Carlisle)..25
Byrne (Salford)..25
Evans (Hull)..24
Ferguson (Wigan)..24

GOALS
(including drop goals)

1970-71
Coslett (St. Helens) 183
Ferguson (Leigh) 166
Holmes (Leeds) 159
Watkins (Salford) 155
Tyrer (Wigan) 141
Stephenson (Dewsbury) 134
Clawson (Hull K.R.) 114
Fox (Wakefield T.) 110
Davies (Huddersfield) 99
Jefferson (Keighley) 98

1971-72
Coslett (St. Helens) 214
Watkins (Salford) 193
Tees (Bradford N.) 173
Dutton (Widnes) 120
Clawson (Hull K.R., Leeds) 120
Gowers (Swinton) 119
Tyrer (Wigan) 117
Larder (Oldham) 114
Whitehead (Warrington) 108
Maloney (York, Hull) 108

1972-73
Watkins (Salford) 221
Coslett (St. Helens) 162
Tees (Bradford N.) 160
Stephenson (Dewsbury) 149
C. Kellett (Featherstone R.) 139
Fox (Wakefield T.) 138
Whitehead (Warrington) 136
Larder (Oldham) 127
Jefferson (Keighley) 120
Quinn (York) 107

1973-74
Watkins (Salford) 183
Whitehead (Warrington) 168
Jefferson (Keighley) 165
Coslett (St. Helens) 134
Mumby (Bradford N.) 131
Dutton (Widnes) 129
Lloyd (Castleford) 121
Quinn (York) 112
Fiddler (Leigh) 111
Holliday (Rochdale H.) 107

1974-75
Fox (Hull K.R.) 146
Coslett (St. Helens) 129
Dutton (Widnes) 122
Lloyd (Castleford) 112
Quinn (York) 112
Hartley (Huddersfield) 110
MacCorquodale (Workington T.) 107
Marshall (Leeds) 107
Mumby (Bradford N.) 96
Fiddler (Salford, Leigh) 85

1975-76
Watkins (Salford) 175
Pimblett (St. Helens) 149
Lloyd (Castleford) 149
Dutton (Widnes) 148
Fairbairn (Wigan) 146
Stacey (Leigh) 137
MacCorquodale (Workington T.) 130
Fox (Hull K.R., York) 102
Marshall (Leeds) 101
Gaitley (New Hunslet) 100

1976-77
Lloyd (Castleford) 163
Quinn (Featherstone R.) 152
Pimblett (St. Helens) 152
Hesford (Warrington) 132
MacCorquodale (Workington T.) 128
Watkins (Salford) 125
Stephenson (Dewsbury) 106
Fairbairn (Wigan) 105
Dutton (Widnes) 97
Woods (Leigh) 90

1977-78
Pimblett (St. Helens) 178
Hesford (Warrington) 158
Woods (Leigh) 149
MacCorquodale (Workington T.) 138
Woods (Widnes) 122
Watkins (Salford) 110
Mumby (Bradford N.) 107
Lloyd (Castleford) 104
Fox (Bradford N.) 95
Oulton (Leeds) 80

1978-79
Lloyd (Hull) 172
Hesford (Warrington) 170
Burke (Widnes) 140
MacCorquodale (Workington T.) 114
Pimblett (St. Helens) 105
Beale (Keighley) 96
Woods (Leigh) 96
Birts (Halifax) 86
Fairbairn (Wigan) 86
Norton (Castleford) 82

1979-80

Quinn (Featherstone R.)..................................163
Hubbard (Hull K.R.)...................................138
Rule (Salford)..134
Hesford (Warrington).................................128
Burke (Widnes) 127
Ball (Barrow)..119
Diamond (Wakefield T.)............................116
Fitzsimons (Oldham).................................108
Parrish (Hunslet)... 98
Birts (Halifax) 97

1980-81

Hesford (Warrington).................................147
Quinn (Featherstone R.).............................123
Diamond (Wakefield T.)............................112
Burke (Widnes) 110
Hubbard (Hull K.R.)...................................109
Ball (Barrow)..104
Birts (Halifax) 100
Beale (Keighley)... 97
Parrish (Oldham) 95
Fairbairn (Wigan)....................................... 94

1981-82

Hopkins (Workington T.) 190
Fairbairn (Hull K.R.) 168
Parrish (Oldham) 164
Woods (Leigh)..158
Rule (Salford)...130
Dick (Leeds)...125
Quinn (Featherstone R.).............................120
Agar (Halifax) 119
Crooks (Hull) 118
Hesford (Warrington).................................116

1982-83

Diamond (Fulham)....................................136
Fitzsimons (Hunslet)..................................121
Crooks (Hull)..120
R. Beardmore (Castleford)..........................117
Hesford (Warrington).................................113
Fenwick (Cardiff C.)..................................111
Jones (Swinton)...110
Whitfield (Wigan).....................................104
Kilner (Bramley)..104
Quinn (Featherstone R.)................................98

1983-84

Hesford (Warrington).................................142
R. Beardmore (Castleford)..........................142
Hallett (Cardiff C.)....................................140
Fitzsimons (Hunslet)..................................131
Woods (Leigh)..124
Whitfield (Wigan) 122
Ball (Barrow)..104
Parrish (Oldham) 101
Agar (Halifax)..94
Tickle (Barrow)...91

1984-85

Day (St. Helens)..157
Fairbairn (Hull K.R.) 141
Wood (Runcorn H.) 126
Steadman (York)..122
Griffiths (Salford)......................................118
Parrish (Oldham) 117
Schofield (Hull) 105
Creasser (Leeds)..102
Agar (Halifax) 87
Jones (Swinton) 87

DROP GOALS

1974-75 Seabourne (Bradford N.) 10
1975-76 Hancock (Hull)....................................10
1976-77 N. Stephenson (Dewsbury) 16
1977-78 Fiddler (Bramley, Leigh) 10
1978-79 Turley (Blackpool B.) 18
1979-80 Dean (Hunslet).....................................18
1980-81 Walker (Whitehaven) 22
1981-82 Agar (Halifax) 17
        Donlan (Leigh) 17
1982-83 Pinner (St. Helens)................................13
1983-84 Hallett (Cardiff C.) 29
1984-85 Wood (Runcorn H.) 28

POINTS

1970-71 Coslett (St. Helens)............................375
1971-72 Watkins (Salford)................................473
1972-73 Watkins (Salford)................................493
1973-74 Watkins (Salford)................................438
1974-75 Fox (Hull K.R.)....................................333
1975-76 Watkins (Salford)................................385
1976-77 Lloyd (Castleford)...............................341
1977-78 Pimblett (St. Helens)...........................381
1978-79 Lloyd (Hull)..373
1979-80 Quinn (Featherstone R.)......................375
1980-81 Hesford (Warrington)...........................310
1981-82 Hopkins (Workington T.)......................446
1982-83 Diamond (Fulham) 308
1983-84 Woods (Leigh) 355
1984-85 Day (St. Helens) 362

.

ALL TIME RECORDS

Most goals in a match:
22 by Jim Sullivan (Wigan) v. Flimby & Fothergill (Challenge Cup), 14th February 1925

Most goals in a season:
DAVID WATKINS holds the record for most goals in a season with 221 — all for Salford — in 1972-73. Watkins played and scored a goal in every match that season as follows:

1972			
Aug.	19	Leeds ....(H)	5
	23	Featherstone R. ....(A)	3
	26	Whitehaven.............................(A)	4
	28	Swinton ....(H)	1
Sept.	1	Oldham ....(LC) (H)	10
	9	Leeds....................................(A)	2
	15	Rochdale H. ....(LC) (H)	11
	17	Leigh ....(A)	6
	24	Barrow.............................(JP) (A)	4
	29	Huyton ....(H)	10
Oct.	3	Oldham...........................(FT) (A)	4
	6	Wigan.............................(LC) (A)	4
	8	Blackpool B. ....(A)	5
	13	Blackpool B. .... (H)	8
	21	Swinton............................(LCF)	5
Nov.	5	Huyton ....(A)	8
	10	Rochdale H. .... (H)	6
	17	Warrington ....(A)	4
	19	New Zealand..........................(H)	10
	24	Dewsbury ....(JP) (H)	4
	26	Workington T. ....(H)	6
Dec.	1	Barrow................................(H)	9
	10	Bradford N. ....(JP) (H)	9
	13	Oldham................................(A)	4
	15	Leigh ....(H)	3
	24	Bradford N. ....(A)	5
	26	Workington T. ....(A)	3
	30	Hull K.R. ....(JP) (A)	5
1973			
Jan.	3	Bradford N............................(H)	6
	7	Rochdale H...........................(A)	2
	12	Featherstone R.......................(H)	4
	28	Featherstone R..........(RL Cup) (A)	4
Feb.	2	Whitehaven...........................(H)	4
	11	Barrow ....(A)	5
	23	St. Helens ....(H)	3
Mar.	7	Widnes................................(A)	3
	9	Dewsbury.............................(H)	3
	16	St. Helens.............................(A)	2
	24	Leeds...........................(JP Final)	2
	30	Warrington ....(H)	1
Apr.	6	Widnes ....(H)	4
	13	Oldham................................(H)	3
	15	Dewsbury ....(A)	2
	17	Wigan.................................(A)	3
	20	Swinton................................(A)	7
	23	Wigan.................................(H)	3
	29	Rochdale H. ....(top 16) (H)	2

	App	Gls
League	34	147
Lancs Cup..............................	4	30
John Player............................	5	24
Tour match	1	10
RL Cup	1	4
Floodlit Cup	1	4
Top 16	1	2
Totals	**47**	**221**

Fastest goals century:
Three players share the record of scoring the fastest 100 goals from the start of a season in terms of number of matches played. They are Bernard Ganley, David Watkins and Steve Quinn, who achieved the century in 18 matches.

Ganley reached 100 goals on 16 November 1957, after playing 17 matches for Oldham and one for Great Britain.

Watkins scored his 100th goal on 17 November 1972, all for Salford.

Quinn scored his 100th goal on 16 December 1979, all for Featherstone Rovers.

Most goals in a career:
JIM SULLIVAN holds the record for most goals in a career with 2,859 between 1921-22 and 1945-46. He scored a century of goals in every season after leaving Welsh Rugby Union for Wigan until the War interrupted the 1939-40 campaign.

The Test full back played all of his club rugby for Wigan apart form War-time appearances with Bradford Northern, Dewsbury and Keighley.

Sullivan's total includes 441 in representative matches, including three tours of Australasia. These figures are accepted by the Record Keepers' Club following research by James Carter and Malcolm Bentley.

Most one-point drop goals in a match:
5 by Danny Wilson (Swinton) v. Hunslet (John Player Special), 6 November 1983.
Peter Wood (Runcorn H.) v.Batley, 21 October 1984.
Paul Bishop (Warrington) at Wigan (Premiership semi-final), 11 May 1986

Most one-point drop goals in a season:
29 by Lyn Hallett (Cardiff C).....................1983-84

Most one-point drop goals in a career:
79 by Harry Pinner (St. Helens) 1974-86

Most tries in a match:
11 by George West (Hull K.R.) v Brookland Rovers Challenge Cup ....4 March 1905

117

Most tries in a career:
BRIAN BEVAN holds the record for most tries in a career with 796 between 1946 and 1964. His season-by-season record is:

1946-47	48
1947-48	57
1948-49	56
1949-50	33
1950-51	68
1951-52	51
1952-53	72
1953-54	67
1954-55	63
1955-56	57
1956-57	17
1957-58	46
1958-59	54
1959-60	40
1960-61	35
1961-62	15
1962-63	10
1963-64	7

Totals

Warrington	740
Blackpool Borough	17
Other Nationalities	26
Other representative matches	13
Grand Total	**796**

The Australian winger played his first game for Warrington on 17 November 1945 and his last on 23 April 1962 before having two seasons at Blackpool Borough. His last match for Borough was on 22 February, 1964.

Most tries in a season:
ALBERT ROSENFELD holds the record for most tries in a season with 80 — all for Huddersfield — in 1913-14.

Rosenfeld's match-by-match record:
1913

Sept.	6	York	(A)	4
	8	Warrington	(H)	2
	13	Leeds	(H)	5
	20	Halifax	(A)	2
	27	Batley	(A)	0
Oct.	4	Oldham	(H)	2
	11	Rochdale H.	(A)	0
	18	Bramley	(YC) (H)	2
	25	Dewsbury	(A)	4
Nov.	1	Halifax	(YC) (A)	2
	8	Wigan	(A)	1
	15	Dewsbury	(YC) (H)	3
	19	Bradford N.	(H)	3
	22	Leeds	(A)	3
	29	Bradford N.	(Halifax, YCF)	1

Dec.	3	Halifax	(H)	3
	6	Hunslet	(A)	2
	13	Rochdale H.	(H)	3
	20	Hull K.R.	(A)	2
	25	Hull	(A)	0
	26	Wakefield T.	(H)	3
	27	Hunslet	(H)	0
1914				
Jan.	1	St. Helens	(A)	0
	3	Warrington	(A)	0
	10	York	(H)	3
	17	Keighley	(A)	2
	24	Dewsbury	(H)	1
	31	Batley	(H)	0
Feb.	7	Oldham	(A)	0
	14	Bramley	(H)	5
	21	Wigan	(H)	3
	28	Swinton Park R.	(RL Cup) (H)	7
Mar.	7	Wakefield T.	(A)	2
	14	Hull K.R.	(RL Cup) (A)	2
	18	Bramley	(A)	3
	21	Widnes	(RL Cup) (H)	0
	25	Keighley	(H)	3
	28	Hull K.R.	(H)	1
	30	Bradford N.	(A)	1
Apr.	4	Hull	(Leeds, RL Cup SF)	0
	11	Hull	(H) did not play	
	13	St. Helens	(H)	0
	20	Hull	(Play-off) (H) did not play	
	25	Salford	(Leeds, Championship final)	0

	App	Tries
League	33	63
Yorks Cup	4	8
RL Cup	4	9
Play Off	1	0
Totals	**42**	**80**

Most points in a season:
LEWIS JONES holds the record for most points in a season with 496 from 194 goals and 36 tries for Leeds and representative teams in 1956-57.

Jones' match-by-match record:

For Leeds
1956

				Gls	Tries	Pts
Aug.	17	Halifax	(H)	3	0	6
	22	Bradford N.	(A)	11	3	31
	25	Wigan	(A)	4	0	8
	27	Featherstone R.	(H)	4	1	11
Sept.	1	Wakefield	(YC) (A)	3	1	9
	8	Dewsbury	(A)	6	0	12
	15	Warrington	(H)	7	0	14
	22	Huddersfield	(A)	3	0	6
	29	York	(H)	6	0	12

Oct.	6	Batley..........................(A)	4	2	14
	13	Australia.......................(H)	Did not play		
	20	Hull K.R. ....(A)	Did not play		
	27	Wigan ....(H)	2	0	4
Nov.	3	Hunslet ....(A)	1	0	2
	10	Barrow.........................(H)	3	2	12
	17	Halifax ....(A)	4	0	8
	24	Keighley.......................(H)	3	3	15
Dec.	1	Barrow ....(A)	4	0	8
	8	Bramley........................(A)	5	0	10
	15	Doncaster ....(H)	1	2	8
	22	Bradford N (abandoned) (H)	1	1	5
	25	Batley..........................(H)	8	1	19
	29	Keighley ....(A)	3	0	6
1957					
Jan.	5	Hull ....(H)	5	2	16
	12	Warrington...................(A)	0	3	9
	19	St. Helens....................(H)	5	1	13
	26	Doncaster....................(A)	Did not play		
Feb.	2	Huddersfield ....(H)	6	0	12
	9	Wigan ....(RL Cup) (H)	2	1	7
	16	York ....(A)	7	1	17
	23	Warrington....(RL Cup) (H)	5	1	13
	27	Castleford.....................(H)	4	1	11
Mar.	9	Halifax ....(RL Cup) (A)	5	0	10
	16	Wakefield T. ....(H)	5	1	13
	20	Bradford N ....(H)	5	1	13
	23	Hull..............................(A)	2	0	4
	30	Whitehaven			
		..........(Odsal, RL Cup SF)	1	0	2
Apr.	3	Wakefield T. ....(A)	3	0	6
	6	St. Helens....................(A)	0	0	0
	12	Hull K.R. ....(H)	Did not play		
	13	Dewsbury ....(H)	6	2	18
	19	Hunslet ....(H)	5	2	16
	20	Featherstone R..............(A)	2	0	4
	22	Castleford....................(A)	2	0	4
	23	Bramley........................(H)	7	1	17
May	4	Oldham ....(Play-off) (A)	3	0	6
	11	Barrow			
		...(Wembley, RL Cup final)	0	0	0

Representative matches
For Great Britain:

Jan.	26	France..............(at Leeds)	9	1	21
Mar.	3	France...........(at Toulouse)	5	1	13
Apr.	10	France.........(at St. Helens)	7	1	17

For The Rest:

Oct.	3	Britain XIII .....(at Bradford)	4	0	8

For RL XIII:

Oct.	29	Australia................(Leigh)	3	0	6

	App	Gls	Tries	Pts
League	36	147	30	384
RL Cup.............................	5	13	2	32
Yorks Cup.........................	1	3	1	9
Play-off.............................	1	3	0	6
Representative.....................	5	28	3	65
Totals	**48**	**194**	**36**	**496**

Most points in a match:
53 (11t, 10g) by George West (Hull K.R.) v. Brookland Rovers (RL Cup)..............................4 March, 1905

Most points in a career:
NEIL FOX holds the record for most points in a career with 6,220 between 1956 and 1979. This total does not include points scored during a spell of club rugby in New Zealand.

Fox was a month short of his 17th birthday when he made his debut for Wakefield Trinity on 10 April, 1956. Apart from a brief time at Bradford Northern Fox had 19 seasons at Wakefield before moving to a succession of clubs in later years.

After a long career as an international centre Fox moved into the forwards and played his last professional match for Bradford in their opening fixture of the 1979-80 season, on 19 August. That match enabled him to join the elite few who have played first team rugby at 40 years of age.

Fox's season-by-season tally is as follows:

	Gls	Tries	Pts
1955-56.............................	6	0	12
1956-57.............................	54	10	138
1957-58.............................	124	32	344
1958-59.............................	148	28	380
1959-60.............................	171	37	453
1960-61.............................	94	20	248
1961-62.............................	183	30	456
1962 Tour			
Australasia..........................	85	19	227
South Africa	19	4	50
1962-63.............................	125	14	292
1963-64.............................	125	21	313
1964-65.............................	121	13	281
1965-66.............................	98	11	229
1966-67.............................	144	16	336
1967-68.............................	98	18	250
1968-69.............................	95	9	217
1969-70.............................	17	5	49
1970-71.............................	110	12	256
1971-72.............................	84	6	186
1972-73.............................	138	8	300
1973-74.............................	62	8	148
1974-75.............................	146(1)	14	333
1975-76.............................	102(1)	4	215
1976-77.............................	79(1)	6	175
1977-78.............................	95(1)	9	216
1978-79.............................	50	4	112
1979-80.............................	2	0	4

A breakdown of Fox's club and representative totals is as follows:

	App	Gls	Tries	Pts
Wakefield T.	574	1,836	272	4,488
Bradford N.	70	85(1)	12	205
Hull K.R.	59	212(2)	16	470
York	13	42	2	90
Bramley....................	23	73	6	164
Huddersfield.............	21	73(1)	5	160
Club Totals	**760**	**2,321(4)**	**313**	**5,577**
Yorkshire.................	17	60	9	147
Britain v. Australia	8	26	3	61
New Zealand.	4	11	1	25
France.........	17	56	10	142
Other representative				
games including tour	22	101	22	268
Representative Totals.	**68**	**254**	**45**	**643**
Grand Totals	**828**	**2,575(4)**	**358**	**6,220**

( ) Figures in brackets are one point drop goals included in total.

Score-a-match:
The following players have appeared and scored in all of their club's matches in one season:

Jim Hoey (Widnes)	1932-33
Billy Langton (Hunslet)	1958-59
Stuart Ferguson (Leigh)	1970-71
David Watkins (Salford).............................	1972-73
David Watkins (Salford).............................	1973-74
John Woods (Leigh)...................................	1977-78
Steve Quinn (Featherstone R.)	1979-80
Mick Parrish (Hunslet)	1979-80
John Gorton (Swinton)..............................	1980-81
Mick Parrish (Oldham)	1981-82
Peter Wood (Runcorn H.)	1984-85

Longest scoring run:
DAVID WATKINS holds the record for the longest scoring run, playing and scoring in 92 consecutive matches for Salford from 19 August 1972 to 25 April 1974. He totalled 403 goals, 41 tries and 929 points.

Longest run of appearances:
KEITH ELWELL holds the record for the longest run of appearances with one club with a total of 239 for Widnes. The consecutive run started at Wembley in the 1977 Challenge Cup final against Leeds on 7 May, and ended after he played in a Lancashire Cup-tie at home to St. Helens on 5 September 1982. He was dropped for the match at Featherstone Rovers a week later. Although he went on as a substitute the record refers to full appearances only.

Elwell played as a substitute in the next match and then made a full appearance before his run of all appearances ended at 242.

Highest score:
Huddersfield 119 v. Swinton Park 2 (RL Cup)
.......28 February 1914

`Most points in all matches in a season:
1,436 by Leigh from 43 matches in 1985-86 as follows:

34 Division Two matches 1,156
2 Lancashire Cup 54
4 John Player Special Trophy 161
3 RL Challenge Cup 65

1,000 points in a League season:
1,156 by Leigh from 34 Division Two matches in 1985-86.
1,126 by Barrow from 34 Division Two matches in 1983-84.
1,005 by St. Helens from 38 matches in one-league system in 1958-59.

Longest unbeaten run:
40 Cup and League matches by Huddersfield in 1914-15, including three draws.

Longest winning run in the League:
31 matches by Wigan. Last 8 matches of 1969-70 and first 23 of 1970-71.
● In 1978-79 Hull won all of their 26 Division Two matches, the only time a club has won all its league matches in one season.

Longest League losing run:
40 Division Two matches by Doncaster between November 1975 and April 1977. This period included a run of 37 Cup and League defeats.
● In 1906-07 Liverpool City lost all 30 of their league matches, the only time a team playing more than 12 league matches has lost them all. Liverpool also lost their two cup ties and dropped out after only one season. Liverpool did manage a home league draw against Bramley but when they were unable to fulfil a return fixture the match was expunged from league records.

Castleford skipper John Joyner hoists aloft the 1986 Silk Cut
Challenge Cup, Lance Todd Trophy winner Bob Beardmore
holding the plinth.

CUPS

RUGBY LEAGUE CHALLENGE CUP

1986 Final

Castleford coach Malcolm Reilly duly produced his pre-written victory speech but only after a dramatic finish as Rugby League provided yet another thrilling Wembley occasion.

The destiny of the 1986 Silk Cut Challenge Cup hung on one kick in the dying minutes of a heart-stopping final.

In the last minute of normal time favourites Hull K.R. clawed their way back with a touchdown near the corner by substitute John Lydiat to take the score to 15-14.

Australian marksman John Dorahy was left with a touchline kick for victory. Players from both sides could not bear to watch as Dorahy — seeking his 100th place kick goal of the season — was hampered in his run up by the closeness of the surrounding track and sent the ball left of the posts. There were still four minutes of injury time left after the try but Castleford held out.

The 1986 Wembley final was a reflection of the two teams' build up. Castleford were full of confidence, based on solid teamwork, having named their side in midweek. Coach Reilly caused a surprise by omitting three players who had figured in all the previous rounds.

Rovers, on the other hand, were well below par and a shadow of the outfit which had so professionally disposed of Leeds in the semi-final replay. Coach Roger Millward did not name his side until the morning of the final. Having already lost Test second row pair Chris Burton and Phil Hogan with broken arms, the Robins struggled all week to get knee-troubled George Fairbairn fit, and were then hit by a stomach bug to Australian prop Peter Johnston and a dose of flu for fellow countryman Dorahy. Then on the eve of the final Gavin Miller, their most effective player

of the season, pulled a hamstring although the injury was kept secret.

Had Dorahy's last ditch attempt been on target it would have been cruel luck for Castleford who had lined up a superbly planned triumph, based on teamwork allied to sufficient individual skill.

Lance Todd Trophy winner Bob Beardmore typified the whole approach. His scrum half role was to work closely with his forwards, but he stood back to send over a 32nd minute drop goal and shortly after the break snatched a demoralising try from a speculative kick through.

Castleford also possessed a matchwinner in centre Tony Marchant who revelled in the big match atmosphere as he did on his tryscoring debut for Great Britain two months earlier. His opening touchdown after 20 minutes was a classic piece of centre play, the 60-yard move featuring the use of wing partner David Plange as a foil to nullify the challenge of Rovers duo Fairbairn and David Laws.

Another thorn in Rovers' side was diminutive Australian winger Jamie Sandy who nearly stayed at home in Brisbane because of fears of terrorism. His nippy running from the wing was a constant source of irritation to the Robins and three players were left in his wake as he flew 40 yards for Castleford's third and final try in the 62nd minute.

The individual brilliance of this trio was backed up by a hard working, cohesive pack of forwards well led by Great Britain training squad members Kevin Beardmore and Kevin Ward.

Rovers were very subdued on attack, even though they also registered three tries. Only the third touchdown was based on teamwork. Kiwi centre Gary Prohm scored his first try a minute before the interval, running 50 yards while suffering from concussion, second row man Andy Kelly having snapped up a pass from Castleford's Keith England. His second in the 67th minute was due entirely to his own strength, a feature of many of his 100-plus tries for Rovers.

Ironically, the two-try hero blotted his copybook in his last match for Rovers before launching a new career with Sydney club Eastern Suburbs. His slow approach to mopping up Bob Beardmore's seemingly harmless kick through allowed the number seven to pounce for a try which took Castleford 11-6 ahead only three minutes after the restart.

Rovers attacking force was dulled from the start when the secret of Miller's hamstring injury was out in the open after only minutes, the usually all-action loose forward being restricted to pedestrian pace. The Friday morning training injury prevented his normal driving runs and he did little more than pass the ball.

The Hull K.R. injury jinx, which also saw international wingman Garry Clark playing with a shoulder harness after a series of dislocations, continued during the afternoon with emergency second row man Des Harrison being stretchered off with severe concussion in the 56th minute.

A crowd of 82,134 paid world record receipts of more than £806,000 to witness Castleford maintain their unbeaten Challenge Cup final record with a fourth Wembley victory, receiving a Silk Cut prize of £16,000. Castleford chairman David Poulter — in his first season — had steered the Wheldon Road club to Wembley success only a couple of months after launching a lifeline fund to offset a financial crisis.

Reilly was well rehearsed for his victory speech which he had written the night before — the ultimate sign of confidence. It began: 'We got the result we came for ...'

All together now! . . . dressing room celebrations for Silk Cut Challenge Cup victors Castleford.

SILK CUT CHALLENGE CUP FINAL
3rd May   **Wembley**

CASTLEFORD 15		**HULL K.R. 14**
Gary Lord	1.	George Fairbairn
David Plange	2.	Garry Clark
Tony Marchant	3.	Mike Smith
Gary Hyde	4.	Gary Prohm
Jamie Sandy	5.	David Laws
John Joyner, Capt.	6.	John Dorahy
Bob Beardmore	7.	Paul Harkin
Kevin Ward	8.	Peter Johnston
Kevin Beardmore	9.	David Watkinson, Capt.
Barry Johnson	10.	Asuquo Ema
Keith England	11.	Andy Kelly
Martin Ketteridge	12.	Des Harrison
Ian French	13.	Gavin Miller
David Roockley	14.	Gordon Smith
Stuart Horton	15.	John Lydiat

T: Marchant, R. Beardmore, Sandy
G: Ketteridge, R. Beardmore (dg)
Substitutions:
Roockley for Lord (63 min.)
Horton for K. Beardmore (75 min.)
Half-time: 7-6
Referee: Robin Whitfield (Widnes)

T: Prohm (2), Lydiat
G: Dorahy
Substitutions:
Lydiat for Harrison (56 min.)
G. Smith for Kelly (68 min.)
Attendance: 82,134
Receipts: £806,676

Scorechart

Minute	Score	Scoreline Castleford	Hull K.R.
20:	Marchant (T)		
	Ketteridge (G)	6	0
27:	Dorahy (PG)	6	2
32:	R. Beardmore (DG)	7	2
39:	Prohm (T)	7	6
43:	R. Beardmore (T)	11	6
62:	Sandy (T)	15	6
67:	Prohm (T)	15	10
79:	Lydiat (T)	15	14
	Scrums	7	8
	Penalties	5	7

Hooker Kevin Beardmore, restored to Castleford's Wembley line up after long-term injury.

Touchdown number two for Hull K.R. centre Gary Prohm on his British club farewell performance.

Looking to off-load, Castleford second row man Keith England.

1986 Round by Round

Amateur clubs returned to the Rugby League Challenge Cup after a five-year break. The three county cup winners were invited to play off for two places in the four-tie preliminary round, Cumbrian victors Kells being given a bye into the competition with Yorkshire's Dudley Hill beating Lancashire's Simms Cross in an elimination game. Kells trailed 20-4 at half-time in their meeting with Hunslet at Elland Road, scoring the only try of the second period to receive a rousing ovation. Man of the Match in the 20-8 defeat was Kells' Paul Messenger, who combined with Ian Clarke to create the try of the tie, a 90-yard effort. Dudley Hill visited the Boulevard and took the lead over Hull after 12 minutes with a try from Man of the Match Gary Brentley, Danny Lockwood adding the goal. Hull's 38-10 victory march included three interception tries, two from Garry Schofield. Leeds visited Swinton where they had not lost for 20 years, that record remaining intact with a 30-8 victory, scoring six tries to one against a Lions side which had won four of their last five home matches. Carlisle beat Mansfield Marksman 20-14 to earn a first round visit to Oldham. Carlisle registered four touchdowns to Mansfield's three with Dean Carroll adding two goals, while the visitors' Carl Sanderson contributed only one.

The shock of the first round was revitalised Doncaster beating Salford 18-12 at mud-bound Tatters Field. With the scores level at 12-12, Doncaster powerhouse prop Kevin Parkhouse scored his second try to put the Dons into the second round for only the second time in 10 years. The Tatters Field game was one of 12 first round ties played on the original date thanks to pitch clearing operations. Controversy reigned with three of the four remaining ties. The League ordered first round ties to be completed after nearly three weeks of postponements due to the Arctic conditions. Dewsbury eventually played their home tie with St. Helens at underground-heated Headingley and went down battling 19-22. Fulham moved their clash with Barrow to Wigan's new electric blanket and lost 26-14 after leading at the interval, Les Quirk and Man of the Match Dave Brown each claiming two tries. Bradford Northern were persuaded to move their encounter with Wakefield Trinity to Headingley for the television cameras and hung on as Trinity came back from 10-0 down to within two points.

Holders Wigan, accompanied by an army of 4,000 fans, went to the soccer ground at Workington to inflict a 56-12 hammering on Workington Town. The Riversiders led 42-0 before John Beattie opened Town's two-try account. Unbeaten since Christmas, Leeds travelled to nearby Halifax to record a 24-4 victory, highlighted by a 50-yard spectacular touchdown from Australian Tony Currie. Thrum Hall fans, who mounted a massive pitch clearing operation, were rewarded only by a Colin Whitfield try. Hull K.R. coach Roger Millward described their 22-6 home defeat of arch rivals Hull as the club's most professional display for more than 20 years, John Dorahy taking the individual honours with the setting up of two of the three tries and five goals from six attempts. Warrington ran in 11 tries in a 62-11 rout of Second Division Sheffield Eagles, scoring a decisive 18 points in a four-minute spell just after the break. Australian loose forward Ian French collected five tries in Castleford's 60-6 runaway win at Hunslet, creating the opening try for David Plange after only nine minutes. Oldham were also in high-scoring mood, running up a 56-10 success over Carlisle at Oldham FC's Boundary Park ground. David Liddiard started the scoring rout after only 18 seconds, snatching three more in an 11-try hammering. Widnes built a 12-0 lead at Featherstone before the Rovers rallied with a Paul Lyman hat-trick to lead 14-12. With Andy Currier sent off, Widnes grabbed victory with 14 minutes to go through a Mick

Burke try. Blackpool Borough reached the second round for the first time in 21 years with a 30-10 home victory over Runcorn Highfield, scoring three tries in each half despite the dismissal of Mick Nanyn. Keighley had Campbell Dews sent off after only three minutes but battled to hold on to a 2-0 interval lead over high-flying Leigh, who had captain Derek Pyke sent off before the break but came back to win 24-2. York had to work hard for an 18-6 victory over Whitehaven at Wiggington Road, a 21st minute try by Australian Rod Pethybridge setting them on the road to victory, the Cumbrians being hit by the sending off of captain Alan Banks. Huddersfield Barracudas tried manfully to recover from two early tries by visitors Rochdale Hornets but eventually went down 10-4, while Bramley's Peter Lister scored the only try of the McLaren Field tie with Batley in a narrow 8-6 success.

In the second round, lowly Doncaster conceded home advantage to Leeds in exchange for £2,500 and 11 free coaches for their fans. The Dons led 10-4 at half-time, thrilling the 7,636 Headingley crowd with tries from Kevin Parkhouse and Man of the Match Kevin Jones before Leeds steadied themselves with four second half tries and a 28-10 victory. Australian Noel Cleal bid farewell to Widnes with a Man of the Match display rounded off with a blockbusting try, one of the Chemics' six against visitors Rochdale Hornets in a 36-20 success. In the televised derby encounter, St. Helens gained a well-deserved interval lead at Central Park, but Wigan hit back, the crucial score being an interception by centre David Stephenson from a stray Neil Holding pass. Wigan twice came from behind to win 24-14. Bramley visited Bradford Northern and led 14-0 at the interval before having Steve Hankins sent off two minutes after the restart. Northern built a 20-14 lead until Bramley skipper and Man of the Match Paul Fletcher scored a try, Shaun Kilner equalising with the goal. In the replay at McLaren Field,

injury-hit Bramley could not repeat the heroics and Northern romped to a 36-2 victory, registering 10 points in the first 13 minutes. Warrington-born Mick Worrall inspired Oldham to a 13-6 triumph after his hometown side had led 6-1. His solo try was followed by two vital goals after taking over from the off-form David Hobbs. Ian French continued to show his top form as Castleford recorded a comfortable 30-6 success at Barrow, Martin Ketteridge hitting five valuable goals. As expected, Hull K.R. showed their superiority in the last quarter at York, running in four tries. Powerful Andy Kelly clinched the Man of the Match award with a strong running performance crowned by two tries. Test man Des Drummond's sensational axing from the Leigh side to entertain Blackpool Borough enabled stand-in John Kerr to take the spotlight, creating touchdowns for Trevor Cogger and Ray Tabern before scoring himself.

In the third round, Leeds met Widnes for the third time in two weeks. After missing five kicks at goal, Test centre David Creasser hit the target with a last second penalty goal to clinch a 10-10 draw. In the Headingley replay, defences were dominant, Leeds going through with a 26th minute penalty from Creasser, a 65th minute Cliff Lyons drop goal and a Creasser penalty in the closing minutes for a 5-0 scoreline. Hull K.R.'s front row proved too powerful for Second Division leaders Leigh, hooker and skipper David Watkinson taking the Man of the Match award ahead of props Peter Johnston and Zook Ema. At 11-10, Rovers Kiwi centre Gary Prohm notched his 100th try for the club to send the Robins into the semi-finals. A beautifully struck drop goal from Silk Cut Award winner Brendan White looked sufficient to secure victory for Bradford Northern at Oldham. Then with only seven minutes left the Liddiard brothers combined, 16-year-old Glen providing the astute pass for full back David to romp between the Northern posts,

Hobbs adding the simple goal for a 6-1 victory. Favourites Wigan were given a shock exit at Central Park by relegation-threatened Castleford. In their worst display of the season, the Riversiders went out 10-2, a second half try by Castleford full back Dave Roockley proving decisive.

In the first semi-final Oldham were denied their first visit to Wembley by a Castleford side who had experienced defeat at this stage three times in the past four years. Man of the Match Bob Beardmore scored two tries and created the third although the Roughyeds were in the game until the final 15 minutes. Their hero was Australian full back David Liddiard who was cast as the villain in Beardmore's clinching second half try when he allowed an up and under to bounce in the in-goal area, the ball bobbing back for Beardmore to touch down. Tony Marchant's try clinched Castleford's booking at Wembley at 18-7. In the second semi-final, Hull K.R. and

Leeds served up a 24-24 thriller, hailed as the best-ever Challenge Cup tie outside of Wembley. Outplayed in the first half, Rovers overcame the 33rd minute dismissal of scrum half Paul Harkin and the loss of second row man Chris Burton with a broken arm nine minutes earlier to pull back from 12-2 down to lead 24-14 on the hour. Leeds replied with tries from Tony Currie and substitute Paul Medley, David Creasser adding a goal. The final nail-biting 12 minutes featured unsuccessful drop goal attempts from John Dorahy and David Ward. A crowd of over 32,000 attended Elland Road for the Thursday night replay with the teams still level at the interval after a scoreless first half. Robins' half back Harkin broke the deadlock with a drop goal before Peter Johnston and John Lydiat scored tries as Rovers broke loose. Kelly added the final touchdown two minutes from time, Dorahy contributing his second goal in the 17-0 victory.

Oldham's dreams of a Wembley debut crashed at Wigan with an 18-7 semi-final defeat by Castleford. Moroccan winger Hussein M'Barki is collared by Keith England as teammates, from the left, Terry Flanagan, Gary Warnecke and Tom Nadiole look on.

1986 RESULTS

Preliminary Round

Carlisle	20	Mansfield M.	14
Hull	38	Dudley Hill (Bradford)	10
Hunslet	20	Kells (Cumbria)	8
Swinton	8	Leeds	30

First Round

Blackpool B.	30	Runcorn H.	10
Bradford N. (at Leeds)	10	Wakefield T.	8
Bramley	8	Batley	6
Dewsbury (at Leeds)	19	St. Helens	22
Doncaster	18	Salford	12
Featherstone R.	14	Widnes	18
Fulham (at Wigan)	14	Barrow	26
Halifax	4	Leeds	24
Huddersfield B.	4	Rochdale H.	10
Hull K.R.	22	Hull	6
Hunslet	6	Castleford	60
Keighley	2	Leigh	24
Oldham (at Oldham FC)	56	Carlisle	10
Warrington	62	Sheffield E.	11
Workington T. (at Workington FC)	12	Wigan	56
York	18	Whitehaven	6

Second Round

Barrow	6	Castleford	30
Bradford N.	20	Bramley	20
Doncaster (at Leeds)	10	Leeds	28
Leigh	31	Blackpool B.	10
Oldham	13	Warrington	6
Widnes	36	Rochdale H.	20
Wigan	24	St. Helens	14
York	6	Hull K.R.	34

Replay

Bramley	2	Bradford N.	36

Third Round

Hull K.R.	25	Leigh	10
Oldham	6	Bradford N.	1
Widnes	10	Leeds	10
Wigan	2	Castleford	10

Replay

Leeds	5	Widnes	0

Semi-Finals

Castleford (at Wigan)	18	Oldham	7
Hull K.R. (at Elland Road, Leeds)	24	Leeds	24

Replay

Hull K.R. (at Elland Road, Leeds)	17	Leeds	0

Final

Castleford (at Wembley)	15	Hull K.R.	14

Mal Reilly, coach of Wembley victors Castleford.

1986 PRIZES

Round	Per Round	Total
Preliminary	8 × £1,100	£8,800
First	16 × £1,100	£17,600
Second	8 × £1,500	£12,000
Third	4 × £2,500	£10,000
Semi-Finals	2 × £4,500	£9,000
Runners-up	1 × £9,000	£9,000
Winners	1 × £16,000	£16,000
Prize Total		£82,400
Development fund		£57,600
Total		£140,000

CHALLENGE CUP ROLL OF HONOUR

Year	Winners		Runners-up		Venue	Attendance	Receipts
1897	Batley	10	St Helens	3	Leeds	13,492	£624.17.7
1898	Batley	7	Bradford	0	Leeds	27,941	£1,586.3.0
1899	Oldham	19	Hunslet	9	Manchester	15,763	£946.16.0
1900	Swinton	16	Salford	8	Manchester	17,864	£1,100.0.0
1901	Batley	6	Warrington	0	Leeds	29,563	£1,644.16.0
1902	Broughton R.	25	Salford	0	Rochdale	15,006	£846.11.0
1903	Halifax	7	Salford	0	Leeds	32,507	£1,834.8.6
1904	Halifax	8	Warrington	3	Salford	17,041	£936.5.6
1905	Warrington	6	Hull K.R.	0	Leeds	19,638	£1,271.18.0
1906	Bradford	5	Salford	0	Leeds	15,834	£920.0.0
1907	Warrington	17	Oldham	3	Broughton	18,500	£1,010.0.0
1908	Hunslet	14	Hull	0	Huddersfield	18,000	£903.0.0
1909	Wakefield T.	17	Hull	0	Huddersfield	23,587	£1,490.0.0
1910	Leeds	7	Hull	7	Huddersfield	19,413	£1,102.0.0
Replay	Leeds	26	Hull	12	Huddersfield	11,608	£657.0.0
1911	Broughton R.	4	Wigan	0	Salford	8,000	£376.0.0
1912	Dewsbury	8	Oldham	5	Leeds	15,271	£853.0.0
1913	Huddersfield	9	Warrington	5	Leeds	22,754	£1,446.9.6
1914	Hull	6	Wakefield T.	0	Halifax	19,000	£1,035.5.0
1915	Huddersfield	37	St. Helens	3	Oldham	8,000	£472.0.0
1920	Huddersfield	21	Wigan	10	Leeds	14,000	£1,936.0.0
1921	Leigh	13	Halifax	0	Broughton	25,000	£2,700.0.0
1922	Rochdale H.	10	Hull	9	Leeds	32,596	£2,964.0.0
1923	Leeds	28	Hull	3	Wakefield	29,335	£2,390.0.0
1924	Wigan	21	Oldham	4	Rochdale	41,831	£3,712.0.0
1925	Oldham	16	Hull K.R.	3	Leeds	28,335	£2,879.0.0
1926	Swinton	9	Oldham	3	Rochdale	27,000	£2,551.0.0
1927	Oldham	26	Swinton	7	Wigan	33,448	£3,170.0.0
1928	Swinton	5	Warrington	3	Wigan	33,909	£3,158.1.11
1929	Wigan	13	Dewsbury	2	Wembley	41,500	£5,614.0.0
1930	Widnes	10	St. Helens	3	Wembley	36,544	£3,102.0.0
1931	Halifax	22	York	8	Wembley	40,368	£3,908.0.0
1932	Leeds	11	Swinton	8	Wigan	29,000	£2,479.0.0
1933	Huddersfield	21	Warrington	17	Wembley	41,874	£6,465.0.0
1934	Hunslet	11	Widnes	5	Wembley	41,280	£6,686.0.0
1935	Castleford	11	Huddersfield	8	Wembley	39,000	£5,533.0.0
1936	Leeds	18	Warrington	2	Wembley	51,250	£7,070.0.0
1937	Widnes	18	Keighley	5	Wembley	47,699	£6,704.0.0
1938	Salford	7	Barrow	4	Wembley	51,243	£7,174.0.0
1939	Halifax	20	Salford	3	Wembley	55,453	£7,681.0.0
1940	*No competition*						
1941	Leeds	19	Halifax	2	Bradford	28,500	£1,703.0.0
1942	Leeds	15	Halifax	10	Bradford	15,250	£1,276.0.0
1943	Dewsbury	16	Leeds	9	Dewsbury	10,470	£823.0.0
	Dewsbury	0	Leeds	6	Leeds	16,000	£1,521.0.0
	Dewsbury won on aggregate 16-15						
1944	Bradford	0	Wigan	3	Wigan	22,000	£1,640.0.0
	Bradford	8	Wigan	0	Bradford	30,000	£2,200.0.0
	Bradford won on aggregate 8-3						
1945	Huddersfield	7	Bradford N.	4	Huddersfield	9,041	£1,184.3.7
	Huddersfield	6	Bradford N.	5	Bradford	17,500	£2,050.0.0
	Huddersfield won on aggregate 13-9						

Year	Winners		Runners-up		Venue	Attendance	Receipts
1946	Wakefield T.	13	Wigan	12	Wembley	54,730	£12,013.13.6
1947	Bradford N.	8	Leeds	4	Wembley	77,605	£17,434.5.0
1948	Wigan	8	Bradford N.	3	Wembley	91,465	£21,121.9.9
1949	Bradford N.	12	Halifax	0	Wembley	95,050	£21,930.5.0
1950	Warrington	19	Widnes	0	Wembley	94,249	£24,782.13.0
1951	Wigan	10	Barrow	0	Wembley	94,262	£24,797.19.0
1952	Workington T.	18	Featherstone R.	10	Wembley	72,093	£22,374.2.0
1953	Huddersfield	15	St. Helens	10	Wembley	89,588	£30,865.12.3
1954	Warrington	4	Halifax	4	Wembley	81,841	£29,706.7.3
Replay	Warrington	8	Halifax	4	Bradford	102,569	£18,623.7.0
1955	Barrow	21	Workington T.	12	Wembley	66,513	£27,453.16.0
1956	St. Helens	13	Halifax	2	Wembley	79,341	£29,424.7.6
1957	Leeds	9	Barrow	7	Wembley	76,318	£32,671.14.3
1958	Wigan	13	Workington T.	9	Wembley	66,109	£33,175.17.6
1959	Wigan	30	Hull	13	Wembley	79,811	£35,718.19.9
1960	Wakefield T.	38	Hull	5	Wembley	79,773	£35,754.16.0
1961	St. Helens	12	Wigan	6	Wembley	94,672	£38,479.11.9
1962	Wakefield T.	12	Huddersfield	6	Wembley	81,263	£33,390.18.4
1963	Wakefield T.	25	Wigan	10	Wembley	84,492	£44,521.17.0
1964	Widnes	13	Hull K.R.	5	Wembley	84,488	£44,840.19.0
1965	Wigan	20	Hunslet	16	Wembley	89,016	£48,080.4.0
1966	St. Helens	21	Wigan	2	Wembley	*98,536	£50,409.0.0
1967	Featherstone R.	17	Barrow	12	Wembley	76,290	£53,465.14.0
1968	Leeds	11	Wakefield T.	10	Wembley	87,100	£56,171.16.6
1969	Castleford	11	Salford	6	Wembley	*97,939	£58,848.1.0
1970	Castleford	7	Wigan	2	Wembley	95,255	£89,262.2.0
1971	Leigh	24	Leeds	7	Wembley	85,514	£84,452.15
1972	St. Helens	16	Leeds	13	Wembley	89,495	£86,414.30
1973	Featherstone R.	33	Bradford N.	14	Wembley	72,395	£125,826.40
1974	Warrington	24	Featherstone R.	9	Wembley	77,400	£132,021.05
1975	Widnes	14	Warrington	7	Wembley	85,098	£140,684.45
1976	St. Helens	20	Widnes	5	Wembley	89,982	£190,129.40
1977	Leeds	16	Widnes	7	Wembley	80,871	£241,488.00
1978	Leeds	14	St. Helens	12	Wembley	*96,000	£330,575.00
1979	Widnes	12	Wakefield T.	3	Wembley	94,218	£383,157.00
1980	Hull K.R.	10	Hull	5	Wembley	*95,000	£448,202.90
1981	Widnes	18	Hull K.R.	9	Wembley	92,496	£591,117.00
1982	Hull	14	Widnes	14	Wembley	92,147	£684,500.00
Replay	Hull	18	Widnes	9	Elland Rd., L'ds	41,171	£180,525.00
1983	Featherstone R.	14	Hull	12	Wembley	84,969	£655,510.00
1984	Widnes	19	Wigan	6	Wembley	80,116	£686,171.00
1985	Wigan	28	Hull	24	Wembley	*97,801	£760,322.00
1986	Castleford	15	Hull K.R.	14	Wembley	82,134	£806,676.00

*Indicates a capacity attendance, the limit being fixed annually taking into account variable factors.

RUGBY LEAGUE CHALLENGE CUP ....
A REVIEW
1963-64
Widnes 13 Randall (2g); R. Chisnall, Briers (1t),
F. Myler (1t), Thompson; Lowe, Owen;
Hurtsfield, Kemel, Collier (1t), Measures,
A. Hughes, V. Karalius
Hull K.R. 5 Kellett (1g); Paul, Major, Elliott,
Blackmore; A. Burwell (1t), Bunting; Tyson,
Flanagan, Mennell, Palmer, Clark, Poole
Referee: R.L. Thomas (Oldham)
1964-65
Wigan 20 Ashby; Boston, Ashton (1g), Holden
(1t), Lake (2t); C. Hill, Parr; Gardiner, Clarke,
McTigue, Evans, A. Stephens, Gilfedder (3g, 1t)
Hunslet 16 Langton (5g); Griffiths (1t), Shelton
(1t), Preece, Lee; Gabbitas, Marchant; Hartley,
Prior, K. Eyre, Ramsey, Gunney, Ward
Referee: J. Manley (Warrington)
1965-66
St. Helens 21 F. Barrow; Vollenhoven,
Murphy (1g), Benyon, Killeen (5g, 1t); Harvey,
Bishop (1t); Halsall, Sayer, Watson, French,
Warlow, Mantle (1t)
Wigan 2 Ashby; Boston, D. Stephens, Ashton,
Lake; C. Hill, Parr; Gardiner, Woosey, McTigue,
A. Stephens, Gilfedder (1g), Major
Referee: H.G. Hunt (Prestbury)
1966-67
Featherstone R. 17 Wrigglesworth; Thomas (1t),
Cotton, Jordan, Greatorex; M. Smith, Dooler (1g);
Tonks, Harris, Dixon, A. Morgan (1t),
Thompson (1t), Smales (1t, 3g)
Barrow 12 Tees (1g); Burgess, Challinor,
Hughes, Murray; Brophy (1t), G. Smith; Kelland,
Redhead, Hopwood, Sanderson, Delooze (2g),
Watson (1t)
Referee: E. Clay (Leeds)
1967-68
Leeds 11 Risman (4g); Alan Smith, Hynes,
Watson, Atkinson (1t); Shoebottom, Seabourne;
Clark, Crosby, K. Eyre, Ramsey, A. Eyre, Batten
Wakefield T 10 Cooper, Hirst (2t), Brooke,
Coetzer, Batty; Poynton, Owen; Jeanes,
Shepherd, D. Fox (2g), Haigh, McLeod, Hawley
Referee: J.P. Hebblethwaite (York)
1968-69
Castleford 11 Edwards; Briggs, Howe (1t),
Thomas, Lowndes; Hardisty (1t), Hepworth (1t);
Hartley, C. Dickinson, J. Ward, Redfearn (1g),
Lockwood, Reilly
Salford 6 K. Gwilliam; Burgess, Whitehead,
Hesketh, Jackson; Watkins, Brennan; Ogden,
Dickens, Bott, Coulman, Dixon, Hill (3g)
Referee: D.S. Brown (Preston)

1969-70
Castleford 7 Edwards; Briggs, Thomas, Stenton,
Lowndes (1t); Hardisty (Hargrave), Hepworth;
Hartley, C. Dickinson, Redfearn (2g), Kirkbride,
Lockwood, Reilly
Wigan 2 Tyrer (1g) (C. Hill); Jones, Francis,
Rowe, Kevin O'Loughlin; D. Hill, Parr;
Ashcroft, Burdell, Hogan, Ashurst, D. Robinson,
Laughton
Referee: G.F. Lindop (Wakefield)
1970-71
Leigh 24 Eckersley (1t, 1g); Ferguson (5g),
Dorrington (1t), Collins, Walsh; A. Barrow,
Murphy (2g) (L. Chisnall); Watts, Ashcroft,
Fiddler (1g), Grimes, Clarkson, Smethurst
Leeds 7 Holmes (2g); Langley, Hynes, Cowan
(Dyl), Atkinson; Wainwright (1t), Seabourne;
J. Burke, Fisher, Barnard, Hick, Haigh, Ramsey
Referee: W.H. Thompson (Huddersfield)
1971-72
St. Helens 16 G. Pimblett; L. Jones (1t), Benyon,
Walsh, Wilson; K. Kelly, Heaton; Rees (1t),
Greenall, J. Stephens, Mantle, E. Chisnall,
Coslett (5g)
Leeds 13 Holmes; Alan Smith, Hynes (Langley),
Dyl, Atkinson; Hardisty, Hepworth; Clawson
(5g), Fisher, Ramsey, Cookson (1t), Haigh, Batten
Referee: E. Lawrinson (Warrington)
1972-73
Featherstone R. 33 C. Kellett (8g); Coventry,
M. Smith (1t) (Hartley) (1t), Newlove (2t),
K. Kellett; Mason, Nash (1g); Tonks, Bridges,
Farrar (1t), Rhodes (Hollis), Thompson, Stone
Bradford N. 14 Tees (4g); Lamb, Stockwell,
Watson, D. Redfearn (1t); Blacker (Treasure),
Seabourne; Hogan, Dunn, Earl (Long), Joyce,
W. Pattinson, Fearnley (1t)
Referee: M.J. Naughton (Widnes)
1973-74
Warrington 24 Whitehead (7g); M. Philbin,
Noonan, Whittle, Bevan; Murphy (2g) (Pickup),
Gordon; D. Chisnall, Ashcroft (1t), Brady
(Wanbon), Wright, Nicholas (1t), B. Philbin
Featherstone R. 9 Box (3g); Dyas, M. Smith,
Hartley, Bray; Newlove (1t), Nash; Tonks,
Bridges, Harris, Rhodes (Busfield), Thompson
(Stone), Bell
Referee: S. Shepherd (Oldham)
1974-75
Widnes 14 Dutton (5g, 1dg); A. Prescott, George,
Aspey, Anderson; Hughes, Bowden; Mills (1t),
Elwell, Sheridan, Foran, Adams, Laughton
Warrington 7 Whitehead (2g); M. Philbin,
Noonan, Reynolds (W. Briggs), Bevan (1t);
Whittle, Gordon; D. Chisnall, Ashcroft, Wanbon,
Conroy, Martyn (Nicholas), B. Philbin
Referee: P. Geraghty (York)

1975-76
St. Helens 20 G. Pimblett (3g, 2dg); L. Jones,
Cunningham (1t), Noonan, Mathias; Benyon
(Glynn 2t), Heaton (1t); Mantle (James),
A. Karalius, Coslett, Nicholls, E. Chisnall, Hull
Widnes 5 Dutton (2g); A. Prescott (D. O'Neill),
Hughes, George, Jenkins; Eckersley, Bowden;
Nelson, Elwell (1dg), Wood, Foran (Sheridan),
Adams, Laughton
Referee: R. Moore (Wakefield)
1976-77
Leeds 16 Murrell; Alan Smith (D. Smith),
Hague, Dyl (1t), Atkinson (1t); Holmes,
Dick (1t, 3g, 1dg); Harrison, Ward, Pitchford,
Eccles, Cookson, Fearnley (Dickinson)
Widnes 7 Dutton (2g); Wright (George), Aspey
(1t), Eckersley, D. O'Neill; Hughes, Bowden;
Ramsey, Elwell, Mills, Dearden (Foran), Adams,
Laughton
Referee: V. Moss (Manchester)
1977-78
Leeds 14 Oulton (1g); D. Smith (1t), Hague, Dyl,
Atkinson (1t); Holmes (1dg), J. Sanderson (Dick);
Harrison (Dickinson), Ward (2dg), Pitchford,
Cookson (1t), Eccles, Crane
St. Helens 12 G. Pimblett (3g), L. Jones,
Noonan, Glynn, Mathias; Francis (1t),
K. Gwilliam; D. Chisnall, Liptrot (1t), James,
Nicholls, Cunningham, Pinner
Referee: W.H. Thompson (Huddersfield)
1978-79
Widnes 12 Eckersley (1dg); Wright (1t), Aspey,
George (Hull), Burke (2g); Hughes (1t), Bowden;
Mills, Elwell (1dg), Shaw, Adams, Dearden
(M. O'Neill), Laughton
Wakefield T. 3 Sheard; Fletcher (1t), K. Smith,
Diamond, Juliff; Topliss, Lampkowski; Burke,
McCurrie, Skerrett, Ashurst, Keith Rayne, Idle
Referee: J.E. Jackson (Pudsey)
1979-80
Hull K.R. 10 Hall; Hubbard (3g, 1t) (Hogan),
M. Smith, Hartley, Sullivan; Millward (1dg),
Agar; Holdstock, Watkinson, Lockwood, Lowe,
Rose (Millington), Casey
Hull 5 Woods; Bray, Walters, Wilby (1t),
Prendiville; Newlove (Hancock), Pickerill;
Tindall, Wileman, Stone (Farrar), Birdsall,
Lloyd (1g), Norton
Referee: G.F. Lindop (Wakefield)
1980-81
Widnes 18 Burke (4g, 1t); Wright, George (1t),
Cunningham (J. Myler), Bentley; Hughes,
Gregory (1t); M. O'Neill (Shaw), Elwell,
Lockwood, L. Gorley, E. Prescott, Adams (1dg)

Hull K.R. 9 Hall; Hubbard (3g), M. Smith,
Hogan, Muscroft; Hartley, Harkin; Holdstock
(Millington), Watkinson, Crooks (Proctor), Lowe,
Burton (1t), Casey
Referee: D.G. Kershaw (Easingwold)
1981-82
Hull 14 Kemble; O'Hara (1t), Day, S. Evans,
Prendivillle; Topliss, Harkin; Skerrett, Wileman,
Stone, Crane (Crooks), Lloyd (4g), Norton (1t)
Widnes 14 Burke (1g), (A. Myler); Wright (1t),
Keiron O'Loughlin, Cunningham (2t), Basnett;
Hughes, Gregory (1g); M. O'Neill, Elwell (1dg),
Lockwood (S. O'Neill), L. Gorley, E. Prescott,
Adams
Referee: G.F. Lindop (Wakefield)
Replay
Hull 18 Kemble (1t); Sullivan, Leuluai, S. Evans,
Prendiville; Topliss (2t), Dean; Tindall, Duke,
Stone, Skerrett, Crooks (1t, 3g), Norton (Crane)
Widnes 9 Burke (3g); Wright (1t), Keiron
O'Loughlin, Cunningham, Basnett; Hughes,
Gregory; M. O'Neill, Elwell, Lockwood,
L. Gorley, E. Prescott, Adams
Referee: G.F. Lindop (Wakefield)
1982-83
Featherstone R. 14 N. Barker; Marsden,
Quinn (4g), Gilbert (Lyman), K. Kellett;
A. Banks, Hudson; Gibbins, Handscombe,
Hankins, D. Hobbs (2t), Slatter (Siddall), Smith
Hull 12 Kemble; O'Hara, S. Evans, Leuluai (1t),
Prendiville; Topliss, Harkin (Day), (Crane);
Skerrett, Bridges, Stone, Rose, Crooks (1t, 3g),
Norton
Referee: M.R. Whitfield (Widnes)
1983-84
Widnes 19 Burke (3g); Wright, Hughes (Hulme),
Lydon (2t), Basnett; Keiron O'Loughlin (1t),
Gregory; S. O'Neill (1dg), Elwell, K. Tamati,
L. Gorley, M. O'Neill (Whitfield), Adams
Wigan 6 Edwards; Ramsdale, Stephenson,
Whitfield (1g), (Elvin), Gill; Cannon, Stephens;
Hemsley (1t), H. Tamati, Case (Juliff), West,
Scott, Pendlebury
Referee: W.H. Thompson (Huddersfield)
1984-85
Wigan 28 Edwards (1t); Ferguson (2t),
Stephenson (1g), Donlan, Gill (1t, 3g);
Kenny (1t), M. Ford; Courtney, Kiss, Case
(Campbell), West, Dunn, Potter
Hull 24 Kemble; James (1t), S. Evans (1t),
Leuluai (2t), O'Hara (Schofield); Ah Kuoi,
Sterling; Crooks (2g), Patrick, Puckering
(Divorty 1t), Muggleton, Rose, Norton
Referee: R. Campbell (Widnes)

THE LANCE TODD TROPHY

The Lance Todd Trophy is presented to the Man of the Match in the Rugby League Challenge Cup Final, the decision being reached by a ballot of members of the Rugby League Writers' Association present at the game.

Lance Todd made his name in Britain as a player with Wigan and as manager of Salford. His untimely death in a road accident on the return journey from a game at Oldham was commemorated by the introduction of the Lance Todd Trophy.

The award was instituted by Australian-born Harry Sunderland, Warrington director Bob Anderton and Yorkshire journalist John Bapty.

Around 1950, the Red Devils' Association at Salford, comprising players and officials who had worked with Todd, raised sufficient funds to provide a trophy and replica for each winner.

The trophy is now sponsored by brewers Greenall Whitley, who help to finance the annual dinner and trophy presentation at the Willows, Salford.

Gerry Helme, of Warrington, is the only player to win the trophy twice; Len Killeen, of St. Helens, is the only winger to earn the title; Hull's Tommy Harris the only hooker; and Ray Ashby and Brian Gabbitas the only players to share the honour.

Following the 1954 replay, it was decided by the Red Devils that in future the trophy would be awarded for the Wembley game. In 1954, Gerry Helme had received the trophy for his performance in the Odsal replay.

The 1986 winner was Castleford scrum half Bob Beardmore, scorer of a try and drop goal.

Lance Todd Trophy winner Bob Beardmore, mobbed by Castleford teammates after scoring a vital 43rd minute try to add to his first half drop goal. Congratulations from, left to right, skipper John Joyner, Barry Johnson and Keith England.

The Lance Todd Trophy Roll of Honour

Year	Winner	Team	Position
1946	Billy Stott	Wakefield Trinity (v Wigan)	Centre
1947	Willie Davies	Bradford Northern (v Leeds)	Stand off
1948	Frank Whitcombe	Bradford Northern (v Wigan)	Prop
1949	Ernest Ward	Bradford Northern (v Halifax)	Centre
1950	Gerry Helme	Warrington (v Widnes)	Scrum half
1951	Cec Mountford	Wigan (v Barrow)	Stand off
1952	Billy Ivison	Workington T. (v Featherstone R.)	Loose forward
1953	Peter Ramsden	Huddersfield (v St. Helens)	Stand off
1954	Gerry Helme	Warrington (v Halifax)	Scrum half
1955	Jack Grundy	Barrow (v Workington Town)	Second row
1956	Alan Prescott	St. Helens (v Halifax)	Prop
1957	Jeff Stevenson	Leeds (v Barrow)	Scrum half
1958	Rees Thomas	Wigan (v Workington Town)	Scrum half
1959	Brian McTigue	Wigan (v Hull)	Second row
1960	Tommy Harris	Hull (v Wakefield Trinity)	Hooker
1961	Dick Huddart	St. Helens (v Wigan)	Second row
1962	Neil Fox	Wakefield Trinity (v Huddersfield)	Centre
1963	Harold Poynton	Wakefield Trinity (v Wigan)	Stand off
1964	Frank Collier	Widnes (v Hull K.R.)	Prop
1965	Ray Ashby	Wigan	Full back
	Brian Gabbitas	Hunslet	Stand off
1966	Len Killeen	St. Helens (v Wigan)	Winger
1967	Carl Dooler	Featherstone Rovers (v Barrow)	Scrum half
1968	Don Fox	Wakefield Trinity (v Leeds)	Prop
1969	Malcolm Reilly	Castleford (v Salford)	Loose forward
1970	Bill Kirkbride	Castleford (v Wigan)	Second row
1971	Alex Murphy	Leigh (v Leeds)	Scrum half
1972	Kel Coslett	St. Helens (v Leeds)	Loose forward
1973	Steve Nash	Featherstone R. (v Bradford N.)	Scrum half
1974	Derek Whitehead	Warrington (v Featherstone Rovers)	Full back
1975	Ray Dutton	Widnes (v Warrington)	Full back
1976	Geoff Pimblett	St. Helens (v Widnes)	Full back
1977	Steve Pitchford	Leeds (v Widnes)	Prop
1978	George Nicholls	St. Helens (v Leeds)	Second row
1979	David Topliss	Wakefield Trinity (v Widnes)	Stand off
1980	Brian Lockwood	Hull K.R. (v Hull)	Prop
1981	Mick Burke	Widnes (v Hull K.R.)	Full back
1982	Eddie Cunningham	Widnes (v Hull)	Centre
1983	David Hobbs	Featherstone Rovers (v Hull)	Second row
1984	Joe Lydon	Widnes (v Wigan)	Centre
1985	Brett Kenny	Wigan (v Hull)	Stand off
1986	Bob Beardmore	Castleford (v Hull K.R.)	Scrum half

CHALLENGE CUP RECORDS

ALL ROUNDS

TEAM

Highest score:
Huddersfield 119 v. *Swinton Park 2. 1914

INDIVIDUAL

Most goals in a match:
22 by Jim Sullivan (Wigan) v. *Flimby and Fothergill
. . . . 1925

Most tries in a match:
11 by George West (Hull K.R.) v. *Brookland Rovers
. . . . 1905

Most points in a match:
53 (11t,10g) by George West (Hull K.R.) as above.

*Amateur teams

FINAL RECORDS

TEAM

Most wins: 10 by Leeds

Most finals: 17 by Wigan

Highest score:
Wakefield T. 38 v. Hull 5. 1960

Widest margin:
Huddersfield 37 v. St. Helens 3. 1915

Biggest attendance:
102,569 Warrington v. Halifax (Replay) at Bradford
. . . . 1954

INDIVIDUAL

Most goals:
8 by Cyril Kellett (Featherstone R.) v. Bradford N.
. . . . 1973

Most tries:
3 by Bob Wilson (Broughton R.) v. Salford. . . . 1902
Stan Moorhouse (Huddersfield) v. Warrington. 1913
Tom Holliday (Oldham) v. Swinton. 1927

Most points:
20 (7g,2t) by Neil Fox (Wakefield T.) v. Hull. . . 1960

WEMBLEY FACTS

WIGAN made a record 13th appearance at Wembley in the 1985 final against Hull, recording their seventh victory at the stadium to equal the Widnes record set a year earlier.

A RECORD 10 overseas players trod the Wembley turf in 1985. Hull fielded six — a record for one club. The Airlie Birds sextet were Australians Peter Sterling and John Muggleton, plus New Zealanders Gary Kemble, James Leuluai, Dane O'Hara and Fred Ah Kuoi. Wigan added Australians John Ferguson and Brett Kenny together with New Zealanders Graeme West and Danny Campbell, who went on as substitute. South African Nick Du Toit was substitute back but did not play.

THE 1985 aggregates of 10 tries and 52 points were both record totals for a Challenge Cup final with Hull's 24 points the most by a losing side. There were also 10 tries in the 1915 final when Huddersfield beat St. Helens 37-3, which is the widest margin. Wakefield Trinity ran up the highest Cup final score when they beat Hull 38-5 in 1960.

WORLD RECORD receipts of £806,676 were taken at the 1986 Final between Castleford and Hull K.R., from a crowd of 82,134.

FIVE players share the record of playing in four Cup-winning sides at Wembley — Alex Murphy, Brian Lockwood, Eric Hughes, Keith Elwell and Mick Adams.
  Murphy was in St. Helens' victorious side of 1961 and as captain led St. Helens (1966), Leigh (1971) and Warrington (1974) to victory. He played in three different positions — stand off, centre and scrum half. Murphy was a scorer in each final with a total of five drop goals and a try.
  Brian Lockwood was in the winning final teams of Castleford (1969 and 1970), Hull K.R. (1980) and Widnes (1981). He also appeared with Widnes in the drawn final of 1982.
  Hughes, Elwell and Adams each played in the Widnes teams that won the Cup in 1975, 1979, 1981 and 1984. They also appeared in the drawn final of 1982.

THE Widnes trio of Eric Hughes, Keith Elwell and Mick Adams also hold the record for most appearances at Wembley . . . seven. In addition to the five finals mentioned above they were on the losing side in 1976 and 1977.

ERIC ASHTON captained a record six teams at Wembley — Wigan in 1958, 1959, 1961, 1963, 1965 and 1966. His record of three wins (in 1958, 1959, 1965) is shared with Derek Turner (Wakefield Trinity 1960, 1962, 1963) and Alex Murphy (St. Helens 1966, Leigh 1971 and Warrington 1974).

THE YOUNGEST player to appear in a Wembley Cup final was Shaun Edwards who was 17 years, 6 months and 19 days when he played full back for Wigan against Widnes in 1984.

THE OLDEST at Wembley was Gus Risman, who at 41 years 29 days led Workington Town to victory over Featherstone Rovers in 1952. He played full back.

THE TALLEST player at Wembley was New Zealand Test star Graeme West who captained Wigan in the 1984 and 1985 finals. He measured 6ft. 5in.

SCHOOLBOYS who have appeared in an Under-11 curtain-raiser at Wembley and gone on to play in the major final at the stadium are Joe Lydon, David Hulme, Mike Ford, Neil Puckering and David Plange. Lydon became the first to achieve the feat with Widnes in the 1984 final against Wigan, followed by Hulme who went on as a 72nd minute substitute. Both had played in the first schoolboys' curtain-raiser in 1975 — Lydon for Wigan, and Hulme for Widnes. Ford played scrum half for Wigan in the 1985 final having represented Oldham in the 1977 curtain-raiser. Puckering played for Hull in the 1977 curtain-raiser and for his home town club in the Challenge Cup final of 1985. Plange was in the Hull Schools team of 1976 and played for Castleford in the 1986 final.

CYRIL KELLETT holds the record for most goals in a Challenge Cup final with his eight for Featherstone Rovers in 1973.

In the most remarkable exhibition of kicking seen at Wembley, the veteran full back was successful with every one of his attempts as Bradford Northern crashed 33-14.

Nine years earlier he scored only one for Hull Kingston Rovers in the 13-5 defeat by Widnes.

NEIL FOX — the record aggregate points scorer of all time — piled up the most points in a Challenge Cup final in 1960. His 20 points helped Wakefield Trinity to a 38-5 defeat of Hull. Fox's points came from two tries and seven goals.

His three drop goals for Trinity in the 12-6 victory over Huddersfield two years later was another extraordinary feat in the days when the drop goal was a rarity.

NO player has scored a hat trick of tries at Wembley, the feat being achieved only three times in the preceding era.

The last to do it was Oldham winger Tom Holliday in the 26-7 defeat of Swinton in 1927.

Bob Wilson, the Broughton Rangers centre and captain, was the first to score three tries, in the 25-0 victory over Salford in 1902.

In between, Stan Moorhouse's three-try feat accounted for all of Huddersfield's points when they beat Warrington 9-5 in 1913. Moorhouse was winger to Harold Wagstaff, recognised as the greatest centre of all time.

MANY great players have gone through an entire career without achieving their ambition of playing at Wembley. Hull's Mike Smith achieved it in his first senior game.

Smith made one of the most remarkable debuts in sporting history when he played in the second row of an injury-hit Boulevard side against Wakefield Trinity in 1960.

In contrast, Freddie Miller signed for Hull in 1932 and

David Hulme, the second of a quintet of under-11 curtain raiser stars to graduate to a senior Wembley appearance.

did not play at Wembley until 1952 ... two years after joining Featherstone Rovers.

A NOTABLE Wembley captain was Gus Risman who led two clubs to victory ... 14 years apart.

He was captain of Salford when they beat Barrow in 1938. At 41, he led Workington Town to their triumph over Featherstone Rovers in 1952.

PROBABLY the unluckiest Challenge Cup finalist was Dai Davies who appeared in four finals and was on the losing side each time.

Three of those occasions were at Wembley with different clubs. He was a loser with Warrington (1933), Huddersfield (1935) and Keighley (1937).

Before the Wembley era he was also in Warrington's beaten team of 1928.

Steve Norton has played at Wembley four times and has yet to be on the winning side. He was in the beaten Hull teams of 1980, 1983 and 1985 in addition to playing in the 1982 drawn final. In 1970 he was a non-playing substitute for Castleford who won the Cup.

Bill Ramsey was on the losing side in four Wembley finals but gained a winner's medal with Leeds in 1968. He picked up losers' medals with Hunslet (1965), Leeds (1971 and 1972) and Widnes (1977).

A TOTAL of 13 current clubs have yet to play at Wembley .... Batley, Blackpool Borough, Bramley, Carlisle, Doncaster, Fulham, Mansfield Marksman, Oldham, Rochdale Hornets, Runcorn Highfield, Sheffield Eagles, Swinton and Whitehaven.

Fate seems to be against Swinton and Oldham. In the five years preceding the move to Wembley, one or the other appeared in the final, twice meeting each other.

Oldham played in four successive finals in that period. Swinton's run of three finals ended when the first Wembley final took place in 1929.

They did get through to the final again three years later .... only for it to be played at Wigan!

CHALLENGE CUP

Wembley Era Semi-Finals

It is generally felt that it is better to have played at Wembley and lost than never to have played there at all. This makes the semi-final stage of the RL Challenge Cup almost as important as the final with no consolation for the losers.

Of the 13 current clubs who have never appeared at Wembley four have been beaten semi-finalists. They are Oldham (four times), Swinton, Rochdale Hornets (twice) and Whitehaven.

Probably the unluckiest are Oldham. They have reached the penultimate stage four times without being able to realise their ambition. Oldham almost made it in 1964. After drawing 5-5 with Hull K.R. they were winning 17-14 in extra time of the replay when bad light stopped play and they were beaten in the third game.

Swinton did win a semi-final in 1932 but the final that year was switched from Wembley to Wigan!

There have been three occasions when Yorkshire has provided all four semi-finalists in one year — in 1962, 1973 and 1983. Only once have all four semi-finalists come from west of the Pennines — in 1930.

Until 1962 the two semi-finals were always played on the same Saturday, but with four Yorkshire clubs competing for the first time it was decided to play one mid-week. Both matches were played at Odsal Stadium, Bradford. The first was on a Wednesday evening — without floodlights — when 43,625 saw Wakefield Trinity beat Featherstone Rovers and on the following Saturday there were 31,423 to see Huddersfield beat Hull K.R.

The following year both semi-finals were again played on the same Saturday, but since then they have been staged on different Saturdays.

Some semi-final facts during the Wembley era are:

Biggest attendance: 69,898 Warrington v. Leeds at Bradford in 1950

Biggest aggregate: 104,453 in 1939 (Only other six-figure aggregate was 102,080 in 1951)

Record receipts: £113,345 Hull K.R. v. Leeds replay at Elland Road, Leeds, in 1986

Lowest attendance: 7,971 Featherstone R. v. Leigh at Leeds in 1974

Highest score and widest margin: Huddersfield 30 v. Leeds 8 in 1933

CHALLENGE CUP SEMI-FINALS

Year	Winners		Runners-up		Venue	Attendance	Receipts
1929	Dewsbury	9	Castleford	3	Huddersfield	25,000	£1,562
	Wigan	7	St. Helens Recs.	7	Swinton	31,000	£2,209
Replay	Wigan	13	St. Helens Recs.	12	Leigh	21,940	£1,437
1930	Widnes	10	Barrow	3	Warrington	25,500	£1,630
	St. Helens	5	Wigan	5	Swinton	37,169	£2,666
Replay	St. Helens	22	Wigan	10	Leigh	24,000	£1,657
1931	Halifax	11	St. Helens	2	Rochdale	21,674	£1,498
	York	15	Warrington	5	Leeds	32,419	£2,329
1932	Leeds	2	Halifax	2	Huddersfield	31,818	£2,456
Replay	Leeds	9	Halifax	2	Wakefield	21,000	£1,417
	Swinton	7	Wakefield T.	4	Rochdale	21,273	£1,369
●	*Final was played at Wigan, not Wembley*						
1933	Huddersfield	30	Leeds	8	Wakefield	36,359	£2,299
	Warrington	11	St. Helens	5	Swinton	30,373	£2,055

Year	Winners		Runners-up		Venue	Attendance	Receipts
1934	Hunslet	12	Huddersfield	7	Wakefield	27,450	£1,797
	Widnes	7	Oldham	4	Swinton	17,577	£1,050
1935	Castleford	11	Barrow	5	Swinton	24,469	£1,534
	Huddersfield	21	Hull	5	Leeds	37,111	£2,753
1936	Leeds	10	Huddersfield	5	Wakefield	37,906	£2,456
	Warrington	7	Salford	2	Wigan	41,538	£2,796
1937	Keighley	0	Wakefield T.	0	Leeds	39,998	£2,793
Replay	Keighley	5	Wakefield T.	3	Huddersfield	14,400	£1,052
	Widnes	13	Wigan	9	Warrington	29,260	£1,972
1938	Barrow	4	Halifax	2	Huddersfield	31,384	£2,431
	Salford	6	Swinton	0	Belle Vue, Manchester	31,664	£2,396
1939	Halifax	10	Leeds	4	Bradford	64,453	£3,645
	Salford	11	Wigan	2	Rochdale	40,000	£2,154
●	*During the war the semi-finals were two-legged and the finals were not played at Wembley*						
1946	Wakefield T.	7	Hunslet	3	Leeds	33,000	£4,991
	Wigan	12	Widnes	5	Swinton	36,976	£4,746
1947	Bradford N.	11	Warrington	7	Swinton	33,474	£4,946
	Leeds	21	Wakefield T.	0	Huddersfield	35,136	£6,339
1948	Bradford N.	14	Hunslet	7	Leeds	38,125	£7,437
	Wigan	11	Rochdale H.	0	Swinton	26,004	£4,206
1949	Bradford N.	10	Barrow	0	Swinton	26,572	£4,646
	Halifax	11	Huddersfield	10	Bradford	61,875	£8,638
1950	Warrington	16	Leeds	4	Bradford	69,898	£9,861
	Widnes	8	Bradford N.	0	Wigan	25,390	£3,936
1951	Barrow	14	Leeds	14	Bradford	57,459	£8,248
Replay	Barrow	28	Leeds	13	Huddersfield	31,078	£5,098
	Wigan	3	Warrington	2	Swinton	44,621	£7,358
1952	Featherstone R.	6	Leigh	2	Leeds	35,621	£6,494
	Workington T.	5	Barrow	2	Wigan	31,206	£4,782
1953	Huddersfield	7	Wigan	0	Bradford	58,722	£10,519
	St. Helens	9	Warrington	3	Swinton	38,059	£7,768
1954	Halifax	18	Hunslet	3	Bradford	46,961	£8,243
	Warrington	8	Leeds	4	Swinton	36,993	£7,596
1955	Barrow	9	Hunslet	6	Wigan	25,493	£4,671
	Workington T.	13	Featherstone R.	2	Leeds	33,499	£7,305
1956	Halifax	11	Wigan	10	Bradford	51,889	£9,054
	St. Helens	5	Barrow	5	Swinton	38,897	£7,793
Replay	St. Helens	10	Barrow	5	Wigan	44,731	£7,750
1957	Barrow	2	Leigh	2	Wigan	34,628	£6,340
Replay	Barrow	15	Leigh	10	Swinton	28,081	£5,695
	Leeds	10	Whitehaven	9	Bradford	49,094	£8,987
1958	Wigan	5	Rochdale H.	3	Swinton	28,597	£6,354
	Workington T.	8	Featherstone R.	2	Bradford	31,517	£6,325
1959	Wigan	5	Leigh	0	Swinton	27,906	£6,068
	Hull	15	Featherstone R.	5	Bradford	52,131	£9,776
1960	Wakefield T.	11	Featherstone R.	2	Bradford	55,935	£10,390
	Hull	12	Oldham	9	Swinton	27,545	£6,093
1961	St. Helens	26	Hull	9	Bradford	42,935	£9,231
	Wigan	19	Halifax	10	Swinton	35,118	£7,557

Year	Winners		Runners-up		Venue	Attendance	Receipts
1962	Wakefield T.	9	Featherstone R.	0	Bradford	43,625	£8,496
	Huddersfield	6	Hull K.R.	0	Bradford	31,423	£6,685
1963	Wakefield T.	5	Warrington	2	Swinton	15,565	£3,530
	Wigan	18	Hull K.R.	4	Leeds	21,420	£6,029
1964	Widnes	7	Castleford	7	Swinton	25,603	£5,541
Replay	Widnes	7	Castleford	5	Wakefield	28,739	£5,313
	Hull K.R.	5	Oldham	5	Leeds	28,823	£7,411
Replay	Hull K.R.	14	Oldham	17	Swinton	27,209	£5,929

● *Score after 80 minutes was 14-14, then bad light caused match to be abandoned after 12 minutes of extra time with Oldham winning 17-14*

Year	Winners		Runners-up		Venue	Attendance	Receipts
Second Replay	Hull K.R.	12	Oldham	2	Huddersfield	28,732	£6,183
1965	Wigan	25	Swinton	10	St. Helens	26,658	£6,384
	Hunslet	8	Wakefield T.	0	Leeds	21,262	£6,090
1966	St. Helens	12	Dewsbury	5	Swinton	13,046	£3,102
	Wigan	7	Leeds	2	Huddersfield	22,758	£5,971
1967	Featherstone R.	16	Leeds	8	Huddersfield	20,052	£6,276
	Barrow	14	Dewsbury	9	Swinton	13,744	£4,560
1968	Leeds	25	Wigan	4	Swinton	30,058	£9,845
	Wakefield T.	0	Huddersfield	0	Bradford	21,569	£6,196
Replay	Wakefield T.	15	Huddersfield	10	Leeds	20,983	£6,425
1969	Castleford	16	Wakefield T.	10	Leeds	21,497	£8,477
	Salford	15	Warrington	8	Wigan	20,600	£7,738
1970	Castleford	6	St. Helens	3	Swinton	18,913	£7,171
	Wigan	19	Hull K.R.	8	Leeds	18,495	£7,862
1971	Leeds	19	Castleford	8	Bradford	24,464	£9,120
	Leigh	10	Huddersfield	4	Wigan	14,875	£5,670
1972	St. Helens	10	Warrington	10	Wigan	19,300	£8,250
Replay	St. Helens	10	Warrington	6	Wigan	32,380	£12,604
	Leeds	16	Halifax	3	Bradford	16,680	£6,851
1973	Featherstone R.	17	Castleford	3	Leeds	15,369	£9,454
	Bradford N.	23	Dewsbury	7	Leeds	14,028	£9,221
1974	Warrington	17	Dewsbury	7	Wigan	11,789	£6,821
	Featherstone R.	21	Leigh	14	Leeds	7,971	£4,461
1975	Widnes	13	Wakefield T.	7	Bradford	9,155	£5,856
	Warrington	11	Leeds	4	Wigan	13,168	£9,581
1976	Widnes	15	Featherstone R.	9	Swinton	13,019	£9,078
	St. Helens	5	Keighley	4	Huddersfield	9,829	£6,113
1977	Leeds	7	St. Helens	2	Wigan	12,974	£11,379
	Widnes	14	Hull K.R.	5	Leeds	17,053	£16,068
1978	Leeds	14	Featherstone R.	9	Bradford	12,824	£11,322
	St. Helens	12	Warrington	8	Wigan	16,167	£13,960
1979	Widnes	14	Bradford N.	11	Swinton	14,324	£16,363
	Wakefield T.	9	St. Helens	7	Leeds	12,393	£14,195
1980	Hull K.R.	20	Halifax	7	Leeds	17,910	£31,650
	Hull	10	Widnes	5	Swinton	18,347	£29,415
1981	Widnes	17	Warrington	9	Wigan	12,624	£20,673
	Hull K.R.	22	St. Helens	5	Leeds	17,073	£30,616
1982	Hull	15	Castleford	11	Leeds	21,207	£41,867
	Widnes	11	Leeds	8	Swinton	13,075	£25,796

Year	Winners		Runners-up		Venue	Attendance	Receipts
1983	Featherstone R.	11	Bradford N.	6	Leeds	10,784	£22,579
	Hull	14	Castleford	7	Elland Rd., L'ds	26,031	£65,498
1984	Wigan	14	York	8	Elland Rd., L'ds	17,156	£52,888
	Widnes	15	Leeds	4	Swinton	14,046	£37,183
1985	Wigan	18	Hull K.R.	11	Elland Rd., L'ds	19,275	£70,192
	Hull	10	Castleford	10	Leeds	20,982	£64,163
Replay	Hull	22	Castleford	16	Leeds	20,968	£65,005
1986	Castleford	18	Oldham	7	Wigan	12,430	£38,296
	Hull K.R.	24	Leeds	24	Elland Rd., L'ds	23,866	£83,757
Replay	Hull K.R.	17	Leeds	0	Elland Rd., L'ds	32,485	£113,345

NON-LEAGUE CLUBS IN THE CHALLENGE CUP

AMATEUR clubs were invited to compete in the 1986 Rugby League Challenge Cup after a five-year break. The League asked for two of the three county cup competition winners to enter the preliminary round. Cumbria Cup winners Kells were given a bye into the draw for the preliminary round, while Yorkshire victors Dudley Hill met Lancashire winners Simms Cross at Bramley in an eliminator, the White Rose side going through.

The Council later decided that in the 1987 Silk Cut Challenge Cup campaign there would be 38 participating teams, the appropriate number of amateur clubs joining the current tally of professional outfits.

In the early years of the Northern Union Challenge Cup — as it was then called — the line between professional and amateurs was less clearly defined.

A variety of Leagues also make it difficult to set non-League clubs apart. Fifty-six clubs appeared in the inaugurating first round of 1897 and four others received byes. The complications continued until 1904 when the League format settled down and non-League clubs had to qualify for the first round.

Not since 1909 when BEVERLEY beat Ebbw Vale 7-2 had a senior team been knocked out by a non-League club although amateur teams twice had victories in the two-leg era of 1946-54.

RECORDS OF NON-LEAGUE CLUBS IN THE RUGBY LEAGUE CHALLENGE CUP SINCE 1904
(Excluding preliminary rounds)
Non-League Clubs in Capitals

Victories over Senior Clubs

1905-06
*FEATHERSTONE ROVERS 23 v. Widnes 2
(second round)

1907-08
WHITEHAVEN RECREATION 13 v. St. Helens 8
(Lost 33-5 at Merthyr Tydfil in second round)

1908-09
BEVERLEY 7 v. Ebbw Vale 2
(Lost 53-2 at Halifax in second round)

1945-46
SHARLSTON 12 v. Workington Town 7
(1st leg) (Workington Town won 2nd leg 16-2)

1947-48
RISEHOW and GILLHEAD 10 v. Keighley 2 (2nd leg)
(Keighley won 1st leg 11-0)

*FEATHERSTONE ROVERS are the only non-League club to appear in the third round when they lost 3-0 at Keighley. In the first round they beat BROOKLAND ROVERS 16-5.

There have been several other instances of non-League clubs meeting in the first round. The last occasion was in 1960 when WALNEY CENTRAL beat LOCK LANE 10-5 before losing at Oldham 55-4 in the second round.

In 1964 THAMES BOARD MILLS received a bye when Bradford Northern disbanded, but lost 48-8 at Blackpool Borough in the second round.

Draws against Senior Clubs

1905-06   VICTORIA RANGERS 0 v. Widnes 0
Widnes won replay 8-3

1906-07   WORKINGTON 3 v. Wakefield Trinity 3
Wakefield Trinity won replay 16-5

1907-08   WIGAN HIGHFIELD 3 v. Bramley 3
Bramley won replay 8-6

1911-12   NORMANTON ST. JOHN'S 6 v. Warrington 6
Warrington won replay 75-0

1921-22   Widnes 5 v. WIGAN HIGHFIELD 5
Widnes won replay 9-4

1951-52   RYLAND RECS 9 v. Whitehaven 9 (2nd leg)
Whitehaven won first leg 16-0

RECORD SCORES

Team

Huddersfield 119 v. SWINTON PARK 2 (1913-14)

● This is the highest score in any competitive match in England.

Non-League teams have provided other sides with club records as follows:

Hull K.R.   73 v. BROOKLAND ROVERS 5 (1905)
Rochdale H. 75 v. BROUGHTON MOOR 13 (1915)
Wigan   116 v. FLIMBY & FOTHERGILL 0
                                        (1925)
Barrow   83 v. MARYPORT 3 (1938)
Blackpool B. 48 v. THAMES BOARD MILLS 8 (1964)
St. Helens 73 v. WARDLEY 0 (1924 at Swinton)

All told, non-League clubs have conceded 50 points or more on 41 occasions but none after 1973-74 (B.A.R.L.A.'s first season).
The lowest score by a senior club was in the 0-0 draw between VICTORIA RANGERS and Widnes in 1906.

Individual

Most tries and points:
11 tries (10g) 53 points by George West (Hull K.R.) v. BROOKLAND ROVERS (1905)

Most goals:
22 by Jim Sullivan (Wigan) v. FLIMBY & FOTHERGILL (1925)

● All three feats are records for any competitive matches in England.

HIGHEST NON-LEAGUE SCORES

FEATHERSTONE ROVERS 23 v. Widnes 2
(second round 1906)

Only other 20 score:

LATCHFORD ALBION 20 v. Wigan 40 (1st leg 1954)
Wigan won second leg 41-2

PILKINGTON RECS. 22 v. Castleford 23 (1978)

NON-LEAGUE CLUBS YEAR-BY-YEAR CUP RECORD

● Non-League clubs in block capitals and all first round ties other than where stated.

1903-04	Broughton R. 26 v. PARTON 0
	Salford 57 v. BROOKLAND ROVERS 0
1904-05	Hull 52 v. LEIGH SHAMROCKS 0
	Hull KR 73 v. BROOKLAND ROVERS 5
	Hunslet 22 v. PARTON 3
	Leeds 20 v. OSSETT 0
	St. Helens 9 v. ROCHDALE R. 2
1905-06	EGERTON 9 v. LEIGH SHAMROCKS 0
	FEATHERSTONE ROVERS 16 v.
	BROOKLAND ROVERS 5
	Keighley 13 v. EGREMONT 0
	VICTORIA RANGERS 0 v. Widnes 0
	Replay
	Widnes 8 v. VICTORIA RANGERS 3
	Second round
	FEATHERSTONE ROVERS 23 v. Widnes 2
	Salford 38 v. EGERTON 5
	Third round
	Keighley 3 v. FEATHERSTONE ROVERS 0
1906-07	Halifax 45 v. MILLOM 0
	Huddersfield 38 v.
	BRIGHOUSE ST JAMES 0
	Keighley 18 v. BROOKLAND ROVERS 0
	RADCLIFFE RANGERS 0 v. York 13
	WHITEHAVEN REC 10 v.
	SAVILLE GREEN 0
	WORKINGTON 3 v. Wakefield T. 3
	Replay
	Wakefield T. 16 v. WORKINGTON 5
	Second round
	WHITEHAVEN REC 0 v. Keighley 14
1907-08	Barrow 28 v. MILLOM 5
	Batley 32 v. BARROW ST GEORGE 5
	BEVERLEY 3 v. Merthyr Tydfil 15
	HALF-ACRE TRINITY 2 v. York 7
	WHITEHAVEN REC 13 v. St. Helens 8
	WIGAN HIGHFIELD 3 v. Bramley 3
	Replay
	Bramley 8 v. WIGAN HIGHFIELD 6
	Second round
	Merthyr Tydfil 33 v.
	WHITEHAVEN REC 5
1908-09	Barrow 36 v. BARROW ST GOERGE 0
	BEVERLEY 7 v. Ebbw Vale 2
	NORMANTON 10 v. Hull 20
	Runcorn 23 v. EGREMONT 5
	PEMBERTON 6 v. Keighley 41
	Second round
	Halifax 53 v. BEVERLEY 2

1909-10 MILLOM 9 v. BROOKLAND ROVERS 4
PURSTON WHITE HORSE 10 v.
Halifax 23
Salford 64 v. YORK IRISH
NATIONAL LEAGUE 0
Warrington 31 v. WIGAN HIGHFIELD 3
Second round
Warrington 37 v. MILLOM 0

1910-11 BROUGHTON MOOR 6 v. Runcorn 23
Dewsbury 47 v. YORK GROVE UNITED 0
NORMANTON ST. JOHN'S 6 v.
Broughton R. 10
PEMBERTON 4 v. Bradford N.12
Widnes 23 v. LANE END UNITED 0

1911-12 BEVERLEY 5 v. Hull KR 34
Dewsbury 36 v. LANE END UNITED 9
MILLOM 0 v. Keighley 11
NORMANTON ST. JOHN'S 6 v.
Warrington 6
Replay
Warrington 75 v.
NORMANTON ST. JOHN'S 0
Wigan 35 v. WIGAN HIGHFIELD 10

1912-13 Bradford N 33 v. PEMBERTON 4
Broughton R 59 v. BARTON 0
ELLAND 2 v. Wakefield T 15
Hull 24 v. SEATON 2
NORMANTON ST. JOHN'S 4 v.
Oldham 17
Rochdale H. 15 v.
FEATHERSTONE ROVERS 3

1913-14 CASTLEFORD 8 v. Wigan 27
ELLAND 2 v.
FEATHERSTONE ROVERS 7
Huddersfield 119 v. SWINTON PARK 2
Hull KR 62 v. MILLOM 0
St. Helens 27 v. WIGAN HIGHFIELD 4
York 45 v. GLASSON RANGERS 0
Second round
FEATHERSTONE ROVERS 3 v. Hull 27

1914-15 BRIGHOUSE RANGERS 0 v.
Salford 26
BROUGHTON MOOR 6 v. WARDLEY 3
FEATHERSTONE ROVERS 0 v.
St Helens 6
Keighley 8 v. ASKHAM 5
WIGAN HIGHFIELD 0 v. Swinton 2
Second round
Rochdale H 75 v. BROUGHTON MOOR 13

1919-20 Bramley 13 v. WIGAN HIGHFIELD 0
FEATHERSTONE ROVERS 2 v.
Broughton R 17
Halifax 55 v. BROOKLAND ROVERS 0
Hull 75 v. BRITISH OIL & CAKE MILLS 2
Leeds 44 v. MILLOM 5
Warrington 9 v. ASKHAM-in-FURNESS 0
Wigan 64 v. HEALEY STREET ADULTS 3

1920-21 ASKHAM 2 v. Bradford N 7
FEATHERSTONE ROVERS 41 v.
PENDLEBURY 0
Oldham 41 v. ELLAND WANDERERS 5
Swinton 25 v. BRITISH OIL &
CAKE MILLS 5
Widnes 41 v. DEARHAM WANDERERS 5
WIGAN HIGHFIELD 10 v. Broughton R 15
Second round
FEATHERSTONE ROVERS 0 v.
Dewsbury 22

1921-22 ASKHAM 15 v. CADISHEAD 5
ELLAND WANDERERS 0 v. Oldham 29
Rochdale H 54 v. BROUGHTON MOOR 2
Swinton 24 v. BRITISH OIL &
CAKE MILLS 5
Widnes 5 v. WIGAN HIGHFIELD 5
Replay
WIGAN HIGHFIELD 4 v. Widnes 9
Second round
Keighley 15 v. ASKHAM 0

1922-23 NORWOOD 3 v. St. Helens 29
Salford 16 v. CASTLEFORD 0
Wakefield T 67 v HENSINGHAM 13
Wigan Highfield 16 v.
CADISHEAD & IRLAM 0
York 40 v. MILLOM 0

1923-24 Barrow 67 v. DEARHAM WANDERERS 3
Broughton R 34 v. HULL ST. PATRICK'S 0
WARDLEY 0 v. St. Helens 73
Warrington 46 v. DALTON 3
Hull KR 24 v. CASTLEFORD 0

1924-25 BARNSLEY UNITED (Hull) 3 v.
DALTON 3
Hunslet 25 v. CASTLEFORD 0
Leeds 27 v. TWELVE APOSTLES 0
Wigan 116 v. FLIMBY & FOTHERGILL 0
Replay
DALTON 3 v.
BARNSLEY UNITED (Hull) 2
Second round
St. Helens Rec 74 v. DALTON 5

1925-26	Barrow 44 v. BARROW CAMBRIDGE ST. 0 CASTLEFORD 12 v. St. Helens Rec 18 HENSINGHAM 0 v. Huddersfield 33 Hull 27 v. PEMBERTON ROVERS 3 Hull KR 28 v. BARNSLEY UNITED (Hull) 0
1926-27	Batley 32 v. COTTINGHAM 5 Dewsbury 20 v. DEARHAM WANDERERS 5 Wigan 51 v. PEMBERTON ROVERS 11
1927-28	Batley 31 v. COTTINGHAM 2 Bradford N 17 v. TWELVE APOSTLES 0 Warrington 43 v. KINSLEY 2 WHITEHAVEN REC 0 v. Swinton 44
1928-29	Castleford 31 v. WHITEHAVEN REC 7 Dewsbury 37 v. COTTINGHAM 0 St Helens 32 v. LINDLEY 2 Wigan Highfield 45 v. UNO'S DABS 0
1929-30	Halifax 74 v. FEATHERSTONE JUNIORS 9 Hull 44 v. BICKERSHAW HORNETS 10 Keighley 6 v. GREAT CLIFTON 5 Leigh 48 v. COTTINGHAM 0
1930-31	Bramley 7 v. GOLDEN LIONS 3 Huddersfield 60 v. BROOKLAND ROVERS 2 LINDLEY 2 v. Rochdale H 13 Wigan Highfield 41 v. FEATHERSTONE JUNIORS 3
1931-32	Barrow 65 v. LINDLEY 5 Dewsbury 27 v. UNO's DABS 10 GREAT CLIFTON 2 v. Broughton R 20
1932-33	ASKERN WELFARE 0 v. Wigan 46 Halifax 42 v. UNO's DABS 5 Hull 37 v. HIGGINSHAW 9 York 35 v. BARROW MARSH HORNETS 6
1933-34	Bramley 20 v. DEARHAM WANDERERS 11 Hull KR 18 v. WIGAN RANGERS 2 London Highfield 32 v. HULL ST MARY'S 2 St. Helens Rec 32 v. PENDLEBURY JUNIORS 3
1934-35	Barrow 28 v. SHARLSTON 3 Castleford 33 v. ASTLEY & TYLDESLEY COLLIERIES 4 MANCHESTER SHIP CANAL 9 v. Dewsbury 28 Rochdale H. 28 v. BARROW MARSH HORNETS 18
1935-36	Leigh 49 v. SEATON 4 Oldham 38 v. HIGGINSHAW 2
1936-37	GOOLE 2 v. Broughton Rangers 14 Widnes 39 v. HIGGINSHAW 2
1937-38	Rochdale H 50 v. GLASSHOUGHTON 2 St. Helens 39 v. PENDLEBURY 0 Barrow 83 v. MARYPORT 3
1938-39	Bradford N 37 v. SEATON 7 SHARLSTON 5 v. Bramley 23 Hunslet 48 v. UNITED GLASS BLOWERS 5 Swinton 46 v. HIGGINSHAW 3
1945-46	HULL JUNIORS 0 v. Bramley 29 Bramley 51 v. HULL JUNIORS 3 Hull KR 18 v. LANGWORTHY JUNIORS 0 LANGWORTHY JUNIORS 7 v. Hull KR 14 KELLS 0 v. Warrington 3 Warrington 27 v. KELLS 0 HIGHER INCE 3 v. Widnes 30 Widnes 42 v. HIGHER INCE 3 SHARLSTON 12 v. Workington Town 7 Workington Town 16 v. SHARLSTON 2
1946-47	WHELDALE COLLIERY 0 v. Halifax 25 Halifax 20 v. WHELDALE COLLIERY 10 PEMBERTON ROVERS 6 v. Liverpool S 27 Liverpool S 20 v. PEMBERTON ROVERS 5 Warrington 46 v. BROOKLAND ROVERS 3 BROOKLAND ROVERS 3 v. Warrington 32 Workington T 48 v. WIDNES DRAGONS 0 WIDNES DRAGONS 5 v. Workington T 21
1947-48	VINE TAVERN 6 v. Bramley 17 Bramley 10 v. VINE TAVERN 2 Keighley 11 v. RISEHOW & GILLHEAD 0 RISEHOW & GILLHEAD 10 v. Keighley 2 Rochdale H 13 v. PEMBERTON ROVERS 0 PEMBERTON ROVERS 0 v. Rochdale H 11 St. Helens 48 v. BUSLINGTHORPE VALE 0 BUSLINGTHORPE VALE 2 v. St. Helens 13
1948-49	NORMANTON 4 v. Belle Vue Rangers 9 Belle Vue Rangers 12 v. NORMANTON 0 Oldham 30 v. BROUGHTON MOOR 0 BROUGHTON MOOR 2 v. Oldham 35 VINE TAVERN 4 v. York 11 York 17 v. VINE TAVERN 3

144

1949-50	WORSLEY BOYS' CLUB 7 v. Hunslet 45
	Hunslet 18 v. WORSLEY BOYS' CLUB 9
	CARDIFF 10 v. Salford 15
	Salford 20 v. CARDIFF 5
	BROUGHTON MOOR 5 v. Wakefield T 28
	Wakefield T 73 v. BROUGHTON MOOR 3
1950-51	LLANELLY 9 v. Barrow 23
	Barrow 39 v. LLANELLY 5
	Batley 41 v. BROUGHTON MOOR 3
	BROUGHTON MOOR 0 v. Batley 36
	Leigh 43 v. LATCHFORD ALBION 0
	LATCHFORD ALBION 0 v. Leigh 19
1951-52	Whitehaven 16. v. RYLANDS RECS 0
	RYLANDS RECS 9 v. Whitehaven 9
1952-53	ORFORD TANNERY 2 v. Warrington 46
	Warrington 46 v. ORFORD TANNERY 8
	Widnes 28 v. HULL DOCKERS (NDLB) 0
	HULL DOCKERS (NDLB) 3 v. Widnes 22
1953-54	LATCHFORD ALBION 20 v. Wigan 40
	Wigan 41 v. LATCHFORD ALBION 2
	Workington T 50 v.
	WHELDALE COLLIERY 2
	WHELDALE COLLIERY 6 v.
	Workington T 32
1954-55	Workington T 43 v. DEWSBURY CELTIC 0
1955-56	Keighley 33 v. TRIANGLE VALVE 8
	Rochdale H 55 v. STANNINGLEY 0
1956-57	Barrow 53 v.
	WAKEFIELD LOCOMOTIVE 12
	Halifax 48 v. WIDNES ST. MARIE'S 0
1957-58	York 50 v. LOCK LANE 5
	Widnes 51 v. ORFORD TANNERY 2
1958-59	York 54 v. ASTLEY &
	TYLDESLEY COLLIERY 2
	Hunslet 55 v. KELLS REC CENTRE 9
1959-60	WALNEY CENTRAL 10 v.
	LOCK LANE 5
	Second round
	Oldham 55 v. WALNEY CENTRAL 4
1960-61	Hull KR 56 v. PILKINGTON RECS 8
	DEWSBURY CELTIC 0 v. Castleford 32
1961-62	Hunslet 53 v. OLDHAM ST ANNE'S 10
	BROOKHOUSE 4 v. Doncaster 7
1962-63	Liverpool C 11 v. ROOSE 0
	IMPERIAL ATHLETIC 4 v. Bramley 15
1963-64	Featherstone R 60 v. STANNINGLEY 4
	THAMES BOARD MILLS — a bye

	Second round
	Blackpool B 48 v.
	THAMES BOARD MILLS 8
1964-65	Blackpool B 27 v. CROSSFIELD RECS 4
	Swinton 48 v. DEWSBURY CELTIC 5
1965-66	Barrow 11 v. CROSSFIELD RECS 2
	Widnes 23 v. BROOKHOUSE 5
1966-67	BLACKBROOK 12 v. York 23
	BRITISH OIL & CAKE MILLS 9 v.
	Liverpool C 20
1967-68	LEIGH MINERS WELFARE 7 v.
	Halifax 24
	BRITISH OIL & CAKE OILS 6 v.
	Castleford 9
1968-69	Wigan 61 v. LEIGH MINERS WELFARE 0
	Wakefield T 50 v. ACKWORTH 7
1969-70	Doncaster 22 v. GLASSON RANGERS 4
	Huddersfield 15 v. LOCK LANE 10
1970-71	Dewsbury 25 v. BRITISH OIL &
	CAKE MILLS 3
	Hunslet 49 v. THAMES BOARD MILLS 5
1971-72	Bramley 19 v. PILKINGTON RECS 5
	DEWSBURY CELTIC 2 v.
	Featherstone Rovers 34
1972-73	MILLOM 5 v. Hunslet 18
	Leigh 27 v. DEWSBURY CELTIC 4
1973-74	LOCK LANE 9 v. Wigan 37
	Leigh 63 v. KIPPAX WHITE SWAN 7
1974-75	DEWSBURY CELTIC 15 v. Hull KR 31
	New Hunslet 9 v. MAYFIELD 5
1975-76	Leigh 37 v. POINTER PANTHERS 8
	Warrington 16 v.
	LEIGH MINERS WELFARE 12
1976-77	BEECROFT & WIGHTMAN 2 v.
	Swinton 10
	PILKINGTON RECS 4 v. Wigan 10
1977-78	DEWSBURY CELTIC 5 v. Wigan 15
	PILKINGTON RECS 22 v. Castleford 23
1978-79	LEIGH MINERS' WELFARE 10 v.
	Leigh 23
	Oldham 23 v. ACE AMATEURS 5
1979-80	ACE AMATEURS 5 v. Widnes 22
	Hull 33 v. MILLOM 10
1980-81	PILKINGTON RECS 7 v. York 18
	Preliminary round
1985-86	Hull 38 v. DUDLEY HILL 10
	Hunslet 20 v. KELLS 8

CHALLENGE CUP PROGRESS CHART

Key: W — Winners. F — Beaten finalists. SF — Semi-final. P — Preliminary round.

	1985-86	1984-85	1983-84	1982-83	1981-82	1980-81	1979-80	1978-79	1977-78	1976-77	1975-76	1974-75	1973-74	1972-73	1971-72	1970-71	1969-70	1968-69	1967-68	1966-67	1965-66
BARROW	2	P	1	2	2	1	2	3	1	2	1	1	1	1	2	1	2	1	1	F	2
BATLEY	1	1	1	1	2	1	1	1	1	1	1	1	1	1	1	1	1	1	1	2	1
BLACKPOOL B.	2	1	1	1	1	1	1	1	1	1	1	1	1	1	1	1	1	1	1	1	1
BRADFORD N.	3	3	3	SF	3	1	3	SF	3	3	2	3	3	F	2	1	1	2	2	1	3
BRAMLEY	2	3	1	1	1	1	1	2	1	1	1	1	2	1	3	3	2	2	2	1	1
CARLISLE	1	1	P	1	1																
CASTLEFORD	W	SF	3	SF	SF	2	2	3	3	3	1	1	1	SF	2	SF	W	W	3	3	1
DEWSBURY	1	1	1	1	1	2	1	2	1	3	1	1	SF	SF	1	2	1	1	1	SF	SF
DONCASTER	2	P	2	1	1	1	1	1	1	1	2	1	1	1	1	1	3	1	1	2	1
FEATHERSTONE R.	1	P	1	W	P	3	1	1	SF	2	SF	1	F	W	2	2	1	2	3	W	2
FULHAM	1	1	2	2	2	1															
HALIFAX	1	2	1	2	3	2	SF	1	1	1	1	1	1	1	SF	1	1	1	2	1	1
HUDDERSFIELD B.	1	1	1	1	1	1	2	3	3	1	1	1	1	1	2	SF	2	2	SF	1	3
HULL	1	F	2	F	W	2	F	3	2	2	1	2	1	2	2	3	1	1	1	3	2
HULL K.R.	F	SF	3	1	2	F	W	2	1	SF	2	3	2	2	1	1	SF	1	1	2	3
HUNSLET	1	3	2	3	1	1	1	1	2	1	2	3	1	2	1	2	1	1	1	1	1
KEIGHLEY	1	1	1	1	2	1	1	1	1	SF	1	1	1	1	2	1	2	3	1	1	
LEEDS	SF	1	SF	2	SF	1	2	1	W	W	3	SF	3	1	F	F	3	3	W	SF	SF
LEIGH	3	2	1	1	3	2	1	2	1	1	3	2	SF	2	2	W	3	1	2	1	2
MANSFIELD M.	P	1																			
OLDHAM	SF	1	2	1	2	3	2	2	2	1	3	3	1	3	1	1	2	2	3	2	1
ROCHDALE H.	2	2	1	1	2	1	2	2	1	2	1	2	2	1	1	2	3	1	1	1	
RUNCORN H.	1	2	1	1	1	1	1	1	1	1	1	1	2	1	1	2	1	1	2	1	
ST. HELENS	2	1	3	3	1	SF	2	SF	F	SF	W	2	3	2	W	2	SF	3	1	1	W
SALFORD	1	2	1	2	1	3	3	1	2	2	2	2	1	1	3	3	F	2	3	1	
SHEFFIELD E.	1	1																			
SWINTON	P	1	P	2	1	1	1	1	2	2	1	1	2	1	3	3	2	1	1	3	2
WAKEFIELD T.	1	2	2	2	3	3	3	F	2	2	1	SF	1	3	3	1	1	SF	F	2	1
WARRINGTON	2	2	2	3	1	SF	3	1	SF	1	3	F	W	3	SF	2	2	SF	1	1	3
WHITEHAVEN	1	1	1	1	1	1	1	1	1	1	1	1	1	1	1	1	1	1	1	1	2
WIDNES	3	3	W	1	F	W	SF	W	3	F	F	W	2	2	1	2	1	3	2	1	2
WIGAN	3	W	F	1	2	1	1	2	2	2	2	3	3	2	2	F	2	SF	2	F	
WORKINGTON T.	1	2	2	3	2	2	1	1	2	3	2	2	2	1	1	1	2	2	1	2	
YORK	2	1	SF	1	1	2	2	1	1	1	2	2	1	1	3	1	1	1	2	2	1

JOHN PLAYER SPECIAL TROPHY

1985-86 Final

Big spenders Wigan collected their third trophy of the season, adding the £11,000 John Player Special Trophy prize to the Lancashire Cup and the new Charity Shield.

But it was an unlucky 13th final as Hull K.R. coach for Roger Millward, robbed of international trio George Fairbairn, Gary Prohm and Phil Hogan through injury and suspension.

Amid the jubilation of the Wigan dressing room, joint coaches Colin Clarke and Alan McInnes declared the international-flavoured Riversiders candidates for Rugby League's Grand Slam. With 11 of the 15 players on duty having full international honours, they took their unbeaten run to 18 matches though their shouts of joy were mixed with sighs of relief.

For battling Rovers took the lead in this defence-orientated final in the 56th minute, and five minutes after Wigan regained their scoreline dominance the Robins stormed back in a nail-biting finale. Rovers sorely missed the powerful attacks of Prohm and Hogan and lost second row man Chris Burton five minutes from time, sent off for an off-the-ball offence on Shaun Wane.

While holders Hull K.R. relinquished the trophy, scrum half Paul Harkin held on to the Man of the Match award he collected 12 months earlier to become the first player to win the individual award twice and the only one from a losing side to receive it outright.

He earned it this time with a much better all-round display than against Hull in the previous final. Then, Harkin's touch-finding was the key factor whereas Wigan were subjected to his distributive skills and the occasional dashing run. The award of £200 and a glass decanter was all the more satisfying at it was achieved under the scrutiny of Great Britain coach Maurice

Bamford only two days after Harkin's omission from the current Test squad.

There was nothing better than Harkin's blind side move at a scrum close to the Wigan line which set up deputy full back John Lydiat's try just before the half-time hooter to leave Hull K.R. trailing only 7-4.

Rovers' well organised defence had conceded a soft try in the 29th minute after Wigan opened the scoring with a rare left-footed drop goal from Australian Test prop Greg Dowling. As the half hour approached, the Robins held back at a play-the-ball on their line and Wane forced himself over between the posts as the defenders wrongly anticipated an up-and-under. David Stephenson tagged on the simple goal.

In the 56th minute Rovers took the lead for the first time with a try in the corner by winger David Laws, created with a long pass from centre partner John Dorahy, the Australian again being unable to add the goal.

Five minutes later Wigan strung together a series of crossfield passes and Steve Ella put fellow half back Mike Ford over for what was to be the winning score. Ironically, Ella was unable to add to his impressive tally of tries and thus failed to be the first player to touchdown in every round of a John Player Special tournament.

Although beaten 7-5 in the scrums, Wigan hooker Nicky Kiss gained two vital strikes against the head. The first gave Wigan unexpected possession directly en route to Ford's clinching try and the second came in the dying seconds to prevent Hull K.R. mounting another wave of pressure in a bid to extend their winning run to 10 matches.

Wigan's multi-nationality line up featured two Australians, a New Zealander and two South Africans including former Springbok winger Ray Mordt, making only his second appearance. He took the eye with a series of strong runs, plus the desire to take a quick line out at one point of the tense encounter!

JOHN PLAYER SPECIAL TROPHY FINAL

11th January   **Elland Road, Leeds**

HULL K.R. 8

John Lydiat	1.	Steve Hampson
Garry Clark	2.	Ray Mordt
Mike Smith	3.	David Stephenson
John Dorahy	4.	Ellery Hanley
David Laws	5.	Henderson Gill
Gordon Smith	6.	Steve Ella
Paul Harkin	7.	Mike Ford
Peter Johnston	8.	Greg Dowling
David Watkinson, Capt.	9.	Nicky Kiss
Asuquo Ema	10.	Shaun Wane
Chris Burton	11.	Graeme West, Capt.
Andy Kelly	12.	Andy Goodway
Gavin Miller	13.	Ian Potter
Ian Robinson	14.	Shaun Edwards
Chris Rudd	15.	Nick Du Toit

WIGAN 11

T: Lydiat, Laws
Substitution:
Robinson for Johnston (74 min.)
Half-time: 4-7
Referee: John Holdsworth (Kippax)
Attendance: 17,573

T: Wane, Ford
G: Stephenson, Dowling (dg)
Substitutions:
Du Toit for Potter (Half-time)
Edwards for Gill (74 min.)

Smiles all round for 1986 John Player Special Trophy winners Wigan.

Kippax referee John Holdsworth on the spot to award the first try of the 1986 final to Wigan's Shaun Wane.

Hull K.R. centre Mike Smith supported by Australians Peter Johnston (left) and John Dorahy, Wigan captain Graeme West covering.

1985-86 Round by Round

Two amateur sides again featured in the four-tie preliminary round. West Hull — who as Cawoods knocked out Halifax in 1977 — made Castleford work hard for a 24-10 victory at the Boulevard. Castleford scambled into an 8-2 interval lead through a Kevin Beardmore try and two goals from brother Bob, while Gary Lord pulled off two try-saving tackles as West Hull missed two easy goal shots. Featherstone amateurs Jubilee earned praise for a battling second half performance but lowly Keighley always had the edge to record a 24-6 success at Lawkholme Lane. Trailing 12-0 at the break, Jubilee camped in the Keighley half for the next 20 minutes to pull back to 12-6 before running out of steam. Visitors Warrington went 14-4 ahead at Featherstone through two Phil Blake tries before Rovers rallied to trail by only four points with six minutes left. Revitalised Rochdale Hornets travelled to Carlisle to secure a comfortable 24-6 victory.

In the first round, Halifax failed to score a try for the first time in the season as holders Hull K.R. staged a top class defensive show to win 11-2. Aided by a 13-6 penalty count, the home side enjoyed territorial advantage but Rovers created the only two clear breaks for Gary Prohm and Garry Clark to touch down. In his comeback from serious injury, Barrow centre Andy Whittle extended his run of nine tries in nine games to score the vital touchdown in the Cumbrians' shock disposal of visitors Leeds by 5-2, Barrow's 11th successive win. Widnes survived a shock defeat by the skin of their teeth up at Whitehaven. After tries by Australian Noel Cleal and winger John Basnett had put the Chemics 12-1 ahead, the Cumbrian Second Division pacesetters came back seven minutes from the end with a Mark Beckwith try, goaled by David Lightfoot. Former Widnes forward Les

Gorley was held on the line as the hooter was blown to deny Whitehaven a surprise success. York and Castleford were level at 10-apiece when the Glassblowers' Tony Spears and Keith England dropped the ball with the line at their mercy. Surefoot home kicker Graham Steadman took his chance of glory by kicking the winning penalty a minute from time.

Keighley were also last gasp winners when two tries in as many minutes gave them a 20-10 victory over Huddersfield when a replay looked certain at 10-10. Second Division leaders Leigh scored with almost every move at Batley, running in 14 tries in a 70-2 runaway victory, their leading try scorers being winger Phil Fox (5) and centre John Henderson (3). Former Leigh chief Alex Murphy made his St. Helens debut as coach at home to Dewsbury, steering his new charges to a 42-6 success. Three brilliant tries in a four-minute spell midway through the second half broke Dewsbury's resistance. For the first half hour, Second Division strugglers Bramley matched Slalom Lager Championship leaders Oldham before the Roughyeds took control with 12 points in eight minutes just before the interval. Australians David Liddiard and Mal Graham scored two tries apiece.

Hunslet's 20-12 home win over Workington Town featured scrum half Graham King's 100th try for the club. Trailing 6-4 to the Cumbrians at half-time, Man of the Match Alan McCurrie led the way in a revival which saw Hunslet in front 14-6 on the hour. Doncaster gained a passage into the second round for the first time in 11 years with a 22-20 victory over Runcorn Highfield at Tatters Field, while scrum half Dean Carroll collected the opening try and four goals to set Bradford Northern on the road to victory at Sheffield. The Eagles never recovered from an early 11-minute spell of relentless Northern pressure which provided an 18-0 lead.

Rochdale Hornets ended their nine-match unbeaten run at Salford. At 12-6 to the Red Devils, full back Kevin Harcombe missed an easy kick at goal and then Hornets conceded a converted try to find themselves trailing 18-6, before pulling back late in the game to 18-12.

Blackpool Borough missed six kicks at goal at home to Wakefield Trinity and were given the order of the boot with a narrow 24-22 defeat. Second Division strugglers Mansfield Marksman restricted Wigan to a 26-0 success at Central Park, the Riversiders receiving injuries to David Stephenson and Nicky Kiss as the irrepressible Steve Ella broke the deadlock with a try just before the interval. Fulham fully deserved their 7-6 half-time lead at home to Warrington. Mark Forster touched down 30 seconds after the break and the Wire secured their hard-earned 20-13 triumph with a further Forster try and one from hooker Carl Webb. Hull romped home 44-0 over Swinton on a frozen Boulevard pitch, John Muggleton scoring a hat-trick of tries, the Man of the Match award being shared by props Geoff Gerard and Neil Puckering.

In the second round, 1,000-1 outsiders Wakefield Trinity twice led Wigan in the opening quarter and trailed only 16-13 at the interval. Hanley scored two brilliant tries as Wigan ran in six, only to concede four touchdowns to their Second Division hosts. York reached the quarter finals for the first time in nine years after surviving a fright from Second Division Keighley. The Wasps did not take the lead until the 73rd minute, Wayne Morrell's try clinching success a minute later. Oldham lost 8-7 at Hull K.R. having had Australian David Liddiard sent off after 32 minutes. Trailing 8-3 visiting scrum half Ray Ashton declined a comfortable shot at goal and took a tap penalty instead, while David Hobbs was unable to add the goal to Hussein M'Barki's 74th minute try. Bradford Northern missed the

flair of John Woods as Widnes ran home 30-6 victors at Naughton Park in the televised tie. After Phil Ford's try put Northern level in the 54th minute, Cleal led the Widnes rush to the line as the Chemics piled up 22 points in the last 11 minutes.

Salford visited Hull and took an 8-4 lead with Man of the Match Paul Fletcher linking up for a try to add to two Clive Griffiths' goals. First half tries from James Leuluai and Andy Gascoigne put the Airlie Birds back in the lead before three second half touchdowns secured a 30-10 success. Lowly Doncaster — 20,000-1 rank outsiders — were unlucky to trail 10-6 at the break at St. Helens, the Saints finally slipping into gear to run in five second half tries in an uncomfortable 36-20 victory. Leigh continued their scoring spree with nine tries and six goals in the 48-6 hammering of Hunslet at Hilton Park. The scoring burst featured a spell of 24 points in 22 minutes, including three tries in four minutes, Man of the Match Henderson collecting a hat-trick of touchdowns. Warrington's Under-21 international Forster picked up four tries in the 34-14 victory over Barrow at Wilderspool, overshadowed only by a world class display from Australian import Les Boyd, a try scorer himself.

In the third round, Second Division leaders Leigh pulled off a shock win at Widnes by 35-31. The Chemics stormed into a 12-0 lead after only four minutes, Leigh levelling the scores at 14-14 after 25 minutes. At 25-25, Widnes had forward Mike O'Neill sent off and the visitors recorded tries by Phil Fox and Des Drummond — his hat-trick and Leigh's 29th try in three rounds. Hull K.R. and York each scored three tries with John Dorahy's five goals breaking the stalemate in a dull 24-16 encounter at Craven Park. Loose forward Gavin Miller sealed victory with a try five minutes from time. Warrington held the lead until seven minutes into the second half in a thrilling tie at Wilderspool, Wigan emerging victors 26-22. The Riversiders ran in five tries to three, Ella scoring one and making two, Great Britain star Andy Goodway enjoying his best game for the club. Hull crashed to a club record defeat of 57-14 at St. Helens. Saints went on the rampage against a disinterested Airlie Bird outfit, skipper Harry Pinner showing masterful distribution allied to the strong running of Roy Haggerty and hat-trick merchant Chris Arkwright. Leading 20-4 at the break, St. Helens ran in a further 20 points in 10 minutes after the restart, Hull staging a mini-revival with two tries from Andy Dannatt.

At the semi-final stage, Australian Test prop Greg Dowling ran in a rare hat-trick in the 36-8 trouncing of neighbours Leigh at St. Helens. Dowling gained the John Player Man of the Match award in Wigan's 13th successive match without defeat, marred only by Colin Whitfield's dismissal in the second half for a high tackle. After Second Division Leigh's exhilerating ten minute opening spell, the gulf between the two sides was too great to bridge. A week later at Headingley — on the last Saturday before Christmas — a crowd of only 3,759 saw Hull K.R. stage a professional display to dispose of St. Helens by 22-4. Man of the Match Miller led the Robins to a successive final, the Saints being restricted to two goals after their 10 tries against Hull in the previous round. Lacking skipper Pinner through injury, Saints were beaten in every department, including a 14-7 scrum deficit. Rovers' tally of four tries included a tremendous effort from winger Clark, preventing Saints from reaching their first John Player final after five semi-final defeats.

1985-86 PRIZES

Round	Per Team			Total
Preliminary	8 ×	£	750	£ 6,000
First	16 ×	£	750	£12,000
Second	8 ×	£	1,000	£ 8,000
Quarter-Finals	4 ×	£	1,500	£ 6,000
Semi-Finals ...	2 ×	£	2,750	£ 5,500
Runners-up ...	1 ×	£	5,500	£ 5,500
Winners	1 ×		£11,000	£11,000

Total Prizes £54,000

Capital Development Fund £26,000

Grand Total £80,000

John Player Special Man of the Match Paul Harkin, with skipper David Watkinson on hand.

RESULTS 1985-86

Preliminary Round

Carlisle	6	Rochdale H.	24
Featherstone R.	10	Warrington	14
Keighley	24	Jubilee (Feath'ne)	6
West Hull	10	Castleford	24
(at Hull)			

First Round

Batley	2	Leigh	70
Barrow	5	Leeds	2
Blackpool B.	22	Wakefield T.	24
Bramley	8	Oldham	46
Doncaster	22	Runcorn H	20
Fulham	13	Warrington	20
Halifax	2	Hull K.R.	11
Hull	44	Swinton	0
Hunslet	20	Workington T.	12
Keighley	20	Huddersfield B.	10
Salford	18	Rochdale H.	12
Sheffield E.	16	Bradford N.	24
St. Helens	42	Dewsbury	6
Whitehaven	7	Widnes	12
Wigan	26	Mansfield M.	0
York	12	Castleford	10

Second Round

Hull	30	Salford	10
Hull K.R.	8	Oldham	7
Leigh	48	Hunslet	6
St. Helens	36	Doncaster	20
Wakefield T.	21	Wigan	30
Warrington	34	Barrow	14
Widnes	30	Bradford N.	6
York	21	Keighley	16

Quarter Finals

Hull K.R.	24	York	16
St. Helens	57	Hull	14
Warrington	22	Wigan	26
Widnes	31	Leigh	35

Semi-Finals

Leigh	8	Wigan	36
(at St. Helens)			
St. Helens	4	Hull K.R.	22
(at Leeds)			

Final

Wigan	11	Hull K.R.	8
(at Elland Road, Leeds)			

JOHN PLAYER SPECIAL TROPHY ROLL OF HONOUR

Season	Winners		Runners-up		Venue	Attendance	Receipts
1971-72	Halifax	22	Wakefield T.	11	Bradford	7,975	£2,545
1972-73	Leeds	12	Salford	7	Huddersfield	10,102	£4,563
1973-74	Warrington	27	Rochdale H.	16	Wigan	9,347	£4,380
1974-75	Bradford N.	3	Widnes	2	Warrington	5,935	£3,305
1975-76	Widnes	19	Hull	13	Leeds	9,035	£6,275
1976-77	Castleford	25	Blackpool B.	15	Salford	4,512	£2,919
1977-78	Warrington	9	Widnes	4	St. Helens	10,258	£8,429
1978-79	Widnes	16	Warrington	4	St. Helens	10,743	£11,709
1979-80	Bradford N.	6	Widnes	0	Leeds	9,909	£11,560
1980-81	Warrington	12	Barrow	5	Wigan	12,820	£21,020
1981-82	Hull	12	Hull K.R.	4	Leeds	25,245	£42,987
1982-83	Wigan	15	Leeds	4	Elland Road, Leeds	19,553	£49,027
1983-84	Leeds	18	Widnes	10	Wigan	9,510	£19,824
1984-85	Hull K.R.	12	Hull	0	Hull City FC	25,326	£69,555
1985-86	Wigan	11	Hull K.R.	8	Elland Road, Leeds	17,573	£66,714

**JOHN PLAYER SPECIAL FINAL ....
A REVIEW**

1971-72
Halifax 22 Hepworth; Rayner, Davies (1t),
Willicombe (1t), Kelly (1t); Burton (5g), Baker
(Sanderson); Dewhirst, Hawksley, Callon (1t),
(Reeves), Fogerty, J. Martin, Halmshaw
Wakefield T. 11 Wraith (Ward); Slater (1t),
Marston, Hegarty, Major; Topliss (1t), Harkin;
Jeanes, Morgan, Lyons, Harrison (Spencer),
Valentine (1t), N. Fox (1g)
Referee: S. Shepherd (Oldham)

1972-73
Leeds 12 Holmes (1g); Alan Smith, Hynes,
Dyl, Atkinson (2t); Hardisty, Hepworth;
Clawson (2g) (Ward), Fisher (Pickup), Jeanes,
Haigh, Cookson, Eccles
Salford 7 Charlton; Colloby, Watkins (2g),
Hesketh, Richards; Gill (P. Ward), Banner;
Ramshaw, J. Ward, Mackay, Grice (Davies),
Kirkbride, Dixon (1t)
Referee: W.H. Thompson (Huddersfield)

1973-74
Warrington 27 Whitehead (6g, 1t); M. Philbin,
Noonan (2t), Reynolds (Pickup), Bevan (1t);
Whittle, Gordon; D. Chisnall, (Nicholas 1t),
Ashcroft, Brady, Wright, Wanbon, B. Philbin
Rochdale H. 16 Crellin; Brelsford (2t), Brophy
(1t), Taylor (1t), Aspinall; Butler (Wood),
Gartland; Holliday (2g), Harris, Whitehead,
Fogerty, Sheffield, Halmshaw
Referee: D.G. Kershaw (York)

1974-75
Bradford N. 3 Carlton (1t); Francis, Ward,
Gant, D. Redfearn; Blacker, Seabourne; Earl,
Jarvis, Jackson, Joyce, Trotter, Fearnley
Widnes 2 Dutton (1g); A. Prescott, D.O'Neill,
Aspey, Anderson; Hughes, Bowden; Mills,
Elwell, Sheridan, Adams, Blackwood,
Laughton
Referee: G.F. Lindop (Wakefield)

1975-76
Widnes 19 Dutton (3g); A. Prescott, George,
Aspey, Jenkins (2t); Hughes, Bowden (1t, 1dg);
Mills, Elwell, Wood, Foran, Sheridan,
Adams (1t)
Hull 13 Stephenson; A. Macklin, Clark, Portz,
Hunter (1t); Hancock, Foulkes (Davidson);
Ramsey, Flanagan, Wardell, Boxall (2g),
Walker, Crane (2t)
Referee: J.V. Moss (Manchester)

1976-77
Castleford 25 Wraith (1t); Fenton, Joyner (1t),
P. Johnson (1t), Briggs; Burton (1t), Stephens
(1t); Khan, Spurr, A. Dickinson, Reilly, Lloyd
(5g), S. Norton

Blackpool B 15 Reynolds; Robinson, Heritage,
Machen (1t), Pitman; Marsh, Newall;
Hamilton, Allen (1t), Egan (3g, 1t), Gamble,
Groves (Hurst), M. Pattinson
Referee: M. J. Naughton (Widnes)

1977-78
Warrington 9 Finnegan; Hesford (3g), Benyon,
Wilson, Bevan (1t); K. Kelly, Gordon; Lester,
Dalgreen, Nicholas, Martyn, B. Philbin, Potter
Widnes 4 Eckersley; Wright, Aspey, George,
Woods (2g); Hughes, Bowden; Ramsey, Elwell,
Shaw (Dearden), Adams, Hull, Laughton
Referee: W.H. Thompson (Huddersfield)

1978-79
Widnes 16 Eckersley; Wright (1t), Aspey,
Hughes, Burke (3g); Moran, Bowden; Mills,
Elwell (2dg), Shaw, Dearden, Hull (1t), Adams
(2dg)
Warrington 4 Finnegan; M. Kelly, Hesford
(2g), Benyon, Sutton; K. Kelly, (Hunter),
Gordon; Lester, Waller, Nicholas, Case,
Martyn, A. Gwilliam
Referee: G.F. Lindop (Wakefield)

1979-80
Bradford N. 6 Mumby (1g); Barends, D.
Redfearn, D. Parker (1t), Gant; Stephenson
(1dg), A. Redfearn; Thompson, Bridges,
Forsyth (I. Van Bellen), Grayshon, G. Van
Bellen (Ferres), Casey
Widnes 0 Eckersley; Wright, Aspey, George,
Burke; Hughes, Bowden; Hogan (Mills),
Elwell, Shaw, L. Gorley, Hull, Adams
Referee: W.H. Thompson (Huddersfield)

1980-81
Warrington 12 Hesford (2g, 2dg); Thackray,
I. Duane, Bevan (2t); M. Kelly; K. Kelly,
A. Gwilliam; Courtney, Waller, Case, Martyn,
Potter, Hunter (Eccles)
Barrow 5 Elliott; McConnell, French, Ball (1g),
Wainwright; Mason (1t), Cairns; D. Chisnall,
Allen (Szymala), Flynn, K. James, Kirkby,
Hadley
Referee: W.H. Thompson (Huddersfield)

1981-82
Hull 12 Banks; O'Hara, Harrison, Leuluai,
Prendiville; Day, Dean (1dg) (K. Harkin);
Skerrett, Wileman (1t), Stone, Crane, L.
Crooks (4g), Norton
Hull K.R. 4 Fairbairn (2g); Hubbard, M.
Smith, Hogan, Muscroft; Hartley, P. Harkin
(Burton); Holdstock (Millington), Watkinson,
S. Crooks, Lowe, Casey, Hall
Referee: G.F. Lindop (Wakefield)

1982-83
Wigan 15 Williams; Ramsdale, Stephenson,
Whitfield (4g, 1dg), Gill (1t) (Juliff 1t); M.
Foy, Fairhurst; Shaw, Kiss, Campbell, West
(Case), Scott, Pendlebury

Leeds 4 Hague; Campbell, Wilkinson, Dyl, Andy Smith; Holmes, Dick (2g); Dickinson, Ward, Burke, Sykes, W. Heron, D. Heron
Referee: R. Campbell (Widnes)
1983-84
Leeds 18 Wilkinson; Prendiville, Creasser (5g), D. Bell, Andy Smith; Holmes (1t), Dick (1t); Keith Rayne, Ward (Squire), Kevin Rayne, Moorby, Laurie, Webb
Widnes 10 Burke (1g); Wright, Keiron O'Loughlin, Lydon (1t), Linton (1t); Hughes, Gregory; S. O'Neill, Elwell, K. Tamati, L. Gorley, Whitfield, Adams
Referee: W.H. Thompson (Huddersfield)
1984-85
Hull K.R. 12 Fairbairn; Clark (1t), Robinson, Prohm (1t), Laws; M. Smith, Harkin; Broadhurst, Watkinson, Ema, Burton, Hogan (1t), Miller
Hull 0 Kemble (Schofield); Evans, Ah Kuoi, Leuluai, O'Hara; Topliss, Sterling; Edmonds (Dannatt), Patrick, Rose, Crooks, Proctor, Divorty
Referee: S. Wall (Leigh)

1981 John Player Man of the Match Tommy Martyn.

JOHN PLAYER SPECIAL MAN OF THE MATCH

Season	Winner	Team	Position
1971-72	Bruce Burton	Halifax (v. Wakefield T.)	Stand off
1972-73	Keith Hepworth	Leeds (v. Salford)	Scrum half
1973-74	Kevin Ashcroft	Warrington (v. Rochdale H.)	Hooker
1974-75	Barry Seabourne	Bradford N. (v. Widnes)	Scrum half
1975-76	Reg Bowden	Widnes (v. Hull)	Scrum half
1976-77	Gary Stephens	Castleford	Scrum half
	Howard Allen	Blackpool B.	Hooker
1977-78	Steve Hesford	Warrington (v. Widnes)	Winger
1978-79	David Eckersley	Widnes (v. Warrington)	Full back
1979-80	Len Casey	Bradford N. (v. Widnes)	Loose forward
1980-81	Tommy Martyn	Warrington (v. Barrow)	Second row
1981-82	Trevor Skerrett	Hull (v. Hull K.R.)	Prop
1982-83	Martin Foy	Wigan (v. Leeds)	Stand off
1983-84	Mark Laurie	Leeds (v. Widnes)	Second row
1984-85	Paul Harkin	Hull K.R. (v. Hull)	Scrum half
1985-86	Paul Harkin	Hull K.R. (v. Wigan)	Scrum half

ROUND BY ROUND
1971-85

1971-72
First round
Barrow 10 v. Swinton 9
Dewsbury 5 v. Hull 5
Huyton 5 v. Keighley 18
Leeds 18 v. Leigh 8
St. Helens 37 v. Featherstone R 7
Bradford N 8 v. Rochdale H 12
Doncaster 4 v. Bramley 16
Hunslet 7 v. Castleford 7
Hull KR 17 v. Salford 14
Batley 5 v. York 11
Warrington 9 v. Halifax 16
Whitehaven 5 v. Oldham 0
Widnes 10 v. Wakefield T 10
Thames Board Mills 7 v. Huddersfield 27
Wigan 33 v. Ace 9
Workington T 0 v. Blackpool B 10
Replays
Castleford 9 v. Hunslet 8
Wakefield T 12 v. Widnes 10
Hull 22 v. Dewsbury 10
Second round
Castleford 11 v. Leeds 13
Barrow 10 v. Huddersfield 6
Halifax 5 v. York 3
Hull KR 11 v. Wigan 18
Whitehaven 0 v. St. Helens 12
Bramley 5 v. Wakefield T 10
Rochdale 4 v. Blackpool B 14
Hull 36 v. Keighley 10
Third round
Halifax 36 v Barrow 13
Leeds 12 v. Wigan 12
St. Helens 33 v. Hull 5
Wakefield T 18 v. Blackpool B 12
Replay
Wigan 5 v. Leeds 12
Semi-finals
Wakefield T 14 v. St. Helens 9
Leeds 7 v. Halifax 15
Final
Halifax 22 v. Wakefield T 11 (at Bradford)

1972-73
First round
Hull KR 20 v. Castleford 10
Batley 26 v. Hunslet 3
Bramley 26 v. Pilkington Recs 5
Halifax 20 v. St. Helens 22
Whitehaven 11 v. Featherstone R 16
Barrow 2 v. Salford 17
Blackpool B 9 v. Leeds 51
Bradford N 32 v. Rochdale H 6
Dewsbury 22 v Dewsbury C 4
Huddersfield 23 v. Warrington 15
Hull 17 v. Oldham 10
Leigh 10 v. Workington T 9
Swinton 29 v. Huyton 10
Wigan 10 v. Wakefield T 34
York 21 v. Keighley 13
Doncaster 7 v. Widnes 22

Second round
Hull 9 v. Wakefield T 4
Salford 19 v. Dewsbury 3
St. Helens 24 v. Featherstone R 8
Leeds 21 v Leigh 3
Bradford N 35 v. York 17
Widnes 21 v. Batley 8
Hull KR 25 v. Bramley 5
Swinton 19 v. Huddersfield 11
Third round
St. Helens 10 v. Widnes 3
Hull 18 v. Leeds 18
Salford 39 v. Bradford N 2
Hull KR 4 v. Swinton 2 (abandoned
after 20 mins)
Replays
Leeds 37 v. Hull 5
Hull KR 30 v. Swinton 6
Semi-finals
Hull KR 13 v. Salford 15
Leeds 19 v. St. Helens 0
Final
Leeds 12 v. Salford 7 (at Huddersfield)

1973-74
First round
Bramley 20 v. Hull 12
Keighley 30 v. Huyton 10
St. Helens 34 v. Featherstone R 16
Whitehaven 26 v. Dewsbury C 3
Wigan 34 v. Batley 0
Bradford N 12 v. Leeds 34
Castleford 88 v. Millom 5
Dewsbury 33 v. Widnes 24
Halifax 20 v. Barrow 5
New Hunslet 11 v. Leigh 26
Rochdale H 18 v. Huddersfield 2
Wakefield T 47 v. Blackpool B 13
Warrington 31 v. Oldham 14
Workington T 20 v. Hull KR 9
York 32 v. Swinton 13
Salford 47 v. Doncaster 17
Second round
Bramley 24 v. Leigh 12
Warrington 18 v. Castleford 9
Halifax 7 v. Dewsbury 16
St. Helens 28 v. Whitehaven 2
Rochdale H 11 v. York 0
Salford 4 v. Leeds 17
Wakefield T 10 v. Workington T 7
Wigan 10 v. Keighley 14
Third round
Wakefield T 18 v St. Helens 18
Keighley 8 v. Bramley 11
Rochdale H. 7 v. Leeds 5
Warrington 20 v. Dewsbury 12
Replay
St. Helens 16 v. Wakefield T 10
Semi-finals
Rochdale H 14 v. Bramley 2
Warrington 20 v. St. Helens 9
Final
Warrington 27 v. Rochdale H 16 (at Wigan)

1974-75
First round
Salford 36 v. Castleford 5
Barrow 5 v. York 14
Bramley 15 v. Hull 6
Leeds 49 v. New Hunslet 10
Wakefield T 44 v. Leigh 10
Whitehaven 32 v. Lock Lane 6
Blackpool B 17 v. Wigan 20
Bradford N 12 v. Dewsbury 8
Doncaster 15 v. Kippax White Swan 6
Halifax 11 v. Keighley 13
Huyton 14 v. Huddersfield 12
Oldham 21 v. Workington T 14
Rochdale H 12 v. Hull KR 16
Swinton 7 v. St. Helens 6
Warrington 36 v. Batley 3
Widnes 10 v. Featherstone R 5.
Second round
Salford 14 v. Bramley 9
Oldham 3 v. Bradford N 12
Keighley 4 v. Leeds 39
Swinton 18 v. Wigan 2
Warrington 33 v. Huyton 6
Whitehaven 14 v. Doncaster 4
Widnes 35 v. Wakefield T 13
York 12 v. Hull KR 26
Third round
Whitehaven 5 v. Warrington 0
Hull KR 25 v. Salford 17
Bradford N 17 v. Leeds 7
Widnes 15 v. Swinton 5
Semi-finals
Whitehaven 6 v. Bradford N 18
Widnes 16 v. Hull KR 14
Final
Bradford N 3 v. Widnes 2 (at Warrington)

1975-76
First round
Castleford 26 v. York 15
Salford 57 v. Mayfield 3
Barrow 16 v. Pilkington Recs 9
Workington T. 16 v. Bramley 9
Wigan 30 v. Keighley 7
Blackpool B 11 v. St. Helens 36
Doncaster 12 v. Hull 23
Huyton 14 v. Oldham 20
Hull KR 33 v. Rochdale H 10
Widnes 27 v. Dewsbury 12
Batley 18 v. Whitehaven 9
Bradford N 12 v. Wakefield T 32
Huddersfield 20 v. Warrington 12
Leigh 12 v. Featherstone R 5
New Hunslet 28 v. Halifax 8
Swinton 7 v. Leeds 23
Second round
Hull KR 23 v. Leigh 8
Wigan 5 v. Widnes 19
Huddersfield 14 v. Barrow 5
Hull 9 v. Leeds 9
Salford 46 v. Oldham 3
St. Helens 47 v Batley 9
Wakefield T 14 v. Castleford 24
Workington T 23 v. New Hunslet 6
Replay
Leeds 11 v. Hull 23

Third round
Hull 9 v. St. Helens 8
Huddersfield 10 v. Castleford 19
Hull KR 14 v. Widnes 18
Salford 16 v. Workington T 8
Semi-finals
Castleford 9 v. Widnes 17
Salford 14 v. Hull 22
Final
Widnes 19 v. Hull 13 (at Leeds)

1976-77
First round
Hull 18 v. Warrington 5
Leeds 34 v. Rochdale H 10
Featherstone R 43 v. Whitehaven 13
Hull KR 7 v. St. Helens 12
Blackpool B 16 v. Barrow 15
Huyton 6 v. York 8
Wigan 33 v. Keighley 0
Workington T 45 v. Doncaster 15
Halifax 24 v. Ovenden 4
Oldham 17 v. Batley 9
New Hunslet 10 v. Castleford 24
Bramley 33 v. Dewsbury 5
Salford 39 v. Ace 15
Bradford N 23 v. Huddersfield 18
Wakefield T 8 v. Widnes 10
Leigh 29 v. Swinton 7
Second round
Leeds 18 v. Salford 17
St. Helens 18 v. Castleford 22
Oldham 13 v. Leigh 28
Blackpool B 7 v. Halifax 3
Widnes 10 v. Featherstone R 0
York 8 v. Wigan 7
Hull 19 v. Bradford N 5
Workington T 17 v. Bramley 13
Third round
Leeds 14 v. Castleford 20
Leigh 17 v. Hull 12
Widnes 13 v. York 10
Workington T 5 v. Blackpool B 11
Semi-finals
Castleford 15 v. Widnes 10
Blackpool B 15 v. Leigh 5
Final
Castleford 25 v. Blackpool B 15 (at Salford)

1977-78
First round
NDLB 4 v. New Hunslet 18
Salford 27 v. Rochdale H 8
Leeds 22 v. Wigan 25
Blackpool B 10 v. Warrington 31
Bradford N 19 v. Bramley 12
Dewsbury 0 v. Castleford 13
Featherstone R 25 v. Hull KR 24
Halifax 8 v. Cawoods 9
Huddersfield 33 v. Whitehaven 13
Keighley 18 v. Hull 16
Leigh 31 v. Doncaster 15
Oldham 16 v. Barrow 8
Swinton 11 v. St. Helens 28
Wakefield T 24 v. Batley 5
Widnes 22 v. Huyton 6
York 12 v. Workington T 20

Second round
Widnes 26 v. Castleford 19
Bradford N 22 v. Workington T 18
Featherstone R 17 v. St. Helens 10
Huddersfield 21 v. Oldham 11
Keighley 5 v. Leigh 14
Wakefield T 31 v. Cawoods 7
Warrington 19 v. Salford 10
Wigan 9 v. New Hunslet 7
Third round
Huddersfield 0 v. Bradford N 11
Featherstone R 11 v. Warrington 14
Wakefield T 12 v. Leigh 9
Widnes 25 v. Wigan 0
Semi-finals
Wakefield T 5 v. Warrington 15
Widnes 14 v. Bradford N 10
Final
Warrington 9 v. Widnes 4 (at St. Helens)

1978-79
First round
Castleford 18 v. Swinton 10
Salford 25 v. Rochdale H 7
Leigh MW 9 v. Halifax 21
St. Helens 16 v. Leeds 11
Barrow 8 v. Bradford N 26
Doncaster 2 v. Wigan 30
Huddersfield 10 v. Widnes 21
Hull KR 67 v. Oldham 11
Keighley 20 v. York 4
Leigh 13 v. Huyton 13
Milford 5 v. Dewsbury 38
New Hunslet 7 v. Hull 17
Wakefield T 27 v. Batley 2
Warrington 14 v. Blackpool B 4
Whitehaven 3 v. Featherstone R 9
Workington T 17 v. Bramley 8
Replay
Huyton 8 v. Leigh 10
Second round
Widnes 11 v. St. Helens 10
Castleford 20 v. Workington T 9
Featherstone R 0 v. Warrington 7
Hull 12 v. Bradford N 18
Hull KR 16 v. Salford 14
Leigh 17 v. Dewsbury 8
Wakefield T 15 v. Halifax 10
Keighley 9 v. Wigan 5
Third round
Bradford N 16 v. Wakefield T 13
Hull KR 23 v. Castleford 10
Keighley 4 v. Widnes 15
Warrington 27 v. Leigh 0
Semi-finals
Widnes 21 v. Bradford N 3
Warrington 9 v. Hull KR 5
Final
Widnes 16 v. Warrington 4 (at St. Helens)

1979-80
First round
Salford 47 v. Huddersfield 5
Wakefield T 25 v. Hull 18
Barrow 13 v. St. Helens 18
Batley 2 v. York 12
Blackpool B 6 v. West Hull 3
Bramley 43 v. Whitehaven 15
Castleford 15 v. Dewsbury 12
Doncaster 0 v. Bradford N 48
Featherstone R 17 v. Halifax 7
Warrington 20 v. Huyton 9
Keighley 21 v. Rochdale H 9
Leigh 16 v. Hull KR 0
Oldham 7 v. Leeds 31
Pilkington Recs 9 v. Wigan 18
Swinton 11 v. Workington T 30
Widnes 17 v. Hunslet 11
Second round
Castleford 24 v. Wigan 10
Keighley 9 v. Bradford N 15
Leeds 7 v. Leigh 14
Salford 23 v. Bramley 9
Wakefield T 21 v. Featherstone R 12
Warrington 20 v. York 15
Widnes 31 v. St. Helens 20
Workington T 43 v. Blackpool B 7
Third round
Warrington 6 v. Widnes 14
Bradford N 25 v. Leigh 11
Castleford 6 v. Salford 13
Wakefield T 26 v. Workington T 5
Semi-finals
Widnes 19 v. Salford 3 (at Warrington)
Bradford N 16 v. Wakefield T 3 (at Leeds)
Final
Bradford N 6 v. Widnes 0 (at Leeds)

1980-81
First round
Hull 12 v. Bradford N 0
Hunslet 15 v. Workington T 5
Batley 4 v. Huddersfield 20
Blackpool B 21 v. Huyton 7
Bramley 10 v. Halifax 11
Castleford 30 v. Pilkington Recs 17
Dewsbury 12 v. Featherstone R 37
Doncaster 10 v. Whitehaven 18
Fulham 9 v. Leeds 3
Keighley 16 v. Hull KR 34
Leigh 38 v. Rochdale H 5
St. Helens 12 v. Warrington 14
Salford 17 v. Wigan 9
Swinton 10 v. Barrow 12
Widnes 20 v. Wakefield T 17
York 14 v. Oldham 9
Second round
Warrington 11 v. Hull KR 7
Barrow 26 v. Hunslet 13
Blackpool B 5 v. Halifax 11
Hull 11 v. York 10
Leigh 17 v. Fulham 9
Salford 8 v. Castleford 15
Whitehaven 22 v. Featherstone R 3
Widnes 25 v. Huddersfield 9

Third round
Castleford 18 v. Widnes 10
Hull 13 v. Whitehaven 0
Leigh 13 v. Barrow 15
Warrington 16 v. Halifax 10
Semi-finals
Warrington 5 v. Castleford 5 (at Wigan)
Barrow 13 v. Hull 10 (at Leeds)
Replay
Warrington 22 v. Castleford 10 (at Leeds)
Final
Warrington 12 v. Barrow 5 (at Wigan)

1981-82
Preliminary round
Leigh 41 v. Blackpool B 4
First round
Workington T 22 v. Bramley 9
Hunslet 8 v. Widnes 44
Warrington 24 v. Fulham 15
Batley 7 v. Featherstone R 16
Carlisle 14 v. Cardiff C 7
Castleford 21 v. Leigh 7
Dewsbury 2 v. Hull KR 34
Halifax 7 v. Hull 26
Huddersfield 19 v. Huyton 17
Keighley 27 v. Wakefield T 22
Leeds 19 v. Wigan 10
Oldham 21 v. Doncaster 7
Whitehaven 11 v. Salford 19
Rochdale H 3 v. Bradford N 19
St. Helens 16 v. Barrow 16
Swinton 32 v. York 5
Replay
Barrow 17 v. St. Helens 0
Second round
Widnes 16 v. Carlisle 10
Castleford 5 v. Hull 23
Leeds 13 v. Warrington 8
Hull KR 18 v. Featherstone R 6
Keighley 10 v. Salford 11
Barrow 8 v. Bradford N 0
Oldham 13 v. Huddersfield 0
Swinton 19 v. Workington T 9
Third round
Barrow 12 v. Hull 14
Oldham 14 v. Leeds 5
Salford 0 v. Swinton 6
Widnes 8 v. Hull KR 9
Semi-finals
Hull 22 v. Oldham 6 (at Leeds)
Hull KR 23 v. Swinton 14 (at Leeds)
Final
Hull 12 v. Hull KR 4 (at Leeds)

1982-83
Preliminary round
Huyton 9 v. Workington T 19
First round
St. Helens 17 v. Fulham 5
Blackpool B 6 v. Batley 5
Cardiff C 7 v. Rochdale H 11
Carlisle 26 v. Doncaster 17
Castleford 10 v. Wigan 16
Dewsbury 11 v. Barrow 28
Featherstone R 14 v. Hull 18
Hull KR 42 v. Whitehaven 3
Keighley 0 v. Bradford N 18
Leeds 17 v. Bramley 7

Leigh 13 v. Oldham 12
Salford 23 v. Hunslet 11
Swinton 13 v. Huddersfield 22
Warrington 19 v. Halifax 8
Widnes 17 v. Wakefield T 12
York 18 v. Workington T 15
Second round
Hull KR 36 v. Leigh 7
Bradford N 12 v. Hull 12
Carlisle 2 v. Widnes 10
Leeds 31 v. York 10
Rochdale H 5 v. Barrow 27
Salford 21 v. Huddersfield 19
Warrington 36 v. Blackpool B 15
Wigan 9 v. St. Helens 5
Replay
Hull 8 v. Bradford N 10
Third round
Salford 4 v. Wigan 5
Barrow 8 v. Leeds 13
Warrington 11 v. Hull KR 10
Widnes 16 v. Bradford N 10
Semi-finals
Leeds 8 v. Widnes 2 (at Huddersfield)
Wigan 15 v. Warrington 14 (at St. Helens)
Final
Wigan 15 v. Leeds 4 (at Elland Rd, Leeds)

1983-84
Preliminary round
Batley 11 v. Doncaster 12
Whitehaven 0 v. Widnes 36
First round
Blackpool B 9 v. Leeds 12
Cardiff C 41 v. Rochdale H 6
Carlisle 10 v. Workington T 5
Castleford 4 v. Hull 8
Dewsbury 14 v. Keighley 17
Doncaster 11 v. Salford 22
Featherstone R 12 v. Fulham 10
Halifax 12 v. Barrow 29
Huddersfield 8 v. Huyton 21
Kent Invicta 7 v. St. Helens 40
Oldham 12 v. Leigh 20
Swinton 17 v. Hunslet 16
Wakefield T 18 v. Warrington 32
Widnes 2 v. Bradford N 1
Wigan 30 v. York 13
Bye: Hull KR drawn at home to Bramley,
who withdrew while in liquidation
Second round
Warrington 10 v. St. Helens 18
Cardiff C 38 v. Huyton 12
Carlisle 17 v. Leigh 68
Featherstone R 20 v. Hull 14
Keighley 8 v. Swinton 23
Leeds 12 v. Hull KR 6
Widnes 18 v. Barrow 6
Wigan 24 v. Salford 15
Third round
Widnes 20 v. Wigan 15
Leigh 12 v. Cardiff C 8
St. Helens 16 v. Featherstone R 12
Swinton 12 v. Leeds 16
Semi-finals
Leeds 18 v. Leigh 11 (at Huddersfield)
Widnes 18 v. St. Helens 4 (at Warrington)
Final
Leeds 18 v. Widnes 10 (at Wigan)

1984-85
Preliminary round
Myson 2 v. Dewsbury 8
Bramley 20 v. Southend I 6
Keighley 24 v. Dudley Hill 10
Sheffield E 17 v. Wakefield T 6
Carlisle 8 v. Bradford N 26
Hunslet 2 v. Workington T 6
First round
Hull KR 32 v. Leigh 5
Bradford N 22 v. Swinton 1
Bramley 12 v. Blackpool B 10
Castleford 42 v. Bridgend 4
Dewsbury 14 v. Salford 8
Featherstone R 17 v. Barrow 12
Fulham 14 v. Hull 36
Leeds 50 v. Sheffield E 2
Rochdale H 10 v. Mansfield M 8
Runcorn H 18 v. Batley 5
St. Helens 60 v. Keighley 8
Warrington 5 v. Halifax 17
Whitehaven 64 v. Doncaster 0
Wigan 50 v. Huddersfield B 6
Workington T 12 v. Widnes 22
York 6 v. Oldham 22
Second round
Leeds 10 v. Wigan 4
Bradford N 12 v. St Helens 12
Bramley 33 v. Whitehaven 5
Dewsbury 31 v. Runcorn H 16
Halifax 20 v. Castleford 18
Hull 26 v. Oldham 14
Hull KR 34 v. Rochdale H 12
Widnes 28 v. Featherstone R 10
Replay
St. Helens 24 v. Bradford N 10
Third round
St. Helens 8 v. Halifax 14
Dewsbury 8 v. Hull 22
Hull KR 14 v. Widnes 6
Leeds 28 v. Bramley 14
Semi-finals
Hull KR 14 v. Halifax 8 (at Leeds)
Hull 18 v. Leeds 6 (at Hull C FC)
Final
Hull KR 12 v. Hull 0 (at Hull C FC)

JOHN PLAYER SPECIAL TROPHY RECORDS

ALL ROUNDS

TEAM
*Highest score: Castleford 88 v. Millom 5
Biggest attendance: 25,326 Hull v. Hull K.R.
(at Hull C. FC)....... Final 1984-85

INDIVIDUAL
*Most goals: 17 by Sammy Lloyd (Castleford)
Most tries: 6 by Vince Gribbin (Whitehaven) v. Doncaster 1984-85
*Most points: 43 (17g,3t) by Sammy Lloyd (Castleford)
*The above records were achieved in the Castleford v. Millom first round tie in 1973-74.

●*BEFORE 1977-78 the competition was known as the Player's No. 6 Trophy, then the John Player Trophy. In 1983-84 it became the John Player Special Trophy. It was not until 1979-80 that semi-finals were played at neutral venues.*

NON-LEAGUE CLUBS IN THE JOHN PLAYER SPECIAL TROPHY
Amateur clubs re-entered the John Player tournament in 1984-85 for the first time since 1980-81, two joining 10 professional clubs in a six-tie preliminary round.

JOHN PLAYER SPECIAL TROPHY FINAL RECORDS

Most final appearances: 6 by Widnes
Most wins: 3 by Warrington
Most tries: No player has scored 3 or more
Most goals: 6 by Derek Whitehead (Warrington) v.
Rochdale H............................. 1973-74
Most points: 15 (6g,1t) by Derek Whitehead (Warrington)
v. Rochdale H......................... 1973-74
Highest score: Warrington 27 v. Rochdale H. 16 1973-74
Widest margin win: Widnes 16 v. Warrington 4 1978-79
Hull K.R. 12 v. Hull 0....1984-85
Biggest attendance: 25,326 Hull v. Hull K.R.
(at Hull C. FC)...............1984-85
Biggest receipts: £69,555 Hull K.R. v. Hull
(at Hull C FC)....................1984-85

From 1971-72 two amateur teams went into the first round draw, except for only one in 1980-81, and their fate varied from the record 88-5 hammering Millom received at Castleford, to Cawoods' historic victory over Halifax — the first time a non-league club had knocked out professionals from either the Challenge Cup or John Player Trophy since 1909. The full list of amateur clubs' results is:

Season						Attendance
1971-72	Wigan	33	v	Ace Amateurs (Hull)	9	2,678
	Thames Board Mill (Warr.)	7	v	Huddersfield	27	1,175
1972-73	Bramley	26	v	Pilkington Recs. (St. Helens)	5	616
	Dewsbury	22	v	Dewsbury Celtic	4	1,897
1973-74	Whitehaven	26	v	Dewsbury Celtic	3	1,276
	Castleford	88	v	Millom (Cumbria)	5	1,031
1974-75	Whitehaven	32	v	Lock Lane (Castleford)	6	537
	Doncaster	15	v	Kippax W.S.	6	453
1975-76	Salford	57	v	Mayfield (Rochdale)	3	3,449
	Barrow	16	v	Pilkington Recs. (St. Helens)	9	612
1976-77	Halifax	24	v	Ovenden (Halifax)	4	3,680
	Salford	39	v	Ace Amateurs (Hull)	15	3,037
1977-78	N.D.L.B. (Hull)	4	v	New Hunslet	18	3,845
	Halifax	8	v	Cawoods (Hull)	9	1,168
1978-79	Leigh Miners Welfare	9	v	Halifax	21	1,621
	Milford (Leeds)	5	v	Dewsbury	38	3,129
1979-80	Pilkington Recs. (St. Helens)	9	v	Wigan	18	6,707
	Blackpool B.	6	v	West Hull	3	555
1980-81	Castleford	30	v	Pilkington Recs. (St. Helens)	17	2,823
1984-85	Myson (Hull)	2	v	Dewsbury	8	1,572
	Keighley	24	v	Dudley Hill (Bradford)	10	1,570
1985-86	Keighley	24	v	Jubilee (Featherstone)	6	1,007
	West Hull	10	v	Castleford	24	2,500

JOHN PLAYER TROPHY PROGRESS CHART

Key: W — Winners. F — Beaten finalists. SF — Semi-final. P — Preliminary round.

	1985-86	1984-85	1983-84	1982-83	1981-82	1980-81	1979-80	1978-79	1977-78	1976-77	1975-76	1974-75	1973-74	1972-73	1971-72
BARROW	2	1	2	3	3	F	1	1	1	1	2	1	1	1	3
BATLEY	1	1	P	1	1	1	1	1	1	1	2	1	1	2	1
BLACKPOOL B.	1	1	1	2	P	2	2	1	1	F	1	1	1	1	3
BRADFORD N.	2	2	1	3	2	1	W	SF	SF	2	1	W	1	3	1
BRAMLEY	1	3	*	1	1	1	2	1	1	2	1	2	SF	2	2
BRIDGEND		1	3	1	1										
CARLISLE	P	P	2	2	2										
CASTLEFORD	1	2	1	1	2	SF	3	3	2	W	SF	1	2	1	2
DEWSBURY	1	3	1	1	1	1	1	2	1	1	1	1	3	2	1
DONCASTER	2	1	1	1	1	1	1	1	1	1	1	2	1	1	1
FEATHERSTONE R.	P	2	3	1	2	2	2	2	3	2	1	1	1	2	1
FULHAM	1	1	1	1	1	2									
HALIFAX	1	SF	1	1	1	3	1	2	1	2	1	1	2	1	W
HUDDERSFIELD	1	1	1	2	2	2	1	1	3	1	3	1	1	2	2
HULL	3	F	2	2	W	SF	1	2	1	3	F	1	1	3	3
HULL K.R.	F	W	2	3	F	2	1	SF	1	1	3	SF	1	SF	2
HUNSLET	2	P	1	1	1	2	1	1	2	1	2	1	1	1	1
KEIGHLEY	2	1	2	1	2	1	2	3	2	1	1	2	3	1	2
LEEDS	1	SF	W	F	3	1	2	1	1	3	2	3	3	W	SF
LEIGH	SF	1	SF	2	1	3	3	3	3	SF	2	1	2	2	1
MANSFIELD M.	1	1													
OLDHAM	2	2	1	1	SF	1	1	1	2	2	2	2	1	1	1
ROCHDALE H.	1	2	1	2	1	1	1	1	1	1	1	1	F	1	2
RUNCORN H.	1	2	2	P	1	1	1	1	1	1	1	2	1	1	1
ST. HELENS	SF	3	SF	2	1	1	2	2	2	2	3	1	SF	SF	SF
SALFORD	2	1	2	3	3	2	SF	2	2	2	SF	3	2	F	1
SHEFFIELD E.	1	1													
SOUTHEND I.		P	1												
SWINTON	1	1	3	1	SF	1	1	1	1	1	1	3	1	3	1
WAKEFIELD T.	2	P	1	1	1	1	SF	3	SF	1	2	2	3	2	F
WARRINGTON	3	1	2	SF	2	W	3	F	W	1	1	3	W	1	1
WHITEHAVEN	1	2	P	1	1	3	1	1	1	1	1	SF	2	1	2
WIDNES	3	3	F	SF	3	3	F	W	F	SF	W	F	1	3	1
WIGAN	W	2	3	W	1	1	2	2	3	2	2	2	2	1	3
WORKINGTON T.	1	1	1	1	2	1	3	2	2	3	3	1	2	1	1
YORK	3	1	1	2	1	2	2	1	1	3	1	2	2	2	2

*Bramley withdrew from the Trophy while in liquidation, opponents Hull K.R. receiving a bye.

PREMIERSHIP TROPHY

1986 Final

Caretaker coach Tony Barrow took Warrington to their first Premiership Trophy success and won himself the full-time role as Wire supremo.

Warrington took their run of consecutive victories to nine with a record Premiership final highest score and winning margin, earning a Slalom Lager prize cheque for £8,000.

Fourth-placed Wire ran in seven tries — the first four from close range — after Slalom Lager Champions Halifax had led 8-4 after eight minutes.

Warrington skipper Les Boyd, the reformed fiery Australian, was awarded the Harry Sunderland Trophy as the star of a formidable front row. The former Test star and recipient of two lengthy suspensions Down Under crowned his first season of British club football with a top class display of controlled aggression and inspiring leadership with the first and last tries.

His scrummaging partners, Kiwi hooker Kevin Tamati and Australian Bob Jackson, also added their names to the scoresheet, just reward for unstinting power drives into the Halifax ranks depleted by the loss of new British cap Neil James with a 29th minute dislocation of the shoulder.

The Wire's back row covered every inch of the Elland Road pitch to complete a dominant pack formation which overwhelmed a Halifax six which had been the backbone of their title success, only loose forward Paul Dixon showing his usual form.

Warrington opened the scoring after two minutes, Boyd powerdriving his way over from Tamati's pass. Teenage stand off Paul Bishop missed the kick, going on to hit five from 10 attempts.

Full back Colin Whitfield opened Halifax's account with a sixth minute penalty goal before the Champions strung together their best move of the afternoon to take the lead for the only time. Dixon was the key man, sweeping onto a pass from the hard working Gary Stephens to sell a neat dummy before charging clear and handing on to captain-coach Chris Anderson to round off a superb 60-yard move. Whitfield added the goal to give Halifax a four-point lead.

Young Bishop, on the eve of departure to join his famous father Tommy in Sydney, forced his way over in the 13th minute to level the scores before putting Warrington ahead 11 minutes later with a penalty goal, Whitfield pulling Halifax level again with his third goal just before the interval.

Warrington had the game sewn up within five minutes of the restart. Front row partners Tamati and Jackson claimed their touchdowns, each goalled by Bishop to open up a 12-point margin. Having relied on battering-ram tactics, the Wire could afford to be more adventurous and opened out to score a superbly worked try for Great Britain Under-21 threequarter Mark Forster, followed by one of the best solo efforts of the season.

Second touchdown for Harry Sunderland Trophy winner Les Boyd.

It went to substitute full back Brian Johnson in the 76th minute. The Australian fielded a Halifax drop out near his own 25-yard line and set off up the middle. A dummy and nimble footwork put him in the clear and he rounded off a 75-yard raid by sweeping between the posts, Bishop again adding the goal.

Just as it had been announced that assistant coach Boyd had earned Man of the Match rating, the stocky number eight rounded off an impressive display with his second try. Having sold a neat dummy, he switched direction to gallop 20 yards to the posts for the seventh and last Wire touchdown.

Bishop's goal took the Warrington tally to a record 38 points, passing the St. Helens score of 36 set only 12 months earlier, the 28-point winning margin surpassing the previous best of 24-2 set by Leeds when they beat Bradford Northern in 1979.

Despite playing behind a beaten pack, veteran scrum half Stephens could not be subdued, his opposite number Andy Gregory once again displaying his tendency to niggle on big occasions, a foul on Dixon as the half-time hooter blew earning him an official caution.

Referee of the Year Fred Lindop disallowed three tries, two against Warrington's Mark Roberts and Billy McGinty for double movements and one for Halifax hooker Seamus McCallion not being able to ground the ball over the line.

Warrington always held the upper hand as they steamed towards their first trophy for nearly four years, captain Boyd becoming only the second overseas player to receive the Harry Sunderland Trophy and Tony Barrow's promotion to first team coach being confirmed amid the dressing room celebrations.

SLALOM LAGER PREMIERSHIP FINAL

18th May   **Elland Road, Leeds**

HALIFAX 10   WARRINGTON 38

Halifax	No.	Warrington
Colin Whitfield	1.	Paul Ford
Eddison Riddlesden	2.	Mark Forster
Tony Anderson	3.	Paul Cullen
Chris Anderson, Capt.	4.	Ronnie Duane
Scott Wilson	5.	Brian Carbert
John Crossley	6.	Paul Bishop
Gary Stephens	7.	Andy Gregory
Mick Scott	8.	Les Boyd, Capt.
Seamus McCallion	9.	Kevin Tamati
Geoff Robinson	10.	Bob Jackson
Brian Juliff	11.	Gary Sanderson
Neil James	12.	Mark Roberts
Paul Dixon	13.	Mike Gregory
Steve Smith	14.	Brian Johnson
Steve Bond	15.	Billy McGinty

T: C. Anderson

G: Whitfield (3)

Substitutions:

Bond for James (29 min.)

Smith for Whitfield (73 min.)

Half-time 10-10

Referee: Fred Lindop (Wakefield)

T: Boyd (2), Bishop, Tamati, Jackson, Johnson, Forster

G: Bishop (5)

Substitutions:

Johnson for Ford (22 min.)

McGinty for Sanderson (67 min.)

Attendance: 13,683

1986 Round by Round

Leeds provided the shock of the first round by becoming the only away side to secure a passage into the semi-finals. The Loiners travelled to St. Helens to record a 38-22 victory against a Saints side which had just completed a record-equalling 13 consecutive Division One wins. Winger Carl Gibson celebrated his Great Britain squad call-up with two of Leeds' six tries.

Six days before their Wembley date with Castleford, Hull K.R. fielded a full strength team at Wigan and looked the better side until losing Phil Hogan with a broken arm after 24 minutes, full back George Fairbairn coming off with an injured knee four minutes later. As Wigan moved into a 10-0 lead, Rovers' Australian prop Peter Johnston was dismissed in the 51st minute and a Joe Lydon drop goal and Ronnie Braithwaite controversial try opened the floodgates. Ellery Hanley grabbed a Premiership record-equalling four tries as Wigan romped home 47-0.

Slalom Lager Champions Halifax rounded off a week of title celebrations with a 32-20 victory over Hull. Man of the Match Chris Anderson collected two tries in a high speed televised encounter, Hull summing up their season by being brilliant, but mostly erratic. John Crossley, who had spent most of the campaign on the Halifax substitute bench, revelled in a full game at stand off.

Fourth-placed Warrington were trailing 8-6 at home to Widnes with two minutes left when young Paul Bishop sprinted down the left to feed centre Ronnie Duane for the clinching touchdown. After an early war of attrition, Widnes looked in command mainly due to John Myler's tactical kicking and brother Tony's distribution.

In the semi-finals, Halifax secured their first victory over Leeds at Thrum Hall since 1964 with only three minutes left, Australian centre Tony Anderson scoring the winning try. After a first half of feuding, play opened up for a thrilling second period, the lead continually changing hands. Warrington travelled to Central Park to gain their first victory over Wigan in eight matches. The in-form Wire dominated the game from the start and half back Bishop hit a record equalling five drop goals as Warrington eased home 23-12, only Wigan's staunch defence preventing a wider margin.

1986 Results

First Round

Halifax	32	Hull	20
St. Helens	22	Leeds	38
Warrington	10	Widnes	8
Wigan	47	Hull K.R.	0

Semi-Finals

Halifax	16	Leeds	13
Wigan	12	Warrington	23

Final

Halifax	10	Warrington	38

(at Elland Road, Leeds)

1986 Prize: Winners £8,000

History

With the reintroduction of two divisions in 1973-74 there was no longer a need for a play-off to decide the championship.

However, it was decided to continue the tradition of an end-of-season play-off, the winners to receive the newly instituted Premiership Trophy.

In the first season of the Premiership, 1974-75, the top 12 Division One clubs and the top four from Division Two went into a first round draw, the luck of the draw operating through to the final, played on a neutral venue.

The following season the play-off was reduced to the top eight clubs in the First Division, the ties being decided on a merit basis i.e. 1st v. 8th, 2nd v. 7th etc. At the semi-final stage the highest placed clubs had the option of when to play at home in the two-legged tie.

In 1978-79 the two-leg system was scrapped and the higher placed clubs had home advantage right through to the neutrally staged final.

·

PREMIERSHIP ROLL OF HONOUR

Year	Winners	Runners-up	Venue	Attendance	Receipts
1975	Leeds 26	St. Helens 11	Wigan...................14,531		£7,795
1976	St. Helens 15	Salford 2	Swinton.................18,082		£13,138
1977	St. Helens 32	Warrington 20	Swinton.................11,178		£11,626
1978	Bradford N...........17	Widnes..................8	Swinton.................16,813		£18,677
1979	Leeds 24	Bradford N. 2	Huddersfield 19,486		£21,291
1980	Widnes 19	Bradford N. 5	Swinton.................10,215		£13,665
1981	Hull K.R. 11	Hull 7	Leeds 29,448		£47,529
1982	Widnes 23	Hull 8	Leeds 12,100		£23,749
1983	Widnes 22	Hull 10	Leeds 17,813		£34,145
1984	Hull K.R. 18	Castleford.............10	Leeds 12,515		£31,769
1985	St. Helens 36	Hull K.R. 16	Elland Rd, Leeds 15,518		£46,950
1986	Warrington 38	Halifax 10	Elland Rd, Leeds 13,683		£50,879

PREMIERSHIP FINAL . . . . A REVIEW

1974-75
Leeds 26 Holmes (2g) (Marshall 3g); Alan Smith
(1t), Hynes (1t, 1dg) (Eccles), Dyl, Atkinson
(2t), Mason (1t), Hepworth; Dickinson, Ward,
Pitchford, Cookson, Batten, Haigh
St. Helens 11 G. Pimblett; L. Jones (1t),
Wilson, Hull, Mathias (1t); Walsh, Heaton (1t);
Warlow (Cunningham), A. Karalius, Mantle
(K. Gwilliam), E. Chisnall, Nicholls, Coslett (1g)
Referee: W.H. Thompson (Huddersfield)
1975-76
St. Helens 15 G. Pimblett (3g); L. Jones, Glynn
(1t), Noonan, Mathias; Benyon, Heaton
(K. Gwilliam); Mantle, A. Karalius (1t), James,
Nicholls, E. Chisnall (1t), Coslett
Salford 2 Watkins (2dg); Fielding, Richards,
Hesketh, Graham; Butler, Nash; Coulman,
Raistrick, Sheffield, Knighton (Turnbull),
Dixon, E. Prescott
Referee: M. J. Naughton (Widnes)
1976-77
St. Helens 32 G. Pimblett (7g, 1t); L. Jones,
Benyon (1t), Cunningham (1t), Mathias (1t),
Glynn (Ashton); K. Gwilliam (1t); D. Chisnall,
Liptrot, James (1t); Nicholls (A. Karalius),
E. Chisnall, Pinner
Warrington 20 Finnegan; Curling, Bevan
(Cunliffe), Hesford (4g), M. Kelly; A. Gwilliam
(1t), Gordon (1t); Weavill (1t), Price, Case,
Martyn (Peers), Lester, B. Philbin (1t)
Referee: G.F. Lindop (Wakefield)
1977-78
Bradford N. 17 Mumby (2g); Barends (1t),
Roe (1t), Austin, D. Redfearn (1t); Wolford (1dg),
A. Redfearn; I. Van Bellen (Fox), Raistrick,
Thompson, Joyce (Forsyth), Trotter, Haigh (1t)
Widnes 8 Eckersley; Wright, Hughes, Aspey (2t),
Woods (1g); Gill, Bowden; Mills, Elwell, Shaw
(Ramsey) (George), Adams, Hull, Laughton
Referee: J.E. Jackson (Pudsey)

1978-79
Leeds 24 Hague; Alan Smith (1t), D. Smith (1t),
Dyl (Fletcher), Atkinson; Dick (7g, 1dg);
J. Sanderson, Harrison, Ward (1t), Pitchford,
Joyce, Eccles (Adams), Cookson
Bradford N. 2 Mumby; D. Parker, Okulicz,
Gant, Spencer; Ferres (1g), A. Redfearn;
Thompson, Bridges, Forsyth (I. Van Bellen),
Trotter (Mordue), Grayshon, Casey
Referee: W.H. Thompson (Huddersfield)
1979-80
Widnes 19 Burke (1g); Wright (1t), George,
Aspey (1t), Bentley (1t); Eckersley (1dg),
Bowden; Shaw, Elwell (1t, 1dg), M. O'Neill,
L. Gorley (1t), Hull (Hogan), Adams
Bradford N. 5 Mumby (1g); MacLean (Ferres),
D. Redfearn (1t), D. Parker, Gant; Stephenson,
A. Redfearn; Thompson, Bridges, Forsyth,
Clarkson (G. Van Bellen), Grayshon, Hale
Referee: W.H. Thompson (Huddersfield)

1980-81
Hull K.R. 11 Proctor; Hubbard (1g), M. Smith
(1t), Hogan (1t), Muscroft; Hartley (1t), Harkin;
Holdstock, Watkinson, Millington, Lowe, Casey,
Hall (Burton)
Hull 7 Woods (2g); Peacham, Elliott, Wilby,
Prendiville; Banks, Dean; Tindall, Wileman,
Stone, Skerrett (Madley), Crane (1t), Norton
Referee: J. Holdsworth (Leeds)
1981-82
Widnes 23 Burke (4g, 1t); Wright (1t), Kieron
O'Loughlin, Cunningham (A. Myler), Basnett
(1t); Hughes (1t), Gregory; M. O'Neill, Elwell,
Lockwood (Whitfield), L. Gorley, E. Prescott,
Adams (1t)
Hull 8 Kemble; O'Hara (Day), Leuluai,
S. Evans, Prendiville; Topliss, Harkin; Tindall,
Wileman (Lloyd), Stone, Skerrett, Crooks
(1t, 2g, 1dg), Norton
Referee: S. Wall (Leigh)

1982-83
Widnes 22 Burke; Linton, Hughes, Lydon (5g), Basnett (2t); A. Myler (1t), Gregory (1t) (Hulme); M. O'Neill, Elwell, L. Gorley, Whitfield (S. O'Neill), Prescott, Adams
Hull 10 Kemble; O'Hara (1t), Day (Solal), Leuluai, S. Evans; Topliss (1t), Dean; Skerrett, Bridges, Stone, Rose, Crooks (2g), Norton (Crane)
Referee: F. Lindop (Wakefield)
1983-84
Hull K.R. 18 Fairbairn; Clark, M. Smith (1t), Prohm (1t), Laws (1t); Dorahy (1t, 1g), Harkin; Holdstock, Rudd, Millington (Robinson), Burton (Lydiat), Broadhurst, Hall

Castleford 10 Roockley; Coen, Marchant, Hyde, Kear (1t); Robinson, R. Beardmore (3g); Ward, Horton, Connell, Crampton, Atkins, Joyner
Referee: R. Campbell (Widnes)
1984-85
St. Helens 36 Veivers (1t); Ledger (2t), Peters, Meninga (2t) (Allen), Day (4g); Arkwright, Holding; Burke (Forber), Ainsworth (1t), P. Gorley, Platt, Haggerty, Pinner (1t)
Hull K.R. 16 Fairbairn (1t, 2g); Clark, Robinson (1t), Prohm, Laws (1t); M. Smith, G. Smith (Harkin); Broadhurst, Watkinson, Ema (Lydiat), Kelly, Hogan, Hall
Referee: S. Wall (Leigh)

THE HARRY SUNDERLAND TROPHY

The trophy, in memory of the famous Queenslander, a former Australian Tour Manager, broadcaster and journalist, is presented to the Man of the Match in the end of season Championship or Premiership final.

The award is donated and judged by the Rugby League Writers' Association and was sponsored by Slalom Lager.

The Harry Sunderland Trophy Roll of Honour

Year	Winner	Team	Position
1965	Terry Fogerty	Halifax (v. St. Helens)	Second row
1966	Albert Halsall	St. Helens (v. Halifax)	Prop
1967	Ray Owen	Wakefield T. (v. St. Helens)	Scrum half
1968	Gary Cooper	Wakefield T. (v. Hull K.R.)	Full back
1969	Bev Risman	Leeds (v. Castleford)	Full back
1970	Frank Myler	St. Helens (v. Leeds)	Stand off
1971	Bill Ashurst	Wigan (v. St. Helens)	Second row
1972	Terry Clawson	Leeds (v. St. Helens)	Prop
1973	Mick Stephenson	Dewsbury (v. Leeds)	Hooker
1974	Barry Philbin	Warrington (v. St. Helens)	Loose forward
1975	Mel Mason	Leeds (v. St. Helens)	Stand off
1976	George Nicholls	St. Helens (v. Salford)	Second row
1977	Geoff Pimblett	St. Helens (v. Warrington)	Full back
1978	Bob Haigh	Bradford N. (v. Widnes)	Loose forward
1979	Kevin Dick	Leeds (v. Bradford N.)	Stand off
1980	Mal Aspey	Widnes (v. Bradford N.)	Centre
1981	Len Casey	Hull K.R. (v. Hull)	Second row
1982	Mick Burke	Widnes (v. Hull)	Full back
1983	Tony Myler	Widnes (v. Hull)	Stand off
1984	John Dorahy	Hull K.R. (v. Castleford)	Stand off
1985	Harry Pinner	St. Helens (v. Hull K.R.)	Loose forward
1986	Les Boyd	Warrington (v. Halifax)	Prop

PREMIERSHIP RECORDS
First staged 1975

ALL ROUNDS

TEAM

Highest score:
Hull K.R. 54 v. Leeds 0................................1984
(Also widest margin)
Biggest attendance:
29,448 Hull v. Hull K.R............Final at Leeds 1981

INDIVIDUAL

Most goals:
9 by Andy Gregory (Widnes) v. Leeds...Round 1 1982
Most points:
22 (7g, 2t) by John Dorahy (Hull K.R.) v. Leeds
............Round 1 1984
Most tries:
4 by David Hall (Hull K.R.) v. Castleford
............Round 1 1983
4 by Phil Ford (Wigan) v. Hull............Round 1 1985
4 by Ellery Hanley (Wigan) v. Hull K.R.
............Round 1 1986

PREMIERSHIP FINAL RECORDS

TEAM
Most final appearances:
4 by Widnes, St. Helens
Most wins:
3 by Widnes, St. Helens
Highest score (and widest margin):
Warrington 38 v. Halifax 10 1986
Biggest attendance:
29,448 Hull v. Hull K.R. (at Leeds) 1981

INDIVIDUAL
Most tries:
No player has scored 3 or more
Most goals:
8 by Kevin Dick (Leeds) v. Bradford N............1979
Most points: 17 (7g, 1t) by Geoff Pimblett (St. Helens)
v. Warrington..........1977

Warrington marksman Paul Bishop — on target five times in 10 attempts — enlists the aid of half back partner Andy Gregory in the windswept Elland Road Stadium.

LANCASHIRE CUP

1985 Final

Big spending Wigan extended their Lancashire Cup records by registering a 17th victory in their 31st final.

The rampaging Riversiders ran in a record 34 points, scoring five tries to Warrington's one, centre David Stephenson contributing a record-equalling seven goals, while missing five other attempts.

Staged in autumn sunshine, the county final had many turning points although the cup always seemed to be heading in Wigan's direction even when the Wire were 8-2 ahead.

Wigan's fine opening spell was marred by poor finishing by newboys Ellery Hanley and Andy Goodway which allowed tries to slip away. Stephenson and Great Britain Under-21 winger Brian Carbert had each kicked a penalty goal when Warrington shot ahead with a brilliant effort.

Scrum half Andy Gregory worked the blind side at a scrum and linked up with Australian full back Brian Johnson who left Wigan trailing on an 80-yard dash to the line, Carbert adding the goal.

It was the only assault on the Wigan line, as the Riversiders built a defensive wall, led by packmen Nick Du Toit and Ian Potter. The Challenge Cup holders replied with two first half tries, hooker Nicky Kiss struggling over and Australian Test stand off Steve Ella dummying his way through for Stephenson to add his second goal for an interval lead of 12-8.

Another Stephenson goal broadened the gap to six points before referee John Holdsworth sent off Warrington loose forward Alan Rathbone after 54 minutes for a late tackle on Potter. Andy Gregory followed him for an early bath 20 minutes later by which time Wigan were cantering to victory, their record points tally being curtailed by a series of blatant obstructions.

It was an afternoon of differing fortunes for the large contingent of Australians on view. Ella took over where Brett Kenny had left off, taking the Man of the Match award with two excellent tries, while Test colleague Greg Dowling was the cornerstone of an efficient Wigan pack.

While Johnson scored that memorable touchdown, team mates Les Boyd, still showing signs of rustiness after his enforced lengthy absence from the game, and high scoring centre Phil Blake, substituted through injury after 27 minutes, were not an effective force.

Wigan's second half burst of tryscoring came from Ella's second touchdown, a 65-yard sprint having been put clear in brilliant fashion by winger Colin Whitfield, Hanley and Shaun Edwards. Ella was run close for the Man of the Match award by team mates Mike Ford, Whitfield and Du Toit.

Acting Wigan skipper Andy Goodway holds aloft the Lancashire Cup.

BURTONWOOD BREWERY LANCASHIRE CUP FINAL

13th October   St. Helens

WARRINGTON 8   **WIGAN 34**

Brian Johnson	1.	Shaun Edwards
Brian Carbert	2.	Gary Henley-Smith
Paul Cullen	3.	David Stephenson
Phil Blake	4.	Ellery Hanley
Rick Thackray	5.	Colin Whitfield
Ken Kelly, Capt.	6.	Steve Ella
Andy Gregory	7.	Mike Ford
Bob Eccles	8.	Greg Dowling
Carl Webb	9.	Nicky Kiss
Robert Jackson	10.	Shaun Wane
Les Boyd	11.	Nick Du Toit
Mike Gregory	12.	Andy Goodway, Capt.
Alan Rathbone	13.	Ian Potter
Mark Forster	14.	Steve Hampson
Kevin Tamati	15.	Brian Case

T: Johnson   T: Ella (2), Kiss, Hanley, Edwards
G: Carbert (2)   G: Stephenson (7)
Substitutions: Substitutions:
Forster for Blake (27 min.)   Case for Wane (27 min.)
Tamati for Boyd (49 min.)   Hampson for Henley-Smith (58 min.)
Half-time: 8-12
Referee: John Holdsworth (Kippax)
Attendance: 19,202

1985 Round by Round

Holders Wigan set out on the defence of the county trophy by beating Second Division Fulham 24-13 at Central Park. The only bright spots for the Wigan fans were newboy Andy Goodway and New Zealand winger Gary Henley-Smith who scored a debutant try after only nine minutes. Great Britain Under-21 skipper Paul Groves was sent off in Salford's 18-14 home victory over derby rivals Swinton. The Red Devils were leading only 9-8 when their hooker was dismissed, but secured victory within minutes with a try from captain John Pendlebury. Bottom of the Second Division side Carlisle held St. Helens to a 26-8 lead at half-time before the Saints unleashed their scoring prowess to run in a total of 13 tries in a 72-8 landslide victory at Knowsley Road. In an all-Cumbria encounter, visitors Whitehaven raced 12-0 ahead before Barrow staged an eight-point comeback.

Runcorn Highfield's weaknesses were exposed by Workington Town, the visitors scoring four first half tries as the foundation for a 38-16 win at Canal Street. Second Division pacesetters Leigh toppled First Division leaders Oldham 40-12 at Hilton Park, new Australian recruit Trevor Cogger joining the list of tryscorers. Blackpool Borough travelled to Warrington to hold a 3-2 half-time lead before the Wire hit a five-minute purple patch to amass 18 points en route to a 30-3 victory, with Andy Gregory voted Man of the Match.

Rochdale Hornets' run of victories was disrupted by a 17-6 home defeat by Widnes, the boot of Mick Burke being decisive with four successful kicks.

In the second round, Wigan gained revenge for an earlier league defeat at the hands of Salford, but only just. Despite home advantage, Wigan only scraped home 22-20 with new skipper Andy Goodway scoring a try and making two others. Trailing 18-2 at the interval, Salford rallied under the inspiration of Australian Neil Baker but ran out of time. Forwards Bob Jackson and Alan Rathbone were the mainstays of Warrington's 38-4 home success over Workington Town, Bob Eccles and Phil Blake each grabbing two tries. Widnes produced another of their famous Houdini acts turning a 14-0 deficit at Leigh into an 18-14 victory, while St. Helens comfortably disposed of Cumbrian Second Division promotion candidates Whitehaven

by 26-8 at Knowsley Road, Sean Day contributing a try and five goals.

In the semi-finals, more than 18,000 fans turned up at Central Park to watch Wigan beat derby rivals St. Helens 30-2. Teenage stand off Shaun Edwards scored two brilliant tries but it was Australian Test man Steve Ella, imported to wear the number six jersey, who stole the spotlight by coming on as a 60th minute substitute to score a debutant try. Injury-hit Saints were further depleted in an undistinguished first half by the loss of Paul Forber with concussion and scrum half Neil Holding with a damaged shoulder. At Wilderspool, Warrington qualified for their first county cup final for three years with an 11-4 victory over Widnes. Australian stand off Phil Blake scored a try by following up his own kick through and then created a touchdown for half back partner Andy Gregory.

Warrington's record buy Andy Gregory meets a four-man Wigan reception committee.

169

1985 RESULTS

First Round

Barrow	8	Whitehaven	12
Leigh	40	Oldham	12
Rochdale H.	6	Widnes	17
Runcorn H.	16	Workington T.	38
Salford	18	Swinton	14
Warrington	30	Blackpool B.	3
St. Helens	72	Carlisle	8
Wigan	24	Fulham	13

Second Round

Leigh	14	Widnes	18
St. Helens	26	Whitehaven	8
Warrington	38	Workington T.	4
Wigan	22	Salford	20

Semi-Finals

Warrington	11	Widnes	4
Wigan	30	St. Helens	2

Final

Warrington (at St. Helens)	8	Wigan	34

Man of the Match Steve Ella.

LANCASHIRE CUP ROLL OF HONOUR

Season	Winners		Runners-up		Venue	Attendance	Receipts
1905-06	Wigan	0	Leigh	0	Broughton	16,000	£400
(replay)	Wigan	8	Leigh	0	Broughton	10,000	£200
1906-07	Broughton R.	15	Warrington	6	Wigan	14,048	£392
1907-08	Oldham	16	Broughton R.	9	Rochdale	14,000	£340
1908-09	Wigan	10	Oldham	9	Broughton	20,000	£600
1909-10	Wigan	22	Leigh	5	Broughton	14,000	£296
1910-11	Oldham	4	Swinton	3	Broughton	14,000	£418
1911-12	Rochdale H.	12	Oldham	5	Broughton	20,000	£630
1912-13	Wigan	21	Rochdale H.	5	Salford	6,000	£200
1913-14	Oldham	5	Wigan	0	Broughton	18,000	£610
1914-15	Rochdale H.	3	Wigan	2	Salford	4,000	£475
1915-16 to 1917-18 *Competition suspended*							
1918-19	Rochdale H.	22	Oldham	0	Salford	18,617	£1,365
1919-20	Oldham	7	Rochdale H.	0	Salford	19,000	£1,615
1920-21	Broughton R.	6	Leigh	3	Salford	25,000	£1,800
1921-22	Warrington	7	Oldham	5	Broughton	18,000	£1,200
1922-23	Wigan	20	Leigh	2	Salford	15,000	£1,200
1923-24	St. Helens Recs.	17	Swinton	0	Wigan	25,656	£1,450
1924-25	Oldham	10	St. Helens Recs.	0	Salford	15,000	£1,116
1925-26	Swinton	15	Wigan	11	Broughton	17,000	£1,115
1926-27	St. Helens	10	St. Helens Recs.	2	Warrington	19,439	£1,192
1927-28	Swinton	5	Wigan	2	Oldham	22,000	£1,275
1928-29	Wigan	5	Widnes	4	Warrington	19,000	£1,150
1929-30	Warrington	15	Salford	2	Wigan	21,012	£1,250

Season	Winners		Runners-up		Venue	Attendance	Receipts
1930-31	St. Helens Recs.	18	Wigan	3	Swinton	16,710	£1,030
1931-32	Salford	10	Swinton	8	Broughton	26,471	£1,654
1932-33	Warrington	10	St. Helens	9	Wigan	28,500	£1,675
1933-34	Oldham	12	St. Helens Recs.	0	Swinton	9,085	£516
1934-35	Salford	21	Wigan	12	Swinton	33,544	£2,191
1935-36	Salford	15	Wigan	7	Warrington	16,500	£950
1936-37	Salford	5	Wigan	2	Warrington	17,500	£1,160
1937-38	Warrington	8	Barrow	4	Wigan	14,000	£800
1938-39	Wigan	10	Salford	7	Swinton	27,940	£1,708
1939-40*	Swinton	5	Widnes	4	Widnes	5,500	£269
	Swinton	16	Widnes	11	Swinton	9,000	£446

Swinton won on aggregate 21-15
1940-41 to 1944-45 *Competition suspended during war-time*

Season	Winners		Runners-up		Venue	Attendance	Receipts
1945-46	Widnes	7	Wigan	3	Warrington	28,184	£2,600
1946-47	Wigan	9	Belle Vue R.	3	Swinton	21,618	£2,658
1947-48	Wigan	10	Belle Vue R.	7	Warrington	23,110	£3,043
1948-49	Wigan	14	Warrington	8	Swinton	39,015	£5,518
1949-50	Wigan	20	Leigh	7	Warrington	35,000	£4,751
1950-51	Wigan	28	Warrington	5	Swinton	42,541	£6,222
1951-52	Wigan	14	Leigh	6	Swinton	33,230	£5,432
1952-53	Leigh	22	St. Helens	5	Swinton	34,785	£5,793
1953-54	St. Helens	16	Wigan	8	Swinton	42,793	£6,918
1954-55	Barrow	12	Oldham	2	Swinton	25,204	£4,603
1955-56	Leigh	26	Widnes	9	Wigan	26,507	£4,090
1956-57	Oldham	10	St. Helens	3	Wigan	39,544	£6,274
1957-58	Oldham	13	Wigan	8	Swinton	42,497	£6,918
1958-59	Oldham	12	St. Helens	2	Swinton	38,780	£6,933
1959-60	Warrington	5	St. Helens	4	Wigan	39,237	£6,424
1960-61	St. Helens	15	Swinton	9	Wigan	31,755	£5,337
1961-62	St. Helens	25	Swinton	9	Wigan	30,000	£4,850
1962-63	St. Helens	7	Swinton	4	Wigan	23,523	£4,122
1963-64	St. Helens	15	Leigh	4	Swinton	21,231	£3,857
1964-65	St. Helens	12	Swinton	4	Wigan	17,383	£3,393
1965-66	Warrington	16	Rochdale H.	5	St. Helens	21,360	£3,800
1966-67	Wigan	16	Oldham	13	Swinton	14,193	£3,558
1967-68	St. Helens	2	Warrington	2	Wigan	16,897	£3,886
(replay)	St. Helens	13	Warrington	10	Swinton	7,577	£2,485
1968-69	St. Helens	30	Oldham	2	Wigan	17,008	£4,644
1969-70	Swinton	11	Leigh	2	Wigan	13,532	£3,651
1970-71	Leigh	7	St. Helens	4	Swinton	10,776	£3,136
1971-72	Wigan	15	Widnes	8	St. Helens	6,970	£2,204
1972-73	Salford	25	Swinton	11	Warrington	6,865	£3,321
1973-74	Wigan	19	Salford	9	Warrington	8,012	£2,750
1974-75	Widnes	6	Salford	2	Wigan	7,403	£2,833
1975-76	Widnes	16	Salford	7	Wigan	7,566	£3,880
1976-77	Widnes	16	Workington T.	11	Wigan	8,498	£6,414
1977-78	Workington T.	16	Wigan	13	Warrington	9,548	£5,038
1978-79	Widnes	15	Workington T.	13	Wigan	10,020	£6,261
1979-80	Widnes	11	Workington T.	0	Salford	6,887	£7,100
1980-81	Warrington	26	Wigan	10	St. Helens	6,442	£8,629
1981-82	Leigh	8	Widnes	3	Wigan	9,011	£14,029
1982-83	Warrington	16	St. Helens	0	Wigan	6,462	£11,732
1983-84	Barrow	12	Widnes	8	Wigan	7,007	£13,160
1984-85	St. Helens	26	Wigan	18	Wigan	26,074	£62,139
1985-86	Wigan	34	Warrington	8	St. Helens	19,202	£56,030

*Emergency War-time competition

171

LANCASHIRE CUP FINAL .... A REVIEW

1963-64
St. Helens 15 Coslett (3g); Killeen (1t),
Vollenhoven (1t), Northey, Harvey; Smith (1t),
A. Murphy; Tembey, Dagnall, Watson, French,
Ashcroft, Major
Leigh 4 Risman; Tyrer (2g), G. Lewis, Collins,
Leadbetter; Rhodes, Entwistle; Robinson,
J. Lewis, Owen, M. Murphy, M. Martyn, Hurt
Referee: R. Gelder (Wilmslow)
1964-65
St. Helens 12 F. Barrow; T. Pimblett, Northey,
Benyon (1t), Killeen (3g); Harvey, Murphy;
Tembey, Dagnall, Warlow, French, Hicks (1t),
Laughton
Swinton 4 Gowers (2g); Harries, Fleet, Buckley,
Speed; Parkinson, Williams; Bate, D. Clarke,
Halliwell, Rees, Simpson, Hurt
Referee: E. Clay (Leeds)
1965-66
Warrington 16 Bootle (2g); Fisher (1t),
Pickavance, Melling (2t), Glover (1t); Aspinall,
Smith; Payne, Oakes, Winslade, Robinson,
Thomas, Hayes
Rochdale H. 5 Pritchard; Pratt, Starkey (1t, 1g),
Chamberlain, Unsworth; Garforth, Fishwick;
Birchall, Ashcroft, Owen, Parr (Drui), Toga,
Baxter
Referee: E. Clay (Leeds)
1966-67
Wigan 16 Ashby; Boston (1t), Ashton (1t),
Holden, Lake; C. Hill, Parr; Gardiner, Clarke (1t),
J. Stephens, Lyon, Gilfedder (2g, 1t), Major
Oldham 13 McLeod; Dolly, McCormack,
Donovan (1t), Simms; Warburton (5g), Canning;
Wilson, Taylor, Fletcher, Smethurst, Irving,
Mooney
Referee: P. Geraghty (York)
1967-68
St. Helens 2 F. Barrow; Vollenhoven, Whittle,
Benyon, A. Barrow; Douglas, Bishop; Warlow,
Sayer, Watson, Hogan, Mantle, Coslett (1g)
Warrington 2 Affleck; Coupe, Melling, Harvey
(Pickavance), Glover; Aspinall (1g), Gordon;
Ashcroft, Harrison, Brady, Parr, Briggs, Clarke
Referee: G.F. Lindop (Wakefield)
Replay
St. Helens 13 F. Barrow; Vollenhoven, Smith,
Benyon, Jones (1t); Douglas (Houghton 2g),
Bishop; Warlow (1t), Sayer, Watson,
E. Chisnall (1t), Mantle, Coslett
Warrington 10 Conroy; Coupe, Melling (1t),
Allen (2g), Glover; Scahill, Gordon (1t); Ashcroft,
Harrison, Price, Parr, Briggs, Clarke
Referee: G.F. Lindop (Wakefield)

1968-69
St. Helens 30 Rhodes; F. Wilson (2t), Benyon,
Myler, Williams (1t); Whittle, Bishop (1t);
Warlow, Sayer, Watson, Rees (1t), E. Chisnall
(1t) Coslett (6g)
Oldham 2 Murphy; Elliott, Larder, McCormack,
Whitehead; Briggs (1g), Canning; K. Wilson,
Taylor, Fletcher (Maders), Irving, McCourt,
Hughes
Referee: W.H. Thompson (Huddersfield)
1969-70
Swinton 11 Gowers; Gomersall, Fleet, Buckley,
Philbin (1t); Davies, Kenny (4g); Bate, D. Clarke,
Mackay, Holliday, Smith, Robinson
Leigh 2 Grainey; Tickle, Warburton, Collins,
Stringer (Brown); Eckersley, Murphy (1g);
D. Chisnall, Ashcroft, Watts, Welding, Lyon,
Fiddler
Referee: E. Clay (Leeds)
1970-71
Leigh 7 Ferguson (2g); Tickle (Canning),
L. Chisnall, Collins, Walsh; Eckersley (1t),
Murphy; D. Chisnall, Ashcroft, Watts, Grimes,
Clarkson, Mooney
St. Helens 4 F. Barrow; L. Jones, Benyon,
Walsh, Wilson; Myler, Whittle; Halsall,
A. Karalius, Rees (Prescott), Mantle, E. Chisnall,
Coslett (2g)
Referee: W.H. Thompson (Huddersfield)
1971-72
Wigan 15 Tyrer (3g); Eastham (1t), Francis (1t),
Fuller, Wright (Gandy); D. Hill, Ayres (1t);
Ashcroft, Clarke, Fletcher, Ashurst, Kevin
O'Loughlin, Laughton
Widnes 8 Dutton; Brown, McLoughlin, Aspey
(1g), Gaydon (1t); D. O'Neill (1t), Bowden;
Warlow, Foran, Doughty, Kirwan, Walsh (Lowe),
Nicholls
Referee: W.H. Thompson (Huddersfield)
1972-73
Salford 25 Charlton (1t); Eastham (1t), Watkins
(1t, 5g), Hesketh, Richards (1t); Gill, Banner (1t);
Mackay, Walker, Ward, Whitehead, Dixon,
Prescott
Swinton 11 Jackson; Fleay (1t), Cooke, Buckley,
Gomersall; Kenny (1g) (M. Philbin), Gowers (3g);
Halsall, Evans, Bate, R. Smith (Holliday), Hoyle,
W. Pattinson
Referee: W.H. Thompson (Huddersfield)
1973-74
Wigan 19 Francis; Vigo, D. Hill, Keiron
O'Loughlin (2t), Wright (1t); Cassidy, Ayres (1g);
Smethurst, Clarke, Gray (4g), Irving,
D. Robinson, Cunningham

Salford 9 Charlton; Fielding, Watkins (1t, 3g), Hesketh, Holland; Gill, Banner; Mackay, Walker, Davies (Grice), Dixon, Kear (Knighton), E. Prescott
Referee: W.H. Thompson (Huddersfield)
1974-75
Widnes 6 Dutton (1g); George (1t), D. O'Neill, Aspey, A. Prescott; Hughes (1dg), Bowden; Mills, Elwell, J. Stephens, Adams, Blackwood, Laughton
Salford 2 Charlton; Fielding (1g), Dixon, Graham, Richards; Taylor, Banner; Mackay, Devlin, Grice, Knighton, Coulman, E. Prescott
Referee: G.F. Lindop (Wakefield)
1975-76
Widnes 16 Dutton (3g, 1dg); A. Prescott (1t), George (1t), Aspey (1t), Jenkins; Hughes, Bowden; Mills, Elwell, Nelson, Foran, Fitzpatrick (Sheridan), Adams
Salford 7 Watkins (2g); Fielding, Butler, Hesketh, Richards (1t); Gill, Nash; Fiddler, Hawksley, Dixon (Mackay), Turnbull, Knighton, E. Prescott
Referee: W.H. Thompson (Huddersfield)
1976-77
Widnes 16 Dutton (4g, 1dg); Wright (1t), Aspey, George (1t), A. Prescott; Eckersley, Bowden (1dg); Ramsey, Elwell, Nelson, Dearden, Adams, Laughton
Workington T. 11 Charlton; Collister, Wilkins (1t), Wright, MacCorquodale (4g); Lauder, Walker; Mills, Banks, Calvin, Bowman, L. Gorley, W. Pattinson (P. Gorley)
Referee: W.H. Thompson (Huddersfield)
1977-78
Workington T. 16 Charlton (Atkinson); Collister, Risman, Wright (1t), MacCorquodale (4g); Wilkins (1t), Walker (2dg); Watts, Banks, Bowman, L. Gorley, W. Pattinson, P. Gorley
Wigan 13 Swann; Vigo, Davies (Burke 1g), Willicombe; Hornby; Taylor, Nulty (1t, 1g); Hogan, Aspinall, Irving, Ashurst (1t), Blackwood, Melling (Regan)
Referee: W.H. Thompson (Huddersfield)
1978-79
Widnes 15 Eckersley; Wright (1t), Aspey, George, Burke (3g); Hughes, Bowden; Mills, Elwell, Shaw, Adams, Dearden (Hull), Laughton (2t)
Workington T. 13 Charlton; Collister, Risman, Wilkins (1t), MacCorquodale (1t, 2g), McMillan, Walker; Beverley, Banks, Bowman, Blackwood, P. Gorley, W. Pattinson (L. Gorley 1t)
Referee: W.H. Thompson (Huddersfield)
1979-80
Widnes 11 Eckersley; Wright, Aspey, Hughes (George), Burke (2g); Moran (1t), Bowden;

Hogan, Elwell (1dg), Shaw, L. Gorley, Dearden, Adams (1t)
Workington T. 0 Charlton; MacCorquodale, Maughan, Thompson, Beck; Rudd, Walker (Roper); Beverley, Banks, Wellbanks (Varty), W. Pattinson, Lewis, Dobie
Referee: W.H. Thompson (Huddersfield)
1980-81
Warrington 26 Finnegan; Thackray (1t), I. Duane, Bevan (1t), Hesford (7g, 1t); K. Kelly, A. Gwilliam; Courtney, Waller, Case, Martyn (1t), Eccles (Potter), Hunter
Wigan 10 Fairbairn (1t, 2g); Ramsdale (1t), Willicombe, Davies, Hornby; M. Foy, Bolton (Coyle); Breheny, Pendlebury (M. Smith), S. O'Neill, Melling, Clough, Hollingsworth
Referee: D. G. Kershaw (York)
1981-82
Leigh 8 Hogan; Drummond, Bilsbury (1t), Donlan (1dg), Worgan; Woods (2g), Green; Wilkinson, Tabern, Cooke, Martyn (Platt), Clarkson, McTigue
Widnes 3 Burke; George, Hughes, Cunningham, Bentley (1t); Moran, Gregory; M. O'Neill, Elwell, Lockwood, L. Gorley, E. Prescott, Adams
Referee: W.H. Thompson (Huddersfield)
1982-83
Warrington 16 Hesford (2g); Fellows (1t), R. Duane, Bevan, M. Kelly (1t); Cullen, K. Kelly (1t); Courtney, Webb, Cooke (D. Chisnall), Eccles (1t), Fieldhouse, Gregory
St. Helens 0 Parkes (Smith); Ledger, Arkwright, Haggerty, Litherland; Peters, Holding; James, Liptrot, Bottell (Mathias), Moorby, P. Gorley, Pinner
Referee: J. Holdsworth (Leeds)
1983-84
Barrow 12 Tickle (1dg); Moore, Whittle, Ball (3g, 1dg), Milby; McConnell (1t), Cairns; Hodkinson, Wall, McJennett, Herbert, Szymala, Mossop
Widnes 8 Burke; Lydon (1t, 2g), Hughes, Keiron O'Loughlin, Basnett; A. Myler, Gregory; S. O'Neill, Elwell, K. Tamati, Whitfield, E. Prescott, Adams
Referee: K. Allatt (Southport)
1984-85
St. Helens 26 Veivers (Haggerty 1t); Ledger, Allen, Meninga (2t), Day (1t, 5g); Arkwright, Holding; Burke, Liptrot, P. Gorley, Platt, Round, Pinner
Wigan 18 Edwards; Ferguson, Stephenson, Whitfield (3g), Gill (1t) (Pendlebury); Cannon, Fairhurst; Courtney, Kiss (1t), Case, West (1t), Wane, Potter
Referee: R. Campbell (Widnes)

173

MAN OF THE MATCH AWARDS

An award for the adjudged man of the match in the Lancashire Cup final was first presented in 1974-75. For four years the award was sponsored by the *Rugby Leaguer* newspaper. From 1978-79 the trophy was presented by Burtonwood Brewery as part of their sponsorship of the Lancashire Cup. Under the auspices of the *Rugby Leaguer*, the choice was made by the Editor, while Burtonwood Brewery invited a panel of the Press to make the decision.

Season	Winner	Team	Position
1974-75	Mike Coulman	Salford (v. Widnes)	Second row
1975-76	Mick George	Widnes (v. Salford)	Centre
1976-77	David Eckersley	Widnes (v. Workington T.)	Stand off
1977-78	Arnold Walker	Workington T. (v. Wigan)	Scrum half
1978-79	Arnold Walker	Workington T. (v. Widnes)	Scrum half
1979-80	Mick Adams	Widnes (v. Workington T.)	Loose forward
1980-81	Tony Waller	Warrington (v. Wigan)	Hooker
1981-82	Ray Tabern	Leigh (v. Widnes)	Hooker
1982-83	Steve Hesford	Warrington (v. St. Helens)	Full back
1983-84	David Cairns	Barrow (v. Widnes)	Scrum half
1984-85	Mal Meninga	St. Helens (v. Wigan)	Centre
1985-86	Steve Ella	Wigan (v. Warrington)	Stand off

LANCASHIRE CUP FINAL RECORDS

TEAM

Most appearances: 31 by Wigan
Most wins: 17 by Wigan
Highest score: Wigan 34 v. Warrington 8 1985
Widest margin: St. Helens 30 v. Oldham 2 1968
Biggest attendance:
42,793 St. Helens v. Wigan (at Swinton) 1953

INDIVIDUAL

Most tries:
4 by Brian Nordgren (Wigan) v. Leigh 1949
Most goals:
7 by Jim Ledgard (Leigh) v. Widnes 1955
   Steve Hesford (Warrington) v. Wigan 1980
   David Stephenson (Wigan) v. Warrington .. 1985
Most points:
17 (7g, 1t) by Steve Hesford (Warrington) v. Wigan
        1980

Australian Test star Steve Ella clashes head on with Ken Kelly (left) and Alan Rathbone.

YORKSHIRE CUP

1985 Final

Hull Kingston Rovers almost allowed the John Smiths Yorkshire Cup to slip from their grasp as a Castleford comeback produced 12 points in the last quarter of a highly entertaining Headingley final.

The Robins were coasting to victory at 22-6 when centre Tony Marchant crashed in for two tries in the 65th and 72nd minute, both goaled by scrum half Bob Beardmore to set up a tense final eight minutes. Marchant almost claimed a hat-trick having been prevented from grounding the ball while over the line on the hour.

Those final few minutes were played out at a stop-go tempo as Rovers tried to close the game up and Castleford frantically bid to open it out.

The Humberside outfit held supreme and received the county cup to complete their collection of trophies since Roger Millward took over as coach in March 1977. Australian centre John Dorahy equalled the record for most goals in a Yorkshire Cup final with five successful shots.

Hull K.R.'s overseas stars stole the show, with the Man of the Match award continuing the recent trend of being won by an Australian, this time the recipient being loose forward Gavin Miller.

New Zealanders Gary Prohm and Gordon Smith were prominent in the 40-yard move which produced Rovers' first try in the 15th minute, Miller touching down and Dorahy adding the goal to an earlier penalty.

Five minutes after the break, Miller dummied to pass to support way behind, the outrageous foil paving the way for a 25-yard dash to touch down for Dorahy to goal.

Only seven minutes later it was again Miller who earned the crowd's appreciation with a barnstorming run which demanded a three-man Castleford tackle, only for the Australian to stretch out a one-handed pass to give winger Garry Clark a clear run to the line, Dorahy's fifth goal providing Rovers with a 22-6 lead with 15 minutes left.

Castleford prop Kevin Ward spearheaded their last-ditch comeback with a powerhouse display which had been evident throughout Rovers' hour-long dominance.

The Glassblowers had been restricted to a Bob Beardmore try and Steve Diamond penalty and even the touchdown had come from a defensive blunder by the Robins. Prop Barry Johnson had put the scrum half through on the halfway line at the end of the first quarter and Beardmore's kick ahead went past full back George Fairbairn. Winger Clark cut across to cover but missed the ball and Beardmore showed excellent footwork to dribble the ball over the line for the touchdown.

It always seemed like a losing battle until Ward's powerhouse charges paved the way for both of Marchant's late tries. A well concealed pass created the first touchdown and eight minutes later the prop plunged forward and in his desperation to reach the Rovers line, lost the ball and while Rovers made a mess of gaining possession Marchant popped up to claim his second score.

Record equalling goalkicker John Dorahy.

175

JOHN SMITHS YORKSHIRE CUP FINAL

27th October   Leeds

CASTLEFORD 18   **HULL K.R.** 22

Castleford	No.	Hull K.R.
Gary Lord	1.	George Fairbairn
David Plange	2.	Garry Clark
Tony Marchant	3.	John Dorahy
Gary Hyde	4.	Gary Prohm
Chris Spears	5.	David Laws
Steve Diamond	6.	Gordon Smith
Bob Beardmore	7.	Paul Harkin
Kevin Ward	8.	Des Harrison
Kevin Beardmore	9.	David Watkinson, Capt.
Barry Johnson	10.	Asuquo Ema
Keith England	11.	Chris Burton
Martin Ketteridge	12.	Phil Hogan
John Joyner, Capt.	13.	Gavin Miller
David Roockley	14.	John Lydiat
Stuart Horton	15.	Andy Kelly

T: Marchant (2), R. Beardmore

G: R. Beardmore (2), Diamond

Half-time: 6-10

Referee: Ron Campbell (Widnes)

Attendance: 12,686

T: Miller (2), Clark

G: Dorahy (5)

Substitutions:

Lydiat for Fairbairn (Half-time)

Kelly for Hogan (73 min.)

1985 Round by Round

For the first time a preliminary round was staged following the inclusion of newcomers Sheffield Eagles. Ironically, the Eagles were drawn to meet Castleford at Wheldon Road going down 38-6. Right wing pair David Plange and Tony Marchant each bagged a brace of tries after Castleford had struggled for the opening 25 minutes before Plange opened their account.

In the first round, Hull lost their three-year grip on the county cup in a dull Humberside derby at Craven Park. Rovers were trailing with seven minutes left when a perfectly judged pass from loose forward Gavin Miller sent Phil Hogan over for his second try, levelling the scores at 10-10. Despite the blustery conditions, Australian John Dorahy added the goal to give Rovers a 12-10 victory. At Headingley, debutant stand off Cliff Lyons scored a hat-trick inside eight minutes in the second half as Keighley crashed 60-12 to a rampaging Leeds side. Loose forward Neil Kelly produced a two-try show for Dewsbury as the home side earned a 14-10 derby triumph over neighbours Batley. Bramley's Peter Lister, an early season try pacesetter, scored a late touchdown to secure a 22-10 home success over Doncaster.

At Wigginton Road, York were left short handed after the dismissal of hooker Peter Phillippo, Featherstone's Calvin Hopkins sealing a 26-18 victory with a try three minutes from time. Hunslet took a 2-0 lead at Castleford with a Gary Rowse penalty goal before the home side ran in 11 tries — four apiece to Tony Marchant and Chris Chapman — to run home 60-2 victors. Halifax emphasised the difference between the two divisions by swamping injury-hit visitors Huddersfield with 10 tries in a 52-14 hammering. Second Division promotion candidates Wakefield Trinity also found the gap too wide at Bradford Northern, going down 40-15 after leading 7-0 at the break. Marching orders were given to Trinity player-coach Len Casey and Northern's young packman Ian Sheldon in separate incidents.

In the second round, Northern's victory at Featherstone was sealed by half backs John Woods and Dean Carroll. A 22-11 success was based on tries from scrum half Carroll in the 37th and 60th minute, while Woods raced the length of the field to notch his side's fourth touchdown. Entertaining Castleford, confident Halifax opened the scoring with a Chris Anderson try. Reduced to 12 men after the sending off of second row man Keith England, Castleford still produced the faster, more effective football to win 24-4. Leeds visited Dewsbury and packman Roy Powell hit his hometown club with an opening try after only nine minutes, the first of nine Loiner touchdowns. Scrum half Mark Conway contributed 16 points with two tries and four goals. Hull K.R. progressed further towards a successive final by disposing of Second Division Bramley 30-6 at Craven Park. Victory was highlighted by two tries from Kiwi Gary Prohm but marred by serious injuries to winger Garry Clark and packman Phil Hogan.

In the semi-finals, Leeds suffered their first defeat of the season, visitors Castleford recording a 14-10 success in a thrilling encounter. Malcolm Reilly's men scored two tries in three minutes midway through the second half to clinch victory, Leeds having held a 10-6 lead. Winger Plange made the initial breakthrough with a 65th minute touchdown, rapidly followed by a Chris Spears score. Hull K.R. went through to a successive county cup final, defeating Bradford Northern 11-5 at Craven Park. Top try scorer Prohm snatched the vital touchdown in the 33rd minute beating two men at the corner after a break by Test forward Chris Burton. Northern were holding a 5-4 lead when the Kiwi struck, newboy Woods kicking two penalties and a drop goal. Northern substitute Mark Fleming was sent off in the 72nd minute.

1985 RESULTS

Preliminary Round

Castleford	38	Sheffield E.	6

First Round

Bradford N.	40	Wakefield T.	15
Bramley	22	Doncaster	10
Batley	10	Dewsbury	14
Castleford	60	Hunslet	2
Halifax	52	Huddersfield	14
Hull K.R.	12	Hull	10
Leeds	60	Keighley	12
York	18	Featherstone R.	26

Second Round

Dewsbury	2	Leeds	48
Featherstone R.	11	Bradford N.	22
Halifax	4	Castleford	24
Hull K.R.	30	Bramley	6

Semi-Finals

Hull K.R.	11	Bradford N.	5
Leeds	10	Castleford	14

Final

Castleford	18	Hull K.R.	22
(at Leeds)			

Man of the Match Gavin Miller.

177

YORKSHIRE CUP ROLL OF HONOUR

Year	Winners		Runners-up		Venue	Attendance	Receipts
1905-06	Hunslet	13	Halifax	3	Bradford P.A.	18,500	£465
1906-07	Bradford	8	Hull K.R.	5	Wakefield	10,500	£286
1907-08	Hunslet	17	Halifax	0	Leeds	15,000	£397
1908-09	Halifax	9	Hunslet	5	Wakefield	13,000	£356
1909-10	Huddersfield	21	Batley	0	Leeds	22,000	£778
1910-11	Wakefield T.	8	Huddersfield	2	Leeds	19,000	£696
1911-12	Huddersfield	22	Hull K.R.	10	Wakefield	20,000	£700
1912-13	Batley	17	Hull	3	Leeds	16,000	£523
1913-14	Huddersfield	19	Bradford N.	3	Halifax	12,000	£430
1914-15	Huddersfield	31	Hull	0	Leeds	12,000	£422
1918-19	Huddersfield	14	Dewsbury	8	Leeds	21,500	£1,309
1919-20	Huddersfield	24	Leeds	5	Halifax	24,935	£2,096
1920-21	Hull K.R.	2	Hull	0	Leeds	20,000	£1,926
1921-22	Leeds	11	Dewsbury	3	Halifax	20,000	£1,650
1922-23	York	5	Batley	0	Leeds	33,719	£2,414
1923-24	Hull	10	Huddersfield	4	Leeds	23,300	£1,728
1924-25	Wakefield T.	9	Batley	8	Leeds	25,546	£1,912
1925-26	Dewsbury	2	Huddersfield	0	Wakefield	12,616	£718
1926-27	Huddersfield	10	Wakefield T.	3	Leeds	11,300	£853
1927-28	Dewsbury	8	Hull	2	Leeds	21,700	£1,466
1928-29	Leeds	5	Featherstone R.	0	Wakefield	13,000	£838
1929-30	Hull K.R.	13	Hunslet	7	Leeds	11,000	£687
1930-31	Leeds	10	Huddersfield	2	Halifax	17,812	£1,405
1931-32	Huddersfield	4	Hunslet	2	Leeds	27,000	£1,764
1932-33	Leeds	8	Wakefield T.	0	Huddersfield	17,685	£1,183
1933-34	York	10	Hull K.R.	4	Leeds	22,000	£1,480
1934-35	Leeds	5	Wakefield T.	5	Dewsbury	22,598	£1,529
Replay	Leeds	2	Wakefield T.	2	Huddersfield	10,300	£745
Replay	Leeds	13	Wakefield T.	0	Hunslet	19,304	£1,327
1935-36	Leeds	3	York	0	Halifax	14,616	£1,113
1936-37	York	9	Wakefield T.	2	Leeds	19,000	£1,294
1937-38	Leeds	14	Huddersfield	8	Wakefield	22,000	£1,508
1938-39	Huddersfield	18	Hull	10	Bradford	28,714	£1,534
1939-40*	Featherstone R.	12	Wakefield T.	9	Bradford	7,077	£403
1940-41*	Bradford N.	15	Dewsbury	5	Huddersfield	13,316	£939
1941-42*	Bradford N.	24	Halifax	0	Huddersfield	5,989	£635
1942-43*	Dewsbury	7	Huddersfield	0	Dewsbury	11,000	£680
	Huddersfield	2	Dewsbury	0	Huddersfield	6,252	£618
	Dewsbury won on aggregate 7-2						
1943-44*	Bradford N.	5	Keighley	2	Bradford	10,251	£757
	Keighley	5	Bradford N.	5	Keighley	8,993	£694
	Bradford N. won on aggregate 10-7						
1944-45*	Hunslet	3	Halifax	12	Hunslet	11,213	£744
	Halifax	2	Hunslet	0	Halifax	9,800	£745
	Halifax won on aggregate 14-3						

Year	Winners		Runners-up		Venue	Attendance	Receipts
1945-46	Bradford N.	5	Wakefield T.	2	Halifax	24,292	£1,934
1946-47	Wakefield T.	10	Hull	0	Leeds	34,300	£3,718
1947-48	Wakefield T.	7	Leeds	7	Huddersfield	24,344	£3,461
Replay	Wakefield T.	8	Leeds	7	Bradford	32,000	£3,251
1948-49	Bradford N.	18	Castleford	9	Leeds	31,393	£5,053
1949-50	Bradford N.	11	Huddersfield	4	Leeds	36,000	£6,365
1950-51	Huddersfield	16	Castleford	3	Leeds	28,906	£5,152
1951-52	Wakefield T.	17	Keighley	3	Huddersfield	25,495	£3,347
1952-53	Huddersfield	18	Batley	8	Leeds	14,705	£2,471
1953-54	Bradford N.	7	Hull	2	Leeds	22,147	£3,833
1954-55	Halifax	22	Hull	14	Leeds	25,949	£4,638
1955-56	Halifax	10	Hull	10	Leeds	23,520	£4,385
Replay	Halifax	7	Hull	0	Bradford	14,000	£2,439
1956-57	Wakefield T.	23	Hunslet	5	Leeds	30,942	£5,609
1957-58	Huddersfield	15	York	8	Leeds	22,531	£4,123
1958-59	Leeds	24	Wakefield T.	20	Bradford	26,927	£3,833
1959-60	Featherstone R.	15	Hull	14	Leeds	23,983	£4,156
1960-61	Wakefield T.	16	Huddersfield	10	Leeds	17,456	£2,937
1961-62	Wakefield T.	19	Leeds	9	Bradford	16,329	£2,864
1962-63	Hunslet	12	Hull K.R.	2	Leeds	22,742	£4,514
1963-64	Halifax	10	Featherstone R.	0	Wakefield	13,238	£2,471
1964-65	Wakefield T.	18	Leeds	2	Huddersfield	13,527	£2,707
1965-66	Bradford N.	17	Hunslet	8	Leeds	17,522	£4,359
1966-67	Hull K.R.	25	Featherstone R.	12	Leeds	13,241	£3,482
1967-68	Hull K.R.	8	Hull	7	Leeds	16,729	£5,515
1968-69	Leeds	22	Castleford	11	Wakefield	12,573	£3,746
1969-70	Hull	12	Featherstone R.	9	Leeds	11,089	£3,419
1970-71	Leeds	23	Featherstone R.	7	Bradford	6,753	£1,879
1971-72	Hull K.R.	11	Castleford	7	Wakefield	5,536	£1,589
1972-73	Leeds	36	Dewsbury	9	Bradford	7,806	£2,659
1973-74	Leeds	7	Wakefield T.	2	Leeds	7,621	£3,728
1974-75	Hull K.R.	16	Wakefield T.	13	Leeds	5,823	£3,090
1975-76	Leeds	15	Hull K.R.	11	Leeds	5,743	£3,617
1976-77	Leeds	16	Featherstone R.	12	Leeds	7,645	£5,198
1977-78	Castleford	17	Featherstone R.	7	Leeds	6,318	£4,528
1978-79	Bradford N.	18	York	8	Leeds	10,429	£9,188
1979-80	Leeds	15	Halifax	6	Leeds	9,137	£9,999
1980-81	Leeds	8	Hull K.R.	7	Huddersfield	9,751	£15,578
1981-82	Castleford	10	Bradford N.	5	Leeds	5,852	£10,359
1982-83	Hull	18	Bradford N.	7	Leeds	11,755	£21,950
1983-84	Hull	13	Castleford	2	Elland Rd, Leeds	14,049	£33,572
1984-85	Hull	29	Hull K.R.	12	Hull C. FC	25,237	£68,639
1985-86	Hull K.R.	22	Castleford	18	Leeds	12,686	£36,327

* Emergency competition.

YORKSHIRE CUP FINAL .... A REVIEW

1963-64
Halifax 10 James (2g); Jackson (1t), Burnett,
C. Dixon, Freeman; Robinson, Marchant; Fox,
Shaw, Scroby, Phillips, Fogerty, Renilson (1t)
Featherstone R. 0 Fennell; Greatorex, Hunt,
Lynch, Jordan; Lingard, Fox; Terry, Fawley,
M. Dixon, Ramshaw, Brown, Clifft
Referee: D.T.H. Davies (Manchester)
1964-65
Wakefield T. 18 Metcalfe; Jones (2t), Thomas,
Fox (2t, 3g), Coetzer; Poynton, Owen;
Campbell, Shepherd, Vines, Haigh, Plumstead,
Holliday
Leeds 2 Dewhurst (1g); Cowan, Broatch,
Gemmell, Wrigglesworth; Shoebottom,
Seabourne; W. Drake, Lockwood,
Chamberlain, Clark, Neumann, J. Sykes
Referee: D.T.H. Davies (Manchester)
1965-66
Bradford N. 17 Scattergood; Williamson (2t),
Brooke (1t), Rhodes, Walker; Stockwell,
Smales; Tonkinson, Morgan, Hill, Ashton,
Clawson (4g), Rae
Hunslet 8 Langton (1g); Lee (1t), Shelton,
Render, Thompson (1t); Preece, Marchant;
Hartley, Prior, Baldwinson, Ramsey, Gunney,
Ward
Referee: W.E. Lawrinson (Warrington)
1966-67
Hull K.R. 25 C. Kellett (5g); Young (1t),
A. Burwell (1t), Moore (1t), Blackmore (1t);
Millward, Bunting; F. Fox, Flanagan (1t),
Tyson, Holliday, Foster, Major
Featherstone R. 12 D. Kellett; Thomas,
Greatorex, Wrigglesworth (1t), Westwood; M.
Smith, Dooler; Dixon, Kosanovic, Forsyth (1t),
A. Morgan, Lyons, Smales (3g)
Referee: B. Baker (Wigan)
1967-68
Hull K.R. 8 Kellett (1g); Young, Moore,
Elliott, A. Burwell (1t); Millward (1t), Cooper;
Holliday, Flanagan, Mennell, Lowe, Hickson
(Foster), Major
Hull 7 Keegan; Oliver, Doyle-Davidson,
Maloney (1g), Stocks; Devonshire, Davidson
(1t, 1g); Harrison, McGlone, Broom, Edson, J.
Macklin, Sykes
Referee: D.T.H. Davies (Manchester)
1968-69
Leeds 22 Risman (5g); Alan Smith (1t), Hynes,
Watson (1t), Atkinson (1t); Shoebottom,
Seabourne; Clark, Crosby, K. Eyre, Ramsey
(Hick 1t), A. Eyre, Batten

Castleford 11 Edwards; Howe, Hill (1t, 2g),
Thomas, Stephens; Hardisty (2g), Hargrave;
Hartley, C. Dickinson, Ward, Small,
Lockwood (Redfearn), Reilly
Referee: J. Manley (Warrington)
1969-70
Hull 12 Owbridge; Sullivan (1t), Gemmell,
Maloney (2g), A. Macklin; Hancock, Davidson;
Harrison, McGlone, J. Macklin (1t), Kirchin,
Forster, Brown (1g)
Featherstone R. 9 C. Kellett (3g); Newlove,
Jordan, M. Smith, Hartley (T. Hudson);
D. Kellett, Nash (1t); Tonks, Farrar, Lyons,
A. Morgan, Thompson, Smales
Referee: R.L. Thomas (Oldham)
1970-71
Leeds 23 Holmes; Alan Smith (2t), Hynes
(4g), Cowan, Atkinson (1t); Wainwright
(Langley), Shoebottom; J. Burke, Dunn (1t),
Cookson, Ramsey (1t), Haigh, Batten
Featherstone R. 7 C. Kellett (2g); M. Smith,
Cotton, Newlove, Hartley (1t); Harding
(Coventry), Hudson; Windmill, D. Morgan,
Lyons, Rhodes, Thompson, Farrar
Referee: D.S. Brown (Preston)
1971-72
Hull K.R. 11 Markham; Stephenson,
Coupland, Kirkpatrick, Longstaff (1t);
Millward (4g), Daley; Wiley, Flanagan,
Millington, Wallis, Palmer (Cooper), Brown
Castleford 7 Edwards; Foster (1t), S. Norton,
Worsley, Lowndes; Hargrave, Stephens;
Hartley, Miller, I. Van Bellen (Ackroyd 2g), A.
Dickinson, Lockwood, Blakeway
Referee: A. Givvons (Oldham)
1972-73
Leeds 36 Holmes (3t); Alan Smith, Hynes
(1g), Dyl (2t), Atkinson (1t); Hardisty (1t),
Hepworth (Langley); Clawson (5g) (Fisher),
Ward, Ramsey, Cookson, Eccles (1t), Batten
Dewsbury 9 Rushton; Ashcroft (1t), Childe,
Day, Yoward; Agar (3g), A. Bates; Bell
(Beverley), M. Stephenson, Lowe, Grayshon,
J. Bates (Lee), Hankins
Referee: M.J. Naughton (Widnes)
1973-74
Leeds 7 Holmes; Langley (1t) (Marshall 1g),
Hynes (1g), Dyl, Atkinson; Hardisty,
Hepworth; Jeanes (Ramsey), Ward, Clarkson,
Eccles, Cookson, Batten
Wakefield T. 2 Wraith (Sheard); D. Smith,
Crook (1g), Hegarty, B. Parker; Topliss,
Bonnar; Valentine, Morgan, Bratt, Knowles
(Ballantyne), Endersby, Holmes
Referee: M.J. Naughton (Widnes)

1974-75
Hull K.R. 16 Smithies; Sullivan (Dunn lt),
Watson (2t), Coupland, Kirkpatrick (1t);
Millward, Stephenson; Millington, Heslop,
Rose, Wallis, N. Fox (2g) (Madley), Brown
Wakefield T. 13 Sheard; D. Smith (1t), Crook
(2g), Hegarty (1t), Archer; Topliss, Bonnar;
Ballantyne, Handscombe, Bratt (1t), Skerrett,
A. Tonks (Goodwin), (Holmes), Morgan
Referee: M.J. Naughton (Widnes)
1975-76
Leeds 15 Marshall; Alan Smith, Hague, Dyl
(1t), Atkinson; Holmes (4g, 1dg), Hynes;
Harrison, Payne, Pitchford, (Dickinson),
Eccles, Batten, Cookson (1t)
Hull K.R. 11 Wallace; Dunn, A. Burwell,
Watson, Sullivan (1t); Turner, Millward (1dg);
Millington, Dickinson, Lyons, Rose, N. Fox
(2g, 1t), Hughes (Holdstock)
Referee: J.V. Moss (Manchester)
1976-77
Leeds 16 Marshall (2g); Hague, Hynes, Dyl
(2t), D. Smith; Holmes, Banner; Dickinson,
Ward, Pitchford, Eccles (1t), Burton, Cookson
(1t)
Featherstone R. 12 Box; Bray (1t), Coventry,
Quinn (3g), K. Kellett; Newlove, Fennell;
Gibbins, Bridges, Farrar, Stone, P. Smith (1t),
Bell (Spells)
Referee: M.J. Naughton (Widnes)
1977-78
Castleford 17 Wraith; Richardson, Joyner,
P. Johnson, Fenton; Burton (2t, 1dg), Pickerill
(Stephens); Fisher (Woodall), Spurr, Weston,
Huddlestone, Reilly, Lloyd (5g)
Featherstone R. 7 Marsden; Evans, Gilbert,
Quinn (1g) (N. Tuffs), K. Kellett; Newlove,
Butler; Townend (1g), Bridges, Farrar,
Gibbins, Stone (P. Smith 1t), Bell
Referee: M.J. Naughton (Widnes)
1978-79
Bradford N. 18 Mumby; Barends, Gant (1t),
D. Parker (1t), D. Redfearn; Slater (Wolford),
A. Redfearn (1t); Thompson, Fisher, Forsyth
(Joyce), Fox (3g), Trotter, Haigh (1t)
York 8 G. Smith (1t); T. Morgan, Day
(Crossley), Foster, Nicholson; Banks (2g),
Harkin; Dunkerley, Wileman, Harris, Rhodes,
Hollis (1dg) (Ramshaw), Cooper
Referee: M.J. Naughton (Widnes)
1979-80
Leeds 15 Hague; Alan Smith (2t), D. Smith
(1t), Dyl, Atkinson; Holmes (J. Sanderson),
Dick (3g); Dickinson, Ward, Pitchford, Eccles,
D. Heron (Adams), Cookson

Halifax 6 Birts (3g); Howard (Snee), Garrod,
Cholmondeley, Waites; Blacker, Langton;
Jarvis (Callon), Raistrick, Ward, Scott, Sharp,
Busfield
Referee: M.J. Naughton (Widnes)
1980-81
Leeds 8 Hague; Alan Smith (1t), D. Smith,
Atkinson, Oulton; Holmes, Dick (2g, 1dg);
Harrison, Ward, Pitchford, Eccles, Cookson
(Carroll), D. Heron
Hull K.R. 7 Robinson; McHugh (1t), M.
Smith, Hogan (2g), Youngman; Hall, Harkin;
Holdstock, Price, Crooks (Rose), Lowe, Casey,
Crane
Referee: R. Campbell (Widnes)
1981-82
Castleford 10 Claughton; Richardson, Fenton,
Hyde (1t), Morris; Joyner (1t), R. Beardmore;
Hardy (P. Norton), Spurr, B. Johnson, Finch
(2g), Ward, Timson
Bradford N. 5 Mumby; Barends, Hale,
A. Parker (1t), Gant; Hanley (1g), A.
Redfearn; Grayshon, Noble, Sanderson (D.
Redfearn), G. Van Bellen (Jasiewicz), Idle,
Rathbone
Referee: M.R. Whitfield (Widnes)
1982-83
Hull 18 Kemble; Evans (1t), Day, Leuluai,
Prendiville (1t); Topliss, Harkin; Skerrett,
Bridges, Stone, Rose (2t), Crooks (2g, 2dg),
Crane (Norton)
Bradford N. 7 Mumby; Barends, Gant,
A. Parker, Pullen (Smith); Whiteman (1t),
Carroll (1g, 2dg); Grayshon, Noble, G. Van
Bellen (Sanderson), Idle, Jasiewicz, Hale
Referee: S. Wall (Leigh)
1983-84
Hull 13 Kemble; Solal, Schofield, Leuluai,
O'Hara (1t); Topliss, Dean; Edmonds,
Wileman, Skerrett, Proctor (1t), Crooks, Crane
(1t, 1dg)
Castleford 2 Coen; Fenton, Marchant, Hyde
(Orum), Kear; Joyner, R. Beardmore (1g);
Connell, Horton, Reilly, Timson, James,
England
Referee: W.H. Thompson (Huddersfield)
1984-85
Hull 29 Kemble·(2t); Leuluai, Schofield (4g,
1dg), Evans (1t), O'Hara; Ah Kuoi, Sterling;
Edmonds, Patrick, Crooks (1t), Norton (1t),
Proctor, Divorty (Rose)
Hull K.R. 12 Fairbairn (1t); Clark, Robinson
(1t), Prohm, Laws; M. Smith, Harkin (Rudd);
Broadhurst, Watkinson, Ema (Hartley),
Burton, Kelly, Hall (1t)
Referee: G.F. Lindop (Wakefield)

THE WHITE ROSE TROPHY

First awarded in 1966, the trophy is presented to the adjudged man of the match in the Yorkshire Cup final.

Donated by the late T.E. Smith, of York, the award is organised by the Yorkshire Federation of Rugby League Supporters' Clubs and judged by a panel of the Press.

The Humberside clubs and Leeds have dominated the trophy, their players winning 16 of 20 awards, including the first 11 in succession.

Season	Winner	Team	Position
1966-67	Cyril Kellett	Hull K.R. (v. Featherstone R.)	Full back
1967-68	Chris Davidson	Hull (v. Hull K.R.)	Scrum half
1968-69	Barry Seabourne	Leeds (v. Castleford)	Scrum half
1969-70	Joe Brown	Hull (v. Featherstone R.)	Loose forward
1970-71	Syd Hynes	Leeds (v. Featherstone R.)	Centre
1971-72	Ian Markham	Hull K.R. (v. Castleford)	Full back
1972-73	John Holmes	Leeds (v. Dewsbury)	Full back
1973-74	Keith Hepworth	Leeds (v. Wakefield T.)	Scrum half
1974-75	Roger Millward	Hull K.R. (v. Wakefield T.)	Stand off
1975-76	Neil Fox	Hull K.R. (v. Leeds)	Second row
1976-77	Les Dyl	Leeds (v. Featherstone R.)	Centre
1977-78	Bruce Burton	Castleford (v. Featherstone R.)	Stand off
1978-79	Bob Haigh	Bradford N. (v. York)	Loose forward
1979-80	Alan Smith	Leeds (v. Halifax)	Winger
1980-81	Kevin Dick	Leeds (v. Hull K.R.)	Scrum half
1981-82	Barry Johnson	Castleford (v. Bradford N.)	Prop
1982-83	Keith Mumby	Bradford N. (v. Hull)	Full back
1983-84	Mick Crane	Hull (v. Castleford)	Loose forward
1984-85	Peter Sterling	Hull (v. Hull K.R.)	Scrum half
1985-86	Gavin Miller	Hull K.R. (v. Castleford)	Loose forward

YORKSHIRE CUP FINAL RECORDS

TEAM
Most appearances: 20 Huddersfield, Leeds
Most wins: 16 Leeds
Highest score: Leeds 36 v. Dewsbury 9............ 1972
Widest margin win: Huddersfield 31 v. Hull 0... 1914
Biggest attendance:
36,000 Bradford N. v. Huddersfield (at Leeds)....1949

INDIVIDUAL
Most tries:
4 by Stan Moorhouse (Huddersfield) v. Leeds.... 1919
Most points:
12 by Moorhouse (as above) plus
      (3g,2t) A. Edwards (Bradford N.) v. Castleford.
                        1948
      (3g,2t) Neil Fox (Wakefield T.) v. Leeds.. 1964
Most goals:
No player has scored more than 5.

1985 CHARITY SHIELD

Wigan lifted the inaugural Rugby League Charity Shield when, as Silk Cut Challenge Cup winners, they comfortably defeated Slalom Lager Champions Hull K.R. in this first-ever professional match on the Isle of Man.

The Riversiders ran in five tries to earn a £4,000 prize cheque from sponsors Okells Brewery and the acclaim of their fans who formed the vast majority of the 4,066 crowd.

Man of the Match Shaun Edwards — revelling in his traditional slot of stand off — and winger Henderson Gill starred in a highly competitive pipeopener to the new season as Wigan provided most of the entertainment for the August Bank Holiday crowd, drenched by driving rain which relented only as the historic encounter kicked off.

Despite the return to Australia of Lance Todd Trophy winner Brett Kenny, Wigan continued as they had left off at Wembley, while league title holders Rovers were often ponderous and uninventive despite a pull of 13-5 in the scrums and 10-6 in the penalty count.

Any suspicion of the Okells Charity Shield being a practice match was soon dispelled in the first hour when Hull K.R. displayed their renowned cast iron tackling to thwart a variety of tricks and ploys from Edwards who made light of the heavy pitch.

Wigan's only score in that period followed a handling error by Rovers stand off Mike Smith which centre Steve Donlan seized upon 30 yards out. Stephenson contributed three goals, to which Rovers' only reply was a John Lydiat penalty to take the score to 10-2 on the hour.

Then the Lancashire side — with Graeme West and South African Nick Du Toit dominant up front — staged a scoring blitz with 18 points in six minutes.

Rovers were forced into a series of handling errors and when Andy Kelly lost the ball, the lively Edwards gathered and kicked ahead and Gill, despite a Lydiat obstruction, followed up to make it unnecessary for referee Ron Campbell to award a penalty try.

Three minutes later Donlan showed speed and perception on a 40-yard dash to the line. The cheering had barely died down when Gill fielded a desperate kick from Lydiat to surge past the entire Rovers team for his second try.

The Robins reserved their best football for five minutes before the final whistle, Phil Hogan and Ian Robinson combining to send in Great Britain winger Garry Clark for their only touchdown.

It was Wigan who had the last word when Hull K.R.'s worrying lack of pace was again exposed by Stephenson and Phil Ford engineering a thrilling 75-yard move with scrum half Mike Ford touching down.

The clubs attended a celebration dinner at their Palace Hotel base before joining the ferry loads of supporters at a successful Rugby League cabaret evening.

Okells Brewery Man of the Match Shaun Edwards.

OKELLS CHARITY SHIELD

25th August **Douglas Bowl, Isle of Man**

HULL K.R. 6		WIGAN 34
George Fairbairn	1.	Steve Hampson
Garry Clark	2.	Phil Ford
Ian Robinson	3.	David Stephenson
Gary Prohm	4.	Steve Donlan
David Laws	5.	Henderson Gill
Mike Smith	6.	Shaun Edwards
Gordon Smith	7.	Mike Ford
Des Harrison	8.	Neil Courtney
David Watkinson, Capt.	9.	Nicky Kiss
Asuquo Ema	10.	Danny Campbell
Andy Kelly	11.	Graeme West, Capt.
Chris Burton	12.	Nick Du Toit
Phil Hogan	13.	Shaun Wane
John Lydiat	14.	Ian Lucas
Chris Rudd	15.	John Mayo

T: Clark
G: Lydiat
Substitutions:
Lydiat for Fairbairn (39 min.)
Rudd for Kelly (59 min.)
Half-time: 0-10
Referee: Ron Campbell (Widnes)
Attendance: 4,066

T: Donlan (2), Gill (2), M. Ford
G: Stephenson (7)
Substitutions:
Mayo for Courtney (62 min.)
Lucas for West (66 min.)

Wigan skipper Graeme West receives the inaugural Okells Brewery Charity Shield from chairman John Cowley.

Hull K.R. substitute John Lydiat sidesteps the grounded Mike Ford and the outstretched Graeme West.

Isle of Man celebrations for a mud-soaked Wigan.

BBC-2 FLOODLIT TROPHY

The BBC-2 Floodlit Trophy competition was launched in 1965 for clubs with flood-lights. Eight clubs competed in the first year and the total had grown to 22 by 1980 when the competition was abolished as part of the BBC's financial cut-backs.

For 15 years the matches became a regular television feature on Tuesday evenings throughout the early winter months.

Although the format changed slightly over the years, it was basically a knockout competition on the lines of the Challenge Cup.

In 1966 the Floodlit Competition was used to introduce the limited tackle rule, then four tackles, which proved such a great success it was adopted in all other matches before the end of the year.

BBC-2 FLOODLIT TROPHY FINALS
(Only the 1967, at Leeds, and 1972, at Wigan, finals were played on neutral grounds)

Season	Winners		Runners-up		Venue	Attendance	Receipts
1965-66	Castleford	4	St. Helens	0	St. Helens	11,510	£1,548
1966-67	Castleford	7	Swinton	2	Castleford	8,986	£1,692
1967-68	Castleford	8	Leigh	5	Leeds	9,716	£2,099
1968-69	Wigan	7	St. Helens	4	Wigan	13,479	£3,291
1969-70	Leigh	11	Wigan	6	Wigan	12,312	£2,854
1970-71	Leeds	9	St. Helens	5	Leeds	7,612	£2,189
1971-72	St. Helens	8	Rochdale H.	2	St. Helens	9,300	£2,493
1972-73	Leigh	5	Widnes	0	Wigan	4,691	£1,391
1973-74	Bramley	15	Widnes	7	Widnes	4,422	£1,538
1974-75	Salford	0	Warrington	0	Salford	4,473	£1,913
Replay	Salford	10	Warrington	5	Warrington	5,778	£2,434
1975-76	St. Helens	22	Dewsbury	2	St. Helens	3,858	£1,747
1976-77	Castleford	12	Leigh	4	Leigh	5,402	£2,793
1977-78	Hull K.R.	26	St. Helens	11	Hull K.R.	10,099	£6,586
1978-79	Widnes	13	St. Helens	7	St. Helens	10,250	£7,017
1979-80	Hull	13	Hull K.R.	3	Hull	18,500	£16,605

BBC2 FLOODLIT TROPHY . . . . A REVIEW
1965-66
Castleford 4 Edwards; C. Battye, M. Battye, Willett (2g); Briggs; Hardisty, Millward; Terry, J. Ward, C. Dickinson, Bryant, Taylor, Small
St. Helens 0 F. Barrow; Vollenhoven, Wood, Benyon, Killeen; Murphy, Prosser; French, Dagnall, Watson, Hicks, Mantle, Laughton
Referee: L. Gant (Wakefield)
1966-67
Castleford 7 Edwards; Howe, Stenton, Willett (1g), Austin (1t); Hardisty, Hepworth (1g); Hartley, C. Dickinson, McCartney, Bryant, Small, Walker
Swinton 2 Gowers; Whitehead (1g), Gomersall, Buckley, Davies; Fleet, G. Williams; Halliwell, D. Clarke, Scott (Cummings), Rees, Simpson, Robinson
Referee: J. Manley (Warrington)
1967-68
Castleford 8 Edwards; Harris, Thomas, Stenton, Willett (4g); Hardisty, Hepworth; Hartley, J. Ward, Walton, Bryant (C. Dickinson), Redfearn, Reilly

Leigh 5 Grainey; Tickle (1t), Lewis, Collins, Walsh; Entwistle, A. Murphy; Whitworth, Ashcroft, Major, Welding, M. Murphy, Gilfed-der (1g)
Referee: G.F. Lindop (Wakefield)
1968-69
Wigan 7 Tyrer (2g); Francis, Ashton, Ashurst, Rowe; C. Hill (1t), Jackson; J. Stephens, Clarke, Mills, Fogerty (Lyon), Kevin O'Loughlin, Laughton
St. Helens 4 Williams; Wilson, Benyon, Myler, Wills; Whittle, Bishop; Warlow, Sayer, Watson, Mantle, Hogan, Coslett (2g)
Referee: E. Clay (Leeds)
1969-70
Leigh 11 Ferguson (3g) (Lewis); Tickle (1t), Dorrington, Collins, Walsh; Eckersley, Murphy (1g); D. Chisnall, Ashcroft, Watts, Welding, Grimes, Lyon
Wigan 6 C. Hill; Wright, Francis (2g), Rowe, Kevin O'Loughlin; D. Hill (1g), Jackson; J. Stephens, Clarke, Ashcroft, Ashurst, Mills, Laughton
Referee: W.H. Thompson (Huddersfield)

1970-71
Leeds 9 Holmes (2g); Alan Smith, Hynes (1t, 1g), Cowan, Atkinson; Wainwright, Shoebottom; J. Burke, Fisher, Barnard, Haigh, Ramsey, Batten
St. Helens 5 F. Barrow; L. Jones (1t), Benyon, Walsh, Wilson; Whittle, Heaton; Rees, A. Karalius, E. Chisnall, Mantle, E. Prescott, Coslett (1g)
Referee: E. Lawrinson (Warrington)
1971-72
St. Helens 8 G. Pimblett; L. Jones, Benyon, Walsh, Wilson; Kelly, Heaton; Rees, A. Karalius, E. Chisnall, E. Prescott, Mantle, Coslett (4g)
Rochdale H. 2 Chamberlain (1g); Brelsford, Crellin, Taylor, Glover; Myler, Gartland; Birchall, P. Clarke, Brown, Welding, Sheffield (Hodkinson), Delooze
Referee: E. Clay (Leeds)
1972-73
Leigh 5 Hogan; Lawson (1t) (Lester), Atkin, Collins, Stacey; A. Barrow, Sayer (Ryding); Grimes, D. Clarke, Fletcher, Fiddler (1g), F. Barrow, Martyn
Widnes 0 Dutton; A. Prescott, Aspey, Blackwood, McDonnell; Lowe, Ashton; Mills, Elwell, Warlow, Foran, Sheridan, Nicholls
Referee: G.F. Lindop (Wakefield)
1973-74
Bramley 15 Keegan; Goodchild (1t), Bollon, Hughes, Austin (1t); T. Briggs, Ward (1g) (Ashman); D. Briggs, Firth, Cheshire, D. Sampson (1t), Idle, Wolford (2g)
Widnes 7 Dutton (2g); D. O'Neill, Hughes, Aspey, Macko (1t); Warburton, Bowden; Hogan, Elwell, Nelson, Sheridan, Blackwood (Foran) Laughton
Referee: D. G. Kershaw (York)
1974-75
Salford 0 Charlton; Fielding, Hesketh, Graham, Richards; Brophy (Taylor), Banner; Coulman, Devlin, Grice, Knighton, Dixon, E. Prescott
Warrington 0 Whitehead; Sutton, Cunliffe (Lowe), Whittle, Bevan; Briggs, Gordon; D. Chisnall, Ashcroft, Wright, Gaskell, Conroy, B. Philbin (Jewitt)
Referee: W.H. Thompson (Huddersfield)
Replay
Salford 10 Stead; Fielding (1t), Watkins (2g), Hesketh, Richards (1t); Gill, Banner; Grice, Walker, Mackay, Dixon, Knighton, E. Prescott

Warrington 5 Cunliffe; Whitehead (1g), Pickup, Whittle, Bevan (1t); Noonan (Briggs), Gordon; D. Chisnall, Ashcroft, Wanbon, Conroy, Nicholas (Brady), B. Philbin
Referee: W.H. Thompson (Huddersfield)
1975-76
St. Helens 22 G. Pimblett (2g); L. Jones, Benyon (1t), Hull (1t), Mathias (2t); Wilson (1t), Heaton (1dg); Mantle, A. Karalius, James, Nicholls, E. Chisnall, Coslett (1g)
Dewsbury 2 Langley; Hegarty, Chalkley, Simpson, Mitchell; N. Stephenson (1g) (Lee), A. Bates; Beverley, Price, Hankins, Halloran (Artis), Bell, Grayshon
Referee: W.H. Thompson (Huddersfield)
1976-77
Castleford 12 Wraith; Fenton, Joyner, P. Johnson, Walsh (1t); Burton (1t), Stephens; Khan, Spurr, A. Dickinson, Reilly, Lloyd (3g), S. Norton
Leigh 4 Hogan; A. Prescott, Stacey, Woods, Walsh (1t); Taylor, Sayer; D. Chisnall, Ashcroft (1dg), Fletcher, Macko, Grimes, Boyd
Referee: J.E. Jackson (Pudsey)
1977-78
Hull K.R. 26 Hall (4g); Dunn (2t), M. Smith (1t), Watson, Sullivan (1t); Hartley (1t), Millward; Millington, Watkinson, Cunningham (Hughes), Lowe, Rose (1t), Casey
St. Helens 11 G. Pimblett (Platt); L. Jones (Courtney), Noonan, Cunningham (1t), Glynn (2t, 1g); Francis, K. Gwilliam; D. Chisnall, Liptrot, James, Hope, A. Karalius, Pinner
Referee: M. J. Naughton (Widnes)
1978-79
Widnes 13 Eckersley; Wright (2t), Hughes, Aspey, P. Shaw; Burke (2g, 1t), Bowden; Hogan, Elwell, Mills, Adams, Dearden, Laughton
St. Helens 7 G. Pimblett (2g), L. Jones, Glynn, Cunningham, Mathias; Francis, Holding; D. Chisnall (1t), Liptrot, James, Nicholls, Knighton (E. Chisnall), Pinner
Referee: J. McDonald (Wigan)
1979-80
Hull 13 Woods; Bray, G. Evans (1t), Coupland, Dennison (1t, 2g); Newlove, Hepworth; Tindall, Wileman, Farrar, Stone, Boxall (Birdsall 1t), Norton
Hull K.R. 3 Robinson; Hubbard (1t), M. Smith, Watson, Sullivan; Hall, Agar; Holdstock, Tyreman, Lockwood, Clarkson (Hartley), Lowe, Hogan (Millington)
Referee: W.H. Thompson (Huddersfield)

CAPTAIN MORGAN TROPHY

This sponsored competition, with a winners' prize of £3,000, lasted only one season. Entry was restricted to the 16 clubs who won their Yorkshire and Lancashire Cup first round ties. The Lancashire contingent was made up to eight by including the side which lost their first round county Cup-tie by the narrowest margin. The first round of the Captain Morgan Trophy was zoned with clubs being drawn against those in their own county. The remainder of the competition was integrated. The final was on a neutral ground as follows:

1973-74   Warrington   4   Featherstone R.   0   Salford   5,259   £2,265

1973-74

Warrington 4 Whitehead (2g); M. Philbin, Noonan, Reynolds (Pickup), Bevan; Whittle, Gordon; D. Chisnall, Ashcroft, Brady, Wanbon (Price), Wright, Mather

Featherstone R. 0 Box; Coventry, M. Smith, Hartley, Bray; Mason, Wood; Tonks, Bridges, Harris, Gibbins (Stone), Rhodes, Bell
Referee: G.F. Lindop (Wakefield)

Queenslander Cavill Heugh, one of title victors Halifax's five Australian imports.

LEAGUE

1985-86 CHAMPIONSHIP

Revitalised Halifax lifted the Slalom Lager Championship Trophy after being quoted as 100-1 outsiders by bookmakers William Hill. It was only their second campaign after gaining promotion from the Second Division — the quickest title win by a promoted club.

The Thrum Hall club had last received the Championship Trophy as top four play-off victors in 1965, their only previous Division One title success being back in 1903.

Halifax's rapid transformation earned them the prestigious rating of Daily Mirror-Lada Cars Team of the Year to add to the Championship Trophy and a Slalom Lager prize cheque for £13,000.

The blue-and-whites were promoted in the 1983-84 season from fourth place, higher placed Barrow, Workington Town and Hunslet all making an immediate return to the lower division. Halifax retained their Championship status by finishing 10th in 1984-85 with 12 wins and two draws in their 30 fixtures.

That season of stabilisation was marked by a massive influx of Australian imports to Thrum Hall. For the 1985-86 campaign, dynamic club president David Brook filled the newly-imposed quota of five overseas players with the recruitment of Australians Joe Kilroy, Cavill Heugh and Geoff Robinson adding to player-coach Chris Anderson and centre Tony Anderson.

There was also an extensive spending spree in the domestic market before and during the season with the purchase of Mick Scott, Brian Juliff and Colin Whitfield from Wigan; scrum half Gary Stephens (Leigh); back row forward Paul Dixon (Huddersfield); winger Wilf George (Widnes); John Crossley (Bradford Northern); and second row man Neil James (Castleford) who was to become Halifax's 28th Great Britain cap.

St. Helens shot from 11th to third place by winning their last 13 matches to equal the Division One record run of successes.

The new look Halifax made a sluggish start, the end of September seeing them in 12th place with only one win and a draw from the opening five games. During the first half of the season, the Slalom Lager Championship table was headed by Hull K.R., Hull, Widnes and, for the whole of December, by Oldham.

Halifax topped the table for the first time on 5th January, adopting a policy of fulfilling league fixtures — hiring both Headingley and Halifax Town's Shay ground — and capitalising on a first round exit from the John Player Special Trophy and the Silk Cut Challenge Cup.

With less than two months left of the Slalom Lager Championship season Halifax were second to Widnes, with Wigan, Leeds and Hull K.R. all with matches in hand and mathematically able to climb over the ambitious Thrum Hall side.

The 2nd March table read:

	P	W	D	L	Pts
Widnes	21	15	2	4	32
Halifax	23	13	5	5	31
Wigan	19	12	2	5	26
Leeds	20	12	2	6	26
Hull K.R.	18	12	1	5	25

As the title race reached its climax, Wigan and Widnes both suffered unexpected defeats, while Leeds fell away after their Silk Cut Challenge Cup semi-final replay defeat by Hull K.R. The Robins, who had qualified for every first-class fixture at that late stage of the season, found themselves at Wembley with nine league fixtures to complete in the final 17 days of the campaign. They won only three of them and thrice fielded complete reserve teams to give their Wembley squad a break.

Halifax entered their final league encounter needing only a draw to secure the title. Visitors Featherstone Rovers were also desperate for points in their penultimate match, staging a relegation battle with York. They finished level at 13-13 amid controversial claims that the match had finished at least three minutes short. The League dismissed demands that the match be declared null and void as both club timekeepers insisted that their official duties had been carried out.

It was Halifax's sixth league draw—a record for any two-division campaign—with Wigan, St. Helens and Warrington all having won one more match than the new champions.

On the new three up-three down system, 1984-85 promoted sides York, Swinton and Dewsbury all made an immediate return to the Second Division, with the fourth promoted side Salford finishing in 10th position with 28 points.

A feature of the 1985-86 season was the Arctic conditions which virtually wiped out the February match programme. The Silk Cut Challenge Cup tournament timetable had to be rescheduled and a host of league matches postponed as the Cup fixtures took precedence. At the height of the bad weather in late February, only 12 fixtures were fulfilled in an 18-day period, nine of those taking advantage of underground heated pitches. The only concession to Slalom Lager Championship clubs was to extend the season by two days to 22nd April. A longer extension was not possible because the first round of the Premiership was scheduled for the weekend of 27th April including a televised game.

The Second Division was to have operated on a two-group formula providing 28 fixtures. The plan was abandoned only four days before the season opened when the League suspended Bridgend for not having a ground and Southend Invicta for not preparing a squad of players. The remaining 18 Second Division clubs agreed to play each other home and away to provide 34 fixtures with the season finishing on 11th May.

Leigh, pre-season 4-5 favourites with bookmakers William Hill, lost only one match en route to the Second Division Championship Bowl and a Slalom Lager prize cheque

of £9,000. They finished 12 points ahead of runners-up Barrow. Wakefield Trinity completed the trio of promoted clubs after two seasons in the lower grade.

The new champions created a Second Division record with 30 successive league victories beating Hull's previous best of 26 in their unbeaten campaign of 1978-79. The Hilton Park side also set a record for most points in a league season with 1,156.

One of the success stories of the season was founded in the Second Division. John Sheridan, appointed in June 1984 as the sixth Doncaster coach in five years, took the Tatters Field side to an all-time high 10th in the table with a club record 16 Division Two victories. Since the reintroduction of two divisions in 1973, Doncaster had never been out of the bottom four, finishing foot of the table on six occasions. The Dons' 611 points were the most scored in any league season and individual records were set by David Noble with most goals and points and by Neil Turner with most tries.

Having set up a new home at the Polytechnic of Central London Stadium, Chiswick, Fulham were rocked by the threat of being wound up by owners Barbara and Roy Close. Hours before the 1st April deadline, former Kent Invicta founder chairman Paul Faires stepped in to rescue the London club, ex-Invicta coach Bill Goodwin taking over from Roy Lester, who had resigned.

As the club was put into voluntary liquidation, the players fulfilled the fixture at Huddersfield without pay on 16th February, their 22nd league match of the season. Fulham's fixtures were then suspended until Faires' rescue act, resuming at home to Doncaster on 6th April. The League had to agree to a week's extension of the Second Division campaign for Fulham to fit in two outstanding home matches with Hunslet and Keighley.

At the end of the season Second Division

clubs expressed a desire to return to a fixture formula which provided 28 matches, six fewer than the 1985-86 campaign.

In May Sheffield Eagles submitted a format for final approval at a special meeting a month later based on the 18 Second Division clubs being divided into six groups of three.

The formula provided 28 matches by each club playing each other home and away expect that Group A would not play Group F, Group B would not meet Group E and Group C would not face Group D.

It was argued that the basic disadvantage of all the clubs not playing each other was outweighed by each club playing six fewer matches, an earlier finish to the Second Division season and the likely promotion candidates playing each other

It was also proposed that a Second Division Premiership be introduced on the same top eight format as operated in the Championship.

The division was decided by the 1985-86 final league placings with the three relegated clubs at the head of the list, as follows:

Group A	York	**Group B**	Whitehaven	**Group C**	Batley
	Swinton		Rochdale H.		Bramley
	Dewsbury		Blackpool B.		Fulham
Group D	Doncaster	**Group E**	Sheffield E.	**Group F**	Runcorn H.
	Carlisle		Hunslet		Keighley
	Workington T.		Huddersfield B.		Mansfield M.

1985-86 Second Division Champions Leigh team and officials, the Championship Bowl resting at the feet of Hilton Park captain Derek Pyke, flanked by chairman Brian Sharples (left) and coach Tommy Dickens (right).

FINAL TABLES 1985-86

SLALOM LAGER CHAMPIONSHIP

	P.	W.	D.	L.	Dr.	FOR Gls.	Trs.	Pts.	Dr.	AGAINST Gls.	Trs.	Pts.	Pts.
Halifax	30	19	6	5	7	66	90	499	5	58	61	365	44
Wigan	30	20	3	7	2	111	138	776	2	51	49	300	43
St. Helens	30	20	2	8	2	112	126	730	7	88	80	503	42
Warrington	30	20	1	9	9	92	118	665	5	68	63	393	41
Widnes	30	19	3	8	6	77	90	520	12	81	70	454	41
Leeds	30	15	3	12	2	88	94	554	6	84	86	518	33
Hull K.R.	30	16	1	13	5	79	86	507	4	73	87	498	33
Hull	30	15	2	13	2	83	112	616	6	81	85	508	32
Oldham	30	13	4	13	4	86	87	524	3	91	91	549	30
Salford	30	14	0	16	8	70	90	508	7	97	90	561	28
Castleford	30	12	1	17	1	89	93	551	3	87	102	585	25
Bradford N.	30	11	1	18	5	92	64	445	10	66	83	474	23
Featherstone R.	30	9	3	18	13	75	64	419	4	82	112	616	21
York	30	9	0	21	9	58	72	413	0	82	107	592	18
Swinton	30	8	0	22	5	63	60	371	2	89	117	648	16
Dewsbury	30	5	0	25	3	53	51	313	7	116	152	847	10

SECOND DIVISION

	P.	W.	D.	L.	Dr.	FOR Gls.	Trs.	Pts.	Dr.	AGAINST Gls.	Trs.	Pts.	Pts.
Leigh	34	33	0	1	4	166	205	1156	5	62	61	373	66
Barrow	34	27	0	7	2	131	187	1012	6	58	69	398	54
Wakefield T.	34	24	1	9	10	101	117	680	3	68	74	435	49
Whitehaven	34	22	0	12	9	91	107	619	9	67	84	479	44
Rochdale H.	34	21	0	13	9	125	126	763	7	73	83	485	42
Blackpool B.	34	20	0	14	7	101	140	769	4	89	97	570	40
Batley	34	18	3	13	9	87	96	567	2	70	77	450	39
Bramley	34	17	1	16	4	98	102	608	9	97	115	663	35
Fulham	34	16	1	17	9	99	118	679	15	103	122	709	33
Doncaster	34	16	1	17	9	103	99	611	2	82	121	650	33
Carlisle	34	15	2	17	13	90	98	585	4	93	123	682	32
Sheffield E.	34	14	1	19	6	83	86	516	11	87	108	617	29
Workington T.	34	13	0	21	2	87	127	684	9	119	119	723	26
Hunslet	34	11	3	20	2	94	101	594	7	116	139	795	25
Huddersfield B.	34	8	4	22	8	73	97	542	11	127	144	841	20
Runcorn H.	34	9	2	23	15	77	80	489	8	101	145	790	20
Keighley	34	9	2	23	7	55	71	401	14	150	151	918	20
Mansfield M.	34	2	1	31	5	61	64	383	4	160	189	1080	5

TWO DIVISION CHAMPIONSHIP ROLL OF HONOUR

	FIRST DIVISION	SECOND DIVISION
1902-03	Halifax	Keighley
1903-04	Bradford	Wakefield Trinity
1904-05	Oldham	Dewsbury
1962-63	Swinton	Hunslet
1963-64	Swinton	Oldham
1973-74	Salford	Bradford Northern
1974-75	St. Helens	Huddersfield
1975-76	Salford	Barrow
1976-77	Featherstone Rovers	Hull
1977-78	Widnes	Leigh
1978-79	Hull Kingston Rovers	Hull
1979-80	Bradford Northern	Featherstone Rovers
1980-81	Bradford Northern	York
1981-82	Leigh	Oldham
1982-83	Hull	Fulham
1983-84	Hull Kingston Rovers	Barrow
1984-85	Hull Kingston Rovers	Swinton
1985-86	Halifax	Leigh

THE UPS AND DOWNS OF TWO DIVISION FOOTBALL

●Figure in brackets indicates position in division.

	RELEGATED	PROMOTED
1902-03	St. Helens (17)	Keighley (1)
	Brighouse (18)	Leeds (2)
1903-04	Keighley (17)	Wakefield Trinity (1)
	Huddersfield (18)	St. Helens (2)
*1904-05	St. Helens (17)	Dewsbury (1)
	Runcorn (18)	Barrow (2)
1962-63	Oldham (15)	Hunslet (1)
	Bramley (16)	Keighley (2)
*1963-64	Keighley (15)	Oldham (1)
	Hull (16)	Leigh (2)
1973-74	Oldham (13)	Bradford Northern (1)
	Hull K.R. (14)	York (2)
	Leigh (15)	Keighley (3)
	Whitehaven (16)	Halifax (4)
1974-75	York (13)	Huddersfield (1)
	Bramley (14)	Hull K.R. (2)
	Rochdale Hornets (15)	Oldham (3)
	Halifax (16)	Swinton (4)

1975-76	Dewsbury (13) Keighley (14) Huddersfield (15) Swinton (16)	Barrow (1) Rochdale Hornets (2) Workington T. (3) Leigh (4)
1976-77	Rochdale Hornets (13) Leigh (14) Barrow (15) Oldham (16)	Hull (1) Dewsbury (2) Bramley (3) New Hunslet (4)
1977-78	Hull (13) New Hunslet (14) Bramley (15) Dewsbury (16)	Leigh (1) Barrow (2) Rochdale Hornets (3) Huddersfield (4)
1978-79	Barrow (13) Featherstone Rovers (14) Rochdale Hornets (15) Huddersfield (16)	Hull (1) New Hunslet (2) York (3) Blackpool Borough (4)
1979-80	Wigan (13) Hunslet (14) York (15) Blackpool Borough (16)	Featherstone Rovers (1) Halifax (2) Oldham (3) Barrow (4)
1980-81	Halifax (13) Salford (14) Workington T. (15) Oldham (16)	York (1) Wigan (2) Fulham (3) Whitehaven (4)
1981-82	Fulham (13) Wakefield T. (14) York (15) Whitehaven (16)	Oldham (1) Carlisle (2) Workington T. (3) Halifax (4)
1982-83	Barrow (13) Workington T. (14) Halifax (15) Carlisle (16)	Fulham (1) Wakefield T. (2) Salford (3) Whitehaven (14)
1983-84	Fulham (13) Wakefield T. (14) Salford (15) Whitehaven (16)	Barrow (1) Workington T. (2) Hunslet (3) Halifax (4)
1984-85	Barrow (13) Leigh (14) Hunslet (15) Workington T. (16)	Swinton (1) Salford (2) York (3) Dewsbury (4)
1985-86	York (14) Swinton (15) Dewsbury (16)	Leigh (1) Barrow (2) Wakefield T. (3)

*Two divisions scrapped following season.

FIRST DIVISION RECORDS
Since reintroduction in 1973

INDIVIDUAL

Match records
Most tries:
5 Roy Mathias (St. Helens) v. Rochdale H. Feb 17, 1974
Roy Mathias (St. Helens) v. Workington T.
  Dec 23, 1979
Parry Gordon (Warrington) v. Dewsbury Mar 3, 1974
Peter Glynn (St. Helens) v. Hull Oct 16, 1977
Steve Fenton (Castleford) v. Dewsbury Jan 27, 1978
Steve Hartley (Hull K.R.) v. Huddersfield Apr 13, 1979
Kevin Meadows (Oldham) at Salford Apr 20, 1984
John Woods (Bradford N.) v. Swinton Oct 13, 1985

Most goals: 13 Geoff Pimblett (St. Helens) v. Bramley
  Mar 5, 1978

Most points: 36 (8g, 5t) John Woods (Bradford N.) v.
  Swinton Oct 13, 1985

Season records
Most tries: 40 Ellery Hanley (Bradford N.) 1984-85
Most goals: 130 Steve Hesford (Warrington) 1978-79
Most points: 295 (101g, 1dg, 23t) John Woods (Leigh)
  1983-84

TEAM
Highest score: Bradford N. 72 v. Hunslet 12 Oct 7, 1984

Widest margin: St. Helens 71 v. Bramley 7 Mar 5, 1978

Highest away score: Carlisle 8 v. Castleford 66
  at Wakefield Apr 7, 1983 (Also widest margin)

In an orthodox away match:
  Workington T. 18 v. Hull 64 Apr 20, 1985
  (Also widest margin)

Most points by losing team:
  Hunslet 40 v. Barrow 41 Sep 9, 1984

Scoreless draw: Wigan 0 v. Castleford 0 Jan 26, 1974

Highest score draw: Widnes 28 v. St. Helens 28
  Apr 23, 1984

Best opening sequence: 13 wins then a draw by Widnes
  1981-82

Longest winning run: 13 by Widnes 1981-82
    13 by St. Helens 1985-86

Longest unbeaten run: 16 by Widnes (won last 12 of
  1973-74, drew first match of 1974-75 and won next three)

Longest losing run: 20 by Whitehaven 1983-84

Longest run without a win: 23, including 3 draws, by
  Whitehaven 1981-82 (Also worst opening sequence)

Biggest attendance: 21,813 Wigan v. St. Helens Dec 26,
1985

100 Division One tries
165 Keith Fielding (Salford)
144 David Smith (Wakefield T., Leeds, Bradford N.)
139 Stuart Wright (Wigan, Widnes)
136 Roy Mathias (St. Helens)
130 John Bevan (Warrington)
126 Steve Hartley (Hull K.R.)
122 Maurice Richards (Salford)
120 David Topliss (Wakefield T., Hull, Oldham)
118 Steve Evans (Featherstone R., Hull)
111 John Joyner (Castleford)
111 David Redfearn (Bradford N.)
107 John Woods (Leigh, Bradford N.)

500 Division One goals
846 Steve Hesford (Warrington)
749 George Fairbairn (Wigan, Hull K.R.)
743 Steve Quinn (Featherstone R.)
647 John Woods (Leigh, Bradford N.)
586 Sammy Lloyd (Castleford, Hull)

1,000 Division One points
1,756 Steve Hesford (Warrington)
1,648 John Woods (Leigh, Bradford N.)
1,618 George Fairbairn (Wigan, Hull K.R.)
1,614 Steve Quinn (Featherstone R.)
1,264 Sammy Lloyd (Castleford, Hull)

*Wigan centre David Stephenson, top Division One goalkicker
and points scorer in 1985-86.*

20 Division One tries in a season
1973-74 36 Keith Fielding (Salford)
        29 Roy Mathias (St. Helens)
        21 David Smith (Wakefield T.)
1974-75 21 Maurice Richards (Salford)
        21 Roy Mathias (St. Helens)
1975-76 26 Maurice Richards (Salford)
        20 David Smith (Wakefield T.)
1976-77 22 David Topliss (Wakefield T.)
        21 Keith Fielding (Salford)
        21 Ged Dunn (Hull K.R.)
        20 David Smith (Leeds)
        20 Stuart Wright (Widnes)
1977-78 26 Keith Fielding (Salford)
        25 Steve Fenton (Castleford)
        24 Stuart Wright (Widnes)
        20 David Smith (Leeds)
        20 Bruce Burton (Castleford)
        20 John Bevan (Warrington)
1978-79 28 Steve Hartley (Hull K.R.)
1979-80 24 Keith Fielding (Salford)
        21 Roy Mathias (St. Helens)
        21 Steve Hubbard (Hull K.R.)
        20 David Smith (Leeds)
1980-81 20 Steve Hubbard (Hull K.R.)
1981-82 David Hobbs (Featherstone R.) was top
        scorer with 19 tries.
1982-83 22 Bob Eccles (Warrington)
        20 Steve Evans (Hull)
1983-84 28 Garry Schofield (Hull)
        23 John Woods (Leigh)
        20 James Leuluai (Hull)
1984-85 40 Ellery Hanley (Bradford N.)
        34 Gary Prohm (Hull K.R.)
        23 Henderson Gill (Wigan)
        22 Barry Ledger (St. Helens)
        22 Mal Meninga (St. Helens)
1985-86 22 Ellery Hanley (Wigan)

Top Division One goalscorers
1973-74 126 David Watkins (Salford)
1974-75 96 Sammy Lloyd (Castleford)
1975-76 118 Sammy Lloyd (Castleford)
1976-77 113 Steve Quinn (Featherstone R.)
1977-78 116 Steve Hesford (Warrington)
1978-79 130 Steve Hesford (Warrington)
1979-80 104 Steve Hubbard (Hull K.R.)
1980-81 96 Steve Diamond (Wakefield T.)
1981-82 110 Steve Quinn (Featherstone R.)
           John Woods (Leigh)
1982-83 105 Bob Beardmore (Castleford)
1983-84 106 Steve Hesford (Warrington)
1984-85 114 Sean Day (St. Helens)
1985-86 85 David Stephenson (Wigan)

Top Division One pointscorer 1985-86
228 (83g, 2dg, 15t) David Stephenson (Wigan)

SECOND DIVISION RECORDS
Since reintroduction in 1973

INDIVIDUAL

Match records
Most tries: 6 Ged Dunn (Hull K.R.) v. New Hunslet
Feb 2, 1975
Most goals: 15 Mick Stacey (Leigh) v. Doncaster
Mar 28, 1976
Most points: 38 (13g, 4t) John Woods (Leigh) v.
Blackpool B. Sep 11, 1977

Season records
Most tries: 48 Steve Halliwell (Leigh) 1985-86
Most goals: 166 Lynn Hopkins (Workington T.)
1981-82
Most points: 395 (163g, 3dg, 22t) Lynn Hopkins
(Workington T.) 1981-82

TEAM

Highest score: Leigh 92 v. Keighley 2 Apr 30, 1986
(Also widest margin)
Highest away: Kent Invicta 8 v. Barrow 80 Apr 8, 1984
Most points by losing team:
Hunslet 38 v. Blackpool B. 32 Sep 22, 1985
Carlisle 32 v. Blackpool B. 33 Oct 27, 1985
Highest score draw: Huddersfield B. 32 v. Keighley 32
Apr 17, 1986
Scoreless draw: Dewsbury 0 v. Rochdale H. 0.
Jan 30, 1983
Longest winning run: 30 by Leigh in 1985-86. Hull won
all 26 matches in 1978-79
Longest losing run: 40 by Doncaster (16 in 1975-76 and
24 in 1976-77)
Biggest attendance: 12,424 Hull v. New Hunslet
May 18, 1979

1985-86 Top Division Two scorers
Most tries: 48 Steve Halliwell (Leigh)
Most goals: 149 Chris Johnson (Leigh)
Most points: 340 (147g, 2dg, 11t) Chris Johnson
(Leigh)

NB. Division One and Two records do not include scores
in abandoned matches that were replayed.

TWO DIVISION SCORING

The most significant change in the scoring pattern last season was a Division One record low total of placed-kick goals since the reintroduction of two divisions in 1973. The figure of 1,294 was a dramatic drop from the record high of 1,508 in the first season of 1973-74.

With the tryscoring total still well above those of early seasons the reduction must be in the number of penalty goals scored.

.The introduction in 1976-77 of the differential penalty rule which prevented kicks at goal for scrum offences had some effect but the goals total remained high until last season. It could be that the low goals total was due to fewer penalties being awarded as teams showed greater discipline and infringed the rules less.

The number of drop goals per season has varied with a succession of rule changes since they were reduced to one point in 1974. Only 48 were scored in Division One during that first season of devaluation but they grew to a peak of 147 in 1980-81. There was an unaccountable fall to 64 in 1982-83 before the hand-over rule pushed the total up to 108, although it fell back to 83 last season.

The fluctuating number of matches in Division Two over the years make comparisons for the lower league difficult.

The following tables show the scoring totals for each two-division season:

DIVISION ONE

Season	Matches each club played	Goals	1-Point drop goals	Tries	Pts
1902-03	34	541	—	692	3,158
1903-04	34	568	—	796	3,524
1904-05	34	659	—	817	3,769
1962-63	30	1,269	—	1,144	5,970
1963-64	30	1,234	—	1,244	6,200
1973-74	30	1,508	—	1,295	6,901
1974-75	30	1,334	48	1,261	6,499
1975-76	30	1,498	53	1,331	7,042
1976-77	30[1]	1,435	91	1,423	7,230
1977-78	30[2]	1,402	99	1,443	7,232
1978-79	30	1,367	119	1,448	7,197
1979-80	30	1,389	131	1,349	6,956
1980-81	30	1,439	147	1,342	7,051
1981-82	30	1,486	132	1,354	7,166
1982-83	30	1,369	64	1,386	6,960
1983-84	30	1,472	108	1,479	8,968
1984-85	30	1,464	84	1,595	9,392
1985-86	30	1,294	83	1,435	8,411

[1] Salford & Leeds played 29 matches — their final match was abandoned and not replayed. This match was expunged from league records.
[2] Featherstone R. & Bradford N. played 29 matches — their final match was cancelled following Featherstone's strike.

DIVISION TWO

Season	Matches each club played	Goals	1-Point drop goals	Tries	Pts
1902-03	34	542	—	723	3,253
1903-04	32	510	—	786	3,378
1904-05	26[1]	369	—	516	2,286
1962-63	26	907	—	856	4,382
1963-64	24[2]	739	—	701	3,581
1973-74	26	1,054	—	955	4,973
1974-75	26	992	36	919	4,777
1975-76	26	1,034	49	963	5,006
1976-77	26	942	78	1,046	5,100
1977-78	26	976	86	1,020	5,098
1978-79	26	971	114	972	4,972
1979-80	26	1,046	106	1,069	5,405
1980-81	28	1,133	123	1,220	6,049
1981-82	32	1,636	150	1,589	8,189
1982-83	32	1,510	103	1,648	8,067
1983-84	34	1,782	254	1,897	11,406
1984-85	28[3]	1,542	226	1,666	9,974
1985-86	34	1,722	130	2,021	11,658

[1] Birkenhead withdrew after 4 matches. These matches were expunged from league records.
[2] Bradford N. withdrew after 13 matches. These matches were expunged from league records.
[3] The 20 clubs played only 28 matches each.

THIRTEEN-SEASON TABLE

St. Helens are the most successful Division One club since the reintroduction of two divisions in 1973 in terms of most points gained. They regained the lead with a record-equalling 13 successive Division One wins at the end of the season to take their 13-season total to 517 points.

But it was Widnes who became the first club to reach the 500-point mark, achieving the target in their 378th Division One match with a 9-5 home victory over Castleford on 26th January.

St. Helens are the only club to have finished in the top eight each season although their only championship win was in 1974-75. In addition to St. Helens and Widnes the only other clubs to have remained in Division One are Castleford, Leeds and Warrington.

Three clubs have spent the entire 13 seasons in Division Two ... Batley, Doncaster and Runcorn Highfield.

Bradford Northern, Hull and Leigh were all Division Two champions who went on to win the Division One title only a few seasons after promotion, while Hull Kingston Rovers and Halifax are other former lower grade clubs who have won the trophy.

Halifax achieved the quickest Division One championship win when they took the title last season in only their second campaign after being promoted.

The highest place gained by a newly-promoted club is third by Hull in 1979-80 after winning the Division Two championship with a 100 per cent record the previous season.

Division One champions who were relegated a few seasons after winning the major title were Salford, Featherstone Rovers and Leigh.

The records of the five clubs who have appeared in Division One throughout the 13 seasons are as follows:

Scrum half Gary Stephens, key man for Slalom Lager Champions Halifax.

	P	W	D	L	F	A	Pts
1. St. Helens	390	250	17	123	7,629	5,023	517
2. Widnes	390	248	17	125	6,572	4,710	513
3. Leeds	389	226	16	147	6,969	5,527	468
4. Warrington	390	216	14	160	6,307	5,399	446
5. Castleford	390	191	23	176	6,917	6,076	405

● Although Bradford Northern and Hull Kingston Rovers have had only 12 seasons in Division One their records compare more favourably with some of the above. Three times champions Rovers have gained 458 points and Northern 418.

Crowd pleasing Australian full back Joe Kilroy registers one of his seven tries for 1985-86 title winners Halifax.

TWO DIVISION FINAL TABLES

Three eras
1902-05, 1962-64, 1973-85

1902-03:

FIRST DIVISION	P.	W.	D.	L.	F.	A.	Pts.
Halifax	34	23	3	8	199	85	49
Salford	34	20	5	9	244	130	45
Swinton	34	18	7	9	254	119	43
Runcorn	34	19	4	11	239	139	42
Broughton R.	34	17	7	10	222	97	41
Oldham	34	20	0	14	200	128	40
Bradford	34	16	5	13	220	161	37
Warrington	34	14	7	13	148	164	35
Hunslet	34	16	3	15	185	220	35
Hull	34	16	2	16	204	192	34
Batley	34	15	4	15	176	214	34
Leigh	34	12	5	17	136	178	29
Widnes	34	13	2	19	131	167	28
Hull K.R.	34	13	2	19	155	215	28
Huddersfield	34	13	2	19	116	196	28
Wigan	34	10	6	18	125	174	26
St. Helens	34	9	2	23	125	309	20
Brighouse R.	34	7	4	23	79	270	18

SECOND DIVISION	P.	W.	D.	L.	F.	A.	Pts.
Keighley	34	27	2	5	270	92	56
Leeds	34	26	1	7	334	98	53
Millom	34	22	3	9	238	118	47
Rochdale H.	34	20	6	8	323	88	46
Holbeck	34	20	5	9	213	83	45
Barrow	34	22	0	12	230	140	44
Wakefield T.	34	18	2	14	263	196	38
Bramley	34	16	4	14	179	151	36
Birkenhead	34	14	6	14	125	140	34
Manningham	34	14	5	15	141	170	33
Lancaster	34	13	4	17	123	214	30
Normanton	34	12	4	18	160	228	28
York	34	11	4	19	111	190	26
South Shields	34	10	2	22	158	264	22
Castleford	34	9	4	21	105	268	22
Dewsbury	34	8	5	21	123	245	21
Morecambe	34	9	2	23	88	220	20
Stockport	34	5	1	28	69	348	11

1903-04:

FIRST DIVISION

	P.	W.	D.	L.	F.	A.	Pts.
Bradford	34	25	2	7	303	96	52
Salford	34	25	2	7	366	108	52
Broughton R.	34	21	4	9	306	142	46
Hunslet	34	22	1	11	250	157	45
Oldham	34	20	3	11	215	110	43
Leeds	34	19	5	10	211	145	43
Warrington	34	17	3	14	214	153	37
Hull K.R.	34	17	2	15	191	167	36
Halifax	34	14	3	17	125	148	31
Wigan	34	11	6	17	177	174	28
Swinton	34	12	4	18	139	215	28
Batley	34	12	3	19	139	241	27
Hull	34	12	3	19	148	258	27
Widnes	34	11	5	18	126	243	27
Leigh	34	10	5	19	174	250	25
Runcorn	34	11	2	21	151	245	24
Keighley	34	8	5	21	129	319	21
Huddersfield	34	10	0	24	160	353	20

CHAMPIONSHIP PLAY-OFF
at Hanson Lane, Halifax

BRADFORD	1	1	5
SALFORD	0	0	0

SECOND DIVISION

	P.	W.	D.	L.	F.	A.	Pts.
Wakefield T.	32	27	1	4	389	57	55
St. Helens	32	23	3	6	328	105	49
Holbeck	32	24	1	7	256	120	49
Rochdale H.	32	22	2	8	319	104	46
York	32	20	1	11	244	97	41
Brighouse R.	32	19	3	10	192	136	41
Castleford	32	18	3	11	185	194	39
Bramley	32	16	4	12	181	180	36
Barrow	32	16	3	13	219	162	35
Pontefract	32	14	6	12	174	150	34
Dewsbury	32	12	3	17	185	205	27
Millom	32	12	2	18	185	209	26
Lancaster	32	8	2	22	129	291	18
Birkenhead	32	7	0	25	75	334	14
South Shields	32	6	1	25	140	336	13
Morecambe	32	5	3	24	72	287	13
Normanton	32	4	0	28	105	411	8

PROMOTION PLAY-OFF
at Huddersfield

ST. HELENS	1	2	7
HOLBECK	0	0	0

1904-05:

FIRST DIVISION

	P.	W.	D.	L.	F.	A.	Pts.
Oldham	34	25	1	8	291	158	51
Bradford	34	23	2	9	294	156	48
Broughton R.	34	22	2	10	295	175	46
Leeds	34	20	4	10	232	150	44
Warrington	34	20	2	12	220	150	42
Salford	34	19	2	13	276	204	40
Wigan	34	18	1	15	230	195	37
Hull	34	15	4	15	224	214	34
Hunslet	34	16	1	17	240	216	33
Halifax	34	15	2	17	204	155	32
Leigh	34	14	3	17	165	209	31
Hull K.R.	34	15	0	19	200	220	30
Swinton	34	13	2	19	155	196	28
Wakefield T.	34	13	2	19	154	211	28
Batley	34	12	3	19	160	228	27
Widnes	34	13	1	20	128	280	27
St. Helens	34	9	1	24	168	351	19
Runcorn	34	7	1	26	133	301	15

SECOND DIVISION

	P.	W.	D.	L.	F.	A.	Pts.
Dewsbury	26	22	2	2	247	48	46
Barrow	26	22	0	4	286	68	44
York	26	18	3	5	205	76	39
Keighley	26	15	2	9	259	94	32
Huddersfield	26	14	2	10	231	143	30
Rochdale H.	26	11	4	11	154	145	26
Millom	26	12	0	14	139	173	24
Pontefract	26	10	1	15	156	175	21
Castleford	26	9	3	14	104	199	21
Normanton	26	9	1	16	105	228	19
Brighouse R.	26	8	1	17	111	169	17
Lancaster	26	8	1	17	106	257	17
Morecambe	26	7	2	17	88	272	16
Bramley	26	5	2	19	95	239	12
Birkenhead	4	0	0	4	0	93	0

Birkenhead resigned from the League after four games. These are not included in the league table.

1962-63:

FIRST DIVISION

	P.	W.	D.	L.	F.	A.	Pts.
Swinton	30	22	1	7	372	231	45
St. Helens	30	19	1	10	525	260	39
Widnes	30	19	1	10	325	301	39
Castleford	30	16	3	11	370	321	35
Wakefield T.	30	16	1	13	432	359	33
Warrington	30	15	2	13	391	337	32
Leeds	30	16	0	14	333	364	32
Wigan	30	14	2	14	476	393	30
Huddersfield	30	14	0	16	298	278	28
Hull K.R.	30	13	1	16	389	387	27
Featherstone R.	30	12	3	15	389	407	27
Workington T.	30	12	3	15	410	441	27
Halifax	30	13	1	16	354	417	27
Hull	30	10	2	18	352	462	22
Oldham	30	9	1	20	288	432	19
Bramley	30	9	0	21	266	580	18

1963-64:

FIRST DIVISION

	P.	W.	D.	L.	F.	A.	Pts.
Swinton	30	25	0	5	401	202	50
Wigan	30	21	2	7	530	294	44
St. Helens	30	20	1	9	418	266	41
Featherstone R.	30	18	1	11	485	364	37
Workington T.	30	18	1	11	436	332	37
Castleford	30	18	0	12	436	338	36
Wakefield T.	30	16	0	14	488	339	32
Halifax	30	15	1	14	368	388	31
Hull K.R.	30	15	0	15	448	368	30
Warrington	30	15	0	15	374	380	30
Hunslet	30	14	0	16	371	487	28
Widnes	30	13	0	17	338	386	26
Leeds	30	10	0	20	323	493	20
Huddersfield	30	10	0	20	264	413	20
Keighley	30	5	0	25	253	599	10
Hull	30	4	0	26	267	551	8

SECOND DIVISION

	P.	W.	D.	L.	F.	A.	Pts.
Hunslet	26	22	0	4	508	214	44
Keighley	26	21	0	5	450	187	42
York	26	16	1	9	418	243	33
Blackpool B.	26	15	0	11	281	247	30
Rochdale H.	26	14	1	11	282	243	29
Barrow	26	14	0	12	413	280	28
Leigh	26	14	0	12	361	264	28
Batley	26	13	1	12	275	322	27
Whitehaven	26	12	2	12	318	306	26
Doncaster	26	10	0	16	283	329	20
Liverpool C.	26	9	1	16	159	328	19
Salford	26	8	1	17	271	442	17
Dewsbury	26	8	0	18	200	345	16
Bradford N.	26	2	1	23	163	632	5

SECOND DIVISION

	P.	W.	D.	L.	F.	A.	Pts.
Oldham	24	21	1	2	508	168	43
Leigh	24	16	2	6	411	224	34
Dewsbury	24	15	2	7	239	220	32
Barrow	24	14	1	9	351	280	29
Bramley	24	14	0	10	300	256	28
Blackpool B.	24	12	1	11	299	303	25
York	24	12	0	12	317	250	24
Rochdale H.	24	8	1	15	209	271	17
Liverpool C.	24	8	1	15	200	261	17
Batley	24	8	0	16	174	304	16
Whitehaven	24	8	0	16	173	341	16
Salford	24	8	0	16	218	392	16
Doncaster	24	7	1	16	182	311	15

*Bradford Northern disbanded after playing 13 matches. They won one and lost 12. For 109, Against 284. These matches were declared null and void.

1973-74:

FIRST DIVISION

	P.	W.	D.	L.	F.	A.	Pts.
Salford	30	23	1	6	632	299	47
St. Helens	30	22	2	6	595	263	46
Leeds	30	20	1	9	554	378	41
Widnes	30	18	1	11	431	329	37
Warrington	30	16	1	13	414	368	33
Dewsbury	30	16	1	13	389	474	33
Wakefield T.	30	16	0	14	470	411	32
Featherstone R.	30	14	2	14	443	397	30
Castleford	30	12	4	14	420	411	28
Rochdale H.	30	13	2	15	379	415	28
Wigan	30	12	3	15	427	364	27
Bramley	30	11	3	16	344	457	25
Oldham	30	12	1	17	341	494	25
Hull K.R.	30	9	2	19	428	552	20
Leigh	30	7	0	23	326	655	14
Whitehaven	30	7	0	23	308	634	14

SECOND DIVISION

	P.	W.	D.	L.	F.	A.	Pts.
Bradford N.	26	24	0	2	607	221	48
York	26	21	0	5	429	219	42
Keighley	26	20	0	6	439	250	40
Halifax	26	18	0	8	460	298	36
Workington T.	26	17	0	9	421	310	34
Hull	26	16	0	10	465	256	32
Swinton	26	15	0	11	405	276	30
Batley	26	12	0	14	286	311	24
Barrow	26	11	0	15	214	291	22
Huddersfield	26	9	0	17	363	394	18
N. Hunslet	26	7	0	19	272	418	14
Blackpool B.	26	7	0	19	272	585	14
Doncaster	26	3	0	23	158	684	6
Huyton	26	2	0	24	182	460	4

1974-75

FIRST DIVISION

	P.	W.	D.	L.	F.	A.	Pts.
St. Helens	30	26	1	3	561	229	53
Wigan	30	21	0	9	517	341	42
Leeds	30	19	1	10	581	359	39
Featherstone R.	30	19	1	10	431	339	39
Widnes	30	18	1	11	382	305	37
Warrington	30	17	1	12	428	356	35
Bradford N.	30	16	1	13	393	376	33
Castleford	30	14	3	13	480	427	31
Salford	30	14	1	15	451	351	29
Wakefield T.	30	12	5	13	440	419	29
Keighley	30	13	0	17	300	424	26
Dewsbury	30	11	0	19	350	506	22
York	30	10	0	20	359	498	20
Bramley	30	9	0	21	338	493	18
Rochdale H.	30	8	0	22	219	400	16
Halifax	30	5	1	24	269	676	11

SECOND DIVISION

	P.	W.	D.	L.	F.	A.	Pts.
Huddersfield	26	21	0	5	489	213	42
Hull K.R.	26	20	1	5	628	249	41
Oldham	26	19	0	7	406	223	38
Swinton	26	17	1	8	399	254	35
Workington T.	26	16	0	10	371	275	32
Whitehaven	26	14	1	11	285	234	29
Huyton	26	12	2	12	301	291	26
Hull	26	12	1	13	344	309	25
Barrow	26	12	2	13	338	315	24
Leigh	26	11	1	14	302	348	23
New Hunslet	26	10	2	14	309	384	22
Blackpool B.	26	7	1	18	261	417	15
Batley	26	4	1	21	197	520	9
Doncaster	26	1	1	24	147	745	3

203

1975-76

FIRST DIVISION

	P.	W.	D.	L.	F.	A.	Pts.
Salford	30	22	1	7	555	350	45
Featherstone R.	30	21	2	7	526	348	44
Leeds	30	21	0	9	571	395	42
St. Helens	30	19	1	10	513	315	39
Wigan	30	18	3	9	514	399	39
Widnes	30	18	1	11	448	369	37
Wakefield T.	30	17	0	13	496	410	34
Hull K.R.	30	17	0	13	446	472	34
Castleford	30	16	1	13	589	398	33
Warrington	30	15	2	13	381	456	32
Bradford N.	30	13	1	16	454	450	27
Oldham	30	11	1	18	380	490	23
Dewsbury	30	10	1	19	287	484	21
Keighley	30	7	0	23	274	468	14
Huddersfield	30	5	0	25	370	657	10
Swinton	30	3	0	27	238	581	6

SECOND DIVISION

	P.	W.	D.	L.	F.	A.	Pts.
Barrow	26	20	3	3	366	213	43
Rochdale H.	26	19	3	4	347	200	41
Workington T.	26	18	4	4	519	228	40
Leigh	26	19	1	6	571	217	39
Hull	26	19	1	6	577	278	39
New Hunslet	26	15	1	10	371	308	31
York	26	12	1	13	447	394	25
Bramley	26	11	1	14	344	370	23
Huyton	26	10	0	16	242	373	20
Whitehaven	26	8	2	16	253	347	18
Halifax	26	7	1	18	322	460	15
Batley	26	6	1	19	228	432	13
Blackpool B.	26	6	1	19	224	460	13
Doncaster	26	2	0	24	195	726	4

1976-77

FIRST DIVISION

	P.	W.	D.	L.	F.	A.	Pts.
Featherstone R.	30	21	2	7	568	334	44
St. Helens	30	19	1	10	547	345	39
Castleford	30	19	1	10	519	350	39
Hull K.R.	30	18	1	11	496	415	37
Warrington	30	18	0	12	532	406	36
Salford	*29	17	1	11	560	402	35
Wigan	30	15	2	13	463	416	32
Bradford N.	30	15	2	13	488	470	32
Leeds	*29	14	2	13	467	439	30
Widnes	30	15	0	15	403	393	30
Wakefield T.	30	13	2	15	487	480	28
Workington T.	30	13	1	16	352	403	27
Rochdale H.	30	11	0	19	367	449	22
Leigh	30	8	1	21	314	634	17
Barrow	30	8	0	22	345	628	16
Oldham	30	7	0	23	322	666	14

*The Salford v. Leeds match was abandoned after a fatal injury to Chris Sanderson (Leeds) and not replayed. Leeds were winning 5-2 after 38 mins. but the match was declared null and void.

SECOND DIVISION

	P.	W.	D.	L.	F.	A.	Pts.
Hull	26	22	1	3	599	238	45
Dewsbury	26	19	2	5	429	199	40
Bramley	26	19	0	7	464	377	38
New Hunslet	26	17	3	6	411	231	37
York	26	17	0	9	422	279	34
Keighley	26	16	1	9	486	235	33
Huddersfield	26	13	0	13	397	329	26
Whitehaven	26	11	1	14	290	346	23
Huyton	26	11	0	15	302	402	22
Halifax	26	10	0	16	301	429	20
Swinton	26	8	2	16	261	406	18
Batley	26	7	1	18	262	461	15
Blackpool B.	26	5	1	20	233	464	11
Doncaster	26	1	0	25	243	704	2

1977-78

FIRST DIVISION

	P.	W.	D.	L.	F.	A.	Pts.
Widnes	30	24	2	4	613	241	50
**Bradford N.	29	21	2	6	500	291	44
St. Helens	30	22	1	7	678	384	45
Hull K.R.	30	16	3	11	495	419	35
Wigan	30	17	1	12	482	435	35
Salford	30	16	0	14	470	446	32
Featherstone R.	29	15	2	12	443	452	32
Leeds	30	15	1	14	512	460	31
Warrington	30	15	0	15	561	367	30
Castleford	30	13	2	15	515	583	28
Workington T.	30	11	4	15	406	519	26
Wakefield T.	30	12	1	17	393	450	25
Hull	30	10	3	17	358	480	23
New Hunslet	30	11	0	19	318	518	22
Bramley	30	5	4	21	281	608	14
Dewsbury	30	2	2	26	207	579	6

**Bradford N. second on percentage as last game was cancelled following Featherstone's strike.

SECOND DIVISION

	P.	W.	D.	L.	F.	A.	Pts.
Leigh	26	21	0	5	538	231	42
Barrow	26	21	0	5	521	234	42
Rochdale H.	26	21	0	5	437	200	42
Huddersfield	26	18	0	8	502	324	36
York	26	16	2	8	447	286	34
Oldham	26	17	0	9	419	325	34
Keighley	26	11	3	12	357	337	25
Swinton	26	11	1	14	369	385	23
Whitehaven	26	10	2	14	277	326	22
Huyton	26	9	2	15	250	352	20
Doncaster	26	9	0	17	304	528	18
Batley	26	5	1	20	233	496	11
Blackpool B.	26	5	1	20	262	543	11
Halifax	26	2	0	24	182	531	4

1978-79

FIRST DIVISION

	P.	W.	D.	L.	F.	A.	Pts.
Hull K.R.	30	23	0	7	616	344	46
Warrington	30	22	0	8	521	340	44
Widnes	30	21	2	7	480	322	44
Leeds	30	19	1	10	555	370	39
St. Helens	30	16	2	12	485	379	34
Wigan	30	16	1	13	484	411	33
Castleford	30	16	1	13	498	469	33
Bradford N.	30	16	0	14	523	416	32
Workington T.	30	13	3	14	378	345	29
Wakefield T.	30	13	1	16	382	456	27
Leigh	30	13	1	16	406	535	27
Salford	30	11	2	17	389	435	24
Barrow	30	9	2	19	368	536	20
Featherstone R.	30	8	1	21	501	549	17
Rochdale H.	30	8	0	22	297	565	16
Huddersfield	30	7	1	22	314	725	15

SECOND DIVISION

	P.	W.	D.	L.	F.	A.	Pts.
Hull	26	26	0	0	702	175	52
New Hunslet	26	21	1	4	454	218	43
York	26	17	1	8	426	343	35
Blackpool B.	26	15	3	8	321	272	33
Halifax	26	15	2	9	312	198	32
Dewsbury	26	15	0	11	368	292	30
Keighley	26	12	2	12	357	298	26
Bramley	26	12	1	13	375	342	25
Oldham	26	10	1	15	297	435	21
Whitehaven	26	8	3	15	297	408	19
Swinton	26	7	2	17	349	452	16
Doncaster	26	7	0	19	259	547	14
Huyton	26	3	3	20	261	513	9
Batley	26	4	1	21	194	479	9

| 1979-80 | | | | | | | | 1980-81 | | | | | | | |

FIRST DIVISION

	P.	W.	D.	L.	F.	A.	Pts.
Bradford N.	30	23	0	7	448	272	46
Widnes	30	22	1	7	546	293	45
Hull	30	18	3	9	454	326	39
Salford	30	19	1	10	495	374	39
Leeds	30	19	0	11	590	390	38
Leigh	30	16	1	13	451	354	33
Hull K.R.	30	16	1	13	539	445	33
St. Helens	30	15	2	13	505	410	32
Warrington	30	15	2	13	362	357	32
Wakefield T.	30	14	2	14	435	466	30
Castleford	30	13	2	15	466	475	28
Workington T.	30	12	2	16	348	483	26
Wigan	30	9	3	18	366	523	21
Hunslet	30	7	1	22	346	528	15
York	30	6	1	23	375	647	13
Blackpool B.	30	5	0	25	230	613	10

SLALOM LAGER CHAMPIONSHIP

	P.	W.	D.	L.	F.	A.	Pts.
Bradford N.	30	20	1	9	447	345	41
Warrington	30	19	1	10	459	330	39
Hull K.R.	30	18	2	10	509	408	38
Wakefield T.	30	18	2	10	544	454	38
Castleford	30	18	2	10	526	459	38
Widnes	30	16	2	12	428	356	34
Hull	30	17	0	13	442	450	34
St. Helens	30	15	1	14	465	370	31
Leigh	30	14	1	15	416	414	29
Leeds	30	14	0	16	388	468	28
Barrow	30	13	0	17	405	498	26
Featherstone R.	30	12	0	18	467	446	24
Halifax	30	11	0	19	385	450	22
Salford	30	10	1	19	473	583	21
Workington T.	30	9	3	18	335	457	21
Oldham	30	7	2	21	362	563	16

SECOND DIVISION

	P.	W.	D.	L.	F.	A.	Pts.
Featherstone R.	26	21	2	3	724	280	44
Halifax	26	19	3	4	463	213	41
Oldham	26	19	3	4	513	276	41
Barrow	26	18	1	7	582	280	37
Whitehaven	26	15	1	10	397	276	31
Dewsbury	26	13	2	11	408	343	28
Rochdale H.	26	9	5	12	315	373	23
Swinton	26	11	1	14	331	436	23
Batley	26	10	2	14	232	370	22
Bramley	26	10	1	15	330	451	21
Keighley	26	10	0	16	342	396	20
Huddersfield	26	10	0	16	363	423	20
Huyton	26	5	0	21	209	555	10
Doncaster	26	1	1	24	196	733	3

SECOND DIVISION

	P.	W.	D.	L.	F.	A.	Pts.
York	28	23	0	5	649	331	46
Wigan	28	20	3	5	597	293	43
Fulham	28	20	0	8	447	237	40
Whitehaven	28	19	1	8	409	250	39
Huddersfield	28	18	1	9	429	310	37
Swinton	28	17	2	9	440	302	36
Keighley	28	14	1	13	445	501	29
Hunslet	28	13	1	14	447	430	27
Bramley	28	13	1	14	433	431	27
Rochdale H.	28	13	0	15	406	418	26
Batley	28	12	0	16	328	405	24
Dewsbury	28	11	1	16	346	364	23
Doncaster	28	5	0	23	250	562	10
Blackpool B.	28	4	1	23	212	419	9
Huyton	28	2	0	26	211	796	4

1981-82

SLALOM LAGER CHAMPIONSHIP

	P.	W.	D.	L.	F.	A.	Pts.
Leigh	30	24	1	5	572	343	49
Hull	30	23	1	6	611	273	47
Widnes	30	23	1	6	551	317	47
Hull K.R.	30	22	1	7	565	319	45
Bradford N.	30	20	1	9	425	332	41
Leeds	30	17	1	12	514	418	35
St. Helens	30	17	1	12	465	415	35
Warrington	30	14	2	14	403	468	30
Barrow	30	13	0	17	408	445	26
Featherstone R.	30	12	1	17	482	493	25
Wigan	30	12	0	18	424	435	24
Castleford	30	10	1	19	486	505	21
Fulham	30	9	1	20	365	539	19
Wakefield T.	30	9	1	20	341	526	19
York	30	4	2	24	330	773	10
Whitehaven	30	2	3	25	224	565	7

1982-83

SLALOM LAGER CHAMPIONSHIP

	P.	W.	D.	L.	F.	A.	Pts.
Hull	30	23	1	6	572	293	47
Hull K.R.	30	21	1	8	496	276	43
Wigan	30	20	3	7	482	270	43
St. Helens	30	19	1	10	516	395	39
Widnes	30	18	2	10	534	357	38
Leeds	30	18	2	10	480	443	38
Castleford	30	18	1	11	629	458	37
Oldham	30	15	2	13	346	320	32
Bradford N.	30	14	2	14	381	314	30
Leigh	30	13	3	14	488	374	29
Warrington	30	13	2	15	423	410	28
Featherstone R.	30	10	4	16	350	447	24
Barrow	30	11	1	18	472	505	23
Workington T.	30	6	2	22	318	696	14
Halifax	30	5	1	24	221	651	11
Carlisle	30	2	0	28	252	751	4

SECOND DIVISION

	P.	W.	D.	L.	F.	A.	Pts.
Oldham	32	30	0	2	734	276	60
Carlisle	32	28	0	4	649	296	56
Workington T.	32	24	0	8	777	311	48
Halifax	32	22	0	10	516	340	44
Salford	32	20	1	11	656	433	41
Hunslet	32	18	1	13	481	452	37
Keighley	32	18	0	14	514	426	36
Cardiff C.	32	17	1	14	566	549	35
Dewsbury	32	16	0	16	357	464	32
Swinton	32	15	0	17	514	418	30
Huddersfield	32	13	1	18	370	523	27
Bramley	32	13	0	19	381	513	26
Rochdale H.	32	10	1	21	361	484	21
Batley	32	8	0	24	357	596	16
Blackpool B.	32	7	0	25	341	608	14
Doncaster	32	5	1	26	319	793	11
Huyton	32	5	0	27	296	707	10

SECOND DIVISION

	P.	W.	D.	L.	F.	A.	Pts.
Fulham	32	27	1	4	699	294	55
Wakefield T.	32	25	2	5	672	381	52
Salford	32	24	0	8	686	363	48
Whitehaven	32	20	3	9	464	298	43
Bramley	32	20	1	11	560	369	41
Hunslet	32	17	5	10	553	448	39
Swinton	32	19	1	12	549	454	39
Cardiff C.	32	17	2	13	572	444	36
Keighley	32	15	5	12	470	423	35
York	32	15	0	17	516	455	30
Blackpool B.	32	13	1	18	381	433	27
Huddersfield	32	13	1	18	397	524	27
Rochdale H.	32	10	5	17	361	469	25
Dewsbury	32	8	1	23	325	507	17
Batley	32	6	1	25	305	719	13
Huyton	32	6	0	26	250	687	12
Doncaster	32	2	1	29	307	799	5

1983-84

SLALOM LAGER CHAMPIONSHIP

	P.	W.	D.	L.	F.	A.	Pts.
Hull K.R.	30	22	2	6	795	421	46
Hull	30	22	1	7	831	401	45
Warrington	30	19	2	9	622	528	40
Castleford	30	18	3	9	686	438	39
Widnes	30	19	1	10	656	457	39
St. Helens	30	18	1	11	649	507	37
Bradford N.	30	17	2	11	519	379	36
Leeds	30	15	3	12	553	514	33
Wigan	30	16	0	14	533	465	32
Oldham	30	15	2	13	544	480	32
Leigh	30	14	0	16	623	599	28
Featherstone R.	30	11	2	17	464	562	24
Fulham	30	9	1	20	401	694	19
Wakefield T.	30	7	0	23	415	780	14
Salford	30	5	0	25	352	787	10
Whitehaven	30	3	0	27	325	956	6

SECOND DIVISION

	P.	W.	D.	L.	F.	A.	Pts.
Barrow	34	32	0	2	1126	332	64
Workington T.	34	24	2	8	714	504	50
Hunslet	34	24	0	10	900	597	48
Halifax	34	23	2	9	722	539	48
Blackpool B.	34	20	3	11	615	466	43
Swinton	34	21	0	13	764	437	42
York	34	19	2	13	743	570	40
Bramley	34	16	2	16	584	545	34
Kent Invicta	34	17	0	17	595	700	34
Huddersfield	34	15	3	16	600	545	33
Cardiff C.	34	15	1	18	710	717	31
Rochdale H.	34	13	3	18	551	667	29
Batley	34	13	0	21	477	738	26
Dewsbury	34	12	0	22	526	698	24
Carlisle	34	12	0	22	539	780	24
Huyton	34	9	2	23	431	760	20
Keighley	34	7	3	24	425	728	17
Doncaster	34	2	1	31	384	1083	5

1984-85

SLALOM LAGER CHAMPIONSHIP

	P.	W.	D.	L.	F.	A.	Pts.
Hull K.R.	30	24	0	6	778	391	48
St. Helens	30	22	1	7	920	508	45
Wigan	30	21	1	8	720	459	43
Leeds	30	20	1	9	650	377	41
Oldham	30	18	1	11	563	439	37
Hull	30	17	1	12	733	550	35
Widnes	30	17	0	13	580	517	34
Bradford N.	30	16	1	13	600	500	33
Featherstone R.	30	15	0	15	461	475	30
Halifax	30	12	2	16	513	565	26
Warrington	30	13	0	17	530	620	26
Castleford	30	12	1	17	552	518	25
Barrow	30	9	1	20	483	843	19
Leigh	30	8	2	20	549	743	18
Hunslet	30	7	1	22	463	952	15
Workington T.	30	2	1	27	297	935	5

SECOND DIVISION

	P.	W.	D.	L.	F.	A.	Pts.
Swinton	28	24	1	3	727	343	49
Salford	28	20	3	5	787	333	43
York	28	21	1	6	717	430	43
Dewsbury	28	21	1	6	539	320	43
Carlisle	28	19	0	9	558	426	38
Whitehaven	28	16	3	9	496	385	35
Batley	28	17	0	11	489	402	34
Fulham	28	16	1	11	521	526	33
Mansfield M.	28	15	0	13	525	398	30
Blackpool B.	28	15	0	13	486	434	30
Wakefield T.	28	12	2	14	450	459	26
Rochdale H.	28	12	2	14	436	466	26
Huddersfield B.	28	12	1	15	476	476	25
Runcorn H.	28	11	1	16	462	538	23
Keighley	28	11	0	17	484	578	22
Bramley	28	9	2	17	439	492	20
Sheffield E.	28	8	0	20	424	582	16
Doncaster	28	6	2	20	353	730	14
Southend I.	28	4	0	24	347	690	8
Brigend	28	1	0	27	258	966	2

CHAMPIONSHIP PLAY-OFFS

Following the breakaway from the English Rugby Union, 22 clubs formed the Northern Rugby Football League. Each club played 42 matches and Manningham won the first Championship as league leaders in 1895-96.

This format was then abandoned and replaced by the Yorkshire Senior and Lancashire Senior Combination leagues until 1901-02 when 14 clubs broke away to form the Northern Rugby League with Broughton Rangers winning the first Championship.

The following season two divisions were formed with the Division One title going to Halifax (1902-03), Bradford (1903-04), who won a play-off against Salford 5-0 at Halifax after both teams tied with 52 points, and Oldham (1904-05).

In 1905-06 the two divisions were merged with Leigh taking the Championship as league leaders. They won the title on a percentage basis as the 31 clubs did not play the same number of matches. The following season the top four play-off was introduced as a fairer means of deciding the title.

The top club played the fourth-placed, the second meeting the third, with the higher club having home advantage. The final was staged at a neutral venue.

It was not until 1930-31 that all clubs played the same number of league matches, but not all against each other, the top four play-off being a necessity until the reintroduction of two divisions in 1962-63.

This spell of two division football lasted only two seasons and the restoration of the Championship table brought about the introduction of a top-16 play-off, this format continuing until the reappearance of two divisions in 1973-74.

Since then the Championship Trophy has been awarded to the leaders of the First Division, with the Second Division champions receiving a silver bowl.

Slalom Lager launched a three-year sponsorship deal of the Championship and the Premiership in 1980-81 in a £215,000 package, extending the deal for another three years from 1983-84 for £270,000. From 1986-87, the sponsorship was taken over by brewers Bass, under the Stones Bitter banner, in a new £400,000 three-year deal.

CHAMPIONSHIP PLAY-OFF FINALS

Season	Winners		Runners-up		Venue	Attendance	Receipts
Top Four Play-Offs							
1906-07	Halifax	18	Oldham	3	Huddersfield	13,200	£722
1907-08	Hunslet	7	Oldham	7	Salford	14,000	£690
Replay	Hunslet	12	Oldham	2	Wakefield	14,054	£800
1908-09	Wigan	7	Oldham	3	Salford	12,000	£630
1909-10	Oldham	13	Wigan	7	Broughton	10,850	£520
1910-11	Oldham	20	Wigan	7	Broughton	15,543	£717
1911-12	Huddersfield	13	Wigan	5	Halifax	15,000	£591
1912-13	Huddersfield	29	Wigan	2	Wakefield	17,000	£914
1913-14	Salford	5	Huddersfield	3	Leeds	8,091	£474
1914-15	Huddersfield	35	Leeds	2	Wakefield	14,000	£750
COMPETITION SUSPENDED DURING WAR TIME							
1919-20	Hull	3	Huddersfield	2	Leeds	12,900	£1,615
1920-21	Hull	16	Hull K.R.	14	Leeds	10,000	£1,320
1921-22	Wigan	13	Oldham	2	Broughton	26,000	£1,825
1922-23	Hull K.R.	15	Huddersfield	5	Leeds	14,000	£1,370
1923-24	Batley	13	Wigan	7	Broughton	13,729	£968
1924-25	Hull K.R.	9	Swinton	5	Rochdale	21,580	£1,504
1925-26	Wigan	22	Warrington	10	St. Helens	20,000	£1,100
1926-27	Swinton	13	St. Helens Recs.	8	Warrington	24,432	£1,803
1927-28	Swinton	11	Featherstone R.	0	Oldham	15,451	£1,136
1928-29	Huddersfield	2	Leeds	0	Halifax	25,604	£2,028
1929-30	Huddersfield	2	Leeds	2	Wakefield	32,095	£2,111
Replay	Huddersfield	10	Leeds	0	Halifax	18,563	£1,319
1930-31	Swinton	14	Leeds	7	Wigan	31,000	£2,100
1931-32	St. Helens	9	Huddersfield	5	Wakefield	19,386	£943
1932-33	Salford	15	Swinton	5	Wigan	18,000	£1,053
1933-34	Wigan	15	Salford	3	Warrington	31,564	£2,114
1934-35	Swinton	14	Warrington	3	Wigan	27,700	£1,710
1935-36	Hull	21	Widnes	2	Huddersfield	17,276	£1,208

Season	Winners		Runners-up		Venue	Attendance	Receipts
1936-37	Salford	13	Warrington	11	Wigan	31,500	£2,000
1937-38	Hunslet	8	Leeds	2	Elland Rd., Leeds	54,112	£3,572
1938-39	Salford	8	Castleford	6	Man. City FC	69,504	£4,301

WAR-TIME EMERGENCY PLAY-OFFS
For the first two seasons the Yorkshire League and Lancashire League champions met in a two-leg final as follows:

1939-40	Swinton	13	Bradford N.	21	Swinton	4,800	£237
	Bradford N.	16	Swinton	9	Bradford	11,721	£570
	Bradford N. won 37-22 on aggregate						
1940-41	Wigan	6	Bradford N.	17	Wigan	11,245	£640
	Bradford N.	28	Wigan	9	Bradford	20,205	£1,148
	Bradford N. won 45-15 on aggregate						

For the remainder of the War the top four in the War League played-off as follows:

1941-42	Dewsbury	13	Bradford N.	0	Leeds	18,000	£1,121
1942-43	Dewsbury	11	Halifax	3	Dewsbury	7,000	£400
	Halifax	13	Dewsbury	22	Halifax	9,700	£683

Dewsbury won 33-16 on aggregate but the Championship was declared null and void because they had played an ineligible player

1943-44	Wigan	13	Dewsbury	9	Wigan	14,000	£915
	Dewsbury	5	Wigan	12	Dewsbury	9,000	£700
	Wigan won 25-14 on aggregate						
1944-45	Halifax	9	Bradford N.	2	Halifax	9,426	£955
	Bradford N.	24	Halifax	11	Bradford	16,000	£1,850
	Bradford N. won 26-20 on aggregate						
1945-46	Wigan	13	Huddersfield	4	Man. C. FC	67,136	£8,387
1946-47	Wigan	13	Dewsbury	4	Man. C. FC	40,599	£5,895
1947-48	Warrington	15	Bradford N.	5	Man. C. FC	69,143	£9,792
1948-49	Huddersfield	13	Warrington	12	Man. C. FC	75,194	£11,073
1949-50	Wigan	20	Huddersfield	2	Man. C. FC	65,065	£11,500
1950-51	Workington T.	26	Warrington	11	Man. C. FC	61,618	£10,993
1951-52	Wigan	13	Bradford N.	6	Huddersfield Town FC	48,684	£8,215
1952-53	St. Helens	24	Halifax	14	Man. C. FC	51,083	£11,503
1953-54	Warrington	8	Halifax	7	Man. C. FC	36,519	£9,076
1954-55	Warrington	7	Oldham	3	Man. C. FC	49,434	£11,516
1955-56	Hull	10	Halifax	9	Man. C. FC	36,675	£9,179
1956-57	Oldham	15	Hull	14	Bradford	62,199	£12,054
1957-58	Hull	20	Workington T.	3	Bradford	57,699	£11,149
1958-59	St. Helens	44	Hunslet	22	Bradford	52,560	£10,146
1959-60	Wigan	27	Wakefield T.	3	Bradford	83,190	£14,482
1960-61	Leeds	25	Warrington	10	Bradford	52,177	£10,475
1961-62	Huddersfield	14	Wakefield T.	5	Bradford	37,451	£7,979

TWO DIVISIONS 1962-63 and 1963-64

Top Sixteen Play-Offs

1964-65	Halifax	15	St. Helens	7	Swinton	20,786	£6,141
1965-66	St. Helens	35	Halifax	12	Swinton	30,634	£8,750
1966-67	Wakefield T.	7	St. Helens	7	Leeds	20,161	£6,702
Replay	Wakefield T.	21	St. Helens	9	Swinton	33,557	£9,800
1967-68	Wakefield T.	17	Hull K.R.	10	Leeds	22,586	£7,697
1968-69	Leeds	16	Castleford	14	Bradford	28,442	£10,130
1969-70	St. Helens	24	Leeds	12	Bradford	26,358	£9,791
1970-71	St. Helens	16	Wigan	12	Swinton	21,745	£10,200
1971-72	Leeds	9	St. Helens	5	Swinton	24,055	£9,513
1972-73	Dewsbury	22	Leeds	13	Bradford	18,889	£9,479

CHAMPIONSHIP FINAL . . . . A 10-YEAR REVIEW

1961-62 HUDDERSFIELD 14 Dyson (4g); Breen, Deighton, Booth, Wicks (1t); Davies, Smales (1t); Slevin, Close, Noble, Kilroy, Bowman, Ramsden

WAKEFIELD T. 5 Round; F. Smith, Skene, N. Fox (1t, 1g), Hirst; Poynton, Holliday; Wilkinson, Kosanovic, Firth, Briggs, Vines, Turner

Referee: N. T. Railton (Wigan)

TWO DIVISIONS — NO PLAY-OFFS 1963 and 1964

1964-65 HALIFAX 15 James (3g); Jackson (1t), Burnett (2t), Kellett, Freeman; Robinson, Daley; Roberts, Harrison, Scroby, Fogerty, Dixon, Renilson

ST. HELENS 7 F. Barrow; Harvey, Vollenhoven, Northey, Killeen (1t, 2g); Murphy, Smith; Tembey (Warlow), Dagnall, Watson, French, Mantle, Laughton

Referee: D. S. Brown (Dewsbury)

1965-66 ST. HELENS 35 F. Barrow; A. Barrow (1t), Murphy (1g), Benyon, Killeen (3t, 6g); Harvey; Bishop; Halsall (3t), Sayer, Watson, French, Warlow (Hitchen), Mantle

HALIFAX 12 Cooper (3g); Jones, Burnett, Dixon, Freeman; Robinson, Baker (1t); Roberts, Harrison, Scroby, Ramshaw (Duffy), Fogerty (1t), Renilson

Referee: J. Manley (Warrington)

1966-67 WAKEFIELD T. 7 Cooper; Hirst, Brooke, N. Fox (2g), Coetzer; Poynton, Owen (1t); Bath, Prior, Campbell, Clarkson, Haigh, D. Fox

ST. HELENS 7 F. Barrow; Vollenhoven, A. Barrow, Smith, Killeen (2g); Douglas, Bishop; Warlow, Sayer, Watson (1t), French, Hogan (Robinson), Mantle

Referee: G. Philpott (Leeds)

Replay: WAKEFIELD T. 21 Cooper; Hirst (1t), Brooke (2t), N. Fox (3g), Coetzer; Poynton (1t), Owen (1t); Bath, Prior, Campbell, Clarkson, Haigh, D. Fox

ST. HELENS 9 F. Barrow; Vollenhoven (1t), A. Barrow, Smith, Killeen (2g); Douglas, Bishop (1g); Warlow, Sayer, Watson, French, Hogan, Mantle

Referee: J. Manley (Warrington)

1967-68 WAKEFIELD T. 17 G. Cooper; Coetzer, Brooke, N. Fox (1t, 2g), Batty; Poynton (1g), Owen (1t); Jeanes (1t), Shepherd, D. Fox (1g), Haigh, McLeod, Hawley

HULL K.R. 10 Wainwright; C. Young, Moore (1t), A. Burwell, Longstaff (1t); Millward (2g), C. Cooper; L. Foster, Flanagan, Mennell, Lowe, Major, F. Foster

Referee: D. S. Brown (Preston)

1968-69 LEEDS 16 Risman (4g); Cowan (1t), Hynes, Watson, Atkinson (1t); Shoebottom, Seabourne (Langley); Clark (Hick), Crosby, K. Eyre, Joyce, Ramsey (1g), Batten

CASTLEFORD 14 Edwards; Briggs, Howe, Thomas, Lowndes; Hardisty (1t, 1g), Hepworth; Hartley, C. Dickinson (1t), J. Ward, Redfearn (3g), Lockwood, Reilly (Fox)

Referee: W. H. Thompson (Huddersfield)

1969-70 ST. HELENS 24 F. Barrow; L. Jones, Benyon, Walsh (1t, 2g), E. Prescott (2t), Myler; Heaton; Halsall, Sayer (1t), Watson, Mantle, E. Chisnall, Coslett (4g)

LEEDS 12 Holmes (3g); Alan Smith (1t), Hynes, Cowan (1t), Atkinson; Shoebottom, Seabourne; J. Burke, Crosby, A. Eyre, Ramsey (Hick), Eccles, Batten

Referee: W. H. Thompson (Huddersfield)

1970-71 ST. HELENS 16 Pimblett; L. Jones, Benyon (1t), Walsh, Blackwood (1t); Whittle, Heaton; J. Stephens, A. Karalius, Rees (Wanbon), Mantle, E. Chisnall, Coslett (5g)

WIGAN 12 Tyrer (1g); Kevin O'Loughlin; Francis, Rowe, Wright; D. Hill, Ayres; Hogan, Clarke, Fletcher, Ashurst (1t, 2g), Robinson (1t) (Cunningham), Laughton

Referee: E. Lawrinson (Warrington)

1971-72 LEEDS 9 Holmes (Hick); Alan Smith, Langley, Dyl, Atkinson (1t); Hardisty, Barham; Clawson (3g), Ward, Fisher (Pickup), Cookson, Eccles, Batten

ST. HELENS 5 Pimblett; L. Jones (Whittle), Benyon, Walsh (1g), Wilson; Kelly, Heaton; Rees, Greenall (1t), J. Stephens, Mantle, E. Chisnall, Coslett

Referee: S. Shepherd (Oldham)

1972-73 DEWSBURY 22 Rushton; Ashcroft, Clark, N. Stephenson (5g, 1t), Day; Agar (1t), A. Bates; Beverley (Taylor), M. Stephenson (2t), Lowe, Grayshon, J. Bates, Whittington

LEEDS 13 Holmes; Alan Smith, Hynes (1g), Dyl (1t), Atkinson; Hardisty, Hepworth; Clawson (1g), Fisher (Ward), Clarkson (Langley), Cookson (1t), Eccles (1t), Haigh

Referee: H. G. Hunt (Prestbury)

LEAGUE LEADERS TROPHY

While the top 16 play-off decided the Championship between 1964 and 1973 it was decided to honour the top club in the league table with a League Leaders Trophy. The winners were:

1964-65   St. Helens
1965-66   St. Helens
1966-67   Leeds
1967-68   Leeds
1968-69   Leeds
1969-70   Leeds
1970-71   Wigan
1971-72   Leeds
1972-73   Warrington

CLUB CHAMPIONSHIP (Merit Table)

With the reintroduction of two divisions, a complicated merit table and Division Two preliminary rounds system produced a 16 club play-off with the Club Championship finalists as follows:

Season	Winners		Runners-up		Venue	Attendance	Receipts
1973-74	Warrington	13	St. Helens	12	Wigan	18,040	£10,032

This format lasted just one season and was replaced by the Premiership.

CLUB CHAMPIONSHIP FINAL .... A REVIEW

1973-74   WARRINGTON 13   Whitehead (2g); M. Philbin (1t), Noonan (1t), Pickup (Lowe), Bevan; Whittle, A. Murphy; D. Chisnall, Ashcroft, Brady (1t), Wanbon (Gaskell), Mather, B. Philbin
ST. HELENS 12   Pimblett; Brown, Wills, Wilson (2t), Mathias; Eckersley, Heaton; Mantle, Liptrot, M. Murphy, E. Chisnall (Warlow), Nicholls, Coslett (3g)
Referee: P. Geraghty (York)

PREMIERSHIP

With the further reintroduction of two divisions in 1973-74, it was declared that the title of Champions would be awarded to the leaders of the First Division.

However, it was also decided to continue the tradition of an end-of-season play-off, the winners to receive the newly instituted Premiership Trophy.

*For full details of the Premiership Trophy see the CUPS section.

Kel Coslett, loose forward for Club Championship finalists St. Helens.

COUNTY LEAGUE

In the early seasons of the code the Lancashire Senior and Yorkshire Senior Competitions, not to be confused with the later reserve leagues, were major leagues. The winners were:

	Lancashire SC	Yorkshire SC
1895-96	Runcorn	Manningham
1896-97	Broughton Rangers	Brighouse Rangers
1897-98	Oldham	Hunslet
1898-99	Broughton Rangers	Batley
1899-00	Runcorn	Bradford
1900-01	Oldham	Bradford
1901-02	Wigan	Leeds

With the introduction of two divisions in 1902-03, the county league competitions were scrapped until they reappeared as the Lancashire League and Yorkshire League in 1907-08. Clubs from the same county played each other home and away to decide the titles. These games were included in the main championship table along with inter- county fixtures. The county leagues continued until 1970, with the exception of war-time interruptions and two seasons when regional leagues with play-offs operated during the 1960s two division era. They were then abolished when a more integrated fixture formula meant clubs did not play all others from the same county, this system later being replaced by the present two division structure.

LANCASHIRE LEAGUE CHAMPIONS

Season	Winners	
1907-08	Oldham	
1908-09	Wigan	
1909-10	Oldham	
1910-11	Wigan	
1911-12	Wigan	
1912-13	Wigan	
1913-14	Wigan	
1914-15	Wigan	
1915-18	Competition Suspended during war-time	
1918-19	Rochdale H.	
1919-20	Widnes	
1920-21	Wigan	
1921-22	Oldham	
1922-23	Wigan	
1923-24	Wigan	
1924-25	Swinton	
1925-26	Wigan	
1926-27	St. Helens R.	
1927-28	Swinton	
1928-29	Swinton	
1929-30	St. Helens	
1930-31	Swinton	
1931-32	St. Helens	
1932-33	Salford	
1933-34	Salford	
1934-35	Salford	
1935-36	Liverpool S.	
1936-37	Salford	
1937-38	Warrington	
1938-39	Salford	
1939-40	Swinton	War Emergency
1940-41	Wigan	Leagues
1941-45	Competition Suspended during war-time	
1945-46	Wigan	
1946-47	Wigan	
1947-48	Warrington	
1948-49	Warrington	
1949-50	Wigan	
1950-51	Warrington	
1951-52	Wigan	
1952-53	St. Helens	
1953-54	Warrington	
1954-55	Warrington	
1955-56	Warrington	
1956-57	Oldham	
1957-58	Oldham	
1958-59	Wigan	
1959-60	St. Helens	
1960-61	Swinton	
1961-62	Wigan	
1962-64	See Regional	

YORKSHIRE LEAGUE CHAMPIONS

Season	Winners	
1907-08	Hunslet	
1908-09	Halifax	
1909-10	Wakefield T.	
1910-11	Wakefield T.	
1911-12	Huddersfield	
1912-13	Huddersfield	
1913-14	Huddersfield	
1914-15	Huddersfield	
1915-18	Competition Suspended during war-time	
1918-19	Hull	
1919-20	Huddersfield	
1920-21	Halifax	
1921-22	Huddersfield	
1922-23	Hull	
1923-24	Batley	
1924-25	Hull K.R.	
1925-26	Hull K.R.	
1926-27	Hull	
1927-28	Leeds	
1928-29	Huddersfield	
1929-30	Huddersfield	
1930-31	Leeds	
1931-32	Hunslet	
1932-33	Castleford	
1933-34	Leeds	
1934-35	Leeds	
1935-36	Hull	
1936-37	Leeds	
1937-38	Leeds	
1938-39	Castleford	
1939-40	Bradford N.	War Emergency
1940-41	Bradford N.	Leagues
1941-45	Competition Suspended during war-time	
1945-46	Wakefield T.	
1946-47	Dewsbury	
1947-48	Bradford N.	
1948-49	Huddersfield	
1949-50	Huddersfield	
1950-51	Leeds	
1951-52	Huddersfield	
1952-53	Halifax	
1953-54	Halifax	
1954-55	Leeds	
1955-56	Halifax	
1956-57	Leeds	
1957-58	Halifax	
1958-59	Wakefield T.	
1959-60	Wakefield T.	
1960-61	Leeds	
1961-62	Wakefield T.	
1962-64	See Regional	

213

LANCASHIRE LEAGUE CHAMPIONS

Season	Winners
1964-65	St. Helens
1965-66	St. Helens
1966-67	St. Helens
1967-68	Warrington
1968-69	St. Helens
1969-70	Wigan

YORKSHIRE LEAGUE CHAMPIONS

Season	Winners
1964-65	Castleford
1965-66	Wakefield T.
1966-67	Leeds
1967-68	Leeds
1968-69	Leeds
1969-70	Leeds

REGIONAL LEAGUES

DURING the 1962-63 and 1963-64 two divisions campaigns the county leagues were replaced by the Eastern and Western Divisions. Each club played four other clubs home and away. There was then a top four play-off to decide the regional championship. The finals were played at neutral venues as follows:

Eastern Division

1962-63	Hull K.R.	13	Huddersfield	10	Leeds	6,751	£1,342
1963-64	Halifax	20	Castleford	12	Huddersfield	10,798	£1,791

Western Division

1962-63	Workington T.	9	Widnes	9	Wigan	13,588	£2,287
Replay	Workington T.	10	Widnes	0	Wigan	7,584	£1,094
1963-64	St. Helens	10	Swinton	7	Wigan	17,363	£3,053

EASTERN DIVISION FINAL . . . . A REVIEW

1962-63 HULL K.R. 13 Kellett (2g); Paul (2t), Major, B. Burwell, Harris (1t); A. Burwell, Bunting; Coverdale, Flanagan, J. Drake, Tyson, Murphy, Bonner
HUDDERSFIELD 10 Dyson (2g); Senior, Booth, Haywood (1t), Stocks; Deighton, Smales (1t); Rowe, Close, Noble, Kilroy, Bowman, Redfearn
Referee: T. W. Watkinson (Manchester)

1963-64 HALIFAX 20 James (4g); Jackson (2t), Burnett, Kellett, Freeman; Robinson (1t), Marchant; Roberts, Shaw, Scott, Dixon (1t), Fogerty, Renilson
CASTLEFORD 12 Edwards; Howe (1t), G. Ward, Small, Gamble; Hardisty, Hepworth; Hirst, C. Dickinson (1t), Clark (3g), Bryant, Walker, Walton
Referee: R. L. Thomas (Oldham)

WESTERN DIVISION FINAL . . . . A REVIEW

1962-63 WORKINGTON T. 9 Lowden (3g); Glastonbury, O'Neil, Brennan, Pretorious (1t); Archer, Roper: Herbert, Ackerley, W. Martin, Edgar, McLeod, Foster
WIDNES 9 Randall (3g); R. Chisnall, Lowe, Thompson (1t), Heyes; F. Myler, Owen; Hurtsfield, Kemel, E. Bate, R. Bate, Measures, V. Karalius
Referee: M. Coates (Pudsey)

Replay WORKINGTON T. 10 Lowden (2g); Glastonbury (1t), O'Neil, Brennan, Pretorious (1t); Archer, Roper; Herbert, Ackerley, W. Martin, Edgar, McLeod, Foster
WIDNES 0 Randall; A. Hughes, Lowe, Thompson, Heyes; F. Myler, Owen; Hurstfield, Kemel, E. Bate, R. Bate, Measures, V. Karalius
Referee: M. Coates (Pudsey)

1963-64 ST. HELENS 10 Coslett (2g); Vollenhoven, Williams, Northey (1t), Killeen; Harvey, Murphy; Tembey, Burdell, Owen, French (1t), Warlow, Laughton
SWINTON 7 Gowers; Speed, Fleet, Parkinson, Stopford (1t); Williams, Cartwright; Bate, D. Clarke, Halliwell, Morgan, Rees, Blan (2g)
Referee: E. Clay (Leeds)

LEAGUE LEADERS .... A REVIEW

The following is a list of the League leaders since the formation of the Northern Union, with the exception of the three eras of two-division football — 1902-05, 1962-64 and 1973-85 — which are comprehensively featured earlier in this section. From 1896 to 1901, the League was divided into a Lancashire Senior Competition and a Yorkshire Senior Competition, winners of both leagues being listed for those seasons. From 1905 to 1930 not all the clubs played each other, the League being determined on a percentage basis.

LSC   —   Lancashire Senior Competition
LL   —   Lancashire League
YSC   —   Yorkshire Senior Competition
YL   —   Yorkshire League
WEL —   War Emergency League
★   Two points deducted for breach of professional rules
†   Decided on a percentage basis after Belle Vue Rangers withdrew shortly before the start of the season.

		P.	W.	D.	L.	F.	A.	Pts.	
1895-96	Manningham	42	33	0	9	367	158	66	
1896-97	Broughton R.	26	19	5	2	201	52	43	LSC
	Brighouse R.	30	22	4	4	213	68	48	YSC
1897-98	Oldham	26	23	1	2	295	94	47	LSC
	Hunslet	30	22	4	4	327	117	48	YSC
1898-99	Broughton R.	26	21	0	5	277	74	42	LSC
	Batley	30	23	2	5	279	75	48	YSC
1899-00	Runcorn	26	22	2	2	232	33	46	LSC
	Bradford	30	24	2	4	324	98	50	YSC
1900-01	Oldham	26	22	1	3	301	67	45	LSC
	Bradford	30	26	1	3	387	100	51★	YSC
1901-02	Broughton R.	26	21	1	4	285	112	43	
1902-05	Two Divisions								
1905-06	Leigh	30	23	2	5	245	130	48	80.00%
1906-07	Halifax	34	27	2	5	649	229	56	82.35%
1907-08	Oldham	32	28	2	2	396	121	58	90.62%
1908-09	Wigan	32	28	0	4	706	207	56	87.50%
1909-10	Oldham	34	29	2	3	604	184	60	88.23%
1910-11	Wigan	34	28	1	5	650	205	57	83.82%
1911-12	Huddersfield	36	31	1	4	996	238	63	87.50%
1912-13	Huddersfield	32	28	0	4	732	217	56	87.50%
1913-14	Huddersfield	34	28	2	4	830	258	58	85.29%
1914-15	Huddersfield	34	28	4	2	888	235	60	88.24%
1915-18	Competitive matches suspended during First World War								
1918-19	Rochdale H.	12	9	0	3	92	52	18	75.00% LL
	Hull	16	13	0	3	392	131	26	81.25% YL
1919-20	Huddersfield	34	29	0	5	759	215	58	85.29%
1920-21	Hull K.R.	32	24	1	7	432	233	49	76.56%
1921-22	Oldham	36	29	1	6	521	201	59	81.94%
1922-23	Hull	36	30	0	6	587	304	60	83.33%
1923-24	Wigan	38	31	0	7	824	228	62	81.57%
1924-25	Swinton	36	30	0	6	499	224	60	83.33%
1925-26	Wigan	38	29	3	6	641	310	61	80.26%
1926-27	St. Helens R.	38	29	3	6	544	235	61	80.26%
1927-28	Swinton	36	27	3	6	439	189	57	79.16%

		P.	W.	D.	L.	F.	A.	Pts.	
1928-29	Huddersfield	38	26	4	8	476	291	56	73.68%
1929-30	St. Helens	40	27	1	12	549	295	55	68.75%
1930-31	Swinton	38	31	2	5	504	156	64	
1931-32	Huddersfield	38	30	1	7	636	368	61	
1932-33	Salford	38	31	2	5	751	165	64	
1933-34	Salford	38	31	1	6	715	281	63	
1934-35	Swinton	38	30	1	7	468	175	61	
1935-36	Hull	38	30	1	7	607	306	61	
1936-37	Salford	38	29	3	6	529	196	61	
1937-38	Hunslet	36	25	3	8	459	301	53	
1938-39	Salford	40	30	3	7	551	191	63	
1939-40	Swinton	22	17	0	5	378	158	34	WEL LL
	Bradford N.	28	21	0	7	574	302	42	WEL YL
1940-41	Wigan	16	15	1	0	297	71	31	WEL LL
	Bradford N.	25	23	1	1	469	126	47	WEL YL
1941-42	Dewsbury	24	19	1	4	431	172	39	81.25% WEL
1942-43	Wigan	16	13	0	3	301	142	26	81.25% WEL
1943-44	Wakefield T.	22	19	0	3	359	97	38	86.36% WEL
1944-45	Bradford N.	20	17	0	3	337	69	34	85.00% WEL
1945-46	Wigan	36	29	2	5	783	219	60	
1946-47	Wigan	36	29	1	6	567	196	59	
1947-48	Wigan	36	31	1	4	776	258	63	
1948-49	Warrington	36	31	0	5	728	247	62	
1949-50	Wigan	36	31	1	4	853	320	63	
1950-51	Warrington	36	30	0	6	738	250	60	
1951-52	Bradford N.	36	28	1	7	758	326	57	
1952-53	St. Helens	36	32	2	2	769	273	66	
1953-54	Halifax	36	30	2	4	538	219	62	
1954-55	Warrington	36	29	2	5	718	321	60	
1955-56	Warrington	34	27	1	6	712	349	55	80.88% †
1956-57	Oldham	38	33	0	5	893	365	66	
1957-58	Oldham	38	33	1	4	803	415	67	
1958-59	St. Helens	38	31	1	6	1005	450	63	
1959-60	St. Helens	38	34	1	3	947	343	69	
1960-61	Leeds	36	30	0	6	620	258	60	
1961-62	Wigan	36	32	1	3	885	283	65	
1962-64	Two Divisions								
1964-65	St. Helens	34	28	0	6	621	226	56	
1965-66	St. Helens	34	28	1	5	521	275	57	
1966-67	Leeds	34	29	0	5	704	373	58	
1967-68	Leeds	34	28	0	6	720	271	56	
1968-69	Leeds	34	29	2	3	775	358	60	
1969-70	Leeds	34	30	0	4	674	314	60	
1970-71	Wigan	34	30	0	4	662	308	60	
1971-72	Leeds	34	28	2	4	750	325	58	
1972-73	Warrington	34	27	2	5	816	400	56	

Peter Fox, now in his 16th full season as a coach and currently serving Leeds and Yorkshire.

COACHES

COACHES

Between June 1985 and June 1986 a total of 17 clubs made first team coaching changes. Six new coaches had their first senior appointments bringing the total of coaches since the start of the 1974-75 season to 167.

This chapter is a compilation of those appointments, featuring a club-by-club coaches register, an index, plus a detailed dossier of the 1985-86 coaches.

CLUB-BY-CLUB REGISTER
The following is a list of coaches each club has had since the start of the 1974-75 season.

BARROW
Frank Foster	May 73 - Apr. 83
Tommy Dawes	May 83 - Feb. 85
Tommy Bishop	Feb. 85 - Apr. 85
Ivor Kelland	May 85 -

BATLEY
Don Fox	Nov. 72 - Oct. 74
Alan Hepworth	Nov. 74 - Apr. 75
Dave Cox	May 75 - June 75
Trevor Walker	June 75 - June 77
Albert Fearnley	June 77 - Oct. 77
Dave Stockwell	Oct. 77 - June 79
*Tommy Smales	June 79 - Oct. 81
Trevor Lowe	Oct. 81 - May 82
Terry Crook	June 82 - Nov. 84
George Pieniazek	Nov. 84 - Nov. 85
Brian Lockwood	Nov. 85 -

*Ex-forward

BLACKPOOL BOROUGH
Tommy Blakeley	Aug. 74 - Apr. 76
Jim Crellin	May 76 - Mar. 77
Joe Egan Jnr.	Mar. 77 - Oct. 77
Albert Fearnley (Mgr)	Nov. 77 - Apr. 79
Bakary Diabira	Nov. 78 - June 79
Graham Rees	June 79 - Mar. 80
Geoff Lyon	July 80 - Aug. 81
Bob Irving	Aug. 81 - Feb. 82
John Mantle	Feb. 82 - Mar. 82
Tommy Dickens	Mar. 82 - Nov. 85
Stan Gittins	Nov. 85 -

BRADFORD NORTHERN
Ian Brooke	Jan. 73 - Sept. 75
Roy Francis	Oct. 75 - Apr. 77
Peter Fox	Apr. 77 - May 85
Barry Seabourne	May 85 -

BRAMLEY
Arthur Keegan	May 73 - Sept. 76
Peter Fox	Sept. 76 - Apr. 77
*Tommy Smales	May 77 - Dec. 77
Les Pearce	Jan. 78 - Oct. 78
Don Robinson	Oct. 78 - May 79
Dave Stockwell	June 79 - June 80
Keith Hepworth	June 80 - May 82
Maurice Bamford	May 82 - Oct. 83
Peter Jarvis	Oct. 83 - Apr. 85
Ken Loxton	Apr. 85 - Dec. 85
Allan Agar	Dec. 85 -

*Ex-forward

CARLISLE
Allan Agar	May 81 - June 82
Mick Morgan	July 82 - Feb. 83
John Atkinson	Feb. 83 - Feb. 86
Alan Kellett	Feb. 86 - May 86

CASTLEFORD
Dave Cox	Apr. 74 - Nov. 74
*Malcolm Reilly	Dec. 74 -

*Shortly after his appointment Reilly returned to Australia to fulfil his contract before resuming at Castleford early the next season.

DEWSBURY
Maurice Bamford	June 74 - Oct. 74
Alan Hardisty	Oct. 74 - June 75
Dave Cox	June 75 - July 77
Ron Hill	July 77 - Dec. 77
Lewis Jones	Dec. 77 - Apr. 78
Jeff Grayshon	May 78 - Oct. 78
Alan Lockwood	Oct. 78 - Oct. 80
Bernard Watson	Oct. 80 - Oct. 82
Ray Abbey	Nov. 82 - Apr. 83
*Tommy Smales	May 83 - Feb. 84
Jack Addy	Feb. 84 -

*Ex-forward

DONCASTER

Ted Strawbridge	Feb. 73 - Apr. 75
Derek Edwards	July 75 - Nov. 76
Don Robson	Nov. 76 - Sept. 77
Trevor Lowe	Sept. 77 - Apr. 79
*Tommy Smales	Feb. 78 - Apr. 79
Billy Yates	Apr. 79 - May 80
Don Vines	Sept. 79 - Jan. 80
Bill Kenny	June 80 - May 81
Alan Rhodes	Aug. 81 - Mar. 83
Clive Sullivan M.B.E.	Mar. 83 - May 84
John Sheridan	June 84 -

*Ex-forward, who shared the coaching post with Trevor Lowe for just over a year.

FEATHERSTONE ROVERS

*Tommy Smales	July 74 - Sept. 74
Keith Goulding	Sept. 74 - Jan. 76
†Tommy Smales	Feb. 76 - May 76
Keith Cotton	June 76 - Dec. 77
Keith Goulding	Dec. 77 - May 78
Terry Clawson	July 78 - Nov. 78
†Tommy Smales	Nov. 78 - Apr. 79
Paul Daley	May 79 - Jan. 81
Vince Farrar	Feb. 81 - Nov. 82
Allan Agar	Dec. 82 - Oct. 85
George Pieniazek	Nov. 85 -

*Ex-forward
†Ex-scrum half

FULHAM

Reg Bowden	July 80 - June 84
Roy Lester	June 84 - Apr. 86
Bill Goodwin	Apr. 86 -

HALIFAX

Derek Hallas	Aug. 74 - Oct. 74
Les Pearce	Oct. 74 - Apr. 76
Alan Kellett	May 76 - Apr. 77
Jim Crellin	June 77 - Oct. 77
Harry Fox	Oct. 77 - Feb. 78
Maurice Bamford	Feb. 78 - May 80
Mick Blacker	June 80 - June 82
Ken Roberts	June 82 - Sept. 82
Colin Dixon	Sept. 82 - Nov. 84
Chris Anderson	Nov. 84 -

HUDDERSFIELD BARRACUDAS

Brian Smith	Jan. 73 - Mar. 76
Keith Goulding	Mar. 76 - Dec. 76
Bob Tomlinson	Jan. 77 - May 77
Neil Fox	June 77 - Feb. 78
*Roy Francis	-
Keith Goulding	May 78 - July 79
Ian Brooke	July 79 - Mar. 80
Maurice Bamford	May 80 - May 81
Les Sheard	June 81 - Nov. 82
Dave Mortimer	Nov. 82 - Aug. 83
Mel Bedford	Aug. 83 - Nov. 83
Brian Lockwood	Nov. 83 - Feb. 85
Chris Forster	Feb. 85 -

*Although Roy Francis was appointed he was unable to take over and Dave Heppleston stood in until the next appointment.

HULL

David Doyle-Davidson	May 74 - Dec. 77
Arthur Bunting	Jan. 78 - Dec. 85
Kenny Foulkes	Dec. 85 - May 86

HULL KINGSTON ROVERS

Arthur Bunting	Feb. 72 - Nov. 75
Harry Poole	Dec. 75 - Mar. 77
Roger Millward M.B.E.	Mar. 77 -

HUNSLET

Paul Daley	Apr. 74 - Aug. 78
Bill Ramsey	Aug. 78 - Dec. 79
Drew Broatch	Dec. 79 - Apr. 81
Paul Daley	Apr. 81 - Nov. 85
Peter Jarvis	Nov. 85 -

KEIGHLEY

Alan Kellett	Jan. 73 - May 75
Roy Sabine	Aug. 75 - Oct. 77
Barry Seabourne	Nov. 77 - Mar. 79
Albert Fearnley (Mgr)	Apr. 79 - Aug. 79
Alan Kellett	Apr. 79 - Apr. 80
Albert Fearnley	May 80 - Feb. 81
Bakary Diabira	Feb. 81 - Sept. 82
Lee Greenwood	Sept. 82 - Oct. 83
Geoff Peggs	Nov. 83 - Sept. 85
Peter Roe	Sept. 85 -

LEEDS

Roy Francis	June 74 - May 75
Syd Hynes	June 75 - Apr. 81
Robin Dewhurst	June 81 - Oct. 83
Maurice Bamford	Nov. 83 - Feb. 85
Malcolm Clift	Feb. 85 - May 85
Peter Fox	May 85 -

LEIGH

Eddie Cheetham	May 74 - Mar. 75
Kevin Ashcroft	June 75 - Jan. 77
Bill Kindon	Jan. 77 - Apr. 77
John Mantle	Apr. 77 - Nov. 78
Tom Grainey	Nov. 78 - Dec. 80
*Alex Murphy	Nov. 80 - June 82
*Colin Clarke	June 82 - Dec. 82
Peter Smethurst	Dec. 82 - Apr. 83
Tommy Bishop	June 83 - June 84
John Woods	June 84 - May 85
Alex Murphy	Feb. 85 - Nov. 85
Tommy Dickens	Nov. 85 -

From Dec. 80 to June 82 Clarke was officially appointed coach and Murphy manager

MANSFIELD MARKSMAN

Mick Blacker	May 84 - Oct. 85
Bill Kirkbride	Nov. 85 - Mar. 86
Steve Dennison	Apr. 86 -

OLDHAM

Jim Challinor	Aug. 74 - Dec. 76
Terry Ramshaw	Jan. 77 - Feb. 77
Dave Cox	July 77 - Dec. 78
Graham Starkey (Mngr)	Jan. 79 - May 81
Bill Francis	June 79 - Dec. 80
Frank Myler	May 81 - Apr. 83
Peter Smethurst	Apr. 83 - Feb. 84
Frank Barrow	Feb. 84 - Feb. 84
Brian Gartland	Mar. 84 - June 84
Frank Myler	June 84 -

ROCHDALE HORNETS

Frank Myler	May 71 - Oct. 74
Graham Starkey	Oct. 74 - Nov. 75
Henry Delooze	Nov. 75 - Nov. 76
Kel Coslett	Nov. 76 - Aug. 79

Tommy Dickens, appointed coach at Leigh in November 1985 after more than three years with Blackpool Borough.

Paul Longstaff	Sept. 79 - May 81
Terry Fogerty	May 81 - Jan. 82
Dick Bonser	Jan. 82 - May 82
Bill Kirkbride	June 82 - Sept. 84
Charlie Birdsall	Sept. 84 - Apr. 86

RUNCORN HIGHFIELD

Terry Gorman	Aug. 74 - May 77
Geoff Fletcher	Aug. 77 -

ST. HELENS

Eric Ashton M.B.E.	May 74 - May 80
Kel Coslett	June 80 - May 82
Billy Benyon	May 82 - Nov. 85
Alex Murphy	Nov. 85 -

SALFORD

Les Bettinson	Dec. 73 - Mar. 77
Colin Dixon	Mar. 77 - Jan. 78
Stan McCormick	Feb. 78 - Mar. 78
Alex Murphy	May 78 - Nov. 80
Kevin Ashcroft	Nov. 80 - Mar. 82
Alan McInnes	Mar. 82 - May 82
Malcolm Aspey	May 82 - Oct. 83
Mike Coulman	Oct. 83 - May 84
Kevin Ashcroft	May 84 -

SHEFFIELD EAGLES

Alan Rhodes	Apr. 84 - May 86

SWINTON

Austin Rhodes	June 74 - Nov. 75
Bob Fleet	Nov. 75 - Nov. 76
John Stopford	Nov. 76 - Apr. 77
Terry Gorman	June 77 - Nov. 78
Ken Halliwell	Nov. 78 - Dec. 79
Frank Myler	Jan. 80 - May 81
Tom Grainey	May 81 - Oct. 83
Jim Crellin	Nov. 83 - May 86

WAKEFIELD TRINITY

Peter Fox	June 74 - May 76
Geoff Gunney	June 76 - Nov. 76
Brian Lockwood	Nov. 76 - Jan. 78
Ian Brooke	Jan. 78 - Jan. 79
Bill Kirkbride	Jan. 79 - Apr. 80
Ray Batten	Apr. 80 - May 81
Bill Ashurst	June 81 - Apr. 82
Ray Batten	May 82 - July 83
Derek Turner	July 83 - Feb. 84
Bob Haigh	Feb. 84 - May 84
Geoff Wraith	May 84 - Oct. 84
David Lamming	Oct. 84 - Apr. 85
Len Casey	Apr. 85 -

WARRINGTON

Alex Murphy	May 71 - May 78
Billy Benyon	June 78 - Mar. 82
Kevin Ashcroft	Mar. 82 - May 84
Reg Bowden	June 84 - Mar. 86
Tony Barrow	Mar. 86 -

WHITEHAVEN

Jeff Bawden	May 72 - May 75
Ike Southward	Aug. 75 - June 76
Bill Smith	Aug. 76 - Oct. 78
Ray Dutton	Oct. 78 - Oct. 79
Phil Kitchin	Oct. 79 - Jan. 82
Arnold Walker	Jan. 82 - May 82
Tommy Dawes	June 82 - May 83
Frank Foster	June 83 - June 85
Phil Kitchin	June 85 -

WIDNES

Vince Karalius	Jan. 72 - May 75
Frank Myler	May 75 - May 78
Doug Laughton	May 78 - Mar. 83
Harry Dawson } Colin Tyrer }	Mar. 83 - May 83
*Vince Karalius } Harry Dawson }	May 83 - May 84
Eric Hughes	June 84 - Jan. 86
Doug Laughton	Jan. 86 -

Dawson quit as coach in March 1984 with Karalius continuing as team manager.

WIGAN

Ted Toohey	May 74 - Jan. 75
Joe Coan	Jan. 75 - Sept. 76
Vince Karalius	Sept. 76 - Sept. 79
Kel Coslett	Oct. 79 - Apr. 80
George Fairbairn	Apr. 80 - May 81
Maurice Bamford	May 81 - May 82
Alex Murphy	June 82 - Aug. 84
Colin Clarke } Alan McInnes }	Aug. 84 - May 86

WORKINGTON TOWN

Ike Southward	Aug. 73 - June 75
Paul Charlton	June 75 - June 76
Ike Southward	June 76 - Feb. 78
Sol Roper	Feb. 78 - Apr. 80
Keith Irving	Aug. 80 - Oct. 80
Tommy Bishop	Nov. 80 - June 82
Paul Charlton	July 82 - Dec. 82
Dave Cox	Mar. 83 - Mar. 83
Harry Archer/Bill Smith	May 83 - June 84
Bill Smith	June 84 - Apr. 85
Jackie Davidson	Apr. 85 - Jan. 86
Keith Davies	Feb. 86 -

YORK

Keith Goulding	Nov. 73 - Sept. 74
Gary Cooper	Dec. 74 - Sept. 76
Mal Dixon	Sept. 76 - Dec. 78
Paul Daley	Jan. 79 - May 79
David Doyle-Davidson	July 79 - July 80
Bill Kirkbride	Aug. 80 - Apr. 82
Alan Hardisty	May 82 - Jan. 83
Phil Lowe	Mar. 83 -

REPRESENTATIVE REGISTER

The following is a list of international and county coaches since 1974-75.

GREAT BRITAIN
Jim Challinor	Dec. 71 - Aug. 74 (Inc. tour)
David Watkins	1977 World Championship
Peter Fox	1978
Eric Ashton	1979 tour
Johnny Whiteley	Aug. 80 - Nov. 82
Frank Myler	Dec. 82 - Aug. 84 (Inc. tour)
Maurice Bamford	Oct. 84 -

ENGLAND
Alex Murphy	Jan. 75 - Nov. 75 (Inc. World Championship tour)
Peter Fox	1976-77
Frank Myler	1977-78
Eric Ashton	1978-79 & 1979-80
Johnny Whiteley	1980-81 & 1981-82
Reg Parker (Mngr)	1984-85

WALES
Les Pearce	Jan. 75 - Nov. 75 (Inc. World Championship tour)
David Watkins / Bill Francis	1976-77
Kel Coslett / Bill Francis	1977-78
Kel Coslett	1978-79 to 1981-82
David Watkins	1982-83, 1984-85

GREAT BRITAIN UNDER-24s
Johnny Whiteley	1976-82
Frank Myler	1983-84

GREAT BRITAIN UNDER-21s
Maurice Bamford	Oct. 84 -

Great Britain coach Maurice Bamford holding team mascot 'Sully.'

CUMBRIA
Ike Southward	1975-76
Frank Foster	1976-77 & 1977-78
Sol Roper	1978-79
Frank Foster	1979-80
Phil Kitchin	1980-81 to 1981-82
Frank Foster	1982-83
Jackie Davidson	1985-86

LANCASHIRE
Alex Murphy	1973-74 to 1977-78
Eric Ashton M.B.E.	1978-79 to 1979-80
Tom Grainey	1980-81 to 1981-82
Doug Laughton	1982-83
Alex Murphy	1985-86

YORKSHIRE
Johnny Whiteley	1970-71 to 1979-80
Arthur Keegan	1980-81
Johnny Whiteley	1981-82 to 1982-83
Peter Fox	1985-86

OTHER NATIONALITIES
Dave Cox	1974-75 to 1975-76

INDEX OF COACHES

The following is an index of the 167 coaches who have held first team coaching posts since the start of the 1974-75 season with the alphabetical listing of clubs they coached in this period.

Ray Abbey (Dewsbury)
Jack Addy (Dewsbury)
Allan Agar (Bramley, Carlisle, Featherstone R.)
Dave Alred (Bridgend)
Chris Anderson (Halifax)
Harry Archer (Workington T.)
Kevin Ashcroft (Leigh, Salford, Warrington)
Eric Ashton M.B.E. (St. Helens)
Bill Ashurst (Wakefield T.)
Mal Aspey (Salford)
John Atkinson (Carlisle)

Maurice Bamford (Bramley, Dewsbury, Halifax, Huddersfield, Leeds, Wigan)
Frank Barrow (Oldham)
Tony Barrow (Warrington) .
Ray Batten (Wakefield T.)
Jeff Bawden (Whitehaven)
Mel Bedford (Huddersfield)
Billy Benyon (St. Helens, Warrington)
Les Bettinson (Salford)
Charlie Birdsall (Rochdale H.)
Tommy Bishop (Barrow, Leigh, Workington T.)
Mick Blacker (Halifax, Mansfield M.)
Tommy Blakeley (Blackpool B.)
Dick Bonser (Rochdale H.)
Reg Bowden (Fulham, Warrington)
Drew Broatch (Hunslet)
Ian Brooke (Bradford N., Huddersfield, Wakefield T.)
Arthur Bunting (Hull, Hull K.R.)

Len Casey (Wakefield T.)
Jim Challinor (Oldham)
Paul Charlton (Workington T.)
Eddie Cheetham (Leigh)
Colin Clarke (Leigh, Wigan)
Terry Clawson (Featherstone R.)
Malcolm Clift (Leeds)
Joe Coan (Wigan)
Gary Cooper (York)
Kel Coslett (Rochdale H., St. Helens, Wigan)

Keith Cotton (Featherstone R.)
Mike Coulman (Salford)
Dave Cox (Batley, Castleford, Dewsbury, Huyton, Oldham, Workington T.)
Jim Crellin (Blackpool B., Halifax, Swinton)
Terry Crook (Batley)

Paul Daley (Featherstone R., Hunslet, York)
Jackie Davidson (Workington T.)
Keith Davies (Workington T.)
Tommy Dawes (Barrow, Whitehaven)
Harry Dawson (Widnes)
Henry Delooze (Rochdale H.)
Steve Dennison (Mansfield M.)
Robin Dewhurst (Leeds)
Bakary Diabira (Blackpool B., Keighley)
Tommy Dickens (Blackpool B., Leigh)
Colin Dixon (Halifax, Salford)
Mal Dixon (York)
David Doyle-Davidson (Hull, York)
Ray Dutton (Whitehaven)

Derek Edwards (Doncaster)
Joe Egan Jnr. (Blackpool B.)

George Fairbairn (Wigan)
Vince Farrar (Featherstone R.)
Albert Fearnley (Batley, Blackpool B., Keighley)
Bob Fleet (Swinton)
Geoff Fletcher (Huyton)
Terry Fogerty (Rochdale H.)
Chris Forster (Huddersfield B.)
Frank Foster (Barrow, Whitehaven)
Kenny Foulkes (Hull)
Don Fox (Batley)
Harry Fox (Halifax)
Neil Fox (Huddersfield)
Peter Fox (Bradford N., Bramley, Leeds, Wakefield T.)
Bill Francis (Oldham)
Roy Francis (Bradford N., Huddersfield, Leeds)

Brian Gartland (Oldham)
Stan Gittins (Blackpool B.)
Bill Goodwin (Fulham, Kent Invicta)
Terry Gorman (Huyton, Swinton)
Keith Goulding (Featherstone R., Huddersfield, York)
Tom Grainey (Leigh, Swinton)
Jeff Grayshon (Dewsbury)
Lee Greenwood (Keighley)
Geoff Gunney (Wakefield T.)

Bob Haigh (Wakefield T.)
Derek Hallas (Halifax)
Ken Halliwell (Swinton)
Alan Hardisty (Dewsbury, York)
Alan Hepworth (Batley)
Keith Hepworth (Bramley)
Ron Hill (Dewsbury)
Eric Hughes (Widnes)
Syd Hynes (Leeds)

Bob Irving (Blackpool B.)
Keith Irving (Workington T.)

Peter Jarvis (Bramley, Hunslet)
Lewis Jones (Dewsbury)

Vince Karalius (Widnes, Wigan)
Arthur Keegan (Bramley)
Ivor Kelland (Barrow)
Alan Kellett (Carlisle, Halifax, Keighley)
Bill Kenny (Doncaster)
Bill Kindon (Leigh)
Bill Kirkbride (Mansfield M., Rochdale H.,
    Wakefield T., York)
Phil Kitchin (Whitehaven)

Dave Lamming (Wakefield T.)
Steve Lane (Kent Invicta)
Doug Laughton (Widnes)
Roy Lester (Fulham)
Alan Lockwood (Dewsbury)
Brian Lockwood (Batley, Huddersfield,
    Wakefield T.)
Paul Longstaff (Rochdale H.)
Phil Lowe (York)
Trevor Lowe (Batley, Doncaster)
Ken Loxton (Bramley)
Geoff Lyon (Blackpool B.)

John Mantle (Blackpool B., Cardiff C., Leigh)
Stan McCormick (Salford)
Alan McInnes (Salford, Wigan)
Roger Millward M.B.E. (Hull K.R.)
Mick Morgan (Carlisle)
David Mortimer (Huddersfield)
Alex Murphy (Leigh, St. Helens, Salford,
    Warrington, Wigan)
Frank Myler (Oldham, Rochdale H., Swinton,
    Widnes)

Les Pearce (Bramley, Halifax)
Geoff Peggs (Keighley)
George Pieniazek (Batley, Featherstone R.)
Harry Poole (Hull K.R.)

Bill Ramsey (Hunslet)
Terry Ramshaw (Oldham)
Graham Rees (Blackpool B.)
Malcolm Reilly (Castleford)
Alan Rhodes (Doncaster, Sheffield E.)
Austin Rhodes (Swinton)
Ken Roberts (Halifax)
Don Robinson (Bramley)
Don Robson (Doncaster)
Peter Roe (Keighley)
Sol Roper (Workington T.)

Roy Sabine (Keighley)
Barry Seabourne (Bradford N., Keighley)
Les Sheard (Huddersfield)
John Sheridan (Doncaster)
Tommy Smales [*Scrum-half*] (Featherstone R.)
Tommy Smales [*Forward*] (Batley, Bramley,
    Dewsbury, Doncaster, Featherstone R.)
Peter Smethurst (Leigh, Oldham)
Bill Smith (Whitehaven, Workington T.)
Brian Smith (Huddersfield)
Ike Southward (Whitehaven, Workington T.)
Graham Starkey (Oldham, Rochdale H.)
Dave Stockwell (Bramley, Batley)
John Stopford (Swinton)
Ted Strawbridge (Doncaster)
Clive Sullivan M.B.E. (Doncaster, Hull)

Bob Tomlinson (Huddersfield)
Ted Toohey (Wigan)
Derek Turner (Wakefield T.)
Colin Tyrer (Widnes)

Don Vines (Doncaster)

Arnold Walker (Whitehaven)
Trevor Walker (Batley)
John Warlow (Bridgend)
David Watkins (Cardiff C.)
Bernard Watson (Dewsbury)
Jeff Woods (Bridgend)
John Woods (Leigh)
Geoff Wraith (Wakefield T.)

Billy Yates (Doncaster)

DOSSIER OF 1985-86 COACHES

The following is a dossier of the coaching and playing careers of coaches holding first team posts during 1985-86 up to the end of May. BF — beaten finalist.

JACK ADDY
Dewsbury: Feb. 84 - (Promotion)
Played for: Dewsbury

ALLAN AGAR
Carlisle: May 81 - June 82 (Promotion)
Featherstone R.: Dec. 82 - Oct. 85
                 (RL Cup winners)
Bramley: Dec. 85 -
Played for: Featherstone R., Dewsbury, New Hunslet, Hull K.R., Wakefield T., Carlisle, Bramley

CHRIS ANDERSON
Halifax   Nov. 84 - (Div. 1 champs, Premier BF)
Played for: Canterbury-Bankstown (Aus.), Widnes, Hull K.R., Halifax

KEVIN ASHCROFT
Leigh: June 75 - Jan. 77 (Promotion, Floodlit Trophy BF)
Salford: Nov. 80 - Mar. 82
Warrington: Mar. 82 - May 84
                 (Lancs. Cup winners)
Salford: May 84 - (Promotion)
Played for: Dewsbury, Rochdale H., Leigh, Warrington, Salford

JOHN ATKINSON
Carlisle: Feb. 83 - Feb. 86
Played for: Leeds, Carlisle

TONY BARROW
Warrington: Mar. 86 - (Premier winners)
Played for: St. Helens, Leigh

BILLY BENYON
Warrington: June 78 - Mar. 82
                 (Lancs. Cup winners, John Player winners and BF)
St. Helens: May 82 - Nov. 85
                 (Lancs. Cup winners and BF, Premier winners)
Played for: St. Helens, Warrington

CHARLIE BIRDSALL
Rochdale H: Sep. 84 - Apr. 86
Played for: Castleford, Rochdale H., Hull, Carlisle

MICK BLACKER
Halifax: June 80 - June 82 (Promotion)
Mansfield M.:   May 84 - Oct. 85
Played for: Bradford N., Halifax, Warrington, Mansfield M.

REG BOWDEN
Fulham: July 80 - June 84 (Div. 2 champs + Promotion)
Warrington: June 84 - Mar. 86 (Lancs. Cup BF)
Played for: Widnes, Fulham, Warrington

ARTHUR BUNTING
Hull K.R.:   Feb. 72 - Nov. 75 (Yorks. Cup BF, Promotion)
Hull: Jan. 78 - Dec. 85 (Div. 1 champs, Div. 2 champs, RL Cup winners and BF (3), Yorks. Cup winners (3), John Player winners and BF, Floodlit Trophy winners, Premier BF (3))
Played for: Bramley, Hull K.R.

LEN CASEY
Wakefield T.:   Apr. 85 - (Promotion)
Played for: Hull, Hull K.R., Bradford N., Wakefield T.

COLIN CLARKE
Leigh: Dec. 80 - Dec. 82 (Div.1 champs, Lancs. Cup winners)
Wigan: Aug. 84 - May 86 (RL Cup winners, Lancs. Cup winners and BF, John Player winners, Charity Shield winners)
Played for: Wigan, Oldham, Salford, Leigh

JIM CRELLIN
Blackpool B.:   May 76 - Mar. 77 (John Player BF)
Halifax: June 77 - Oct. 77
Swinton: Nov. 83 - May 86 (Div. 2 champs)
Played for: Workington T., Oldham, Rochdale H.

225

PAUL DALEY
New Hunslet: Apr. 74 - Aug. 78 (Promotion)
York: Jan. 79 - May 79 (Promotion)
Featherstone R.: May 79 - Jan. 81 (Div. 2 champs)
Hunslet: Apr. 81 - Nov. 85 (Promotion)
Played for: Halifax, Bradford N., Hull K.R., Hunslet

JACKIE DAVIDSON
Workington T.: Apr. 85 - Jan. 86
Played for: Whitehaven

KEITH DAVIES
Workington T.: Feb. 86 -
Played for: Workington T.

STEVE DENNISON
Mansfield M.: Apr. 86 -
Played for: Hull, Mansfield M.

TOMMY DICKENS
Blackpool B.: Mar. 82 - Nov. 85
Leigh: Nov. 85 - (Div. 2 champs)
Played for: Leigh, Warrington, Widnes

GEOFF FLETCHER
Runcorn H.: Aug. 77 -
Played for: Leigh, Oldham, Wigan, Workington T., Runcorn H.

CHRIS FORSTER
Huddersfield B.: Feb. 85 —
Played for: Huddersfield, Hull, Bramley

KENNY FOULKES
Hull: Dec. 85 - May 86
Played for: Castleford, Hull

PETER FOX
Featherstone R.: Jan. 71 - May 74 (RL Cup winners & BF)
Wakefield T.: June 74 - May 76 (Yorks. Cup BF)
Bramley: Sept. 76 - Apr. 77 (Promotion)
Bradford N.: Apr. 77 - May 85 (Div. 1 champs (2), Yorks. Cup winners and BF (2), Premier winners and BF (2), John Player winners)
Leeds: May 85 -
England: 1977 (2 matches)
Great Britain: 1978 (3 Tests v. Australia)
Yorkshire: 1985-86
Played for: Featherstone R., Batley, Hull K.R., Wakefield T.

STAN GITTINS
Blackpool B.: Nov. 85 -
Played for: Batley, Swinton

BILL GOODWIN
Kent Invicta: Apr. 83 - Nov. 83
Kent Invicta: Aug. 84 - May 85
Fulham: Apr. 86 -
Played for: Doncaster, Featherstone R., Batley

ERIC HUGHES
Widnes: June 84 - Jan. 86
Played for: Widnes, St. Helens

PETER JARVIS
Bramley: Oct. 83 - Apr. 85
Hunslet: Nov. 85 -
Played for: Hunslet, Bramley, Halifax, Huddersfield

IVOR KELLAND
Barrow: May 85 - (Promotion)
Played for: Barrow

ALAN KELLETT
Keighley: Jan. 68 - Feb. 70
Bradford N.: May 70 - Oct. 70
Keighley: Jan. 73 - May 75 (Promotion)
Halifax: May 76 - Apr. 77
Keighley: Apr. 79 - Apr. 80
Carlisle: Feb. 86 - May 86
Played for: Oldham, Halifax, Bradford N., Keighley

BILL KIRKBRIDE
Wakefield T.: Jan. 79 - Apr. 80 (RL Cup BF)
York: Aug. 80 - Apr. 82 (Div. 2 champs)
Rochdale H.: June 82 - Sept. 84
Mansfield M.: Nov. 85 - Mar. 86
Played for: Workington T., Halifax, Castleford, Salford, Leigh (on loan), S. Suburbs (Aus.), Wakefield T., York, Rochdale H.

DOUG LAUGHTON
Widnes: May 78 - Mar. 83 (RL Cup winners (2) and BF, Lancs. Cup winners (2) and BF, John Player winners and BF, Premier winners (2))
Widnes: Jan. 86 -
Played for: Wigan, St. Helens, Widnes

ROY LESTER
Fulham: June 84 - Apr. 86
Played for: Warrington, Leigh, Fulham

BRIAN LOCKWOOD
Wakefield T.: Nov. 76 - Jan. 78
Huddersfield: Nov. 84 - Feb. 85
Batley: Nov. 85 -
Played for: Castleford, Balmain (Aus.), Canterbury-Bankstown (Aus.), Wakefield T., Hull K.R., Widnes, Oldham

PHIL LOWE
York: Mar. 83 - (Promotion)
Played for: Hull K.R., Manly (Aus.)

KEN LOXTON
Bramley: Apr. 85 - Dec. 85
Played for: Huddersfield, Keighley, Halifax, Bramley

ALAN McINNES
Salford: Mar. 82 - May 82
Wigan: Aug 84 - May 86 (RL Cup winners, Lancs. Cup winners and BF, John Player winners, Charity Shield winners)

ROGER MILLWARD M.B.E.
Hull K.R.: Mar. 77 - (Div. 1 champs (3), RL Cup winners and BF (2), John Player winners and BF (2), Premier winners (2) and BF, Yorks. Cup winners and BF (2), Floodlit Trophy winners and BF, Charity Shield BF)
Played for: Castleford, Hull K.R., Cronulla (Aus.)

A pensive Frank Myler, a veteran of 15 years of top flight coaching.

ALEX MURPHY
Leigh: Nov. 66 - May 71 (RL Cup winners, Lancs. Cup winners and BF, Floodlit Trophy winners and BF)
Warrington: May 71 - May 78 (League Leaders, Club Merit winners, RL Cup winners and BF, John Player winners (2), Floodlit Trophy BF, Capt. Morgan winners, Premier BF)
Salford: May 78 - Nov. 80
Leigh: Nov. 80 - June 82 (Div. 1 champs, Lancs. Cup winners)
Wigan: June 82 - Aug. 84 (John Player winners, RL Cup BF)
Leigh: Feb. 85 - Nov. 85
St. Helens: Nov. 85 -
Lancashire: 1973-74 to 1977-78; 1985-86 Champions (2)
England: 1975 (including World Championship (European Champions))
Played for: St. Helens, Leigh, Warrington

FRANK MYLER
Rochdale H.: May 71 - Oct. 74 (John Player BF, Floodlit Trophy BF)
Widnes: May 75 - May 78 (Div. 1 champs, RL Cup BF (2), Lancs. Cup winners (2), John Player winners and BF, Premier BF)
Swinton: Jan. 80 - May 81
Oldham: May 81 - May 83 (Div. 2 champs)
Oldham: June 84 -
Great Britain Under-24s: 1983
England: 1978 — (European Champions)
Great Britain: 1983-84 and 1984 tour
Played for: Widnes, St. Helens, Rochdale H.

GEOFF PEGGS
Keighley: Nov. 83 - Sept. 85
Played for: Bramley, Rochdale H.

GEORGE PIENIAZEK
Batley: Nov. 84 - Nov. 85
Featherstone R.: Nov. 85 -
Played for: Bramley, Keighley, Wakefield T., Batley

227

MALCOLM REILLY
Castleford: Dec. 74 - (Yorks. Cup winners (2) and BF (2), Floodlit Trophy winners, John Player winners, Premier BF, RL Cup winners)
Played for: Castleford, Manly (Aus.)

ALAN RHODES
Doncaster: Aug. 81 - Mar. 83
Sheffield E.:   Apr. 84 - May 86
Played for: Featherstone R., York, Castleford, Doncaster

PETER ROE
Keighley: Sept. 85 -
Played for: Keighley, Bradford N., York, Hunslet, Queanbeyan (Aus.)

BARRY SEABOURNE
Keighley: Nov. 77 - Mar. 79
Bradford N.:   May 85 -
Played for: Leeds, Bradford N., Keighley.

JOHN SHERIDAN
Doncaster: June 84 -
Played for: Castleford

Castleford coach Mal Reilly and assistant Dave Sampson issue 'cool it' instructions only minutes away from earning a 1986 Wembley appearance.

Kiwi captain Mark Graham, watched over by James Leuluai.

1985 KIWIS

1985 KIWIS

The polish of the top ranked Kiwis was dulled by Britain's rejuvenated Lions. New coach Maurice Bamford stemmed the tide of 10 successive defeats by Test sides from Australia and New Zealand to square the three-match series and earn Great Britain a share of the new Whitbread Trophy.

The Test arena was filled with action, drama and controversy as New Zealand snatched victory in the final three minutes of the first Whitbread Trophy Bitter Test; Great Britain coasted to a 25-8 success in the second encounter and British substitute Lee Crooks hit a last ditch touchline penalty goal equaliser in a blood-and-thunder decider.

New Zealand's 11th tour of Britain, already scheduled to be the shortest ever with a 13-match itinerary, was reduced to 12 fixtures by the postponement of the Lancashire game at Oldham due to frost.

The 1985 Kiwis recorded eight victories and a draw, amassing 249 points and conceding 153, on an eventful tour which drew the best crowds for a New Zealand tour for 20 years.

The dozen matches attracted a total of 107,347 spectators, compared with the 1980 total of 90,904 from 14 games and the 1971 tally of 20 fixtures pulling in 101,600 fans.

The average attendance for the 1985 Kiwi tour was 8,946 compared with the 1980 figure of 6,394. The trio of Tests — all televised live in both Britain and New Zealand — attracted 50,306, an average of 16,769 . . . nearly double the 1980 Test average of 8,706.

The biggest gate on the 1985 tour was 22,209 at Elland Road, Leeds, for the third and final Whitbread Trophy Bitter Test, with record receipts of nearly £90,000. Wigan's opening crowd of 12,856 produced the best club attendance.

The Riversiders were the only club side to topple the Kiwis, their other defeats coming at the hands of Great Britain and Yorkshire.

Wingman Mark Bourneville made the most full appearances with nine, missing only the three Tests. Bourneville, who had previously served Leigh for a season, attracted the attention of St. Helens along with forward Adrian Shelford, while the Saints succeeded in obtaining the signature of former Southend Invicta centre Mark Elia, the tour's top try scorer with eight touchdowns.

Olsen Filipaina also made nine appearances, including two as substitute, to finish as top goal and points scorer with 20 successful shots for 40 points.

Tour records were created in the match at St. Helens. The 46-8 victory over a full strength Saints was the highest-ever score by a touring Kiwi side in Britain with the nine goals by Filipaina a match record by any New Zealand tourist.

The Kiwis arrived at their Harrogate base with their world rating intact after imposing an 18-0 World Cup defeat on Australia following two last minute defeats. The 24-strong tour party included Filipaina — the star of the summer Australasian series — a fear of flying having been mastered. Also available for Test duty only were the eight British-based Kiwi Test players, although Graeme West and Kevin Tamati were released for a tour match as Test build-up.

New Zealand called on 20 players for Test duty, awarding new caps to Sam Stewart, Ricky Cowan, Darrell Williams and Wayne Wallace.

One of the disappointments of the dramatic tour was skipper Mark Graham's curtailment by injury to only four appearances, including the first and third Tests. The scorer of three tries — including the only touchdown of the deciding Test — Graham was justifying his tag of the world's greatest forward in the first Test at Headingley when he was forced to retire having inspired the Kiwis to a 14-6 lead with his 28th minute try.

The 11th hour announcement of his

withdrawal from the second Test line-up spurred an already confident Great Britain as much as it demoralised his fellow Kiwis. His return for the Elland Road World Cup qualifier was a vital factor in New Zealand's face-saving operation, scoring a controversial try and producing the Kiwis' most outstanding individual performance.

Another let down was the lacklustre form of Filipaina. Only his goalkicking kept him on the scoresheet and his lack of traditional attacking prowess eventually cost him his Test role as stand off.

Elsewhere, world class form was produced by Dean Bell, Clayton Friend, the Sorensen brothers and, in the early stages, Hugh McGahan.

As with any tour, new faces took the spotlight as the itinerary progressed. Stewart, Williams and Wallace fully justified their Test caps, while utility back Shane Cooper, top scoring centre Elia and back row forward James Goulding showed promise for the future reshaping of the New Zealand Test side.

This forward planning was a key exercise on the 1985 tour as most of the highly successful Kiwi squad of the past five years were approaching retirement from top class football together. Indeed, Filipaina, Ah Kuoi and Kevin Tamati all announced the end of their illustrious Test careers after the tour.

An unwanted feature of the British section of the tour was the presence of physical tactics in the Kiwi gameplan. Their disciplinary record of four dismissals and four sin bin sessions included Gerry Kershaw's much criticised sending off of three Kiwis along with two Hull players at the Boulevard.

However, an over-reliance on hard line ploys was evident throughout the tour, coming to the fore in the fixture with Leeds and boiling over in the torrid third Test, when Britain's patience finally snapped and

the police felt forced to come on to the field to stop a prolonged brawl.

The international reputations of Australian referee Barry Gomersall and respective coaches Bamford and Graham Lowe were all affected by the Whitbread Trophy Bitter Tests.

Gomersall — invited back by the British authorities for his second Test series in eight months — compounded his well known relaxed image by allowing two crucial touchdowns in the first Test despite video evidence of forward passes, while in the third Test he used his controversial style of turning a blind eye to a brawl. It was a method which was to backfire on him, especially when he eventually gained control and sent two players to the sin bin including Kurt Sorensen who had already been sidelined for five minutes for a late high tackle which had led to Britain's Andy Goodway being stretchered off.

Lowe had arrived in Britain wearing the mantle of the world's top coach. But his quiet, studious facade soon took on a worried look as the crown began to slip when his charges only just managed a last ditch record fourth successive Test win against Britain at Headingly.

By that time, Great Britain's new supremo Bamford had begun to make his undoubted motivational skills evident at world level. In his first major Test battle since his shock appointment a year earlier, the much travelled Bamford had restored national pride and inner confidence to a morale-battered British side.

An intensive build-up programme of week-long training camps and warm-up matches, in liaison with assistant Phil Larder and manager Les Bettinson, was packaged in a new-style strip and national symbol, flag-waving plus new-found self belief.

The Anglo-Kiwi Tests were sponsored for the first time by Whitbread Trophy Bitter in a £170,000 two-year deal and a feature of the £230,000 back-up promotional campaign was the introduction of Man of the Match awards for both sides. The first Test awards went to loose forwards Harry Pinner and McGahan; the second Test honours to record-breaking try scorer Garry Schofield and debutant Stewart; the third Test prizes to Crooks and skipper Graham.

The Whitbread Trophy Bitter Man of the Series awards went to Great Britain's debutant prop forward John Fieldhouse and his opposite number Dane Sorensen.

Graham, Joe Ropati and Ross Taylor received injuries in Britain which prevented their travelling on to France and replacements Marty Crequer and Brent Todd flew out to join the tour party before leaving this country.

The Kiwis went on to win all their seven tour matches in France including the two Tests at Marseilles and Perpignan, both by 22-0, the second Test being a World Cup qualifier.

1985 KIWIS
Left to Right:
Back Row: Tamati, Wallace, Taylor, Stewart, O'Callaghan, Ropati, K. Sorensen, Cooper, Bell.
Middle Row: Graham Lowe (Coach), Bourneville, Shelford, O'Regan, McGahan, Wright, Cowan, Williams, Elia, Horo, Glen Gallagher (Physio).
Front Row: Jim Campbell (Manager), Gibb, D. Sorensen, Graham (Captain), Filipaina, Goulding, Friend, Tom McKeown (Business Manager).

TOUR RESULTS

Date		Result	Score	Opposition	Venue	Attendance
Oct.	6th	L	8-14	Wigan	Wigan	12,856
	9th	W	16-12	Great Britain U-21s	Bradford	2,285
	13th	W	20-10	Hull K.R.	Hull K.R.	6,630
	15th	W	32-6	Cumbria	Whitehaven	5,212
	19th	W	24-22	GREAT BRITAIN	Leeds	12,591
	23rd	L	8-18	Yorkshire	Bradford	3,745
	27th	W	46-8	St. Helens	St. Helens	7,897
	29th	W	16-10	Leeds	Leeds	4,829
Nov.	2nd	L	8-25	GREAT BRITAIN	Wigan	15,506
	4th	W	32-12	Widnes	Widnes	5,181
	9th	D	6-6	GREAT BRITAIN	Elland Rd, Leeds	22,209
	13th	P'poned (frost)		Lancashire	Oldham	
	17th	W	33-10	Hull	Hull	8,406

TOUR SUMMARY

					FOR				AGAINST			
P.	W.	D.	L.	T.	G.	DG.	Pts.	T.	G.	DG.	Pts.
12	8	1	3	42	40	1	249	20	35	3	153

TEST SUMMARY

					FOR				AGAINST			
P.	W.	D.	L.	T.	G.	DG.	Pts.	T.	G.	DG.	Pts.
3	1	1	1	7	5	0	38	7	12	1	53

TOUR RECORDS

Biggest attendance: 22,209 third Test at Elland Rd, Leeds

Highest score and widest margin victory: 46-8 v. St. Helens

Highest score and widest margin defeat: 8-25 v. Great Britain, second Test

Most tries in a match: 2 by Mark Elia v. St. Helens and Hull; Sam Stewart v. Cumbria; Mark Bourneville v. Hull

Most goals and points in a match: 9 goals and 18 points by Olsen Filipaina v. St. Helens

Most tries on tour: 8 by Mark Elia

Most goals and points on tour: 20 goals and 40 points by Olsen Filipaina

Most appearances: 9 by Mark Bourneville, and Olsen Filipaina (including two as substitute)

Sent off: Mark Bourneville v. Leeds (not guilty)
Clayton Friend v. Hull (sending off sufficient)
Howie Tamati v Hull (sending off sufficient)
Olsen Filipaina v. Hull (sending off sufficient)

Sin bin: Kevin Tamati v. Great Britain, first Test (5 min.)
Kurt Sorensen v. Great Britain Under 21s (10 min.)
Kurt Sorensen v. Great Britain, third Test (5 min. and 10 min.)

Opponents sent off: Bill Pattinson (Cumbria) 2 matches
Lee Crooks (Hull) sending off sufficient
Shaun Patrick (Hull) sending off sufficient

Opponents' sin bin: Jeff Grayshon (Great Britain, third Test)

TOUR PARTY

Manager: Jim Campbell

Business Manager: Tom McKeown

Coach: Graham Lowe

Physiotherapist: Glen Gallaher

Doctor: Lloyd Drake

Manager Jim Campbell

Coach Graham Lowe

PLAYER	CLUB	App	Sub	T	G	Pts
BELL, Dean	Eastern Suburbs (A)	7	1	2	—	8
BOURNEVILLE, Mark	Mt. Albert, Auckland	9	—	3	—	12
COOPER, Shane	Mt. Albert, Auckland	5	3	3	—	12
COWAN, Ricky	Mt. Albert, Auckland	5	1	—	—	—
*CREQUER, Marty	Canterbury	1	—	1	—	4
ELIA, Mark	Te Atatu, Auckland	8	—	8	—	32
FILIPAINA, Olsen	Eastern Suburbs (A)	7	2	—	20	40
FRIEND, Clayton	Manukau, Auckland	8	—	3	—	12
GIBB, Glen	Runanga, West Coast	3	—	—	—	—
GOULDING, James	Richmond, Auckland	6	—	—	—	—
GRAHAM, Mark	North Sydney (A)	4	—	3	—	12
HORO, Shane	Waring City Tigers, Waikato	5	—	3	—	12
McGAHAN, Hugh	Eastern Suburbs (A)	7	1	3	—	12
O'CALLAGHAN, Vaun	Waikato	3	—	1	7	18
O'REGAN, Ron	City Newton, Auckland	5	2	1	—	4
ROPATI, Joe	Otahuhu, Auckland	5	1	—	8	16
SHELFORD, Adrian	Hornby, Canterbury	4	3	2	—	8
SORENSEN, Dane	Cronulla (A)	5	1	—	1	2
SORENSEN, Kurt	Cronulla (A)	6	1	2	—	8
STEWART, Sam	Wellington	7	—	4	—	16
TAMATI, Howie	Taranaki	6	—	—	—	—
TAYLOR, Ross	Hornby, Canterbury	3	—	1	—	4
*TODD, Brett	Canterbury	—	1	—	—	—
WALLACE, Wayne	Hornby, Canterbury	6	—	—	—	—
WILLIAMS, Darrell	Mt. Albert, Auckland	8	—	—	—	—
WRIGHT, Owen	Manukau, Auckland	6	2	—	4(1)	9
British-based players						
AH KUOI, Fred	Hull	2	1	—	—	—
KEMBLE, Gary	Hull	2	1	—	—	—
LEULUAI, James	Hull	3	—	1	—	4
O'HARA, Dane	Hull	3	—	1	—	4
PROHM, Gary	Hull K.R.	3	—	—	—	—
TAMATI, Kevin	Warrington	2	1	—	—	—
WEST, Graeme	Wigan	2	—	—	—	—

Key: * Replacements (A) Australia ( ) drop goal

Great Britain Test squad, left to right. Back row: Arkwright, Myler, Potter, Burke, Goodway, Crooks, Watkinson. Middle row: Phil Larder (Asst. Coach), K. Beardmore, Drummond, Hanley, Fieldhouse, Hulme, Mike Stabler (Physio). Front row: R. Beardmore, Fox, Les Bettinson (Manager), Pinner, Maurice Bamford (Coach), Lydon, Schofield.

Make a wish! . . . British stars John Fieldhouse (left) and Deryck Fox hang on to Kiwi pack star Kurt Sorensen in the third Test.

MATCH BY MATCH

6th October

WIGAN	14
NEW ZEALAND	8

1. O'Callaghan (Shelford)
2. Ropati
3. Elia (Filipaina)
4. O'Regan
5. Bourneville
6. Cooper
7. Friend
8. D. Sorensen
9. H. Tamati
10. K. Sorensen
11. Graham
12. Wright
13. McGahan

T: Cooper
G: O'Callaghan (2)

Wigan:
Edwards; Henley-Smith, Stephenson, Hanley, Whitfield (Hampson); Ella, Ford; Case, Kiss (Courtney), Wane, Du Toit, Goodway, Potter

T: Edwards, Goodway
G: Stephenson (3)

Referee: Ron Campbell (Widnes)
Attendance: 12,856

Continuous torrential rain affected both the attendance and the scoreline in this opening tour encounter at Central Park. Nearly 13,000 fans braved the elements, two-thirds of the anticipated turnout, to witness a Wigan victory with two of the three tries influenced by the downpour.

The Riversiders recorded the first score of the tour with a well-worked move involving Hanley, whose early ball enabled centre partner Stephenson to sprint through and delay a pass to Edwards to score by the posts. Stephenson landed the goal and two penalties before O'Callaghan struck a penalty goal.

The adverse conditions played a part in Edwards' misfielding a Friend up and under and Cooper touched down, O'Callaghan adding the goal to make it 10-8. The tourists lost possession at crucial times in a second half display of brilliant support play before the weather helped Wigan clinch victory. Ella's kick was kept in play by the inexperienced O'Callaghan who slid well over the touchline for Goodway to dribble the ball skilfully 35 yards before launching himself for the clinching touchdown.

9th October

Bradford

GT BRITAIN U-21s	12
NEW ZEALAND	16

1. Williams
2. Bourneville
3. Ropati
4. Filipaina
5. Horo
6. Cooper
7. Gibb
8. D. Sorensen (K. Sorensen)
9. Wallace
10. Goulding
11. Wright
12. Stewart
13. McGahan

T: McGahan, Horo
G: Filipaina (4)

Great Britain Under-21s:
Lyon (Widnes); Dalton (Whitehaven), Creasser (Leeds), Forster (Warrington), Carbert (Warrington); Edwards (Wigan), Ford (Wigan); Dannatt (Hull), Groves (Salford), Wane (Wigan), Powell (Leeds), Lyman (Featherstone R.), Divorty (Hull). Substitutions: Hulme (Widnes) for Creasser, Westhead (Leigh) for Lyman.

T: Edwards, Forster
G: Carbert (2)

Referee: Derek Fox (Wakefield)
Attendance: 2,285

New Zealand gained the expected victory but Great Britain's young Lions commanded praise and self-satisfaction with a promising display of battling forward play and direct running from the backs.

Discipline was also a key feature of the Under-21s as they levelled the tries at two apiece and fell behind only to two Filipaina penalty goals.

Hull loose forward Divorty stood out in a hard-working pack to take the Whitbread Trophy Bitter Man of the Match award for the home side, making his mark with tactical kicking and two defence splitting passes that led to both Britain's tries and looking at least the equal of the tourists' Man of the Match, his opposite number McGahan.

Outstanding also for the Under-21s were the only current Test squad member Edwards — a try scorer at stand off — prop Dannatt, centre Forster and substitute back Hulme.

13th October

HULL K.R. 10
NEW ZEALAND 20

1. Williams
2. Bourneville
3. Horo
4. Ropati
5. Elia
6. Filipaina
7. Friend
8. Cowan
9. H. Tamati
10. K. Sorensen
11. Graham
12. Goulding (O'Regan)
13. McGahan (D. Sorensen)

T: Graham, Elia, Friend
G: Ropati (4)

Hull K.R.:
Lydiat; S. Smith, Robinson, Prohm, Laws; Dorahy, G. Smith, (Rudd); P. Johnston, Watkinson, Ema, Kelly, Hogan (Harrison), Miller

T: S. Smith
G: Dorahy (3)

Referee: John McDonald (Wigan)
Attendance: 6,630

A controversial 56th minute try helped New Zealand gain an unimpressive victory over the League Champions. With a touch judge on the field following a two-man fight, Rovers were guilty of not playing to the whistle as referee McDonald allowed play to continue with Kiwi centre Elia weaving his way through an uninterested home defence to touch down under the posts.

Ropati's goal put the visitors 14-8 ahead at a time when Rovers were in with a shout, having built up a 6-2 lead with a Dorahy penalty goal and a try by winger Steve Smith with the first touch of the ball on his debut.

New Zealand sealed victory with a last minute try from scrum half Friend, goaled by Ropati, although their lacklustre performance confirmed the need for Test inclusion of British-based players, particularly Hull K.R. centre Prohm.

The visitors objected to an 18-7 penalty count against them, especially a 9-0 second half count, the respective Man of the Match awards going to Hull K.R.'s Hogan and debutant Kiwi tourist Cowan.

15th October

Whitehaven

CUMBRIA 6
NEW ZEALAND 32

1. O'Callaghan (Ropati)
2. Bourneville
3. Bell
4. O'Regan
5. Elia
6. Cooper
7. Gibb
8. Cowan
9. Wallace
10. Taylor
11. Shelford
12. Goulding (Wright)
13. Stewart

T: Stewart (2), Shelford, Cooper, Taylor, Elia
G: Ropati (3), O'Callaghan

Cumbria:
Stoddart (Whitehaven); Dalton (Whitehaven), Jones (Workington T.), Whittle (Barrow), Beck (Workington T.); Smith (Workington T.), Cairns (Barrow); Henney (Fulham), Banks (Whitehaven), Simpson (Whitehaven), Hetherington (Whitehaven), W. Pattinson (Workington T.), Huddart (Carlisle). Substitutions: Pape (Carlisle) for Stoddart; Nixon (Workington T.) for Huddart.

G: Smith (3)

Referee: Kevin Allatt (Southport)
Attendance: 5,212

New Zealand's second string side recorded a flattering victory as Cumbria's hopes of repeating their 1980 Kiwi tour success were dashed by the loss of two key players.

Urged on by a bumper crowd of 5,000-plus, Cumbria were disrupted while leading 2-0 from a Smith penalty by full back Stoddart having to leave the field after 20 minutes with a facial injury.

New Zealand capitalised on the enforced Cumbrian reshuffle with quick tries from Stewart and Taylor, O'Callaghan adding a goal. Two further penalties from Smith, who missed a simple kick from under the posts, left Cumbria trailing only 10-6 at the interval.

Elia streaked in at the corner to stretch the visitors' lead before Cumbria were dealt a second blow with the dismissal of second row man Pattinson for a high tackle. The Kiwis emphasised their overall strength and numerical supremacy by running in three late tries from Cooper, Stewart and Shelford, substitute Ropati adding all three goals.

237

FIRST TEST

Great Britain crashed to their 10th successive Australasian Test defeat after being only three minutes away from glory in one of the best-ever international contests.

Despite being second best to the Kiwis, Britain produced a memorable length of the field move for winger Joe Lydon to streak over and add the goal to put the new look home side 22-18 ahead with only eight minutes left.

As coach Maurice Bamford's promised new era looked like dawning, New Zealand refused to lie down and star packman Kurt Sorensen burst through to send the supporting James Leuluai over by the posts for Olsen Filipaina to hit his second goal from five attempts and secure victory.

The suspicion of a forward pass in the build up to both spectacular tries could not detract from this thrilling, tense encounter which enthralled the Headingley crowd of 12,000-plus and a live television audience of millions in both Britain and New Zealand.

The Kiwis' last minute salvation was ironic retribution for their own double defeat by Australia four months earlier when the Kangaroos secured success in the dying minutes in both the first and second Tests.

This first Whitbread Trophy Bitter Test will be remembered for the re-emergence of Great Britain as an international force under new coach Bamford and for that unforgettable Lydon touchdown.

The long-range move confirmed the pre-match theory that Britain would be most dangerous out wide. What appeared to be the winning try started with Des Drummond fielding the ball five yards from the corner flag on his right wing. The Leigh star rounded opposite number Dane O'Hara and weaved to the 25-yard line, linking with scrum half Deryck Fox and substitute forward Chris Arkwright who fed the ball to potential match-winner Ellery Hanley.

The world's most expensive player set off on a 50-yard touchline dash beating Kiwi winger Dean Bell and holding off Leuluai before lobbing a high pass to Lydon who streaked for the posts.

Britain had opened in spectacular style with an Andy Goodway try and Mick Burke goal giving them a morale-boosting 6-0 lead after only three minutes. It then looked like the same old story when skipper Mark Graham inspired the visitors with a towering performance which brought three tries in 19 minutes, one for himself and touchdowns for wingers O'Hara and Bell.

A superb individual try from the irrepressible Hanley, with Burke again adding the goal, put Britain back in the picture at the break at 12-14.

Britain's hopes of victory rose immediately after the restart when New Zealand's mainspring Graham was forced to withdraw through injury, although Britain's forward power was also reduced when prop Lee Crooks departed in the 55th minute.

Skipper Harry Pinner took the official Man of the Match award for Britain, mainly for his first half display, being pushed close by stand off Tony Myler who served up his best performance in the red, white and blue jersey.

New Zealand's decision to play Hull centre Leuluai at full back almost backfired as he dropped Pinner's speculative up and under for Goodway to score and failed to field another while under pressure. The Kiwis back division was far more balanced when Gary Kemble took over the number one role after the break with Leuluai reverting to his poaching role to grab the winning try.

There were only four punished fouls, one earning substitute Kiwi forward Kevin Tamati five minutes in the sin bin, and only six scrums. A 1947 Test between the same two countries at the same venue produced more than 70 scrummages!

FIRST WHITBREAD TROPHY BITTER TEST

19th October   **Headingley, Leeds**

GREAT BRITAIN 22		**NEW ZEALAND 24**
Mick Burke (Widnes)	1.	James Leuluai
Des Drummond (Leigh)	2.	Dean Bell
Garry Schofield (Hull)	3.	Fred Ah Kuoi
Ellery Hanley (Wigan)	4.	Gary Prohm
Joe Lydon (Widnes)	5.	Dane O'Hara
Tony Myler (Widnes)	6.	Olsen Filipaina
Deryck Fox (Featherstone R.)	7.	Clayton Friend
Lee Crooks (Hull)	8.	Kurt Sorensen
David Watkinson (Hull K.R.)	9.	Howie Tamati
John Fieldhouse (Widnes)	10.	Dane Sorensen
Andy Goodway (Wigan)	11.	Mark Graham, Capt.
Ian Potter (Wigan)	12.	Owen Wright
Harry Pinner (St. Helens), Capt.	13.	Hugh McGahan
David Hulme (Widnes)	14.	Gary Kemble
Chris Arkwright (St. Helens)	15.	Kevin Tamati

T: Goodway, Hanley, Lydon
G: Burke (3), Lydon (2)
Substitution:
Arkwright for Crooks (55 min.)
Half-time: 12-14
Referee: Barry Gomersall (Australia)
Attendance: 12,591

T: O'Hara, Bell, Graham,
K. Sorensen, Leuluai
G: Filipaina (2)
Substitutions:
Kemble for Ah Kuoi (Half-time)
K. Tamati for Graham (41 min.)

Scorechart

Minute	Score	*Scoreline* GB	NZ
3:	Goodway (T)		
	Burke (G)	6	0
9:	O'Hara (T)	6	4
24:	Bell (T)	6	8
28:	Graham (T)		
	Filipaina (G)	6	14
37:	Hanley (T)		
	Burke (G)	12	14
55:	Burke (PG)	14	14
59:	K. Sorensen (T)	14	18
67:	Lydon (PG)	16	18
72:	Lydon (T)		
	Lydon (G)	22	18
77:	Leuluai (T)		
	Filipaina (G)	22	24
	Scrums	4	2
	Penalties	11	8

Kiwi Man of the Match Hugh McGahan.

239

23rd October

Bradford

YORKSHIRE 18
NEW ZEALAND 8

1. Williams
2. Bourneville
3. Ropati (Bell)
4. Elia
5. Horo
6. O'Regan
7. Cooper
8. Cowan (Wright)
9. Wallace
10. Taylor
11. Shelford
12. Goulding
13. Stewart

T: Elia
G: Ropati, Wright

Yorkshire:
Mumby (Bradford N.); Gibson (Batley), Creasser (Leeds), Schofield (Hull), Mason (Bramley); Hanley (Wigan), Fox (Featherstone R.); Grayshon (Bradford N.), Noble (Bradford N.), Skerrett (Hull), Crooks (Hull), Goodway (Wigan), Heron (Leeds). Substitutes: Steadman (York) for Creasser, Lyman (Featherstone R.) for Skerrett.

T: Hanley, Goodway, Gibson
G: Fox (2), Schofield (dg), Hanley (dg)

Referee: John Holdsworth (Kippax)
Attendance: 3,745

Yorkshire fielded five stars from Great Britain's first Test side against New Zealand's second string, the Kiwis being subjected to their second tour defeat in six matches.

Scrum half Fox made up for a disappointing first Test by taking the Man of the Match award, making two of the three White Rose tries and adding two goals. Goodway also improved on his Test showing and scored the opening try, while Wigan team mate Hanley returned to Odsal for the first time since his transfer to notch a try and a rare drop goal.

On a freezing night, New Zealand had little to offer other than Ropati's brilliant solo try from centre Elia. The injection of Test players Bell and Wright as substitutes did not lift the disappointing standard.

The victory completed a notable double for Yorkshire coach Peter Fox, adding to his surprise scalp of Lancashire in the Rodstock War of the Roses. The White Rose props had differing fortunes, Grayshon justifying his claim for Test inclusion and Skerrett being ruled out of consideration by suffering a fractured cheekbone.

27th October

ST HELENS 8
NEW ZEALAND 46

1. Williams
2. Bourneville
3. Bell
4. Elia
5. Ropati (Cooper)
6. Filipaina
7. Friend
8. K. Sorensen
9. Wallace
10. Taylor (Shelford)
11. Cowan
12. Stewart
13. McGahan

T: Elia (2), Friend, K. Sorensen, McGahan, Shelford, Stewart
G: Filipaina (9)

St. Helens:
Veivers; Ledger, Conlon, French, Meadows; Arkwright, Holding; Greinke, Liptrot, Forber (Round), Platt (Loughlin), Haggerty, Pinner

T: Haggerty
G: Conlon (2)

Referee: Fred Lindop (Wakefield)
Attendance: 7,897

With only five current Test stars in their ranks, New Zealand secured their biggest-ever tour victory, scoring seven tries to one.

Saints were at virtual full strength, with county player Forber standing in for the injured Gorley, but their tackling showed a marked deterioration in the second half when already 14-6 behind.

The Kiwis masterful display was marred only by the loss of prop Taylor with a badly broken arm, an injury which was to rule him out of the rest of the European tour.

Kurt Sorensen and McGahan were outstanding in the pack, with Stewart staking a claim for a Test spot. Filipaina staged an exhibition of goalkicking, hitting a record nine successful shots, his only miss striking the upright!

Australian centre Conlon scored two goals for the Saints whose try came from second row man Haggerty, the only player to match the tourists.

29th October

LEEDS   10
NEW ZEALAND   16

1. Williams
2. Bourneville
3. Bell
4. Elia
5. Horo (Cooper)
6. Filipaina
7. Friend
8. Cowan
9. H. Tamati ⌐
10. Shelford
11. West
12. Wright (O'Regan)
13. Stewart

T: Friend, Horo, Stewart
G: Filipaina (2)

Leeds:
Gill (Clark); Currie, Creasser, Wilson, Francis; Lyons, Conway; Keith Rayne, Ward, Hill, Powell, Webb (Moorby), Heron

T: Lyons
G: Creasser (3)

Referee: Jim Smith (Halifax)
Attendance: 4,829

New Zealand secured their sixth tour victory but won no friends in a physical performance which resulted in the sending off of winger Bourneville and three Leeds players being taken off injured, two on stretchers.

Bourneville claimed mistaken identity after being dismissed after Creasser had been felled in an off-the-ball incident. A few minutes earlier centre Wilson was carried off with a dislocated knee while second row man Webb had hobbled off with a twisted knee as early as the fifth minute.

The home side fought back to within two points having trailed 12-2 at the interval in a torrid game where the Kiwis' tactics incensed the Headingley supporters.

Referee Smith awarded a penalty count of 21-10 to Leeds and the Kiwis also had to weather a second half fightback by Leeds who trailed 12-10 for most of the period, the visitors making the game secure with a Stewart try with four minutes to go.

Experienced hooker Howie Tamati, on duty at Headingley.

241

SECOND TEST

Great Britain's long awaited return to winning ways against a side from Down Under was highlighted by a record breaking display of try scoring by 20-year-old Hull centre Garry Schofield.

After a lacklustre performance in the first Test, Schofield bagged all four tries to equal the British Test record and establish a new points record against New Zealand.

The emphatic victory ended a 10-match run of defeats against either New Zealand or Australia and confirmed the vast improvement in style which had been promised in the Headingley Test two weeks earlier.

Even allowing for the demoralising absence through injury of Kiwi skipper Mark Graham, this was Britain's finest hour. In only his fourth Test encounter, coach Maurice Bamford produced a winning gameplan worthy of worldwide recognition.

A defensive net was slackened only once when Kiwi winger Dean Bell touched down, a much improved Deryck Fox topping the tackle count with 31, just ahead of David Watkinson, Ian Potter and Jeff Grayshon.

Bamford's encouragement of freedom of expression on attack paid off in style and although Schofield took the scoring honours, the glory was spread among world-rated talent in British colours, particularly Ellery Hanley, Tony Myler and Harry Pinner.

It will always be a matter of conjecture whether Graham's last minute withdrawal with an ankle injury was the vital factor between the Kiwis' expected victory and the overwhelming defeat, but it was difficult to see one man resisting the rampant young Lions with their new found confidence.

Once again key figures such as Olsen Filipaina and loose forward Hugh McGahan failed to make any impact, while former captain Graeme West looked short of match fitness at Test level.

But this was always going to be Britain's day as they ended New Zealand's longest winning run against them of four matches. Building on their restored pride from the Headingley encounter, Bamford's charges displayed true patriotism in the pre-match ceremonies and the Union Jack started its journey up the victory flag pole as early as the 15th minute.

Joe Lydon and Filipaina had scored a penalty goal apiece before Schofield notched the first of his quartet of touchdowns. From a scrum, long passes from Fox and Myler gave Hanley space to manoeuvre and his clever inside pass sent the Airlie Bird centre 25 yards to the line, having to hold off three defenders to put the ball down.

Lydon added another penalty five minutes later and on the half hour second row man Potter intercepted a loose Kiwi pass for Fieldhouse to show surprising speed and put Schofield clear, taking the scoreline to 12-2 at the break.

In his half-time pep talk, coach Bamford instructed his players to imagine they were trailing and the determination to score again paid off within two minutes of the restart. Pinner and Potter opened the way for Myler and the stand off's superb one-handed inside pass set Schofield off again on a 45-yard run to the posts for Lydon's goal to make it 18-2.

Britain's one defensive slip came in the 55th minute when Bell rounded substitute full back Edwards and Filipaina added the simple kick. Britain replied with a 64th minute Pinner drop goal.

With four minutes left, Schofield grabbed the spotlight — and the records — with his fourth try following a top class break by Pinner and a smart pass from Hanley, Lydon adding his fourth goal.

Britain's dressing room overflowed with champagne . . . and a few tears including those shed by the emotional Bamford and his shock selection, veteran prop Jeff Grayshon, called up for his 12th cap at the age of 36 years and 8 months.

SECOND WHITBREAD TROPHY BITTER TEST

2nd November   **Wigan**

GREAT BRITAIN 25   **NEW ZEALAND 8**

Mick Burke (Widnes)	1.	Gary Kemble
Des Drummond (Leigh)	2.	Dean Bell
Garry Schofield (Hull)	3.	James Leuluai
Ellery Hanley (Wigan)	4.	Gary Prohm
Joe Lydon (Widnes)	5.	Dane O'Hara
Tony Myler (Widnes)	6.	Olsen Filipaina, Capt.
Deryck Fox (Featherstone R.)	7.	Clayton Friend
Jeff Grayshon (Leeds)	8.	Kurt Sorensen
David Watkinson (Hull K.R.)	9.	Howie Tamati
John Fieldhouse (Widnes)	10.	Dane Sorensen
Andy Goodway (Wigan)	11.	Graeme West
Ian Potter (Wigan)	12.	Sam Stewart
Harry Pinner (St. Helens), Capt.	13.	Hugh McGahan
Shaun Edwards (Wigan)	14.	Fred Ah Kuoi
Chris Burton (Hull K.R.)	15.	Ricky Cowan

T: Schofield (4)   T: Bell
G: Lydon (4), Pinner (dg)   G: Filipaina (2)
Substitutions: Substitutions:
Edwards for Burke (43 min.)   Ah Kuoi for West (48 min.)
Burton for Goodway (74 min.)   Cowan for Stewart (70 min.)
Half-time: 12-2
Referee: Barry Gomersall (Australia)
Attendance: 15,506

Scorechart

		Scoreline	
Minute	*Score*	*GB*	*NZ*
8:	Lydon (PG)	2	0
12:	Filipaina (PG)	2	2
15:	Schofield (T)	6	2
20:	Lydon (PG)	8	2
30:	Schofield (T)	12	2
42:	Schofield (T)		
	Lydon (G)	18	2
55:	Bell (T)		
	Filipaina (G)	18	8
64:	Pinner (dg)	19	8
76:	Schofield (T)		
	Lydon (G)	25	8
	Scrums	6	3
	Penalties	11	9

Kiwi Man of the Match Sam Stewart.

4th November

WIDNES	12
NEW ZEALAND	32

1. O'Callaghan
2. Horo
3. Williams
4. Elia
5. Bourneville
6. Cooper
7. Gibb
8. K. Tamati (Todd)
9. Wallace
10. Shelford
11. Wright
12. Goulding
13. O'Regan

T: O'Regan, Horo, Cooper, Elia, Bourneville, O'Callaghan
G: O'Callaghan (4)

Widnes:
Lyon (Dowd); Currier, Stockley, Linton, George; D. Hulme, Sephton; Barrow, Elwell, M. O'Neill, Cleal, Eyres, J. Myler (P. Hulme)

T: Eyres, George
G: J. Myler, Dowd

Referee: John Kendrew (Castleford)
Attendance: 5,181

New Zealand recorded victory number seven with an exciting six-try performance against a Widnes side weakened by the absence of four current Test stars.

The Kiwi tourists shot into a commanding lead with three tries in a stunning 11-minute early spell. O'Regan raced in for the first after good work by Cooper and minutes later Horo completed a fine four-man movement to touchdown. O'Regan then returned the compliment to Cooper with a well-timed pass to send the stand off over, O'Callaghan adding the goal. Myler's penalty made it 14-2 to the Kiwis at the interval.

New Zealand went further ahead with two tries in the first five minutes after the break, Elia beating four men on the way to the line, then winger Bourneville racing 80 yards to touch down, O'Callaghan adding both goals.

A Widnes mini-revival saw tries from Eyres and George, substitute Dowd contributing a goal, before O'Callaghan completed the scoring with a late try and penalty goal.

Olsen Filipaina, top goal and points scorer on the tour.

Whitbread Trophy Bitter Tests Men of the Series award winners, John Fieldhouse (left) and Dane Sorensen.

The last gasp penalty shot by Lee Crooks which levelled the third Test and the series.

THIRD TEST

A towering touchline penalty goal in the last minute by substitute forward Lee Crooks squared a torrid third Test and earned a revitalised Great Britain a share of the new Whitbread Trophy.

The last ditch goalkick crowned an afternoon of high drama staged before 22,000 fervent fans and featuring acts of controversy, violence and old fashioned blood-and-thunder Test football.

But the scenario also had two unwanted "stars" as a pair of police officers entered the field when an ugly 63rd minute brawl involving 10 players showed no signs of ending as Australian referee Barry Gomersall adopted a policy of turning a blind eye.

A reshaped New Zealand side — with strong runners Dean Bell in the centre and Gary Prohm at loose forward — was expected to rely on a gameplan of direct, high speed support play. Instead the Kiwis, intent on retaining their challenge for world supremacy by collecting a further two World Cup points, dragged the showpiece occasion down with incessant violent tactics.

Controversy seeped through the 80 minutes. At the end of the first quarter Britain's Andy Goodway was stretchered off after a high, off-the-ball tackle by Kurt Sorensen. Following consultation with the touch judge, referee Gomersall sent the Kiwi to the sin bin for five minutes, while Goodway took no further part in the game, Crooks coming on eventually to turn the match for Britain.

The only try of a tense encounter came in the 32nd minute. Skipper Mark Graham — the Kiwis' Man of the Match — played the ball to himself and scrambled over amid claims that he had not touched down fairly. Gomersall awarded the try and later revealed that it would have been a penalty touchdown anyway because of John Fieldhouse's interference at the play-the-ball. Dane Sorensen's success in his unlikely role of goalkicker gave

the Kiwis a 6-0 interval lead.

The appearance of substitute Crooks had added a new dimension to Britain's forward play and his Man of the Match performance included penalty goals in the 48th and 56th minute to leave the home side trailing only 4-6 as the last quarter of play began.

Then came the moment when the British players' patience snapped and the 35-second brawl erupted. When Gomersall eventually intervened — along with the policemen — the referee sent Jeff Grayshon and, amazingly, Kurt Sorensen to the sin bin for 10 minutes. British hooker David Watkinson went off for five stitches to an eye wound, Pinner and Potter also needing sewing up after the final whistle.

Chief Supt. William Speight justified his presence on the field, commenting: "There was a serious incident taking place on the playing area and there appeared to be no apparent end to it".

Man-in-the-middle Gomersall explained: "It is my stated policy to let play carry on when there is a brawl. If all 26 players had been involved then I would have intervened immediately but Britain had the ball and a three-to-two advantage. After a brawl like that I was not particular about who went to the sin bin. It could have been any two".

The penalty count was 20-7 in Britain's favour, including nine for foul play, double the combined total for the other two Tests.

Crooks was being announced as Britain's best player as he teed the ball up for his high tension last ditch kick at goal, 30 yards out near the best stand touchline. The memorable on-target boot further justified his individual award in a pack which featured a bulwark front row of veteran Grayshon, Watkinson and Man of the Series Fieldhouse.

Britain had completed their transformation from international also-rans despite the absence of pivot Tony Myler through injury which forced Ellery Hanley's switch from centre to stand off.

THIRD WHITBREAD TROPHY BITTER TEST

9th November   **Elland Road, Leeds**

GREAT BRITAIN 6   NEW ZEALAND 6

Mick Burke (Widnes)	1.	Gary Kemble
Des Drummond (Leigh)	2.	Darrell Williams
Garry Schofield (Hull)	3.	Dean Bell
Shaun Edwards (Wigan)	4.	James Leuluai
Joe Lydon (Widnes)	5.	Dane O'Hara
Ellery Hanley (Wigan)	6.	Fred Ah Kuoi
Deryck Fox (Featherstone R.)	7.	Clayton Friend
Jeff Grayshon (Leeds)	8.	Kevin Tamati
David Watkinson (Hull K.R.)	9.	Wayne Wallace
John Fieldhouse (Widnes)	10.	Dane Sorensen
Andy Goodway (Wigan)	11.	Mark Graham, Capt.
Ian Potter (Wigan)	12.	Kurt Sorensen
Harry Pinner (St. Helens), Capt.	13.	Gary Prohm
Chris Arkwright (St. Helens)	14.	Olsen Filipaina
Lee Crooks (Hull)	15.	Hugh McGahan

G: Crooks (3)   T: Graham

Substitutions: G: D. Sorensen

Crooks for Goodway (23 min.)   Substitutions:

Arkwright for Watkinson (63 min.)   Filipaina for Ah Kuoi (71 min.)

Half-time: 0-6   McGahan for K. Tamati (71 min.)

Referee: Barry Gomersall (Australia)

Attendance: 22,209

Scorechart

		Scoreline	
Minute	*Score*	*GB*	*NZ*
32:	Graham (T)		
	D. Sorensen (G)	0	6
48:	Crooks (PG)	2	6
56:	Crooks (PG)	4	6
79:	Crooks (PG)	6	6
	Scrums	7	7
	Penalties	20	7

Kiwi Test debutant Darrell Williams.

17th November

HULL	10
NEW ZEALAND	33

1. Williams
2. Bourneville
3. Bell
4. Elia
5. Crequer
6. Filipaina
7. Friend
8. Wright
9. H. Tamati
10. Goulding (Shelford)
11. McGahan
12. Stewart
13. O'Regan (Cooper)

T: Elia (2), Bourneville (2), Crequer, McGahan
G: Wright (3, 1dg), Filipaina

Hull:
Kemble; Eastwood, Schofield (Hick), Leuluai, O'Hara; Evans, Gascoigne; Gerard, Patrick, Puckering, Muggleton, Crooks, Divorty

T: Schofield
G: Schofield, Crooks, Hick

Referee: Gerry Kershaw (Easingwold)
Attendance: 8,406

Referee Gerry Kershaw was at the centre of a sensational and controversial finish to the New Zealand tour when he sent off five players — three Kiwis and two from Hull.

The quintet were all dismissed in a first half which also saw Hull's Test centre Schofield stretchered off with a suspected broken leg. After a drama-ridden match in which the Kiwis pulled back from 10-0 down to canter home 33-10, a hastily convened disciplinary committee ruled that all five players were guilty but that sending off was sufficient.

The game was not a rough-house affair and referee Kershaw was fiercely criticised for over-reaction by sending off first Crooks and Friend, and then Patrick and Tamati, for fighting, to be followed by Filipaina for dangerous kicking.

New Zealand completely dominated the second half despite being one man light after the dismissals which the Easingwold man-in-the-middle justified with the comment: "It was Kershaw's Law which won the day after the interval when we saw the New Zealanders display some fine footballing skills without foul play".

NEW ZEALAND APPENDIX

In addition to full tours, World Cup parties made occasional appearances against club sides as follows, the Kiwis score first:

1960

Halifax	won	18-12

1970

Salford	won	8-7
Bradford N.	won	28-17
Barrow	won	14-10

1972

Leeds	lost	6-11
Huddersfield	won	32-2
Salford	lost	4-50

1975

Barrow	won	24-0
Keighley	won	20-8

RECORDS AGAINST CLUB SIDES:

Highest score and widest margin win: 46-8 v. St. Helens in 1985-86

Biggest defeat: 4-50 v. Salford (1972 World Cup tour)

Biggest attendance: 30,000 v. Wigan in 1907-08

INDIVIDUAL RECORDS
(Club and representative matches)

Most tries on tour: 23 by H. Avery in 1926-27

Most goals on tour: 63 by D. White in 1951-52

Most points on tour: 141 (60g, 7t) by H. Messenger in 1907-08

Most appearances on tour: 33 by H. Turtill in 1907-08

Australian Test centre Steve Rogers, three European tours among a 24-cap haul.

AUSTRALIA

The following is a list of Test matches involving Australia. For Tests versus Great Britain see the GREAT BRITAIN section.

Australia v. France			
2 Jan. 1938	W	35-6	Paris
16 Jan. 1938	W	16-11	Marseilles
9 Jan. 1949	W	29-10	Marseilles
23 Jan. 1949	W	10-0	Bordeaux
11 Jun. 1951	L	15-26	Sydney
30 Jun. 1951	W	23-11	Brisbane
21 Jul. 1951	L	14-35	Sydney
27 Dec. 1952	W	16-12	Paris
11 Jan. 1953	L	0-5	Bordeaux
25 Jan. 1953	L	5-13	Lyons
11 Jun. 1955	W	20-8	Sydney
2 Jul. 1955	L	28-29	Brisbane
27 Jul. 1955	L	5-8	Sydney
1 Nov. 1956	W	15-8	Paris
23 Dec. 1956	W	10-6	Bordeaux
13 Jan. 1957	W	25-21	Lyons
31 Oct. 1959	W	20-19	Paris
20 Dec. 1959	W	17-2	Bordeaux
20 Jan. 1960	W	16-8	Roanne
11 Jun. 1960	D	8-8	Sydney
2 Jul. 1960	W	56-6	Brisbane
16 Jul. 1960	L	5-7	Sydney
8 Dec. 1963	L	5-8	Bordeaux
22 Dec. 1963	W	21-9	Toulouse
18 Jan. 1964	W	16-8	Paris
13 Jun. 1964	W	20-6	Sydney
4 Jul. 1964	W	27-2	Brisbane
18 Jul. 1964	W	35-9	Sydney
17 Dec. 1967	D	7-7	Marseilles
24 Dec. 1967	L	3-10	Carcassone
7 Jan. 1968	L	13-16	Toulouse
9 Dec. 1973	W	21-9	Perpignan
16 Dec. 1973	W	14-3	Toulouse
26 Nov. 1978	L	10-13	Carcassone
10 Dec. 1978	L	10-11	Toulouse
4 Jul. 1981	W	43-3	Sydney
18 Jul. 1981	W	17-2	Brisbane
5 Dec. 1982	W	15-4	Avignon
18 Dec. 1982	W	23-9	Narbonne

	Played	Won	Drawn	Lost	Pts for	Pts against
TOTALS	39	25	2	12	688	388

Australia v. New Zealand			
9 May 1908	L	10-11	Sydney
30 May 1908	L	12-24	Brisbane
6 Jun. 1908	W	14-9	Sydney
12 Jun. 1909	L	11-19	Sydney
26 Jun. 1909	W	10-5	Brisbane
3 Jul. 1909	W	25-5	Sydney
23 Aug. 1919	W	44-21	Wellington
30 Aug. 1919	L	10-26	Christchurch
6 Sep. 1919	W	34-23	Auckland
13 Sep. 1919	W	32-2	Auckland
28 Sep. 1935	L	14-22	Auckland
2 Oct. 1935	W	29-8	Auckland
5 Oct. 1935	W	31-8	Auckland
29 May 1948	L	19-21	Sydney
12 Jun. 1948	W	13-4	Brisbane
17 Sep. 1949	L	21-26	Wellington
8 Oct. 1949	W	13-10	Auckland
9 Jun. 1952	W	25-13	Sydney
28 Jun. 1952	L	25-49	Brisbane
2 Jul. 1952	L	9-19	Sydney
27 Jun. 1953	L	5-25	Christchurch
4 Jul. 1953	L	11-12	Wellington
18 Jul. 1953	W	18-16	Auckland
9 Jun. 1956	W	12-9	Sydney
23 Jun. 1956	W	8-2	Brisbane
30 Jun. 1956	W	31-14	Sydney
13 Jun. 1959	W	9-8	Sydney
27 Jun. 1959	W	38-10	Brisbane
4 Jul. 1959	L	12-28	Sydney
1 Jul. 1961	L	10-12	Auckland
8 Jul. 1961	W	10-8	Auckland
8 Jun. 1963	W	7-3	Sydney
22 Jun. 1963	L	13-16	Brisbane
29 Jun. 1963	W	14-0	Sydney
19 Jun. 1965	W	13-8	Auckland
26 Jun. 1965	L	5-7	Auckland
10 Jun. 1967	W	22-13	Sydney
1 Jul. 1967	W	35-22	Brisbane
8 Jul. 1967	W	13-9	Sydney
1 Jun. 1969	W	20-10	Auckland
7 Jun. 1969	L	14-18	Auckland
26 Jun. 1971	L	3-24	Auckland

8 Jul. 1972	W	36-11	Sydney
15 Jul. 1972	W	31-7	Brisbane
24 Jun. 1978	W	24-2	Sydney
15 Jul. 1978	W	38-7	Brisbane
22 Jul. 1978	W	33-16	Sydney
1 Jun. 1980	W	27-6	Auckland
15 Jun. 1980	W	15-6	Auckland
3 Jul. 1982	W	11-8	Brisbane
17 Jul. 1982	W	20-2	Sydney
12 Jun. 1983	W	16-4	Auckland
9 Jul. 1983	L	12-19	Brisbane
18 Jun. 1985	W	26-20	Brisbane
30 Jun. 1985	W	10-6	Auckland
7 Jul. 1985	L	0-18	Auckland

	Played	Won	Drawn	Lost	Pts for	Pts against
TOTALS	56	37	0	19	1,023	731

Australia v. Papua-New Guinea

| 2 Oct. 1982 | W | 38-2 | Port Moresby |

Australia v. South Africa

| 20 Jul. 1963 | W | 34-6 | Brisbane |
| 27 Jul. 1963 | W | 54-21 | Sydney |

*The Australian players who defeated Great Britain 25-8 in the First Test in Sydney in June 1984, left to right:
Back Row: Dowling, Brown, Miles, Conlon, Young, Close. Middle Row: Murray, Kenny, Niebling, Boustead.
Front row: Conescu, Price, Lewis (Captain), Pearce, Jack.*

AUSTRALIA TEAMS . . .
A 20-year review
The following is a compendium of Australia Test and World Cup teams since 1965. Only playing substitutes are included on the teamsheet.

Key: *: Captain (WC): World Cup t: try g:goal dg: drop goal

1965 New Zealand
Auckland: 19 June

Won 13-8

Johns 2g
Cleary
Gasnier
Langlands
Irvine 2t
Lisle
Smith
Quinn
*Walsh
Weier 1t
Veivers, M.
Morgan, John
Hambly

1965 New Zealand
Auckland: 26 June

Lost 5-7

Johns 1g
Cleary
Gasnier
Langlands
Irvine 1t
Lisle
Smith
Weier
*Walsh
Quinn
Morgan, John
Veivers, M.
Hambly

1966 Great Britain
Sydney: 25 June

Lost 13-17

Barnes 5g
Irvine
Langlands
McDonald
King
Banks 1t
Smith
Weier
*Walsh
Crowe
Bradstreet
Crema
Raper

1966 Great Britain
Brisbane: 16 July

Won 6-4

Barnes 3g
Irvine
Langlands
Greaves
King
Gleeson
Smith
Wittenberg
*Walsh
Kelly
Veivers, M.
Thornett, R.
Lynch

1966 Great Britain
Sydney: 23 July

Won 19-14

Johns 2g
Irvine 3t
Dimond
Greaves
King 1t
Gleeson
Smith
Wittenberg
*Walsh
Kelly
Veivers, M.
Beetson
Lynch 1t
Sub: Thornett, R.

1967 New Zealand
Sydney: 10 June

Won 22-13

Langlands 1t, 2g
Irvine 1t
*Gasnier 1t
Greaves
Hanigan 2t
Gleeson 1t
Smith
Kelly
Fitzsimmons
Gallagher, P.
Thomson, A.
Tutty
Raper

1967 New Zealand
Brisbane: 1 July

Won 35-22

Langlands 1t, 1g
Irvine 2t
*Gasnier
McDonald 2t, 6g
Hanigan 1t
Gleeson
Smith
Kelly
Buman
Gallagher, P.
Lynch
Thomson, A.
Raper 1t

1967 New Zealand
Sydney: 8 July

Won 13-9

Langlands
Irvine 1t
*Gasnier
McDonald 2t, 2g
King
Gleeson
Smith
Gallagher, P.
Buman
Kelly
Connell
Lynch
Raper

1967 Great Britain
Leeds: 21 Oct.

Lost 11-16

Johns
McDonald
Langlands 1t, 4g
*Gasnier
King
Gleeson
Smith
Manteit
Kelly
Gallagher, P.
Lynch
Rasmussen
Raper

1967 Great Britain
White City, London: 3 Nov.
Won 17-11
Johns
Greaves
Langlands 1t, 4g
McDonald
King 1t
Branson
Gleeson
Gallagher, N.
Kelly
*Gallagher, P.
Lynch
Rasmussen
Coote 1t

1967 Great Britain
Swinton: 9 Dec.
Won 11-3
Johns
King 1t
Langlands 1g
Greaves
McDonald
Gleeson
Smith
Gallagher, P.
Kelly
Manteit
Rasmussen
Coote 1t
*Raper
Sub: Branson 1t

1967 France
Marseilles: 17 Dec.
Drew 7-7
Johns 1t, 1g
King
Langlands 1g
Greaves
Irvine
Branson
Smith
Manteit
Kelly
Gallagher, P.
Rasmussen
Coote
*Raper
Sub: Lynch

1967 France
Carcassonne: 24 Dec.
Lost 3-10
Johns
King
Greaves 1t
Langlands
McDonald
Branson
Smith
Rasmussen
Gallagher, N.
Gallagher, P.
Lynch
Coote
*Raper

1968 France
Toulouse: 7 Jan.
Lost 13-16
Johns 1g
King
Greaves 2t
Langlands 1t, 1g
McDonald
Branson
Smith
Gallagher, P.
Kelly
Rasmussen
Thomson, A.
Coote
*Raper

1968 Great Britain (WC)
Sydney: 25 May
Won 25-10
Simms 8g
Rhodes
Greaves
Langlands
King
Branson
Smith 1t
Wittenberg
Jones
Beetson
Thornett, R.
Coote 1t
*Raper 1t

1968 New Zealand (WC)
Brisbane: 1 June
Won 31-12
Simms 8g
Rhodes 1t
Greaves
Langlands
King 2t
Branson
Smith
Wittenberg
Jones 1t
Rasmussen
Thornett, R.
Coote 1t
*Raper
Sub: Fulton

1968 France (WC)
Brisbane: 8 June
Won 37-4
Simms 5g
James
Rhodes
Greaves 1t
Williamson 2t
Fulton 2t
Smith 1t, 3g
Wittenberg
Fitzsimmons
Beetson
Manteit
Coote 1t
*Raper

1968 France (WC)
Sydney: 10 June
Won 20-2
Simms 4g
Williamson 2t
Langlands
Greaves 1t
Rhodes
Fulton
Smith
Wittenberg
Jones
Beetson
Thornett, R.
Coote 1t
*Raper
Sub: Rasmussen

1969 New Zealand
Auckland: 1 June
Won 20-10
Johns 4g
Cootes 1t
Langlands
McDonald
Honan
Pittard 1t
Ward
Wittenberg
Walters
*Sattler
Costello
McCarthy
Coote 2t

1969 New Zealand
Auckland: 7 June
Lost 14-18
Johns 4g
Cootes
Langlands
McDonald
Honan
Pittard
Ward
Wittenberg
Walters
*Sattler
Weiss
McCarthy 1t
Coote 1t

1970 Great Britain
Brisbane: 6 June
Won 37-15
*Langlands 9g
King 2t
McDonald 1t
Brass
Cootes
Hawthorne 2g
Smith
Morgan, Jim 2t
Walters
Wittenberg
Lynch
Beetson
Coote
Sub: Weiss

1970 Great Britain
Sydney: 20 June
Lost 7-28
Laird
Cootes
Brass
McDonald 1g
King 1t
Hawthorne 1g
Smith
*Sattler
Fitzsimmons
Wittenberg
Beetson
Weiss
Coote

1970 Great Britain
Sydney: 4 July
Lost 17-21
McKean 7g
McDonald
Brass
Fulton
King
*Hawthorne
Grant, R.
Beetson
Walters
Morgan, Jim
Costello
McCarthy 1t
Coote

1970 New Zealand (WC)
Wigan: 21 Oct.
Won 47-11
Simms 10g, 1t
Branighan 1t
Cootes 2t
Fulton 1t
Williamson
Pittard
Smith 1t
O'Neill
Walters
O'Reilly
McCarthy 1t
Sait
*Coote 1t
Sub: Turner 1t

1970 Great Britain (WC)
Leeds: 24 Oct.
Lost 4-11
Simms 1g
Williamson
Branighan
Fulton 1g
Harris
Pittard
*Smith
O'Neill
Walters
O'Reilly
McCarthy
Sait
Sullivan

1970 France (WC)
Bradford: 1 Nov.
Lost 15-17
Simms 3g
Branighan
Cootes 2t
Fulton 1t
Williamson
Pittard
Smith
McTaggart
Walters
O'Reilly
McCarthy
Sait
*Coote
Subs: Turner
Sullivan

1970 Great Britain (WC)
Leeds: 7 Nov.
Won 12-7
Simms 3g
Williamson 1t
Cootes 1t
Sait
Harris
Fulton
Smith
O'Neill
Turner
O'Reilly
Costello
McCarthy
*Coote
Subs: Branighan
Walters

1971 New Zealand
Auckland: 26 June
Lost 3-24
*Langlands
Branighan
Fulton
Sait
Williamson
Branson
Grant, R.
Sattler
Fitzsimmons
O'Reilly
Costello
McCarthy
Campbell 1t

1972 New Zealand
Sydney: 8 July
Won 36-11
*Langlands 6g
Harris
Starling 1t
Fulton 1t
Ambrum 2t
Pickup
Raudonikis
Beetson
Walters
O'Reilly
McCarthy 2t
Elford
Sullivan 2t

1972 New Zealand
Brisbane: 15 July
Won 31-7
*Langlands
Stewart 5g
Starling 2t
Fulton 2t
Ambrum
Pickup
Raudonikis 1t
Beetson
Walters
O'Reilly
McCarthy
Elford 2t
Sullivan
Subs: Murphy
    Goodwin

1972 Great Britain (WC)
Perpignan: 29 Oct.
Lost 21-27
*Langlands 4g
Harris
Branighan
Starling
Knight
Fulton 3t
Raudonikis 1t
Beetson
Walters
O'Neill
Elford
McCarthy 1dg
Sullivan
Subs: Ward
    Sait

1972 New Zealand (WC)
Paris: 1 Nov.
Won 9-5
*Langlands
Grant, J.
Branighan 1g
Starling
Knight
Fulton 1t, 1dg
Ward 1t
O'Reilly
Walters
O'Neill
Sullivan
Elford
Sait
Sub: Stevens

1972 France (WC)
Toulouse: 5 Nov.
Won 31-9
*Langlands
Grant, J.
Harris 2t
Starling
Branighan 5g
Fulton 1t
Ward
O'Neill 1t
Walters 1t
O'Reilly
Stevens
Beetson
Sait 2t

1972 Great Britain (WC)
Lyon: 11 Nov.
Drew 10-10
*Langlands
Branighan 2g
Starling
Harris
Grant, J.
Fulton
Ward
O'Neill 1t
Walters
O'Reilly
Beetson 1t
Stevens
Sullivan

1973 Great Britain
Wembley: 3 Nov.
Lost 12-21
*Langlands 3g
Goodwin
Fulton 1t
Starling
Branighan 1t
Pickup
Raudonikis
O'Reilly
Walters
Beetson
McCarthy
Maddison
Sait

1973 Great Britain
Leeds: 24 Nov.
Won 14-6
Eadie 5g
Williamson
Starling
Branighan
Waite
Fulton 1dg
Raudonikis
O'Reilly
Walters
Beetson
*McCarthy 1t
Stevens
Sait
Sub: Maddison

255

1973 Great Britain
Warrington: 1 Dec.
Won 15-5
Eadie
Williamson
Starling 1t
Branighan
Waite
Fulton 1t
*Raudonikis
O'Reilly
Walters 1t
Beetson
Maddison 2t
Stevens
Sait
Sub: Pickup

1973 France
Perpignan: 9 Dec.
Won 21-9
Branighan 2g
Williamson
Fulton 2t
Cronin 1g
Waite
Pickup
*Raudonikis
Beetson
Lang
O'Neill
Pierce
Walters
Starling 1t
Sub: Goodwin 2t

1973 France
Toulouse: 16 Dec.
Won 14-3
Branighan 1t
Goodwin
Cronin 1t, 1g
Starling
Waite
Fulton 1t
Pickup
*Beetson
Walters
O'Reilly
Maddison 1t
Stevens
Sait

1974 Great Britain
Brisbane: 15 June
Won 12-6
*Langlands 4g
Orr 1t
Fulton 1dg
Cronin
Waite
Richardson
Raudonikis
Beetson
Walters
O'Reilly
Sait
Higgs
Coote

1974 Great Britain
Sydney: 6 July
Lost 11-16
Eadie
Orr
Fulton 1t
Cronin 1g
Waite
Richardson
Raudonikis
*Beetson
Lang 1t
O'Reilly
Stevens
Sait
Coote 1t
Subs: Branighan
McCarthy

1974 Great Britain
Sydney: 20 July
Won 22-18
*Langlands 1t, 5g
Williamson 1t
Fulton
Cronin
Branighan
Pickup
Raudonikis
Beetson
Turner
O'Neill
Stevens
McCarthy 1t
Coote 1t

1975 New Zealand (WC)
Brisbane: 1 June
Won 36-8
*Langlands 2t
Anderson
Fulton 1t
Cronin 2t, 6g
Fahey
Pickup
Strudwick
Randall 1t
Lang
Wright
Stevens
Platz, L. 1t
Coote
Subs: Branighan 1t
Sait

1975 Wales (WC)
Sydney: 14 June
Won 30-13
*Langlands 1t
Harris 1t
Fulton 1t
Cronin 9g
Rhodes
Pickup
Raudonikis 1t
O'Neill
Lang
Randall
Stevens
Platz, L.
Sait
Sub: Donnelly

1975 France (WC)
Brisbane: 22 June
Won 26-6
*Langlands
Harris 2t
Cronin 1t, 4g
Fulton 2t
Rhodes
Pickup 1t
Raudonikis
Donnelly
Lang
Beetson
Randall
Platz, L.
Coote

1975 England (WC)
Sydney: 28 June
Drew 10-10
*Langlands
Rhodes
Fulton
Cronin 2g
Harris
Pickup
Raudonikis
Beetson
Lang
Randall
Stevens
Platz, L.
Coote 1t
Subs: Anderson 1t
　　　Donnelly

1975 New Zealand (WC)
Auckland: 27 Sept.
Won 24-8
Eadie
Rhodes
Cronin 1t, 6g
*Brass
Schubert 1t
Peard
Mayes
Veivers, G.
Piggins
Mackay
Platz, L.
Higgs 1t
Quayle 1t
Subs: Raudonikis
　　　Fitzgerald

1975 Wales (WC)
Swansea: 19 Oct.
Won 18-6
Eadie
McMahon
Cronin 3g
Rogers
Schubert 3t
Peard 1t
Mayes
*G. Beetson
Piggins
Veivers, G.
Randall
Higgs
Quayle
Subs: Porter
　　　Mackay

1975 France (WC)
Perpignan: 26 Oct
Won 41-2
Eadie 7g, 1t
Rhodes 1t
Rogers 2t
Brass
Porter
Peard 1t
Raudonikis 1t
*Beetson
Lang
Randall 1t
Platz, L. 1t
Higgs 1t
Pierce
Sub: Schubert

1975 England (WC)
Wigan: 1 Nov.
Lost 13-16
Eadie
Schubert 3t
Brass
Cronin 2g
Rhodes
Peard
Mayes
*Beetson
Piggins
Mackay
Higgs
Randall
Pierce
Sub: Rogers

1977 New Zealand (WC)
Auckland: 29 May
Won 27-12
Eadie
Harris 1t
Cronin 6g
Thomas 1t
McMahon 2t
Peard 1t
Raudonikis
*Veivers, G.
Geiger
Fitzgerald
Randall
Higgs
Pierce

1977 France (WC)
Sydney: 11 June
Won 21-9
Eadie 2t
McMahon 1t
Cronin 3g
Thomas
Fahey
Peard
Raudonikis
Veivers, G. 1t
Geiger
Fitzgerald 1t
Randall
*Beetson
Reddy
Subs: Gartner
　　　Higgs

1977 Great Britain (WC)
Brisbane: 18 June
Won 19-5
Eadie 2t
McMahon
Cronin 5g
Thomas
Fahey
Peard
Raudonikis
Fitzgerald
Geiger
Veivers, G.
*Beetson
Randall 1t
Pierce
Sub: Higgs

1977 Great Britain (WC)
Sydney: 25 June
Won 13-12
Eadie
McMahon 1t
Cronin 2g
Gartner 1t
Harris
Peard
Kolc 1t
Veivers, G.
Geiger
Randall
*Beetson
Higgs
Pierce
Sub: Fitzgerald

257

1978 New Zealand
Sydney: 24 June
Won 24-2
Eadie
Fahey 1t
Cronin 6g
Rogers 1t
Boustead 1t
*Fulton
Morris, S.
Olling
Peponis 1t
Thomson, I.
Pierce
Reddy
Price
Sub: Oliphant

1978 New Zealand
Brisbane: 15 July
Won 38-7
Dorahy
Boustead 2t
Cronin 7g
Rogers 1t
Glover 2t
*Fulton
Oliphant
Donnelly
Lang
Olling
Platz, G.
Reddy 1t
Price 2t

1978 New Zealand
Sydney: 22 July
Won 33-16
Dorahy 1t
Glover
Cronin 9g
Rogers
Boustead 1t
*Fulton 2t
Raudonikis
Morris, R.
Krilich
Young
Pierce 1t
Reddy
Price

1978 Great Britain
Wigan: 21 Oct.
Won 15-9
Eadie
Boustead 1t
Rogers
Cronin 4g
Anderson
*Fulton 1t, 1dg
Raudonikis
Young
Krilich
Olling
Gerard
Reddy
Price

1978 Great Britain
Bradford: 5 Nov.
Lost 14-18
Eadie
Boustead
Rogers 1t, 2g
Cronin 2g
Anderson
*Fulton
Raudonikis
Olling
Krilich
Young
Gerard
Reddy
Price 1t
Subs: Thompson
　　　Boyd

1978 Great Britain
Leeds: 18 Nov.
Won 23-6
Eadie
Boustead
Rogers
Cronin 5g
Anderson
*Fulton 1dg
Raudonikis 1t
Young
Peponis 1t
Morris, R.
Gerard 1t
Boyd 1t
Price
Subs: Thompson
　　　Thomson, I.

1978 France
Carcassone: 26 Nov.
Lost 10-13
Eadie 1t
Boustead
Cronin 1t, 2g
Martin
Anderson
*Fulton
Raudonikis
Morris, R.
Peponis
Young
Gerard
Boyd
Price

1978 France
Toulouse: 10 Dec.
Lost 10-11
Eadie
Boustead 1t
Rogers 1t
Cronin 2g
Anderson
*Fulton
Raudonikis
Thomson, I.
Hilditch
Young
Gerard
Reddy
Price

1979 Great Britain
Brisbane: 16 June
Won 35-0
Eadie
Corowa 1t
Rogers
Cronin 10g
Boustead 2t
Thompson
Raudonikis
Young
*Peponis
Morris, R.
Reddy
Boyd
Price 2t

1979 Great Britain
Sydney: 30 June
Won 24-16
Eadie
Corowa
Rogers 1t
Cronin 2t, 6g
Boustead
Thompson
Raudonikis
Young
*Peponis
Morris, R.
Reddy 1t
Boyd
Price

1979 Great Britain
Sydney: 14 July
Won 28-2
Eadie 1t
Anderson
Cronin 8g
Rogers
Fahey
Thompson
Raudonikis
Young
*Peponis
Morris, R.
Reddy 1t
Boyd 1t
Price 1t

1980 New Zealand
Auckland: 1 June
Won 27-6
Dowling, Gary
Boustead 1t
Cronin 6g
Brentnall
Anderson
Thompson 2t
Raudonikis
Morris, R.
*Peponis
Young 1t
Reddy 1t
Boyd
Price

1980 New Zealand
Auckland: 15 June
Won 15-6
Dowling, Gary
Quinn, G.
Cronin 1t, 3g
Brentnall
Anderson
Thompson
Raudonikis
Young
*Peponis
Morris, R.
Boyd 1t
Reddy 1t
Price

1981 France
Sydney: 4 July
Won 43-3
Brentnall 1t
Ribot 1t
Cronin 8g
*Rogers 1t
Boustead 1t
Lewis
Mortimer 2t
Hilditch
Masterman 1t
Young
Boyd
McCabe 2t
Price
Subs: Sigsworth
       Morris, R.

1981 France
Brisbane: 18 July
Won 17-2
Brentnall
Ribot
*Rogers
Cronin 4g
Fahey 2t
Lewis
Mortimer
Hilditch
Masterman
Morris, R. 1t
McCabe
Boyd
Price
Sub: Ayliffe

1982 New Zealand
Brisbane: 3 July
Won 11-8
Brentnall
Ribot
Cronin 4g
Rogers
Boustead
Lewis
Mortimer
Young
*Krilich
Morris, R.
Hancock
Boyd
Vautin
Sub: Muggleton 1t

1982 New Zealand
Sydney: 17 July
Won 20-2
Brentnall 1t
Boustead 1t
Cronin 4g
Meninga
Ribot
Lewis 1t
Mortimer
Young
*Krilich
Hancock
Muggleton
Boyd
Price 1t
Subs: Rogers
       Morris, R.

1982 Papua-New Guinea
Port Moresby: 2 Oct.
Won 38-2
Brentnall 2t
Boustead 1t
Rogers 1t
Meninga 1t, 4g
Ribot 4t
Kenny 1t
Mortimer
Young
*Krilich
Hancock
Muggleton
Reddy
Price
Subs: Murray
       Brown, R.

1982 Great Britain
Hull City FC: 30 Oct.

Won 40-4

Brentnall
Boustead 1t
Meninga 1t, 8g
Rogers
Grothe 1t
Kenny 1t
Sterling
Young
*Krilich
Boyd 1t
Pearce 1t
Reddy 1t
Price 1t

1982 Great Britain
Wigan: 20 Nov.

Won 27-6

Brentnall
Boustead
Meninga 1t, 6g
Rogers 1t
Grothe 1t
Kenny
Sterling 1t
Young
*Krilich
Boyd
Pearce
Reddy
Price 1t
Subs: Lewis
      Brown, R.

1982 Great Britain
Leeds: 28 Nov.

Won 32-8

Brentnall
Boustead 1t
Meninga 7g
Rogers 1t
Ribot 1t
Kenny 1t
Sterling
Boyd
*Krilich 1t
Morris, R.
McCabe
Reddy
Pearce 1t
Subs: Lewis
      Brown, R.

1982 France
Avignon: 5 Dec.

Won 15-4

Brentnall
Boustead
Rogers
Kenny
Meninga 3g
Lewis
Sterling
Young
*Krilich
Morris, R.
McCabe
Boyd
Pearce 1t
Sub: Grothe 2t

1982 France
Narbonne: 18 Dec.

Won 23-9

Brentnall
Boustead
Rogers
Meninga 1t, 4g
Grothe 2t
Kenny 1t
Sterling
Young
*Krilich
Boyd
McCabe
Reddy 1t
Pearce

1983 New Zealand
Auckland: 12 June

Won 16-4

Brentnall
Boustead
Meninga 4g
Rogers 1t
Grothe 1t
Lewis
Sterling
Brown, D.
*Krilich
Gerard
Fullerton-Smith
McCabe
Vautin
Subs: Murray
      Jarvis

1983 New Zealand
Brisbane: 9 July

Lost 12-19

Scott
Boustead
Meninga 2g
Miles
Grothe 1t
Lewis
Mortimer
Tessman
*Krilich
Brown, D.
Fullerton-Smith
Vautin
Price
Subs: Ella 1t
      Brown, R.

1984 Great Britain
Sydney: 9 June

Won 25-8

Jack
Boustead 1t
Miles
Kenny
Conlon 4g
*Lewis 1t, 1dg
Murray 1t
Brown, D.
Conescu
Dowling, Greg
Niebling
Pearce
Price 1t
Sub: Young

1984 Great Britain
Brisbane: 26 June

Won 18-6

Jack
Boustead
Meninga 1t, 3g
Miles
Grothe 1t
*Lewis
Murray
Brown, D.
Conescu
Dowling, Greg
Niebling
Vautin
Pearce 1t
Subs: Mortimer
      Fullerton-Smith

1984 Great Britain
Sydney: 7 July
Won 20-7
Jack 1t
Boustead
Meninga 4g
Miles
Grothe 1t
*Lewis
Mortimer
Niebling
Conescu 1t
Dowling, Greg
Fullerton-Smith
Pearce
Price
Subs: Kenny
      Brown, D.

1985 New Zealand
Brisbane: 18 June
Won 26-20
Jack
Ribot 2t, 1g
Close 1t
Meninga 2g
Ferguson
*Lewis
Murray
Dowling, Greg
Conescu
Roach 1t
Cleal 1t
Wynn, P.
Pearce
Sub: Tunks

1985 New Zealand
Auckland: 30 June
Won 10-6
Jack
Ribot 1t, 1g
Close
Meninga 2g
Ferguson
*Lewis
Murray
Dowling, Greg
Conescu
Roach
Vautin
Wynn, P.
Pearce
Subs: Ella
      Cleal

1985 New Zealand
Auckland: 7 July
Lost 0-18
Jack
Ribot
Meninga
Ella
Ferguson
*Lewis
Hasler
Tunks
Elias
Roach
Vautin
Wynn, P.
Pearce
Subs: Close
      Dowling

Australian Test stalwart Bobby Fulton, a veteran of four World Cups and two European tours.

AUSTRALIA REGISTER . . .
1965-85

The following is an index of players who have appeared for Australia, toured or been members of a World Cup squad since 1965. Where a player began his international career before 1965 his preceding record is also given.

Appearances refer to Test and World Cup matches only. For matches in France the year given is for the first half of the season.

World Cup matches are in bold letters in the list of *Appearances*. Substitute appearances are in lower case letters. In 1975 the World Cup was in two sections — 1 refers to the first part in Australasia, 2 refers to the second part in Britain and France.

Key: B - Britain, E - England, F - France, NSW - New South Wales, NZ - New Zealand, PNG - Papua-New Guinea, SA - South Africa, W - Wales.

AMBRUM, George (NSW)
Appearances: 1972 NZ2
ANDERSON, Chris (NSW)
Tours: Britain 1978,1982; NZ 1980
World Cup: 1975 (1)
Appearances: **1975 NZ,e**; 1978 B3,F2; 1979 B; 1980 NZ2
AYLIFFE, Royce (NSW)
Appearances: 1981 f

BANKS, Gary (NSW)
Appearances: 1966 B
BARNES, Keith (NSW)
Tours: Britain 1959
World Cup: 1957,1960
Appearances: **1957 NZ**; 1959 NZ2,B3,F3; 1960 F3, **NZ,B**; 1962 B; 1966 B2
BEATH, Barry (NSW)
Tours: NZ 1965,1971
BEETSON, Arthur (NSW)
Tours: Britain 1973
World Cup: 1968,1972,1975(1&2),1977
Appearances: 1966 B; **1968 B,F2**; 1970 B3; 1972 NZ2, **B2,F**; 1973 B3,F2; 1974 B3; **1975 F2,E2,W**; **1977 F,B2**
BENNETT, Wayne (Queensland)
Tours: NZ 1971
BOUSTEAD, Kerry (Queensland, NSW)
Tours: Britain 1978,1982; NZ 1980
Appearances: 1978 NZ3,B3,F2; 1979 B2; 1980 NZ; 1981 F; 1982 NZ2,PNG,B3,F2; 1983 NZ2; 1984 B3

BOYD, Les (NSW)
Tours: Britain 1978,1982; NZ 1980
Appearances: 1978 Bb,F; 1979 B3; 1980 NZ2; 1981 F2; 1982 NZ2,B3,F2
BRADSTREET, Bill (NSW)
Appearances: 1966 B
BRANIGHAN, Ray (NSW)
Tours: Britain 1973; NZ 1971
World Cup: 1970,1972,1975(1)
Appearances: **1970 NZ,Bb,F**; 1971 NZ; **1972 B2,NZ,F**; 1973 B3,F2; 1974 Bb; **1975 nz**
BRANSON, Tony (NSW)
Tours: Britain 1967; NZ 1971
World Cup: 1968
Appearances: 1967 Bb,F3; **1968 B,NZ**; 1971 NZ
BRASS, John (NSW)
World Cup: 1975(2)
Appearances: 1970 B3; **1975 NZ,F,E**
BRENTNALL, Greg (NSW)
Tours: Britain 1982; NZ 1980
Appearances: 1980 NZ2; 1981 F2; 1982 NZ2,PNG,B3,F2; 1983 NZ
BROWN, Dave (NSW)
Appearances: 1983 NZ2; 1984 B2b
BROWN, Johnny (Queensland)
World Cup: 1970
BROWN, Ray (NSW)
Tours: Britain 1982
Appearances: 1982 png,b2; 1983 nz
BUMAN, Allan (NSW)
Tours: NZ 1965   *Appearances:* 1967 NZ2

CAMPBELL, Keith (NSW)
Tours: NZ 1971
Appearances: 1971 NZ
CAVANAGH, Noel (Queensland)
Tours: NZ 1965
CLEAL, Noel (NSW)
Tours: NZ 1985
Appearances: 1985 NZnz
CLEARY, Michael (NSW)
Tours: Britain 1963; NZ 1965,1969
Appearances: 1962 B; 1963 NZ F; 1964 F3; 1965 NZ2
CLOSE, Chris (Queensland)
Tours: NZ 1980,1985
Appearances: 1985 NZnz
CONESCU, Greg (Queensland)
Tours: Britain 1982; NZ 1985
Appearances: 1984 B3; 1985 NZ2
CONLON, Ross (NSW)
Appearances: 1984 B
CONNELL, Geoff (Queensland)
Appearances: 1967 NZ
COOTE, Ron (NSW)
Tours: Britain 1967; NZ 1969
World Cup: 1968,1970,1975(1)
Appearances: 1967 B2,F3; **1968 B,NZ,F2**; 1969 NZ2; 1970 B3; **1970 NZ,F,B**; 1974 B3; **1975 NZ,F,E**

COOTES, John (NSW)
Tours: NZ 1969
World Cup: 1970
Appearances: 1969 NZ2; 1970 B2; **1970 NZ,F,B**
COROWA, Larry (NSW)
Tours: Britain 1978
Appearances: 1979 B2
COSTELLO, Ron (NSW)
Tours: NZ 1969,1971
World Cup: 1970
Appearances: 1969 NZ; 1970 B; **1970 B;** 1971 NZ
CREAR, Steve (Queensland)
World Cup: 1977
CREMA, Angelo (Queensland)
Appearances: 1966 B
CRONIN, Michael (NSW)
Tours: Britain 1973,1978; NZ 1980
World Cup: 1975(1&2),1977
Appearances: 1973 F2; 1974 B3; **1975 NZ2,W2,E2,F;**
1977 NZ,F,B2; 1978 NZ3,B3,F2; 1979 B3;
1980 NZ2; 1981 F2; 1982 NZ2
CROWE, Ron (NSW)
Tours: NZ 1961
Appearances: 1961 NZ2; 1964 F2; 1966 B

DENMAN, Jeff (Queensland)
Tours: NZ 1969
DIMOND, Peter (NSW)
Tours: Britain 1963
Appearances: 1958 B2; 1962 B; 1963 B3,F3; 1966 B
DONNELLY, John (NSW)
World Cup: 1975(1)
Appearances: 1975 F,e,w; 1978 NZ
DORAHY, John (NSW)
Appearances: 1978 NZ2
DOWLING, Gary (NSW)
Tours: NZ 1980
Appearances: 1980 NZ2
DOWLING, Greg (Queensland)
Tours: NZ 1985
Appearances: 1984 B3; 1985 NZ2 nz

EADIE, Graham (NSW)
Tours: Britain 1973,1978
World Cup: 1975(2),1977
Appearances: 1973 B2; 1974 B; **1975 NZ,W,F,E;**
1977 B2,NZ,F; 1978 NZ,B3,F2; 1979 B3
ELFORD, John (NSW)
World Cup: 1972
Appearances: 1972 NZ2; **1972 B,NZ**
ELIAS, Ben (NSW)
Tours: NZ 1985
Appearances; 1985 NZ
ELLA, Steve (NSW)
Tours: Britain 1982; NZ 1985
Appearances: 1983 nz; 1985 NZ nz

FAHEY, Terry (NSW)
World Cup: 1975(1),1977
Appearances: **1975 NZ; 1977 F,B;** 1978 NZ; 1979 B;
1981 F
FERGUSON, John (NSW)
Tours: NZ 1985
Appearances: 1985 NZ3
FITZGERALD, Denis (NSW)
World Cup: 1975(1),1977
Appearances: **1975 NZ; 1977 NZ,F,Bb**
FITZSIMMONS, Brian (Queensland)
Tours: NZ 1969,1971
World Cup: 1968
Appearances: 1967 NZ; **1968 F;** 1970 B; 1971 NZ
FULLERTON-SMITH, Wally (Queensland)
Tours: NZ 1985
Appearances: 1983 NZ3; 1984 Bb
FULTON, Bobby (NSW)
Tours: Britain 1973,1978; NZ 1971
World Cup: 1968,1970,1972,1975(1)
Appearances: **1968 nz,F2;** 1970 B; **1970 B2,NZ,F;**
1971 NZ; 1972 NZ2; **1972 B2,NZ,F;** 1973 B3,F2;
1974 B3; **1975 NZ,W,F,E;** 1978 NZ3,B3,F2

GALLAGHER, Noel (Queensland)
Tours: Britain 1967
Appearances: 1967 B,F
GALLAGHER, Peter (Queensland)
Tours: Britain 1963,1967
Appearances: 1963 NZ3,SA2,B,F2; 1967 NZ3,B3,F3
GARTNER, Russel (NSW)
World Cup: 1977
Appearances: **1977 B,f**
GASNIER, Reg (NSW)
Tours: Britain 1959,1963,1967; NZ 1961,1965
World Cup: 1960
Appearances: 1959 NZ3,B3,F3; **1960 F,NZ,B;** 1960 F3;
1961 NZ2; 1962 B2; 1963 NZ3,SA2,B3,F3; 1964 F3;
1965 NZ2; 1967 NZ3,B
GEIGER, Nick (Queensland)
World Cup: 1977
Appearances: **1977 B2,NZ,F**
GERARD, Geoff (NSW)
Tours: Britain 1978
Appearances: 1978 B3,F2; 1983 NZ
GIBBS, Johnny (NSW)
Tours: Britain 1978
GLEESON, John (Queensland)
Tours: Britain 1963,1967; NZ 1965
Appearances: 1964 F2; 1966 B2; 1967 NZ3,B3
GLOVER, Neville (NSW)
Appearances: 1978 NZ2
GOLDSPINK, Kevin (NSW)
Tours: Britain 1967
GOODWIN, Ted (NSW)
Tours: Britain 1973
Appearances: 1972 nz; 1973 B,Ff

GRANT, Bob (NSW)
Tours: NZ 1971
Appearances: 1970 B; 1971 NZ
GRANT, John (Queensland)
World Cup: 1972
Appearances: **1972 NZ,F,B**
GREAVES, Johnny (NSW)
Tours: Britain 1967
World Cup: 1968
Appearances: 1966 B2; 1967 NZ,B2,F3; **1968 B,NZ,F2**
GROTHE, Eric (NSW)
Tours: Britain 1982
Appearances: 1982 B2,Ff; 1983 NZ2; 1984 B2

HAMBLY, Brian (NSW)
Tours: Britain 1959,1963; NZ 1965
World Cup: 1960
Appearances: 1959 B3,F3; 1960 F2; **1960 F,NZ,B**; 1963 NZ2,B2,F3; 1964 F; 1965 NZ2
HAMILTON, Bill (NSW)
Tours: Britain 1973
HANCOCK, Rohan (Queensland)
Tours: Britain 1982; NZ 1980
Appearances: 1982 NZ2 PNG
HANIGAN, Les (NSW)
Tours: Britain 1967
Appearances; 1967 NZ2
HARRIS, Mark (NSW)
World Cup: 1970,1972,1975(1),1977
Appearances: **1970 B2**; 1972 NZ; **1972 B2,F; 1975 W,F,E; 1977 NZ,B**
HASLER, Des (NSW)
Tours: NZ 1985
Appearances: 1985 NZ
HAWTHORNE, Phil (NSW)
Appearances: 1970 B3
HIGGS, Ray (Queensland-NSW)
World Cup: 1975(2),1977
Appearances; 1974 B; **1975 NZ,W,F,E; 1977 NZ,f,bB**
HILDITCH, Ron (NSW)
Tours: Britain 1978
Appearances: 1978 F; 1981 F2
HONAN, Bob (NSW)
Tours: NZ 1969
Appearances: 1969 NZ2

IRVINE, Ken (NSW)
Tours: Britain 1959,1963,1967; NZ 1961,1965
World Cup: 1960
Appearances: 1959 F; 1960 F3; **1960 F,NZ**; 1961 NZ2; 1962 B3; 1963 NZ3,SA2,B3,F2; 1964 F3; 1965 NZ2; 1966 B3; 1967 NZ3,F
JACK, Gary (NSW)
Tours: NZ 1985
Appearances: 1984 B3; 1985 NZ3
JAMES, Brian (NSW)
World Cup: 1968
Appearances: **1968 F**

JARVIS, Pat (NSW)
Appearances: 1983 nz
JOHNS, Les (NSW)
Tours: Britain 1963, 1967; NZ 1965, 1969
Appearances: 1963 SA2; 1964 F; 1965 NZ2; 1966 B; 1967 B3,F3; 1969 NZ2
JONES, Fred (NSW)
World Cup: 1968,1972
Appearances: **1968 B,NZ,F**
JUNEE, Kevin (NSW)
Tours: Britain 1967

KELLY, Noel (NSW)
Tours: Britain 1959,1963,1967
World Cup: 1960
Appearances: 1959 NZ3; 1960 F; **1960 F,NZ,B**; 1963 NZ,SA2,B3,F3; 1964 F2; 1966 B2; 1967 NZ3,B3,F2
KENNY, Brett (NSW)
Tours: Britain 1982
Appearances: 1982 PNG,B3,F2; 1984 Bb
KING, Johnny (NSW)
Tours: Britain 1967
World Cup: 1968
Appearances: 1966 B3; 1967 NZ,B3,F3; **1968 B,NZ**; 1970 B3
KNEEN, Steve (NSW)
Tours: Britain 1978
KNIGHT, Stephen (NSW)
World Cup: 1972
Appearances: **1972 B,NZ**
KOLC, John (NSW)
World Cup: 1977
Appearances: **1977 B**
KRILICH, Max (NSW)
Tours: Britain 1978,1982
Appearances: 1978 NZ,B2; 1982 NZ2,PNG,B3,F2

LAIRD, Ray (Queensland)
Appearances: 1970 B
LANG, John (Queensland, NSW)
Tours: Britain 1973; NZ 1980
World Cup: 1975 (1&2)
Appearances: 1973 F; 1974 B; **1975 NZ,W,F2,E**; 1978 NZ
LANGLANDS, Graeme (NSW)
Tours: Britain 1963,1967,1973; NZ 1965,1969,1971
World Cup: 1968,1972,1975(1)
Appearances: 1963 NZ3,SA2,B3,F2; 1964 F2; 1965 NZ2; 1966 B2; 1967 NZ3,B3,F3; **1968 F,B,NZ**; 1969 NZ2; 1970 B; 1971 NZ; 1972 NZ2; **1972 B2,NZ,F**; 1973 B; 1974 B2; **1975 NZ,W,F,E**
LEIS, Jim (NSW)
Tours: NZ 1980
LEWIS, Wally (Queensland)
Tours: Britain 1982; NZ 1985
Appearances: 1981 F2; 1982 NZ2,b2,F; 1983 NZ2; 1984 B3; 1985 NZ3

LISLE, Jimmy (NSW)
Tours: Britain 1963; NZ 1965
Appearances: 1962 B; 1964 F3; 1965 NZ2
LYE, Graeme (NSW)
Tours: NZ 1969
LYNCH, Ron (NSW)
Tours: Britain 1967; NZ 1961
Appearances: 1961 NZ2; 1962 B; 1966 B2;
    1967 NZ2,B2,Ff; 1970 B

MACKAY, Ian (NSW)
World Cup: 1975(2)
Appearances: **1975 NZ,E,w**
McCABE, Paul (NSW)
Tours: Britain 1982
Appearances: 1981 F2; 1982 B,F2; 1983 NZ
McCARTHY, Bob (NSW)
Tours: Britain 1973; NZ 1969,1971
World Cup: 1970,1972
Appearances: 1969 NZ2; 1970 B; **1970 NZ,B2,F;**
    1971 NZ; 1972 NZ2; **1972 B**; 1973 B2; 1974 Bb
McDONALD, John (Queensland, NSW)
Tours: Britain 1967; NZ 1969
Appearances: 1966 B; 1967 NZ2,B3,F2; 1969 NZ2;
    1970 B3
McKEAN, Allan (NSW)
Appearances: 1970 B
McKINNON, Don (NSW)
Tours: Britain 1982
McMAHON, Allan (NSW)
Tours: Britain 1978
World Cup: 1975(2),1977
Appearances: **1975 W; 1977 NZ,F,B2**
McTAGGART, Barry (NSW)
World Cup: 1970
Appearances: **1970 F**
MADDISON, Ken (NSW)
Tours: Britain 1973
Appearances: 1973 B2b,F
MANTEIT, Dennis (Queensland)
Tours: Britain 1967; NZ 1969
World Cup: 1968
Appearances: 1967 B2,F; **1968 F**
MARTIN, Steve (NSW)
Tours: Britain 1978; NZ 1980
Appearances: 1978 F
MASTERMAN, Jeff (NSW)
Appearances: 1981 F2
MAYES, Johnny (NSW)
World Cup: 1975(2)
Appearances: **1975 NZ,W,E**
MENINGA, Mal (Queensland)
Tours: Britain 1982; NZ 1985
Appearances: 1982 NZ,PNG,B3,F2; 1983 NZ2; 1984 B2;
    1985 NZ3
MILES, Gene (Queensland)
Tours: Britain 1982
Appearances: 1984 B3

MOORE, Brian (NSW)
Tours: Britain 1967
MORGAN, Jim (NSW)
Appearances: 1970 B2
MORGAN, John (NSW)
Tours: NZ 1965
Appearances: 1965 NZ2
MORRIS, Rod (Queensland, NSW)
Tours: Britain 1978,1982; NZ 1980
Appearances: 1978 NZ,B,F; 1979 B3; 1980 NZ2;
    1981 Ff; 1982 NZnz,B,F
MORRIS, Steve (NSW)
Appearances: 1978 NZ
MORTIMER, Steve (NSW)
Tours: Britain 1982
Appearances: 1981 F2; 1982 NZ2 PNG; 1983 NZ; 1984 Bb
MUGGLETON, John (NSW)
Tours: Britain 1982
Appearances: 1982 NZnz PNG
MURPHY, Jim (Queensland)
Tours: NZ 1971
Appearances: 1972 nz
MURRAY, Mark (Queensland)
Tours: Britain 1982; NZ 1985
Appearances: 1982 png; 1983 nz; 1984 B2; 1985 NZ2

NIEBLING, Bryan (Queensland)
Appearances: 1984 B3

O'CONNOR, Michael (NSW)
Tours: NZ 1985
OLIPHANT, Greg (Queensland)
Tours: Britain 1978
Appearances: 1978 NZnz
OLLING, Graeme (NSW)
Tours: Britain 1978
Appearances: 1978 NZ2,B2
O'NEILL, John (NSW)
Tours: Britain 1973
World Cup: 1970,1972,1975(1)
Appearances: **1970 NZ,B2; 1972 B2,NZ,F**; 1973 F;
    1974 B; **1975 W**
O'REILLY, Bob (NSW)
Tours: Britain 1973; NZ 1971
World Cup: 1970,1972
Appearances: **1970 NZ,B2,F**; 1971 NZ; 1972 NZ2;
    1972 NZ,F,B; 1973 B3,F; 1974 B2
ORR, Warren (Queensland)
Tours: Britain 1973
Appearances: 1974 B2

PANNOWITZ, Terry (NSW)
Tours: NZ 1965
PEARCE, Wayne (NSW)
Tours: Britain 1982; NZ 1985
Appearances: 1982 B3,F2; 1984 B3; 1985 NZ3

PEARD, John (NSW)
World Cup: 1975(2),1977
Appearances: **1975 NZ,W,F,E; 1977 NZ,F,B2**
PEPONIS, George (NSW)
Tours: Britain 1978; NZ 1980
Appearances: 1978 NZ,B,F; 1979 B3; 1980 NZ2
PICKUP, Tim (NSW)
Tours: Britain 1973
World Cup: 1975(1)
Appearances: 1972 NZ2; 1973 Bb,F2; 1974 B;
   1975 NZ,W,F,E
PIERCE, Greg (NSW)
Tours: Britain 1973,1978
World Cup: 1975(2),1977
Appearances: 1973 F; **1975 F,E; 1977 NZ,B2**; 1978 NZ2
PIGGINS, George (NSW)
World Cup: 1975(2)
Appearances: **1975 NZ,W,E**
PITTARD, Denis (NSW)
Tours: NZ 1969
World Cup: 1970
Appearances: 1969 NZ2; **1970 NZ,B,F**
PLATZ, Greg (Queensland)
Appearances: 1978 NZ
PLATZ, Lew (Queensland)
World Cup: 1975(1&2)
Appearances: **1975 NZ2,F2,W,E**
PORTER, Jim (NSW)
World Cup: 1975(2)
Appearances: **1975 F,w**
PRICE, Ray (NSW)
Tours: Britain 1978,1982; NZ 1980
Appearances: 1978 NZ3,B3,F2; 1979 B3; 1980 NZ2;
   1981 F2; 1982 NZ,PNG,B2; 1983 NZ; 1984 B2

QUAYLE, John (NSW)
World Cup: 1975(2)
Appearances: **1975 NZ,W**
QUINN, Graham (NSW)
Tours: NZ 1980
Appearances; 1980 NZ
QUINN, Paul (NSW)
Tours; Britain 1963; NZ 1965
Appearances: 1963 SA,B2,F; 1964 F; 1965 NZ2

RANDALL, Terry (NSW)
Tours: Britain 1973
World Cup: 1975(1&2),1977
Appearances: **1975 NZ,W2,F2,E2; 1977 NZ,F,B2**
RAPER, Johnny (NSW)
Tours: Britain 1959,1963,1967
World Cup: 1960,1968
Appearances: 1959 NZ3,B,F2; 1960 F3; **1960 F,NZ**;
   1962 B2; 1963 NZ3,SA2,B3,F2; 1964 F3; 1966 B;
   1967 NZ3,B2,F3; **1968 B,NZ,F2**

RASMUSSEN, Elton (Queensland, NSW)
Tours: Britain 1959,1967; NZ 1961
World Cup: 1960,1968
Appearances: 1959 B,F; 1960 F3; **1960 B**; 1961 NZ2;
   1962 B2; 1967 B3,F3; **1968 NZ,f**
RAUDONIKIS, Tom (NSW)
Tours: Britain 1973,1978; NZ 1971,1980
World Cup: 1972,1975(1&2),1977
Appearances: 1972 NZ2; **1972 B**; 1973 B3F; 1974 B3;
   1975 W,F2,E,nz; 1977 NZ,F,B; 1978 NZ,B3,F2;
   1979 B3; 1980 NZ2
REDDY, Rod (NSW)
Tours: Britain 1978,1982; NZ 1980
World Cup: 1977
Appearances: **1977 F**; 1978 NZ3,B2,F; 1979 B3;
   1980 NZ2; 1982 PNG,B3,F
RHODES, Johnny (NSW, Queensland)
World Cup: 1968,1975(1&2)
Appearances: **1968 B,NZ,F2; 1975 W,F2,E2,NZ**
RIBOT, John (NSW, Queensland)
Tours: Britain 1982; NZ 1985
Appearances: 1981 F2; 1982 NZ2,PNG,B; 1985 NZ3
RICHARDSON, Geoff (Queensland)
Appearances: 1974 B2
ROACH, Steve (NSW)
Tours: NZ 1985
Appearances: 1985 NZ3
ROBSON, Ian (Queensland)
Tours: NZ 1969
ROGERS, Steve (NSW)
Tours: Britain 1973,1978,1982
World Cup: 1975(2)
Appearances: **1975 NZ,F,e**; 1978 NZ3,B3,F; 1979 B3;
   1981 F2; 1982 NZnz,PNG,B3,F2; 1983 NZ

SADDLER, Ron (NSW)
Tour: Britain 1967
SAIT, Paul (NSW)
Tours: Britain 1973; NZ 1971
World Cup: 1970,1972,1975(1)
Appearances: **1970 NZ,B2, F**; 1971 NZ; **1972 b,NZ,F**;
   1973 B3,F; 1974 B2; **1975 nz,W**
SATTLER, John (NSW)
Tours: Britain 1967; NZ 1969,1971
Appearances: 1969 NZ2; 1970 B; 1971 NZ
SCHUBERT, Ian (NSW)
Tours: Britain 1978,1982
World Cup: 1975(2)
Appearances: **1975 NZ,W,f,E**
SCOTT, Colin (Queensland)
Appearances: 1983 NZ
SIGSWORTH, Phil (NSW)
Appearances: 1981 f
SIMMS, Eric (NSW)
World Cup: 1968,1970
Appearances: **1968 B,NZ,F2; 1970 NZ,B2,F**

SMITH, Billy (NSW)
Tours: Britain 1967; NZ 1965
World Cup: 1968,1970
Appearances: 1964 F3; 1965 NZ2; 1966 B3;
    1967 NZ3,B2,F3; **1968 F2,B,NZ**; 1970 B2;
    1970 NZ,B2,F
STARLING, Geoff (NSW)
Tours: Britain 1973; NZ 1971
World Cup: 1972
Appearances: 1972 NZ2; **1972 B2,NZ,F**; 1973 B3,F2
STERLING, Peter (NSW)
Tours: Britain 1982
Appearances: 1982 B3,F2; 1983 NZ
STEVENS, Gary (NSW)
Tours: Britain 1973
World Cup: 1972,1975(1)
Appearances: 1972 nz,F,B; 1973 B2,F; 1974 B2;
    1975 NZ,W,E
STEWART, Wayne (Queensland)
Appearances: 1972 NZ
STRUDWICK, Ross (Queensland)
World Cup: 1975(1)
Appearances: **1975 NZ**
SULLIVAN, Gary (NSW)
World Cup: 1970,1972
Appearances: **1970 B,f**; 1972 NZ2; **1972 B2,NZ**

TESSMAN, Brad (Queensland)
Appearances: 1983 NZ
THOMAS, Mark (Queensland)
World Cup: 1977
Appearances: **1977 NZ,F,B**
THOMPSON, Alan (NSW)
Tours: Britain 1978; NZ 1980
Appearances: 1978 b2; 1979 B3; 1980 NZ2
THOMSON, Alan (NSW)
Tours: Britain 1967
Appearances: 1967 NZ2,F
THOMSON, Ian (NSW)
Tours: Britain 1978
Appearances: 1978 NZ,b,F
THORNETT, Dick (NSW)
Tours: Britain 1963
World Cup: 1968
Appearances: 1963 SA2, B3,F; 1964 F3; 1966 Bb;
    1968 B,NZ,F
TUNKS, Peter (NSW)
Tours: NZ 1985
Appearances: 1985 NZ nz
TURNER, Ron (NSW)
World Cup: 1970
Appearances: **1970 nz,f,B**; 1974 B
TUTTY, Dennis (NSW)
Appearances: 1967 NZ

VAUTIN, Paul (NSW)
Tours: NZ 1985
Appearances: 1982 NZ; 1983 NZ2; 1984 B; 1985 NZ2

VEIVERS, Greg (Queensland)
World Cup: 1975(2), 1977
Appearances: **1975 NZ,W; 1977 NZ,F,B2**
VEIVERS, Mick (Queensland, NSW)
Tours: NZ 1965
Appearances: 1962 B2; 1965 NZ2; 1966 B2

WAITE, David (NSW)
Tours: Britain 1973
Appearances: 1973 B2,F2; 1974 B2
WALKER, Bruce (NSW)
Tours: Britain 1978
WALSH, Ian (NSW)
Tours: Britain 1959,1963; NZ 1961,1965
Appearances: 1959 B3,F3; 1961 NZ2; 1962 B3;
    1963 NZ3,SA,B3,F; 1964 F; 1965 NZ2; 1966 B3
WALTERS, Elwyn (NSW)
Tours: Britain 1967,1973; NZ 1969
World Cup: 1970,1972
Appearances: 1969 NZ2; 1970 B2; **1970 NZ, Bb, F**;
    1972 NZ2; **1972 B2,NZ,F**; 1973 B3,F2; 1974 B
WARD, Dennis (NSW)
Tours: Britain 1973; NZ 1969
World Cup: 1972
Appearances: 1969 NZ2; **1972 Bb,NZ,F**
WEIER, Lloyd (NSW)
Tours: NZ 1965
Appearances: 1965 NZ2; 1966 B
WEISS, Col (Queensland)
Tours: NZ 1969
Appearances: 1969 NZ; 1970 Bb
WELLINGTON, Gary (Queensland)
Tours: NZ 1965
WILLIAMSON, Lionel (Queensland, NSW)
Tours: Britain 1973. NZ 1971
World Cup: 1968,1970
Appearances: **1968 F2; 1970 NZ,B2,F**; 1971 NZ;
    1973 B2,F; 1974 B
WITTENBERG, John (Queensland, NSW)
Tours: NZ 1969
World Cup: 1968
Appearances: 1966 B2; **1968 B,NZ,F2**; 1969 NZ2; 1970 B2
WRIGHT, David (Queensland)
World Cup: 1975(1)
Appearances: **1975 NZ**
WYNN, Graeme (NSW)
Tours: NZ 1980
WYNN, Peter (NSW)
Tours: NZ 1985
Appearances: 1985 NZ3

YAKICH, Nick (NSW)
Tours: NZ 1965
YOUNG, Craig (NSW)
Tours: Britain 1978,1982; NZ 1980
Appearances: 1978 NZ,B3,F2; 1979 B3; 1980 NZ2;
    1981 F; 1982 NZ2,PNG,B2,F2; 1984 b

AUSTRALIA TOURS OF BRITAIN

1908-09 TOUR

MATCH RESULTS

Mid-Rhondda	won	20-6	7,500
Bradford N.	won	12-11	4,000
Rochdale H	won	5-0	3,000
York	drew	5-5	3,000
Salford	drew	9-9	6,100
Runcorn	won	9-7	3,000
Cumberland League (W'haven)	**won**	**52-10**	**4,000**
Leigh	lost	11-14	6,000
Dewsbury	lost	0-15	2,000
Yorkshire (Hull)	**won**	**24-11**	**3,500**
Hunslet	won	12-11	6,000
Aberdare	won	37-10	5,000
Warrington	lost	3-10	5,000
Northern RL (Everton)	**won**	**10-9**	**6,000**
Hull KR	lost	16-21	7,000
Lancashire (Wigan)	**won**	**20-6**	**4,000**
Barrow	won	21-5	6,500
Halifax	lost	8-12	6,000
Swinton	won	10-9	1,500
BRITAIN (QPR, London)	**drew**	**22-22**	**2,000**
Treherbert	won	6-3	4,000
Wakefield T	lost	13-20	3,000
Leeds	won	14-10	12,000
Oldham	lost	5-11	12,000
England (Huddersfield)	**lost**	**9-14**	**7,000**
Widnes	won	13-2	1,000
†Wigan	lost	7-10	4,000
Batley	lost	5-12	2,000
Welsh League (Merthyr Tydfil)	**lost**	**13-14**	**6,000**
Ebbw Vale	won	9-8	5,000
†Wigan	lost	8-16	8,000
BRITAIN (Newcastle)	**lost**	**5-15**	**22,000**
Keighley	drew	8-8	1,000
Hull	lost	8-9	10,000
England (Glasgow)	**drew**	**17-17**	**3,000**
Cumberland (Carlisle)	**lost**	**2-11**	**2,000**
Broughton R	lost	12-14	12,000
St. Helens	lost	0-9	1,500
Warrington	drew	8-8	7,000
BRITAIN (Birmingham)	**lost**	**5-6**	**9,000**
Huddersfield	lost	3-5	9,677
Barrow	lost	3-11	6,000
Merthyr Tydfil	lost	13-15	4,000
England (Everton)	**lost**	**7-14**	**4,500**
Lancashire (Leigh)	**won**	**14-9**	**4,000**

●The tourists also played an exhibition match against Widnes at Southport on January 1, winning 55-3, but this is not included in tour records.

†There were two matches against Wigan because the first was marred by fog.

SUMMARY

Played 45   Won 17   Drew 6   Lost 22

For
Tries 113   Goals 87   Points 513

Against
Tries 106   Goals 78   Points 474

Lost Test series 2-0 with one drawn

Attendance total: 250,777

TOUR PARTY

Manager: J. Giltinan   Captain: D. Lutge

	App	Tries	Gls	Pts
J. Abercrombie	31	2	6	18
T. Anderson	5	0	0	0
E. Anlezark	17	1	0	3
W. Bailey	3	3	0	9
M. Bolewski	33	2	0	6
A. Burdon	25	3	0	9
A. Butler	23	4	1	14
W. Cann	8	0	0	0
F. Cheadle	7	0	0	0
A. Conlon	7	3	2	13
E. Courtney	27	8	0	24
J. Davis	6	0	0	0
S. Deane	27	6	0	18
J. Devereux	30	17	3	57
A. Dobbs	5	0	0	0
D. Frawley	22	10	0	30
R. Graves	21	2	0	6
A. Halloway	29	5	0	15
W. Hardcastle	6	1	0	3
C. Hedley	17	1	1	5
W. Heidke	25	3	0	9
A. Hennessy	7	0	0	0
L. Jones	5	1	0	3
D. Lutge	5	0	0	0
T. McCabe	20	4	0	12
H. Messenger	32	10	65	160
P. Moir	4	2	0	6
A. Morton	23	4	9	30
W. Noble	3	0	0	0
L. O'Malley	35	5	0	15
S. Pearce	32	2	0	6
A. Rosenfeld	15	5	0	15
J. Rosewall	1	0	0	0
P. Walsh	29	9	0	27

MEMO

First match on October 3, last match March 8.

All three Test matches were played on soccer grounds outside the Northern Union area in a move to expand the game, but it was not a success.

The party included Herbert "Dally" Messenger who had toured the previous season with New Zealand.

Among the players who were to sign for English clubs was Albert Rosenfeld who scored a record 80 tries in a season while with Huddersfield.

1911-12 TOUR

MATCH RESULTS

Midlands — South (Coventry)	won	20-11	3,000
Yorkshire (Sheffield)	won	33-13	4,000
Broughton R	won	18-8	12,000
Lancashire (Blackburn)	won	25-12	5,000
Wales (Ebbw Vale)	won	28-20	7,000
Widnes	won	23-0	5,000
St. Helens	won	16-5	12,000
England (Fulham)	won	11-6	6,000
Hunslet	drew	3-3	4,000
Northern RL (Everton)	won	16-3	6,000
Wigan	lost	2-7	25,000
Swinton	won	28-9	4,000
Hull	won	26-7	6,000
BRITAIN (Newcastle)	won	19-10	6,500
Oldham	lost	8-14	10,000
Leigh	won	13-12	6,000
Wakefield T	won	24-10	5,000
Cumberland (Maryport)	won	5-2	6,000
Barrow	won	44-8	6,500
Runcorn	won	23-7	2,000
Huddersfield	lost	7-21	17,000
England (Nottingham)	lost	3-5	3,000
Salford	won	6-3	4,000
York	won	16-8	1,500
BRITAIN (Edinburgh)	drew	11-11	6,000
Wales and West of England (Bristol)	won	23-3	1,000
Rochdale H	won	18-6	4,500
Halifax	won	23-5	10,000
Warrington	won	34-6	8,500
BRITAIN (Birmingham)	won	33-8	4,000
Leeds	won	8-6	1,000
Hull K.R.	won	5-2	7,000
Barrow	won	22-5	1,500
Batley	lost	5-13	4,000
Northern RL (Wigan)	won	20-12	2,000

SUMMARY

Played 35   Won 28   Drew 2   Lost 5

For
Tries 149   Goals 86   Points 619

Against
Tries 63   Goals 46   Points 281

Won Test series 2-0 with one drawn

Attendance total: 216,000

The Australians also played an exhibition match against Runcorn at Southport on December 25, winning 54-6 but this is not included in tour records.

TOUR PARTY

Managers: J. Quinlan and C. Ford
Captain: C. McKivat

	App	Tries	Gls	Pts
T. Berecry	12	12	0	36
A. Broomham	19	5	0	15
P. Burge	4	1	0	3
W. Cann	21	10	3	36
E. Courtney	25	4	0	12
R. Craig	30	8	2	28
S. Darmody	6	0	9	18
V. Farnsworth	28	18	0	54
W. Farnsworth	14	1	0	3
A. Francis (NZ)	24	9	49	125
C. Fraser	20	0	12	24
D. Frawley	11	13	3	45
H. Gilbert	29	20	2	64
G. Gillett (NZ)	4	0	0	0
H. Hallett	29	12	1	38
A. Halloway	12	0	0	0
P. McCue	22	6	0	18
C. McKivat	31	10	0	30
C. McMurtie	8	3	0	9
J. Murray	7	1	0	3
W. Neill	7	0	0	0
W. Noble	21	1	0	3
C. Russell	24	9	5	37
C. Savoury (NZ)	4	1	0	3
R. Stuart	2	0	0	0
C. Sullivan	16	1	0	3
R. Williams	19	3	0	9
F. Woodward (NZ)	6	1	0	3

MEMO

First match on September 23, last match on January 31.

The tour party included the following New Zealanders: Francis, Gillett, Savoury and Woodward.

A star of the party was Gilbert who later signed for Hull and became the first overseas player to captain an RL Challenge Cup-winning side, in 1914.

Often regarded as the best-ever touring party, they were the first Australian squad to remain unbeaten in a Test series in this country.

The Tests were again played on soccer grounds outside the Northern Union area, again without success.

1921-22 TOUR

MATCH RESULTS

Salford	won	48-3	9,000
Keighley	won	29-0	5,500
Hull KR	won	26-6	13,000
Bradford N	won	53-3	3,000
BRITAIN (Leeds)	**lost**	**5-6**	**32,000**
Widnes	won	28-4	11,000
Broughton R	won	18-6	17,000
England (Arsenal)	**lost**	**4-5**	**12,000**
Wigan	won	14-6	24,308
Leeds	won	11-5	14,000
Wakefield T	won	29-3	6,000
Batley	won	33-7	6,000
Warrington	lost	5-8	16,000
York	lost	3-9	5,000
BRITAIN (Hull)	**won**	**16-2**	**21,504**
Bramley	won	92-7	1,500
Rochdale H	won	16-2	12,000
Swinton	lost	0-9	6,000
Huddersfield	won	36-2	12,000
St. Helens	won	16-8	6,000
Oldham	won	16-5	15,000
Lancashire League (Everton)	**won**	**29-6**	**17,000**
Barrow	won	24-15	8,000
Yorkshire (Wakefield)	**won**	**24-8**	**6,000**
Wales (Pontypridd)	**won**	**21-16**	**13,000**
Lancashire (Warrington)	**lost**	**6-8**	**6,000**
Dewsbury	lost	6-13	6,000
Leigh	won	17-4	5,000
Hull	won	21-10	12,000
Widnes	won	17-8	12,000
Halifax	won	35-6	12,000
Hunslet	won	19-10	3,174
Cumberland (Workington)	**won**	**25-12**	**5,000**
BRITAIN (Salford)	**lost**	**0-6**	**21,000**
Oldham	lost	5-15	6,000
St. Helens Recs	won	16-5	5,000

SUMMARY

Played 36   Won 27   Lost 9

For
Tries 187   Goals 101   Points 763

Against
Tries 44   Goals 58   Points 248

Lost Test series 2-1

Attendance total: 384,986

TOUR PARTY

Managers: S. Ball and W. Cann
Captain: L. Cubitt

	App	Tries	Gls	Pts
C. Blinkhorn	29	39	0	117
N. Broadfoot	4	2	0	6
E. Brown	4	1	0	3
F. Burge	23	33	6	111
H. Caples	24	7	0	21
G. Carstairs	17	7	2	25
J. Craig	24	10	14	58
L. Cubitt	4	1	0	3
C. Fraser	23	2	1	8
B. Gray	5	2	0	6
H. Horder	25	35	11	127
J. Ives	6	1	0	3
A. Johnston	12	3	1	11
B. Laing (NZ)	10	4	0	12
R. Latta	22	7	0	21
E. McGrath	16	1	2	7
R. Norman	21	2	13	32
S. Pearce	21	0	0	0
H. Peters	4	2	0	6
N. Potter	10	1	0	3
C. Prentice	25	3	2	13
W. Richards	15	4	0	12
F. Ryan	24	6	0	18
W. Schultz	24	1	0	3
D. Thompson	26	3	49	107
R. Townsend	13	2	0	6
R. Vest	26	7	0	21
J. Watkins	11	1	0	3

MEMO

First match on September 17, last match on January 21.

Three players dominated the tryscoring on this tour. Blinkhorn, a winger, scored a tour record 39 tries and Burge's 33 tries were the most by a forward on tour. Horder, another winger, scored 35 tries.

Blinkhorn's total included a tour record nine against Bramley, who were beaten 92-7 — another tour record. Horder also got five as the tourists ran in 24 tries despite being penalised 18 times to Bramley's three. The half-time score was 43-5.

"Sandy" Pearce, a hooker, who was in the first tour party of 1908, returned at 41 years of age, to play 21 matches including two Tests.

1929-30 TOUR

MATCH RESULTS

Rochdale H	won	36-3	6,521
York	won	32-11	4,729
Batley	won	27-5	6,000
Widnes	won	37-13	6,400
Broughton R	won	21-8	6,514
Lancashire (Warrington)	**won**	**29-14**	**24,000**
Wakefield T	lost	3-14	9,786
Keighley	won	15-9	3,000
BRITAIN (Hull KR)	**won**	**31-8**	**20,000**
Castleford	won	53-2	4,000
Huddersfield	won	18-8	18,560
Leigh	won	19-16	8,000
Barrow	won	13-10	10,000
Leeds	lost	7-8	10,000
Hull	won	35-2	10,000
Oldham	won	18-10	18,000
BRITAIN (Leeds)	**lost**	**3-9**	**31,402**
Bradford N	won	26-17	7,000
St. Helens	drew	18-18	9,500
Yorkshire (Wakefield)	**won**	**25-12**	**7,011**
Halifax	won	58-9	8,440
Swinton	lost	5-9	9,000
Northern League (Wigan)	**lost**	**5-18**	**9,987**
Cumberland (Workington)	**lost**	**5-8**	**3,500**
Glamorgan and Monmouth-	**won**	**39-9**	**3,000**
shire (White City, Cardiff)			
St. Helens Recs	won	22-8	9,000
Northern League (Newcastle)	**won**	**32-22**	**9,690**
Warrington	lost	8-17	12,826
Hunslet	lost	3-18	12,000
Hull KR	won	10-5	12,000
Wigan	won	10-9	8,000
(Abandoned after 65 min — waterlogged)			
BRITAIN (Swinton)	**drew**	**0-0**	**34,709**
Salford	won	21-5	8,000
BRITAIN (Rochdale)	**lost**	**0-3**	**16,743**
Wales (Wembley)	**won**	**26-10**	**16,000**

SUMMARY

Played 35   Won 24   Drew 2   Lost 9

For

Tries 164   Goals 109   Points 710

Against

Tries 67   Goals 73   Points 347

Lost Test series 2-1, and one drawn

Attendance total: 393,318

TOUR PARTY

Managers: J. Dargan and H. Sunderland
Captain: T. Gorman   Coach: A. Hennessy

	App	Tries	Gls	Pts
V. Armbruster	19	6	0	18
G. Bishop	15	4	0	12
W. Brogan	20	2	0	6
J. Busch	19	2	0	6
D. Dempsey	10	0	0	0
A. Edwards	9	3	0	9
C. Fifield	22	8	0	24
H. Finch	10	16	18	84
T. Gorman	22	2	0	6
A. Henderson	7	0	0	0
J. Holmes	12	5	0	15
A. Justice	13	2	0	6
H. Kadwell	8	2	5	16
J. Kingston	26	18	0	54
F. Laws	15	2	5	16
P. Madsen	17	1	0	3
P. Maher	12	4	0	12
F. McMillan	26	0	4	8
W. Prigg	16	4	0	12
A. Ridley	7	11	0	33
E. Root	15	3	0	9
L. Sellars	8	1	0	3
W. Shankland	23	24	17	106
W. Spencer	22	23	0	69
W. Steinohrt	21	0	0	0
G. Treweeke	22	6	0	18
J. Upton	19	10	4	38
E. Weissel	20	5	56	127

MEMO

First match on September 7, last match on January 18.
This was the tour that featured a fourth Test match. The unique extra Test followed a 0-0 draw in the third match after Britain had lost the first and won the second.

Demands for a deciding Test match were answered with a Wednesday afternoon fixture at Rochdale on January 15. A late try by Stan Smith snatched Britain a 3-0 victory.

This was also the first tour in which Australia appointed an official coach to join the party, the position going to Arthur Hennessy.

1933-34 TOUR

MATCH RESULTS

St. Helens Recs	won	13-9	8,880
Leigh	won	16-7	4,600
Hull K.R.	won	20-0	7,831
Bramley	won	53-6	1,902
Oldham	won	38-6	15,281
Yorkshire (Leeds)	**won**	**13-0**	**10,309**
Barrow	won	24-5	12,221
Lancashire (Warrington)	**won**	**33-7**	**16,576**
Wigan	won	10-4	15,712
Castleford	won	39-6	4,250
Halifax	won	16-5	10,358
BRITAIN (Belle Vue, Man'r)	**lost**	**0-4**	**34,000**
Bradford N	lost	5-7	3,328
Warrington	lost	12-15	16,431
Hunslet	won	22-18	6,227
Salford	lost	9-16	15,761
Widnes	won	31-0	6,691
Wakefield T	won	17-6	5,596
Bradford N	won	10-7	9,937
Northern League (York)	**lost**	**5-7**	**3,158**
Swinton	lost	4-10	13,341
BRITAIN (Leeds)	**lost**	**5-7**	**29,618**
Keighley	won	14-7	3,800
Huddersfield	won	13-5	7,522
London Highfield	won	20-5	10,541
Broughton R	won	19-0	5,527
Leeds	won	15-7	5,295
St. Helens	won	20-11	5,735
Rochdale H	won	26-4	3,603
Cumberland (Whitehaven)	**lost**	**16-17**	**5,800**
BRITAIN (Swinton)	**lost**	**16-19**	**10,990**
York	won	15-7	6,500
Hull	won	19-5	16,341
Wales (Wembley)	**won**	**51-19**	**10,000**
England (Paris)	**won**	**63-13**	**5,000**
Oldham	won	38-5	4,000
England (Gateshead)	**lost**	**14-19**	**15,576**

SUMMARY

Played 37   Won 27   Lost 10

For
Tries 162   Goals 134   Points 754

Against
Tries 47   Goals 77   Points 295

Lost Test series 3-0

Attendance total: 368,238

TOUR PARTY

Managers: H. Sunderland and W. Webb
Captain: F. McMillan

	App	Tries	Gls	Pts
D. Brown	32	19	114	285
F. Curran	12	0	0	0
D. Dempsey	12	1	0	3
H. Denny	8	0	0	0
F. Doonar	11	2	0	6
J. Doyle	21	7	0	21
A. Folwell	21	2	0	6
F. Gardner	20	13	2	43
J. Gibbs	19	10	0	30
F. Gilbert	4	2	0	6
M. Glasheen	2	1	0	3
V. Hey	26	14	0	42
F. Laws	15	1	5	13
J. Little	4	0	0	0
M. Madsen	25	2	0	6
F. McMillan	21	1	3	9
L. Mead	15	2	5	16
F. Neumann	9	1	0	3
F. O'Connor	16	7	0	21
C. Pearce	27	6	1	20
S. Pearce	24	12	4	44
W. Prigg	32	16	0	48
A. Ridley	27	25	0	75
W. Smith	16	3	0	9
R. Stehr	26	4	0	12
V. Thicknesse	18	3	0	9
J. Why	17	8	0	24

●R. Morris was taken ill en route to England and died in hospital in Malta.

MEMO

First match on August 26, last match on January 13.

Dave Brown scored 114 goals and 285 points on this tour, two records which still stand. The centre's points total, which included 19 tries, came from 32 matches.

The tourists helped launch the game in France by playing England in Paris on December 31, winning 63-13.

Vic Hey was one of the tour's biggest successes, later returning to England and becoming a great favourite at Leeds.

An extra fixture to the official programme of matches was a seven-a-side match against England at Roundhay Park, Leeds.

1937 TOUR

MATCH RESULTS

Leigh	won	11-9	5,000
York	won	15-6	5,000
Newcastle	won	37-0	4,000
Lancashire (Warrington)	**lost**	**5-7**	**16,250**
Halifax	lost	2-12	14,500
Yorkshire (Bradford)	**won**	**8-4**	**7,570**
Wakefield T	won	17-10	8,696
Rochdale H	won	6-0	2,400
BRITAIN (Leeds)	**lost**	**4-5**	**31,949**
Widnes	drew	13-13	4,201
Hull	won	22-12	15,000
Bradford N	won	19-6	5,748
Salford	lost	8-11	12,000
Wigan	won	25-23	9,800
Oldham	won	10-6	15,000
BRITAIN (Swinton)	**lost**	**3-13**	**31,724**
Liverpool S	won	28-9	1,500
Huddersfield	lost	7-17	9,383
Swinton	lost	3-5	4,113
Warrington	lost	6-8	12,637
Leeds	lost	8-21	5,000
St. Helens XIII	won	15-7	2,000
Barrow	lost	8-12	8,153
BRITAIN (Huddersfield)	**won**	**13-3**	**9,093**
Broughton R	lost	0-13	3,000

SUMMARY

Played 25   Won 13   Drew 1   Lost 11

For
Tries 67   Goals 46   Points 293

Against
Tries 40   Goals 56   Points 232

Lost Test series 2-1

Attendance total: 243,717

TOUR PARTY

Managers: H. Sunderland and R. Savage
Captain: W. Prigg

	App	Tries	Gls	Pts
J. Beaton	18	3	28	65
E. Collins	2	1	0	3
F. Curran	11	4	0	12
L. Dawson	17	6	0	18
P. Fairall	8	0	0	0
J. Gibbs	12	0	0	0
F. Gilbert	13	2	4	14
F. Griffiths	6	0	0	0
C. Hazelton	8	3	0	9
L. Heidke	14	1	0	3
E. Lewis	12	2	0	6
G. McLennan	11	1	0	3
R. McKinnon	19	5	6	27
D. McLean	5	0	0	0
H. Narvo	15	5	0	15
F. Nolan	5	0	0	0
E. Norman	16	3	0	9
A. Norval	10	6	0	18
H. Pierce	15	3	0	9
W Prigg	18	7	0	21
J. Reardon	19	7	0	21
H. Robison	9	2	0	6
R. Stehr	12	0	0	0
R. Thompson	5	1	2	7
L. Ward	18	1	0	3
G. Whittle	7	0	0	0
B. Williams	11	3	0	9
P. Williams	9	1	6	15

● J. Pearce was injured in New Zealand and although he continued the trip did not play in England. H. Narvo replaced him.

MEMO

First match on September 18, last match on December 25.

This was Harry Sunderland's third trip as manager and Wally Prigg completed his hat-trick as a player, this time captaining the squad.

For the first time Australia made a brief tour of France, including two Tests which they won.

A reduced number of matches and a less adventurous style resulted in a drop in tryscoring with no player scoring more than 10 on the tour.

AUSTRALIA

1948 TOUR

MATCH RESULTS

Huddersfield	lost	3-22	26,017
Belle Vue Rangers	won	14-9	7,535
Hull	won	13-3	16,616
Wakefield T	won	26-19	20,040
Leigh	won	24-12	12,968
Salford	won	13-2	16,627
Castleford	won	10-8	14,004
BRITAIN (Leeds)	**lost**	**21-23**	**36,529**
Cumberland (Whitehaven)	**lost**	**4-5**	**8,818**
St. Helens	lost	8-10	20,175
Dewsbury	won	14-4	13,614
Hull K.R.	lost	12-17	7,614
Wigan	lost	11-16	28,554
Barrow	won	11-5	13,143
Leeds	won	15-2	13,542
Warrington	lost	7-16	26,879
BRITAIN (Swinton)	**lost**	**7-16**	**36,354**
Bradford N	won	21-7	13,287
Workington T	lost	7-10	13,253
Swinton	won	21-0	5,849
Wales (Swansea)	**won**	**12-5**	**9,161**
Yorkshire (Leeds)	**lost**	**2-5**	**5,310**
Halifax	won	10-8	6,520
Oldham	won	27-7	14,798
Lancashire (Wigan)	**lost**	**8-13**	**11,788**
Widnes	won	18-8	10,761
BRITAIN (Bradford)	**lost**	**9-23**	**42,000**

SUMMARY

Played 27 Won 15 Lost 12

For
Tries 76 Goals 60 Points 348

Against
Tries 57 Goals 52 Points 275

Lost Test series 3-0

Attendance total: 451,756

TOUR PARTY

Managers: W. Buckley and E. Simmonds
Captain: C. Maxwell

	App	Tries	Gls	Pts
F. de Belin	10	1	0	3
I. Benton	6	0	0	0
E. Brosnan	12	0	0	0
V. Bulgin	11	0	1	2
C. Churchill	16	0	1	2
L. Cowie	15	5	0	15
R. Dimond	9	2	0	6
K. Froome	12	2	21	48
A. Gibbs	13	1	0	3
J. Graves	15	6	24	66
D. Hall	15	5	0	15
N. Hand	11	1	0	3
J. Hawke	17	7	0	21
J. Holland	17	3	0	9
B. Hopkins	9	0	8	16
J. Horrigan	16	13	5	49
F. Johnson	3	0	0	0
R. Lulham	13	8	0	24
P. McMahon	18	10	0	30
D. McRitchie	8	1	0	3
C. Maxwell	9	2	0	6
N. Mulligan	15	1	0	3
W. O'Connell	15	1	0	3
L. Pegg	10	1	0	3
J. Rayner	19	2	0	6
K. Schubert	17	1	0	3
W. Thompson	11	1	0	3
W. Tyquin	9	2	0	6

MEMO

First match on September 18, last match on January 29.

The final match was to have been the third Test at Bradford on December 18 but fog caused a postponement and the party left to tour France.

They lost only one of 10 matches in France and returned for the third Test against Britain on January 29. Although Britain had already retained the Ashes there was a record crowd for a Test against Australia in this country of 42,000.

Britain won the Test series 3-0, but several of Australia's best players were playing for English clubs. Three different captains were used in the Tests, Wally O'Connell, Col Maxwell and Bill Tyquin.

A surprise omission from the party was Len Smith who had led Australia in the previous Test series against New Zealand. He was expected to be an automatic choice as centre and captain.

This was the first tour by Clive Churchill who was to become one of Australia's greatest full-backs. He was on tour again as a player in 1952 and 1956, and also coached the 1959 squad.

1952 TOUR

MATCH RESULTS

Keighley	won	54-4	7,431
Hull	won	28-0	15,364
Barrow	won	26-2	16,045
Whitehaven	won	15-5	9,253
Oldham	drew	7-7	19,370
Halifax	won	39-7	18,773
Wigan	won	23-13	16,223
St. Helens	lost	8-26	17,205
Featherstone R	won	50-15	3,700
BRITAIN (Leeds)	**lost**	**6-19**	**34,505**
Bradford N	won	20-6	29,287
Warrington	won	34-10	21,478
Leigh	won	34-5	8,409
Swinton	won	31-8	10,269
Hunslet	won	49-2	3,273
Workington T	won	27-15	11,341
Doncaster	won	41-13	2,452
Huddersfield	won	27-9	25,494
BRITAIN (Swinton)	**lost**	**5-21**	**32,421**
Wakefield T	won	58-8	7,239
Hull K.R.	won	31-6	5,817
Lancashire (Warrington)	**won**	**36-11**	**5,863**
Leeds	won	45-4	20,335
Yorkshire (Huddersfield)	**won**	**55-11**	**3,737**
Dewsbury	won	22-7	2,485
Widnes	won	18-7	7,411
BRITAIN (Bradford)	**won**	**27-7**	**30,509**

SUMMARY

Played 27   Won 23   Drew 1   Lost 3

For
Tries 176   Goals 144   Points 816

Against
Tries 42   Goals 61   Points 248

Lost Test series 2-1

Attendance total: 385,689

TOUR PARTY

Managers: D. McLean and N. Robinson
Captain: C. Churchill

	App	Tries	Gls	Pts
F. Ashton	14	7	0	21
R. Bull	9	1	0	3
B. Carlson	14	19	2	61
C. Churchill	17	2	17	40
A. Collinson	17	9	0	27
H. Crocker	11	2	0	6
B. Davies	16	7	0	21
C. Donohoe	11	4	0	12
R. Duncan	12	8	0	24
D. Flannery	11	15	0	45
C. Geelan	15	8	0	24
C. Gill	14	1	0	3
D. Hall	17	3	0	9
G. Hawick	9	4	0	12
N. Hazzard	16	5	0	15
K. Holman	10	8	7	38
K. Kearney	12	0	0	0
K. McCaffery	8	8	0	24
D. McGovern	6	10	0	30
A. Paul	13	7	4	29
N. Pidding	15	17	79	209
J. Rooney	12	1	0	3
T. Ryan	13	16	0	48
K. Schubert	14	0	0	0
F. Stanmore	15	3	0	9
T. Tyrrell	13	7	0	21
H. Wells	7	2	0	6
R. Willey	10	2	35	76

MEMO

First match on September 6, last match on December 13.

This was the most free-scoring tour squad of all time. They opened with a 54-4 defeat of Keighley and went on to score a record 816 points from 27 matches.

They also scored half centuries against Featherstone Rovers, Wakefield Trinity and Yorkshire.

The only club side to beat them was St. Helens, Oldham forcing a draw.

After losing the first two Tests, Australia finished with a third Test victory in a brawling match which gained notoriety as "The Battle of Odsal".

For the first time an Australian tour match was televised, when BBC covered the opening match at Keighley. The whole of the first Test match was also televised.

Australia used 23 players in the Test matches with only Clive Churchill, Brian Davies, Noel Hazzard and Duncan Hall playing in all three.

Captained by Willie Horne, Britain used 17 players in the Tests with nine playing in all three.

1956 TOUR

MATCH RESULTS

Liverpool C	won	40-12	4,712
Leeds	lost	13-18	24,459
Hull-Hull KR	won	37-14	17,172
Barrow	won	25-11	9,988
Whitehaven	lost	11-14	10,840
Bradford N	won	23-11	2,743
Warrington	lost	17-21	15,613
League XIII (Leigh)	**won**	**19-15**	**7,811**
York	won	20-18	6,842
Oldham	lost	2-21	8,458
Huddersfield	won	20-10	12,127
BRITAIN (Wigan)	**lost**	**10-21**	**22,473**
Hunslet	won	27-11	4,451
St. Helens	lost	2-44	15,579
BRITAIN (Bradford)	**won**	**22-9**	**23,634**
Halifax	lost	3-6	2,254
Wigan	won	32-4	15,854
Wakefield T	lost	12-17	3,381
BRITAIN (Swinton)	**lost**	**0-19**	**17,542**

SUMMARY

Played 19   Won 10   Lost 9

For
Tries 69   Goals 64   Points 335

Against
Tries 58   Goals 61   Points 296

Lost Test series 2-1

Attendance total: 225,933

TOUR PARTY

Managers: C. Fahy and C. Connell
Captain: K. Kearney

	App	Tries	Gls	Pts
D. Adams	8	6	0	18
R. Banks	13	3	0	9
R. Bull	14	2	0	6
C. Churchill	9	0	11	22
G. Clifford	9	1	34	71
G. Connell	9	6	1	20
B. Davies	10	5	1	17
L. Doyle	10	2	0	6
D. Flannery	11	8	0	24
D. Furner	10	0	3	6
E. Hammerton	8	0	0	0
K. Holman	10	5	2	19
I. Johnston	6	3	0	9
K. Kearney	11	0	0	0
W. Marsh	12	3	0	9
D. McGovern	8	5	0	15
I. Moir	10	7	0	21
K. O'Brien	7	2	0	6
B. Orrock	3	0	0	0
K. O'Shea	11	2	0	6
T. Payne	8	0	0	0
R. Poole	12	6	0	18
N. Provan	9	0	0	0
B. Purcell	6	0	12	24
T. Tyquin	10	2	0	6
A. Watson	13	1	0	3

MEMO

First match on October 10, last match on December 15.

A disappointing tour with no player totalling more than 10 tries during a programme reduced to fewer than 20 matches for the first time.

They were badly hit by a series of injuries to Norman Provan, one of their greatest ever forwards, which caused him to miss all three Test matches.

Alan Prescott led Britain and was one of nine players to appear in all three Tests.

Clive Churchill, regarded as one of the legendary figures of Australian rugby, ended an illustrious international career against Britain after the first Test.

Ken Kearney returned as captain of the tour squad after having played for Leeds.

1959 TOUR

MATCH RESULTS

Leeds	won	44-20	14,629
Rochdale H	won	27-14	10,155
Warrington	won	30-24	17,112
Lancashire (St. Helens)	**lost**	**22-30**	**15,743**
Salford	won	22-20	11,008
Yorkshire (York)	**lost**	**15-47**	**7,338**
Widnes	won	45-15	9,381
Oldham	won	25-14	17,630
Leigh	lost	17-18	11,932
St. Helens	won	15-2	29,156
BRITAIN (Swinton)	**won**	**22-14**	**35,224**
Whitehaven-Workington T	won	13-8	7,463
Barrow	lost	9-12	8,488
Hull-Hull KR	won	29-9	15,944
Bradford N	won	29-8	4,126
Halifax	won	17-5	8,274
Featherstone R	lost	15-23	7,671
Wigan	lost	9-16	24,466
BRITAIN (Leeds)	**lost**	**10-11**	**30,184**
Swinton	won	25-24	5,021
Wakefield T	lost	10-20	17,615
Huddersfield	won	21-7	2,349
Hunslet	won	12-11	8,061
BRITAIN (Wigan)	**lost**	**12-18**	**26,089**

SUMMARY

Played 24 Won 15 Lost 9

For
Tries 93 Goals 108 Points 495

Against
Tries 68 Goals 93 Points 390

Lost Test series 2-1

Attendance total: 345,059

TOUR PARTY

Managers: J. Argent and E. Keefer
Captain: K. Barnes Coach: C. Churchill

	*App	Tries	Gls	Pts
K. Barnes	12	0	52	104
D. Beattie	15	0	0	0
R. Boden	11	4	0	12
A. Brown	6	2	0	6
R. Budgen	5	4	0	12
P. Burke	8	4	0	12
B. Carlson	15	10	39	108
D. Chapman	12	1	0	3
B. Clay	14	2	0	6
W. Delamare	11	2	0	6
R. Gasnier	12	14	0	42
B. Hambly	12	5	0	15
K. Irvine	13	7	0	21
N. Kelly	9	2	0	6
E. Lumsden	16	8	0	24
R. Mossop	19	0	0	0
B. Muir	13	1	0	3
G. Parcell	12	1	0	3
D. Parish	9	3	16	41
J. Paterson	12	2	0	6
J. Raper	8	7	0	21
E. Rasmussen	13	3	1	11
J. Riley	11	2	0	6
I. Walsh	15	1	0	3
H. Wells	16	6	0	18
W. Wilson	13	2	0	6

*Including substitute appearances

MEMO

First match September 12, last match December 12.
Australia again flattered to deceive. After winning the first Test they went down in the other two, but only a late try and goal robbed them of the Ashes in the second Test.
Reg Gasnier made a sensational first tour and went on to become probably Australia's greatest centre of all time.
Gasnier scored three tries on his Test match debut and was a prominent figure in the other two.
Australia used only 15 players for the three Test matches, led each time by Keith Barnes.
The second Test saw the start of Neil Fox's long career for Britain. In the third Test the big centre scored 15 of Britain's 18 points with six goals and a try.

AUSTRALIA

1963 TOUR

MATCH RESULTS

Warrington	won	28-20	20,090
Huddersfield	won	6-5	13,398
Yorkshire (Hull KR)	lost	**5-11**	**10,324**
Leeds	won	13-10	16,641
Lancashire (Wigan)	lost	**11-13**	**15,068**
St. Helens	won	8-2	21,284
Featherstone R	lost	17-23	7,898
Oldham	won	12-4	11,338
Leigh	won	33-7	9,625
Hull-Hull KR XIII	won	23-10	10,481
BRITAIN (Wembley)	**won**	**28-2**	**13,946**
Rochdale H	won	3-0	8,637
Hunslet	won	17-13	4,400
Wakefield T	won	29-14	15,821
Cumberland (Workington)	**won**	**21-0**	**8,229**
Barrow	won	18-5	10,130
BRITAIN (Swinton)	**won**	**50-12**	**30,833**
Castleford	lost	12-13	7,887
Wigan	won	18-10	11,746
Widnes	won	20-9	6,509
Swinton	drew	2-2	11,947
BRITAIN (Leeds)	lost	**5-16**	**20,497**

SUMMARY

Played 22 Won 16 Drew 1 Lost 5

For
Tries 75 Goals 77 Points 379

Against
Tries 31 Goals 54 Points 201

Won Test series 2-1

Attendance total: 286,729

TOUR PARTY

Managers: J. Lynch and A. Sparkes
Captain: A. Summons

	*App	Tries	Gls	Pts
J. Cleary	7	0	0	0
M. Cleary	13	6	0	18
K. Day	9	0	0	0
P. Dimond	15	6	0	18
P. Gallagher	12	0	0	0
R. Gasnier	10	11	0	33
J. Gleeson	5	0	0	0
R. Hambly	13	1	0	3
E. Harrison	12	3	0	9
K. Irvine	17	17	2	55
L. Johns	10	2	24	54
N. Kelly	14	1	0	3
G. Langlands	16	11	51	135
J. Lisle	8	0	0	0
B. Muir	13	1	0	3
P. Quinn	15	1	0	3
J. Raper	13	2	0	6
B. Rushworth	11	5	0	15
K. Ryan	4	0	0	0
K. Smyth	8	1	0	3
F. Stanton	10	1	0	3
A. Summons	7	0	0	0
K. Thornett	11	1	0	3
R. Thornett	15	4	0	12
I. Walsh	16	1	0	3
G. Wilson	7	0	0	0

*Including substitute appearances

MEMO

First match September 14, last match November 30.

One of the most successful of all touring teams to Britain, the Australians returned home with the Ashes for the first time since 1911-12.

They clinched the series in the second Test with a record victory over Britain of 50-12. Britain were reduced to 11 men during the match because of injuries, but Australia had already displayed their superiority.

In the first Test at Wembley Australia won 28-2 with Reg Gasnier scoring another hat-trick of tries, the match watched by the Duke of Edinburgh.

Britain made several changes for the third Test which they won 16-5. This was a brawling affair at Headingley with referee Eric Clay sending off Australia's Brian Hambly and Barry Muir, plus Britain's Cliff Watson.

Although Arthur Summons was captain and coach of the squad, he did not play against Britain, Ian Walsh leading Australia in all three Tests.

The only club teams to beat Australia were Castleford and Featherstone Rovers but the Kangaroos also lost to Lancashire and Yorkshire.

1967 TOUR

MATCH RESULTS

Warrington	won	16-7	11,642
Yorkshire (Wakefield)	**lost**	**14-15**	**19,370**
Hull K.R.	lost	15-27	11,252
Lancashire (Salford)	**won**	**14-2**	**9,369**
Wigan	lost	6-12	22,770
Rochdale H	won	25-2	2,676
BRITAIN (Leeds)	**lost**	**11-16**	**22,293**
St. Helens	lost	4-8	17,275
Wakefield T	won	33-7	10,056
BRITAIN, (W'City, London)	**won**	**17-11**	**17,445**
Castleford	lost	3-22	6,137
Oldham	won	18-8	3,174
Widnes	won	33-11	9,828
Barrow	drew	10-10	8,418
Cumberland (Workington)	**lost**	**15-17**	**7,545**
Swinton	won	12-9	5,640
Leeds	won	7-4	5,522
Halifax	won	22-2	5,285
Bradford N	won	7-3	14,173
BRITAIN (Swinton)	**won**	**11-3**	**13,615**

SUMMARY

Played 20 Won 12 Drew 1 Lost 7

For
Tries 57 Goals 61 Points 293

Against
Tries 30 Goals 53 Points 196

Won Test series 2-1

Attendance total: 223,485

TOUR PARTY

Managers: J. Drewes and H. Schmidt
Captain: R. Gasnier

	*App	Tries	Gls	Pts
A. Branson	12	3	0	9
R. Coote	13	5	0	15
N. Gallagher	10	0	0	0
P. Gallagher	11	1	0	3
R. Gasnier	5	1	0	3
J. Gleeson	11	2	1	8
J. Greaves	10	2	0	6
K. Goldspink	9	0	0	0
L. Hanigan	8	2	0	6
K. Irvine	13	8	5	34
L. Johns	10	1	5	13
K. Junee	6	2	1	8
N. Kelly	12	0	0	0
J. King	13	8	0	24
G. Langlands	14	3	36	81
R. Lynch	12	2	0	6
J. McDonald	11	4	10	32
D. Manteit	11	2	0	6
B. Moore	7	4	0	12
J. Raper	9	0	0	0
E. Rasmussen	13	0	0	0
R. Saddler	9	0	0	0
J. Sattler	9	0	0	0
W. Smith	11	3	3	15
A. Thomson	9	2	0	6
E. Walters	5	2	0	6

*Including substitute appearances

MEMO

First match September 30, last match December 9.

Australia retained the Ashes with victory in the third Test at a frostbound Swinton. Heavy snow fell during the match in which Arthur Keegan's tackling at full back kept Australia's winning margin down to 11-3.

Britain had won the first Test at Headingley, but lost the second at White City, London.

Reg Gasnier's great international career ended in the first Test when he received a broken leg, a match which was Roger Millward's first Test against Australia.

In Gasnier's absence, Peter Gallagher captained Australia in the second Test and Johnny Raper took over for the third.

Australia recovered after losing five of their first eight matches although they later crashed 22-3 at Castleford.

AUSTRALIA

1973 TOUR

MATCH RESULTS

Salford	won	15-12	11,064
Wakefield T	won	13-9	5,863
Dewsbury	won	17-3	5,685
Castleford	won	*18-10	2,419
Widnes	won	25-10	5,185
Oldham	won	44-10	2,895
Cumbria (Whitehaven)	**won**	**28-2**	**3,666**
Bradford N	won	50-14	5,667
BRITAIN (Wembley)	**lost**	**12-21**	**9,874**
Hull K.R.	won	25-9	5,150
Huddersfield	won	32-2	1,333
Leigh	won	31-4	2,607
St. Helens	lost	7-11	10,013
Featherstone R	won	18-13	5,659
BRITAIN (Leeds)	**won**	**14-6**	**16,674**
BRITAIN (Warrington)	**won**	**15-5**	**10,019**

*Australia's score includes penalty under 7-point try rule although this was not within International Rules.

SUMMARY

Played 16   Won 14   Lost 2

For
Tries 81   Goals 60   Drop goals 1   Points 364

Against
Tries 18   Goals 42   Drop goals 3   Points 141

Won Test series 2-1

Attendance total: 103,773

Graham Eadie

280

TOUR PARTY

Managers: C. Gibson and A. Bishop
Captain-coach: Graeme Langlands

	*App	Tries	Gls	Pts
A. Beetson	13	3	0	9
R. Branighan	11	6	0	18
M. Cronin	9	6	23	64
G. Eadie	10	4	10	32
R. Fulton	11	16	0(1)	49
E. Goodwin	7	5	0	15
W. Hamilton	7	1	0	3
J. Lang	6	1	0	3
G. Langlands	8	4	27	66
R. McCarthy	8	4	0	12
K. Maddison	12	5	0	15
J. O'Neill	4	0	0	0
R. O'Reilly	12	0	0	0
W. Orr	6	2	0	6
T. Pickup	9	2	0	6
G. Pierce	6	0	0	0
T. Randall	5	1	0	3
T. Raudonikis	9	3	0	9
S. Rogers	6	2	0	6
P. Sait	11	2	0	6
G. Starling	11	7	0	21
G. Stevens	7	1	0	3
D. Waite	10	4	0	12
E. Walters	12	2	0	6
D. Ward	7	0	0	0
L. Williamson	8	0	0	0

*Including substitute appearances
( )One point drop goal

MEMO

First match September 30, last match December 1.

After losing the series Down Under in 1970, Australia returned to power despite being convincingly beaten in the first Test at Wembley.

They won the second Test at Headingley and regained the Ashes with a 15-5 victory at Warrington on a frostbound pitch. Australia scored five tries to one to win much more easily than the score suggests.

St. Helens were the only club side to beat the tourists, with Bradford Northern suffering the biggest defeat by 50-14.

A serious hand injury ruled out tour captain Graeme Langlands for the second and third Tests, giving the chance for Graham Eadie to emerge as a new Test star at full back.

Other stars of the tour were Bobby Fulton and Arthur Beetson, while centres Steve Rogers and Mick Cronin were to gain valuable experience as stars of the future.

1978 TOUR

MATCH RESULTS

Blackpool B	won	39-1	2,700
Cumbria (Barrow)	**won**	**47-4**	**5,964**
Britain Under-24 (Hull KR)	**won**	**30-8**	**6,418**
Bradford N	won	21-11	15,755
Warrington	lost	12-15	10,143
Wales (Swansea)	**won**	**8-3**	**4,250**
Leeds	won	25-19	9,781
BRITAIN (Wigan)	**won**	**15-9**	**17,644**
Widnes	lost	10-11	12,202
Hull	won	34-2	10,723
Salford	won	14-2	6,155
BRITAIN (Bradford)	**lost**	**14-18**	**26,447**
Wigan	won	28-2	10,645
St. Helens	won	26-4	16,352
York	won	29-2	5,155
BRITAIN (Leeds)	**won**	**23-6**	**29,627**

SUMMARY

Played 16   Won 13   Lost 3

For
Tries 79   Goals 68   Drop goals 2   Points 375

Against
Tries 12   Goals 39   Drop goals 3   Points 117

Won Test series 2-1

Attendance total: 189,961

TOUR PARTY

Managers: P. Moore and J. Caldwell
Captain: R. Fulton   Coach: F. Stanton

	*App	Tries	Gls	Pts
C. Anderson	9	3	0	9
K. Boustead	10	2	0	6
L. Boyd	8	3	0	9
L. Corowa	5	4	0	12
M. Cronin	11	2	46	98
G. Eadie	10	4	0	12
R. Fulton	12	9	0(2)	29
G. Gerard	11	3	0	9
J. Gibbs	2	1	0	3
R. Hilditch	5	1	0	3
S. Kneen	5	2	0	6
M. Krilich	6	0	0	0
A. McMahon	8	6	1	20
S. Martin	8	1	0	3
R. Morris	9	2	0	6
G. Oliphant	3	0	0	0
G. Olling	7	2	0	6
G. Peponis	6	6	0	18
G. Pierce	4	0	0	0
R. Price	10	2	0	6
T. Raudonikis	11	4	0	12
R. Reddy	10	3	0	9
S. Rogers	12	8	21	66
I. Schubert	8	3	0	9
A. Thompson	13	4	0	12
I. Thomson	10	0	0	0
B. Walker	6	2	0	6
C. Young	11	2	0	6

*Including substitute appearances
( )One point drop goal

MEMO

First match September 30, last match November 18.

Australia's dominance continued despite going down to Britain's "Dad's Army" pack in the second Test at Odsal.

The Kangaroos had a narrow first Test win but retained the Ashes with a runaway success in the third Test at Headingley.

The only club teams to beat the tourists were Warrington and Widnes.

Defence was the tourists' strong point. They did not concede a try until their fourth match and finished with only 12 against them in 16 matches.

The tourists did much to revive interest in international rugby with attendances showing a big increase over the previous tour.

It was a magnificent farewell to touring for Australia's captain Bobby Fulton, but a sad end to the wonderful Test career of Britain's captain Roger Millward.

Rod Reddy

1982 TOUR

MATCH RESULTS

Hull KR	won	30-10	10,742
Wigan	won	13-9	12,158
Barrow	won	29-2	6,282
St. Helens	won	32-0	8,190
Leeds	won	31-4	11,570
Wales (Cardiff)	**won**	**37-7**	**5,617**
BRITAIN (Hull C FC)	**won**	**40-4**	**26,771**
Leigh	won	44-4	7,680
Bradford N	won	13-6	10,506
Cumbria (Carlisle)	**won**	**41-2**	**5,748**
Fulham	won	22-5	10,432
Hull	won	13-7	16,049
BRITAIN (Wigan)	**won**	**27-6**	**23,216**
Widnes	won	19-6	9,790
BRITAIN (Leeds)	**won**	**32-8**	**17,318**

SUMMARY

Played 15   Won 15   Lost 0

For
Tries 97   Goals 66   Points 423

Against
Tries 7   Goals 29   Drop goals 1   Points 80

Won Test series 3-0

Attendance total: 182,069

Wally Lewis

TOUR PARTY

Managers: F. Farrington and T. Drysdale
Captain: M. Krilich   Coach: F. Stanton

	App	Tries	Gls	Pts
C. Anderson	7	3	0	9
K. Boustead	8 + 1	8	0	24
L. Boyd	10	3	0	9
G. Brentnall	9	1	0	3
R. Brown	5 + 4	0	0	0
G. Conescu	2 + 2	1	0	3
S. Ella	7 + 1	9	3	33
E. Grothe	7	7	0	21
R. Hancock	4	0	0	0
B. Kenny	8	2	0	6
M. Krilich	8	1	0	3
W. Lewis	7 + 5	3	9	27
P. McCabe	8	7	0	21
D. McKinnon	5	3	1	11
M. Meninga	10	6	50	118
G. Miles	6	1	0	3
R. Morris	6 + 2	0	0	0
S. Mortimer	5	2	0	6
J. Muggleton	6 + 2	4	0	12
M. Murray	4 + 1	3	0	9
W. Pearce	9	4	0	12
R. Price	6 + 2	2	0	6
J. Ribot	8	10	0	30
R. Reddy	8	1	0	3
S. Rogers	9 + 3	8	3	30
I. Schubert	7	2	0	6
P. Sterling	8	5	0	15
C. Young	8	1	0	3

+ indicates substitute appearance

MEMO

First match October 10, last match November 28.

The young 28-man squad — only two players were over 30 — rewrote the record books by displaying a showcase of skill, strength and speed that was to thrill millions worldwide and set alarm bells ringing throughout the British game.

The 1982 Kangaroos became the first touring party from any country to win all their matches in Britain and the first tourists to win all three Tests in Britain, their total of 99 points being the most scored in an Anglo-Aussie Test series in either country.

The tourists amassed 97 tries and conceded only seven in their 15-match programme in which they piled up 27 points or more on 10 occasions.

Tour stars such as triple record breaker Mal Meninga, inspiring captain Max Krilich, mercurial Peter Sterling, artistic Brett Kenny and rampaging Wayne Pearce captivated the British public, the average tour gate of 12,138 being the best for 20 years.

AUSTRALIA APPENDIX

In addition to full tours, World Cup parties made occasional appearances as follows, Australia score first:

1960	St. Helens	lost	12-15	12,750
1970	St. Helens	lost	10-37	15,570
1972	St. Helens	won	24-9	10,000
	Wigan	drew	18-18	6,000
	Bradford N	won	29-16	2,820
1975	Salford	won	44-6	5,357
	St. Helens	won	32-7	10,170
	Oldham	won	20-10	3,575
	York	won	45-4	4,082
	England (Leeds)	won	25-0	7,680

AUSTRALIA TOURS OF FRANCE

Each tour immediately followed trip to Britain

	P	W	D	L	F	A
1937-38	10	9	—	1	267	80
Won Test series 2-0						
1948-49	10	9	—	1	279	71
Won Test series 2-0						
1952-53	13	10	—	3	301	125
Lost Test series 2-1						
1956-57	9	8	1	—	207	110
Won Test series 3-0						
1959-60	11	9	—	2	277	120
Won Test series 3-0						
1963-64	14	12	—	2	328	111
Won Test series 2-1						
1967-68	7	4	1	2	105	53
Lost Test series 2-0, one drawn						
1973-74	3	3	—	—	59	24
Won Test series 2-0						
1978-79	6	3	—	3	116	73
Lost Test series 2-0						
1982-83	7	7	—	—	291	20
Won Test series 2-0						

● During their tour of Britain in 1933-34 Australia beat England 63-13 in Paris in an exhibition game.
● The 1960 World Cup squad played an extra game against France, winning 37-12. The 1970 squad beat France 7-4 and France B 36-8. In 1975, Rouergue were beaten 35-4.

RECORDS AGAINST CLUB SIDES

Highest score: 92-7 v. Bramley in 1921-22
(Also widest margin win)
Biggest defeat: 2-44 v. St. Helens in 1956
Biggest attendance: 29,287 v. Bradford N in 1952

INDIVIDUAL RECORDS

Club and representative matches
Most tries on tour: 39 by C. Blinkhorn in 1921-22
Most goals and points on tour: 114g-285pts (19t) by D. Brown in 1933-34
Most appearances on tour: 35 by L. O'Malley in 1908-09

AUSTRALIA TOURS OF NEW ZEALAND

	P	W	D	L	F	A
1919	9	8	—	1	443	101
Won Test series 3-1						
1935	6	5	—	1	173	81
Won Test series 2-1						
1937	3	1	—	2	32	40
En route to Britain, the Australians played two non-Test matches against New Zealand and also lost against the Maoris.						
1949	10	9	—	1	299	123
Drew Test series 1-1						
1953	9	7	—	2	366	98
Lost Test series 2-1						
1961	9	7	—	2	215	68
Drew Test series 1-1						
1965	8	7	—	1	159	58
Drew Test series 1-1						
1969	6	4	—	2	137	78
Drew Test series 1-1						
1971	3	1	—	2	52	53
Lost Test series 1-0						
1980	7	5	1	1	158	48
Won Test series 2-0						
1985	6	5	—	1	192	44
Won Test series 2-1 including one Test win in Australia						

● The 1975 World Cup squad beat Auckland 17-6. The 1977 squad beat South Island 68-5 and lost 19-15 to Auckland.

AUSTRALIA TOUR SQUADS TO NEW ZEALAND
Captains in bold

1919

A. Halloway

F. Burge
L. Cubitt
C. Fraser
H. Gilbert
A. Halloway
H. Horder
A. Johnston
J. Kerwick
R. Latta
R. Norman
C. O'Donnell
A. Oxford
B. Paten
N. Potter
C. Prentice
J. Robinson
F. Ryan
W. Schultz
T. Sweeney
D. Thompson
C. Thorogood
R. Townsend
R. Vest
J. Watkins

Managers: C. Upton
W. Webb

1935

D. Brown

H. Bichel
D. Brown
E. Collins
F. Curran
P. Fairall
J. Gibbs
F. Gilbert
S. Goodwin
R. Hines
E. Lewis
W. Mahon
R. McKinnon
E. Norman
S. Pearce
W. Prigg
M. Shields
R. Stehr
V. Thicknesse
L. Ward
J. Whittle

Managers: W. Chareling
H. Sunderland

1949

K. Froome

V. Bulgin
R. Bull
C. Churchill
L. Cowie
F. de Belin
K. Froome
J. Graves
R. Griffiths
K. Hansen
J. Hawke
J. Holland
I. Johnston
M. McCoy
P. McMahon
N. Mulligan
W. O'Connell
J. Rayner
R. Roberts
K. Schubert
F. Stanmore
A. Thompson
W. Thompson

Managers: A. Thompson
F. Moynihan

1953

C. Churchill

F. Ashton
R. Banks
R. Bull
B. Carlson
C. Churchill
L. Cowie
H. Crocker
B. Davies
B. Drew
C. Gill
G. Hawick
K. Holman
A. Hornery
K. Kearney
K. McCaffery
D. McGovern
A. Paul
N. Pidding
A. Watson
H. Wells

Managers: D. Locke
G. McLeod

1961

B. Carlson

D. Beattie
R. Beaven
B. Carlson
R. Crowe
K. Day
F. Drake
R. Gasnier
R. Gehrke
A. Gill
K. Irvine
E. Lumsden
R. Lynch
B. Muir
W. Owen
D. Parish
J. Paterson
E. Rasmussen
J. Sinclair
A. Summons
I. Walsh

Managers: J. Kessey
J. Allen

1965

I. Walsh

B. Beath
A. Buman
N. Cavanagh
M. Cleary
R. Gasnier
J. Gleeson
B. Hambly
K. Irvine
L. Johns
G. Langlands
J. Lisle
J. Morgan
T. Pannowitz
P. Quinn
W. Smith
M. Veivers
I. Walsh
L. Weier
G. Wellington
N. Yakich

Managers: A. Stehr
D. Green

1969

J. Sattler

M. Cleary
R. Coote
J. Cootes
R. Costello
J. Denman
B. Fitzsimmons
R. Honan
L. Johns
G. Langlands
G. Lye
D. Manteit
R. McCarthy
J. McDonald
D. Pittard
I. Robson
J. Sattler
E. Walters
D. Ward
C. Weiss
J. Wittenberg

Managers: E. Burns
          J. Lynch
Coach: H. Bath

1971

G. Langlands

B. Beath
W. Bennett
R. Branighan
A. Branson
K. Campbell
R. Costello
B. Fitzsimmons
R. Fulton
R. Grant
G. Langlands
R. McCarthy
J. Murphy
R. O'Reilly
T. Raudonikis
P. Sait
J. Sattler
G. Starling
L. Williamson

Managers: R. Dunn
          R. Stafford
Coach: H. Bath

1980

G. Peponis

C. Anderson
K. Boustead
L. Boyd
G. Brentnall
C. Close
M. Cronin
G. Dowling
R. Hancock
J. Lang
J. Leis
S. Martin
R. Morris
G. Peponis
R. Price
G. Quinn
T. Raudonikis
R. Reddy
A. Thompson
G. Wynn
C. Young

Managers: T. Bellow
          J. Caldwell
Coach: F. Stanton

1985

W. Lewis

N. Cleal
C. Close
G. Conescu
G. Dowling
B. Elias
S. Ella
J. Ferguson
W. Fullerton-Smith
D. Hasler
G. Jack
W. Lewis
M. Meninga
M. Murray
M. O'Connor
W. Pearce
J. Ribot
S. Roach
P. Tunks
P. Vautin
P. Wynn

Managers: J. Garrahy
          D. Barnhill
Coach: T. Fearnley

1963 Kangaroo Dick Thornett touches down in the 50-12 romp against Britain in the Second Test at Swinton.

AUSTRALIA WORLD CUP SQUADS

1954 in France

C. Churchill

R. Banks
R. Bull
C. Churchill
M. Crocker
B. Davies
P. Diversi
D. Flannery
D. Hall
G. Hawick
K. Holman
K. Kearney
K. McCaffery
I. Moir
K. O'Shea
N. Pidding
N. Provan
A. Watson
H. Wells

Managers: J. McMahon
          S. O'Neill
Coach: V. Hey

1957 in Australia

R. Poole

K. Barnes
B. Carlson
B. Clay
B. Davies
G. Hawick
K. Holman
K. Kearney
W. Marsh
K. McCaffery
I. Moir
K. O'Shea
R. Poole
N. Provan
R. Ritchie
D. Schofield
T. Tyquin
A. Watson
H. Wells

Manager: N. C. Robinson
Coach: R. Poole

1960 in Britain

K. Barnes

K. Barnes
D. Beattie
R. Boden
A. Brown
R. Budgen
B. Carlson
R. Gasnier
B. Hambly
K. Irvine
N. Kelly
L. Morgan
R. Mossop
B. Muir
G. Parcell
J. Raper
W. Rayner
E. Rasmussen
H. Wells

Managers: J. O'Toole
          P. Duggan
Coach: K. Barnes

1968 in Australia and New Zealand

J. Raper

A. Beetson
A. Branson
R. Coote
B. Fitzsimmons
R. Fulton
J. Greaves
B. James
F. Jones
J. King
G. Langlands
D. Manteit
J. Raper
E. Rasmussen
J. Rhodes
E. Simms
W. Smith
R. Thornett
L. Williamson
J. Wittenberg

Managers: A. M. Kingston
Coach: H. Bath

1970 in Britain

R. Coote

R. Branighan
J. Brown
R. Coote
J. Cootes
R. Costello
R. Fulton
M. Harris
R. McCarthy
B. McTaggart
J. O'Neill
R. O'Reilly
D. Pittard
P. Sait
E. Simms
W. Smith
G. Sullivan
R. Turner
E. Walters
L. Williamson

Managers: K. Arthurson
          J. B. Quinn
Coach: H. Bath

1972 in France

G. Langlands

A. Beetson
E. Branighan
J. Elford
R. Fulton
J. Grant
M. Harris
F. Jones
S. Knight
G. Langlands
R. McCarthy
J. O'Neill
R. O'Reilly
T. Raudonikis
P. Sait
G. Starling
G. Stevens
G. Sullivan
E. Walters
D. Ward

Managers: A. M. Kingston
          J. Clark
Coach: H. Bath

1975 First phase In Australia	1975 Second phase in New Zealand, Britain and France	1977 in Australia and New Zealand
G. Langlands	**A. Beetson**	**A. Beetson**
C. Anderson	A. Beetson	A. Beetson
A. Beetson	J. Brass	S. Crear
R. Branighan	M. Cronin	M. Cronin
R. Coote	G. Eadie	G. Eadie
M. Cronin	D. Fitzgerald	T. Fahey
J. Donnelly	R. Higgs	D. Fitzgerald
T. Fahey	J. Lang	R. Gartner
R. Fulton	I. Mackay	E. Geiger
M. Harris	A. McMahon	M. Harris
J. Lang	J. Mayes	R. Higgs
G. Langlands	J. Peard	J. Kolc
J. O'Neill	G. Pierce	A. McMahon
T. Pickup	G. Piggins	J. Peard
L. Platz	L. Platz	G. Pierce
T. Randall	J. Porter	T. Randall
T. Raudonikis	J. Quayle	T. Raudonikis
J. Rhodes	T. Randall	R. Reddy
P. Sait	T. Raudonikis	M. Thomas
G. Stevens	J. Rhodes	G. Veivers
R. Strudwick	S. Rogers	
D. Wright	I. Schubert	Manager: C. Brown
	G. Veivers	D. Hall
Manager: R. Stafford		Coach: T. Fearnley
Coach: G. Langlands	Manager: R. Abbott	
	J. Cairns	
	Coach: G. Langlands	

Kangaroo loose forward Ray Price touches down in the 40-4 hammering of Great Britain at Boothferry Park, Hull, in 1982.

RECORDS IN TEST AND WORLD CUP MATCHES

For Australia

Highest score: 56-6 v. France, Second Test at Brisbane July 2, 1960 (Also widest margin win)

Most tries in a match: 4 by J. Ribot v. Papua-New Guinea at Port Moresby Oct. 2, 1982

Most goals in a match: 10 by K. Barnes v. France, Second Test at Brisbane July 2, 1960
10 by E. Simms v. New Zealand, World Cup at Wigan Oct. 10, 1970
10 by M. Cronin v. Britain, First Test at Brisbane June 16, 1979

Most points in a match: 23(10g,1t) by E. Simms v. New Zealand, World Cup at Wigan Oct. 10, 1970

Most appearances: 45 by G. Langlands (1963-1975)

Most career tries: 34 by K. Irvine (1959-1967)

Most career goals: 141 by M. Cronin (1973-1982)

Most career points: 309(141g,9t) by M. Cronin (1973-1982)

Biggest attendance: 70,204 v. Britain, First Test at Sydney June 6, 1932

Against Australia

Highest score: 49-25 v. New Zealand, Second Test at Brisbane June 28, 1952

Most tries in a match: 4 by J. Leytham (Britain) Second Test at Brisbane July 2, 1910

Most goals in a match: 11 by D. White (New Zealand) Second Test at Brisbane June 28, 1952

Most points in a match: 22 by D. White (as above).

Great Britain's Lee Crooks and Kiwi skipper Mark Graham, Men of the Match in the 1985 third Whitbread Trophy Bitter Test.

GREAT BRITAIN

GREAT BRITAIN

1985-86 TEST REVIEW

Great Britain's report card after Maurice Bamford's first full season as coach would probably read: 'Has made impressive progress, but still room for improvement'.

Revitalised Britain earned a season's tally of only one defeat in five Tests. Two draws — against New Zealand and France — were gained in the new-style World Cup.

Bamford succeeded in restoring national pride in a close-knit Test squad, nicknamed 'The Family'. Including playing substitutes, only 17 players were used in the three Whitbread Trophy Bitter Tests with New Zealand. Two more were called up for the first French encounter and a further five for the return fixture, mainly because of injuries, bringing the 1985-86 total of Test players to 24, including seven debutants.

After nine successive defeats at the hands of Australia and New Zealand, the drawn series against the highly-rated Kiwis was greeted with deserved acclaim. A last minute controversial try robbed Britain of a shock victory at Headingley in the first Test. With growing confidence, the British swept to a 25-8 success at Wigan two weeks later, centre Garry Schofield collecting a record haul of four tries and 16 points. Seven days later, the World Cup-rated decider at Elland Road attracted more than 22,000 fans and finished in a bruising 6-6 draw with British substitute forward Lee Crooks grabbing the headlines as the last minute goalkicking hero.

The three Whitbread Trophy Bitter Tests are fully chronicled in the 1985 KIWIS section.

Bamford's usually meticulous preparations were ruined by Arctic-style weather as Britain set off to Avignon for the first Test against France, a World Cup qualifier. Heavy snow and frost restricted the British squad to a video session at Huddersfield and an indoor training stint on the day of departure. In France, their only session was carried out on a small soccer pitch.

The side showed two changes from the Kiwi Tests, Wigan duo Henderson Gill and Shaun Wane returning from injury to replace the unfit Joe Lydon and the unavailable Andy Goodway.

In unaccustomed sunny conditions, Britain were lucky to hang on for a draw after a disappointing performance which severely dented their World Cup hopes.

Bamford's charges squandered an undeserved 10-2 interval lead, the French controlling the game for long spells despite being beaten 15-5 in the scrums. After full back Gilles Dumas levelled the scores with a 62nd minute penalty, both teams missed chances to win the game in the dying minutes with penalty shots.

The scorer of all the French points, Dumas miscued a simple drop goal attempt in the 68th minute before sending a penalty kick wide with seconds remaining. Hull prop Crooks, the hero of the hour three months earlier, also missed another chance of glory with a difficult 45-yard penalty kick with three minutes to go.

The tension of those final minutes was one of the few highlights of a disappointing Test, only the third draw in 43 Anglo-French encounters.

Australian referee Kevin Roberts sent three players for 10-minute stays in the sin bin, French prop Max Chantal and Widnes stand off Tony Myler for tripping and Crooks for kicking out in the tackle.

Britain led 10-2 at the interval from an Ellery Hanley try, goalled by Crooks to add to his earlier brace of penalties, Dumas having opened the scoring with a second minute penalty goal.

The visitors could have had the game sewn up two minutes after the restart. Ace poacher Schofield popped up to collect a Crooks ball to touch down under the French posts, only for the pass to be ruled forward. France roared back four minutes later for Dumas to put in an enterprising kick for winger Pascal Laroche to pick up and return the ball to the blond full back for an exciting touchdown to bring the scoreline to 10-8 with the the successful goalkick.

Few British players enhanced their reputations in the lacklustre display and the Whitbread Trophy Bitter Man of the Match award went to Wigan second row man Ian Potter for a brave tackling display. Despite five stitches in a scalp wound, Potter finished as top tackler with 23, ahead of hardworking scrum half Deryck Fox with 20.

A fortnight later, the British team which kicked off at Wigan showed seven changes, two positional. Ruled out through injury were Hanley, Mick Burke, Jeff Grayshon and skipper Harry Pinner, while Gill and Wigan teammate Wane were omitted.

In came fit-again Lydon and new caps Tony Marchant (Castleford), David Laws (Hull K.R.), Kevin Rayne (Leeds) and Halifax second row man Neil James, a non-playing substitute at Avignon. Andy Platt of St. Helens came in as forward substitute and made a late appearance.

Led for the first time by hooker David Watkinson, Britain gained a confidence-boosting 24-10 victory over a French side which again was praised for combining typical Gallic flair on attack with a more controlled gameplan under the influence of Australian coach Tas Baitieri.

Thrum Hall second row man James claimed the Whitbread Trophy Bitter Man of the Match award for an outstanding debut performance, highlighted by a 50th minute try. The Test triumph rounded off a remarkable comeback for the 24-year-old packman who was on the verge of quitting the game before being transferred from Castleford to Halifax.

The £5,000 bargain buy formed a highly promising second row pairing with Rayne, at last emerging from the shadow of his twin brother Keith. Another debutant partner-ship showing potential was on the left wing where Laws settled better than on his debut for Yorkshire on the same ground six months earlier, and centre Marchant crowned a top defensive show with a strong running try in the 62nd minute.

Britain's official tackle count put him joint top with 22, an extraordinary tally for a threequarter. Skipper Watkinson finished level in a competitive display of leadership by example.

After the torrid scenes of the Kiwis series in which Britain gained praise for their shows of self discipline, Bamford's peace-keeping orders were followed once again and only four penalties were conceded.

PREPARATION SQUAD

At the end of April, Great Britain coach Maurice Bamford named a 29-man squad to undertake a summer training programme in preparation for the visit of the 1986 Australian tourists in October and November.

The named squad was: Kevin Beardmore (Castleford), Darren Bloor (Salford), Mick Burke (Widnes), Chris Burton (Hull K.R.), Lee Crooks (Hull), Des Drummond (Leigh), Ronnie Duane (Warrington), George Fairbairn (Hull K.R.), John Field-house (Widnes), Deryck Fox (Featherstone R.), Carl Gibson (Leeds), Jeff Grayshon (Leeds), Andy Gregory (Warrington), Ellery Hanley (Wigan), David Heron (Leeds), Neil James (Halifax), David Laws (Hull K.R.), Joe Lydon (Wigan), Tony Marchant (Castleford), Tony Myler (Widnes), Brian Noble (Bradford N.), Harry Pinner (St. Helens), Ian Potter (Wigan), Kevin Rayne (Leeds), Garry Schofield (Hull), Trevor Skerrett (Hull), Mike Smith (Hull K.R.), Kevin Ward (Castleford), David Watkinson (Hull K.R.).

At the end of the season, Skerrett with-drew because of work commitments and Bamford added Bob Beardmore (Castleford) and Wigan duo Shaun Edwards and Shaun Wane.

Ace try scorer Ellery Hanley touches down for Great Britain in the First Kiwi Test at Headingley, Leeds.

Great Britain stand off Tony Myler in full flight against the 1985 Kiwis, clubmate John Fieldhouse in support.

Determined defence by Great Britain winger Des Drummond in the First Anglo-French Test in Avignon.

Man of the Match-rated running from Great Britain debutant Neil James in the Second French Test at Wigan, support on hand from Deryck Fox (left) and Ian Potter.

293

FIRST WHITBREAD TROPHY BITTER TEST

16th February   **Avignon**

GREAT BRITAIN 10   **FRANCE 10**

Mick Burke (Widnes)	1.	Gilles Dumas (St. Gaudens)
Des Drummond (Leigh)	2.	Didier Couston (Le Pontet)
Garry Schofield (Hull)	3.	Alain Maury (Villeneuve)
Ellery Hanley (Wigan)	4.	Philippe Fourquet (Toulouse)
Henderson Gill (Wigan)	5.	Pascal Laroche (Villeneuve)
Tony Myler (Widnes)	6.	Dominique Espugna (Lezignan)
Deryck Fox (Featherstone R.)	7.	Patrick Entat (Avignon)
Lee Crooks (Hull)	8.	Max Chantal (Villeneuve)
David Watkinson (Hull K.R.)	9.	Patrick Baco (XIII Catalan)
Shaun Wane (Wigan)	10.	Serge Titeux (Le Pontet)
Ian Potter (Wigan)	11.	Guy Laforgue (XIII Catalan) Capt.
John Fieldhouse (Widnes)	12.	Marc Palanque (Le Pontet)
Harry Pinner (St. Helens) Capt.	13.	Thierry Bernabe (Le Pontet)
Shaun Edwards (Wigan)	14.	Denis Berge (Le Pontet)
Neil James (Halifax)	15.	Jean-Luc Rabot (Villeneuve)

T: Hanley   T: Dumas
G: Crooks (3)   G: Dumas (3)
Half-time: 10-2   Substitutions:
Manager: Les Bettinson   Rabot for Titeux (36 min.)
Coach: Maurice Bamford   Berge for Laroche (75 min.)
Referee: Kevin Roberts (Sydney)   Attendance: 4,000

Scorechart

		Scoreline	
Minute	Score	GB	France
2:	Dumas (P)	0	2
15:	Crooks (P)	2	2
35:	Crooks (P)	4	2
39:	Hanley (T)		
	Crooks (G)	10	2
46:	Dumas (T)		
	Dumas (G)	10	8
62:	Dumas (P)	10	10
	Scrums	15	5
	Penalties	7	11

Ian Potter, Whitbread Trophy Bitter Man of the Match in Avignon.

SECOND WHITBREAD TROPHY BITTER TEST

1st March **Wigan**

GREAT BRITAIN 24

Joe Lydon (Wigan)	1.	
Des Drummond (Leigh)	2.	
Garry Schofield (Hull)	3.	
Tony Marchant (Castleford)	4.	
David Laws (Hull K.R.)	5.	
Tony Myler (Widnes)	6.	
Deryck Fox (Featherstone R.)	7.	
Lee Crooks (Hull)	8.	
David Watkinson (Hull K.R.) Capt.	9.	
John Fieldhouse (Widnes)	10.	
Kevin Rayne (Leeds)	11.	
Neil James (Halifax)	12.	
Ian Potter (Wigan)	13.	
Shaun Edwards (Wigan)	14.	
Andy Platt (St. Helens)	15.	

T: Schofield, Drummond, James,
  Marchant
G: Crooks (2), Schofield (2)
Substitution:
Platt for Fieldhouse (73 min.)
Half-time: 12-4
Manager: Les Bettinson
Coach: Maurice Bamford

FRANCE 10

Gilles Dumas (St. Gaudens)
Didier Couston (Le Pontet)
Denis Berge (Le Pontet)
Philippe Fourquet (Toulouse)
Pascal Laroche (Villeneuve)
Dominique Espugna (Lezignan)
Patrick Entat (Avignon)
Max Chantal (Villeneuve)
Patrick Baco (XIII Catalan)
Serge Titeux (Le Pontet)
Guy Laforgue (XIII Catalan) Capt.
Marc Palanque (Le Pontet)
Thierry Bernabe (Le Pontet)
Serge Pallares (XIII Catalan)
Jean-Luc Rabot (Villeneuve)
T: Couston (2)
G: Dumas
Substitutions:
Rabot for Chantal (66 min.)
Pallares for Espugna (70 min.)
Referee: Kevin Roberts (Sydney)
Attendance: 8,112

Scorechart

			Scoreline	
Minute	*Score*	*GB*	*France*	
10:	Crooks (P)	2	0	
14:	Couston (T)	2	4	
17:	Schofield (T)			
	Crooks (G)	8	4	
33:	Drummond (T)	12	4	
50:	James (T)			
	Schofield (G)	18	4	
62:	Marchant (T)	22	4	
65:	Couston (T)			
	Dumas (G)	22	10	
69:	Schofield (P)	24	10	
	Scrums	9	8	
	Penalties	12	4	

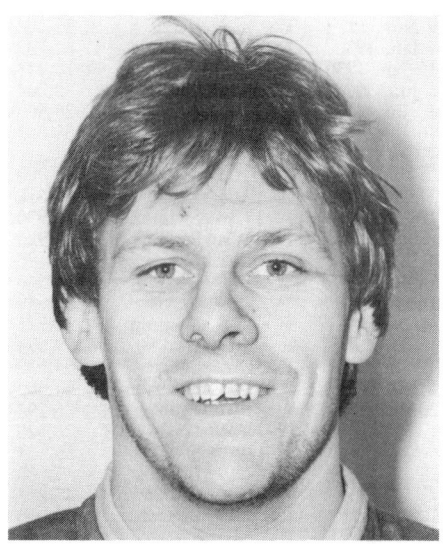

Great Britain Test debutant Kevin Rayne.

TESTS

● Although early Tests were played under the titles of Northern Union or England, it is acceptable to regard them as Great Britain.

W-Win, D-Drawn, L-Lost refer to Great Britain.

GREAT BRITAIN v. AUSTRALIA

Date	Result	Score	Venue	Attendance
12 Dec. 1908	D	22-22	QPR, London	2,000
23 Jan. 1909	W	15-5	Newcastle	22,000
15 Feb. 1909	W	6-5	Birmingham	9,000
18 Jun. 1910	W	27-20	Sydney	42,000
†2 Jul. 1910	W	22-17	Brisbane	18,000
8 Nov. 1911	L	10-19	Newcastle	6,500
16 Dec. 1911	D	11-11	Edinburgh	6,000
1 Jan. 1912	L	8-33	Birmingham	4,000
27 Jun. 1914	W	23-5	Sydney	40,000
29 Jun. 1914	L	7-12	Sydney	55,000
4 Jul. 1914	W	14-6	Sydney	34,420
26 Jun. 1920	L	4-8	Brisbane	28,000
3 Jul. 1920	L	8-21	Sydney	40,000
10 Jul. 1920	W	23-13	Sydney	32,000
1 Oct. 1921	W	6-5	Leeds	32,000
5 Nov. 1921	L	2-16	Hull	21,504
14 Jan. 1922	W	6-0	Salford	21,000
23 Jun. 1924	W	22-3	Sydney	50,000
28 Jun. 1924	W	5-3	Sydney	33,842
12 Jul. 1924	L	11-21	Brisbane	36,000
23 Jun. 1928	W	15-12	Brisbane	39,200
14 Jul. 1928	W	8-0	Sydney	44,548
21 Jul. 1928	L	14-21	Sydney	37,000
5 Oct. 1929	L	8-31	Hull K.R.	20,000
9 Nov. 1929	W	9-3	Leeds	31,402
4 Jan. 1930	D	0-0	Swinton	34,709
15 Jan. 1930	W	3-0	Rochdale	16,743
6 Jun. 1932	W	8-6	Sydney	70,204
18 Jun. 1932	L	6-15	Brisbane	26,500
16 Jul. 1932	W	18-13	Sydney	50,053
7 Oct. 1933	W	4-0	Belle Vue, Manchester	34,000
11 Nov. 1933	W	7-5	Leeds	29,618
16 Dec. 1933	W	19-16	Swinton	10,990
29 Jun. 1936	L	8-24	Sydney	63,920
4 Jul. 1936	W	12-7	Brisbane	29,486
18 Jul. 1936	W	12-7	Sydney	53,546
16 Oct. 1937	W	5-4	Leeds	31,949
13 Nov. 1937	W	13-3	Swinton	31,724
18 Dec. 1937	L	3-13	Huddersfield	9,093
17 Jun. 1946	D	8-8	Sydney	64,527
6 Jul. 1946	W	14-5	Brisbane	40,500
20 Jul. 1946	W	20-7	Sydney	35,294
9 Oct. 1948	W	23-21	Leeds	36,529
6 Nov. 1948	W	16-7	Swinton	36,354
29 Jan. 1949	W	23-9	Bradford	42,000
12 Jun. 1950	W	6-4	Sydney	47,215
1 Jul. 1950	L	3-15	Brisbane	35,000
22 Jul. 1950	L	2-5	Sydney	47,178
4 Oct. 1952	W	19-6	Leeds	34,505
8 Nov. 1952	W	21-5	Swinton	32,421
13 Dec. 1952	L	7-27	Bradford	30,509
12 Jun. 1954	L	12-37	Sydney	65,884
3 Jul. 1954	W	38-21	Brisbane	46,355
17 Jul. 1954	L	16-20	Sydney	67,577
17 Nov. 1956	W	21-10	Wigan	22,473
1 Dec. 1956	L	9-22	Bradford	23,634
15 Dec. 1956	W	19-0	Swinton	17,542
14 Jun. 1958	L	8-25	Sydney	68,777
5 Jul. 1958	W	25-18	Brisbane	32,965
19 Jul. 1958	W	40-17	Sydney	68,720
17 Oct. 1959	L	14-22	Swinton	35,224
21 Nov. 1959	W	11-10	Leeds	30,184
12 Dec. 1959	W	18-12	Wigan	26,089
9 Jun. 1962	W	31-12	Sydney	70,174
30 Jun. 1962	W	17-10	Brisbane	34,766
14 Jul. 1962	L	17-18	Sydney	42,104
16 Oct. 1963	L	2-28	Wembley	13,946
9 Nov. 1963	L	12-50	Swinton	30,833
30 Nov. 1963	W	16-5	Leeds	20,497
25 Jun. 1966	W	17-13	Sydney	57,962
16 Jul. 1966	L	4-6	Brisbane	45,057
23 Jul. 1966	L	14-19	Sydney	63,503
21 Oct. 1967	W	16-11	Leeds	22,293
3 Nov. 1967	L	11-17	White City, London	17,445
9 Dec. 1967	L	3-11	Swinton	13,615
6 Jun. 1970	L	15-37	Brisbane	42,807
20 Jun. 1970	W	28-7	Sydney	60,962
4 Jul. 1970	W	21-17	Sydney	61,258
3 Nov. 1973	W	21-12	Wembley	9,874
24 Nov. 1973	L	6-14	Leeds	16,674
1 Dec. 1973	L	5-15	Warrington	10,019
15 Jun. 1974	L	6-12	Brisbane	30,280
6 Jul. 1974	W	16-11	Sydney	48,006
20 Jul. 1974	L	18-22	Sydney	55,505
21 Oct. 1978	L	9-15	Wigan	17,644
5 Nov. 1978	W	18-14	Bradford	26,447
18 Nov. 1978	L	6-23	Leeds	29,627
16 Jun. 1979	L	0-35	Brisbane	23,051
30 Jun. 1979	L	16-24	Sydney	26,837
14 Jul. 1979	L	2-28	Sydney	16,844
30 Oct. 1982	L	4-40	Hull City AFC	26,771
20 Nov. 1982	L	6-27	Wigan	23,216
28 Nov. 1982	L	8-32	Leeds	17,318
9 Jun. 1984	L	8-25	Sydney	30,190
26 Jun. 1984	L	6-18	Brisbane	26,534
7 Jul. 1984	L	7-20	Sydney	18,756

	Played	Won	Drawn	Lost	Tries	Goals	Dr	Pts for
Great Britain	96	49	4	43	236	244	4	1203
Australia	96	43	4	49	265	298	5	1406

† 1910 Tour:
Australian records do not recognise this as a Test match, while most British sources claim this second Test win clinched the series and there was no need for a third Test.

Britain played two matches against Australasian sides which included New Zealanders. These are accepted as Tests by Australia. Both were played at Sydney, the first on July 9 was drawn 13-13, the second on July 13 was won by Australasia 32-15.

GREAT BRITAIN-AUSTRALIA TEST MATCH RECORDS

Britain

Highest score: 40-17 Third Test at Sydney July 19, 1958 (Also widest margin win)
Most tries in a match: 4 by J. Leytham (Wigan) Second Test at Brisbane July 2, 1910
Most goals in a match: 10 by B. L. Jones (Leeds) Second Test at Brisbane July 3, 1954
Most points in a match: 20 by B. L. Jones (as above)
20 (7g,2t) by R. Millward (Hull KR) Second Test at Sydney June 20, 1970.
Biggest attendance: 42,000 Third Test at Bradford Jan. 29, 1949

Australia

Highest score: 50-12 Second Test at Swinton, Nov 9, 1963 (Also widest margin win)
Most tries in a match:* 3 by J. Devereux, First Test at QPR, London, Dec 12, 1908
3 by R. Gasnier, First Test at Swinton, Oct 17, 1959
3 by R. Gasnier, First Test at Wembley, Oct 16, 1963
3 by K. Irvine, Second Test at Swinton, Nov 9, 1963
3 by K. Irvine, Third Test at Sydney, July 23, 1966
Most goals in a match: 10 by M. Cronin, First Test at Brisbane, June 16, 1979

Most points in a match: 20 by M. Cronin (as above)
20 (7g,2t) by G. Langlands at Swinton, Nov 9, 1963
Biggest attendance: 70,204 First Test at Sydney, June 6, 1932

● In a World Cup match at Perpignan, France, on October 29, 1972, R. Fulton scored three tries.

GREAT BRITAIN v. NEW ZEALAND

Date	Result		Venue	Attendance
25 Jan. 1908	W	14-6	Leeds	8,182
8 Feb. 1908	L	6-18	Chelsea	14,000
15 Feb. 1908	L	5-8	Cheltenham	4,000
30 Jul. 1910	W	52-20	Auckland	16,000
1 Aug. 1914	W	16-13	Auckland	15,000
31 Jul. 1920	W	31-7	Auckland	34,000
7 Aug. 1920	W	19-3	Christchurch	10,000
14 Aug. 1920	W	11-10	Wellington	4,000
2 Aug. 1924	L	8-16	Auckland	22,000
6 Aug. 1924	L	11-13	Wellington	6,000
9 Aug. 1924	W	31-18	Dunedin	14,000
2 Oct. 1926	W	28-20	Wigan	14,500
13 Nov. 1926	W	21-11	Hull	7,000
15 Jan. 1927	W	32-17	Leeds	6,000
4 Aug. 1928	L	13-17	Auckland	28,000
18 Aug. 1928	W	13-5	Dunedin	12,000
25 Aug. 1928	W	6-5	Christchurch	21,000
30 Jul. 1932	W	24-9	Auckland	25,000
13 Aug. 1932	W	25-14	Christchurch	5,000
20 Aug. 1932	W	20-18	Auckland	6,500
8 Aug. 1936	W	10-8	Auckland	25,000
15 Aug. 1936	W	23-11	Auckland	17,000
10 Aug. 1946	L	8-13	Auckland	10,000
4 Oct. 1947	W	11-10	Leeds	28,445
8 Nov. 1947	L	7-10	Swinton	29,031
20 Dec. 1947	W	25-9	Bradford	42,680
29 Jul. 1950	L	10-16	Christchurch	10,000
12 Aug. 1950	L	13-20	Auckland	20,000
6 Oct. 1951	W	21-15	Bradford	37,475
10 Nov. 1951	W	20-19	Swinton	29,938
15 Dec. 1951	W	16-12	Leeds	18,649
24 Jul. 1954	W	27-7	Auckland	22,097
31 Jul. 1954	L	14-20	Greymouth	4,240
14 Aug. 1954	W	12-6	Auckland	6,186
8 Oct. 1955	W	25-6	Swinton	21,937
12 Nov. 1955	W	27-12	Bradford	24,443
17 Dec. 1955	L	13-28	Leeds	10,438
26 Jul. 1958	L	10-15	Auckland	25,000
9 Aug. 1958	W	32-15	Auckland	25,000
30 Sept. 1961	L	11-29	Leeds	16,540
21 Oct. 1961	W	23-10	Bradford	19,980
4 Nov. 1961	W	35-19	Swinton	22,536
28 Jul. 1962	L	0-19	Auckland	14,976
11 Aug. 1962	L	8-27	Auckland	16,411
25 Sept. 1965	W	7-2	Swinton	8,541
23 Oct. 1965	W	15-9	Bradford	15,740
6 Nov. 1965	D	9-9	Wigan	7,919
6 Aug. 1966	W	25-8	Auckland	14,494
20 Aug. 1966	W	22-14	Auckland	10,657
11 Jul. 1970	W	19-15	Auckland	15,948
19 Jul. 1970	W	23-9	Christchurch	8,600
25 Jul. 1970	W	33-16	Auckland	13,137
25 Sept. 1971	L	13-18	Salford	3,764
16 Oct. 1971	L	14-17	Castleford	4,108
6 Nov. 1971	W	12-3	Leeds	5,479
27 Jul. 1974	L	8-13	Auckland	10,466
4 Aug. 1974	W	17-8	Christchurch	6,316
10 Aug. 1974	W	20-0	Auckland	11,574
21 Jul. 1979	W	16-8	Auckland	9,000
5 Aug. 1979	W	22-7	Christchurch	8,500
11 Aug. 1979	L	11-18	Auckland	7,000
18 Oct. 1980	D	14-14	Wigan	7,031
2 Nov. 1980	L	8-12	Bradford	10,946
15 Nov. 1980	W	10-2	Leeds	8,210
14 Jul. 1984	L	0-12	Auckland	10,238
22 Jul. 1984	L	12-28	Christchurch	3,824
28 Jul. 1984	L	16-32	Auckland	7,967
19 Oct. 1985	L	22-24	Leeds	12,591
2 Nov. 1985	W	25-8	Wigan	15,506
9 Nov. 1985	D	6-6	Elland Rd, Leeds	22,209

	Played	Won	Lost	Drawn	Tries	Goals	Dr	Pts for
Great Britain	70	43	24	3	254	205	3	1186
New Zealand	70	24	43	3	163	204	0	916

GREAT BRITAIN-NEW ZEALAND TEST MATCH RECORDS

Britain

Highest score: *52-20 First Test at Auckland, July 30, 1910 (Also widest margin win)

Most tries in a match: 4 by W. Boston (Wigan) First Test at Auckland, July 24, 1954
4 by G. Schofield (Hull) Second Test at Wigan, Nov 2, 1985

Most goals in a match: *7 by N. Fox (Wakefield T.) Third Test at Swinton, Nov 4, 1961
7 by E. Fraser (Warrington) Second Test at Auckland, Aug 9, 1958

Most points in a match: *16 (4t) by G. Schofield (Hull) Second Test at Wigan, Nov 2, 1985

Biggest attendance: 42,680 Third Test at Bradford, Dec 20, 1947

* In a World Cup match at Pau, France, on November 4, 1972, Britain won 53-19 with J. Holmes (Leeds) scoring 26 points from 10 goals and two tries.

In a World Cup match at Sydney on June 8, 1968, Bev Risman scored 7 goals.

New Zealand

Highest score: 32-16 Third Test at Auckland, July 28, 1984

Widest margin win: 19-0 First Test at Auckland, July 28, 1962

    27-8 Second Test at Auckland, Aug 11, 1962

No player has scored three tries or more in a Test.

Most goals and points: *7g-14pts by D. White Second Test at Greymouth, July 31, 1954

    J. Fagan, First Test at Headingley, Sep 30, 1961

    E. Wiggs, Second Test at Auckland, Aug 20, 1966

Biggest attendance: 34,000 First Test at Auckland, July 31, 1920

* In a World Cup match at Sydney, Australia, on June 25, 1957, W. Sorenson also scored 7 goals, 14 points.

● Results since France were given Test match status.

GREAT BRITAIN v. FRANCE

26 Jan. 1957	W	45-12	Leeds	20,221	22 Jan. 1967	W	16-13	Carcassonne	10,650
3 Mar. 1957	D	19-19	Toulouse	16,000	4 Mar. 1967	L	13-23	Wigan	7,448
10 Apr. 1957	W	29-14	St. Helens	23,250	11 Feb. 1968	W	22-13	Paris	8,000
3 Nov. 1957	W	25-14	Toulouse	15,000	2 Mar. 1968	W	19-8	Bradford	14,196
23 Nov. 1957	W	44-15	Wigan	19,152	30 Nov. 1968	W	34-10	St. Helens	6,080
2 Mar. 1958	W	23-9	Grenoble	20,000	2 Feb. 1969	L	9-13	Toulouse	10,000
14 Mar. 1959	W	50-15	Leeds	22,000	7 Feb. 1971	L	8-16	Toulouse	14,960
5 Apr. 1959	L	15-24	Grenoble	8,500	17 Mar. 1971	W	24-2	St. Helens	7,783
6 Mar. 1960	L	18-20	Toulouse	15,308	6 Feb. 1972	W	10-9	Toulouse	11,508
26 Mar. 1960	D	17-17	St. Helens	14,000	12 Mar. 1972	W	45-10	Bradford	7,313
11 Dec. 1960	W	21-10	Bordeaux	8,000	20 Jan. 1974	W	24-5	Grenoble	5,500
28 Jan. 1961	W	27-8	St Helens	18,000	17 Feb. 1974	W	29-0	Wigan	10,105
17 Feb. 1962	L	15-20	Wigan	17,277	6 Dec. 1981	W	37-0	Hull	13,173
11 Mar. 1962	L	13-23	Perpignan	14,000	20 Dec. 1981	L	2-19	Marseilles	6,500
2 Dec. 1962	L	12-17	Perpignan	5,000	20 Feb. 1983	W	20-5	Carcassonne	3,826
3 Apr. 1963	W	42-4	Wigan	19,487	6 Mar. 1983	W	17-5	Hull	6,055
8 Mar. 1964	W	11-5	Perpignan	4,326	29 Jan. 1984	W	12-0	Avignon	4,000
18 Mar. 1964	W	39-0	Leigh	4,750	17 Feb. 1984	W	10-0	Leeds	7,646
6 Dec. 1964	L	8-18	Perpignan	15,000	1 Mar. 1985	W	50-4	Leeds	6,491
23 Jan. 1965	W	17-7	Swinton	9,959	17 Mar. 1985	L	16-24	Perpignan	5,000
16 Jan. 1966	L	13-18	Perpignan	6,000	16 Feb. 1986	D	10-10	Avignon	4,000
5 Mar. 1966	L	4-8	Wigan	14,004	1 Mar. 1986	W	24-10	Wigan	8,112

	Played	Won	Drawn	Lost	Tries	Goals	Dr	Pts for
Great Britain	44	28	3	13	190	185	0	958
France	44	13	3	28	85	115	3	496

GREAT BRITAIN-FRANCE TEST MATCH RECORDS

Britain

Highest score:	50-15 at Leeds, March 14, 1959
	50-4 at Leeds, March 1, 1985 (also widest margin win)
Most tries in a match:	4 by A. Murphy (St. Helens) at Leeds, March 14, 1959
Most goals in a match:	10 by B. Ganley (Oldham) at Wigan, November 23, 1957
Most points in a match:	21 (9g, 1t) by B.L. Jones (Leeds) at Leeds, January 26, 1957
	21 (9g,1t) by N. Fox (Wakefield T.) at Wigan, April 3, 1963
	21 (9g,1t) by N. Fox (Wakefield T.) at Leigh, March 18, 1964
Biggest attendance:	23,250 at St. Helens, April 10, 1957

France

Highest score:	24-15 at Grenoble, April 5, 1959
	24-16 at Perpignan, March 17, 1985
Widest margin win:	19-2 at Marseilles, December 20, 1981
Most tries in a match:	3 by D. Couston at Perpignan, March 17, 1985
Most goals in a match:	7 by P. Lacaze at Wigan, March 4, 1967
Most points in a match:	14 by P. Lacaze (as above).
	14 (4g,2t) by G. Benausse at Wigan, February 17, 1962
●Biggest attendance:	20,000 at Grenoble, March 2, 1958

●In a World Cup match at Toulouse on November 7, 1954, there were 37,471

Additional Great Britain v. France

Pre-Test status

22 May 1952	L	12-22	Paris	16,466
24 May 1953	L	17-28	Lyons	
27 Apr. 1954	W	17-8	Bradford	14,153
11 Dec. 1955	L	5-17	Paris	18,000
11 Apr. 1956	W	18-10	Bradford	10,453

Other match

31 July 1982	L	7-8	Venice	1,500

GREAT BRITAIN v PAPUA NEW GUINEA

5 Aug. 1985	W	38-20	Mt. Hagen	7,510

Leeds scoring maestro Lewis Jones, joint holder of the Great Britain record for most points against France.

GREAT BRITAIN IN THE WORLD CUP

A — Australia, Fr — France, GB — Great Britain, NZ — New Zealand

1954 in France   *Winners:* Great Britain

30 Oct.	Fr	22 NZ	13	Paris	13,240
31 Oct.	GB	28 A	13	Lyons	10,250
7 Nov.	GB	13 Fr	13	Toulouse	37,471
7 Nov.	A	34 NZ	15	Marseilles	20,000
11 Nov.	GB	26 NZ	6	Bordeaux	14,000
11 Nov.	A	5 Fr	15	Nantes	13,000

Play off

13 Nov.	GB	16 Fr	12	Paris	30,368

Final Table

	P.	W.	D.	L.	F.	A.	Pts.
Great Britain	3	2	1	0	67	32	5
France	3	2	1	0	50	31	5
Australia	3	1	0	2	52	58	2
New Zealand	3	0	0	3	34	82	0

1957 in Australia   *Winners:* Australia

15 June	GB	23 Fr	5	Sydney	50,007
15 June	A	25 NZ	5	Brisbane	29,636
17 June	GB	6 A	31	Sydney	57,955
17 June	NZ	10 Fr	14	Brisbane	28,000
22 June	A	26 Fr	9	Sydney	35,158
25 June	GB	21 NZ	29	Sydney	14,263

Final Table

	P.	W.	D.	L.	F.	A.	Pts.
Australia	3	3	0	0	82	20	6
Great Britain	3	1	0	2	50	65	2
New Zealand	3	1	0	2	44	60	2
France	3	1	0	2	28	59	2

1960 in England   *Winners:* Great Britain

24 Sept.	GB	23 NZ	8	Bradford	20,577
24 Sept.	A	13 Fr	12	Wigan	20,278
1 Oct.	A	21 NZ	15	Leeds	10,773
1 Oct.	GB	33 Fr	7	Swinton	22,923
8 Oct.	A	3 GB	10	Bradford	32,773
8 Oct.	NZ	9 Fr	0	Wigan	2,876

Final Table

	P.	W.	D.	L.	F.	A.	Pts.
Great Britain	3	3	0	0	66	18	6
Australia	3	2	0	1	37	37	4
New Zealand	3	1	0	2	32	44	2
France	3	0	0	3	19	55	0

1968 in Australia and New Zealand   *Winners:* Australia

25 May	A	25 GB	10	Sydney	62,256
25 May	Fr	15 NZ	10	Auckland	18,000
1 June	A	31 NZ	12	Brisbane	23,608
2 June	Fr	7 GB	2	Auckland	15,760
8 June	A	37 Fr	4	Brisbane	32,600
8 June	GB	38 NZ	14	Sydney	14,105

Final Table

	P.	W.	D.	L.	F.	A.	Pts.
Australia	3	3	0	0	93	26	6
France	3	2	0	1	26	49	4
Great Britain	3	1	0	2	50	46	2
New Zealand	3	0	0	3	36	84	0

Play off final

10 Jun.	A	20 Fr	2	Sydney	54,290

1970 in England   *Winners:* Australia

21 Oct.	A	47 NZ	11	Wigan	9,586
24 Oct.	GB	11 A	4	Leeds	15,084
25 Oct.	NZ	16 Fr	15	Hull	3,824
28 Oct.	GB	6 Fr	0	Castleford	8,958
31 Oct.	GB	27 NZ	17	Swinton	5,609
1 Nov.	Fr	17 A	15	Bradford	6,215

Final Table

	P.	W.	D.	L.	F.	A.	Pts.
Great Britain	3	3	0	0	44	21	6
Australia	3	1	0	2	66	39	2
France	3	1	0	2	32	37	2
New Zealand	3	1	0	2	44	89	2

Play off Final

7 Nov.	A	12 GB	7	Leeds	18,776

301

1972 in France   Winners: Great Britain

28 Oct.	Fr	20 NZ	9	Marseilles	20,748
29 Oct.	GB	27 A	21	Perpignan	6,324
1 Nov.	A	9 NZ	5	Paris	8,000
1 Nov.	GB	13 Fr	4	Grenoble	5,321
4 Nov.	GB	53 NZ	19	Pau	7,500
5 Nov.	A	31 Fr	9	Toulouse	10,332

Final Table

	P.	W.	D.	L.	F.	A.	Pts.
Great Britain	3	3	0	0	93	44	6
Australia	3	2	0	1	61	41	4
France	3	1	0	2	33	53	2
New Zealand	3	0	0	3	33	82	0

Play off Final

| 11 Nov. | GB | 10 A | 10 | Lyon | 4,231 |

No further score after extra-time so Great Britain took the championship because they had scored the greater number of points in the qualifying League table.

1977 in Australia
New Zealand   *Winners:* Australia

29 May	A	27 NZ	12	Auckland	18,000
5 June	GB	23 Fr	4	Auckland	10,000
11 June	A	21 Fr	9	Sydney	13,231
12 June	GB	30 NZ	12	C'church	7,000
18 June	A	19 GB	5	Brisbane	27,000
19 June	NZ	28 Fr	20	Auckland	8,000

Final Table

	P.	W.	D.	L.	F.	A.	Pts.
Australia	3	3	0	0	67	26	6
Great Britain	3	2	0	1	58	35	4
New Zealand	3	1	0	2	52	77	2
France	3	0	0	3	33	72	0

Play off Final

| 25 June | A | 13 GB | 12 | Sydney | 24,457 |

● For details of the 1975 World Championship see ENGLAND AND WALES section.

GREAT BRITAIN REPRESENTATION CLUB-BY-CLUB

Only six of last season's clubs have not had a player selected for Great Britain in Test or World Cup matches — Blackpool Borough, Bramley and Doncaster, plus newcomers Carlisle, Mansfield Marksman and Sheffield Eagles. Of the extinct clubs only Broughton Rangers (later Belle Vue Rangers), Merthyr Tydfil, St. Helens Recs and the old Runcorn had players selected for Britain.

Wigan hold the record for most players selected with a remarkable number of 70. Of those players, seven once lined up in a Test together — another record. They were backs Martin Ryan, Gordon Ratcliffe, Ernie Ashcroft, Jack Hilton and Tommy Bradshaw; plus forwards Ken Gee and Joe Egan. Hilton scored both Britain's tries in the 6-4 victory over Australia at Sydney on 12 June, 1950.

Mick Sullivan gained Test honours with four clubs — Huddersfield (16), Wigan (19), St. Helens (10) and York (1). Billy Boston gained the most Test honours with a single club, making all 31 of his appearances for Britain while with Wigan.

The following is a club-by-club register of Great Britain players. The figure in brackets after a player's name is the number of Great Britain appearances he made while serving the club under whose entry he is listed, and the number after the + sign indicates playing substitute. This is followed by the time span between his first and last British cap while at that club.

BARROW (19 players)
W. Burgess (16) 1924-29
W. Burgess (13) 1962-68
D. Cairns (2) 1984
C. Camilleri (2) 1980
C. Carr (7) 1924-26
F. Castle (4) 1952-54
R. Francis (1) 1947
H. Gifford (2) 1908
D. Goodwin (5) 1957-58
J. Grundy (12) 1955-57
P. Hogan (4 + 1) 1977-78
W. Horne (8) 1946-52
P. Jackson (27) 1954-58
J. Jones (1) 1946
B. Knowelden (1) 1946
E. Szymala (1 + 1) 1981
E. Toohey (3) 1952
L. Λ. Troup (2) 1936
J. Woods (1) 1933

BATLEY (4 players)
N. Field (1) 1963
F. Gallagher (8) 1924-26
C. Gibson (+ 1) 1985
J. Oliver (4) 1928

BRADFORD NORTHERN (26 players)
D. Barends (2) 1979
E. Batten (4) 1946-47
I. Brooke (5) 1966
L. Casey (5) 1979
W. T. H. Davies (3) 1946-47
A. Fisher (8) 1970-78
T. Foster (3) 1946-48
J. Grayshon (11) 1979-82
E. Hanley (10 + 1) 1984-85
R. Jasiewicz (1) 1984
J. Kitching (1) 1946
A. Mann (2) 1908
K. Mumby (11) 1982-84
B. Noble (11) 1982-84
T. Price (1) 1970
J. Rae (1) 1965
W. Ramsey (+ 1) 1974
A. Rathbone (4 + 1) 1982-85
A. Redfearn (1) 1979
D. Redfearn (6 + 1) 1972-74
T. Smales (3) 1965
H. Smith (2) 1926
J. Thompson (1) 1978
K. Traill (8) 1950-54
E. Ward (20) 1946-52
F. Whitcombe (2) 1946

BROUGHTON/BELLE VUE RANGERS (8 players)
W. Bentham (2) 1924
L. Clampitt (3) 1907-14
E. Gwyther (6) 1947-51
A. Hogg (1) 1907
S. McCormick (2) 1948
D. Phillips (1) 1950
J. Price (2) 1921
J. Ruddick (3) 1907-10

CASTLEFORD (21 players)
A. Atkinson (11) 1929-36
K. Beardmore (+ 1) 1984
W. Bryant (4 + 1) 1964-67
A. Croston (1) 1937
B. Cunniffe (1) 1937
W. J. Davies (1) 1933
D. Edwards (3 + 2) 1968-71
A. Hardisty (12) 1964-70
D. Hartley (9) 1968-70
K. Hepworth (11) 1967-70
J. Joyner (14 + 2) 1978-84
B. Lockwood (7) 1972-74
A. Marchant (1) 1986
R. Millward (1) 1966
S. Norton (2 + 1) 1974
M. Reilly (9) 1970
P. Small (1) 1962
G. Stephens (5) 1979
D. Walton (1) 1965
J. Ward (3) 1963-64
K. Ward (1) 1984

DEWSBURY (6 players)
A. Bates (2 + 2) 1974
F. Gallagher (4) 1920-21
J. Ledgard (2) 1947
R. Pollard (1) 1950
M. Stephenson (5 + 1) 1971-72
H. Street (4) 1950

FEATHERSTONE ROVERS (13 players)
T. Askin (6) 1928
K. Bridges (3) 1974
T. Clawson (2) 1962
M. Dixon (2) 1962-64
S. Evans (5 + 3) 1979-80
Deryck Fox (7) 1985-86
Don Fox (1) 1963
D. Hobbs (7 + 1) 1984
G. Jordan (2) 1964-67
A. Morgan (4) 1968
S. Nash (16) 1971-74
P. Smith (1 + 5) 1977-84
J. Thompson (19 + 1) 1970-77

FULHAM (1 player)
J. Dalgreen (1) 1982

HALIFAX (28 players)
A. Ackerley (2) 1952-58
A. Bassett (2) 1946
J. Beames (2) 1921
N. Bentham (2) 1929
H. Beverley (2) 1937
O. Burgham (1) 1911
A. Daniels (3) 1952-55
W. T. Davies (1) 1911
C. Dixon (1) 1968
P. Eccles (1) 1907
T. Fogerty (+ 1) 1966
A. Halmshaw (1) 1971
N. James (1) 1986
R. Lloyd (1) 1920
A. Milnes (2) 1920
S. Prosser (1) 1914
D. Rees (1) 1926
C. Renilson (7 + 1) 1965-68
J. Riley (1) 1910
K. Roberts (10) 1963-66
A. Robinson (3) 1907-08
D. Schofield (1) 1955
J. Shaw (5) 1960-62
J. C. Stacey (1) 1920
J. Thorley (4) 1954
J. Wilkinson (6) 1954-55
F. Williams (2) 1914
D. Willicombe (1) 1974

HUDDERSFIELD (24 players)
J. Bowden (3) 1954
K. Bowman (3) 1962-63
B. Briggs (1) 1954
S. Brogden (9) 1929-33
J. Chilcott (3) 1914
D. Clark (11) 1911-20
D. Close (1) 1967
R. Cracknell (2) 1951
J. Davies (2) 1911
F. Dyson (1) 1959
B. Gronow (7) 1911-20
F. Longstaff (2) 1914
K. Loxton (1) 1971
S. Moorhouse (2) 1914
R. Nicholson (3) 1946-48
J. Rogers (7) 1914-21
K. Senior (2) 1965-67
T. Smales (5) 1962-64
M. Sullivan (16) 1954-57
G. Thomas (8) 1920-21
D. Valentine (15) 1948-54
R. Valentine (1) 1967
H. Wagstaff (12) 1911-21
H. Young (1) 1929

HULL (30 players)
W. Batten (1) 1921
H. Bowman (8) 1924-29
F. Boylen (1) 1908
R. Coverdale (4) 1954
M. Crane (1) 1982
L. Crooks (7+2) 1982-86
A. Dannatt (2) 1985
G. Divorty (2) 1985
J. Drake (1) 1960
W. Drake (1) 1962
S. Evans (2) 1982
V. Farrar (1) 1978
R. Gemmell (2) 1968-69
T. E. Gwynne (3) 1928-29
T. Harris (25) 1954-60
M. Harrison (7) 1967-73
W. Holder (1) 1907
A. Keegan (9) 1966-69
E. Morgan (2) 1921
S. Norton (9) 1978-82
W. Proctor (+1) 1984
P. Rose (1) 1982
G. Schofield (10) 1984-86
T. Skerrett (6) 1980-82
W. Stone (8) 1920-21
C. Sullivan (17) 1967-73
H. Taylor (3) 1907
R. Taylor (2) 1921-26
D. Topliss (1) 1982
J. Whiteley (15) 1957-62

HULL KINGSTON ROVERS (25 players)
C. Burton (6+1) 1982-85
A. Burwell (7+1) 1967-69
L. Casey (7+2) 1977-83
G. Clark (3) 1984-85
A. Dockar (1) 1947
G. Fairbairn (3) 1981-82
J. Feetham (1) 1929
P. Flanagan (14) 1962-70
F. Foster (1) 1967
D. Hall (2) 1984
P. Harkin (+1) 1985
S. Hartley (3) 1980-81
P. Hogan (2+2) 1979
R. Holdstock (2) 1980
W. Holliday (8+1) 1964-67
D. Laws (1) 1986
B. Lockwood (1+1) 1978-79
P. Lowe (12) 1970-78
R. Millward (27+1) 1967-78
H. Poole (1) 1964
P. Rose (1+3) 1974-78
M. Smith (10+1) 1979-84
B. Tyson (3) 1963-67
D. Watkinson (9+1) 1979-86
C. Young (5) 1967-68

Leeds utility star John Holmes, holder of 20 Great Britain caps.

HUNSLET (23 players)
W. Batten (9) 1907-11
H. Beverley (4) 1936-37
A. Burnell (3) 1951-54
H. Crowther (1) 1929
J. Evans (4) 1951-52
K. Eyre (1) 1965
B. Gabbitas (1) 1959
G. Gunney (11) 1954-65
D. Hartley (2) 1964
J. Higson (2) 1908
D. Jenkins (1) 1929
A. Jenkinson (2) 1911
W. Jukes (6) 1908-10
B. Prior (1) 1966
W. Ramsey (7) 1965-66
B. Shaw (5) 1956-60
G. Shelton (7) 1964-66
F. Smith (9) 1910-14
S. Smith (4) 1954
C. Thompson (2) 1951
L. White (7) 1932-33
R. Williams (3) 1954
H. Wilson (3) 1907

KEIGHLEY (1 player)
T. Hollindrake (1) 1955

LEEDS (60 players)
L. Adams (1) 1932
J. Atkinson (26) 1968-80
J. Bacon (11) 1920-26
R. Batten (3) 1969-73
J. Birch (1) 1907
S. Brogden (7) 1936-37
J. Brough (5) 1928-36
G. Brown (6) 1954-55
M. Clark (5) 1968
T. Clawson (3) 1972
D. Creasser (2) 1985
W. A. Davies (2) 1914
K. Dick (2) 1980
R. Dickinson (2) 1985
L. Dyl (11) 1974-82
A. Fisher (3) 1970-71
R. Gemmell (1) 1964
J. Grayshon (2) 1985
R. Haigh (3+1) 1970-71
D. Hallas (2) 1961
F. Harrison (3) 1911
D. Heron (1+1) 1982
J. Holmes (14+6) 1971-82
S. Hynes (12+1) 1970-73
J. W. Jarman (2) 1914
D. Jeanes (3) 1972
D. Jenkins (1) 1947
B. L. Jones (15) 1954-57
K. Jubb (2) 1937
J. Lowe (1) 1932
I. Owens (4) 1946
S. Pitchford (4) 1977
H. Poole (2) 1966
R. Powell (+1) 1985
D. Prosser (1) 1937
Keith Rayne (4) 1984
Kevin Rayne (1) 1986
B. Risman (5) 1968
D. Robinson (5) 1956-60
D. Rose (4) 1954
B. Seabourne (1) 1970
B. Shaw (1) 1961
M. Shoebottom (10+2) 1968-71
B. Simms (1) 1962
A. Smith (10) 1970-73
S. Smith (10) 1929-33
J. Stevenson (15) 1955-58
S. Stockwell (3) 1920-21
A. Terry (1) 1962
A. Thomas (4) 1926-29
P. Thomas (1) 1907
J. Thompson (12) 1924-32
A. Turnbull (1) 1951
D. Ward (12) 1977-82
W. Ward (1) 1910
F. Webster (3) 1910
R. Williams (9) 1948-51
H. Woods (1) 1937
G. Wriglesworth (5) 1965-66
F. Young (1) 1908

Oldham loose forward Terry Flanagan capped four times.

LEIGH (19 players)
K. Ashcroft (5) 1968-70
J. Cartwright (7) 1920-21
D. Chisnall (2) 1970
J. Darwell (5) 1924
S. Donlan (+2) 1984
D. Drummond (22) 1980-86
P. Foster (3) 1955
C. Johnson (1) 1985
F. Kitchen (2) 1954
J. Ledgard (9) 1948-54
G. Lewis (1) 1965
M. Martyn (2) 1958-59
W. Mooney (2) 1924
S. Owen (1) 1958
C. Pawsey (7) 1952-54
W. Robinson (2) 1963
Joe Walsh (1) 1971
W. Winstanley (2) 1910
J. Woods (7+3) 1979-83

MERTHYR TYDFIL (1 player)
D. Jones (2) 1907

OLDHAM (38 players)
A. Avery (4) 1910-11
C. Bott (1) 1966
A. Brough (2) 1924
T. Clawson (9) 1973-74
A. Davies (20) 1955-60
E. Davies (3) 1920
T. Flanagan (4) 1983-84
D. Foy (3) 1984-85
B. Ganley (3) 1957-58
A. Goodway (11) 1983-85
W. Hall (4) 1914
H. Hilton (7) 1920-21
D. Holland (4) 1914
R. Irving (8+3) 1967-72
K. Jackson (2) 1957
E. Knapman (1) 1924
S. Little (10) 1956-58
T. Llewellyn (2) 1907
J. Lomas (2) 1911
W. Longworth (3) 1908
L. McIntyre (1) 1963
T. O'Grady (5) 1954
J. Oster (1) 1929
D. Parker (2) '1964
D. Phillips (3) 1946
F. Pitchford (2) 1958-62
T. Rees (1) 1929
S. Rix (9) 1924-26
R. Sloman (5) 1928
A. Smith (6) 1907-08
I. Southward (7) 1959-62
L. Thomas (1) 1947
D. Turner (11) 1956-58
G. Tyson (4) 1907-08
T. White (1) 1907
C. Winsdale (1) 1959
A. Wood (4) 1911-14
M. Worrall (3) 1984

ROCHDALE HORNETS (8 players)
J. Baxter (1) 1907
J. Bennett (6) 1924
J. Bowers (1) 1920
T. Fogerty (1) 1974
E. Jones (4) 1920
M. Price (2) 1967
J. Robinson (2) 1914
T. Woods (2) 1911

RUNCORN (2 players)
J. Jolley (3) 1907
R. Padbury (1) 1908

**RUNCORN HIGHFIELD/
HUYTON/LIVERPOOL/WIGAN
HIGHFIELD (4 players)**
R. Ashby (1) 1964
W. Belshaw (6) 1936-37
N. Bentham (6) 1928
H. Woods (5) 1936

ST. HELENS (42 players)
C. Arkwright (+2) 1985
L. Aston (3) 1947
W. Benyon (5+1) 1971-72
T. Bishop (15) 1966-69
F. Carlton (1) 1958
E. Chisnall (4) 1974
E. Cunningham (1) 1978
R. Dagnall (4) 1961-65
D. Eckersley (2+2) 1973-74
A. Ellaby (13) 1928-33
L. Fairclough (6) 1926-29
A. Fildes (4) 1932
A. Frodsham (3) 1928-29
P. Gorley (2+1) 1980-81
D. Greenall (6) 1951-54
M. Hicks (1) 1965
N. Holding (4) 1984
R. Huddart (12) 1959-63
L. Jones (1) 1971
A. Karalius (4+1) 1971-72
V. Karalius (10) 1958-61
K. Kelly (2) 1972
B. Ledger (1) 1985
J. Mantle (13) 1966-73
S. McCormick (1) 1948
T. McKinney (1) 1957
R. Mathias (1) 1979
G. Moses (9) 1955-57
A. Murphy (26) 1958-66
F. Myler (9) 1970
G. Nicholls (22) 1973-79
H. Pinner (5+1) 1980-86
A. Platt (+2) 1985-86
A. Prescott (28) 1951-58
A. Rhodes (6) 1957-61
J. Stott (1) 1947
M. Sullivan (10) 1961-62
J. Tembey (2) 1963-64
A. Terry (10) 1958-61
John Walsh (4+1) 1972
J. Warlow (3+1) 1964-68
C. Watson (29+1) 1963-71

ST. HELENS RECS (5 players)
F. Bowen (3) 1928
A. Fildes (11) 1926-29
J. Greenall (1) 1921
J. Owen (1) 1921
J. Wallace (1) 1926

SALFORD (27 players)
W. Burgess (1) 1969
P. Charlton (17+1) 1970-74
M. Coulman (2+1) 1971
G. Curran (6) 1946-48
E. Curzon (1) 1910
T. Danby (3) 1950
C. Dixon (11+2) 1969-74
A. Edwards (7) 1936-37
J. Feetham (7) 1932-33
K. Fielding (3) 1974-77
K. Gill (5+2) 1974-77
J. Gore (1) 1926
C. Hesketh (21+2) 1970-74
B. Hudson (8) 1932-37
E. Jenkins (9) 1933-37
J. Lomas (5) 1908-10
T. McKinney (7) 1951-54
A. Middleton (1) 1929
S. Nash (8) 1977-82
M. Richards (2) 1974
A. Risman (17) 1932-46
J. Spencer (1) 1907
J. Ward (1) 1970
S. Warwick (2) 1907
D. Watkins (2+4) 1971-74
W. Watkins (7) 1933-37
W. Williams (2) 1929-32

SWINTON (15 players)
T. Armitt (8) 1933-37
A. Buckley (7) 1963-66
F. Butters (2) 1929
W. Davies (1) 1968
B. Evans (10) 1926-33
F. Evans (4) 1924
J. Evans (3) 1926
K. Gowers (14) 1962-66
H. Halsall (1) 1929
M. Hodgson (16) 1929-37
R. Morgan (2) 1963
W. Rees (11) 1926-29
D. Robinson (12) 1965-67
J. Stopford (12) 1961-66
J. Wright (1) 1932

**WAKEFIELD TRINITY
(22 players)**
I. Brooke (8) 1967-68
N. Fox (29) 1959-69
R. Haigh (2) 1968-70
W. Horton (14) 1928-33
D. Jeanes (5) 1971-72
B. Jones (3) 1964-66
H. Kershaw (2) 1910
F. Mortimer (2) 1956
H. Murphy (1) 1950
H. Newbould (1) 1910
J. Parkin (17) 1920-29
C. Pollard (1) 1924
E. Pollard (2) 1932

H. Poynton (3) 1962
D. Robinson (5) 1954-55
G. Round (8) 1959-62
T. Skerrett (4) 1979
S. Smith (1) 1929
D. Topliss (3) 1973-79
D. Turner (13) 1959-62
D. Vines (3) 1959
J. Wilkinson (7) 1959-62

WARRINGTON (38 players)
J. Arkwright (6) 1936-37
K. Ashcroft (+1) 1974
W. Aspinall (1) 1966
W. Belshaw (2) 1937
N. Bentham (2) 1929
J. Bevan (6) 1974-78
T. Blinkhorn (1) 1929
E. Brooks (3) 1908
J. Challinor (3) 1958-60
N. Courtney (+1) 1982
W. Cunliffe (11) 1920-26
G. Dickenson (1) 1908
W. Dingsdale (3) 1929-33
R. Duane (3) 1983-84
R. Eccles (1) 1982
J. Featherstone (6) 1948-52
E. Fraser (16) 1958-61
L. Gilfedder (5) 1962-63
R. Greenough (1) 1960
G. Helme (12) 1948-54
K. Holden (1) 1963
A. Johnson (6) 1946-47
K. Kelly (2) 1980-82
T. McKinney (3) 1955
J. Miller (6) 1933-36
A. Murphy (1) 1971
A. Naughton (2) 1954
T. O'Grady (1) 1961
H. Palin (2) 1947
K. Parr (1) 1968
A. Pimblett (3) 1948
R. Price (9) 1954-57
R. Ryan (5) 1950-52
R. Ryder (1) 1952
F. Shugars (1) 1910
G. Skelhorne (7) 1920-21
G. Thomas (1) 1907
D. Whitehead (3) 1971

WHITEHAVEN (5 players)
V. Gribbin (1) 1985
W. Holliday (1) 1964
R. Huddart (4) 1958
P. Kitchin (1) 1965
A. Walker (1) 1980

WIDNES (32 players)
M. Adams (11+2) 1979-84
J. Basnett (1) 1984
K. Bentley (1) 1980
M. Burke (14+1) 1980-86
F. Collier (1) 1964
R. Dutton (6) 1970
K. Elwell (3) 1977-80
J. Fieldhouse (5) 1985-86
R. French (4) 1968
L. Gorley (4+1) 1980-82
A. Gregory (8+1) 1981-84
I. Hare (1) 1967
F. Higgins (6) 1950-51
H. Higgins (2) 1937
E. Hughes (8) 1978-82
A. Johnson (4) 1914-20
G. Kemel (2) 1965
V. Karalius (2) 1963
D. Laughton (4) 1973-79
J. Lydon (9+1) 1983-85
T. McCue (6) 1936-46
J. Measures (2) 1963
J. Mills (6) 1974-79
A. Myler (11) 1983-86
F. Myler (14+1) 1960-67
G. Nicholls (7) 1971-72
D. O'Neill (2+1) 1971-72
M. O'Neill (3) 1982-83
G. Shaw (1) 1980
N. Silcock (12) 1932-37
J. Warlow (3) 1971
S. Wright (7) 1977-78

WIGAN (70 players)
R. Ashby (1) 1965
E. Ashcroft (11) 1947-54
E. Ashton (26) 1957-63
W. Ashurst (3) 1971-72
F. Barton (1) 1951
J. Barton (2) 1960-61
J. Bennett (1) 1926
D. Bevan (1) 1952
W. Blan (3) 1951
D. Bolton (23) 1957-63
W. Boston (31) 1954-63
T. Bradshaw (6) 1947-50
F. Carlton (1) 1962
B. Case (4) 1984
W. Cherrington (1) 1960
C. Clarke (7) 1965-73
A. Coldrick (4) 1914
F. Collier (1) 1963
J. Cunliffe (4) 1950-54
S. Edwards (2+1) 1985
J. Egan (14) 1946-50
R. Evans (4) 1961-62
G. Fairbairn (14) 1977-80
T. Fogerty (1) 1967
P. Ford (1) 1985
W. Francis (4) 1967-77

D. Gardiner (1) 1965
K. Gee (17) 1946-51
H. Gill (5) 1981-86
A. Goodway (3) 1985
J. Gray (5 + 3) 1974
E. Hanley (4) 1985-86
C. Hill (1) 1966
D. Hill (1) 1971
J. Hilton (4) 1950
T. Howley (6) 1924
W. Hudson (1) 1948
D. Hurcombe (8) 1920-24
B. Jenkins (12) 1907-14
K. Jones (2) 1970
R. Kinnear (1) 1929
N. Kiss (1) 1985
D. Laughton (11) 1970-71
J. Lawrenson (3) 1948
J. Leytham (5) 1907-10
J. Lydon (1) 1986
B. McTigue (25) 1958-63
J. Miller (1) 1911

J. Morley (2) 1936-37
I. Potter (5) 1985-86
J. Price (4) 1924
R. Ramsdale (8) 1910-14
G. Ratcliffe (3) 1947-50
J. Ring (2) 1924-26
D. Robinson (1) 1970
M. Ryan (4) 1947-50
W. Sayer (7) 1961-63
J. Sharrock (4) 1910-11
N. Silcock (3) 1954
R. Silcock (1) 1908
D. Stephenson (2) 1982
J. Sullivan (25) 1924-33
M. Sullivan (19) 1957-60
G. Thomas (1) 1914
J. Thomas (8) 1907-11
S. Wane (2) 1985-86
E. Ward (3) 1946-47
L. White (2) 1947
D. Willicombe (2) 1974
W. Winstanley (3) 1911

WORKINGTON TOWN
(9 players)
E. Bowman (4) 1977
P. Charlton (1) 1965
B. Edgar (11) 1958-66
N. Herbert (6) 1961-62
W. Martin (1) 1962
V. McKeating (2) 1951
A. Pepperell (2) 1950-51
I. Southward (4) 1958
G. Wilson (3) 1951

YORK (7 players)
E. Dawson (1) 1956
H. Field (3) 1936
G. Smith (3) 1963-64
J. Stevenson (4) 1959-60
M. Sullivan (1) 1963
B. Watts (5) 1954-55
L. White (4) 1946

GREAT BRITAIN TEAMS
. . . A 20-year review

The following is a compendium of Great Britain Test and World Cup teams since the 1966-67 season.

Initials are included where more than one celebrated player shared a surname in the same era. Only playing substitutes are included on the teamsheet.

(WC): World Cup   t: try   g: goal
dg: drop goal   * captain

1966 France
Wigan: 5 March
Lost 4-8

Gowers (Swinton) 2g
Burgess, W (Barrow)
Shelton (Hunslet)
Buckley (Swinton)
Stopford (Swinton)
Millward (Castleford)
*Murphy, A (St. Helens)
Bott (Oldham)
Prior (Hunslet)
Watson (St. Helens)
Ramsey (Hunslet)
Mantle (St. Helens)
Robinson, D (Swinton)
Sub: Holliday (Hull KR)

1966 Australia
Sydney: 25 June
Won 17-13

Keegan (Hull) 3g
Burgess, W (Barrow) 1t
Brooke (Bradford)
Buckley (Swinton)
Stopford (Swinton)
Hardisty (Castleford) 1t
Bishop (St. Helens) 1g
*Edgar (Workington)
Flanagan (Hull KR)
Watson (St. Helens) 1t
Bryant (Castleford)
Mantle (St. Helens)
Robinson, D (Swinton)

1966 France
Perpignan: 16 Jan
Lost 13-18

Gowers (Swinton)
Jones, B (Wakefield) 1t
Shelton (Hunslet)
*Fox, N (Wakefield) 2g
Stopford (Swinton) 1t
Hill, C (Wigan)
Murphy, A (St. Helens) 1t
Roberts (Halifax)
Clarke (Wigan)
Watson (St. Helens)
Holliday (Hull KR)
Mantle (St. Helens)
Robinson, D (Swinton)

1966 Australia
Brisbane: 16 July
Lost 4-6

Keegan (Hull) 2g
Burgess, W (Barrow)
Brooke (Bradford)
Myler (Widnes)
Wriglesworth (Leeds)
Hardisty (Castleford)
Bishop (St. Helens)
*Edgar (Workington)
Flanagan (Hull KR)
Watson (St. Helens)
Ramsey (Hunslet)
Mantle (St. Helens)
Robinson, D (Swinton)

1966 Australia
Sydney: 23 July
Lost 14-19
Gowers (Swinton) 4g
Burgess, W (Barrow)
Brooke (Bradford)
Buckley (Swinton)
Wriglesworth (Leeds)
Hardisty (Castleford) 2t
Bishop (St. Helens)
*Edgar (Workington)
Flanagan (Hull KR)
Watson (St. Helens)
Ramsey (Hunslet)
Mantle (St. Helens)
Robinson, D (Swinton)
Sub: Bryant (Castleford)

1966 New Zealand
Auckland: 6 Aug
Won 25-8
Gowers (Swinton) 5g
Burgess, W (Barrow) 1t
Brooke (Bradford) 1t
Buckley (Swinton)
Wriglesworth (Leeds)
Hardisty (Castleford)
Bishop (St. Helens)
Roberts (Halifax)
Clarke (Wigan) 1t
Watson (St. Helens) 1t
Ramsey (Hunslet)
*Poole (Leeds)
Robinson, D (Swinton)
Sub: Myler (Widnes) 1t

1966 New Zealand
Auckland: 20 Aug
Won 22-14
Gowers (Swinton) 5g
Burgess, W (Barrow) 1t
Brooke (Bradford) 2t
Myler (Widnes)
Wriglesworth (Leeds)
Aspinall (Warrington) 1t
Bishop (St. Helens)
Roberts (Halifax)
Flanagan (Hull KR)
Watson (St. Helens)
Ramsey (Hunslet)
*Poole (Leeds)
Robinson, D (Swinton)
Sub: Fogerty (Halifax)

1967 France
Carcassonne: 22 Jan
Won 16-13
Keegan (Hull)
Hare (Widnes)
Myler (Widnes)
Fox, N (Wakefield) 2g
Sullivan, C (Hull) 2t
*Hardisty (Castleford) 2t
Hepworth (Castleford)
Harrison, M (Hull)
Clarke (Wigan)
Tyson, B (Hull KR)
Irving (Oldham)
Fogerty (Wigan)
Robinson, D (Swinton)

1967 France
Wigan: 4 March
Lost 13-23
Keegan (Hull) 1t
Burgess, W (Barrow)
Myler (Widnes)
Fox, N (Wakefield) 2g
Senior (Huddersfield)
*Hardisty (Castleford) 1t
Hepworth (Castleford)
Harrison, M (Hull)
Close (Huddersfield)
Watson (St. Helens)
Irving (Oldham)
Bryant (Castleford)
Robinson, D (Swinton) 1t

1967 Australia
Leeds: 21 Oct
Won 16-11
Keegan (Hull)
Young, C (Hull KR) 1t
Brooke (Wakefield)
Price, M (Rochdale)
Burgess (Barrow)
Millward (Hull KR) 3g,1t
Bishop (St. Helens) 1g
*Holliday (Hull KR) 1g
Flanagan (Hull KR)
Watson (St. Helens)
Irving (Oldham)
Mantle (St. Helens)
Robinson, D (Swinton)

1967 Australia
White City (London): 3 Nov
Lost 11-17
Keegan (Hull)
Young, C (Hull KR)
Brooke (Wakefield)
Fox, N (Wakefield) 3g
Francis, W (Wigan)
Millward (Hull KR)
Bishop (St. Helens) 1t,1g
*Holliday (Hull KR)
Flanagan (Hull KR)
Watson (St. Helens)
Irving (Oldham)
Mantle (St. Helens)
Foster, F (Hull KR)

1967 Australia
Swinton: 9 Dec
Lost 3-11
Keegan (Hull)
Young, C (Hull KR)
Brooke (Wakefield)
Price, M (Rochdale) 1t
Jordan (Featherstone)
Millward (Hull KR)
Bishop (St. Helens)
*Holliday (Hull KR)
Flanagan (Hull KR)
Watson (St. Helens)
Irving (Oldham)
Valentine, R (Huddersfield)
Robinson, D (Swinton)
Sub: Burwell (Hull KR)
      Renilson (Halifax)

1968 France
Paris: 11 Feb
Won 22-13
Risman, B (Leeds) 5g,2t
Young, C (Hull KR)
Brooke (Wakefield)
*Fox, N (Wakefield)
Burwell (Hull KR) 1t
Millward (Hull KR) 1t
Bishop (St. Helens)
Clark, M (Leeds)
Flanagan (Hull KR)
Watson (St. Helens)
French (Widnes)
Morgan, A (Featherstone)
Renilson (Halifax)
Sub: Edwards, D (Castleford)

1968 France
Bradford: 2 March
Won 19-8
Risman, B (Leeds) 2g
Young, C (Hull KR) 1t
Brooke (Wakefield)
*Fox, N (Wakefield)
Burwell (Hull KR) 2t
Millward (Hull KR) 1t
Bishop (St. Helens)
Clark, M (Leeds)
Flanagan (Hull KR)
Watson (St. Helens)
French (Widnes)
Morgan, A (Featherstone) 1t
Renilson (Halifax)

1968 Australia (WC)
Sydney: 25 May
Lost 10-25
*Risman, B (Leeds) 2g
Brooke (Wakefield) 1t
Burwell (Hull KR)
Shoebottom (Leeds)
Sullivan, C (Hull) 1t
Millward (Hull KR)
Bishop (St. Helens)
Clark, M (Leeds)
Ashcroft, K (Leigh)
Watson (St. Helens)
French (Widnes)
Haigh (Wakefield)
Renilson (Halifax)

1968 France (WC)
Auckland: 2 June
Lost 2-7
*Risman, B (Leeds) 1g
Sullivan, C (Hull)
Brooke (Wakefield)
Burwell (Hull KR)
Atkinson, J (Leeds)
Millward (Hull KR)
Bishop (St. Helens)
Clark, M (Leeds)
Flanagan (Hull KR)
Watson (St. Helens)
Morgan, A (Featherstone)
Haigh (Wakefield)
Renilson (Halifax)
Sub: Warlow (St. Helens)

1968 New Zealand (WC)
Sydney: 8 June
Won 38-14
*Risman, B (Leeds) 7g
Sullivan, C (Hull) 3t
Brooke (Wakefield) 1t
Burwell (Hull KR) 2t
Atkinson, J (Leeds)
Millward (Hull KR)
Bishop (St. Helens)
Clark, M (Leeds)
Flanagan (Hull KR)
Warlow (St. Helens)
French (Widnes)
Morgan, A (Featherstone) 1t
Renilson (Halifax)
Sub: Shoebottom (Leeds) 1t
Watson (St. Helens)

1968 France
St. Helens: 30 Nov
Won 34-10
Keegan (Hull)
Burgess, W (Barrow) 3t
Fox, N (Wakefield) 5g
Gemmell (Hull) 2t
Burwell (Hull KR) 1t
Davies, W (Swinton)
*Bishop (St. Helens)
Hartley, D (Castleford)
Ashcroft, K (Leigh) 1t
Warlow (St. Helens)
Dixon, C (Halifax) 1t
Parr (Warrington)
Renilson (Halifax)

1969 France
Toulouse: 2 Feb
Lost 9-13
Keegan (Hull)
Burgess, W (Salford)
Fox, N (Wakefield) 3g
Gemmell (Hull)
Burwell (Hull KR)
Shoebottom (Leeds)
*Bishop (St. Helens)
Hartley, D (Castleford)
Ashcroft, K (Leigh)
Watson (St. Helens)
Dixon, C (Salford) 1t
Mantle (St. Helens)
Batten, R (Leeds)

1970 Australia
Brisbane: 6 June
Lost 15-37
Price, T (Bradford) 3g
Sullivan, C (Hull)
*Myler (St. Helens)
Shoebottom (Leeds)
Atkinson, J (Leeds)
Hardisty (Castleford)
Hepworth (Castleford)
Chisnall, D (Leigh)
Flanagan (Hull KR) 1t
Watson (St. Helens) 1t
Laughton (Wigan) 1t
Robinson, D (Wigan)
Reilly (Castleford)
Sub: Irving (Oldham)

1970 Australia
Sydney: 20 June
Won 28-7
Edwards, D (Castleford)
Smith, A (Leeds)
Hynes (Leeds) 1g
*Myler (St. Helens)
Atkinson, J (Leeds) 1t
Millward (Hull KR) 7g,2t
Hepworth (Castleford)
Hartley, D (Castleford)
Fisher (Bradford) 1t
Watson (St. Helens)
Laughton (Wigan)
Thompson, J (Featherstone)
Reilly (Castleford)
Sub: Shoebottom (Leeds)

1970 Australia
Sydney: 4 July
Won 21-17
Shoebottom (Leeds)
Smith, A (Leeds)
Hynes (Leeds) 1t
*Myler (St. Helens)
Atkinson, J (Leeds) 2t
Millward (Hull KR) 3g,1t
Hepworth (Castleford)
Hartley, D (Castleford) 1t
Fisher (Bradford)
Watson (St. Helens)
Laughton (Wigan)
Thompson, J (Featherstone)
Reilly (Castleford)

1970 New Zealand
Auckland: 11 July
Won 19-15
Shoebottom (Leeds)
Smith, A (Leeds)
Hynes (Leeds) 2g,1t
*Myler (St. Helens)
Atkinson, J (Leeds) 1t
Millward (Hull KR) 1t
Seabourne (Leeds)
Hartley, D (Castleford)
Fisher (Bradford)
Watson (St. Helens)
Laughton (Wigan) 2t
Thompson, J (Featherstone)
Reilly (Castleford)

1970 New Zealand
Christchurch: 19 July
Won 23-9
Dutton (Widnes) 4g
Smith, A (Leeds)
Hynes (Leeds)
*Myler (St. Helens) 1t
Atkinson, J (Leeds)
Millward (Hull KR) 2t
Hepworth (Castleford)
Hartley, D (Castleford)
Fisher (Bradford)
Watson (St. Helens)
Laughton (Wigan) 1t
Thompson, J (Featherstone)
Reilly (Castleford) 1t

1970 New Zealand
Auckland: 25 July
Won 33-16
Dutton (Widnes) 5g
Smith, A (Leeds) 1t
Hesketh (Salford) 1t
*Myler (St. Helens)
Atkinson, J (Leeds)
Millward (Hull KR) 1g
Hepworth (Castleford) 1t
Watson (St. Helens) 1t
Fisher (Bradford)
Ward, J (Salford)
Irving (Oldham)
Lowe, P (Hull KR) 2t
Reilly (Castleford)
Sub: Hynes (Leeds) 1t

1970 Australia (WC)
Leeds: 24 Oct
Won 11-4
Dutton (Widnes) 3g
Smith, A (Leeds)
Hynes (Leeds) 1t,1g
*Myler (St. Helens)
Atkinson, J (Leeds)
Shoebottom (Leeds)
Hepworth (Castleford)
Hartley, D (Castleford)
Fisher (Bradford)
Watson (St. Helens)
Laughton (Wigan)
Thompson, J (Featherstone)
Reilly (Castleford)

1970 France (WC)
Castleford: 28 Oct
Won 6-0
Dutton (Widnes) 3g
Jones, K (Wigan)
Hynes (Leeds)
*Myler (St. Helens)
Atkinson, J (Leeds)
Shoebottom (Leeds)
Hepworth (Castleford)
Hartley, D (Castleford)
Ashcroft, K (Leigh)
Watson (St. Helens)
Laughton (Wigan)
Thompson, J (Featherstone)
Reilly (Castleford)

1970 New Zealand (WC)
Swinton: 31 Oct
Won 27-17
Dutton (Widnes) 6g
Jones, K (Wigan)
Hynes (Leeds) 1t
Hesketh (Salford) 1t
Atkinson, J (Leeds) 1t
Shoebottom (Leeds)
Hepworth (Castleford)
Chisnall, D (Leigh)
Ashcroft, K (Leigh)
Watson (St. Helens) 1t
Haigh (Leeds)
Thompson, J (Featherstone)
*Laughton (Wigan) 1t
Sub: Charlton (Salford)

1970 Australia (WC)
Leeds: 7 Nov
Lost 7-12
Dutton (Widnes) 1g
Smith, A (Leeds)
Hynes (Leeds) 1g
*Myler (St. Helens)
Atkinson, J (Leeds) 1t
Shoebottom (Leeds)
Hepworth (Castleford)
Hartley, D (Castleford)
Fisher (Leeds)
Watson (St. Helens)
Laughton (Wigan)
Thompson, J (Featherstone)
Reilly (Castleford)
Sub: Hesketh (Salford)
Haigh (Leeds)

1971 France
Toulouse: 7 Feb
Lost 8-16
Whitehead (Warrington) 1g
Smith, A (Leeds) 1t
*Hynes (Leeds)
Benyon (St. Helens)
Atkinson, J (Leeds)
Hill, D (Wigan)
Shoebottom (Leeds)
Jeanes (Wakefield) 1t
Fisher (Leeds)
Warlow (Widnes)
Mantle (St. Helens)
Haigh (Leeds)
Laughton (Wigan)
Sub: Hesketh (Salford)
Thompson, J (Featherstone)

1971 France
St. Helens: 17 March
Won 24-2
Whitehead (Warrington) 1t,3g
Smith, A (Leeds) 1t
Hesketh (Salford)
Benyon (St. Helens) 1t
Atkinson, J (Leeds)
Millward (Hull KR) 2t
Nash (Featherstone)
Warlow (Widnes)
Fisher (Leeds)
Watson (St. Helens)
Mantle (St. Helens)
Thompson, J (Featherstone) 1t
*Laughton (Wigan)
Sub: Watkins, D (Salford)
Coulman (Salford)

310

1971 New Zealand

Salford: 25 Sep

Lost 13-18

Whitehead (Warrington) 2g
Jones, L (St. Helens)
Benyon (St. Helens) 1t
Hesketh (Salford) 1t
Sullivan, C (Hull)
*Millward (Hull KR)
Nash (Featherstone)
Warlow (Widnes)
Karalius, A (St. Helens)
Jeanes (Wakefield)
Ashurst (Wigan) 1t
Coulman (Salford)
Mantle (St. Helens)
Sub: Edwards, D (Castleford)

1971 New Zealand

Castleford: 16 Oct

Lost 14-17

Edwards, D (Castleford)
Sullivan, C (Hull) 1t
Watkins, D (Salford) 1g
Hesketh (Salford)
Walsh, Joe (Leigh) 1t
*Millward (Hull KR) 1t
Murphy, A (Warrington)
Harrison, M (Hull)
Karalius, A (St. Helens)
Coulman (Salford) 1t
Dixon, C (Salford)
Mantle (St. Helens)
Haigh (Leeds)
Sub: Benyon (St. Helens)
     Stephenson, M (Dewsbury)

1971 New Zealand

Leeds: 6 Nov

Won 12-3

Edwards, D (Castleford)
Sullivan, C (Hull)
Hesketh (Salford)
Holmes (Leeds) 2g,2dg
Atkinson, J (Leeds) 2t
*Millward (Hull KR)
Loxton (Huddersfield)
Harrison, M (Hull)
Karalius, A (St. Helens)
Jeanes (Wakefield)
Irving (Oldham)
Nicholls (Widnes)
Halmshaw (Halifax)
Sub: O'Neill, D (Widnes)

1972 France

Toulouse: 6 Feb

Won 10-9

Charlton (Salford)
*Sullivan, C (Hull) 1t
Holmes (Leeds) 2g
Benyon (St. Helens) 1t
Atkinson, J (Leeds)
Kelly (St. Helens)
Nash (Featherstone)
Harrison, M (Hull)
Karalius, A (St. Helens)
Jeanes (Wakefield)
Ashurst (Wigan)
Lowe, P (Hull KR)
Nicholls (Widnes)

1972 France

Bradford: 12 March

Won 45-10

Charlton (Salford) 1t
*Sullivan, C (Hull) 1t
Holmes (Leeds) 1t,6g
Benyon (St. Helens) 1t
Atkinson, J (Leeds) 1t
Kelly (St. Helens)
Nash (Featherstone)
Harrison, M (Hull)
Stephenson, M (Dewsbury) 1t
Jeanes (Wakefield) 1t
Ashurst (Wigan) 2t
Lowe, P (Hull KR) 1t
Nicholls (Widnes)
Sub: Walsh, John (St. Helens) 1t
     Irving (Oldham)

1972 Australia (WC)

Perpignan: 29 Oct

Won 27-21

Charlton (Salford)
*Sullivan, C (Hull) 1t
Hesketh (Salford)
Walsh, John (St. Helens)
Atkinson, J (Leeds) 1t
O'Neill, D (Widnes) 1t
Nash (Featherstone)
Clawson (Leeds) 6g
Stephenson, M (Dewsbury) 1t
Jeanes (Leeds)
Lockwood (Castleford)
Lowe, P (Hull KR) 1t
Nicholls (Widnes)
Sub: Holmes (Leeds)

1972 France (WC)

Grenoble: 1 Nov

Won 13-4

Charlton (Salford)
*Sullivan, C (Hull) 1t
Hesketh (Salford)
Walsh, John (St. Helens)
Atkinson, J (Leeds)
O'Neill, D (Widnes)
Nash (Featherstone)
Clawson (Leeds) 2g
Stephenson, M (Dewsbury)
Lockwood, B (Castleford)
Dixon, C (Salford)
Lowe, P (Hull KR) 2t
Nicholls (Widnes)

1972 New Zealand (WC)

Pau: 4 Nov

Won 53-19

Charlton (Salford) 1t
*Sullivan, C (Hull) 1t
Hesketh (Salford) 1t
Walsh, John (St. Helens)
Atkinson, J (Leeds) 2t
Holmes (Leeds) 10g,2t
Nash (Featherstone) 1t
Jeanes (Leeds) 1t
Stephenson, M (Dewsbury) 1t
Lockwood (Castleford)
Irving (Oldham)
Lowe, P (Hull KR)
Nicholls (Widnes) 1t
Sub: Redfearn, D (Bradford)
     Karalius, A (St. Helens)

1972 Australia (WC)

Lyon: 11 Nov

Drew 10-10

Charlton (Salford)
*Sullivan, C (Hull) 1t
Hesketh (Salford)
Walsh, John (St. Helens)
Atkinson, J (Leeds)
Holmes (Leeds)
Nash (Featherstone)
Clawson (Leeds) 2g
Stephenson, M (Dewsbury) 1t
Jeanes (Leeds)
Lockwood, B (Castleford)
Lowe, P (Hull KR)
Nicholls (Widnes)
Sub: Irving (Oldham)

1973 Australia
Wembley: 3 Nov
Won 21-12
Charlton (Salford)
*Sullivan (Hull)
Hynes (Leeds)
Hesketh (Salford)
Atkinson, J (Leeds)
Topliss (Wakefield)
Nash (Featherstone) 1dg
Clawson (Oldham) 4g
Clarke (Wigan) 1t
Lockwood (Castleford) 1t
Nicholls (St. Helens)
Lowe, P (Hull KR) 2t
Batten (Leeds)

1974 France
Grenoble: 20 Jan
Won 24-5
Charlton (Salford)
Fielding (Salford) 3t
Willicombe (Halifax) 1t
Hesketh (Salford)
Redfearn, D (Bradford)
Gill, K (Salford) 1t
Bates, A (Dewsbury)
Clawson (Oldham) 3g
Bridges (Featherstone)
Lockwood (Castleford)
Dixon, C (Salford)
Nicholls (St. Helens)
*Laughton (Widnes) 1t
Sub: Watkins, D (Salford)
　　 Gray (Wigan)

1974 Australia
Sydney: 6 July
Won 16-11
Charlton (Salford)
Dyl (Leeds)
Eckersley (St. Helens)
*Hesketh (Salford)
Millward (Hull KR)
Gill, K (Salford) 1t
Nash (Featherstone)
Mills (Widnes)
Gray (Wigan) 3g,1dg
Thompson, J (Featherstone)
Dixon, C (Salford) 1t
Chisnall, E (St. Helens) 1t
Nicholls (St. Helens)
Sub: Norton (Castleford)

1973 Australia
Leeds: 24 Nov
Lost 6-14
Charlton (Salford)
*Sullivan (Hull)
Hynes (Leeds)
Hesketh (Salford)
Atkinson, J (Leeds)
Topliss (Wakefield)
Nash (Featherstone)
Clawson (Oldham) 3g
Clarke (Wigan)
Lockwood (Castleford)
Mantle (St. Helens)
Lowe, P (Hull KR)
Batten, R (Leeds)
Sub: Eckersley (St. Helens)
　　 Dixon, C (Salford)

1974 France
Wigan: 17 Feb
Won 29-0
Charlton (Salford) 2t
Fielding (Salford)
Willicombe (Wigan) 1t
Hesketh (Salford)
Redfearn, D (Bradford) 2t
Gill, K (Salford)
Bates, A (Dewsbury)
Clawson (Oldham) 2g
Bridges (Featherstone)
Fogerty (Rochdale)
Dixon, C (Salford)
Nicholls (St. Helens)
*Laughton (Widnes) 1t
Sub: Watkins, D (Salford) 1g
　　 Gray (Wigan) 1t,1g

1974 Australia
Sydney: 20 July
Lost 18-22
Charlton (Salford)
Richards (Salford) 1t
Dyl (Leeds) 1t
*Hesketh (Salford)
Bevan, J (Warrington)
Gill, K (Salford)
Nash (Featherstone)
Clawson (Oldham)
Gray (Wigan) 6g
Thompson, J (Featherstone)
Dixon, C (Salford)
Chisnall, E (St. Helens)
Nicholls (St. Helens)
Sub: Millward (Hull KR)
　　 Rose, P (Hull KR)

1973 Australia
Warrington: 1 Dec
Lost 5-15
Charlton (Salford)
Smith, A (Leeds)
Hynes (Leeds)
Hesketh (Salford)
*Sullivan, C (Hull)
Eckersley (St. Helens)
Millward (Hull KR) 1t,1g
Clawson (Oldham)
Clarke (Wigan)
Harrison, M (Hull)
Nicholls (St. Helens)
Lowe, P (Hull KR)
Laughton (Widnes)
Sub: Watkins, D (Salford)
　　 Dixon, C (Salford)

1974 Australia
Brisbane: 15 June
Lost 6-12
Charlton (Salford)
Redfearn, D (Bradford)
Watkins, D (Salford) 1g
*Hesketh (Salford)
Bevan, J (Warrington)
Millward (Hull KR)
Nash (Featherstone)
Clawson (Oldham) 2g
Bridges (Featherstone)
Mills (Widnes)
Dixon, C (Salford)
Thompson, J (Featherstone)
Nicholls (St. Helens)
Sub: Eckersley (St. Helens)
　　 Gray (Wigan)

1974 New Zealand
Auckland: 27 July
Lost 8-13
Charlton (Salford)
Redfearn, D (Bradford)
Dyl (Leeds)
*Hesketh (Salford)
Bevan, J (Warrington) 1t
Gill, K (Salford)
Nash (Featherstone) 1t
Clawson (Oldham) 1g
Gray (Wigan)
Thompson, J (Featherstone)
Dixon, C (Salford)
Norton (Castleford)
Nicholls (St. Helens)
Sub: Ashcroft (Warrington)

312

1974 New Zealand
Christchurch: 4 Aug
Won 17-8
Charlton (Salford)
Redfearn, D (Bradford) 1t
Dyl (Leeds) 1t
Dixon, C (Salford)
Richards (Salford)
*Hesketh (Salford) 1t
Nash (Featherstone)
Mills (Widnes)
Gray (Wigan) 4g
Thompson, J (Featherstone)
Chisnall, E (St. Helens)
Norton (Castleford)
Nicholls (St. Helens)
Sub: Bates, A (Dewsbury)

1974 New Zealand
Auckland: 10 Aug
Won 20-0
Charlton (Salford)
Redfearn, D (Bradford)
Willicombe (Wigan)
Dyl (Leeds) 1t
Bevan, J (Warrington) 2t
*Hesketh (Salford) 1t
Nash (Featherstone)
Clawson (Oldham)
Gray (Wigan) 4g
Thompson, J (Featherstone)
Chisnall, E (St. Helens)
Dixon, C (Salford)
Nicholls (St. Helens)
Sub: Bates, A (Dewsbury)
     Ramsey (Bradford)

1977 France (WC)
Auckland: 5 June
Won 23-4
Fairbairn (Wigan) 7g
Fielding (Salford)
Holmes (Leeds)
Dyl (Leeds) 1t
Wright, S (Widnes) 1t
*Millward (Hull KR) 1t
Nash (Salford)
Thompson, J (Featherstone)
Ward, D (Leeds)
Pitchford, S (Leeds)
Bowman, E (Workington)
Nicholls (St. Helens)
Hogan (Barrow)
Sub: Gill, K (Salford)
     Casey (Hull KR)

1977 New Zealand (WC)
Christchurch: 12 June
Won 30-12
Fairbairn (Wigan) 6g
Wright, S (Widnes) 2t
Holmes (Leeds)
Dyl (Leeds)
Francis, W (Wigan)
*Millward (Hull KR) 1t
Nash (Salford)
Thompson, J (Featherstone)
Ward, D (Leeds)
Pitchford, S (Leeds)
Bowman, E (Workington) 1t
Nicholls (St. Helens) 1t
Hogan (Barrow) 1t
Sub: Casey (Hull KR)

1977 Australia (WC)
Brisbane: 18 June
Lost 5-19
Fairbairn (Wigan) 1g
Wright, S (Widnes)
Francis, W (Wigan)
Dyl (Leeds)
Fielding (Salford)
*Millward (Hull KR) 1t
Nash (Salford)
Thompson, J (Featherstone)
Ward, D (Leeds)
Pitchford, S (Leeds)
Bowman, E (Workington)
Nicholls (St. Helens)
Hogan (Barrow)
Sub: Holmes (Leeds)
     Smith, P (Featherstone)

1977 Australia (WC)
Sydney: 25 June
Lost 12-13
Fairbairn (Wigan) 3g
Wright, S (Widnes)
Holmes (Leeds)
Dyl (Leeds)
Francis, W (Wigan)
*Millward (Hull KR)
Nash (Salford)
Thompson, J (Featherstone)
Elwell (Widnes)
Pitchford, S (Leeds) 1t
Bowman, E (Workington)
Casey (Hull KR)
Hogan (Barrow)
Sub: Gill, K (Salford) 1t
     Smith, P (Featherstone)

1978 Australia
Wigan: 21 Oct
Lost 9-15
Fairbairn (Wigan) 3g
Wright, S (Widnes)
Hughes (Widnes)
Cunningham (St. Helens)
Bevan, J (Warrington) 1t
*Millward (Hull KR)
Nash (Salford)
Thompson, J (Bradford)
Ward, D (Leeds)
Rose, P (Hull KR)
Nicholls (St. Helens)
Casey (Hull KR)
Norton (Hull)
Sub: Holmes (Leeds)
     Hogan (Barrow)

1978 Australia
Bradford: 5 Nov
Won 18-14
Fairbairn (Wigan) 6g
Wright, S (Widnes) 2t
Joyner (Castleford)
Dyl (Leeds)
Atkinson, J (Leeds)
*Millward (Hull KR)
Nash (Salford)
Mills (Widnes)
Fisher (Bradford)
Lockwood (Hull KR)
Nicholls (St. Helens)
Lowe, P (Hull KR)
Norton (Hull)
Sub: Holmes (Leeds)
     Rose, P (Hull KR)

1978 Australia
Leeds: 18 Nov
Lost 6-23
Fairbairn (Wigan)
Wright, S (Widnes)
Joyner (Castleford)
Bevan, J (Warrington) 1t
Atkinson, J (Leeds)
*Millward (Hull KR) 1t
Nash (Salford)
Mills (Widnes)
Fisher (Bradford)
Farrar (Hull)
Nicholls (St. Helens)
Lowe, P (Hull KR)
Norton (Hull)
Sub: Holmes (Leeds)
     Rose, P (Hull KR)

313

1979 Australia
Brisbane: 16 June
Lost 0-35
Woods, J (Leigh)
Barends (Bradford)
Joyner (Castleford)
Hughes (Widnes)
Mathias (St. Helens)
Holmes (Leeds)
Stephens (Castleford)
Mills (Widnes)
Ward, D (Leeds)
Skerrett (Wakefield)
Nicholls (St. Helens)
*Laughton (Widnes)
Norton (Hull)
Sub: Evans, S (Featherstone)
    Hogan (Hull KR)

1979 New Zealand
Auckland: 21 July
Won 16-8
Fairbairn (Wigan) 1t,2g
Evans, S (Featherstone) 1t
Joyner (Castleford)
Smith, M (Hull KR) 1t
Hughes (Widnes) 1t
Holmes (Leeds)
Stephens (Castleford)
Casey (Bradford)
Ward, D (Leeds)
*Nicholls (St. Helens)
Hogan (Hull KR)
Grayshon (Bradford)
Adams, M (Widnes)
Sub: Lockwood (Hull KR)

1980 New Zealand
Wigan: 18 Oct
Drew 14-14
*Fairbairn (Wigan) 4g
Camilleri (Barrow) 1t
Joyner (Castleford)
Smith, M (Hull KR) 1t
Bentley (Widnes)
Hartley, S (Hull KR)
Dick (Leeds)
Holdstock (Hull KR)
Watkinson (Hull KR)
Skerrett (Hull)
Gorley, L (Widnes)
Grayshon (Bradford)
Casey (Hull KR)
Sub: Pinner (St. Helens)

1979 Australia
Sydney: 30 June
Lost 16-24
Fairbairn (Wigan)
Barends (Bradford)
Joyner (Castleford) 1t
Woods, J (Leigh) 5g
Hughes (Widnes) 1t
Holmes (Leeds)
Stephens (Castleford)
*Nicholls (St. Helens)
Ward, D (Leeds)
Skerrett (Wakefield)
Casey (Bradford)
Grayshon (Bradford)
Adams, M (Widnes)
Sub: Evans, S (Featherstone)
    Watkinson (Hull KR)

1979 New Zealand
Christchurch: 5 Aug
Won 22-7
Fairbairn (Wigan) 5g
Evans, S (Featherstone) 1t
Joyner (Castleford)
Smith, M (Hull KR)
Hughes (Widnes) 1t
Holmes (Leeds)
Stephens (Castleford)
*Nicholls (St. Helens)
Ward, D (Leeds)
Skerrett (Wakefield)
Casey (Bradford) 1t
Grayshon (Bradford) 1t
Adams, M (Widnes)

1980 New Zealand
Bradford: 2 Nov
Lost 8-12
*Fairbairn (Wigan) 4g
Drummond (Leigh)
Joyner (Castleford)
Smith, M (Hull KR)
Camilleri (Barrow)
Kelly (Warrington)
Dick (Leeds)
Holdstock (Hull KR)
Elwell (Widnes)
Shaw, G (Widnes)
Casey (Hull KR)
Grayshon (Bradford)
Pinner (St. Helens)
Sub: Evans, S (Featherstone)
    Gorley, L (Widnes)

1979 Australia
Sydney: 14 July
Lost 2-28
Fairbairn (Wigan) 1g
Evans, S (Featherstone)
Joyner (Castleford)
Woods, J (Leigh)
Hughes (Widnes)
Topliss (Wakefield)
Redfearn, A (Bradford)
*Nicholls (St. Helens)
Ward, D (Leeds)
Casey (Bradford)
Hogan (Hull KR)
Grayshon (Bradford)
Norton (Hull)
Sub: Holmes (Leeds)
    Adams, M (Widnes)

1979 New Zealand
Auckland: 11 Aug
Lost 11-18
Fairbairn (Wigan) 1g
Evans, S (Featherstone)
Joyner (Castleford)
Smith, M (Hull KR) 1t
Hughes (Widnes) 1t
Holmes (Leeds)
Stephens (Castleford) 1t
Skerrett (Wakefield)
Ward, D (Leeds)
*Nicholls (St. Helens)
Casey (Bradford)
Grayshon (Bradford)
Adams, M (Widnes)
Sub: Woods, J (Leigh)
    Hogan (Hull KR)

1980 New Zealand
Leeds: 15 Nov
Won 10-2
Burke (Widnes) 2g
Drummond (Leigh) 2t
Joyner (Castleford)
Evans, S (Featherstone)
Atkinson, J (Leeds)
Woods, J (Leigh)
Walker (Whitehaven)
Skerrett (Hull)
Elwell (Widnes)
*Casey (Hull KR)
Gorley, P (St. Helens)
Adams, M (Widnes)
Norton (Hull)

1981 France
Hull: 6 Dec
Won 37-0
Fairbairn (Hull KR) 1g
Drummond (Leigh) 2t
Smith, M (Hull KR)
Woods, J (Leigh) 1t, 7g
Gill (Wigan) 3t
Hartley (Hull KR) 1t
Gregory (Widnes)
Grayshon (Bradford)
*Ward, D (Leeds)
Skerrett (Hull)
Gorley, L (Widnes)
Gorley, P (St. Helens)
Norton (Hull)
Sub: Burke (Widnes)
 Szymala (Barrow)

1982 Australia
Wigan: 20 Nov
Lost 6-27
Mumby (Bradford) 3g
Drummond (Leigh)
Smith, M (Hull KR)
Stephenson, D (Wigan)
Gill (Wigan)
Holmes (Leeds)
Kelly, K (Warrington)
*Grayshon (Bradford)
Dalgreen (Fulham)
Skerrett (Hull)
Eccles (Warrington)
Burton (Hull KR)
Heron, D (Leeds)
Sub: Woods, J (Leigh)
 Rathbone (Bradford)

1983 France
Hull: 6 March
Won 17-5
Mumby (Bradford) 4g
Drummond (Leigh)
Joyner (Castleford)
Duane, R (Warrington) 1t
Lydon (Widnes)
Myler, A (Widnes)
Gregory (Widnes) 1t
O'Neill, M (Widnes)
Noble (Bradford)
Goodway (Oldham)
*Casey (Hull KR)
Rathbone (Bradford)
Flanagan (Oldham)
Sub: Smith, P (Featherstone) 1t

1981 France
Marseilles: 20 Dec
Lost 2-19
Burke (Widnes)
Drummond (Leigh)
Smith, M (Hull KR)
Woods, J (Leigh) 1g
Gill (Wigan)
Hartley (Hull KR)
Gregory (Widnes)
*Grayshon (Bradford)
Watkinson (Hull KR)
Skerrett (Hull)
Gorley, L (Widnes)
Szymala (Barrow)
Norton (Hull)
Sub: Gorley, P (St. Helens)

1982 Australia
Leeds: 28 Nov
Lost 8-32
Fairbairn (Hull KR)
Drummond (Leigh)
Stephenson, D. (Wigan)
Smith, M (Hull KR)
Evans (Hull) 1t
*Topliss (Hull)
Gregory (Widnes)
O'Neill, M (Widnes)
Noble (Bradford)
Rose (Hull)
Smith, P (Featherstone)
Crooks (Hull) 2g, 1dg
Crane (Hull)
Sub: Courtney (Warrington)

1984 France
Avignon: 29 Jan
Won 12-0
*Mumby (Bradford)
Drummond (Leigh)
Duane, R (Warrington)
Foy, D (Oldham) 1t
Clark (Hull KR)
Lydon (Widnes)
Cairns (Barrow)
Rayne, Keith (Leeds)
Watkinson (Hull KR)
Goodway (Oldham) 1t
Worrall, M (Oldham)
Hobbs, D (Featherstone)
Hall (Hull KR)
Sub: Hanley (Bradford)
 Crooks (Hull) 2g

1982 Australia
Hull City FC: 30 Oct
Lost 4-40
Fairbairn (Hull KR)
Drummond (Leigh)
Hughes (Widnes)
Dyl (Leeds)
Evans, S (Hull)
Woods, J (Leigh)
*Nash (Salford)
Grayshon (Bradford)
Ward, D (Leeds)
Skerrett (Hull)
Gorley, L (Widnes)
Crooks (Hull) 2g
Norton (Hull)
Sub: D. Heron (Leeds)

1983 France
Carcassonne: 20 Feb
Won 20-5
Burke (Widnes) 1g
Drummond (Leigh)
Joyner (Castleford) 1t
Duane, R (Warrington)
Lydon (Widnes) 1t, 3g
Myler, A (Widnes)
Gregory (Widnes)
O'Neill, M (Widnes)
Noble (Bradford) 1t
Goodway (Oldham) 1t
*Casey (Hull KR)
Rathbone (Bradford)
Flanagan (Oldham)
Sub: Woods, J (Leigh)
 Smith, P (Featherstone)

1984 France
Leeds: 17 Feb
Won 10-0
Mumby (Bradford)
Clark (Hull KR)
Joyner (Castleford)
Schofield (Hull)
Basnett (Widnes)
Hanley (Bradford)
Cairns (Barrow)
Rayne, Keith (Leeds)
*Noble (Bradford)
Ward, K (Castleford)
Jasiewicz (Bradford)
Hobbs, D (Featherstone) 5g
Hall (Hull KR)
Sub: Smith, M (Hull KR)
 Smith, P (Featherstone)

315

1984 Australia

Sydney: 9 June

Lost 8-25

Burke (Widnes) 2g
Drummond (Leigh)
Schofield (Hull) 1t
Mumby (Bradford)
Hanley (Bradford)
Foy, D (Oldham)
Holding (St. Helens)
Crooks (Hull)
*Noble (Bradford)
Goodway (Oldham)
Burton (Hull KR)
Worrall, M (Oldham)
Adams (Widnes)
Sub: Lydon (Widnes)
    Hobbs, D (Featherstone)

1984 Australia

Brisbane: 26 June

Lost 6-18

Burke (Widnes) 1g
Drummond (Leigh)
Schofield (Hull) 1t
Mumby (Bradford)
Hanley (Bradford)
Myler, A (Widnes)
Holding (St. Helens)
Rayne, Keith (Leeds)
*Noble (Bradford)
Crooks (Hull)
Burton (Hull KR)
Goodway (Oldham)
Worrall (Oldham)
Sub: Gregory (Widnes)
    Adams (Widnes)

1984 Australia

Sydney: 7 July

Lost 7-20

Burke (Widnes) 1g
Drummond (Leigh)
Schofield (Hull)
Mumby (Bradford)
Hanley (Bradford) 1t
Myler, A (Widnes)
Holding (St. Helens) 1dg
Hobbs, D (Featherstone)
*Noble (Bradford)
Case (Wigan)
Burton (Hull KR)
Goodway (Oldham)
Adams (Widnes)

1984 New Zealand

Auckland: 14 July

Lost 0-12

Burke (Widnes)
Drummond (Leigh)
Schofield (Hull)
Mumby (Bradford)
Hanley (Bradford)
Smith, M (Hull KR)
Holding (St. Helens)
Hobbs, D (Featherstone)
*Noble (Bradford)
Case (Wigan)
Burton (Hull KR)
Goodway (Oldham)
Adams (Widnes)

1984 New Zealand

Christchurch: 22 July

Lost 12-28

Burke (Widnes) 2g
Drummond (Leigh)
Hanley (Bradford) 1t
Mumby (Bradford)
Lydon (Widnes)
Myler, A (Widnes) 1t
Gregory (Widnes)
Hobbs, D (Featherstone)
*Noble (Bradford)
Case (Wigan)
Burton (Hull KR)
Goodway (Oldham)
Adams (Widnes)
Sub: Joyner (Castleford)
    Beardmore, K (Castleford)

1984 New Zealand

Auckland: 28 July

Lost 16-32

Burke (Widnes) 4g
Drummond (Leigh)
Hanley (Bradford) 1t
Mumby (Bradford) 1t
Lydon (Widnes)
Myler, A (Widnes)
Gregory (Widnes)
Hobbs, D (Featherstone)
*Noble (Bradford)
Case (Wigan)
Adams (Widnes)
Goodway (Oldham)
Flanagan (Oldham)
Sub: Donlan (Leigh)
    Joyner (Castleford)

1984 Papua New Guinea

Mount Hagen: 5 Aug

Won 38-20

Burke (Widnes) 1t, 5g
Drummond (Leigh) 2t
Hanley (Bradford) 1t
Mumby (Bradford) 1t
Lydon (Widnes)
Myler, A (Widnes)
Gregory (Widnes)
Rayne, Keith (Leeds) 1t
*Noble (Bradford)
Goodway (Oldham)
Flanagan (Oldham)
Hobbs, D (Featherstone) 1t
Adams (Widnes)
Sub: Donlan (Leigh)
    Proctor (Hull)

1985 France

Leeds: 1 March

Won 50-4

Edwards (Wigan)
Ledger (St. Helens)
Creasser (Leeds) 8g
Gribbin (Whitehaven) 1t
Gill (Wigan) 1t
Hanley (Bradford) 2t
Fox (Featherstone) 2t, 1g
Dickinson (Leeds)
Watkinson (Hull KR) 1t
Dannatt (Hull)
*Goodway (Oldham)
Rathbone (Bradford)
Divorty (Hull) 1t
Sub: Gibson (Batley)
    Platt (St. Helens)

1985 France

Perpignan: 17 March

Lost 16-24

Johnson, C (Leigh)
Clark (Hull KR)
Creasser (Leeds) 1g
Foy, D (Oldham) 1t
Ford, P (Wigan) 2t
*Hanley (Bradford)
Fox (Featherstone)
Dickinson (Leeds)
Kiss (Wigan)
Wane (Wigan)
Dannatt (Hull)
Rathbone (Bradford)
Divorty (Hull) 1g
Sub: Harkin (Hull KR)
    Powell (Leeds)

1985 New Zealand
Leeds: 19 Oct
Lost 22-24
Burke (Widnes) 3g
Drummond (Leigh)
Schofield (Hull)
Hanley (Wigan) 1t
Lydon (Widnes) 1t,2g
Myler, A (Widnes)
Fox (Featherstone)
Crooks (Hull)
Watkinson (Hull KR)
Fieldhouse (Widnes)
Goodway (Wigan) 1t
Potter (Wigan)
*Pinner (St. Helens)
Sub: Arkwright (St. Helens)

1985 New Zealand
Wigan: 2 Nov
Won 25-8
Burke (Widnes)
Drummond (Leigh)
Schofield (Hull) 4t
Hanley (Wigan)
Lydon (Widnes) 4g
Myler, A (Widnes)
Fox (Featherstone)
Grayshon (Leeds)
Watkinson (Hull KR)
Fieldhouse (Widnes)
Goodway (Wigan)
Potter (Wigan)
*Pinner (St. Helens) 1dg
Sub: Edwards (Wigan)
Burton (Hull KR)

1985 New Zealand (Also WC)
Elland Rd, Leeds: 9 Nov
Drew 6-6
Burke (Widnes)
Drummond (Leigh)
Schofield (Hull)
Edwards (Wigan)
Lydon (Widnes)
Hanley (Wigan)
Fox (Featherstone)
Grayshon (Leeds)
Watkinson (Hull KR)
Fieldhouse (Widnes)
Goodway (Wigan)
Potter (Wigan)
*Pinner (St. Helens)
Sub: Arkwright (St. Helens)
Crooks (Hull) 3g

1986 France (Also WC)
Avignon: 16 Feb
Drew 10-10
Burke (Widnes)
Drummond (Leigh)
Schofield (Hull)
Hanley (Wigan) 1t
Gill (Wigan)
Myler, A (Widnes)
Fox (Featherstone)
Crooks (Hull) 3g
Watkinson (Hull KR)
Wane (Wigan)
Potter (Wigan)
Fieldhouse (Widnes)
*Pinner (St. Helens)

1986 France
Wigan: 1 Mar
Won 24-10
Lydon (Wigan)
Drummond (Leigh) 1t
Schofield (Hull) 1t,2g
Marchant (Castleford) 1t
Laws (Hull KR)
Myler, A (Widnes)
Fox (Featherstone)
Crooks (Hull) 2g
*Watkinson (Hull KR)
Fieldhouse (Widnes)
Rayne, Kevin (Leeds)
James (Halifax) 1t
Potter (Wigan)
Sub: Platt (St. Helens)

Harry Pinner, 1985-86 Great Britain captain.

317

GREAT BRITAIN RECORDS

Most appearances
46	Mick Sullivan*
31	Billy Boston
29 + 1	Cliff Watson
29	George Nicholls
29	Neil Fox
28 + 1	Roger Millward
28	Alan Prescott
27	Phil Jackson
27	Alex Murphy
26	Eric Ashton
26	John Atkinson
25	Brian McTigue
25	Jim Sullivan
25	Tommy Harris

*Mick Sullivan's record number of appearances include a record run of 36 successive matches. In addition he played in two matches against France before they were given Test status.

Most tries
40, Mick Sullivan, also scoring two against France before they were given Test status

Most goals and points
93 goals, (14 tries), 228 points, Neil Fox.

Longest Test careers
14 years   — Gus Risman
1932 to 1946 (17 appearances)
13 years 9 months — Billy Batten
1908 to 1921 (10 appearances)
13 years 6 months — Alex Murphy
1958 to 1971 (27 appearances)
12 years 9 months — Roger Millward
1966 to 1978 (28 + 1 appearances)
12 years 6 months — John Atkinson
1968 to 1980 (26 appearances)
12 years 6 months — Terry Clawson
1962 to 1974 (14 appearances)

Youngest Test player
Shaun Edwards was 18 years 135 days old when he made his Great Britain Test debut against France at Leeds on 1 March, 1985. Born on 17 October, 1966, he beat the previous record held by Roger Millward (born 16 September, 1947) who was not quite 18 years 6 months old when he made his debut for Britain against France at Wigan on 5 March, 1966. Five months earlier Millward was a non-playing substitute for the second Test against New Zealand.

Oldest Test player
Jeff Grayshon (born 4 March, 1949), was 36 years 8 months when he played in his last Test for Britain, against New Zealand at Elland Road, Leeds, on 9 November, 1985.

Record team changes

The record number of team changes made by the Great Britain selectors is 10. This has happened on three occasions — all against Australia — and in the first two cases resulted in unexpected victories.

In 1929, Britain crashed 31-8 to Australia in the first Test at Hull KR and retained only three players for the second Test at Leeds where they won 9-3.

After their biggest ever defeat of 50-12 in the 1963 second Test at Swinton, Britain dropped nine players and were forced to make another change when Vince Karalius was injured and replaced by Don Fox. Britain stopped Australia making a clean sweep of the series by winning 16-5 at Leeds in the last Test.

Following the 40-4 first Test defeat at Hull City's soccer ground in 1982, the selectors again made 10 changes, not including substitutes. The changes made little difference this time as Britain went down 27-6 in the second Test at Wigan.

Britain have never fielded the same team for three or more successive Tests.

GREAT BRITAIN REGISTER

The following is a record of the 551 players who have appeared for Great Britain in 236 Test and World Cup matches.

It does not include matches against France before 1957, the year they were given official Test match status.

Figures in brackets are the total of appearances, with the plus sign indicating substitute appearances, e.g. (7 + 3).

For matches against touring teams, the year given is for the first half of the season.

World Cup matches are in bold letters except when also classified as Test matches. Substitute appearances are in lower case letters.

A - Australia, F - France, NZ - New Zealand, P - Papua New Guinea.

ACKERLEY, A (2) Halifax: 1952 A; 1958 NZ
ADAMS, L (1) Leeds: 1932 A
ADAMS, M (11 + 2) Widnes: 1979 Aa, NZ3; 1980 NZ; 1984 A2a, NZ3, P
ARKWRIGHT, C (+2) St. Helens: 1985 nz2
ARKWRIGHT, J (6) Warrington: 1936 A2, NZ; 1937 A3
ARMITT, T (8) Swinton: 1933 A; 1936 A2, NZ2; 1937 A3
ASHBY, R (2) Liverpool: 1964 F; Wigan: 1965 F
ASHCROFT, E (11) Wigan: 1947 NZ2; 1950 A3, NZ; 1954 A3, NZ2
ASHCROFT, K (5 + 1) Leigh: **1968 A**; 1968 F; 1969 F; **1970 F,NZ**; Warrington: 1974 nz
ASHTON, E (26) Wigan: **1957 A,NZ**; 1958 A2,NZ2; 1959 F, A3; 1960 F2; **1960 NZ,A**; 1961 NZ3; 1962 F3,A3; 1963 F,A2
ASHURST, W (3) Wigan: 1971 NZ; 1972 F2
ASKIN, T (6) Featherstone R: 1928 A3,NZ3
ASPINALL, W (1) Warrington: 1966 NZ
ASTON, L (3) St. Helens: 1947 NZ3
ATKINSON, A (11) Castleford: 1929 A3; 1932 A3,NZ3; 1933 A; 1936 A
ATKINSON, J (26) Leeds: **1968 F,NZ**; 1970 A3,NZ3; **1970 A2,F,NZ**; 1971 F2,NZ; 1972 F2; **1972 A2,F,NZ**; 1973 A2; 1978 A2; 1980 NZ
AVERY, A (4) Oldham: 1910 A,NZ; 1911 A2

BACON, J (11) Leeds: 1920 A3,NZ3; 1921 A3; 1924 A; 1926 NZ
BARENDS, D (2) Bradford N: 1979 A2
BARTON, F (1) Wigan: 1951 NZ
BARTON, J. (2) Wigan: 1960 F; 1961 NZ
BASNETT, J. (1) Widnes: 1984 F
BASSETT, A (2) Halifax: 1946 A2
BATES, A (2+2) Dewsbury: 1974 F2,nz2
BATTEN, E (4) Bradford N: 1946 A2,NZ; 1947 NZ
BATTEN, R. (3) Leeds: 1969 F; 1973 A2
BATTEN, W (10) Hunslet: 1907 NZ; 1908 A3; 1910 A2,NZ; 1911 A2; Hull: 1921 A
BAXTER, J (1) Rochdale H: 1907 NZ
BEAMES, J (2) Halifax: 1921 A2

BEARDMORE, K (+1) Castleford; 1984 nz
BELSHAW, W (8) Liverpool S: 1936 A3,NZ2; 1937 A; Warrington: A2
BENNETT, J (7) Rochdale H: 1924 A3,NZ3; Wigan. 1926 NZ
BENTHAM, N (10) Wigan H: 1928 A3,NZ3; Halifax: 1929 A2; Warrington: 1929(cont) A2
BENTHAM, W (2) Broughton R: 1924 NZ2
BENTLEY, K (1) Widnes: 1980 NZ
BENYON, W (5+1) St. Helens: 1971 F2,NZ,nz; 1972 F2
BEVAN, D (1) Wigan: 1952 A
BEVAN, J (6) Warrington: 1974 A2,NZ2; 1978 A2
BEVERLEY, H (6) Hunslet: 1936 A3; 1937 A; Halifax: A2
BIRCH, J (1) Leeds: 1907 NZ
BISHOP, T (15) St. Helens: 1966 A3,NZ2; 1967 A3; 1968 F3; **1968 A,F,NZ**; 1969 F
BLAN, W (3) Wigan: 1951 NZ3
BLINKHORN, T (1) Warrington: 1929 A
BOLTON, D (23) Wigan: 1957 F3; 1958 F,A2; 1959 F,A3; 1960 F2; 1961 NZ3; 1962 F2,A,NZ2; 1963 F,A2
BOSTON, W (31) Wigan: 1954 A2,NZ3; 1955 NZ; 1956 A3; 1957 F5; **1957 F,A**; 1958 F; 1959 A; 1960 F; **1960 A**; 1961 F,NZ3; 1962 F2,A3,NZ; 1963 F
BOTT, C (1) Oldham: 1966 F
BOWDEN, J (3) Huddersfield: 1954 A2,NZ
BOWEN, F (3) St. Helens Rec: 1928 NZ3
BOWERS, J (1) Rochdale H: 1920 NZ
BOWMAN, E (4) Workington T: **1977 F, NZ, A2**
BOWMAN, H (8) Hull: 1924 NZ2; 1926 NZ2; 1928 A2,NZ; 1929 A
BOWMAN, K (3) Huddersfield: 1962 F; 1963 F,A
BOYLEN, F (1) Hull: 1908 A
BRADSHAW, T (6) Wigan: 1947 NZ2; 1950 A3,NZ
BRIDGES, K (3) Featherstone R: 1974 F2,A
BRIGGS, B (1) Huddersfield: 1954 NZ
BROGDEN, S (16) Huddersfield: 1929 A; 1932 A3,NZ3; 1933 A2; Leeds: 1936 A3,NZ2; 1937 A2

BROOKE, I (13) Bradford N: 1966 A3,NZ2; Wakefield: 1967 A3; 1968 F2; **1968 A,F,NZ**
BROOKS, E (3) Warrington: 1908 A3
BROUGH, A (2) Oldham: 1924 A,NZ
BROUGH, J (5) Leeds: 1928 A2,NZ2; 1936A
BROWN, G (6) Leeds: **1954 F2,NZ,A**; 1955 NZ2
BRYANT, W (4+1) Castleford: 1964 F2; 1966 Aa; 1967 F
BUCKLEY, A (7) Swinton: 1963 A; 1964 F; 1965 NZ; 1966 F,A2,NZ
BURGESS, W (16) Barrow: 1924 A3,NZ3; 1926 NZ3; 1928 A3,NZ2; 1929 A2
BURGESS, W (14) Barrow: 1962 F; 1963 A; 1965 NZ2; 1966 F,A3,NZ2; 1967 F,A; 1968 F; Salford: 1969 F
BURGHAM, O (1) Halifax: 1911 A
BURKE, M (14+1) Widnes: 1980 NZ; 1981 fF; 1983 F; 1984 A3, NZ3, P; 1985 NZ3; 1986 F
BURNELL, A (3) Hunslet: 1951 NZ2; 1954 NZ
BURTON, C (6+1) Hull KR: 1982 A; 1984 A3, NZ2; 1985 nz
BURWELL, A (7+1) Hull KR: 1967 a; 1968 F3; **1968 A,F,NZ**; 1969 F
BUTTERS, F (2) Swinton: 1929 A2

CAIRNS, D (2) Barrow: 1984 F2
CAMILLERI, C (2) Barrow: 1980 NZ2
CARLTON, F (2) St. Helens: 1958 NZ; Wigan: 1962 NZ
CARR, C (7) Barrow: 1924 A2,NZ2; 1926 NZ3
CARTWRIGHT, J (7) Leigh: 1920 A,NZ3; 1921 A3
CASE, B (4) Wigan: 1984 A, NZ3
CASEY, L (12+2) Hull KR: **1977 f,nz,A**; 1978 A; Bradford N: 1979 A2,NZ3; Hull KR: 1980 NZ3; 1983 F2
CASTLE, F (4) Barrow: 1952 A3; 1954 A
CHALLINOR, J (3) Warrington: 1958 A,NZ; **1960 F**
CHARLTON, P (18+1) Workington T: 1965 NZ; Salford: **1970 nz**; 1972 F2; **1972 A2,F,NZ**; 1973 A3; 1974 F2,A3,NZ3
CHERRINGTON, N (1) Wigan: 1960 F
CHILCOTT, J (3) Huddersfield: 1914 A3
CHISNALL, D (2) Leigh: 1970 A; **1970 NZ**
CHISNALL, E (4) St. Helens: 1974 A2,NZ2
CLAMPITT, L (3) Broughton R: 1907 NZ; 1911 A; 1914 NZ
CLARK, D (11) Huddersfield: 1911 A2; 1914 A3; 1920 A3,NZ3
CLARK, G (3) Hull KR: 1984 F2; 1985 F
CLARK, M (5) Leeds: 1968 F2; **1968 A,F,NZ**
CLARKE, C (7) Wigan: 1965 NZ; 1966 F,NZ; 1967 F; 1973 A3
CLAWSON, T (14) Featherstone R: 1962 F2; Leeds: **1972 A2,F**; Oldham: 1973 A3; 1974 F2,A2,NZ2
CLOSE, D (1) Huddersfield: 1967 F
COLDRICK, A (4) Wigan: 1914 A3,NZ
COLLIER, F (2) Wigan: 1963 A; Widnes: 1964 F

COULMAN, M (2+1) Salford: 1971 f,NZ2
COURTNEY, N (+1) Warrington: 1982 a
COVERDALE, R (4) Hull: **1954 F2,NZ,A**
CRACKNELL, R (2) Huddersfield: 1951 NZ2
CRANE, M (1) Hull: 1982 A
CREASSER, D (2) Leeds: 1985 F2
CROOKS, L (7+2) Hull: 1982 A2; 1984 f, A2; 1985 NZ nz; 1986 F2
CROSTON, A (1) Castleford: 1937 A
CROWTHER, H (1) Hunslet: 1929 A
CUNNIFFE, B (1) Castleford: 1937 A
CUNNINGHAM, E (1) St. Helens: 1978 A
CUNLIFFE, J (4) Wigan: 1950 A,NZ; 1951 NZ; 1954 A
CUNLIFFE, W (11) Warrington: 1920 A,NZ2; 1921 A3; 1924 A3,NZ; 1926 NZ
CURRAN, G (6) Salford: 1946 A,NZ; 1947 NZ; 1948 A3
CURZON, E (1) Salford: 1910 A

DAGNALL, R (4) St.Helens: 1961 NZ2; 1964 F; 1965 F
DALGREEN, J (1) Fulham: 1982 A
DANBY, T (3) Salford: 1950 A2,NZ
DANIELS, A (3) Halifax: 1952 A2; 1955 NZ
DANNATT, A (2) Hull: 1985 F2
DARWELL, J (5) Leigh: 1924 A3,NZ2
DAVIES, A (20) Oldham: 1955 NZ; 1956 A3; **1957 F,A**; 1957 F2; 1958 F,A2,NZ2; 1959 F2,A; **1960 NZ,F,A**; 1960 F
DAVIES, E (3) Oldham: 1920 NZ3
DAVIES, J (2) Huddersfield: 1911 A2
DAVIES, W.A (2) Leeds: 1914 A,NZ
DAVIES, W.J (1) Castleford: 1933 A
DAVIES, W.T (1) Halifax: 1911 A
DAVIES, W.T.H (3) Bradford N: 1946 NZ; 1947 NZ2
DAVIES, W (1) Swinton: 1968 F
DAWSON, E (1) York: 1956 A
DICK, K (2) Leeds: 1980 NZ2
DICKENSON, G (1) Warrington: 1908 A
DICKINSON, R (2) Leeds: 1985 F2
DINGSDALE, W (3) Warrington: 1929 A2; 1933 A
DIVORTY, G (2) Hull: 1985 F2
DIXON, C (12+2) Halifax: 1968 F; Salford: 1969 F; 1971 NZ; **1972 F**; 1973 a2; 1974 F2,A3,NZ3
DIXON, M (2) Featherstone R: 1962 F; 1964 F
DOCKAR, A (1) Hull KR: 1947 NZ
DONLAN, S (+2) Leigh: 1984 nz, p
DRAKE, J (1) Hull: 1960 F
DRAKE, W (1) Hull: 1962 F
DRUMMOND, D (22) Leigh: 1980 NZ2; 1981 F2; 1982 A3; 1983 F2; 1984 F, A3, NZ3, P; 1985 NZ3; 1986 F2
DUANE, R (3) Warrington: 1983 F2; 1984 F
DUTTON, R (6) Widnes: 1970 NZ2; **1970 A2,F,NZ**
DYSON, F (1) Huddersfield: 1959 A

DYL, L (11) Leeds: 1974 A2,NZ3; **1977 F,NZ,A2**; 1978 A; 1982 A

ECCLES, P (1) Halifax: 1907 NZ
ECCLES, R (1) Warrington: 1982 A
ECKERSLEY, D (2+2) St.Helens: 1973 Aa; 1974 Aa
EDGAR, B (11) Workington T: 1958 A,NZ; 1961 NZ; 1962 A3,NZ; 1965 NZ; 1966 A3
EDWARDS, A (7) Salford: 1936 A3,NZ2; 1937 A2
EDWARDS, D (3+2) Castleford: 1968 f; 1970 A; 1971 NZ2nz
EDWARDS, S (2+1) Wigan: 1985 F,nzNZ
EGAN, J (14) Wigan: 1946 A3; 1947 NZ3; 1948 A3; 1950 A3,NZ2
ELLABY, A (13) St.Helens: 1928 A3,NZ2; 1929 A2; 1932 A3,NZ2; 1933 A
ELWELL, K (3) Widnes: **1977 A;** 1980 NZ2
EVANS, B (10) Swinton: 1926 NZ; 1928 NZ; 1929 A; 1932 A2,NZ3; 1933 A2
EVANS, F (4) Swinton: 1924 A2,NZ2
EVANS, J (4) Hunslet: 1951 NZ; 1952 A3
EVANS, J (3) Swinton: 1926 NZ3
EVANS, R (4) Wigan: 1961 NZ2; 1962 F,NZ
EVANS, S (7+3) Featherstone R: 1979 Aa2,NZ3, 1980 NZnz; Hull: 1982 A2
EYRE, K (1) Hunslet: 1965 NZ

FAIRBAIRN, G (17) Wigan: **1977 F,NZ,A2**; 1978 A3; 1979 A2,NZ3; 1980 NZ2; Hull KR: 1981 F; 1982 A2
FAIRCLOUGH, L (6) St.Helens: 1926 NZ; 1928 A2,NZ2; 1929 A
FARRAR, V (1) Hull: 1978 A
FEATHERSTONE, J (6) Warrington: 1948 A; 1950 NZ2; 1952 A3
FEETHAM, J (8) Hull KR: 1929 A; Salford: 1932 A2,NZ2; 1933 A3
FIELD, H (3) York: 1936 A,NZ2
FIELD, N (1) Batley: 1963 A
FIELDHOUSE, J (5) Widnes: 1985 NZ3; 1986 F2
FIELDING, K (3) Salford: 1974 F2; **1977 F**
FILDES, A (15) St.Helens Recs: 1926 NZ2; 1928 A3,NZ3; 1929 A3; St.Helens: 1932 A,NZ3
FISHER, A (11) Bradford N: 1970 A2,NZ3; **1970 A;** Leeds: **A;** 1971 F2; Bradford N: 1978 A2
FLANAGAN, P (14) Hull KR: 1962 F; 1963 F; 1966 A3,NZ; 1967 A3; 1968 F,NZ; 1970 A
FLANAGAN, T (4) Oldham: 1983 F2; 1984 NZ, P
FOGERTY, T (2+1) Halifax: 1966 nz; Wigan: 1967 F; Rochdale H: 1974 F
FORD, P (1) Wigan: 1985 F
FOSTER, F (1) Hull KR: 1967 A
FOSTER, P (3) Leigh: 1955 NZ3
FOSTER, T (3) Bradford N: 1946 NZ; 1948 A2
FOX, Deryck (7) Featherstone R: 1985 F2, NZ3; 1986 F2
FOX, Don (1) Featherstone R: 1963 A

FOX, N (29) Wakefield T: 1959 F,A2; 1960 F3; 1961 NZ2; 1962 F3,A3,NZ2; 1963 A2,F; 1964 F; 1965 F; 1966 F; 1967 F2,A; 1968 F3; 1969 F
FOY, D (3) Oldham: 1984 F, A; 1985 F
FRANCIS, R (1) Barrow: 1947 NZ
FRANCIS, W (4) Wigan: 1967 A; **1977 NZ,A2**
FRASER, E (16) Warrington: 1958 A3,NZ2; 1959 F2,A; 1960 F3; **1960 F,NZ**; 1961 F,NZ2
FRENCH, R (4) Widnes: 1968 F2; **1968 A,NZ**
FRODSHAM, A (3) St.Helens: 1928 NZ2; 1929 A

GABBITAS, B (1) Hunslet: 1959 F
GALLAGHER, F (12) Dewsbury: 1920 A3; 1921 A; Batley: 1924 A3,NZ3; 1926 NZ2
GANLEY, B (3) Oldham: 1957 F2; 1958 F
GARDINER, D (1) Wigan: 1965 NZ
GEE, K (17) Wigan: 1946 A3,NZ; 1947 NZ3; 1948 A3; 1950 A3,NZ2; 1951 NZ2
GEMMELL, R (3) Leeds: 1964 F; Hull: 1968 F; 1969 F
GIBSON, C (+1) Batley: 1985 f
GIFFORD, H (2) Barrow: 1908 A2
GILFEDDER, L (5) Warrington: 1962 A,NZ2,F; 1963 F
GILL, H (5) Wigan: 1981 F2; 1982 A; 1985 F; 1986 F
GILL, K (5+2) Salford: 1974 F2,A2,NZ; **1977 f,a**
GOODWAY, A (14) Oldham: 1983 F2; 1984 F, A3, NZ3, P; 1985 F; Wigan: 1985 NZ3
GOODWIN, D (5) Barrow: 1957 F2; 1958 F,NZ2
GORE, J (1) Salford: 1926 NZ
GORLEY, L (4+1) Widnes: 1980 NZnz; 1981 F2; 1982 A
GORLEY, P (2+1) St.Helens: 1980 NZ; 1981 Ff
GOWERS, K (14) Swinton: 1967 F,A3; 1964 F2; 1965 NZ2; 1966 F2,A,NZ2
GRAY, J (5+3) Wigan: 1974 f2,A2a,NZ3
GRAYSHON, J (13) Bradford N: 1979 A2,NZ3; 1980 NZ2; 1981 F2; 1982 A2; Leeds: 1985 NZ2
GREENALL, D (6) St.Helens: 1951 NZ3; 1952 A2; 1954 NZ
GREENALL, J (1) St.Helens Rec: 1921 A
GREENOUGH, R (1) Warrington: **1960 NZ**
GREGORY, A (8+1) Widnes: 1981 F2; 1982 A; 1983 F2; 1984 a, NZ2, P
GRIBBIN, V (1) Whitehaven: 1985 F
GRONOW, B (7) Huddersfield: 1911 A2, 1920 A2, NZ3
GRUNDY, J (12) Barrow: 1955 NZ3; 1956 A3; 1957 F3; **1957 F,A,NZ**
GUNNEY, G (11) Hunslet: 1954 NZ3; 1956 A; 1957 F3; **1957 F,NZ**; 1964 F; 1965 F
GWYNNE, T. E (3) Hull: 1928 A,NZ; 1929 A
GWYTHER, E (6) Belle Vue R: 1947 NZ2; 1950 A3; 1951 NZ

HAIGH, R (5+1) Wakefield T: **1968 A,F**; Leeds: **1970 NZ,a**; 1971 F,NZ

HALL, D (2) Hull KR: 1984 F2
HALL, W (4) Oldham: 1914 A3,NZ
HALLAS, D (2) Leeds: 1961 F,NZ
HALMSHAW, A (1) Halifax: 1971 NZ
HALSALL, H (1) Swinton: 1929 A
HANLEY, E (14+1) Bradford N: 1984 fF, A3, NZ3,
P; 1985 F2; Wigan: 1985 NZ3; 1986 F
HARDISTY, A (12) Castleford: 1964 F3; 1965 F,NZ;
1966 A3,NZ; 1967 F2; 1970 A
HARE, I (1) Widnes: 1967 F
HARKIN, P (+1) Hull KR: 1985 f
HARRIS, T (25) Hull: 1954 NZ2; 1956 A3; 1957 F5;
1957 F,A; 1958 A3,NZ,F; 1959 F2,A3; 1960 F2;
1960 NZ
HARRISON, F (3) Leeds: 1911 A3
HARRISON, M (7) Hull: 1967 F2; 1971 NZ2; 1972
F2; 1973 A
HARTLEY, D (11) Hunslet: 1964 F2; Castleford:
1968 F; 1969 F; 1970 A2,NZ2; **1970 A2,F**
HARTLEY, S (3) Hull KR: 1980 NZ; 1981 F2
HELME, G (12) Warrington: 1948 A3; 1954 A3,NZ2;
1954 F2,A,NZ
HEPWORTH, K (11) Castleford: 1967 F2; 1970
A3,NZ2; **1970 A2,F,NZ**
HERBERT, N (6) Workington T: 1961 NZ; 1962
F,A3,NZ
HERON, D (1+1) Leeds: 1982 aA
HESKETH, C (21+2) Salford: 1970 NZ; **1970 NZ,a**;
1971 Ff,NZ3; **1972 A2,F,NZ**; 1973 A3; 1974
F2,A3,NZ3
HICKS, M (1) St.Helens: 1965 NZ
HIGGINS, F (6) Widnes: 1950 A3,NZ2; 1951 NZ
HIGGINS, H (2) Widnes: 1937 A2
HIGSON, J (2) Hunslet: 1908 A2
HILL, C (1) Wigan: 1966 F
HILL, D (1) Wigan: 1971 F
HILTON, H (7) Oldham: 1920 A3,NZ3; 1921 A
HILTON, J (4) Wigan: 1950 A2,NZ2
HOBBS, D (7+1) Featherstone R: 1984 F2, Aa,
NZ3, P
HODGSON, M (16) Swinton: 1929 A2; 1932
A3,NZ3; 1933 A3; 1936 A3,NZ; 1937 A
HOGAN, P (6+3) Barrow: **1977 F,NZ,A2**; 1978 a;
Hull KR: 1979 Aa,NZ,nz
HOGG, A (1) Broughton R: 1907 NZ
HOLDEN, K (1) Warrington: 1963 A
HOLDER, W (1) Hull: 1907 NZ
HOLDING, N (4) St. Helens: 1984 A3, NZ
HOLDSTOCK, R (2) Hull KR: 1980 NZ2
HOLLAND, D (4) Oldham: 1914 A3,NZ
HOLLIDAY, W (9+1) Whitehaven: 1964 F; Hull
KR: 1965 F,NZ3; 1966 Ff; 1967 A3
HOLLINDRAKE, T (1) Keighley: 1955 NZ
HOLMES, J (14+6) Leeds: 1971 NZ; 1972 F2; **1972
Aa,NZ**; **1977 F,NZ,Aa**; 1978 a3; 1979 A2a,NZ3;
1982 A
HORNE, W (8) Barrow: 1946 A3; 1947 NZ; 1948 A;
1952 A3

HORTON, W (14) Wakefield T: 1928 A3,NZ3; 1929
A; 1932 A3,NZ; 1933 A3
HOWLEY, T (6) Wigan: 1924 A3,NZ3
HUDDART, R (16) Whitehaven: 1958 A2,NZ2;
St.Helens: 1959 A; 1961 NZ3; 1962 F2,A3,NZ2;
1963 A
HUDSON, B (8) Salford: 1932 NZ; 1933 A2; 1936
A,NZ2; 1937 A2
HUDSON, W (1) Wigan: 1948 A
HUGHES, E (8) Widnes: 1978 A; 1979 A3,NZ3;
1982 A
HURCOMBE, D (8) Wigan: 1920 A2,NZ; 1921 A;
1924 A2,NZ2
HYNES, S (12+1) Leeds: 1970 A2,NZ2nz; **1970
A2,F,NZ**; 1971 F; 1973 A3

IRVING, R (8+3) Oldham: 1967 F2,A3; 1970 a,NZ;
1971 NZ; 1972 f; **1972 NZ,a**

JACKSON, K (2) Oldham: 1957 F2
JACKSON, P (27) Barrow: 1954 A3,NZ3; **1954
F2,A,NZ**; 1955 NZ3; 1956 A3; **1957 F,NZ**; 1957
F5; 1958 F,A2,NZ
JAMES, N (1) Halifax: 1986 F
JARMAN, J.W. (2) Leeds: 1914 A2
JASIEWICZ, R (1) Bradford N: 1984 F
JEANES, D (8) Wakefield T: 1971 F,NZ2; 1972 F2;
Leeds: **1972 A2,NZ**
JENKINS, B (12) Wigan: 1907 NZ3; 1908 A3; 1910
A,NZ; 1911 A2, 1914 A,NZ
JENKINS, D (1) Hunslet: 1929 A
JENKINS, D (1) Leeds: 1947 NZ
JENKINS, E (9) Salford: 1933 A; 1936 A3,NZ2;
1937 A3
JENKINSON, A (2) Hunslet: 1911 A2
JOHNSON, A (4) Widnes: 1914 A,NZ; 1920 A2
JOHNSON, A (6) Warrington: 1946 A2,NZ;
1947 NZ3
JOHNSON, C (1) Leigh: 1985 F
JOLLEY, J (3) Runcorn: 1907 NZ3
JONES, B (3) Wakefield T: 1964 F; 1965 F; 1966 F
JONES, B.L (15) Leeds: 1954 A3,NZ3; 1955 NZ3;
1957 F3; **1957 F,A,NZ**
JONES, D (2) Merthyr: 1907 NZ2
JONES, E (4) Rochdale H: 1920 A,NZ3
JONES, J (1) Barrow: 1946 NZ
JONES, K (2) Wigan: **1970 F,NZ**
JONES, L (1) St.Helens: 1971 NZ
JORDAN, G (2) Featherstone R: 1964 F; 1967 A
JOYNER, J (14+2) Castleford: 1978 A2; 1979
A3,NZ3; 1980 NZ3; 1983 F2; 1984 F, nz2
JUBB, K (2) Leeds: 1937 A2
JUKES, W (6) Hunslet: 1908 A3; 1910 A2,NZ

KARALIUS, A (4+1) St.Helens: 1971 NZ3; 1972 F;
1972 nz

KARALIUS, V (12) St.Helens: 1958 A2,NZ2; 1959 F; **1960 NZ,F,A**; 1960 F; 1961 F; Widnes: 1963 A2

KEEGAN, A (9) Hull: 1966 A2; 1967 F2,A3; 1968 F; 1969 F

KELLY, K (4) St.Helens: 1972 F2; Warrington: 1980 NZ; 1982 A

KEMEL, G (2) Widnes: 1965 NZ2

KERSHAW, H (2) Wakefield T: 1910 A,NZ

KINNEAR, R (1) Wigan: 1929 A

KISS, N (1) Wigan: 1985 F

KITCHEN, F (2) Leigh: **1954 A,NZ**

KITCHIN, P (1) Whitehaven: 1965 NZ

KITCHING, J (1) Bradford N: 1946 A

KNAPMAN, E (1) Oldham: 1924 NZ

KNOWELDEN, B (1) Barrow: 1946 NZ

LAUGIITON, D (15) Wigan: 1970 A3,NZ2; **1970 A2,F,NZ**; 1971 F2; Widnes: 1973 A; 1974 F2; 1979 A

LAWRENSON, J (3) Wigan: 1948 A3

LAWS, D (1) Hull KR: 1986 F

LEDGARD, J (11) Dewsbury: 1947 NZ2; Leigh: 1948 A; 1950 A2,NZ; 1951 NZ; **1954 F2,A,NZ**

LEDGER, B (1) St. Helens: 1985 F

LEWIS, G (1) Leigh: 1965 NZ

LEYTHAM, J (5) Wigan: 1907 NZ2; 1910 A2,NZ

LITTLE, S (10) Oldham: 1956 A; 1957 F5; **1957 F,A,NZ**; 1958 F

LLEWELLYN, T (2) Oldham: 1907 NZ2

LLOYD, R (1) Halifax: 1920 A

LOCKWOOD, B (8 + 1) Castleford: **1972 A2,F,NZ**; 1973 A2; 1974 F; Hull KR: 1978 A; 1979 nz

LOMAS, J (7) Salford: 1908 A2; 1910 A2,NZ; Oldham: 1911 A2

LONGSTAFF, F (2) Huddersfield: 1914 A,NZ

LONGWORTH, W (3) Oldham: 1908 A3

LOWE, J (1) Leeds: 1932 NZ

LOWE, P (12) Hull KR: 1970 NZ; 1972 F2; **1972 A2,F,NZ**; 1973 A3, 1978 A2

LOXTON, K (1) Huddersfield: 1971 NZ

LYDON, J (10 + 1) Widnes: 1983 F2; 1984 F, a, NZ2, P; 1985 NZ3; Wigan: 1986 F

MANN, A (2) Bradford N: 1908 A2

MANTLE, J (13) St.Helens: 1966 F2,A3; 1967 A2; 1969 F; 1971 F2,NZ2; 1973 A

MARCHANT, A (1) Castleford: 1986 F

MARTIN, W (1) Workington T: 1962 F

MARTYN, M (2) Leigh: 1958 A; 1959 A

McCORMICK, S (3) Belle Vue R: 1948 A2; St.Helens: A

McCUE, T (6) Widnes: 1936 A; 1937 A; 1946 A3,NZ

McINTYRE, L (1) Oldham: 1963 A

McKEATING, V (2) Workington T: 1951 NZ2

McKINNEY, T (11) Salford: 1951 NZ; 1952 A2; 1954 A3,NZ; Warrington: 1955 NZ3; St.Helens: **1957 NZ**

McTIGUE, B (25) Wigan: 1958 A2,NZ2; 1959 F2,A3; 1960 F2; **1960 NZ,F,A**; 1961 F,NZ3; 1962 F,A3,NZ2; 1963 F

MATHIAS, R (1) St.Helens: 1979 A

MEASURES, J (2) Widnes: 1963 A2

MIDDLETON, A (1) Salford: 1929 A

MILLER, J (1) Wigan: 1911 A

MILLER, J (6) Warrington: 1933 A3; 1936 A,NZ2

MILLS, J (6) Widnes: 1974 A2,NZ; 1978 A2; 1979 A

MILLWARD, R (28 + 1) Castleford: 1966 F; Hull KR: 1967 A3; 1968 F2; **1968 A,F,NZ**; 1970 A2,NZ3; 1971 F,NZ3; 1973 A; 1974 A2a; **1977 F,NZ,A2**; 1978 A3

MILNES, A (2) Halifax: 1920 A2

MOONEY, W (2) Leigh: 1924 NZ2

MOORHOUSE, S (2) Huddersfield: 1914 A,NZ

MORGAN, A (4) Featherstone R: 1968 F2; **1968 F,NZ**

MORGAN, E (2) Hull: 1921 A2

MORGAN, R (2) Swinton: 1963 F,A

MORLEY, J (2) Wigan: 1936 A; 1937 A

MORTIMER, F (2) Wakefield T: 1956 A2

MOSES, G (9) St.Helens: 1955 NZ2; 1956 A; 1957 F3; **1957 F,A,NZ**

MUMBY, K (11) Bradford N: 1982 A; 1983 F; 1984 F2, A3, NZ3, P

MURPHY, A (27) St.Helens: 1958 A3,NZ; 1959 F2,A; **1960 NZ,F,A**; 1960 F; 1961 F,NZ3; 1962 F,A3; 1963 A2; 1964 F; 1965 F,NZ; 1966 F2; Warrington: 1971 NZ

MURPHY, H (1) Wakefield T: 1950 A

MYLER, A (11) Widnes: 1983 F2; 1984 A2, NZ2, P; 1985 NZ2; 1986 F2

MYLER, F (23 + 1) Widnes: **1960 NZ,F,A**; 1960 F; 1961 F; 1962 F; 1963 A; 1964 F; 1965 F,NZ; 1966 A,NZnz; 1967 F2; St.Helens: 1970 A3,NZ3; **1970 A2,F**

NASH, S (24) Featherstone R: 1971 F,NZ; 1972 F2; **1972 A2,F,NZ**; 1973 A2; 1974 A3,NZ3; Salford: **1977 F,NZ,A2**; 1978 A3; 1982 A

NAUGHTON, A (2) Warrington: **1954 F2**

NEWBOULD, H (1) Wakefield T: 1910 A

NICHOLLS, G (29) Widnes: 1971 NZ; 1972 F2; **1972 A2,F,NZ**; St.Helens: 1973 A2; 1974 F2,A3,NZ3; **1977 F,NZ,A**; 1978 A3; 1979 A3,NZ3

NICHOLSON, R (3) Huddersfield: 1946 NZ; 1948 A2

NOBLE, B (11) Bradford N: 1982 A; 1983 F2; 1984 F, A3, NZ3, P

NORTON, S (11 + 1) Castleford: 1974 a,NZ2; Hull: 1978 A3; 1979 A2; 1980 NZ; 1981 F2; 1982 A

O'GRADY, T (6) Oldham: 1954 A2,NZ3; Warrington: 1961 NZ

OLIVER, J (4) Batley: 1928 A3,NZ

323

O'NEILL, D (2 + 1) Widnes: 1971 nz; **1972 A,F**
O'NEILL, M (3) Widnes: 1982 A; 1983 F2
OSTER, J (1) Oldham: 1929 A
OWEN, J (1) St.Helens Recs: 1921 A
OWEN, S (1) Leigh: 1958 F
OWENS, I (4) Leeds: 1946 A3,NZ

PADBURY, R (1) Runcorn: 1908 A
PALIN, H (2) Warrington: 1947 NZ2
PARKER, D (2) Oldham: 1964 F2
PARKIN, J (17) Wakefield T: 1920 A2,NZ3; 1921 A2;1924 A3,NZ; 1926 NZ2; 1928 A,NZ; 1929 A2
PARR, K (1) Warrington: 1968 F
PAWSEY, C (7) Leigh: 1952 A3; 1954 A2,NZ2
PEPPERELL, A (2) Workington T: 1950 NZ; 1951 NZ
PHILLIPS, D (4) Oldham: 1946 A3, Belle Vue R: 1950 A
PIMBLETT, A (3) Warrington: 1948 A3
PINNER, H (5 + 1) St.Helens: 1980 nzNZ; 1985 NZ3; 1986 F
PITCHFORD, F (2) Oldham: 1958 NZ; 1962 F
PITCHFORD, S (4) Leeds: **1977 F,NZ,A2**
PLATT, A (+2) St. Helens: 1985 f; 1986 F
POLLARD, C (1) Wakefield T: 1924 NZ
POLLARD, E (2) Wakefield T: 1932 A2
POLLARD, R (1) Dewsbury: 1950 NZ
POOLE, H (3) Hull KR: 1964 F; Leeds: 1966 NZ2
POTTER, I (5) Wigan: 1985 NZ3; 1986 F2
POWELL, R (+1) Leeds: 1985 f
POYNTON, H (3) Wakefield T: 1962 A2,NZ
PRESCOTT, A (28) St.Helens: 1951 NZ2; 1952 A3; 1954 A3,NZ3; 1955 NZ3; 1956 A3; 1957 F5; **1957 F,A,NZ**; 1958 F,A2
PRICE, J (6) Broughton R: 1921 A2; Wigan: 1924 A2,NZ2
PRICE, M (2) Rochdale H: 1967 A2
PRICE, R (9) Warrington: 1954 A,NZ2; 1955 NZ; 1956 A3; 1957 F2
PRICE, T (1) Bradford N: 1970 A
PRIOR, B (1) Hunslet: 1966 F
PROCTOR, W (+1) Hull: 1984 p
PROSSER, D (1) Leeds: 1937 A
PROSSER, S (1) Halifax: 1914 A

RAE, J (1) Bradford N: 1965 NZ
RAMSDALE, R (8) Wigan: 1910 A2; 1911 A2; 1914 A3,NZ
RAMSEY, W (7 + 1) Hunslet: 1965 NZ2; 1966 F,A2,NZ2; Bradford N; 1974 nz
RATCLIFFE, G (3) Wigan: 1947 NZ; 1950 A2
RATHBONE, A (4 + 1) Bradford N: 1982 a; 1983 F2; 1985 F2
RAYNE, KEITH (4) Leeds: 1984 F2, A, P
PAYNE, KEVIN (1) Leeds: 1986 F
REDFEARN, A (1) Bradford N: 1979 A
REDFEARN, D (6 + 1) Bradford N: **1972 nz**; 1974 F2,A,NZ3

REES, D (1) Halifax: 1926 NZ
REES, T (1) Oldham: 1929 A
REES, W (11) Swinton: 1926 NZ2; 1928 A3,NZ3; 1929 A3
REILLY, M (9) Castleford: 1970 A3,NZ3; **1970 A2,F**
RENILSON, C (7 + 1) Halifax: 1965 NZ; 1967 a; 1968 F3; **1968 A,F,NZ**
RHODES, A (4) St.Helens: **1957 NZ; 1960 F,A**; 1961 NZ
RICHARDS, M (2) Salford: 1974 A,NZ
RILEY, J (1) Halifax: 1910 A
RING, J (2) Wigan: 1924 A; 1926 NZ
RISMAN, A (17) Salford: 1932 A,NZ3; 1933 A3; 1936 A2,NZ2; 1937 A3; 1946 A3
RISMAN, B (5) Leeds: 1968 F2; **1968 A,F,NZ**
RIX, S (9) Oldham: 1924 A3,NZ3; 1926 NZ3
ROBERTS, K (10) Halifax: 1963 A; 1964 F2; 1965 F,NZ3; 1966 F,NZ2
ROBINSON, A (3) Halifax: 1907 NZ; 1908 A2
ROBINSON, Dave (13) Swinton: 1965 NZ; 1966 F2,A3,NZ2; 1967 F2,A2; Wigan: 1970 A
ROBINSON, Don (10) Wakefield T: **1954 F2,NZ,A**; 1955 NZ; Leeds: 1956 A2; 1959 A2; 1960 F
ROBINSON, J (2) Rochdale H: 1914 A2
ROBINSON, W (2) Leigh: 1963 F,A
ROGERS, J (7) Huddersfield: 1914 A; 1920 A3; 1921 A3
ROSE, D (4) Leeds: **1954 F2,A,NZ**
ROSE, P (2 + 3) Hull KR: 1974 a; 1978 Aa2; Hull: 1982 A
ROUND, G (8) Wakefield T: 1959 A; 1962 F2,A3,NZ2
RUDDICK, J (3) Broughton R: 1907 NZ2; 1910 A
RYAN, M (4) Wigan: 1947 NZ; 1948 A2; 1950 A
RYAN, R (5) Warrington: 1950 A,NZ2; 1951 NZ; 1952 A
RYDER, R (1) Warrington: 1952 A

SAYER, W (7) Wigan: 1961 NZ; 1962 F,A3,NZ; 1963 A
SCHOFIELD, D (1) Halifax: 1955 NZ
SCHOFIELD, G (10) Hull: 1984 F, A3, NZ; 1985 NZ3; 1986 F2
SEABOURNE, B (1) Leeds: 1970 NZ
SENIOR, K (2) Huddersfield: 1965 NZ; 1967 F
SHARROCK, J (4) Wigan: 1910 A2,NZ; 1911 A
SHAW, B (6) Hunslet: 1956 A2; **1960 F,A**; 1960 F; Leeds: 1961 F
SHAW, G (1) Widnes: 1980 NZ
SHAW, J (5) Halifax: **1960 F,A**; 1960 F; 1961 F; 1962 NZ
SHELTON, G (7) Hunslet: 1964 F2; 1965 NZ3; 1966 F2
SHOEBOTTOM, M (10 + 2) Leeds: **1968 A,nz**; 1969 F; 1970 A2a,NZ; **1970 A2,F,NZ**; 1971 F
SHUGARS, F (1) Warrington: 1910 NZ
SILCOCK, N (12) Widnes: 1932 A2,NZ2; 1933 A3; 1936 A3; 1937 A2

SILCOCK, N (3) Wigan: 1954 A3
SILCOCK, R (1) Wigan: 1908 A
SIMMS, B (1) Leeds: 1962 F
SKELHORNE, G (7) Warrington: 1920 A,NZ3;
1921 A3
SKERRETT, T (10) Wakefield T: 1979 A2,NZ2;
Hull: 1980 NZ2; 1981 F2; 1982 A2
SLOMAN, R (5) Oldham: 1928 A3,NZ2
SMALES, T (8) Huddersfield: 1962 F; 1963 F,A;
1964 F2; Bradford N: 1965 NZ3
SMALL, P (1) Castleford: 1962 NZ
SMITH, A (6) Oldham: 1907 NZ3; 1908 A3
SMITH, A (10) Leeds: 1970 A2,NZ3; **1970 A2**; 1971
F2; 1973 A
SMITH, F (9) Hunslet: 1910 A,NZ; 1911 A3; 1914
A3,NZ
SMITH, G (3) York: 1963 A; 1964 F2
SMITH, H (2) Bradford N: 1926 NZ2
SMITH, M (10+1) Hull KR: 1979 NZ3; 1980 NZ2;
1981 F2; 1982 A2; 1984 f,NZ
SMITH, P (1+5) Featherstone R: **1977 a2;**1982 A;
1983 f2; 1984 f
SMITH, S (11) Wakefield T: 1929 A; Leeds: A2;
1932 A3,NZ3; 1933 A2
SMITH, S (4) Hunslet: **1954 A,NZ,F2**
SOUTHWARD, I (11) Workington T: 1958 A3,NZ;
Oldham: 1959 F2,A2; 1960 F2; 1962 NZ
SPENCER, J (1) Salford: 1907 NZ
STACEY, J.C (1) Halifax: 1920 NZ
STEPHENS, G (5) Castleford: 1979 A2,NZ3
STEPHENSON, D (2) Wigan: 1982 A2
STEPHENSON, M (5+1) Dewsbury: 1971 nz; 1972
F; **1972 A2,F,NZ**
STEVENSON, J (19) Leeds: 1955 NZ3; 1956 A3;
1957 F5; **1957 F,A,NZ**; 1958 F; York: 1959 A2;
1960 F2
STOCKWELL, S (3) Leeds: 1920 A; 1921 A2
STONE, W (8) Hull: 1920 A3,NZ3; 1921 A2
STOPFORD, J (12) Swinton: 1961 F; 1963 F,A2;
1964 F2; 1965 F,NZ2; 1966 F2,A
STOTT, J (1) St.Helens: 1947 NZ
STREET, H (4) Dewsbury: 1950 A3,NZ
SULLIVAN, C (17) Hull: 1967 F; **1968 A,F,NZ**;
1970 A; 1971 NZ3; 1972 F2; **1972 A2,F,NZ**;
1973 A3
SULLIVAN, J (25) Wigan: 1924 A3,NZ; 1926 NZ3;
1928 A3,NZ3; 1929 A3; 1932 A3,NZ3; 1933 A3
SULLIVAN, M (46) Huddersfield: **1954 F2,NZ,A**;
1955 NZ3; 1956 A3; 1957 F3; **1957 F,A,NZ**;
Wigan: 1957 F2; 1958 F,A3,NZ2; 1959 F2,A3;
1960 F3; **1960 F,NZ,A**; St.Helens: 1961 F,NZ2;
1962 F3,A3,NZ; York: 1963 A
SZYMALA, E (1+1) Barrow: 1981 fF

TAYLOR, H (3) Hull: 1907 NZ3
TAYLOR, R (2) Hull: 1921 A; 1926 NZ
TEMBEY, J (2) St.Helens: 1963 A; 1964 F

TERRY, A (11) St.Helens: 1958 A2; 1959 F2,A3;
1960 F; 1961 F,NZ; Leeds: 1962 F
THOMAS, A (4) Leeds: 1926 NZ2; 1929 A2
THOMAS, G (1) Warrington: 1907 NZ
THOMAS, G (9) Wigan: 1914 A; Huddersfield: 1920
A3,NZ2; 1921 A3
THOMAS, J (8) Wigan: 1907 NZ; 1908 A3; 1910
A2,NZ; 1911 A
THOMAS, L (1) Oldham: 1947 NZ
THOMAS, P (1) Leeds: 1907 NZ
THOMPSON, C (2) Hunslet: 1951 NZ2
THOMPSON, J (12) Leeds: 1924 A,NZ2; 1928
A,NZ; 1929 A; 1932 A3,NZ3
THOMPSON, J (20+1) Featherstone R: 1970
A2,NZ2; **1970 A2,F,NZ**; 1971 Ff; 1974 A3,NZ3;
1977 F,NZ,A2; Bradford N: 1978 A
THORLEY, J (4) Halifax: **1954 F2,NZ,A**
TOOHEY, E (3) Barrow: 1952 A3
TOPLISS, D (4) Wakefield T: 1973 A2; 1979 A;
Hull: 1982 A
TRAILL, K (8) Bradford N: 1950 NZ2; 1951 NZ;
1952 A3; 1954 A,NZ
TROUP, L A (2) Barrow: 1936 NZ2
TURNBULL, A (1) Leeds: 1951 NZ
TURNER, D (24) Oldham: 1956 A2; 1957 F5; **1957
F,A,NZ**; 1958 F; Wakefield: 1959 A; 1960 F3;
1960 NZ,A; 1961 F,NZ; 1962 A2,NZ2,F
TYSON, B (3) Hull KR: 1963 A; 1965 F; 1967 F
TYSON, G (4) Oldham: 1907 NZ; 1908 A3

VALENTINE, D (15) Huddersfield: 1948 A3; 1951
NZ; 1952 A2; 1954 A3,NZ2; **1954 F2,NZ,A**
VALENTINE, R (1) Huddersfield: 1967 A
VINES, D (3) Wakefield T: 1959 F2,A

WAGSTAFF, H (12) Huddersfield: 1911 A2; 1914
A3,NZ; 1920 A2,NZ2; 1921 A2
WALKER, A (1) Whitehaven: 1980 NZ
WALLACE, J (1) St.Helens Recs: 1926 NZ
WALSH, Joe (1) Leigh: 1971 NZ
WALSH, John (4+1) St.Helens: 1972 f; **1972
A2,F,NZ**
WALTON, D (1) Castleford: 1965 F
WANE, S (2) Wigan: 1985 F; 1986 F
WARD, D (12) Leeds: **1977 F,NZ,A**; 1978 A; 1979
A3,NZ3;1981 F; 1982 A
WARD, Edward (3) Wigan: 1946 A2; 1947 NZ
WARD, Ernest (20) Bradford N: 1946 A3,NZ; 1947
NZ2; 1948 A3; 1950 A3,NZ2; 1951 NZ3;
1952 A3
WARD, J (4) Castleford: 1963 A; 1964 F2; Salford:
1970 NZ
WARD, K (1) Castleford: 1984 F
WARD, W (1) Leeds: 1910 A
WARLOW, J (6+1) St.Helens: 1964 F; **1968 f,NZ**;
1968 F; Widnes: 1971 F2,NZ
WARWICK, S (2) Salford: 1907 NZ2

WATKINS, D (2 + 4) Salford: 1971 f,NZ; 1973 a; 1974 f2,A

WATKINS, W (7) Salford: 1933 A; 1936 A2,NZ2; 1937 A2

WATKINSON, D (9 + 1) Hull KR: 1979 a; 1980 NZ; 1981 F; 1984 F; 1985 F, NZ3; 1986 F2

WATSON, C (29 + 1) St.Helens: 1963 A2; 1966 F2,A3,NZ2; 1967 F,A3; 1968 F2; **1968 A,F,nz**; 1969 F; 1970 A3,NZ3; **1970 A2,F,NZ**; 1971 F

WATTS, B (5) York: **1954 F2,NZ,A**; 1955 NZ

WEBSTER, F (3) Leeds: 1910 A2,NZ

WHITCOMBE, F (2) Bradford N: 1946 A2

WHITE, L (7) Hunslet: 1932 A3,NZ2; 1933 A2

WHITE, L (6) York: 1946 A3,NZ; Wigan: 1947 NZ2

WHITE, T (1) Oldham: 1907 NZ

WHITEHEAD, D (3) Warrington: 1971 F2,NZ

WHITELEY, J (15) Hull: **1957 A**; 1958 A3,NZ; 1959 F2,A2; 1960 F; **1960 NZ,F**; 1961 NZ2; 1962 F

WILKINSON, J (13) Halifax: 1954 A,NZ2; 1955 NZ3; Wakefield T: 1959 A; 1960 F2; **1960 NZ,F,A**; 1962 NZ

WILLIAMS, F (2) Halifax: 1914 A2

WILLIAMS, R (12) Leeds: 1948 A2; 1950 A2,NZ2; 1951 NZ3; Hunslet: 1954 A2,NZ

WILLIAMS, W (2) Salford: 1929 A; 1932 A

WILLICOMBE, D (3) Halifax: 1974 F; Wigan: F,NZ

WILSON, G (3) Workington T: 1951 NZ3

WILSON, H (3) Hunslet: 1907 NZ3

WINSLADE, C (1) Oldham: 1959 F

WINSTANLEY, W (5) Leigh: 1910 A,NZ; Wigan: 1911 A3

WOOD, A (4) Oldham: 1911 A2; 1914 A,NZ

WOODS, H (6) Liverpool S: 1936 A3,NZ2; Leeds: 1937 A

WOODS, J (1) Barrow: 1933 A

WOODS, J (7 + 3) Leigh: 1979 A3,nz; 1980 NZ; 1981 F2; 1982 Aa; 1983 f

WOODS, T (2) Rochdale H: 1911 A2

WORRALL, M (3) Oldham: 1984 F, A2

WRIGHT, J (1) Swinton: 1932 NZ

WRIGHT, S (7) Widnes: **1977 F,NZ,A2**; 1978 A3

WRIGLESWORTH, G (5) Leeds: 1965 NZ; 1966 A2,NZ2

YOUNG, C (5) Hull KR: 1967 A3; 1968 F2

YOUNG, F (1) Leeds: 1908 A

YOUNG, H (1) Huddersfield: 1929 A

GREAT BRITAIN WORLD CUP SQUADS

Captains in bold

1954 IN FRANCE

D. Valentine (Huddersfield)
W. Banks (Huddersfield)
H. Bradshaw (Huddersfield)
G. Brown (Leeds)
R. Coverdale (Hull)
G. Helme (Warrington)
P. Jackson (Barrow)
F. Kitchen (Leigh)
J. Ledgard (Leigh)

A. Naughton (Warrington)
D. Robinson (Wakefield T)
D. Rose (Leeds)
R. Rylance (Huddersfield)
S. Smith (Hunslet)
M. Sullivan (Huddersfield)
J. Thorley (Halifax)
B. Watts (York)
J. Whiteley (Hull)

Manager: G. Shaw (Castleford)

1957 IN AUSTRALIA

A. Prescott (St. Helens)
E. Ashton (Wigan)
W. Boston (Wigan)
A. Davies (Oldham)
J. Grundy (Barrow)
G. Gunney (Hunslet)
T. Harris (Hull)
P. Jackson (Barrow)
L. Jones (Leeds)

S. Little (Oldham)
T. McKinney (St. Helens)
G. Moses (St. Helens)
R. Price (Warrington)
A. Rhodes (St. Helens)
J. Stevenson (Leeds)
M. Sullivan (Huddersfield)
D. Turner (Oldham)
J. Whiteley (Hull)

Managers: W. Fallowfield (RL Secretary) and H. Rawson (Hunslet)

1960 IN ENGLAND

E. Ashton (Wigan)
W. Boston (Wigan)
J. Challinor (Warrington)
A. Davies (Oldham)
E. Fraser (Warrington)
R. Greenough (Warrington)
T. Harris (Hull)
V. Karalius (St. Helens)
B. McTigue (Wigan)

A. Murphy (St. Helens)
F. Myler (Widnes)
A. Rhodes (St. Helens)
B. Shaw (Hunslet)
J. Shaw (Halifax)
M. Sullivan (Wigan)
D. Turner (Wakefield T)
J. Whiteley (Hull)
J. Wilkinson (Wakefield T)

Manager: W. Fallowfield (RL Secretary)

1968 IN AUSTRALIA AND NEW ZEALAND

B. Risman (Leeds)
J. Atkinson (Leeds)
K. Ashcroft (Leigh)
T. Bishop (St. Helens)
I. Brooke (Wakefield T)
A. Burwell (Hull KR)
M. Clark (Leeds)
D. Edwards (Castleford)
P. Flanagan (Hull KR)

R. French (Widnes)
R. Haigh (Wakefield T)
R. Millward (Hull KR)
A. Morgan (Featherstone R)
C. Renilson (Halifax)
M. Shoebottom (Leeds)
C. Sullivan (Hull)
J. Warlow (St. Helens)
C. Watson (St. Helens)
C. Young (Hull KR)

Manager: W. Fallowfield (RL Secretary)

Coach: C. Hutton (Hull KR)

1970 IN ENGLAND

F. Myler (St. Helens)
K. Ashcroft (Leigh)
J. Atkinson (Leeds)
P. Charlton (Salford)
D. Chisnall (Leigh)
R. Dutton (Widnes)
A. Fisher (Bradford N & Leeds)
R. Haigh (Leeds)
D. Hartley (Castleford)
C. Hesketh (Salford)

K. Hepworth (Castleford)
S. Hynes (Leeds)
K. Jones (Wigan)
D. Laughton (Wigan)
M. Reilly (Castleford)
M. Shoebottom (Leeds)
A. Smith (Leeds)
J. Thompson (Featherstone R)
C. Watson (St. Helens)

Manager: J. Harding (Leigh)

Coach: J. Whiteley (Hull KR)

1972 IN FRANCE

C. Sullivan (Hull)
J. Atkinson (Leeds)
P. Charlton (Salford)
T. Clawson (Leeds)
C. Dixon (Salford)
C. Hesketh (Salford)
J. Holmes (Leeds)
R. Irving (Oldham)
D. Jeanes (Leeds)
A. Karalius (St. Helens)

Manager: W. Spaven (Hull KR)

B. Lockwood (Castleford)
P. Lowe (Hull KR)
S. Nash (Featherstone R)
G. Nicholls (Widnes)
D. O'Neill (Widnes)
D. Redfearn (Bradford N)
M. Stephenson (Dewsbury)
D. Topliss (Wakefield T)
John Walsh (St. Helens)

Coach: J. Challinor (St. Helens)

1977 IN AUSTRALIA AND NEW ZEALAND

R. Millward (Hull KR)
E. Bowman (Workington T)
L. Casey (Hull KR)
L. Dyl (Leeds)
K. Elwell (Widnes)
G. Fairbairn (Wigan)
K. Fielding (Salford)
W. Francis (Wigan)
K. Gill (Salford)
A. Hodkinson (Rochdale H)

Manager: R. Parker (Blackpool B)

P. Hogan (Barrow)
J. Holmes (Leeds)
S. Lloyd (Castleford)
S. Nash (Salford)
G. Nicholls (St. Helens)
S. Pitchford (Leeds)
P. Smith (Featherstone R)
J. Thompson (Featherstone R)
D. Ward (Leeds)
S. Wright (Widnes)

Coach: D. Watkins (Salford)

● For details of the 1975 World Championship Squads see ENGLAND AND WALES section.

A rampaging Neil Puckering at Whitehaven.

UNDER-21s

Great Britain's young Lions experienced an up and down season. A creditable 16-12 defeat at the hands of the New Zealand tourists was followed by a 19-6 trouncing by the French Under-24s, beaten two weeks later 6-2 at Whitehaven.

The opening match of the Under-21s' Whitbread Trophy Bitter programme was at Odsal, Bradford, in October, the second match of the Kiwi tour. The British produced a mixture of battling forward play and sudden bursts of direct running among the backs.

Discipline was also a strong point in the narrow loss as they refused to get rattled despite some fierce forward exchanges. Hull's Gary Divorty stood out in the hardworking British pack to take the home team's Whitbread Trophy Bitter Man of the Match award with an artistic loose forward display.

He made his mark with tactical kicking and two defence-splitting passes that led to both Britain's tries from Shaun Edwards and Mark Forster. Club team-mate Andy Dannatt and Edwards also stood out in a promising team effort, Warrington winger Brian Carbert adding two goals.

Three months later the Under-21s travelled to St. Esteve to meet the French Espoirs, an Under-24 selection. Previously defeated only once — back in 1966 — in 17 meetings at under-24 and under-21 level, the junior Lions crashed to a disappointing 13-point margin defeat.

Britain were a distinct second best to a revitalised French outfit featuring six players who were to go on to claim a Test cap a month later.

Blond full back Gilles Dumas took the Man of the Match award with a brilliant display highlighted by a haul of 11 points from five goals and a drop goal.

The St. Gaudens star opened the scoring with two penalties inside the first six minutes before new Under-21 skipper Shaun Wane crashed over for an equalising try. Dumas added two more long range penalty goals to further punish an undisciplined British outfit who failed to find sustained attacking rhythm.

Dumas started the second half with a drop goal before prop Gilles Dorval crossed for a 48th minute try, a Brian Carbert penalty 15 minutes later cutting the French lead to 13-6.

Eight minutes from time, the French dominance was confirmed with a try from busy scrum half Patrick Entat, plus the almost inevitable goal from Dumas.

The visitors contributed little on attack and the British Whitbread Trophy Bitter Man of the Match award went to tough tackling second row man Paul Lyman ahead of fellow top defender Roy Powell.

Two weeks later in Cumbria, France battled against an improved British side and freezing conditions to prove that their newfound style of Gallic support play combined with Australian-influenced defence was no flash in the pan.

Dumas again opened the scoring with a 26th minute penalty and it was not until after the break that Britain settled into any sort of pattern. Lacking the suspended Shaun Wane and fielding two newcomers in Rochdale Hornets full back Kevin Harcombe and Leigh hooker Gary Hughes, Britain made the vital breakthrough after 53 minutes.

Stand-off David Creasser's long pass created the space for Warrington winger Carbert to touch down. Britain produced a powerful finishing quarter when Leeds barnstorming prop Brendan Hill came on for Hull's Neil Puckering, who had earlier spent 10 minutes in the sin bin.

Carbert added a penalty goal in the 69th minute to put Britain back on the victory trail, debutant Harcombe taking Britain's Whitbread Trophy Bitter Man of the Match award.

9th October   Bradford

GREAT BRITAIN 12   **NEW ZEALAND 16**

David Lyon (Widnes)	1.	Darren Williams
Jimmy Dalton (Whitehaven)	2.	Mark Bourneville
David Creasser (Leeds)	3.	Joe Ropati
Mark Forster (Warrington)	4.	Olsen Filipaina, Capt.
Brian Carbert (Warrington)	5.	Shaun Horo
Shaun Edwards (Wigan)	6.	Shane Cooper
Mike Ford (Wigan)	7.	Glen Gibb
Andy Dannatt (Hull)	8.	Dane Sorensen
Paul Groves (Salford), Capt.	9.	Wayne Wallace
Shaun Wane (Wigan)	10.	James Goulding
Roy Powell (Leeds)	11.	Owen Wright
Paul Lyman (Featherstone R.)	12.	Sam Stewart
Gary Divorty (Hull)	13.	Hugh McGahan
David Hulme (Widnes)	14.	Ron O'Regan
John Westhead (Leigh)	15.	Kurt Sorensen

T: Edwards, Forster

G: Carbert (2)

Substitutions:

Westhead for Lyman (35 min.)

Hulme for Creasser (46 min.)

Manager: Les Bettinson

Coach: Maurice Bamford

T: McGahan, Horo

G: Filipaina (4)

Substitution:

K. Sorensen for D. Sorensen (46 min.)

Half-time: 6-10

Referee: Derek Fox (Wakefield)

Attendance: 2,285

19th January   St. Esteve

GREAT BRITAIN 6   **FRANCE 19**

David Lyon (Widnes)	1.	Gilles Dumas (St. Gaudens)
Jimmy Dalton (Whitehaven)	2.	Didier Paillares (X111 Catalan)
David Creasser (Leeds)	3.	Philippe Lapeyre (Albi)
Mark Forster (Warrington)	4.	Jean-Philippe Pougeau (Paris-Chat)
Brian Carbert (Warrington)	5.	Didier Couston (Le Pontet)
David Hulme (Widnes)	6.	Dominique Espugna (Lezignan)
Mike Ford (Wigan)	7.	Patrick Entat (Avignon)
Andy Dannatt (Hull)	8.	Thierry Brencz (Albi)
Neil Puckering (Hull)	9.	Patrick Baco (X111 Catalan)
Shaun Wane (Wigan), Capt.	10.	Gilles Dorval (Paris-Chat)
Roy Powell (Leeds)	11.	Pierre Montgaillard (X111 Catalan), Capt.
Paul Lyman (Featherstone R.)	12.	Francis Cunnac (Albi)
Gary Divorty (Hull)	13.	Mathieu Khedimi (St. Esteve)
Mark Beckwith (Whitehaven)	14.	Vincent Baloup (Toulouse)
John Westhead (Leigh)	15.	Franck Romano (Carpentras)

T: Wane

G: Carbert

Substitutions:

Westhead for Dannatt (Half-time)

Beckwith for Ford (69 min.)

Manager: Les Bettinson

Coach: Maurice Bamford

Attendance: 3,000

T: Dorval, Entat

G: Dumas (5, 1dg)

Substitutions:

Romano for Cunnac (61 min.)

Baloup for Couston (74 min.)

Half-time: 4-8

Referee: Fred Lindop (Wakefield)

2nd February Whitehaven

GREAT BRITAIN 6		FRANCE 2
Kevin Harcombe (Rochdale H.)	1.	Gilles Dumas (St. Gaudens)
Jimmy Dalton (Whitehaven)	2.	Didier Paillares (X111 Catalan)
Mark Beckwith (Whitehaven)	3.	Philippe Lapeyre (Albi)
Mark Forster (Warrington)	4.	Jean-Philippe Pougeau (Paris-Chat)
Brian Carbert (Warrington)	5.	Vincent Baloup (Toulouse)
David Creasser (Leeds)	6.	Dominique Espugna (Lezignan)
David Hulme (Widnes)	7.	Patrick Entat (Avignon)
Roy Powell (Leeds)	8.	Thierry Brencz (Albi)
Gary Hughes (Leigh)	9.	Patrick Baco (X111 Catalan)
Neil Puckering (Hull)	10.	Gilles Dorval (Paris-Chat)
Gary Divorty (Hull), Capt.	11.	Pierre Montgaillard (X111 Catalan), Capt.
John Westhead (Leigh)	12.	Franck Romano (Carpentras)
Paul Lyman (Featherstone R.)	13.	Mathieu Khedimi (St. Esteve)
David Lyon (Widnes)	14.	Didier Couston (Le Pontet)
Brendan Hill (Leeds)	15.	Gilbert Allieres (Toulouse)

T: Carbert
G: Carbert
Substitution:
Hill for Puckering (58 min.)
Manager: Les Bettinson
Coach: Maurice Bamford
Referee: Julien Rascagneres (Perpignan)

G: Dumas
Substitutions:
Allieres for Khedimi (58 min.)
Couston for Pougeau (75 min.)
Half-time: 0-2
Attendance: 2,539

GREAT BRITAIN UNDER-21s RESULTS

25 Nov. 1984 W 24-8 v. F Castleford
16 Dec. 1984 W 8-2 v. F Albi
 9 Oct. 1985 L 12-16 v. NZ Bradford
19 Jan. 1986 L 6-19 v. F St. Esteve
 2 Feb. 1986 W 6-2 v. F Whitehaven

Key: A - Australia, F - France,
NZ - New Zealand

GREAT BRITAIN UNDER-21s REGISTER

The following is a register of appearances for Great Britain Under-21s since this classification of match was introduced in 1984.

Figures in brackets are the total appearances, with the plus sign indicating substitute appearances, e.g. (3 + 1).

Away matches are in bold letters. Substitute appearances are in lower case letters.

ALLEN, S. (1) St. Helens: 1984 F

BECKWITH, M. (1 + 1) Whitehaven: 1986 f, F

CARBERT, B. (3) Warrington: 1985 NZ; 1986 **F**, F
CLARK, G. (2) Hull K.R.: 1984 F, **F**
CONWAY, M. (1) Leeds: 1984 F
CREASSER, D. (5) Leeds: 1984 F, **F**; 1985 NZ; 1986 **F**, F
CROOKS, L. (2) Hull 1984 F, **F**
CURRIER, A. (2) Widnes: 1984 F, **F**

DALTON, J. (3) Whitehaven: 1985 NZ; 1986 **F**, F
DANNATT, A. (4) Hull: 1984 F, **F**; 1985 NZ; 1986 **F**
DIVORTY, G. (4) Hull: 1984 F; 1985 NZ; 1986 **F**, F

EDWARDS, S. (2) Wigan: 1984 F; 1985 NZ

FORD, M. (2) Wigan: 1985 NZ; 1986 **F**
FORSTER, M. (3) Warrington: 1985 NZ; 1986 **F**, F
FOX, D. (1) Featherstone R.: 1984 **F**

GREGORY, M. (1) Warrington: 1984 **F**
GRIBBIN, V. (1 + 1) Whitehaven: 1984 f, **F**;
GROVES, P. (3) Salford: 1984 F, **F**; 1985 NZ

HARCOMBE, K. (1) Rochdale H.: 1986 F
HILL, B. (+1) Leeds: 1986 f
HUGHES, G. (1) Leigh: 1986 F
HULME, D. (2+1) Widnes: 1985 nz; 1986 **F**, F

LYMAN, P. (3) Featherstone R.: 1985 NZ; 1986 **F**, F
LYON, D. (2) Widnes: 1985 NZ; 1986 F

POWELL, R. (5) Leeds: 1984 F, **F**; 1985 NZ; 1986 **F**, F
PROCTOR, W. (+1) Hull: 1984 f
PUCKERING, N. (2) Hull: 1986 **F**, F

RIPPON, A. (1) Swinton: 1984 **F**
ROUND, P. (1+1) St. Helens: 1984 F, f

SCHOFIELD, G. (2) Hull: 1984 **F**, F

WANE, S. (3) Wigan: 1984 **F**; 1985 NZ; 1986 F
WESTHEAD, J. (1+2) Leigh: 1985 nz; 1986 f, **F**

Wingman Jimmy Dalton on home ground at Whitehaven.

GREAT BRITAIN
UNDER-24s RESULTS

3 Apr. 1965	W 17-9	v. F	Toulouse
20 Oct. 1965	W 12-5	v. F	Oldham
26 Nov. 1966	L 4-7	v. F	Bayonne
17 Apr. 1969	W 42-2	v. F	Castleford
14 Nov. 1976	W 19-2	v. F	Hull K.R.
5 Dec. 1976	W 11-9	v. F	Albi
12 Nov. 1977	W 27-9	v. F	Hull
18 Dec. 1977	W 8-4	v. F	Tonneins
4 Oct. 1978	L 8-30	v. A	Hull K.R.
14 Jan. 1979	W 15-3	v. F	Limoux
24 Nov. 1979	W 14-2	v. F	Leigh
13 Jan. 1980	W 11-7	v. F	Carcassonne
5 Nov. 1980	L 14-18	v. NZ	Fulham
10 Jan. 1981	W 9-2	v. F	Villeneuve
16 Jan. 1982	W 19-16	v. F	Leeds
21 Feb. 1982	W 24-12	v. F	Tonneins
16 Jan. 1983	W 19-5	v. F	Carpentras
11 Nov. 1983	W 28-23	v. F	Villeneuve
4 Dec. 1983	W 48-1	v. F	Oldham

GREAT BRITAIN
UNDER-24s REGISTER
Since reintroduction in 1976

The following is a register of appearances for Great Britain Under-24s since this classification of match was reintroduced in 1976.

Figures in brackets are the total appearances, with the plus sign indicating substitute appearances, e.g. (7+3).

Away matches are in bold letters. Substitute appearances are in lower case letters.

ARKWRIGHT, C. (1) St. Helens: 1982 F
ASHTON, R. (3) Oldham: 1983 **F**, **F**, F

BANKS, B. (1) York: 1979 **F**
BELL, K. (2) Featherstone R.: 1977 F, **F**
BENTLEY, K. (+1) Widnes: 1980 nz
BURKE, M. (5) Widnes: 1979 F; 1980 **F**, NZ; 1982 F; 1983 **F**
BURTON, B. (2) Castleford: 1976 F, **F**

CAIRNS, D. (2) Barrow: 1979 F; 1982 **F**
CASE, B. (3 + 1) Warrington: 1979 **F**; 1980 NZ: 1981 **F**; 1982 f
CLARK, G. (3) Hull K.R.: 1983 **F, F,** F
CRAMPTON, J. (4) Hull: 1976 F, **F**; 1977 F, **F**
CROOKS, L. (1) Hull: 1983 F

DICKINSON, R. (5) Leeds: 1976 F, **F**; 1977 F, **F**; 1978 A
DRUMMOND, D. (5) Leigh: 1979 F; 1980 **F**; 1981 **F**; 1982 F, **F**
DUANE, R. (2) Warrington: 1983 **F, F**
DUNN, B. (2) Wigan: 1983 **F,** F

ECCLES, R. (2) Warrington: 1978 A; 1979 F
ENGLAND, K. (+1) Castleford: 1983 f
EVANS, S. (3) Featherstone R.: 1980 NZ; 1981 **F**; Hull: 1982 **F**

FENNELL, D. (1) Featherstone R.: 1978 A
FENTON, S. (6) Castleford: 1977 F, **F**; 1979 F; 1980 **F**, NZ; 1981 **F**
FIELDHOUSE, J. (1 + 1) Warrington: 1983 **F**, f
FLANAGAN, T. (5) Oldham: 1980 NZ; 1981 **F**; 1983 **F, F,** F
FORD, Phil (1) Warrington: 1982 **F**
FOX, V. (1) Whitehaven: 1980 NZ
FOY, D. (2) Oldham: 1983 **F,** F

GIBBINS, M. (2) Featherstone R.: 1977 F, **F**
GILBERT, J. (2 + 1) Featherstone R.: 1977 F; 1977 f; 1981 **F**
GILL, H. (1) Wigan: 1982 F
GOODWAY, A. (2) Oldham: 1983 **F,** F
GREGORY, A. (1) Widnes: 1982 F

HALL, D. (+1) Hull K.R.: 1976 f
HANLEY, E. (2) Bradford N.: 1982 F; 1983 F
HARKIN, P. (1) Hull K.R.: 1981 **F**
HARTLEY, I. (1) Workington T.: 1979 **F**
HOBBS, D. (2) Featherstone R.: 1982 F, **F**
HOGAN, P. (2) Barrow: 1978 A; Hull K.R.: 1979 **F**
HOLDING, N. (4) St. Helens: 1979 **F**; 1980 **F**, NZ; 1983 **F**
HOLDSTOCK, R. (3) Hull K.R.: 1978 A; 1979 F; 1980 **F**
HORNBY, J. (2) Wigan: 1978 A; 1979 **F**
HYDE, G. (1 + 1) Castleford: 1980 NZ; 1982 f

JAMES, K. (1) Bramley: 1980 **F**
JOHNSON, B. (2) Castleford: 1982 F, **F**
JOYNER, J. (4 + 1) Castleford: 1976 f; 1977 F, **F**; 1978 A; 1979 **F**

LEDGER, B. (2) St. Helens: 1983 **F,** F
LIPTROT, G. (4) St. Helens: 1977 F, **F**; 1978 A; 1979 **F**
LYDON, J. (3) Widnes: 1983 **F, F,** F

MASKILL, C. (1) Wakefield T.: 1983 **F**
MOLL, D. (1) Keighley: 1983 **F**
MUMBY, K. (6) Bradford N.: 1976 F, **F**; 1977 F, **F**; 1978 A; 1981 **F**
MUSCROFT, P. (3) New Hunslet: 1976 F, **F**; 1978 A
MYLER, A. (3) Widnes: 1982 **F**; 1983 **F,** F
MYLER, J. (1 + 1) Widnes: 1982 f; **F**

NOBLE, B. (4) Bradford N.: 1982 F, **F**; 1983 **F,** F
NULTY, J. (2) Wigan: 1976 F, **F**

O'NEILL, M. (3 + 2) Widnes: 1980 nz; 1982 F, f; 1983 **F, F**
O'NEILL, P. (3) Salford: 1980 **F**, NZ; 1981 **F**
O'NEILL, S. (2) Wigan: 1979 **F**; 1981 **F**

PINNER, H. (4 + 4) St. Helens: 1976 F, **F**; 1977 f, f; 1978 a; 1979 f, **F**; 1980 **F**
POTTER, I. (4) Warrington: 1979 **F**; 1981 **F**; Leigh: 1982 F, **F**
PROCTOR, W. (1) Hull: 1983 **F**

RATHBONE, A. (+1) Leigh: 1979 f
RAYNE, Keith (2) Wakefield T.: 1979 F; 1980 **F**
RICHARDSON, T. (1) Castleford: 1979 **F**
ROE, P. (4) Bradford N.: 1976 F, **F**; 1977 F, **F**
RUDD, I. (1 + 1) Workington T.: 1979 f; 1980 **F**

SCHOFIELD, G. (+2) Hull: 1983 f, f
SHEPHERD, M. (2) Huddersfield: 1977 F, **F**
SKERRETT, T. (1) Wakefield T.: 1977 F
SMITH, D. (2) Leeds: 1976 F, **F**
SMITH, Malcolm (1) Wigan: 1979 F
SMITH, Mike (7) Hull K.R.: 1976 F, **F**; 1977 **F**; 1978 A; 1979 **F**, F; 1980 **F**
SMITH, P. (1) Featherstone R.: 1978 A
SMITH, R. (+1) Salford: 1983 f
STEPHENSON, D. (5) Salford: 1979 F; 1980 **F**, NZ; 1982 F; Wigan: 1982 **F**
SWANN, M. (1) Leigh: 1979 F
SYZMALA, E. (2) Barrow: 1976 F, **F**

THACKRAY, R. (1) Warrington: 1980 NZ
TIMSON, A. (2) Castleford: 1982 F, **F**
TURNBULL, S. (2) Salford: 1976 F, **F**

VAN BELLEN, G. (2) Bradford N.: 1980 NZ; 1982 **F**

WARD, D. (+2) Leeds: 1976 f, f
WARD, K. (3) Castleford: 1980 **F**, NZ; 1981 **F**
WHITFIELD, C. (1) Salford: 1981 **F**
WILKINSON, A. (1) Leigh: 1977 **F**
WOOD, J. (2) Widnes: 1977 F, **F**
WOODS, J. (5) Leigh: 1977 F, **F**; 1978 A; 1979 F, F
WORRALL, M. (3) Oldham: 1983 **F, F,** F

ENGLAND & WALES

The following is a register of England and Wales appearances since the reintroduction of European and World Championship matches in 1975, but does not include England's challenge match against Australia played after the 1975 World Championship.

Figures in brackets are the total appearances since 1975, with the plus sign indicating substitute appearances, e.g. (7 + 3).

A few players also played in the 1969-70 European Championship and this is shown as an additional total outside bracket, e.g. (11)2.

World championship matches are in bold letters. Substitute appearances are in lower case letters.

A - Australia, E - England, F - France, NZ - New Zealand, W - Wales.

ENGLAND REGISTER
Since reintroduction in 1975

ADAMS, M. (3 + 2) Widnes: 1975 **NZ, a**; 1978 F; 1979 W; 1981 w
ARKWRIGHT, C. (+ 1) St. Helens: 1984 w
ATKINSON, J. (7)4 Leeds: 1975 W, **F, W, NZ, W**; 1978 F, W

BANKS, B (+ 1) York: 1979 f
BEARDMORE, K. (1) Castleford: 1984 W
BEVERLEY, H. (1) Workington T: 1979 W
BRIDGES, K. (7) Featherstone R: 1975 **NZ, A, W, F, NZ, A**; 1977 W
BURKE, M. (1) Widnes: 1984 W

CAIRNS, D. (1) Barrow: 1984 W
CASE, B. (1) Warrington: 1981 F
CASEY, L. (5) Hull K.R.: 1978 F, W; 1980 W; 1981 F, W
CHARLTON, P. (1) Salford: 1975 **F**
CHISNALL, D. (3 + 1) Warrington: 1975 w, **F, W, NZ**
CHISNALL, E. (3 + 1) St. Helens: 1975 F, **W, NZ, a**
CLARK, G. (1) Hull K.R.: 1984 W
COOKSON, P. (2) Leeds: 1975 **NZ, A**
COULMAN, M. (5) Salford: 1975 F, W, **W, A**; 1977 F
CUNNINGHAM, J. (2) Barrow: 1975 F, W

DONLAN, S. (1) Leigh: 1984 W
DRUMMOND, D. (5) Leigh: 1980 W, F; 1981 F, W; 1984 W
DUNN, G. (6) Hull K.R.: 1975 W, **A, F, NZ, A**; 1977 F
DYL, L. (12 + 1) Leeds: 1975 F, W, **F, W, NZ, A, nz** A; 1977 W, F; 1978 F, W; 1981 W
ECKERSLEY, D. (+ 5) St. Helens: 1975 f, **w, f**; Widnes: 1977 w; 1978 w
ELWELL, K. (2) Widnes: 1978 F, W
EVANS, S. (3) Featherstone R: 1979 F; 1980 W, F

FAIRBAIRN, G. (15) Wigan: 1975 **W, NZ, A, W, F, NZ, A**; 1977 W, F; 1978 F; 1980 W, F; 1981 F, W; Hull K.R.: 1981 W

FARRAR, V. (1) Featherstone R: 1977 F
FENTON, S. (2) Castleford: 1981 F, W
FIELDING, K. (7) Salford: 1975 F, **F, W, NZ, A, W, F**
FORSYTH, C. (3) Bradford N: 1975 **W, F, NZ**

GILL, H. (1) Wigan: 1981 **W**
GILL, K. (9 + 2) Salford: 1975 W, **F, w, NZ, a, W, F, NZ, A**; 1977 W, F
GLYNN, P. (2) St. Helens: 1979 W, F
GOODWAY, A. (1) Oldham: 1984 W
GORLEY, L. (1 + 1) Workington T: 1977 W. Widnes: 1981 w
GORLEY, P. (2 + 1) St. Helens: 1980 W, f; 1981 W
GRAY, J. (3) Wigan: 1975 F, W, **F**
GRAYSHON, J. (9 + 1) Dewsbury: 1975 **W, F, NZ, A**; 1977 W. Bradford N: 1979 W, F; 1980 w, F; 1981 W
HANLEY, E. (1) Bradford N.: 1984 W
HARRISON, M. (2) Leeds: 1978 F, W
HOBBS, D. (1) Featherstone R.: 1984 W
HOGAN, B. (5) Wigan: 1975 **W, F, NZ, A**; 1977 W
HOGAN, P. (1) Hull K.R.: 1979 F
HOLDING, N. (1) St. Helens: 1980 W
HOLDSTOCK, R. (3) Hull K.R.: 1980 W, F; 1981 W
HOLMES, J. (5 + 2) Leeds: 1975 **W, F, NZ, A**; 1977 W, f; 1978 f
HUDDART, M. (1) Whitehaven: 1984 W
HUGHES, E. (8 + 1) Widnes: 1975 **W, F, NZ, a**; 1977 F; 1978 F, W; 1979 W, F
IRVING, R. (3) Wigan: 1975 **W, F, A**

JACKSON, P. (2) Bradford N.: 1975 W, **F**
JONES, L. (1) St. Helens: 1977 W
JOYNER, J. (4) Castleford: 1980 W, F; 1981 F, W
KELLY, A. (1) Hull K.R.: 1984 W
KELLY, K. (3) Warrington: 1979 W; 1981 F, W
LAUGHTON, D. (1) Widnes: 1977 W
LEDGER, B. (+ 1) St. Helens: 1984 w

LIPTROT, G. (2) St. Helens: 1979 W, F
LOCKWOOD, B. (2)+1 Hull K.R.: 1979 W, F
LOWE, P. (3)2 Hull K.R.: 1977 F; 1978 F; 1981 W

MARTYN, T. (4+1) Warrington: 1975 W, **F, w**;
1979 W, F
MILLINGTON, J. (2) Hull K.R.: 1975 F; 1981 W
MILLWARD, R. (13)3+1 Hull K.R.: 1975 F, W,
F, W, A, W, F, NZ, A; 1977 W, F; 1978 F, W
MORGAN, M. (3+3) Wakefield T: 1975 f, W, **f, W,
nz, A**
MUMBY, K. (2) Bradford N: 1979 W, F
MURPHY, M. (1) Oldham: 1975 F

NASH, S. (7) Featherstone R: 1975 **W, NZ, A.**
Salford: 1978 F, W; 1981 W, W
NICHOLLS, G. (7+4) St. Helens: 1975 F, **F, W, NZ,
A, w, nz, f**; 1977 f; 1978 F, W
NOONAN, D. (3) Warrington: 1975 W, **F, W**
NORTON, S. (11) Castleford: 1975 **W, NZ, A, W, F,
NZ, A**; 1977 F. Hull: 1978 W; 1981 W, W

O'NEILL, S. (1) Wigan: 1981 F

PATTINSON, W. (1+1) Workington T: 1981 f, W
PHILBIN, B. (1) Warrington: 1975 **F**
PIMBLETT, G. (1) St. Helens: 1978 W
PINNER, H. (3) St. Helens: 1980 W, F; 1981 F
POTTER, I. (2) Warrington: 1981 F, W

RAYNE, Keith (2) Wakefield T: 1980 W, F

REDFEARN, A. (2) Bradford N: 1979 F; 1980 F
REDFEARN, D. (2) Bradford N: 1975 F, **A**
REILLY, M. (+1)2 Castleford: 1977 w
RICHARDSON, T. (1) Castleford: 1981 W
ROSE, P. (2) Hull K.R.: 1977 F; 1978 W

SCHOFIELD, G. (1) Hull: 1984 W
SHEARD, L. (1) Wakefield T: 1975 W
SMITH, D. (1) Leeds: 1977 F
SMITH, K. (1) Wakefield T: 1979 W
SMITH, M. (5) Hull K.R.: 1980 W, F; 1981 F, W, W
SMITH, P. (1) Featherstone R: 1980 F
STEPHENS, G. (1) Castleford: 1979 W
SZYMALA, E. (+1) Barrow: 1979 f

THOMPSON, J. (2+1)1 Featherstone R: 1975 **A**;
1977 W. Bradford N: 1978 w
TINDALL, K. (1) Hull: 1979 F
TOPLISS, D. (1) Wakefield T: 1975 F

WADDELL, H. (1) Blackpool B.: 1984 W
WALKER, A. (1) Whitehaven: 1981 W
WALSH, J. (3) St. Helens: 1975 F, **NZ, A**
WARD, D. (6) Leeds: 1977 F; 1980 W, F;
1981 F, W, W
WATKINSON, D (+1) Hull K.R.: 1977 w
WOODS, J. (3+4) Leigh: 1979 w, F; 1980 w, F;
1981 f, w, W
WRIGHT, S. (7) Wigan: 1975 **NZ.** Widnes: 1977 W;
1978 F, W; 1979 W, F; 1980 W

WALES REGISTER
Since reintroduction in 1975

BANNER, P. (9) Salford: 1975 F, E, **F, E, NZ.**
Featherstone R: 1975 (cont.) **E, A, NZ, F**
BAYLISS, S. (1) St. Helens: 1981 E
BEVAN, J. (17) Warrington: 1975 F, E, **E, A, NZ, F**;
1977 E; 1978 A; 1979 F, E; 1980 F, E;
1981 F, E, E; 1982 A
BOX, H. (5) Featherstone R: 1979 F, E; 1980 F, E.
Wakefield T: 1981 F
BUTLER, B. (2+2) Swinton: 1975 **F, nz.** Warrington:
1975 (cont.) f; 1977 F

CAMBRIANI, A. (3) Fulham: 1981 F, E, E
CAMILLERI, C. (3) Barrow: 1980 F. Widnes:
1982 A. Bridgend: 1984 E
COSLETT, K. (8)2 St. Helens: 1975 F, E, **F, E, A,
NZ, E, A**
CUNNINGHAM, E (8) St. Helens: 1975 **E, A, E, A**;
1977 E; 1978 F, E, A
CUNNINGHAM, T. (2) Warrington: 1979 F, E
CURLING, D. (+1) Warrington: 1977 f

DAVID, T. (2) Cardiff C: 1981 E; 1982 A

DAVIES, F. (1) New Hunslet: 1978 E
DAVIES, M. (1) Bridgend: 1984 E
DIAMOND, S. (2+1) Wakefield T: 1980 F, e; 1981 F
DIXON, C. (10)3 Salford: 1975 F, E, **F, E, NZ, A**;
1977 E, F; 1978 F. Hull K.R.: 1981 E
EVANS, R. (5) Swinton: 1975 E, **F, F**; 1978 F;
Salford: 1978 E
FENWICK, S. (2) Cardiff C: 1981 E; 1982 A
FISHER, A. (10)4 Leeds: 1975 F, **E, A, NZ.**
Castleford: 1975 (cont.) **E, A, NZ**; 1977 E, F.
Bradford N: 1978 A
FLOWERS, N. (4) Wigan: 1980 F, E; 1981 E.
Bridgend: 1984 E
FORD, Phil (1) Warrington: 1984 E
FRANCIS, W. (19) Wigan: 1975 F, E, **F, E, A, NZ,
E, A, NZ, F**; 1977 E, F. St. Helens: 1978 F, E,
A; 1979 F, E. Oldham: 1980 F, E

GALLACHER, S. (3+1) Keighley: 1975 f, E, **NZ, F**
GREGORY, B. (3) Wigan: 1975 **E, NZ, F**
GRIFFITHS, C. (+2) St. Helens: 1980 f; 1981 f

HALLETT, L. (2) Cardiff C: 1982 A. Bridgend:
1984 E
HERDMAN, M. (2 + 1) Fulham: 1981 e, E; 1982 A
HOPKINS, L. (1) Workington T: 1982 A

JAMES, M. (11) St. Helens: 1975 **E**; 1978 F, E, A;
1979 F, E; 1980 F, E; 1981 F, E, E
JOHNS, G. (+ 2) Salford: 1979 f. Blackpool B: 1984 e
JONES, C. (1 + 3) Leigh: 1975 **nz, F**; 1978 f, e
JULIFF, B. (8) Wakefield T: 1979 F, E; 1980 F, E;
1981 F, E: Wigan: 1982 A; 1984 E

McJENNETT, M. (2 + 1) Barrow: 1980 F; 1982 a;
1984 E
MANTLE, J. (11 + 1)3 St. Helens: 1975 F, E, **F, e, A,
NZ, E, A, NZ, F**; 1977 E; 1978 E
MATHIAS, R. (20) St. Helens: 1975 F, E, **F, E, A,
NZ, A, NZ, F**; 1977 E, F; 1978 F, E, A;
1979 F, E; 1980 F, E; 1981 F, E
MILLS, J. (13)4 Widnes: 1975 F, E, **E, A, NZ, A,
NZ**; 1977 E, F; 1978 F, E, A; 1979 E
MURPHY, M. (4 + 1) Bradford N: 1975 **F, NZ, F**;
1977 f. St. Jacques, France: 1979 F

NICHOLAS, M. (4 + 2) Warrington: 1975 F, e;
1977 E, F; 1978 F; 1979 e

O'BRIEN, C. (1) Bridgend: 1984 E
OWEN, G. (2) Oldham: 1981 E, F
OWEN, R. (+ 2) St. Helens: 1981 f, e

PARRY, D. (6) Blackpool B: 1980 F, E; 1981 F, E, E;
1982 A
PREECE, C. (1) Bradford N: 1984 E
PRENDIVILLE, P. (4 + 2) Hull: 1979 e; 1980 E;
1981 F, e; 1982 A; 1984 E
PRITCHARD, G. (1 + 2) Barrow: 1978 f, e;
Cardiff C.: 1981 E

RICHARDS, M. (2)1 Salford: 1975 **F**; 1977 E
RINGER, P. (2) Cardiff C: 1981 E; 1982 A
RISMAN, J. (2 + 1) Workington T: 1978 F; 1979 f, E
ROWE, P. (4 + 3)2 Blackpool B: 1975 **a, e, a**.
Huddersfield: 1977 E, F; 1979 F, E
RULE, S. (1) Salford: 1981 E

SELDON, C. (1 + 1) St. Helens: 1980 f, E
SHAW, G. (7) Widnes: 1978 F, A; 1980 F, E; 1981 E.
Wigan: 1982 A; 1984 E
SKERRETT, T. (7) Wakefield T: 1978 A; 1979 F, E;
1980 F. Hull: 1981 F, E; 1984 E
SULLIVAN, C. (10)4 Hull K.R.: 1975 **E, A, NZ, E**;
1977 F; 1978 F, E, A; 1979 F, E

TREASURE, D. (5) Oldham: 1975 **E, A, NZ, E**;
1977 F
TURNER, G. (3 + 3) Hull K.R.: 1975 e, **A**, e, **A**, f.
Hull: 1978 E

WALLACE, R. (+ 1) York: 1975 f
WALTERS, G. (2 + 1) Hull: 1980 E. 1981 E.
Bridgend 1984 e
WANBON, R. (3)3 + 1 Warrington: 1975 **E, A, NZ**
WATKINS, D. (14) Salford: 1975 F, E, **F, E, A, NZ,
E, A, NZ, F**; 1977 E; 1978 E, A; 1979 F
WILKINS, R. (1 + 1) Workington T: 1977 e, F
WILLIAMS, B. (1) Cardiff C: 1982 A
WILLICOMBE, D. (11) + 2 Wigan: 1975 F, E, **F, E,
A, NZ, NZ, F**; 1978 F, E, A
WILSON, D. (4) Swinton: 1981 F, E, E; 1984 E
WILSON, F. (7 + 2)4 St. Helens: 1975 F, E, **F, e, a,
E, A, NZ, F**
WOODS, P. (10) Widnes: 1977 E, F; 1978 F, E, A.
Rochdale H: 1979 F, E. Hull: 1980 E; 1981 F, E

1975 WORLD CHAMPIONSHIP

Winners: Australia (home and away basis)

Date					Venue	Attendance
2 Mar.	France	14	Wales	7	Toulouse	7,563
16 Mar.	England	20	France	2	Leeds	10,842
1 June	Australia	36	New Zealand	8	Brisbane	10,000
10 June	Wales	12	England	7	Brisbane	6,000
14 June	Australia	30	Wales	13	Sydney	25,386
15 June	New Zealand	27	France	0	Christchurch	2,500
21 June	New Zealand	17	England	17	Auckland	12,000
22 June	Australia	26	France	6	Brisbane	9,000
28 June	New Zealand	13	Wales	8	Auckland	18,000
28 June	Australia	10	England	10	Sydney	33,858
20 Sept.	England	22	Wales	16	Warrington	5,034
27 Sept.	New Zealand	8	Australia	24	Auckland	18,000

continued

11 Oct.	France	2	England	48	Bordeaux	1,581
17 Oct.	France	12	New Zealand	12	Marseilles	18,000
19 Oct.	Wales	6	Australia	18	Swansea	11,112
25 Oct.	England	27	New Zealand	12	Bradford	5,507
26 Oct.	France	2	Australia	41	Perpignan	10,440
1 Nov.	England	16	Australia	13	Wigan	9,393
2 Nov.	Wales	25	New Zealand	24	Swansea	2,645
6 Nov.	Wales	23	France	2	Salford	2,247

Final Table

	P	W	D	L	For	Against	Pts
Australia	8	6	1	1	198	69	13
England	8	5	2	1	167	84	12
Wales	8	3	-	5	110	130	6
New Zealand	8	2	2	4	121	149	6
France	8	1	1	6	40	204	3

1975 World Championship squads for Australasian section

ENGLAND
R. Millward (Hull K.R.)
J. Atkinson (Leeds)
J. Bridges (Featherstone R.)
D. Chisnall (Warrington)
E. Chisnall (St. Helens)
P. Cookson (Leeds)
M. Coulman (Salford)
G. Dunn (Hull K.R.)
L. Dyl (Leeds)
G. Fairbairn (Wigan)
K. Fielding (Salford)
K. Gill (Salford)
P. Gordon (Warrington)
T. Martyn (Warrington)
M. Morgan (Wakefield T.)
S. Nash (Featherstone R.)
G. Nicholls (St. Helens)
D. Noonan (Warrington)
S. Norton (Castleford)
J. Walsh (St. Helens)
Manager: W. Oxley (Barrow)
Coach: A.J. Murphy (Warrington)

WALES
D. Watkins (Salford)
P. Banner (Salford)
B. Butler (Swinton)
K. Coslett (St. Helens)
E. Cunningham (St. Helens)
C. Dixon (Salford)
R. Evans (Swinton)
A. Fisher (Leeds)
W. Francis (Wigan)
J. Mantle (St. Helens)
R. Mathias (St. Helens)
J. Mills (Widnes)
M. Nicholas (Warrington)
P. Rowe (Blackpool B.)
C. Sullivan (Hull K.R.)
D. Treasure (Oldham)
G. Turner (Hull K.R.)
R. Wanbon (Warrington)
D. Willicombe (Wigan)
F. Wilson (St. Helens)
Manager: R. Simpson (Castleford)
Coach: L. Pearce (Halifax)

Veteran prop Mick Morgan, an 11th hour Yorkshire hero.

WAR OF THE ROSES

WAR OF THE ROSES

Champion of the underdog Peter Fox masterminded an outstanding victory by his patched-up Yorkshire side against a Lancashire outfit packed with Test stars in the inaugural Rodstock War of the Roses clash at Wigan.

In the first-ever county of origin Roses battle, Fox's makeshift side containing three Second Division players swept aside the undistinguished challenge of a home side featuring 10 Great Britain players, plus two from the current international training squad.

The Rodstock Man of the Match award went to Yorkshire scrum half Deryck Fox who created two of their five tries and added three goals, outplaying his Test contender Lancashire skipper Andy Gregory.

Pack stars for the visitors were two inspired choices by coach Fox. Leeds prop Brendan Hill celebrated his 21st birthday four days early, marking his county debut with a series of storming runs and effective ball distribution. But it was an 11th hour shock call up for Oldham prop Mick Morgan which set Yorkshire on the road to unexpected success.

Celebrating a testimonial for 20 years as a professional player and only 19 days away from his 37th birthday, Morgan produced a classic display of close range ball work before being given a standing ovation on his 73rd minute substitution.

Yorkshire opened the scoring after nine minutes when a speculative kick by second row man David Hobbs bounced off Red Rose winger Joe Lydon to centre Gary Hyde, who pounced for a try. It was again a kick which paved the way for Yorkshire's second touchdown 23 minutes later, Fox chipping through to regather and feed winger David Laws who sent in fellow debutant Andy Mason for the first of his two tries.

A well-placed angled goal from Fox extended the underdogs' lead to 10-0 before home captain Gregory struck with a solo try in the 38th minute, taking a quick penalty tap to scamper 20 yards through a surprised Yorkshire defence. Full back Mick Burke added the goal for an interval scoreline of 10-6 to the visitors.

Strong running by Warrington's Bob Eccles brought him a try four minutes after the break and equalised the scores only for Yorkshire to rally in a storming finish highlighted by three further tries.

Morgan's renowned ball play opened the way for touchdowns by forward colleagues Hobbs and David Heron. Then, despite his tireless running, scrum half Fox still had the energy to break clear in the 78th minute to seal Yorkshire's victory by sending Mason tearing in for the final try.

Despite the loss of a host of original selections — including Harry Pinner, Alan Rathbone, Jeff Grayshon, Ellery Hanley, Lee Crooks and Mike Smith — the War of the Roses, the first of a three-year £10,000 sponsorship by the Rodstock group of companies, caught the public's imagination with an attendance of 6,743, the biggest for a meeting of the two counties since 1968.

Victorious Yorkshire captain John Joyner.

RODSTOCK WAR OF THE ROSES

11th September   Wigan

LANCASHIRE 10		**YORKSHIRE 26**
Mick Burke (Widnes)	1.	Andy Kay (Hunslet)
Barry Ledger (St. Helens)	2.	Carl Gibson (Batley)
David Stephenson (Wigan)	3.	Gary Hyde (Castleford)
Keiron O'Loughlin (Salford)	4.	Andy Mason (Bramley)
Joe Lydon (Widnes)	5.	David Laws (Hull K.R.)
Tony Myler (Widnes)	6.	John Joyner (Castleford), Capt.
Andy Gregory (Warrington), Capt.	7.	Deryck Fox (Featherstone R.)
Mike O'Neill (Widnes)	8.	Brendan Hill (Leeds)
Carl Webb (Warrington)	9.	David Watkinson (Hull K.R.)
Paul Forber (St. Helens)	10.	Mick Morgan (Oldham)
Bob Eccles (Warrington)	11.	David Hobbs (Oldham)
John Fieldhouse (Widnes)	12.	Chris Burton (Hull K.R.)
John Pendlebury (Salford)	13.	David Heron (Leeds)
Shaun Edwards (Wigan)	14.	Paul Lyman (Featherstone R.)
Shaun Wane (Wigan)	15.	Andy Dannatt (Hull)

T: Gregory, Eccles   T: Mason (2), Heron, Hobbs, Hyde
G: Burke   G: Fox (3)
Substitutions: Substitutions:
Edwards for Gregory (Half-time)   Lyman for Watkinson (Half-time)
Wane for Forber (50 min.)   Dannatt for Morgan (73 min.)
Coach: Alex Murphy   Coach: Peter Fox
Half-time: 6-10
Referee: Fred Lindop (Wakefield)
Attendance: 6,743

Jubilant Yorkshire, first-ever holders of the Rodstock Rosebowl.

341

LANCASHIRE v. YORKSHIRE RESULTS
.All county championship matches except where stated.

Date	Result		Score	Venue	Attendance
7 Dec. 1895	Yorkshire	won	8 - 0	Oldham	9,059
29 Feb. 1896	Lancashire	won	8 - 3	Huddersfield	5,300
21 Nov. 1896	Lancashire	won	7 - 3	Oldham	15,000
20 Nov. 1897	Yorkshire	won	7 - 6	Bradford P.A.	11,000
5 Nov. 1898	Yorkshire	won	20 - 9	Salford	8,000
4 Nov. 1899	Lancashire	won	16 - 13	Halifax	9,000
3 Nov. 1900	Lancashire	won	24 - 5	Rochdale	18,000
15 Feb. 1902	Yorkshire	won	13 - 8	Hull	15,000
15 Nov. 1902	Lancashire	won	13 - 0	Salford	14,000
14 Nov. 1903	Lancashire	won	8 - 0	Leeds	11,000
12 Nov. 1904	Yorkshire	won	14 - 5	Oldham	8,500
4 Nov. 1905	Lancashire	won	8 - 0	Hull	8,000
3 Nov. 1906	Lancashire	won	19 - 0	Salford	5,000
2 Nov. 1907	Yorkshire	won	15 - 11	Halifax	7,000
31 Oct. 1908	Lancashire	won	13 - 0	Salford	5,000
4 Nov. 1909	Yorkshire	won	27 - 14	Hull	6,000
7 Nov. 1910	Lancashire	won	17 - 3	Wigan	2,000
25 Jan. 1912	Lancashire	won	13 - 12	Halifax	3,199
16 Dec. 1912	Yorkshire	won	20 - 8	Oldham	4,000
10 Dec. 1913	Yorkshire	won	19 - 11	Huddersfield	3,500
24 Sept. 1919	Lancashire	won	15 - 5	Broughton	5,000
21 Oct. 1920	Yorkshire	won	18 - 3	Hull	7,000
4 Oct. 1921	Yorkshire	won	5 - 2	Rochdale	4,000
7 Dec. 1922	Match drawn	—	11 - 11	Hull K.R.	8,000
8 Dec. 1923	Lancashire	won	6 - 5	Oldham	8,000
29 Nov. 1924	Lancashire	won	28 - 9	Halifax	6,000
12 Dec. 1925	Lancashire	won	26 - 10	St. Helens	13,000
30 Oct. 1926	Lancashire	won	18 - 13	Wakefield	9,000
29 Oct. 1927	Lancashire	won	35 - 19	Warrington	12,000
3 Nov. 1928	Lancashire	won	33 - 10	Halifax	6,520
22 Mar. 1930	Lancashire	won	18 - 3	Rochdale	4,000
18 Oct. 1930	Yorkshire	won	25 - 15	Wakefield	9,000
17 Oct. 1931	Lancashire	won	11 - 8	Warrington	10,049
29 Oct. 1932	Yorkshire	won	30 - 3	Wakefield	4,000
25 Sept. 1933	Yorkshire	won	15 - 12	Oldham	2,000
*9 Jan. 1935	Match drawn	—	5 - 5	Leeds	1,500
12 Oct. 1935	Lancashire	won	16 - 5	Widnes	6,700
21 Oct. 1936	Lancashire	won	28 - 6	Castleford	7,648
12 Feb. 1938	Lancashire	won	10 - 9	Rochdale	3,653
*26 Oct. 1938	Match drawn	—	10 - 10	Leeds	3,000
10 Nov. 1945	Lancashire	won	17 - 16	Swinton	11,059
9 Nov. 1946	Yorkshire	won	13 - 10	Hunslet	5,000
12 Nov. 1947	Lancashire	won	22 - 10	Wigan	6,270

Date	Result		Score	Venue	Attendance
3 May 1949	Lancashire	won	12 - 3	Halifax	7,000
5 Oct. 1949	Lancashire	won	22 - 13	Warrington	15,000
18 Oct. 1950	Yorkshire	won	23 - 15	Huddersfield	6,547
10 Oct. 1951	Yorkshire	won	15 - 5	Leigh	11,573
28 Apr. 1953	Yorkshire	won	16 - 8	Hull	8,400
14 Oct. 1953	Lancashire	won	18 - 10	Leigh	12,870
6 Oct. 1954	Yorkshire	won	20 - 10	Bradford	8,500
26 Sept. 1955	Lancashire	won	26 - 10	Oldham	8,000
26 Sept. 1956	Lancashire	won	35 - 21	Hull	8,500
23 Sept. 1957	Yorkshire	won	25 - 11	Widnes	6,200
24 Sept. 1958	Yorkshire	won	35 - 19	Hull K.R.	5,000
29 Oct. 1958	Yorkshire	won	16 - 15	Leigh	8,500
11 Nov. 1959	Yorkshire	won	38 - 28	Leigh	6,417
31 Aug. 1960	Lancashire	won	21 - 20	Wakefield	15,045
9 Oct. 1961	Lancashire	won	14 - 12	Leigh	4,970
26 Sept. 1962	Yorkshire	won	22 - 8	Wakefield	7,956
11 Sept. 1963	Lancashire	won	45 20	St. Helens	11,200
23 Sept. 1964	Yorkshire	won	33 - 10	Hull	7,100
10 Nov. 1965	Yorkshire	won	16 - 13	Swinton	5,847
21 Sept. 1966	Lancashire	won	22 - 17	Leeds	10,528
24 Jan. 1968	Lancashire	won	23 - 17	Widnes	8,322
25 Sept. 1968	Yorkshire	won	10 - 5	Hull K.R.	6,656
3 Sept. 1969	Lancashire	won	14 - 12	Salford	4,652
13 Jan. 1971	Yorkshire	won	32 - 12	Castleford	2,000
24 Feb. 1971	Yorkshire	won	34 - 8	Castleford	4,400
29 Sept. 1971	Yorkshire	won	42 - 22	Leigh	4,987
11 Oct. 1972	Yorkshire	won	32 - 18	Castleford	2,474
19 Sept. 1973	Lancashire	won	17 - 15	Widnes	3,357
25 Sept. 1974	Yorkshire	won	20 - 14	Keighley	1,219
16 Oct. 1974	Lancashire	won	29 - 11	Widnes	3,114
20 Dec. 1975	Yorkshire	won	17 - 7	Wigan	700
1 Mar. 1977	Yorkshire	won	18 - 13	Castleford	2,730
††19 Oct. 1977	Lancashire	won	33 - 8	Widnes	5,056
27 Sept. 1978	Lancashire	won	23 - 7	Widnes	4,283
12 Sept. 1979	Yorkshire	won	19 - 16	Castleford	2,738
24 Sept. 1980	Lancashire	won	17 - 9	Widnes	1,593
9 Sept. 1981	Yorkshire	won	21 - 15	Castleford	1,222
23 May 1982	Yorkshire	won	22 - 21	Leigh	1,738
WR11 Sept. 1985	Yorkshire	won	26-10	Wigan	6,743

* Match abandoned but result stands   †War-time fixture   ††Queen's Jubilee match   WR War of the Roses
● There were also a few Lancashire-Yorkshire matches played during the First World War but not of a competitive nature.

SUMMARY
Lancashire won 41   Yorkshire won 38   Drawn 3

LANCASHIRE v. YORKSHIRE RECORDS

LANCASHIRE
Highest score:	45-20 at St. Helens, 11 Sept. 1963
Widest margin win:	As above and 33-8 at Widnes, 19 Oct. 1977
Most tries in a match:	No player has scored more than 3
Most goals in a match:	9 by L. Gilfedder (Wigan) at St. Helens, 11 Sept. 1963
Most points in a match:	18 by L. Gilfedder (Wigan) as above
Biggest home attendance:	18,000 at Rochdale, 3 Nov. 1900

OTHER RECORDS (not involving Yorkshire)
Highest score:	60-12 v. Cumberland at Wigan, 10 Sept. 1958
Most tries in a match:	4 by T. O'Grady (Oldham) v. Cumberland at Wigan, 6 Sept. 1956
	4 by W. Burgess (Barrow) v. Cumberland at Widnes, 12 Sept. 1962
Most goals in a match:	12 by E. Fraser (Warrington) v. Cumberland at Wigan, 10 Sept. 1958
Most points in a match:	24 by E. Fraser (Warrington) as above
Biggest home attendance:	24,000 v. Australia at Warrington, 26 Sept. 1929

YORKSHIRE
Highest score:	42-22 at Leigh, 29 Sept. 1971
Widest margin win:	30-3 at Wakefield, 29 Oct. 1932
Most tries in a match:	No player has scored more than 3
Most goals in a match:	10 by V. Yorke (York) at Hull K.R., 24 Sept. 1958
Most points in a match:	20 by V. Yorke (York) as above
Biggest home attendance:	15,045 at Wakefield, 31 Aug. 1960

OTHER RECORDS (not involving Lancashire)
Highest score:	51-12 v. Cumberland at Hunslet, 17 Oct. 1923
Highest against:	55-11 v. Australia at Huddersfield, 26 Nov. 1952
Most tries in a match:	5 by J. Parkin (Wakefield T.) v. Cumberland at Halifax, 14 Nov. 1921
Most goals in a match:	10 also by N. Fox (Wakefield T.) v. Australia at York, 28 Sept. 1959
Most points in a match:	23 by N. Fox (Wakefield T.) as above
Biggest home attendance:	19,376 v. Australia at Wakefield, 4 Oct. 1967

LANCASHIRE TEAMS
. . . A 20-year review. Initials are included where more than one celebrated player shared a surname in the same era. Only playing substitutes are listed.

1966 Yorkshire	1966 Cumberland	1967 Cumberland
Leeds: 21 Sept.	Warrington: 12 Oct.	Workington: 12 Sept.
Won 22-17	Lost 14-18	Won 19-6
Tyrer (Leigh) 5g	Gowers (Swinton) 4g	F. Barrow (St. Helens)
Burgess (Barrow)	Burgess (Barrow)	Burgess (Barrow) 2t
F. Myler (Widnes)	F. Myler (Widnes)	Hesketh (Salford)
Benyon (St. Helens)	Benyon (St. Helens)	F. Myler (St. Helens) 1t
Glover (Warrington) 2t	Glover (Warrington)	Glover (Warrington)
Aspinall (Warrington) 1t	Aspinall (Warrington)	Aspinall (Warrington) 1t, 2g
Bishop (St. Helens) 1t	Williams (Swinton)	Bishop (St. Helens) 1t
Halsall (St. Helens)	Halsall (St. Helens)	Halsall (St. Helens)
Kemel (Widnes)	Kemel (Widnes)	Burdell (Salford)
Kelland (Barrow)	Kelland (Barrow)	Brady (Warrington)
French (St. Helens)	French (St. Helens)	Sanderson (Barrow)
Tomlinson (Barrow)	Tomlinson (Barrow)	Parr (Warrington)
Robinson (Swinton)	Robinson (Swinton) 2t	Clarke (Warrington)
		Sub: Laughton (Wigan)

1967 Australia
Salford: 11 Oct.

Lost 2-14

F. Barrow (St. Helens)
Burgess (Barrow)
Hesketh (Salford)
F. Myler (St. Helens)
Glover (Warrington)
Aspinall (Warrington)
Bishop (St. Helens)
Halliwell (Barrow) 1g
Burdell (Salford)
Brady (Warrington)
Sanderson (Barrow)
Parr (Warrington)
Clarke (Warrington)
Subs: Tees (Barrow)
      S. Whitehead (Salford)

1968 Cumberland
St. Helens: 6 Nov.

Won 24-19

Dutton (Widnes) 3g
Burgess (Barrow) 2t
Hesketh (Salford)
Gemmell (Hull) 2t
Tickle (Leigh)
Brophy (Barrow)
Bishop (St. Helens)
J. Stephens (Wigan)
Sayer (St. Helens)
Brown (Rochdale)
E. Chisnall (St. Helens) 2t
Welding (Leigh)
Robinson (Swinton)
Sub: D. O'Neill (Widnes)

1970 Cumberland
Barrow: 11 Nov.

Won 28-5

John Walsh (St. Helens) 5g
S. Wright (Wigan) 1t
Benyon (St. Helens)
Hesketh (Salford) 1t
Joe Walsh (Leigh)
F. Myler (St. Helens) 2t
Boylan (Widnes)
D. Chisnall (Leigh)
Ashcroft (Leigh) 1t
Brown (Rochdale)
E. Prescott (St. Helens) 1t
E. Chisnall (St. Helens)
Laughton (Wigan)
Subs: Martin Murphy (Oldham)
      Nicholls (Widnes)

1968 Yorkshire
Widnes: 24 Jan.

Won 23-17

Tyrer (Wigan) 4g
Burgess (Barrow)
Buckley (Swinton)
F. Myler (St. Helens)
Glover (Warrington) 1t
D. O'Neill (Widnes) 2t
Bishop (St. Helens)
Halliwell (Barrow) 1t
Burdell (Salford)
Fletcher (Oldham) 1t
Fogerty (Wigan)
French (Widnes)
Laughton (Wigan)
Sub: Warburton (Oldham)

1969 Yorkshire
Salford: 3 Sept.

Won 14-12

Dutton (Widnes) 4g
Jones (St. Helens)
Hesketh (Salford)
Benyon (St. Helens)
Murray (Barrow) 1t
W. Davies (Swinton)
Gordon (Warrington)
J. Stephens (Wigan)
Taylor (Oldham)
Fletcher (Wigan)
Nicholls (Widnes)
Welding (Leigh)
Laughton (Wigan) 1t
Subs: Tees (Rochdale)
      B. Hogan (Wigan)

1971 Yorkshire
Castleford: 13 Jan.

Lost 12-32

Dutton (Widnes) 3g
S. Wright (Wigan)
Benyon (St. Helens)
D. O'Neill (Widnes)
Joe Walsh (Leigh)
W. Davies (Swinton) 1t
A. Murphy (Leigh)
Mick Murphy (Barrow)
Clarke (Wigan)
Brown (Rochdale)
E. Chisnall (St. Helens)
E. Prescott (St. Helens)
Laughton (Wigan) 1t
Subs: Boylan (Widnes)
      Nicholls (Widnes)

1968 Yorkshire
Hull K.R.: 25 Sept.

Lost 5-10

Dutton (Widnes) 1g
D. Whitehead (Oldham)
Benyon (St. Helens)
Glover (Warrington)
Jones (St. Helens)
D. O'Neill (Widnes)
Williams (Swinton)
Halliwell (Salford)
Taylor (Oldham)
Fletcher (Oldham)
French (Widnes)
S. Whitehead (Salford)
Lyon (Wigan)
Subs: Hesketh (Salford) 1t
      J. Stephens (Wigan)

1969 Cumberland
Workington: 24 Sept.

Won 30-10

Dutton (Widnes) 6g
Burgess (Salford)
Hesketh (Salford)
F. Myler (St. Helens)
Murray (Barrow)
A. Murphy (Leigh) 3t
Gordon (Warrington) 1t
J. Stephens (Wigan)
Ashcroft (Leigh)
Sanderson (Barrow)
Robinson (Swinton) 1t
Welding (Leigh)
Laughton (Wigan) 1t
Sub: D. Hill (Wigan)

1971 Yorkshire (Play-off)
Castleford: 24 Feb.

Lost 8-34

Tyrer (Wigan) 1g
Joe Walsh (Leigh)
Buckley (Swinton)
Hesketh (Salford)
Jones (St. Helens) 1t
D. O'Neill (Widnes)
Boylan (Widnes)
J. Stephens (St. Helens)
Ashcroft (Leigh)
B. Hogan (Wigan)
Nicholls (Widnes) 1t
Cramant (Swinton)
Robinson (Wigan)
Subs: Eckersley (Leigh)
      Clarke (Wigan)

345

1971 Cumberland
Workington: 15 Sept.
Lost 7-17
Dutton (Widnes) 2g
Keiron O'Loughlin (Wigan)
Benyon (St. Helens) 1t
Eckersley (Leigh)
Fuller (Wigan)
D. O'Neill (Widnes)
Boylan (Leigh)
D. Chisnall (Warrington)
A. Karalius (St. Helens)
Brown (Rochdale)
Cunningham (Wigan)
Wills (Huyton)
Nicholls (Widnes)
Subs: Whittle (St. Helens)
    Welding (Rochdale)

1971 Yorkshire
Leigh: 29 Sept.
Lost 22-42
Dutton (Widnes) 5g
Jones (St. Helens)
Benyon (St. Helens)
Hesketh (Salford)
Joe Walsh (Leigh)
D. O'Neill (Widnes)
Kenny (Swinton) 1t
J. Stephens (St. Helens) 1t
A. Karalius (St. Helens)
Mick Murphy (Barrow)
Lester (Leigh)
Ashurst (Wigan)
Clark (Oldham) 1t
Subs: Eckersley (Leigh)
    Welding (Rochdale) 1t

1972 Cumberland
Warrington: 27 Sept.
Won: 26-16
Martin Murphy (Oldham)
Hodgkinson (Oldham)
Benyon (St. Helens)
John Walsh (St. Helens) 1t, 4g
E. Hughes (Widnes)
K. Kelly (St. Helens) 1t
Banner (Salford)
Halsall (Swinton)
A. Karalius (St. Helens) 2t
J. Stephens (St. Helens)
E. Prescott (Salford)
B. Gregory (Warrington) 1t
Nicholls (Widnes) 1t
Subs: Hesketh (Salford)
    Birchall (Rochdale)

1972 Yorkshire
Castleford: 11 Oct.
Lost 18-32
Dutton (Widnes) 2g
Hodgkinson (Oldham) 1t
Benyon (St. Helens)
John Walsh (St. Helens) 1g
E. Hughes (Widnes) 1t
D. O'Neill (Widnes) 1t
Banner (Salford)
Halsall (Swinton)
A. Karalius (St. Helens)
J. Stephens (St. Helens) 1t
E. Chisnall (St. Helens)
B. Gregory (Warrington)
Ashurst (Wigan)

1973 Cumbria
Barrow: 5 Sept.
Won 18-6
D. Whitehead (Warrington) 3g
Brelsford (Rochdale)
Benyon (St. Helens) 1t
Hesketh (Salford)
E. Hughes (Widnes) 1t
Eckersley (St. Helens)
Gordon (Warrington)
Fiddler (Leigh) 1t
Evans (Swinton)
Brady (Warrington)
Nicholls (St. Helens)
Welding (Rochdale)
Laughton (Widnes)
Sub: Noonan (Warrington) 1t

1973 Yorkshire
Widnes: 19 Sept.
Won 17-15
D. Whitehead (Warrington) 3g
Brelsford (Rochdale)
Benyon (St. Helens) 1t
Hesketh (Salford)
E. Hughes (Widnes)
Eckersley (St. Helens)
Gordon (Warrington)
Fiddler (Leigh) 1g
Evans (Swinton)
Brady (Warrington)
Nicholls (St. Helens) 1t
Welding (Rochdale)
E. Prescott (Salford) 1t
Subs: Noonan (Warrington)
    Briggs (Warrington)

1974 Other Nationalities
Salford: 11 Sept.
Won 14-13
D. Whitehead (Warrington) 1g
S. Wright (Wigan)
John Walsh (St. Helens)
Noonan (Warrington)
Jones (St. Helens)
Whittle (Warrington) 1t
Gordon (Warrington)
D. Chisnall (Warrington)
Evans (Swinton)
Fiddler (Leigh) 3g
Nicholls (St. Helens)
E. Prescott (Salford)
B. Philbin (Warrington)
Sub: B. Gregory (Oldham) 1t

1974 Cumbria
Warrington: 18 Sept.
Won 29-4
D. Whitehead (Warrington) 4g, 1t
S. Wright (Wigan) 1t
Noonan (Warrington) 2t
Hesketh (Salford)
E. Hughes (Widnes) 1t
Whittle (Warrington)
Nulty (Wigan)
D. Chisnall (Warrington) 1t
Evans (Swinton)
Fiddler (Leigh)
Robinson (Wigan)
B. Gregory (Oldham)
T. Martyn (Leigh) 1t

1974 Yorkshire
Keighley: 25 Sept.
Lost 14-20
D. Whitehead (Warrington) 4g
S. Wright (Wigan)
John Walsh (St. Helens)
Hesketh (Salford) 1t
E. Hughes (Widnes)
Whittle (Warrington)
Gordon (Warrington)
D. Chisnall (Warrington)
Evans (Swinton)
Fiddler (Leigh)
T. Martyn (Leigh) 1t
B. Gregory (Oldham)
B. Philbin (Warrington)
Sub: Robinson (Wigan)

1974 Yorkshire (Play-off)
Widnes: 16 Oct.

Won 29-11

Dutton (Widnes) 7g
S. Wright (Wigan) 1t
Hesketh (Salford) 1t
Noonan (Warrington) 2t
E. Hughes (Widnes)
Gill (Salford) 1t
Gordon (Warrington)
D. Chisnall (Warrington)
Ashcroft (Warrington)
Brady (Warrington)
Nicholls (St. Helens)
E. Prescott (Salford)
B. Philbin (Warrington)
Subs: Aspey (Widnes)
　　　 T. Martyn (Leigh)

1975 Yorkshire
Wigan: 20 Dec.

Lost 7-17

Dutton (Widnes) 2g
Jones (St. Helens)
Butler (Salford)
George (Widnes)
E. Hughes (Widnes)
Gill (Salford)
Bowden (Widnes)
B. Hogan (Wigan)
Evans (Swinton)
Hodkinson (Rochdale)
Turnbull (Salford) 1t
T. Martyn (Warrington)
Adams (Widnes)
Subs: Benyon (St. Helens)
　　　 Nelson (Widnes)

1977 Yorkshire (Jubilee)
Widnes: 19 Oct.

Won 33-8

Pimblett (St. Helens) 5g
Jones (St. Helens)
Aspey (Widnes) 1t
Woods (Leigh) 2t, 2g
S. Wright (Widnes) 1t
Gill (Salford)
Bowden (Widnes)
Wilkinson (Leigh) 1t
Elwell (Widnes) 1t
Gourley (Rochdale)
Adams (Widnes) 1dg
Nicholls (St. Helens)
E. Prescott (Salford)
Sub: Macko (Leigh)

1975 Other Nationalities
St. Helens: 25 Nov.

Won 36-7

Dutton (Widnes) 6g
J. Davies (Leigh)
Pimblett (St. Helens)
Butler (Salford)
George (Widnes)
Gill (Salford) 1t
Bowden (Widnes) 1t
B. Hogan (Wigan)
Elwell (Widnes) 1t
Nelson (Widnes)
Nicholls (St. Helens) 1t
T. Martyn (Warrington) 2t
Adams (Widnes) 1t
Subs: Eckersley (St. Helens)
　　　 Hodkinson (Rochdale) 1t

1977 Cumbria
Leigh: 2 Feb.

Won 18-14

M. Hogan (Leigh)
Fielding (Salford) 1t
Stacey (Leigh)
Butler (Salford)
S. Wright (Widnes) 1t
Gill (Salford)
Bowden (Widnes)
Coulman (Salford) 1t
Elwell (Widnes)
Wilkinson (Leigh)
T. Martyn (Warrington)
Adams (Widnes)
Boyd (Leigh)
Sub: Hesford (Warrington) 1t, 3g

1978 Yorkshire
Widnes: 27 Sept.

Won 23-7

Fairbairn (Wigan) 4g
Fielding (Salford) 2t
Aspey (Widnes)
Cunningham (St. Helens) 1t
Bevan (Warrington) 1t
K. Kelly (Warrington) 1t
Bowden (Widnes)
D. Chisnall (St. Helens)
Elwell (Widnes)
Hodkinson (Rochdale)
Adams (Widnes)
Nicholls (St. Helens)
E. Prescott (Salford)
Subs: Glynn (St. Helens)
　　　 Pinner (St. Helens)

1975 Cumbria
Workington: 6 Dec.

Won 22-17

Dutton (Widnes) 5g
Davies (Leigh) 1t
Butler (Salford) 1t
George (Widnes)
Jones (St. Helens)
Gill (Salford)
Bowden (Widnes) 2t
B. Hogan (Wigan)
Elwell (Widnes)
Hodkinson (Rochdale)
Nicholls (St. Helens)
T. Martyn (Warrington)
Adams (Widnes)
Subs: Eckersley (St. Helens)
　　　 Turnbull (Salford)

1977 Yorkshire
Widnes: 1 March

Lost 13-18

Fairbairn (Wigan) 3g
Fielding (Salford)
Hughes (Widnes) 1t
Hesford (Warrington)
S. Wright (Widnes)
Gill (Salford)
Bowden (Widnes)
Hodkinson (Rochdale)
Elwell (Widnes) 1dg
J. Wood (Widnes)
T. Martyn (Warrington) 1t
Adams (Widnes)
Boyd (Leigh)
Subs: Aspey (Widnes)
　　　 Pinner (St. Helens)

1978 Cumbria
Whitehaven: 11 Oct.

Lost 15-16

Glynn (St. Helens) 3g
S. Wright (Widnes) 2t
Aspey (Widnes)
E. Hughes (Widnes)
Jones (St. Helens)
K. Kelly (Warrington)
Bowden (Widnes)
D. Chisnall (St. Helens)
Liptrot (St. Helens)
Hodkinson (Rochdale)
Adams (Widnes)
Nicholls (Widnes)
E. Prescott (Salford)
Subs: Keiron O'Loughlin (Wigan) 1t
　　　 Pinner (St. Helens)

347

Rodstock Man of the Match Deryck Fox receiving a Mick Morgan short ball, with hooker David Watkinson in support.

Lancashire tryscorer Bob Eccles in full flight.

1979 Cumbria
St. Helens: 5 Sept.
Won 23-15
Eckersley (Widnes) 2g
Arkwright (St. Helens) 1t
Woods (Leigh) 1t, 3g
E. Hughes (Widnes) 2t
Hornby (Wigan)
K. Kelly (Warrington)
Bowden (Widnes)
B. Hogan (Wigan)
Elwell (Widnes)
S. O'Neill (Wigan)
W. Melling (Wigan)
Nicholls (St. Helens)
Pinner (St. Helens) 1dg
Subs: Glynn (St. Helens)
E. Prescott (Salford)

1979 Yorkshire
Castleford: 12 Sept.
Lost 16-19
Eckersley (Widnes) 1t
Arkwright (St. Helens)
Keiron O'Loughlin (Wigan)
E. Hughes (Widnes)
Glynn (St. Helens)
Burke (Widnes) 3g
Bowden (Widnes)
S. O'Neill (Wigan)
Elwell (Widnes)
Gourley (Salford)
Adams (Widnes)
W. Melling (Wigan)
Pinner (St. Helens) 2t, 1dg
Subs: Hull (Widnes)
E. Prescott (Salford)

1980 Cumbria
Barrow: 3 Sept.
Lost 16-19
Burke (Widnes) 2g
Bilsbury (Leigh) 1t
Stephenson (Salford)
Glynn (St. Helens)
Bentley (Widnes)
Woods (Leigh) 2t
Holding (St. Helens)
M. O'Neill (Widnes)
Elwell (Widnes)
Eccles (Warrington) 1t
Dearden (Widnes)
Gittins (Leigh)
Adams (Widnes)
Sub: Flanagan (Oldham)

1980 Yorkshire
Widnes: 24 Sept.
Won 17-9
C. Whitfield (Salford) 4g
Bentley (Widnes)
Bilsbury (Leigh) 1t
M. Foy (Wigan)
Hornby (Wigan) 1t
Woods (Leigh)
Holding (St. Helens) 1t
M. O'Neill (Widnes)
Liptrot (St. Helens)
Eccles (Warrington)
S. O'Neill (Wigan)
Dearden (Widnes)
Adams (Widnes)
Subs: A. Fairhurst (Leigh)
Gittins (Leigh)

1981 Yorkshire
Castleford: 9 Sept.
Lost 15-21
C. Whitfield (Salford) 3g
Drummond (Leigh) 2t
Stephenson (Salford)
M. Foy (Wigan)
Bentley (Widnes) 1t
K. Kelly (Warrington)
A. Gregory (Widnes)
M. O'Neill (Widnes)
Kiss (Wigan)
Case (Warrington)
Potter (Warrington)
Adams (Widnes)
Pinner (St. Helens)
Sub: Donlan (Leigh)

1981 Cumbria
Wigan: 16 Sept.
Lost 15-27
C. Whitfield (Salford) 3g
Drummond (Leigh) 1t
George (Widnes)
Glynn (St. Helens) 1t
Bentley (Widnes)
K. Kelly (Warrington) 1t
Peters (St. Helens)
Hodkinson (Wigan)
Kiss (Wigan)
M. O'Neill (Widnes)
Potter (Warrington)
Case (Warrington)
Pinner (St. Helens)
Subs: Kirwan (Oldham)
Yates (Salford)

1982 Yorkshire
Leigh: 26 May
Lost 21-22
Burke (Widnes) 1t, 6g
Drummond (Leigh)
Stephenson (Wigan) 1t
Woods (Leigh)
Basnett (Widnes)
A. Myler (Widnes) 1t
A. Gregory (Widnes)
M. O'Neill (Widnes)
Kiss (Wigan)
Wilkinson (Leigh)
Potter (Leigh)
F. Whitfield (Widnes)
Flanagan (Oldham)
Sub: Fieldhouse (Warrington)

1982 Cumbria
Workington: 30 May
Won 46-8
Burke (Widnes) 8g
Meadows (St. Helens) 3t
Stephenson (Wigan) 2t
Donlan (Leigh) 3t
Basnett (Widnes)
Keiron O'Loughlin (Widnes)
A. Gregory (Widnes)
M. O'Neill (Widnes) 1t
Kiss (Wigan)
Wilkinson (Leigh)
Potter (Leigh)
Tabern (Leigh) 1t
Flanagan (Oldham)
Subs: C. Whitfield (Wigan)
Fieldhouse (Warrington)

1985 Yorkshire
Wigan: 11 Sept.
Lost 10-26
Burke (Widnes) 1g
Ledger (St. Helens)
Stephenson (Wigan)
Keiron O'Loughlin (Salford)
Lydon (Widnes)
A. Myler (Widnes)
A. Gregory (Warrington) 1t
M. O'Neill (Widnes)
Webb (Warrington)
Forber (St. Helens)
Eccles (Warrington) 1t
Fieldhouse (Widnes)
Pendlebury (Salford)
Subs: Edwards (Wigan)
Wane (Wigan)

349

LANCASHIRE REGISTER

The following is a register of current players who have appeared for Lancashire. Each played at least one first team game last season.

ARKWRIGHT, C. (2) St. Helens

BASNETT, J. (2) Widnes
BEVAN, J. (1) Warrington
BURKE, M. (5) Widnes

CASE, B. (2) Warrington

DONLAN, S. (1+1) Leigh
DRUMMOND, D. (3) Leigh

ECCLES, R. (3) Warrington
EDWARDS, S. (+1) Wigan
ELWELL, K. (9) Widnes

FAIRBAIRN, G. (2) Wigan
FAIRHURST, A. (+1) Leigh
FIELDHOUSE, J. (1+2) Warrington +2, Widnes
FLANAGAN, T. (2+1) Oldham
FLETCHER, G. (3) Oldham 2, Wigan
FORBER, P. (1) St. Helens
FOY, M. (2) Wigan

GITTINS, T. (1+1) Leigh
GLYNN, P. (4+2) St. Helens
GREGORY, A. (4) Widnes 3, Warrington

HESFORD, S. (1+1) Warrington
HODKINSON, A. (7) Rochdale H. 6, Wigan
HOLDING, N. (2) St. Helens

KELLY, K. (6) St. Helens, Warrington 5
KIRWAN, P. (+1) Oldham
KISS, N. (4) Wigan

LEDGER, B. (1) St. Helens
LIPTROT, G. (2) St. Helens
LYDON, J. (1) Widnes

MEADOWS, K. (1) St. Helens
MYLER, A. (2) Widnes

O'LOUGHLIN, Keiron (4+1) Wigan 2+1, Widnes, Salford
O'NEILL, M. (7) Widnes
O'NEILL, S. (3) Wigan

PENDLEBURY, J. (1) Salford
PETERS, S. (1) St. Helens
PINNER, H. (4+3) St. Helens
POTTER, I. (4) Warrington 2, Leigh 2
PRESCOTT, E. (9+2) Salford 7+2, St. Helens 2

STEPHENSON, D. (5) Salford 2, Wigan 3

TABERN, R. (1) Leigh

WANE, S. (+1) Wigan
WEBB, C. (1) Warrington
WHITFIELD, C. (3+1) Salford 3, Wigan +1
WHITFIELD, F, (1) Widnes
WOODS, J. (5) Leigh
WRIGHT, S. (10) Wigan 6, Widnes 4

YORKSHIRE TEAMS

. . . A 20-year review. Initials are included where more than one celebrated player shared a surname in the same era. Only playing substitutes are listed.

1966 Cumberland	**1966 Lancashire**	**1967 Australia**
Workington: 7 Sept.	Leeds: 21 Sept.	Wakefield: 4 Oct.
Drew 17-17	Lost 17-22	Won 15-14
Keegan (Hull)	Keegan (Hull)	Keegan (Hull)
Goodchild (Doncaster)	Goodchild (Doncaster)	Young (Hull KR)
Brooke (Bradford)	Brooke (Bradford)	Wriglesworth (Bradford)
N. Fox (Wakefield) 4g	N. Fox (Wakefield) 4g,1t	N. Fox (Wakefield) 3g,1t
Wriglesworth (Leeds) 2t	Wriglesworth (Leeds)	Francis (Wigan)
Shoebottom (Leeds) 1t	Shoebottom (Leeds)	Millward (Hull KR) 1t
Dooler (Featherstone)	Dooler (Featherstone)	Dooler (Featherstone) 1t
F. Fox (Hull KR)	Denis Hartley (Castleford)	Harrison (Hull)
Flanagan (Hull KR)	Flanagan (Hull KR)	Close (Huddersfield)
Scroby (Halifax)	Scroby (Halifax)	Hill (Bradford)
Ramshaw (Halifax)	Ramshaw (Halifax) 2t	Clarkson (Wakefield)
Clawson (Bradford)	Clawson (Bradford)	Small (Castleford)
Major (Hull KR)	Poole (Leeds)	Major (Hull KR)
Sub: Stockwell (Bradford)	Sub: Bryant (Castleford)	Sub: A. Morgan (Featherstone)

1967 Cumberland
Castleford: 25 Oct.

Won 34-23

Keegan (Hull) 2g
Goodchild (Halifax) 2t
Stockwell (Bradford)
Longstaff (Huddersfield)
Francis (Wigan) 4t
Millward (Hull KR) 1t,3g
K. Hepworth (Castleford) 1t
Clark (Leeds)
Close (Huddersfield)
Scroby (Halifax)
Bryant (Castleford)
Clarkson (Wakefield)
Major (Hull KR)
Sub: Ramsey (Hunslet)

1968 Lancashire
Hull KR: 25 Sept.

Won 10-5

Keegan (Hull) 1t
Francis (Wigan)
Hynes (Leeds)
Wriglesworth (Bradford)
Atkinson (Leeds)
Millward (Hull KR) 2g
Seabourne (Leeds) 1t
Denis Hartley (Castleford)
C. Dickinson (Castleford)
J. Ward (Castleford)
P. Lowe (Hull KR)
A. Morgan (Featherstone)
Reilly (Castleford)

1970 Cumberland
Whitehaven: 14 Sept.

Lost 15-21

Edwards (Castleford)
Slater (Wakefield)
Shoebottom (Leeds)
Watson (Leeds)
Lamb (Bradford) 1t
Wolford (Bramley)
Davidson (Hull)
Denis Hartley (Castleford)
M. Stephenson (Dewsbury) 1t
Clawson (Hull KR) 3g
Lockwood (Castleford)
J. Thompson (Featherstone) 1t
Batten (Leeds)
Subs: Firth (Hull)

1968 Lancashire
Widnes: 24 Jan.

Lost 17-23

Keegan (Hull)
Young (Hull KR)
A. Burwell (Hull KR)
N. Fox (Wakefield) 4g
Atkinson (Leeds) 1t
Millward (Hull KR) 1t
Seabourne (Leeds)
Clark (Leeds)
Close (Huddersfield)
Walton (Castleford)
Ramshaw (Bradford) 1t
Ramsey (Leeds)
Major (Hull KR)
Sub: A. Hepworth (Bradford)

1969 Lancashire
Salford: 3 Sept.

Lost 12-14

Keegan (Hull)
A. Smith (Leeds)
Hynes (Leeds)
A. Burwell (Hull KR)
Francis (Wigan)
Millward (Hull KR) 2g
K.Hepworth (Castleford) 1t
Denis Hartley (Castleford)
C. Dickinson (Castleford)
Macklin (Hull) 1g
P. Lowe (Hull KR) 1t
Lockwood (Castleford)
Batten (Leeds)
Subs: Edwards (Castleford)
A. Morgan (Featherstone)

1971 Lancashire
Castleford: 13 Jan.

Won 32-12

Jefferson (Keighley) 6g
A. Smith (Leeds) 2t
Hynes (Leeds) 1t
N. Stephenson (Dewsbury) 2t
Atkinson (Leeds)
Topliss (Wakefield)
Shoebottom (Leeds) 1g
Clawson (Hull KR)
C. Dickinson (Castleford)
Jeanes (Wakefield)
Haigh (Leeds)
J. Thompson (Featherstone)
Batten (Leeds) 1t

1968 Cumberland
Whitehaven: 11 Sept.

Won 23-10

Keegan (Hull)
Hurl (Hunslet)
A. Burwell (Hull KR) 1t
Wriglesworth (Bradford) 2t
Atkinson (Leeds) 1t
Millward (Hull KR) 4g,1t
Seabourne (Leeds)
Clark (Leeds)
C. Dickinson (Castleford)
Scroby (Halifax)
Ramsey (Leeds)
A. Morgan (Featherstone)
Reilly (Castleford)

1969 Cumberland
Hull KR: 1 Oct.

Won 42-3

Keegan (Hull) 1t
Lowndes (Castleford) 1t
Moore (Hull KR) 3t
A. Burwell (Hull KR)
T. Thompson (Hunslet) 1t
Millward (Hull KR) 6g, 2t
Davidson (Hull) 1t
Harrison (Hull)
M. Stephenson (Dewsbury)
J. Ward (Castleford)
Haigh (Wakefield) 1t
J. Thompson (Featherstone)
Doyle (Batley)

1971 Lancashire (Play-off)
Castleford: 24 Feb.

Won 34-8

Jefferson (Keighley) 1t,1g
Slater (Wakefield) 2t
Stenton (Castleford)
N. Stephenson (Dewsbury) 3g, 2t
Young (York)
Hardisty (Castleford) 1g
K. Hepworth (Castleford)
Clawson (Hull KR)
C. Dickinson (Castleford)
Jeanes (Wakefield) 1t
Lockwood (Castleford)
Irving (Oldham) 1t
Halmshaw (Halifax)
Sub: Topliss (Wakefield) 1t
M. Stephenson (Dewsbury)

1971 Lancashire
Leigh: 29 Sept.
Won 42-22
Edwards (Castleford)
Slater (Wakefield)
Watson (Bradford) 1t
N. Stephenson (Dewsbury) 5g,1t
Lamb (Bradford) 1t
Millward (Hull KR) 4g,1t
Nash (Featherstone) 1t
Harrison (Hull)
M. Stephenson (Dewsbury)
Jeanes (Wakefield)
Boxall (Hull)
Irving (Oldham)
Halmshaw (Halifax) 1t
Subs: Topliss (Wakefield) 1t
      Farrar (Featherstone) 1t

1971 Cumberland
Wakefield: 20 Oct.
Won 17-12
Edwards (Castleford)
Slater (Wakefield)
Watson (Bradford) 2t
N. Stephenson (Dewsbury) 2t
Lamb (Bradford)
Millward (Hull KR) 1g
A. Bates (Dewsbury)
Harrison (Hull)
M. Stephenson (Dewsbury)
Farrar (Featherstone)
Boxall (Hull) 1t
Irving (Oldham)
Halmshaw (Halifax)

1972 Cumberland
Whitehaven: 13 Sept.
Lost: 14-23
Rushton (Dewsbury)
A. Smith (Leeds)
Dyl (Leeds)
N. Stephenson (Dewsbury) 4g
D. Redfearn (Bradford)
Millward (Hull KR)
Nash (Featherstone) 2t
Clawson (Leeds)
M. Stephenson (Dewsbury)
Jeanes (Wakefield)
Cookson (Leeds)
J. Bates (Dewsbury)
Halmshaw (Halifax)
Subs: Wraith (Wakefield)
      Irving (Oldham)

1972 Lancashire
Castleford: 11 Oct.
Won 32-18
Jefferson (Keighley) 7g
Lamb (Bradford) 2t
Worsley (Castleford) 1t
Pickup (Huddersfield) 1t
D. Redfearn (Bradford) 1t
Blacker (Bradford)
A. Bates (Dewsbury)
Naylor (Batley)
M. Stephenson (Dewsbury)
T. Lowe (Dewsbury)
Irving (Oldham) 1t
Lockwood (Castleford)
Norton (Castleford)
Subs: Wraith (Wakefield)
      C. Dickinson (Castleford)

1973 Cumberland (Play-off)
Leeds: 17 Jan.
Won 20-7
Jefferson (Keighley) 4g
Lamb (Bradford)
Worsley (Castleford)
Dyl (Leeds)
D. Redfearn (Bradford) 1t
Topliss (Wakefield) 1t
Hudson (Hull KR)
Dixon (York) 1t
M. Stephenson (Dewsbury)
Lyons (Wakefield) 1t
Irving (Oldham)
Lockwood (Castleford)
Batten (Leeds)
Subs: N. Stephenson (Dewsbury)
      B. Kear (Featherstone)

1973 Cumbria
Bramley: 12 Sept.
Won 37-12
Jefferson (Keighley) 7g, 1t
A. Smith (Leeds) 3t
Newlove (Featherstone)
Dyl (Leeds)
Atkinson (Leeds)
Topliss (Wakefield) 1t
Nash (Featherstone) 1g
Ballantyne (Wakefield)
M. Morgan (Wakefield) 1t
Davies (Huddersfield)
Irving (Wigan)
J. Thompson (Featherstone) 1t
Stone (Featherstone)
Sub: Idle (Bramley)

1973 Lancashire
Widnes: 19 Sept.
Lost 15-17
Jefferson (Keighley) 3g
A. Smith (Leeds) 1t
Hynes (Leeds)
Holmes (Leeds)
Atkinson (Leeds) 1t
Topliss (Wakefield)
Nash (Featherstone)
Harrison (Hull)
M. Morgan (Wakefield)
Davies (Huddersfield) 1t
Grayshon (Dewsbury)
J. Thompson (Featherstone)
Stone (Featherstone)
Subs: J. Bates (Dewsbury)

1974 Cumbria
Workington: 10 Sept.
Lost 7-10
Jefferson (Keighley) 2g
Lamb (Bradford)
Dave Hartley (Featherstone) 1t
M. Smith (Featherstone)
D. Redfearn (Bradford)
Topliss (Wakefield)
Nash (Featherstone)
Harrison (Leeds)
Spurr (Castleford)
Farrar (Featherstone)
Grayshon (Dewsbury)
J. Bates (Dewsbury)
Norton (Castleford)
Subs: Burton (Halifax)
      Ramsey (Bradford)

1974 Other Nationalities
Hull KR: 18 Sept.
Won 22-15
Marshall (Leeds) 5g
D. Redfearn (Bradford)
Hughes (Bramley)
M. Smith (Featherstone) 1t
Atkinson (Leeds) 1t
Burton (Halifax) 1t
A. Bates (Dewsbury)
Harrison (Leeds)
Farrar (Featherstone)
Ramsey (Bradford) 1t
Grayshon (Dewsbury)
J. Thompson (Featherstone)
Norton (Castleford)
Subs: Langley (Leeds)
      J. Bates (Dewsbury)

1974 Lancashire
Keighley: 25 Sept.
Won 20-14
Marshall (Leeds) 4g
D. Redfearn (Bradford)
Hughes (Bramley)
Roe (Keighley)
Atkinson (Leeds) 1t
Millward (Hull KR) 1t
A. Bates (Dewsbury) 1t
Dixon (York)
Raistrick (Keighley)
Irving (Wigan) 1t
Grayshon (Dewsbury)
Idle (Bramley)
Norton (Castleford)
Subs: Clark (N. Hunslet)
      J. Bates (Dewsbury)

1974 Lancashire (Play-off)
Widnes: 16 Oct.
Lost 11-29
Sheard (Wakefield)
Lamb (Bradford)
Roe (Keighley) 1t
Burton (Halifax) 1g
Atkinson (Leeds) 1t
Topliss (Wakefield)
A. Bates (Dewsbury)
Dixon (York)
Raistrick (Keighley)
Millington (Hull KR)
Grayshon (Dewsbury)
Irving (Wigan)
Norton (Castleford) 1t

1975 Cumbria
Dewsbury: 19 Nov.
Won 10-7
Wraith (Castleford)
D. Smith (Wakefield) 1t
Holmes (Leeds) 1t, 2g
Dyl (Leeds)
Dunn (Hull KR)
Newlove (Featherstone)
Millward (Hull KR)
Beverley (Dewsbury)
Bridges (Featherstone)
J. Thompson (Featherstone)
Grayshon (Dewsbury)
Irving (Wigan)
Norton (Castleford)
Subs: N. Stephenson (Dewsbury)
      M. Morgan (Wakefield)

1975 Other Nationalities
Bradford: 6 Dec.
Drew 16-16
Wraith (Castleford)
D. Smith (Wakefield) 1t
Holmes (Leeds) 2g
N. Stephenson (Dewsbury)
Dunn (Hull KR)
Newlove (Featherstone)
Nash (Salford)
Beverley (Dewsbury)
Bridges (Featherstone) 1t
J. Thompson (Featherstone) 2t
Grayshon (Dewsbury)
Irving (Wigan)
Norton (Castleford)
Subs: Topliss (Wakefield)
      M. Morgan (Wakefield)

1975 Lancashire
Wigan: 20 Dec.
Won 17-7
Langley (Dewsbury)
D. Smith (Wakefield)
Holmes (Leeds) 4g
Dyl (Leeds)
Atkinson (Leeds) 1t
Topliss (Wakefield)
Stephens (Castleford)
Millington (Hull KR)
Bridges (Featherstone)
Farrar (Featherstone)
Grayshon (Dewsbury)
M. Morgan (Wakefield) 2t
Norton (Castleford)
Subs: Hancock (Hull)
      J. Thompson (Featherstone)

1977 Cumbria
Whitehaven: 15 Feb.
Drew 12-12
Wraith (Castleford)
Muscroft (N. Hunslet)
Joyner (Castleford) 1t
Roe (Bradford)
Atkinson (Leeds)
Topliss (Wakefield) 1t
Stephens (Castleford)
J. Thompson (Featherstone)
D. Ward (Leeds)
A. Dickinson (Castleford)
Grayshon (Dewsbury)
Lloyd (Castleford) 3g
M. Morgan (Wakefield)

1977 Lancashire
Castleford: 1 Mar.
Won 18-13
Mumby (Bradford) 1g
Muscroft (N. Hunslet) 1t
Crook (Wakefield)
Francis (Wigan)
Atkinson (Leeds)
Topliss (Wakefield)
Stephens (Castleford)
J. Thompson (Featherstone)
D. Ward (Leeds) 1t
Farrar (Featherstone)
Rose (Hull KR) 1t
P. Lowe (Hull KR)
Norton (Castleford)
Subs: N. Stephenson (Dewsbury) 1t
      Lloyd (Castleford) 2g

1977 Cumbria (Jubilee)
York: 5 Oct.
Won 28-10
Banks (York)
D. Smith (Leeds) 2t
Marston (York) 1t
Quinn (Featherstone) 5g
Atkinson (Leeds) 2t
Hancock (Hull)
Shepherd (Huddersfield)
Beverley (Dewsbury)
Bridges (Featherstone)
Farrar (Featherstone)
M. Morgan (York)
Boxall (Hull) 1t
Bell (Featherstone)
Subs: Hague (Leeds)
      Branch (Huddersfield)

1977 Lancashire (Jubilee)
Widnes: 19 Oct.
Lost 8-33
Mumby (Bradford)
D. Smith (Leeds)
Hague (Leeds)
Quinn (Featherstone) 1g
Atkinson (Leeds) 1t
Francis (Wigan)
Nash (Salford)
J. Thompson (Bradford)
Bridges (Featherstone)
Farrar (Featherstone)
M. Morgan (York) 1t
Branch (Huddersfield)
Bell (Featherstone)
Subs: Hancock (Hull)
      Griffiths (N. Hunslet)

1978 Cumbria

Hull: 20 Sept.

Won 37-9

Mumby (Bradford) 4g
T. Morgan (York)
Joyner (Castleford) 1t
N. Stephenson (Dewsbury) 1t, 1g
Atkinson (Leeds)
Francis (St. Helens) 2t
Nash (Salford)
Harrison (Leeds)
Dalgreen (Warrington) 1t
Pitchford (Leeds) 1t
Casey (Hull KR) 1t
P. Lowe (Hull KR) 1t
Crane (Leeds) 1t
Subs: Topliss (Wakefield)
     Farrar (Hull)

1979 Lancashire

Castleford: 12 Sept.

Won 19-16

Box (Featherstone) 3g
Fletcher (Wakefield)
Joyner (Castleford)
Evans (Featherstone)
Fenton (Castleford)
Burton (Castleford) 1t
Stephens (Castleford)
Beverley (Workington)
Raistrick (Halifax) 1t, 1dg
Gibbins (Featherstone)
Branch (Huddersfield) 1t
Hankins (Dewsbury)
Adams (Leeds) 1t
Subs: Johnson (Castleford)
     R. Dickinson (Leeds)

1981 Lancashire

Castleford: 9 Sept.

Won 21-15

Mumby (Bradford) 1t
Richardson (Castleford)
Joyner (Castleford) 2t
Dyl (Leeds) 1t
Fenton (Castleford)
Holmes (Leeds)
Nash (Salford)
Grayshon (Bradford)
D. Ward (Leeds) 1t
Millington (Hull KR)
Finch (Castleford) 3g
P. Smith (Featherstone)
Norton (Hull)

1978 Lancashire

Widnes: 27 Sept.

Lost 7-23

Mumby (Bradford)
Muscroft (N. Hunslet)
Joyner (Castleford)
M. Smith (Hull KR) 1t
D. Redfearn (Bradford)
Francis (St. Helens)
Stephens (Castleford)
Ballantyne (Castleford)
Wileman (York)
Pitchford (Leeds)
Lloyd (Hull) 2g
P. Smith (Featherstone)
Branch (Huddersfield)
Subs: Topliss (Wakefield)
     Farrar (Hull)

1980 Cumbria

Hull KR: 17 Sept.

Lost 16-17

Wraith (Castleford)
Fletcher (Wakefield) 1t
Joyner (Castleford)
Quinn (Featherstone) 4g
Fenton (Castleford)
Hague (Leeds)
Dick (Leeds) 1t, 2dg
Holdstock (Hull KR)
Spurr (Castleford)
Skerrett (Hull)
Grayshon (Bradford)
Kevin Rayne (Wakefield)
Norton (Hull)
Sub: D. Heron (Leeds)

1981 Cumbria

Whitehaven: 23 Sept.

Lost 10-20

Box (Wakefield)
Richardson (Castleford)
Hague (Leeds)
Quinn (Featherstone) 1g
A. Parker (Bradford) 1t
Holmes (Leeds)
Nash (Salford)
R. Dickinson (Leeds)
D. Ward (Leeds)
Standidge (Halifax)
Finch (Castleford) 1t, 1g
Idle (Bradford)
Bell (Featherstone)
Subs: Evans (Featherstone)
     White (York)

1979 Cumbria

Workington: 29 Aug.

Lost 13-17

Box (Featherstone)
Fletcher (Wakefield) 1t
M. Parrish (Hunslet) 3g
Banks (York) 1t
Fenton (Castleford)
Evans (Featherstone)
Dean (Hunslet) 1dg
Tindall (Hull)
Wileman (Hull)
Gibbins (Featherstone)
Grayshon (Bradford)
Hankins (Dewsbury)
Bell (Featherstone)
Sub: G. Smith (York)

1980 Lancashire

Widnes: 24 Sept.

Lost 9-17

Wraith (Castleford)
Fletcher (Wakefield) 1t
Joyner (Castleford)
Quinn (Featherstone) 3g
Fenton (Castleford)
Topliss (Wakefield)
Stephens (Castleford)
Holdstock (Hull KR)
Watkinson (Hull KR)
Skerrett (Hull)
Grayshon (Bradford)
Kevin Rayne (Wakefield)
Norton (Hull)
Subs: Wilby (Hull)
     D. Heron (Leeds)

1982 Cumbria

Castleford: 23 May

Won 22-7

Mumby (Bradford)
Richardson (Castleford) 3t
Joyner (Castleford) 2t
Day (Hull)
Gant (Bradford)
Holmes (Leeds)
Dick (Leeds) 1t, 2g
Tindall (Hull)
D. Ward (Leeds)
R. Dickinson (Leeds)
G. Van Bellen (Bradford)
Casey (Hull KR)
Norton (Hull)
Subs: Dyl (Leeds)
     D. Hobbs (Featherstone)

1982 Lancashire
Leigh: 26 May
Won 22-21
Mumby (Bradford)
Pryce (York) 3t
Joyner (Castleford)
Day (Hull)
Gant (Bradford)
Holmes (Leeds)
Dick (Leeds) 1t, 3g, 1dg
Tindall (Hull)
D. Ward (Leeds)
R. Dickinson (Leeds)
G. Van Bellen (Bradford)
P. Smith (Featherstone)
K. Ward (Castleford) 1t
Subs: Dyl (Leeds)
    Keith Rayne (Leeds)

1985 Lancashire
Wigan: 11 Sept.
Won 26-10
Kay (Hunslet)
Gibson (Batley)
Hyde (Castleford) 1t
Mason (Bramley) 2t
Laws (Hull K.R.)
Joyner (Castleford)
Fox (Featherstone) 3g
Hill (Leeds)
Watkinson (Hull K.R.)
M. Morgan (Oldham)
D. Hobbs (Oldham) 1t
Burton (Hull K.R.)
D. Heron (Leeds) 1t
Subs: Lyman (Featherstone)
    Dannatt (Hull)

1985 New Zealand
Bradford: 23 Oct.
Won 18-8
Mumby (Bradford)
Gibson (Batley) 1t
Creasser (Leeds)
Schofield (Hull) 1dg
Mason (Bramley)
Hanley (Wigan) 1t, 1dg
Fox (Featherstone) 2g
Grayshon (Bradford)
Noble (Bradford)
Skerrett (Hull)
Crooks (Hull)
Goodway (Wigan) 1t
D. Heron (Leeds)
Subs: Steadman (York)
    Lyman (Featherstone)

YORKSHIRE REGISTER

The following is a register of current players who have appeared for Yorkhire. Each played at least one first team game last season.

BELL, K. (4) Featherstone R.
BEVERLEY, H. (4) Dewsbury 3, Workington T. 1
BOX, H. (2) Featherstone R. 1, Wakefield T. 1
BURTON, C. (1) Hull K.R.

CASEY, L. (2) Hull K.R.
CREASSER, D. (1) Leeds
CROOKS, L. (1) Hull

DANNATT, A (+1) Hull
DICK, K. (3) Leeds
DICKINSON, R. (3+1) Leeds

EVANS, S. (2+1) Featherstone R.

FENTON, S. (5) Castleford
FINCH, D. (2) Castleford
FLETCHER, A. (4) Wakefield T.
FOX, D. (2) Featherstone R.

GIBBINS, M. (2) Featherstone R.
GIBSON, C. (2) Batley
GOODWAY, A. (1) Wigan
GRAYSHON, J. (14) Dewsbury 9, Bradford N. 5

HAGUE, N. (3+1) Leeds
HANKINS, S. (2) Dewsbury
HANLEY, E. (1) Wigan
HERON, D. (2+2) Leeds
HILL, B. (1) Leeds
HOBBS, D. (1+1) Featherstone R. +1, Oldham
HUDSON, T. (1) Hull K.R.
HYDE, G. (1) Castleford

IDLE, G. (1+1) Bramley +1, Bradford N.

JOHNSON, Phil. (+1) Castleford
JOYNER, J. (10) Castleford

KAY, A. (1) Hunslet

LAWS, D. (1) Hull K.R.
LYMAN, P. (+2) Featherstone R.

MASON, A. (2) Bramley
MILLINGTON, J. (3) Hull KR
MORGAN, M. (7+2) Wakefield T. 4+2, York 2, Oldham
MUMBY, K. (8) Bradford N.

NOBLE, B. (1) Bradford N.
NORTON, S. (13) Castleford 9, Hull 4

PARRISH, M. (1) Hunslet
PITCHFORD, S. (2) Leeds
PRYCE, G. (1) York

QUINN, S. (5) Featherstone R.

RAYNE, Keith (+1) Leeds
RAYNE, Kevin (2) Wakefield T.
REDFEARN, D. (7) Bradford N.
REILLY, M. (2) Castleford
RICHARDSON, T. (3) Castleford
ROE, P. (3) Keighley 2, Bradford N.
ROSE, P. (1) Hull K.R.

SCHOFIELD, G. (1) Hull
SKERRETT, T. (3) Hull
SMITH, G. (+1) York
SMITH, M. (1) Hull K.R.
SMITH, P. (3) Featherstone R.
SPURR, R. (2) Castleford
STEADMAN, G. (+1) York
STEPHENS, G. (6) Castleford
STEPHENSON, N (7+3) Dewsbury

TOPLISS, D. (10+5) Wakefield T.

VAN BELLEN, G. (2) Bradford N.

WARD, D. (6) Leeds
WARD, K. (1) Castleford
WATKINSON, D. (2) Hull K.R.
WHITE, B. (+1) York
WOLFORD, J. (1) Bramley

COUNTY CHAMPIONSHIP TITLES
(including joint titles)

Lancashire 34
Yorkshire 24
Cumbria 16
Cheshire 1

Season	County	Season	County
1895-96	Lancashire	1937-38	Lancashire
1896-97	Lancashire	1938-39	Lancashire
1897-98	Yorkshire	1945-46	Lancashire
1898-99	Yorkshire	1946-47	Yorkshire
1899-1900	Lancashire	1947-48	Lancashire
1900-01	Lancashire	1948-49	Cumberland
1901-02	Cheshire	1949-50	Undecided
1902-03	Lancashire	1950-51	Undecided
1903-04	Lancashire	1951-52	Yorkshire
1904-05	Yorkshire	1952-53	Lancashire
1905-06	Lancashire / Cumberland	1953-54	Yorkshire
		1954-55	Yorkshire
1906-07	Lancashire	1955-56	Lancashire
1907-08	Cumberland	1956-57	Lancashire
1908-09	Lancashire	1957-58	Yorkshire
1909-10	Cumberland / Yorkshire	1958-59	Yorkshire
		1959-60	Cumberland
1910-11	Lancashire	1960-61	Lancashire
1911-12	Cumberland	1961-62	Cumberland
1912-13	Yorkshire	1962-63	Yorkshire
1913-14	Undecided	1963-64	Cumberland
1919-20	Undecided	1964-65	Yorkshire
1920-21	Yorkshire	1965-66	Cumberland
1921-22	Yorkshire	1966-67	Cumberland
1922-23	Lancashire / Yorkshire	1967-68	Lancashire
		1968-69	Yorkshire
1923-24	Lancashire	1969-70	Lancashire
1924-25	Lancashire	1970-71	Yorkshire
1925-26	Lancashire	1971-72	Yorkshire
1926-27	Lancashire	1972-73	Yorkshire
1927-28	Cumberland	1973-74	Lancashire
1928-29	Lancashire	1974-75	Lancashire
1929-30	Lancashire	1975-76	Yorkshire
1930-31	Yorkshire	1976-77	Yorkshire
1931-32	Lancashire	1977-78	Not Held
1932-33	Cumberland	1978-79	Lancashire
1933-34	Cumberland	1979-80	Lancashire
1934-35	Cumberland	1980-81	Cumbria
1935-36	Lancashire	1981-82	Cumbria
1936-37	Lancashire	1982-83	Yorkshire

Test threequarter Joe Lydon, the first £100,000 purchase, moving from Widnes to hometown Wigan.

TRANSFERS

1985-86 TRANSFER REVIEW

Transfer deals soared to record heights last season as Wigan twice broke the top fee barrier, including the first £100,000 pay out and a record £65,000 sum for a forward.

The record deal for a Rugby Union recruit was also smashed as Bradford Northern signed one of the 15-a-side code's greatest-ever players for £80,000.

There had been a slump in the transfer market since Hull K.R. signed Test full back George Fairbairn from Wigan for £72,500 in June 1981, but that record went in the opening days of the season. Ellery Hanley's refusal to play for Bradford Northern in the opening match set off a pay dispute which ended with Wigan signing the Great Britain Test back in a sensational £150,000 package deal on 16th September.

The Riversiders handed over £85,000 — breaking the cash record — with Test backs Steve Donlan and Phil Ford joining the Odsal club. The duo were valued at a total of £65,000, the transfer fees paid by Wigan the previous season, Ford from Warrington for £40,000 and Donlan from Leigh for £25,000.

The previous cash-plus-player record deal was estimated to be £75,000 when Test scrum half Andy Gregory moved from Widnes to Warrington in January 1985, Test forward John Fieldhouse moving in the opposite direction.

Unlike the Hanley deal, which had been expected over a 14-day period, Wigan's capture of Lydon for £100,000 was a shock move, the Central Park club completing the signing only hours before the Silk Cut Challenge Cup deadline on 20th January. Lydon had not asked for a transfer, Widnes needing to enter the transfer market as sellers to ease pressing financial problems. Eric Hughes quit as Widnes coach because of not being consulted on the move.

Even before the season began Wigan had paid a record £65,000 for a forward, signing Andy Goodway from Oldham on 29th July. Goodway, who was experiencing a summer stay with Sydney club Manly-Warringah, was on the transfer list at his own request, Oldham placing a £100,000 price tag on the Great Britain packman.

The previous record fee for a forward was £60,000 when Andy Kelly moved from Wakefield Trinity to Hull K.R. in June 1982.

There were a total of eight £30,000 or more transfer deals between June 1985 and May 1986 inclusive, twice as many as in the previous year. The other five were: £65,000 for John Woods, Leigh to Bradford Northern; £50,000 for Graham Steadman, York to Featherstone Rovers, and for Carl Gibson, Batley to Leeds; £40,000 for Alan Rathbone, Bradford Northern to Warrington; £35,000 for John Gilbert, Featherstone Rovers to Widnes.

The overall total of transfers between clubs remained fairly static with 185 against 180 the previous year.

There were an additional 123 moves on loan — including players returning to their original clubs — three fewer than in 1984-85.

Bradford Northern's capture of Terry Holmes was regarded as one of the biggest-ever Rugby Union signings with the £80,000 contract easily a record for a 15-a-side player. The Wales captain and British Lions scrum half put his name to a three-year contract on 3rd December in a blaze of publicity. Unfortunately he dislocated a shoulder on his debut, put it out again in an A-team comeback match and missed the rest of the season.

The previous record fee for a Rugby

Union player was the £27,500 Clive Griffiths, the former Llanelli and Wales full back, received from St. Helens in August 1979.

Another major Rugby Union signing during the season was Whitehaven's capture of Rob Ackerman, the Wales and British Lions centre who had left Cardiff for London Welsh. Ackerman signed a three-year contract reported to be worth £40,000 and backed by Whitehaven club sponsors British Nuclear Fuels.

Two Rugby Union captures to make an impact on the international sporting and political scenes were Wigan's signing of South African Springbok winger Ray Mordt and forward Rob Louw, signed in front of the BBC Grandstand cameras on 14th December for a total of £75,000. Their switch of codes and countries gave rise to a minimal amount of anti-apartheid protest.

There were a total of 10 Rugby Union converts during the season compared with the previous season's tally of 15.

The amateur Rugby League ranks provided 139 new recruits for the professional sector compared with the 1984-85 campaign tally of 200.

Australian and New Zealand players again made the biggest impact on the domestic scene despite the limitations of the new quota system. After protests of mass importation from the Professional Players Association, the Department of Employment insisted that the League introduce a quota system and an agreed limit of five graded overseas players per club was brought in for the 1985-86 season. This was to be reduced to four per club for 1986-87 and to three for 1987-88 and thereafter to be a permanent quota of three per club. The League ruled that an overseas player was to be defined as anyone not eligible to play for

Great Britain, eligibility for British selection being birthright.

Four clubs — Hull, Hull K.R., Warrington and Wigan — were given special dispensation to have one extra quota player for the seasons 1985-86 and 1986-87 because they had recruited New Zealand players on long-term contracts before the lifting of the Anglo-Aussie transfer restriction.

Wigan, inevitably, led the way with the signing of Australian Test stars stand off Steve Ella and prop Greg Dowling, both living up to their high reputations.

Les Boyd at Warrington and Noel Cleal at Widnes were other Australian Test packmen to make a huge impact.

The most unfortunate Australian recruit was Steve Rogers, the great Test centre, who played only 13 minutes of his Widnes debut before breaking a leg at Wigan on 22nd September, an injury which was to end his brilliant career.

Other incoming Australian Test players were Dave Brown (Barrow), Ross Conlon (St. Helens) and Geoff Gerard (Hull). New Zealand Test stars joining English clubs were Mark Elia (St. Helens) and Kurt Sorensen (Widnes).

Signings from Australia dropped from 71 to 68, with New Zealand recruits shooting up from 11 to 27.

The total of Australian players registered with English clubs during the season was 82 compared with 84 the previous season. There were 42 New Zealanders registered against 35 a year earlier.

The following is a list of the 127 overseas players registered with English clubs during 1985-86, the influx of Australians on short-term stays still causing some anomalies in the League's registration system.

★ Test players as at 1st June 1986.

AUSTRALIA (82)

*Anderson, Chris	(Halifax)
Anderson, Tony	(Halifax)
Austin, Greg	(Rochdale H.)
Austin, Tony	(Rochdale H.)
Baker, Neil	(Salford)
Battese, Brian	(Salford)
Bilbie, Giles	(Mansfield M.)
Blake, Phil	(Warrington)
*Boyd, Les	(Warrington)
Brockwell, Simon	(Leigh)
*Brown, Dave	(Barrow)
Carter, Matt	(York)
*Cleal, Noel	(Widnes)
Cogger, Trevor	(Leigh)
*Conlon, Ross	(St. Helens)
Cowan, Murray	(Widnes, Workington T., Batley)
Currie, Tony	(Leeds)
Davis, Mike	(Fulham, Leigh)
Deane, Duane	(Hunslet)
Dews, Campbell	(Keighley)
Dreier, Col	(York)
*Dorahy, John	(Hull K.R.)
Dorrough, Scott	(Featherstone R.)
*Dowling, Greg	(Wigan)
Duffy, Don	(Fulham)
Dwyer, Tim	(Barrow)
*Ella, Steve	(Wigan)
Elliott, Tony	(Barrow)
French, Brett	(St. Helens)
French, Ian	(Castleford)
*Gerard, Geoff	(Hull)
Gerard, Graham	(Wakefield T.)
Gerard, Greg	(Castleford)
Gould, Phil	(York)
Graham, Mal	(Oldham)
Grienke, Gary	(St. Helens)
Halliwell, Steve	(Leigh)
Haynes, Les	(Dewsbury)
Heugh, Cavill	(Halifax)
Hooper, Michael	(Mansfield M.)
Jackson, Bob	(Warrington)
Johnson, Brian	(Warrington)
Johnston, Lindsey	(Hull K.R.)
Johnston, Peter	(Hull K.R.)
Kellaway, Bob	(Bradford N.)
Key, Andrew	(Fulham)
Khunnaman, Paul	(Sheffield E.)
Kilroy, Joe	(Halifax)
Leery, Geoff	(Dewsbury)
Lewis, Mike	(Warrington)
Liddiard, David	(Oldham)
Liddiard, Glen	(Oldham)
Lumby, Ashley	(Bradford N.)
Lyons, Cliff	(Leeds)
Marketo, Mike	(York)
Martin, Peter	(York)
Mayoh, Peter	(Leigh)
McKenzie, Phil	(Rochdale H.)
Miller, Gavin	(Hull K.R.)
*Muggleton, John	(Hull)
Nissen, Glen	(Fulham)
O'Dwyer, James	(Hunslet)
O'Riley, Paul	(Fulham)
Penola, Colin	(Oldham, Hunslet)
Pethybridge, Rod	(Featherstone R., York)
Pobjie, Michael	(Salford)
Robinson, Geoff	(Halifax)
*Rogers, Steve	(Widnes)
Sandy, Jamie	(Castleford)
Schaefer, Derek	(Rochdale H.)
Schofield, Derek	(Rochdale H.)
Sherwood, Mitchell	(Sheffield E.)
Smith, Greg	(Barrow)
Thomas, Michael	(Carlisle)
Thompson, Garry	(Bradford N.)
Veivers, Phil	(St. Helens)
Warnecke, Gary	(Oldham)
Webb, Terry	(Leeds)
Willey, Sean	(York)
Windshuttle, Ross	(York)
Wood, Mark	(Widnes)
Wright, Scott	(Sheffield E.)

NEW ZEALAND (42)

*Ah Kuoi, Fred	(Hull)
Bancroft, Phil	(Rochdale H.)
Barlow, Glenn	(Hunslet)
Barrow, Scott	(Widnes)
Benioni, Kuku	(Hunslet, Huddersfield B.)
Burgoyne, Paddy	(Featherstone R., Sheffield E.)
Campbell, Danny	(Wigan, Leigh)

Clark, Trevor	(Leeds)
Clarke, Jeff	(Leigh)
*Elia, Mark	(St. Helens)
Fisher, Adam	(Keighley)
Green, John	(Keighley)
Grima, Joe	(Swinton)
Henley-Smith, Gary	(Wigan, Fulham)
Henson, Bob	(Leigh)
Hiley, Greg	(Mansfield M.)
Howells, Steve	(Dewsbury)
*Kemble, Gary	(Hull)
Kemble, Steve	(Hunslet)
Kete, Ivan	(Fulham)
Kuiti, Mike	(Rochdale)
*Leuluai, James	(Hull)
Mather, Steve	(Keighley)
Mita, Chris	(Dewsbury)
Moore, Andrew	(Wakefield T.)
Moore, Brent	(Blackpool B.)
Muller, Roby	(Salford, Swinton)
Nicholson, Grant	(Mansfield M.)
*O'Hara, Dane	(Hull)
*Prohm, Gary	(Hull K.R.)
Ramsey, Neville	(Bradford N., Wakefield T.)
Roiall, Mark	(Featherstone R., Sheffield E.)
Schaumkell, Kevin	(Sheffield E.)
Sefuive, David	(Dewsbury)
*Smith, Gordon	(Hull K.R.)
*Sorensen, Kurt	(Widnes)
Subritzsky, Peter	(Blackpool B.)
Swanston, Don	(Wakefield T.)
*Tamati, Kevin	(Warrington)
Townsend, Glen	(Fulham)
Tuimavave, Paddy	(Swinton)
*West, Graeme	(Wigan)

SOUTH AFRICA (3)

Du Toit, Nick	(Wigan)
Louw, Rob	(Wigan)
Mordt, Ray	(Wigan)

MOROCCO (1)

M'Barki, Hussein	(Oldham)

BRITONS DOWN UNDER

The number of British players given clearance to play Down Under during the summer of 1986 was 19, nine fewer than the previous year.

The short-term contract exports included current Great Britain Test stars Des Drummond, Garry Schofield, Tony Marchant, Tony Myler, Deryck Fox and Lee Crooks.

The following is a list of players granted a clearance before 1st June to play in Australia and New Zealand with the names of clubs they were due to join. In some cases no advance notice was given of prospective clubs.

TO AUSTRALIA (18)

Burney, Stephen	(Whitehaven)	Wests, Sydney
Crooks, Lee	(Hull)	Wests, Sydney
Drummond, Des	(Leigh)	Manly, Sydney
Fox, Deryck	(Featherstone R.)	Wests, Sydney
Gelling, Bryan	(Leigh)	Bateman Bay, Brisbane
Henderson, John	(Leigh)	Wests, Sydney
Huddart, Milton	(Carlisle)	Canberra
Kendall, David	(Barrow)	—
Kendall, Gary	(Barrow)	—
Keyworth, Mark	(Dewsbury)	Stanthorpe, Toowoomba
Lydiat, John	(Hull K.R.)	Ipswich
Marchant, Tony	(Castleford)	Wynumm-Manly, Brisbane
Myler, Tony	(Widnes)	Balmain, Sydney
Rigby, Colin	(Widnes)	—
Rowbottom, Mark	(Swinton)	Stanthorpe, Toowoomba
Schofield, Garry	(Hull)	Balmain, Sydney
Sherratt, Ian	(Bradford N.)	Stanthorpe, Toowoomba
Thackray, Rick	(Warrington)	Manly, Sydney

TO NEW ZEALAND (1)

Atherton, Wayne	(Leigh)	—

RECORD TRANSFERS

The first £1,000 transfer came in 1921 when Harold Buck joined Leeds from Hunslet, although there were reports at the time that another player was involved in the deal to make up the four-figure transfer. Other claims for the first £1,000 transfer are attached to Stan Brogden's move from Bradford Northern to Huddersfield in 1929.

The following list gives an indication of how transfer fees have grown this century (straight cash deals only):

Season	Player	Position	From	To	Fee
1901-02	Jim Lomas	Centre	Bramley	Salford	£100
1910-11	Jim Lomas	Centre	Salford	Oldham	£300
1912-13	Billy Batten	Centre	Hunslet	Hull	£600
1921-22	Harold Buck	Wing	Hunslet	Leeds	£1,000
1929-30	Stanley Smith	Wing	Wakefield T.	Leeds	£1,075
1933-34	Stanley Brogden	Wing/centre	Huddersfield	Leeds	£1,200
1937-38	Billy Belshaw	Full back	Liverpool S.	Warrington	£1,450
1946-47	Bill Davies	Full back/centre	Huddersfield	Dewsbury	£1,650
1947-48	Bill Hudson	Forward	Batley	Wigan	£2,000
1947-48	Jim Ledgard	Full back	Dewsbury	Leigh	£2,650
1948-49	Ike Owens	Forward	Leeds	Castleford	£2,750
1948-49	Ike Owens	Forward	Castleford	Huddersfield	£2,750
1948-49	Stan McCormick	Wing	Belle Vue R.	St. Helens	£4,000
1949-50	Albert Naughton	Centre	Widnes	Warrington	£4,600
1950-51	Bruce Ryan	Wing	Hull	Leeds	£4,750
1950-51	Joe Egan	Hooker	Wigan	Leigh	£5,000
1950-51	Harry Street	Forward	Dewsbury	Wigan	£5,000
1957-58	Mick Sullivan	Wing	Huddersfield	Wigan	£9,500
1958-59	Ike Southward	Wing	Workington T.	Oldham	£10,650
1960-61	Mick Sullivan	Wing	Wigan	St. Helens	£11,000
1960-61	Ike Southward	Wing	Oldham	Workington T.	£11,002 10s
1968-69	Colin Dixon	Forward	Halifax	Salford	£12,000
1969-70	Paul Charlton	Full back	Workington T.	Salford	£12,500
1972-73	Eric Prescott	Forward	St. Helens	Salford	£13,500
1975-76	Steve Nash	Half back	Featherstone R.	Salford	£15,000
1977-78	Bill Ashurst	Forward	Wigan	Wakefield T.	£18,000
1978-79	Clive Pickerill	Half back	Castleford	Hull	£20,000
1978-79	Phil Hogan	Forward	Barrow	Hull K.R.	£35,000
1979-80	Len Casey	Forward	Bradford N.	Hull K.R.	£38,000
1980-81	Trevor Skerrett	Forward	Wakefield T.	Hull	£40,000
1980-81	George Fairbairn	Full back	Wigan	Hull K.R.	£72,500
1985-86	Ellery Hanley	Centre/stand-off	Bradford N.	Wigan	£85,000
1985-86	Joe Lydon	Centre	Widnes	Wigan	£100,000

MOST MOVES

Geoff Clarkson extended his record number of transfers to 12 when he left Leigh for Featherstone Rovers on 27th October 1983. He played for 10 different English clubs and had a brief spell in Australia.

Clarkson, born on 12th August 1943 was 40
years old when he finished playing regular first team rugby in 1983-84. He turned professional with Wakefield Trinity in 1966 after gaining Yorkshire County forward honours with Wakefield Rugby Union Club.

Clarkson's club career in England is as follows:

1966 — Wakefield T.
1968 — Bradford N.
1970 — Leigh
1971 — Warrington
1972 — Leeds
1975 — York
1976 — Bramley
1978 — Wakefield T. and Hull K.R.
1980 — Bradford N. and Oldham
1981 — Leigh
1983 — Featherstone R.

1985-86 SIGNINGS

The following is a register of signings by clubs between June 1985 and May 1986 inclusive. The right-hand column lists the club from which the player was recruited (ARL Amateur Rugby League, RU — Rugby Union).

In some instances a player who wishes to retain his amateur status is not registered although he may be named in the club's list of appearances.

Although this is a register of signings, it is possible to trace a club's transfers by scrutinising the right hand column.

Indicates where clubs have agreed to a player being signed 'on loan', a temporary transfer, the Rugby Football League prohibiting a subsequent transfer within 28 days. Where a player on loan has not been retained his return to his original club is also marked.

Oldham recruited full back David Liddiard (left) from Sydney club Parramatta, his 16-year-old brother Glen (right) starring for local amateur side Saddleworth before joining the Watersheddings club.

BARROW

Signed	Player	Club From
19.7.85	Mason, Mel	Whitehaven
6.8.85	Moses, Graham	Barrow Island ARL
27.8.85	Brown, Dave	Easts, Aus.
31.8.85	McNichol, Tony	Holker Pioneers ARL
2.9.85	Dwyer, Tim	Brothers, Aus.
2.9.85	Smith, Greg	Brothers, Aus.
13.9.85	Williams, Stewart	Salford
21.9.85	Turley, Norman	Runcorn H.
26.9.85	Elliott, Tony	Caloundra, Aus.
14.2.86	Blacker, Brian	Huddersfield B.
21.2.86	Gleave, Mark	Warrington
27.3.86	*Van Bellen, Gary	Bradford N.
4.4.86	*Fairhurst, Jimmy	Wigan
22.4.86	Morrison, Stephen	Holker Pioneers ARL

BATLEY

Signed	Player	Club From
1.6.85	James, Kevin	Barrow
18.6.85	Riding, David	Batley Boys ARL
18.6.85	Williams, Andrew	Batley Boys ARL
21.6.85	Durham, Stephen	Stanley Rangers ARL
8.8.85	Bartle, Phillip	Stanley Rangers ARL
28.8.85	Senior, Paul	Batley Boys ARL
1.10.85	Pickerill, Neil	Huddersfield B.
28.11.85	Iveson, Derek	George Hotel ARL
8.12.85	Davies, Tom	Wakefield T.
9.1.86	Cunningham, Eddie	Widnes
26.3.86	Cowan, Murray	Workington T.

BLACKPOOL BOROUGH

Signed	Player	Club From
21.8.85	Swann, Malcolm	Wakefield T.
22.8.85	Subritzky, Peter	Mangakino, NZ
26.9.85	Platt, Billy	Fulham
6.10.85	Howard, Paul	St. Helens
11.11.85	Moore, Brent	Mangakino, NZ
19.12.85	Sanderson, Mark	Rochdale H.
23.1.86	Howarth, Roy	Leigh
19.4.86	Yates, Mal	Warrington

BRADFORD NORTHERN

Signed	Player	Club From
11.6.85	*Van Bellen, Gary	Hunslet
27.6.85	*Carroll, Dean	Carlisle
6.8.85	Woods, John	Leigh
13.8.85	Lumby, Ashley	Brisbane Souths, Aus.
27.8.85	Potter, Martin	Bradford N. Colts
31.8.85	Fleming, Martin	Lock Lane ARL
3.9.85	Thompson, Garry	Brisbane Souths, Aus.
9.9.85	Chambers, Shaun	Redhill ARL
16.9.85	Ford, Phil	Wigan
16.9.85	Donlan, Steve	Wigan
23.9.85	Ramsey, Neville	Ngaruawahia, NZ
29.9.85	White, Brendan	York
30.9.85	*Pennant, Audley	Castleford
1.10.85	*Atherton, Michael	Sheffield E.
15.10.85	Kamis, Andy	Hull K.R. Colts
28.11.85	Grayshon, Paul	Bradford N. Colts
3.12.85	Holmes, Terry	Cardiff RU
19.12.85	Pridgeon, David	Bradford N. Colts
4.2.86	Barnett, Stephen	Apperly Bridge ARL
18.3.86	*Preece, Chris	Halifax
27.3.86	*Sykes, Andy	York
7.5.86	*Van Bellen, Gary,	Barrow
14.5.86	Simpson, Robert	Bradford N. Colts
15.5.86	*Hale, Gary	Doncaster
21.5.86	Race, Wayne	Bradford & Bingley RU

BRAMLEY

Signed	Player	Club From
20.8.85	Hankins, Steve	Featherstone R.
6.9.85	Downs, David	Jubilee ARL
10.9.85	Box, Harold	Wakefield T.
3.10.85	*Bowman, Chris	York
31.10.85	*Coen, Darren	Castleford
11.1.86	Coventry, Paul	Featherstone R.
14.1.86	Agar, Allan	Featherstone R.
21.1.86	*Tansley, Ian	York
15.3.86	Robinson, Graeme	Carlisle
25.3.86	Burgess, Mark	Rochdale H.

CARLISLE

Signed	Player	Club From
8.8.85	Stockley, John	Fulham
28.9.85	Thomason, Malcolm	Broughton Red Rose ARL
28.9.85	Little, Alan	Caledonian ARL
28.9.85	*O'Byrne, Mick	Halifax
28.9.85	Tunstall, Brian	Hensingham ARL
30.11.85	*Youngman, Wally	Wakefield T.
10.12.85	Elliott, David	Barrow
18.12.85	Carroll, Dean	Bradford N.
2.1.86	Kirkby, Steve	Barrow
11.1.86	Thomas, Michael	Penrith, Aus.
11.1.86	Loynes, Dean	Mansfield M.
20.1.86	Peacham, Tony	Northern Dairies ARL

CASTLEFORD

Signed	Player	Club From
26.6.85	Southernwood, Roy	Travellers Saints ARL
9.8.85	Diamond, Steve	Hunslet
26.8.85	Shillito, Alan	Halifax
26.8.85	*Pennant, Audley	Bradford N.
28.8.85	Gerard, Greg	Huddersfield B.
30.8.85	Plange, David	Doncaster
19.9.85	French, Ian	Wynnum Manly, Aus.
18.10.85	Sandy, Jamie	Brisbane Easts, Aus.
22.10.85	Hill, Ken	Travellers Saints ARL
25.10.85	Blackburn, John	Castleford Colts
25.11.85	Thornton, Wayne	Castleford Colts
20.1.86	*Coen, Darren	Bramley
12.2.86	Irwin, Shaun	Redhill ARL
15.5.86	*Jones, Kevin	Doncaster

DEWSBURY

Signed	Player	Club From
20.6.85	Madden, Michael	Batley Boys ARL
9.7.85	Howley, Patrick	Dewsbury Moor ARL
23.8.85	Mita, Chris	Pt. Chevalier, NZ
26.8.85	Leary, Geoff	Batemans Bay, Aus.
27.8.85	Sefuive, David	Richmond Rovers, NZ
16.9.85	Howells, Steve	Mount Albert, NZ
9.10.85	Haynes, Les	Aus.
29.11.85	Janicwiez, Paul	Illingworth ARL
6.12.85	Bailey, Dennis	Queenswood ARL
17.1.86	*Cook, Mark	Mansfield M.
6.3.86	*Sharp, Greg	Mansfield M.

DONCASTER

Signed	Player	Club From
2.8.85	*Plange, David	Castleford
27.8.85	Pickett, John	Hunslet
28.8.85	Harrison, Peter	Leeds
29.8.85	Roache, Mark	Castleford
26.9.85	Green, John	Bradford N.
3.10.85	*Turner, Richard	Leeds
2.11.85	*Jones, Kevin	Castleford
7.1.86	*Hale, Gary	Bradford N.
14.1.86	Barratt, Dale	Doncaster Colts
14.1.86	Robinson, Kevin	Castleford
14.1.86	Gibbon, Mark	Askern Miners ARL
14.1.86	Foster, Ben	Askern Miners ARL
14.1.86	Ford, Brian	Askern Miners ARL
16.1.86	Parkhouse, Kevin	Askern Welfare ARL
16.1.86	Carr, Alan	Askern Welfare ARL
16.1.86	Turner, Neil	Wheatley Hills RU
16.1.86	Morris, Geoff	Rochdale H.
16.1.86	Pickerill, Clive	Wakefield T.
16.1.86	Freeman, Lawrence	Askern Miners ARL
27.2.86	O'Toole, Tony	Featherstone R.
3.4.86	Hardy, Alan	Mansfield M.
10.4.86	Ellis, David	Keighley
13.4.86	Timson, Andy	Rochdale H.

FEATHERSTONE ROVERS

Signed	Player	Club From
11.6.85	Bibb, Chris	Lock Lane ARL
1.7.85	Pethybridge, Rod	Wests, Aus.
22.7.85	Hunter, Martin	Travellers Saints ARL
10.11.85	Chappell, Chris	Duke of York ARL
13.11.85	*Marsh, Richard	Huddersfield B.
22.11.85	Hird, Adrian	Featherstone R. Colts
19.12.85	Harrison, Karl	Bramley
23.12.85	Campbell, Mark	Featherstone M.W. ARL
17.1.86	Wright, Craig	Huddersfield B.
17.1.86	Robinson, Tim	Doncaster
18.1.86	Heselwood, David	Barrow
7.2.86	Steadman, Graham	York
13.2.86	Langton, Terry	Mansfield M.
14.2.86	*Crooks, Martin	Leeds
14.2.86	*Massa, Mark	Leeds
6.3.86	Barker, Alan	Jubilee ARL
11.3.86	Kellett, Brian	Jubilee ARL
12.3.86	Kelly, Neil	Dewsbury
14.4.86	Oakley, Graham	Travellers Saints ARL
26.4.86	Wild, Paul	Featherstone Welfare ARL

FULHAM

Signed	Player	Club From
27.8.85	Nissen, Glen	Penrith, Aus.
29.8.85	Key, Andrew	Grafton Ghosts ARL
10.9.85	Mordell, Bob	Southend I.
14.9.85	Platt, Alan	Oldham
21.9.85	O'Riley, Paul	Guildford, Aus.
27.9.85	Feighan, Frank	Southend I.
28.9.85	Glover, Mike	Bridgend
22.11.85	Bullough, Dave	Bramley
19.12.85	Henley-Smith, Gary	Wigan
19.12.85	Herdman, Martin	Halifax
19.1.86	Johnson, Nick	Leeds University ARL
19.1.86	Meachin, Colin	Salford
7.3.86	Worgan, Graham	Leigh
7.3.86	*Yates, Mal	Warrington
5.4.86	Rexson, Ian	Peckham ARL
5.4.86	Briscoe, Phil	Southend I.
5.4.86	Gibson, Russell	Streatham Celtic ARL
5.4.86	Cooper, Tony	Southend I.

HALIFAX

Signed	Player	Club From
1.6.85	*Goodall, Adrian	Keighley
1.6.85	*Whitehouse, Nigel	Mansfield M.
22.7.85	Robinson, Geoff	Canterbury-Bankstown, Aus.
23.7.85	Kilroy, Joe	Brisbane Easts, Aus.
23.7.85	Heugh, Cavill	Brisbane Easts, Aus.
29.7.85	Scott, Mick	Wigan
31.7.85	Stephens, Gary	Leigh
16.8.85	*White, Brendan	York
16.8.85	Dixon, Paul	Huddersfield B.
28.8.85	James, Neil	Castleford
5.9.85	Juliff, Brian	Wigan

1.10.85	Fairbank, Frank	Elland ARL
2.10.85	*Waites, Keith	Hunslet
9.10.85	*McCurrie, Alan	Oldham
10.10.85	Crossley, John	Bradford N.
18.10.85	Bell, Peter	David Brown ARL
22.10.85	Simpson, Andy	Oulton ARL
31.10.85	*O'Byrne, Mick	Carlisle
2.1.86	*Marshall, Nigel	Keighley
16.1.86	Whitfield, Colin	Wigan
16.1.86	*Preece, Chris	Bradford N.
16.1.86	Clayforth, Shaun	Redhill ARL
16.1.86	Dobell, David	Redhill ARL
16.1.86	Moore, Darren	Redhill ARL
16.1.86	Stephenson, Billy	David Brown ARL
13.2.86	George, Wilf	Widnes

HUDDERSFIELD BARRACUDAS

Signed	Player	Club From
12.7.85	Wood, Neil	Keighley
27.8.85	Pollard, Gordon	Oldham
29.8.85	Humphreys, Lee	Halifax
1.9.85	Charlton, Mark	Huddersfield Colts
5.9.85	Hooper, Trevor	York
8.9.85	Meehan, Gary	Bradford N.
8.9.85	Kenworthy, Simon	Underbank ARL
29.9.85	*Marsh, Richard	Featherstone R.
29.9.85	Nelson, David	Leeds
3.10.85	Cockerham, Paul	Sheepscar WMC ARL
17.10.85	Platt, Billy	Blackpool B.
17.10.85	McGovern, Terry	Swinton
8.12.85	Benioni, Kuku	Hunslet
19.12.85	Boothroyd, Alan	David Brown ARL
2.1.86	Campbell, Mark	Sheffield E.
2.1.86	*Marshall, Nigel	Halifax
2.4.86	Cook, Billy	Bramley
17.4.86	Munro, Geoff	Oldham

HULL

Signed	Player	Club From
25.6.85	Hobson, Alan	Travellers Saints ARL
15.7.85	Gerard, Geoff	Penrith, Aus.
30.8.85	Gascoigne, Andy	Bramley
16.9.85	*Gaitley, Bob	Carlisle
22.10.85	Hick, Steve	Hull Colts
20.12.85	Brand, Michael	Scunthorpe RU
1.1.86	*Banks, Barry	Hunslet
10.5.86	*Harkin, Kevin	Wakefield T.
10.5.86	*Dennison, Steve	Mansfield M.

HULL KINGSTON ROVERS

Signed	Player	Club From
12.8.85	Johnston, Peter	Canterbury-Bankstown, Aus.
16.9.85	Johnston, Lindsey	Easts, Aus.
2.1.86	Hutchinson, Carl	Negas ARL
17.1.86	Wilson, Ian	York
20.1.86	*Tosney, Andrew	Wakefield T.
27.3.86	*Hall, David	Wakefield T.
6.5.86	*Holdstock, Roy	Wakefield T.

HUNSLET

Signed	Player	Club From
4.6.85	*Rowe, Danny	Huddersfield B.
4.6.85	*Smith, Stewart	Rochdale H.
4.6.85	*Britton, Steve	Doncaster
20.6.85	*Pickett, John	Doncaster
21.6.85	Hirst, John	Huddersfield B.
21.6.85	Lunn, Martin	Huddersfield B.
14.7.85	*Lean, Neil	Bramley
7.8.85	Rowse, Gary	Keighley
22.8.85	*Waites, Keith	Halifax
17.9.85	Benioni, Kuku	Otara, NZ
17.9.85	Kemble, Steve	Ellerslie, NZ
17.9.85	Barlow, Glenn	Ellerslie, NZ
28.9.85	Nicholson, Steve	Mansfield M.
3.10.85	Deane, Duane	West Tamworth, Aus.
5.10.85	Wilson, Warren	Bramley Social ARL
18.10.85	Cawood, Gary	Halifax
25.10.85	O'Dwyer, James	Manly-Warringah, Aus.
5.11.85	Walker, Steve	Bramley
15.11.85	McCurrie, Alan	Oldham
19.11.85	Crampton, Jimmy	Castleford
6.12.85	Dufton, Stephen	Dewsbury
17.12.85	Newsome, Mark	Hunslet Colts
27.12.85	Warrener, Stanley	West Hunslet ARL
29.12.85	Humphreys, Lee	Huddersfield B.
29.12.85	*Birkby, Ian	Oldham
3.1.86	*Hunt, Ian	Keighley
3.1.86	*Hirst, John	Keighley
9.1.86	Penola, Colin	Oldham
21.1.86	Webb, Darren	Hunslet Boys ARL
28.1.86	Goodyear, George	Hunslet Parkside ARL
3.3.86	Allen, Michael	Keighley
18.3.86	Kitchen, Phillip	Keighley
19.3.86	*Cooper, Glen	Mansfield M.
10.5.86	Nickle, Sonny	Hunslet Parkside ARL

KEIGHLEY

Signed	Player	Club From
3.6.85	*Sellers, Les	Bramley
8.6.85	*Moll, David	Halifax
9.7.85	Ragan, Mark	De la Salle College ARL
9.7.85	*Shillito, Alan	Halifax
1.8.85	Green, John	Addington, NZ
1.8.85	Mather, Steve	Addington, NZ
1.8.85	Fisher, Adam	Addington, NZ
17.8.85	*Hunt, Ian	Hunslet
17.8.85	Hirst, John	Hunslet
3.9.85	Roe, Peter	Hunslet
8.9.85	Goodier, Frank	Green Dragon ARL
8.9.85	Turner, Fred	Rosebridge ARL
17.9.85	*Marshall, Nigel	Halifax
20.9.85	*Townsend, Jeff	York
21.10.85	*Johnson, Billy	Swinton
14.11.85	Pitts, John	Batley
21.11.85	Dews, Campbell	Brisbane North, Aus.
6.12.85	*McDermott, Paul	Sheffield E.
7.1.86	Walsh, Tim	Keighley Celtic ARL
8.3.86	Farmer, Nick	Oulton ARL
8.3.86	Page, Steve	Mansfield M.
26.3.86	*Waites, Keith	Halifax

LEEDS

Signed	Player	Club From
4.6.85	*Harrison, Peter	Doncaster
6.6.85	*Turner, Richard	Doncaster
20.8.85	Lyons, Cliff	Gundagai, Aus.
28.8.85	Staniland, Andrew	Roundhay RU
13.10.85	Smithson, Martyn	Lock Lane ARL
30.10.85	Grayshon, Jeff	Bradford N.
18.1.86	Gibson, Carl	Batley
21.1.86	Pratt, Richard	Batley Boys ARL
14.5.86	*Turner, Richard	Doncaster
16.5.86	*Crooks, Martin	Featherstone R.
16.5.86	*Massa, Mark	Featherstone R.

LEIGH

Signed	Player	Club From
26.6.85	*Bilsbury, Terry	Rochdale H.
13.7.85	Mayoh, Peter	North Sydney, Aus.
16.7.85	Cogger, Trevor	Wests, Aus.
16.7.85	Halliwell, Steve	Parramatta, Aus.
18.8.85	Gelling, Bryan	St. Helens
20.8.85	Kerr, John	Warrington
27.8.85	Henson, Bob	City Newton, NZ
27.8.85	Brockwell, Simon	North Sydney, Aus.
27.9.85	Grundy, Darryl	Blackpool B.
8.10.85	Walkden, Gary	Blackbrook ARL
6.1.86	Riding, Colin	Leigh Colts
12.1.86	O'Toole, David	Leigh East ARL
16.1.86	Campbell, Danny	Wigan
8.4.86	Evans, Stuart	Leigh Miners ARL
25.4.86	Collier, Andy	Leigh Miners ARL

MANSFIELD MARKSMAN

Signed	Player	Club From
20.6.85	Blackmore, Peter	Redhill ARL
24.6.85	Cook, Mark	Batley Boys ARL
16.8.85	Edgington, David	Lock Lane ARL
17.9.85	Wilkes, Calvin	Southend I.
23.9.85	Hiley, Greg	Mangere East, NZ
23.9.85	Nicholson, Grant	Mangere East, NZ
9.10.85	Hooper, Michael	Canterbury-Bankstown, Aus.
3.11.85	Bilbie, Giles	Lakes United, Aus.
15.11.85	Scanlon, Andy	Southend I.
16.11.85	*Whiteman, Keith	Wakefield T.
22.11.85	O'Byrne, Mick	Halifax
28.11.85	Goodall, Adrian	Halifax
30.11.85	Hughes, Brian	Rochdale H.
12.12.85	Hardy, Alan	Rochdale H.
5.1.86	Stevens, Darren	Wests, Aus.
10.1.86	Rose, Tony	Huddersfield B.
17.1.86	Barrett, David	Swinton
17.1.86	Farrar, Andrew	Hunslet
17.1.86	*Cook, Mark	Dewsbury
17.1.86	*Sharp, Greg	Dewsbury

Leeds' Australian import Cliff Lyons who delayed his move to Sydney Club Manly in a vain bid to reach Wembley.

18.1.86	Simpkin, Kevin	Rochdale H.
18.1.86	*Sanderson, Carl	Carlisle
19.1.86	Duffy, Andy	Rochdale H.
19.1.86	Ellis, Ken	Doncaster
11.2.86	Fletcher, Andrew	Wakefield T.
18.2.86	*Cooper, Glen	Hunslet
18.2.86	Welsh, Paul	Sheffield E.
14.3.86	Whitehead, Craig	Rochdale H.
22.3.86	Humphreys, Lee	Hunslet
27.3.86	*Willis, Chris	Rochdale H.

367

OLDHAM

Signed	Player	Club From
6.9.85	M'Barki, Hussein	Warrington
12.9.85	Penola, Colin	Southend I.
26.9.85	Finch, David	Castleford
26.9.85	Warnecke, Gary	Wests, Aus.
29.9.85	Graham, Mal	Wests, Newcastle, Aus.
10.10.85	Liddiard, David	Parramatta, Aus.
26.10.85	Bardsley, Michael	Tameside ARL
13.11.85	*McCurrie, Alan	Halifax
13.12.85	Liddiard, Glen	Saddleworth Rangers ARL
14.5.85	Clawson, Neil	Featherstone R.
15.5.85	*Birkby, Ian	York

ROCHDALE HORNETS

Signed	Player	Club From
23.6.85	*Garside, Brett	Fulham
24.6.85	*Fitzpatrick, Paul	Runcorn H.
24.6.85	*Morris, Geoff	Doncaster
8.8.85	Timson, Andy	Castleford
9.8.85	Wood, David	Wigan
9.8.85	Dunn, Brian	Wigan
14.8.85	Harcombe, Kevin	Doncaster
18.8.85	Mellor, Ian	Folly Lane ARL
18.8.85	Hardy, Alan	Carlisle
18.8.85	Fitzsimons, Eric	Hunslet
24.8.85	Duane, Ian	Warrington
28.8.85	Evans, David	GM Police ARL
10.9.85	Nash, Steve	Salford
17.9.85	Austin, Greg	North Sydney, Aus.
17.9.85	Austin, Tony	North Sydney, Aus.
17.9.85	McKenzie, Phil	Illawarra, Aus.
2.10.85	Schofield, Derek	Mullumbimby, Aus.
7.10.85	Schaefer, Derek	Aus.
14.10.85	Kuiti, Mike	Upper Hutt, NZ
23.10.85	Bancroft, Phil	Halswell, NZ
18.12.85	Idle, Graham	Hunslet
23.12.85	Fellows, Paul	Warrington
30.12.85	*Willis, Chris	Mansfield M.
11.2.86	Meachin, Colin	Fulham
28.2.86	Shaw, Glyn	Warrington
3.3.86	Stapleton, John	Swinton

RUNCORN HIGHFIELD

Signed	Player	Club From
20.8.85	*Fitzpatrick, Paul	Rochdale H.
28.8.85	Turley, Norman	Blackpool B.
28.8.85	Dainty, Gary	Mansfield M.
28.8.85	Blackwood, Bob	Bridgend
30.8.85	Garritty, Tony	Widnes
4.10.85	Egan, Martin	Rosebridge ARL
3.2.86	*Blythin, Kevin	Whitehaven
12.2.86	Henney, Harold	Fulham
25.2.86	Hunter, Clive	Swinton

ST. HELENS

Signed	Player	Club From
18.6.85	Lee, Mark	St. Helens Colts
3.7.85	*Bottell, Gary	Barrow
18.7.85	Donegan, Austin	UGB ARL
29.7.85	*Gelling, Bryan	Leigh
15.8.85	French, Brett	Wynnum Manly, Aus.
4.9.85	Grienke, Gary	Brisbane Souths, Aus.
2.10.85	Conlon, Ross	Balmain, Aus.
17.11.85	Elia, Mark	Te Atatu, NZ
24.11.85	McCormack, Kevin	Widnes Tigers ARL
30.12.85	Jones, Paul	Leigh Easts ARL
18.1.86	Ogden, Tony	Oldham
30.1.86	Kerr, Steve	Sutton Oak ARL
31.1.86	Souto, Peter	Widnes
5.2.86	Hughes, Eric	Widnes
13.2.86	Doherty, Paul	St. Patricks ARL

SALFORD

Signed	Player	Club From
10.6.85	*Williams, Stewart	Wigan
16.6.85	Baker, Neil	Souths, Aus.
2.7.85	Corless, Michael	Leigh Miners ARL
3.7.85	Battese, Brian	Souths, Aus.
10.8.85	Telford, Neil	Blackpool B.
20.8.85	Fizackerley, John	Thotto Heath ARL
30.8.85	O'Loughlin, Keiron	Widnes
12.9.85	Herbert, Steve	Barrow
19.9.85	Muller, Roby	City Newton, NZ
19.9.85	Pobjie, Michael	Souths, Aus.
10.10.85	*Gribbin, Vince	Whitehaven
6.11.85	Moylan, Steve	Warrington

SHEFFIELD EAGLES

Signed	Player	Club From
1.6.85	Wileman, Vic	Grimethorpe ARL
2.6.85	Nason, Kevin	Moorends ARL
12.8.85	Dickinson, Andy	Halifax
23.8.85	*Atherton, Michael	Bradford N.
26.8.85	Farrell, Kevin	Keighley
27.8.85	Bridgeman, Derek	Queens Park ARL
3.9.85	Cholmondeley, David	Southend I.
29.9.85	Lake, Ernie	Moorends ARL
20.10.85	Walton, David	Halifax
1.11.85	Glancy, John	Selby ARL
2.11.85	Herdman, Martin	Halifax
6.12.85	*McDermott, Paul	Keighley
16.12.85	Schaumkell, Kevin	NZ
17.12.85	Burgoyne, Paddy	NZ
17.1.86	Lane, Steve	Roanne, France
17.1.86	Wright, Scott	Easts, Aus.
17.1.86	Sherwood, Mitchell	Easts, Aus.
17.1.86	Khunnaman, Paul	Easts, Aus.
19.1.86	Smith, Gary	York
22.3.86	Ferres, Steve	Batley
19.4.86	Box, Harold	Bramley

SWINTON

Signed	Player	Club From
6.6.85	Oxendale, Adrian	Saddleworth R. ARL
8.8.85	Topping, Simon	St. Patricks ARL
30.9.85	Hewitt, Tony	Rosebridge ARL
1.10.85	Cassidy, Frank	Rosebridge ARL
14.10.85	Tuimavave, Paddy	Mt. Albert, NZ
14.10.85	Grimo, Joe	Ponsonby, NZ
15.10.85	Scott, Terry	St. Patricks ARL
15.10.85	Berry, John	Crown Springs ARL
27.10.85	Mooney, James	Rosebridge ARL
29.10.85	Whitehead, Sean	Saddleworth ARL
12.11.85	Evans, Terry	Crossfields ARL
14.12.85	*Johnson, Billy	Keighley
20.12.85	*Hunter, Clive	Whitehaven
22.1.86	Muller, Roby	Salford
25.3.86	Ainsworth, Gary	Leigh
31.3.86	*Jones, Ken	Wakefield T.
13.4.86	Swann, Malcolm	Blackpool B.

WAKEFIELD TRINITY

Signed	Player	Club From
1.6.85	Wainman, Stuart	West Hull ARL
1.8.85	*Harkin, Kevin	Hull
7.8.85	Millington, John	Hull K.R.
30.9.85	Hickman, Kevin	NDLB ARL
30.9.85	Gerard, Graham	Parramatta, Aus.
3.10.85	*Davies, Tom	Huddersfield B.
10.10.85	*Whiteman, Keith	Mansfield M.
23.10.85	Swanston, Don	Christchurch, NZ
24.10.85	Moore, Andrew	Christchurch, NZ
31.10.85	*Youngman, Wally	Carlisle
1.11.85	Lazenby, Tracy	Hull K.R.
10.1.86	Whiteman, Keith	Mansfield M.
11.1.86	*Hall, David	Hull K.R.
11.1.86	*Holdstock, Roy	Hull K.R.
1.3.86	*Jones, Ken	Swinton
4.3.86	*Parkes, Brian	St. Helens
20.4.86	Green, Jimmy	Blackpool B.
15.5.86	*Tosney, Andrew	Hull K.R.

WARRINGTON

Signed	Player	Club From
1.6.85	Boyd, Les	Manly-Warringah, Aus.
20.6.85	Rawlinson, Tommy	Runcorn H.
21.6.85	Copewell, Eric	Widnes Tigers ARL
27.6.85	Rathbone, Alan	Bradford N.
15.7.85	Blake, Phil	Manly-Warringah, Aus.
9.8.85	Tamati, Kevin	Widnes
26.9.85	Lewis, Mike	Cootamundra, Aus.
26.9.85	Johnson, Brian	St. George, Aus.
21.11.85	Abram, Darren	Thatto Heath ARL
17.12.85	Sanderson, Gary	Thatto Heath ARL
26.12.85	Lowe, Kevin	Rochdale H.
9.1.86	Harmon, Neil	Blackbrook ARL
29.3.86	Peters, Steve	St. Helens
29.3.86	Meadows, Kevin	St. Helens
29.3.86	Thornley, Tony	Woolston Rovers ARL
17.4.86	*Yates, Mal	Fulham

WHITEHAVEN

Signed	Player	Club From
24.7.85	McCartney, Duncan	Egremont Rangers ARL
24.7.85	Cole, Kevin	Broughton Red Rose ARL
24.7.85	Hetherington, Gary	Kells ARL
24.7.85	Preston, Gary	Kells ARL
24.7.85	*Stewart, Joe	Carlisle
24.7.85	*Tomlinson, Brian	Carlisle
24.7.85	Thomson, Alan	Carlisle
26.7.85	House, Stephen	St. Benedicts RU
26.7.85	Cunningham, Tony	Hessingham ARL
9.8.85	Fearon, Neil	Glasson ARL
21.9.85	Ditchburn, Tom	Flimby ARL
1.10.85	Dinsdale, Edwin	Kells ARL
3.10.85	*Hunter, Clive	Swinton
4.10.85	*Todd, Colin	Workington T.
4.11.85	*Gribbin, Vince	Salford
3.1.86	*Blythin, Kevin	Runcorn H.
17.1.86	McDermott, Paul	Sheffield E.
18.1.86	Thompson, Ian	Workington T.
27.2.86	Bottell, Gary	St. Helens
25.3.86	Gorley, Peter	St. Helens
10.4.86	Ackerman, Rob	London Welsh RU

Kiwi Test star Kurt Sorensen, a long-term contract capture for Widnes.

WIDNES

Signed	Player	Club From
21.8.85	Barrow, Scott	Canterbury, NZ
17.9.85	Cowan, Murray	Wests, Aus.
19.9.85	Rogers, Steve	Cronulla, Aus.
17.10.85	Souto, Peter	Fulham
22.10.85	Cleal, Noel	Manly-Warringah, Aus.
14.12.85	Sorensen, Kurt	Cronulla, Aus.
15.1.86	Wood, Mark	Werielda, Aus.
7.2.86	Gilbert, John	Featherstone R.
28.3.86	*Moran, Dave	Workington T.
16.4.86	Eyres, Andrew	Blackbrook ARL

WIGAN

Signed	Player	Club From
19.6.85	*Flowers, Ness	Bridgend
28.7.85	Dowling, Greg	Wynnum Manly, Aus.
29.7.85	Goodway, Andy	Oldham
12.8.85	Ella, Steve	Parramatta, Aus.
16.9.85	Hanley, Ellery	Bradford N.
20.10.85	Russell, Richard	St. Patricks, ARL
22.10.85	Stott, Phil	Vale of Lune RU
14.12.85	Louw, Rob	South Africa RU
14.12.85	Mordt, Ray	South Africa RU
10.1.86	Lydon, Joe	Widnes
4.2.86	Collier, Andrew	Wigan Colts
14.5.86	*Fairhurst, Jimmy	Barrow

WORKINGTON TOWN

Signed	Player	Club From
23.6.85	*Hogg, Graeme	Barrow
23.6.85	Bailey, Stephen	Egremont ARL
23.7.85	*Todd, Colin	Barrow
25.10.85	Cowan, Murray	Widnes
1.11.85	Burgess, Glen	Clifton ARL
3.11.85	Sullivan, Joe	Glasson ARL
13.11.85	*Todd, Colin	Whitehaven
19.12.85	Stafford, Peter	Wigton ARL
9.1.86	*Moran, Dave	Widnes
15.1.86	Courty, David	Ellenborough ARL
17.1.86	Frazer, Neil	Whitehaven
19.1.86	Lowden, David	Glasson ARL

YORK

Signed	Player	Club From
28.6.85	*Hooper, Trevor	Huddersfield B.
14.8.85	Willey, Sean	Manly-Warringah, Aus.
15.8.85	Gould, Philip	Canterbury-Bankstown, Aus.
30.8.85	Marketo, Mike	Balmain, Aus.
3.9.85	*Bowman, Chris	Bramley
10.9.85	Martin, Peter	North Sydney, Aus.
30.9.85	*White, Brendan	Halifax
19.10.85	Carter, Matt	Parramatta, Aus.
30.11.85	Pethybridge, Rod	Featherstone R.
26.12.85	*Sykes, Andy	Barrow
30.1.86	*Townend, Jeff	Keighley
8.3.86	*Tansley, Ian	Bramley
27.3.86	*Birkby, Ian	Hunslet
31.3.86	Windshuttle, Ross	Manly-Warringah, Aus.
31.3.86	Dreier, Col	Manly-Warringah, Aus.

Greenalls Man of Steel 1986, Gavin Miller.

AWARDS

THE 1986 MAN OF STEEL AWARDS

Launched in the 1976-77 season, the Rugby Football League's official awards are presented to the Man of Steel, the personality judged to have made the most impact on the season; the First and Second Division Players of the Year, decided by a ballot of the players; the Young Player of the Year, under-21 at the start of the season; the Coach of the Year and Referee of the Year.

Having been sponsored by Trumanns Steel for the first seven years, the awards were taken over by Greenall Whitley in 1983-84 who last season presented a record £6,000 in prizes in front of a capacity audience at the Variety Centre, Salford.

Greenalls Man of Steel

Hull K.R. loose forward Gavin Miller became the first overseas star to win the prestigious title of Man of Steel, the personality judged to have made the most impact on the season.

The former Eastern Suburbs and Cronulla packman received a cheque for £1,500 and a silver champagne goblet worth £300.

In his second campaign at Craven Park, Miller was voted Rovers' Player of the Year after dominating their Man of the Match awards.

He also collected the White Rose Trophy as Man of the Match in the John Smiths Yorkshire Cup final and a twin Silk Cut Award in the double Challenge Cup semi-final epic with Leeds.

The Greenalls Man of Steel citation praised Miller's 'dominance of matches across Rugby League country with his professionalism and vast array of skills'.

Award ceremony acclaim for 1986 Greenalls Man of Steel Gavin Miller from 10th anniversary past winners, from the left, Alan Agar, David Ward, Mick Morgan, George Nicholls, Doug Laughton and Ellery Hanley.

Greenalls First Division
Player of the Year
Australian import Gavin Miller topped the poll of fellow Slalom Lager Championship players, votes being cast in a twin ballot in January and April.

Miller, who arrived at Craven Park relatively unheralded from Sydney, produced a host of Man of the Match performances, scoring 13 tries in 40 appearances for the Robins.

Miller's dominance of the pack scene in Britain raised speculation that the former Cronulla skipper could have been in the running for a Kangaroo tour spot despite his temporary emigration.

Greenalls Second Division
Player of the Year
Prop forward Derek Pyke, captain of runaway Second Division champions Leigh, collected the most votes of fellow players.

The Hilton Park outfit lost only one of the 34 league matches en route to the Second Division Championship Bowl and a Slalom Lager £9,000 prize cheque, finishing 12 points ahead of runners-up Barrow.

Their record breaking campaign featured Pyke's leadership and ball handling inspiration, plus his contribution of 10 touchdowns in a record tryscoring bonanza.

Greenalls Young Player of the Year
Wigan's 19-year-old record junior signing Shaun Edwards added a Man of Steel award to his vast array of honours.

Having already been capped at every level for Great Britain, Edwards furthered his international career during 1985-86 with two appearances for Britain against the Kiwis, two non-playing substitute Test roles against France, a tryscoring appearance for the Under-21s against New Zealand and captaincy of Great Britain Colts in France.

Edwards opened the season at stand off for Wigan with a Man of the Match performance in the inaugural Okells Charity Shield encounter on the Isle of Man before turning out for Lancashire in the first-ever Rodstock War of the Roses match. Switching to scrum half in the second half of the season, he scored 14 tries in 35 Wigan fixtures.

Greenalls Coach of the Year
In his first full season at Halifax, Chris Anderson became the first overseas team boss to lift the Coach of the Year title.

Appointed in November 1984, Anderson took the Thrum Hall side to their first Championship success for 21 years, losing only five matches in a 30-game programme.

Halifax started the Slalom Lager Championship campaign as 100-1 outsiders for the title and £13,000 prize cheque. Anderson welded together a hybrid of astute overseas recruits and a crop of domestic bargain buys, while missing only two of their 37 matches in a season in which he contributed 12 tries.

Greenalls Referee of the Year
Wakefield man-in-the-middle Fred Lindop collected his hat-trick of Referee of the Year awards, having lifted the title in 1980 and 1982.

His 1986 nomination was the ninth in 10 years of Man of Steel award ceremonies. During the season, Lindop had travelled to France to take charge of the Great Britain Under-21 international in Perpignan and was appointed for his third Premiership final.

● Each of the five category winners received a cheque for £500 and an inscribed silver wine goblet worth £200.

THE MAN OF STEEL AWARDS ROLL OF HONOUR

	Man of Steel	1st Division Player	2nd Division Player	Young Player	Coach	Referee
1977	David Ward (Leeds)	Mal Reilly (Castleford)	Ged Marsh (Blackpool B.)	David Ward (Leeds)	Eric Ashton MBE (St. Helens)	Billy Thompson (Huddersfield)
1978	George Nicholls (St. Helens)	George Nicholls (St. Helens)	John Woods (Leigh)	John Woods (Leigh)	Frank Myler (Widnes)	Billy Thompson (Huddersfield)
1979	Doug Laughton (Widnes)	Mick Adams (Widnes)	Steve Norton (Hull)	Steve Evans (Featherstone R.)	Doug Laughton (Widnes)	Mick Naughton (Widnes)
1980	George Fairbairn (Wigan)	Mick Adams (Widnes)	Steve Quinn (Featherstone R.)	Roy Holdstock (Hull K.R.)	Peter Fox (Bradford N.)	Fred Lindop (Wakefield)
1981	Ken Kelly (Warrington)	Ken Kelly (Warrington)	John Crossley (York)	Des Drummond (Leigh)	Billy Benyon (Warrington)	John Holdsworth (Leeds)
1982	Mick Morgan (Carlisle)	Steve Norton (Hull)	Mick Morgan (Carlisle)	Des Drummond (Leigh)	Arthur Bunting (Hull)	Fred Lindop (Wakefield)
1983	Allan Agar (Featherstone R.)	Keith Mumby (Bradford N.)	Steve Nash (Salford)	Brian Noble (Bradford N.)	Arthur Bunting (Hull)	Robin Whitfield (Widnes)
1984	Joe Lydon (Widnes)	Joe Lydon (Widnes)	David Cairns (Barrow)	Joe Lydon (Widnes)	Tommy Dawes (Barrow)	Billy Thompson (Huddersfield)
1985	Ellery Hanley (Bradford N.)	Ellery Hanley (Bradford N.)	Graham Steadman (York)	Lee Crooks (Hull)	Roger Millward MBE (Hull K.R.)	Ron Campbell (Widnes)
1986	Gavin Miller (Hull K.R.)	Gavin Miller (Hull K.R.)	Derek Pyke (Leigh)	Shaun Edwards (Wigan)	Chris Anderson (Halifax)	Fred Lindop (Wakefield)

NOMINEES:

1977   *1st Division Player:* Bruce Burton (Castleford), Vince Farrar (Featherstone R.). *2nd Division Player:* Jeff Grayshon (Dewsbury), Keith Hepworth (Hull). *Young Player:* Jimmy Crampton (Hull), Harry Pinner (St. Helens). *Coach:* Keith Cotton (Featherstone R.), Mal Reilly (Castleford). *Referee:* Joe Jackson (Pudsey), Mick Naughton (Widnes).

1978   *1st Division Player:* Roger Millward (Hull K.R.), Harry Pinner (St. Helens). *2nd Division Player:* Phil Hogan (Barrow), Mick Morgan (York). *Young Player:* Neil Hague (Leeds), Keith Mumby (Bradford N.). *Coach:* Eric Ashton MBE (St. Helens), John Mantle (Leigh). *Referee:* Ron Campbell (Widnes), Fred Lindop (Wakefield).

1979   *1st Division Player:* Brian Lockwood (Hull K.R.), Tommy Martyn (Warrington). *2nd Division Player:* Barry Banks (York), John Wolford (Dewsbury). *Young Player:* Mick Burke (Widnes), John Woods (Leigh). *Coach:* Billy Benyon (Warrington), Arthur Bunting (Hull). *Referee:* Fred Lindop (Wakefield), Billy Thompson (Huddersfield).

1980   *1st Division Player:* Len Casey (Hull K.R.), George Fairbairn (Wigan). *2nd Division Player:* Mick Blacker (Halifax), John Wolford (Dewsbury). *Young Player:* Steve Hubbard (Hull K.R.), Harry Pinner (St. Helens). *Coach:* Maurice Bamford (Halifax), Arthur Bunting (Hull). *Referee:* Ron Campbell (Widnes), Billy Thompson (Huddersfield).

1981   *1st Division Player:* Mick Adams (Widnes), Tommy Martyn (Warrington). *2nd Division Player:* Arnie Walker (Whitehaven), Danny Wilson (Swinton). *Young Player:* Paul Harkin (Hull K.R.), Keith Mumby (Bradford N.). *Coach:* Reg Bowden (Fulham), Peter Fox (Bradford N.). *Referee:* Ron Campbell (Widnes), Fred Lindop (Wakefield).

1982   *1st Division Player:* Jeff Grayshon (Bradford N.), Andy Gregory (Widnes). *2nd Division Player:* Denis Boyd (Carlisle), Alan Fairhurst (Swinton). *Young Player:* Lee Crooks (Hull), Andy Gregory (Widnes). *Coach:* Doug Laughton (Widnes), Alex Murphy/Colin Clarke (Leigh). *Referee:* Gerry Kershaw (York), Billy Thompson (Huddersfield).

1983   *1st Division Player:* Bob Eccles (Warrington), David Topliss (Hull). *2nd Division Player:* Tommy David (Cardiff C.), Mike Lampkowski (Wakefield T.). *Young Player:* Ronnie Duane (Warrington), Andy Goodway (Oldham). *Coach:* Alex Murphy (Wigan), Frank Myler (Oldham). *Referee:* John Holdsworth (Leeds), Fred Lindop (Wakefield).

1984   *1st Division Player:* Garry Schofield (Hull), John Woods (Leigh). *2nd Division Player:* Lynn Hopkins (Workington T.), John Wolford (Hunslet). *Young Player:* Gary Divorty (Hull), Garry Schofield (Hull). *Coach:* Arthur Bunting (Hull), Roger Millward MBE (Hull K.R.). *Referee:* Derek Fox (Wakefield), Fred Lindop (Wakefield).

1985   *1st Division Player:* Harry Pinner (St. Helens), Gary Prohm (Hull K.R.). *2nd Division Player:* Terry Langton (Mansfield M.), Peter Wood (Runcorn H.). *Young Player:* Deryck Fox (Featherstone R.), Andy Platt (St. Helens). *Coach:* Arthur Bunting (Hull), Colin Clarke/Alan McInnes (Wigan). *Referee:* Fred Lindop (Wakefield), Stan Wall (Leigh).

1986   *1st Division Player:* Steve Ella (Wigan), John Fieldhouse (Widnes). *2nd Division Player:* John Henderson (Leigh), Graham King (Hunslet). *Young Player:* Paul Lyman (Featherstone R.), Roy Powell (Leeds). *Coach:* Roger Millward MBE (Hull K.R.), John Sheridan (Doncaster). *Referee:* John Holdsworth (Kippax), Robin Whitfield (Widnes).

GREENALL WHITLEY — SUNDAY PEOPLE AWARDS

Sponsored by brewers Greenall Whitley and promoted by the Sunday People newspaper, the scheme featured Men of the Month awards. In the 1985-86 season, the monthly winners each received tankards and £150. The traditional Personality of the Year award was suspended in 1983-84 because of Greenall Whitley's takeover of the Man of Steel awards and replaced in 1984-85 by a £500 Clubman of the Year award.

The Greenall Whitley-Sunday People Awards Roll of Honour

	1977-78	1978-79	1979-80	1980-81	1981-82
PERSONALITY OF THE YEAR					
	Reg Bowden (Widnes)	Doug Laughton (Widnes)	George Fairbairn (Wigan)	Reg Bowden (Fulham)	Des Drummond (Leigh)
MEN OF THE MONTH					
Sept.	J. Woods (Leigh)	J. Mills (Widnes)	I. Ball (Barrow)	P. Harkin (Hull K.R.)	D. Drummond (Leigh)
Oct.	G. Vigo (Wigan)	B. Lockwood (Hull K.R.)	K. Gill (Salford)	G. Hyde (Castleford)	A. Gregory (Widnes)
Nov.	P. Fox (Bradford N.)	D. Laughton (Widnes)	S. Quinn (Featherstone R.)	K. Kelly (Warrington)	S. Norton (Hull)
Dec.	M. Adams (Widnes)	N. Holding (St. Helens)	G. Fairbairn (Wigan)	B. Benyon (Warrington)	J. Grayshon (Bradford N.)
Jan.	W. Ashurst (Wigan)	C. Stone (Hull)	M. Adams (Widnes)	B. Case (Warrington)	M. Morgan (Carlisle)
Feb.	Not awarded — Bad weather	G. Wraith (Castleford)	R. Holdstock (Hull K.R.)	A. Agar (Wakefield T.)	D. Drummond (Leigh)
Mar.	E. Cunningham (St. Helens)	S. Evans (Featherstone R.)	S. Norton (Hull)	M. Adams (Widnes)	L. Hopkins (Workington T.)
Apr.	J. Holmes (Leeds)	K. Kelly (Warrington)	G. Munro (Oldham)	K. Mumby (Bradford N.)	J. Woods (Leigh)
May.	G. Pimblett (St. Helens)	J. Sanderson (Leeds)	M. Aspey (Widnes)	S. Norton (Hull)	M. Adams (Widnes)
SPECIAL AWARDS	Keith Fielding (Superstars) Colin Welland (BBC Documentary)			Roger Millward (Hull K.R. on retirement as a player)	

1982-83	1983-84	1984-85	1985-86

PERSONALITY OF THE YEAR

David Topliss —
(Hull)

CLUBMAN OF THE YEAR

Geoff Fletcher   Roger Millward MBE
(Runcorn H.)   (Hull K.R.)

MEN OF THE MONTH

	1982-83	1983-84	1984-85	1985-86
Sept.	D. Heron (Leeds)	E. Hanley (Bradford N.)	E. Hanley (Bradford N.)	P. Lister (Bramley)
Oct.	M. Meninga (Australia)	G. Smith (Hull K.R.)	M. Meninga (St. Helens)	N. Du Toit (Wigan)
Nov.	F. Stanton (Australia)	J. Basnett (Widnes)	B. Ledger (St. Helens)	J. Fieldhouse (Widnes)
Dec.	B. Eccles (Warrington)	J. Lydon (Widnes)	C. Anderson (Halifax)	S. Ella (Wigan)
Jan.	A. Murphy (Wigan)	M. Bamford (Leeds)	P. Harkin (Hull K.R.)	A. Myler (Widnes)
Feb.	N. Holding (St. Helens)	R. Beardmore (Castleford)	B. Kenny (Wigan)	Not awarded — Bad weather
Mar.	T. Hudson (Featherstone R.)	N. Holding (St. Helens)	H. Gill (Wigan)	K. Ward (Castleford)
Apr.	D. Topliss (Hull)	G. Schofield (Hull)	G. Prohm (Hull K.R.)	E. Hanley (Wigan)
May.	A. Agar (Featherstone R.)	—	—	T. Barrow (Warrington)

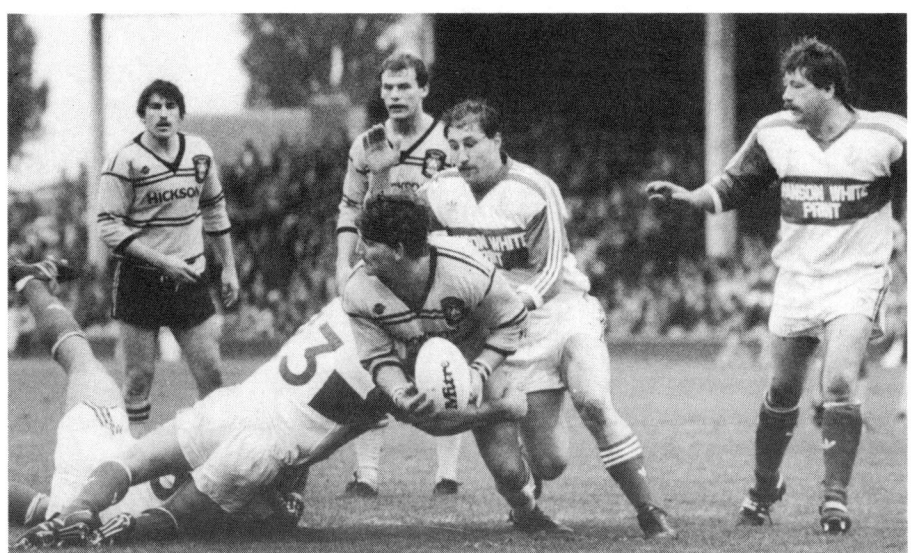

Castleford prop forward Kevin Ward, recipient of the Greenall Whitley — Sunday People Man of the Month award for March 1986.

GREENALL WHITLEY-SUNDAY PEOPLE TOP SCORERS AWARDS

Launched in the 1976-77 season, the scheme was designed to reward the top try and goal scorers.

Sponsored by brewers Greenall Whitley and promoted by the Sunday People newspaper, the awards were worth £25 a try and £5 a goal in the 1985-86 season.

Free-scoring Leigh provided both chart toppers in Australian-based centre Steve Halliwell with 49 touchdowns — the most by a centre in any season — and full back Chris Johnson, on target 173 times.

Halliwell collected £1,225 prize money while setting the new tryscoring record for a centre, beating the previous best of 45 touchdowns by Huddersfield's Tommy Gleeson in 1913-14 and equalled by Hull K.R.'s Gary Prohm in 1984-85. Great Britain international Johnson received £865 for his top markmanship.

Greenall Whitley - Sunday People Top Scorers Awards Roll of Honour

Top Tries

1976-77	1977-78	1978-79	1979-80	1980-81
Stuart Wright (Widnes): 31	Stuart Wright (Widnes): 33	Steve Hartley (Hull K.R.): 35	Keith Fielding (Salford): 30 Steve Hubbard (Hull K.R.): 30	John Crossley (York): 35

1981-82	1982-83	1983-84	1984-85	1985-86
John Jones (Work'ton T.): 31	Bob Eccles (Warrington): 37	Garry Schofield (Hull): 38	Ellery Hanley (Bradford N.): 55	Steve Halliwell (Leigh): 49

Top Goals

1976-77	1977-78	1978-79	1979-80	1980-81
Sammy Lloyd (Castle'd): 163	Geoff Pimblett (St. Helens): 178	Sammy Lloyd (Hull): 172	Steve Quinn (F'stone R.): 163	Steve Hesford (Warrington): 147

1981-82	1982-83	1983-84	1984-85	1985-86
Lynn Hopkins (Work'ton T.): 190	Steve Diamond (Fulham): 136	Bob Beardmore (Castleford): 142 Steve Hesford (Warrington): 142	Sean Day (St. Helens): 157	Chris Johnson (Leigh): 173

DAILY EXPRESS — FRIGIDAIRE AWARDS

Launched in the 1978-79 season in conjunction with Hepworth Tailoring, was taken over by Frigidaire in 1984-85, the awards being decided by a ballot of Daily Express readers.

In the 1985-86 season, the Player of the Year received a cheque for £1,000 and a silver salver. Periodic awards were presented during the season, each worth £200.

The Daily Express-Frigidaire Roll of Honour

PLAYER OF THE YEAR

1978-79	1979-80	1980-81	1981-82	1982-83	1983-84
Doug Laughton (Widnes)	Steve Norton (Hull)	Mick Adams (Widnes)	George Fairbairn (Hull K.R.)	David Topliss (Hull)	Garry Schofield (Hull)

1984-85	1985-86
Ellery Hanley (Bradford N.)	Gavin Miller (Hull K.R.)

PERIODIC AWARDS

1978-79	1979-80	1980-81	1981-82	1982-83	1983-84
Keith Smith (Wakefield T.)	John Woods (Leigh)	Steve Quinn (Featherstone R.)	Des Drummond (Leigh)	Trevor Skerrett (Hull)	Bob Beardmore (Castleford)
Neil Holding (St. Helens)	Alan Smith (Leeds)	Fred Ah Kuoi (New Zealand)	Jeff Grayshon (Bradford N.)	Lee Crooks (Hull)	Ian Ball (Barrow)
Reg Bowden (Widnes)	Steve Quinn (Featherstone R.)	Des Drummond (Leigh)	Steve Norton (Hull)	Mal Meninga (Australia)	Mick Burke (Widnes)
Roger Millward (Hull K.R.)	Harry Pinner (St. Helens)	Ken Kelly (Warrington)	George Fairbairn (Hull K.R.)	Garry Clark (Hull K.R.)	Brian Noble (Bradford N.)
Doug Laughton (Widnes)	George Fairbairn (Wigan)	Tommy Martyn (Warrington)	Trevor Skerrett (Hull)	Terry Flanagan (Oldham)	Keith Rayne (Leeds)
Sammy Lloyd (Hull)	Alan Redfearn (Bradford N.)	Steve Hesford (Warrington)	Des Drummond (Leigh)	Brian Noble (Bradford N.)	Ken Kelly (Warrington)
		Mick Adams (Widnes)		Terry Hudson (Featherstone R.)	Garry Schofield (Hull)

1984-85	1985-86
Mal Meninga (St. Helens)	Deryck Fox (Featherstone R.)
Mike Smith (Hull K.R.)	Steve Ella (Wigan)
Andy Goodway (Oldham)	John Fieldhouse (Widnes)
John Wolford (Hunslet)	Gavin Miller (Hull K.R.)
Brett Kenny (Wigan)	Kurt Sorensen (Widnes)
Mike Ford (Wigan)	David Heron (Leeds)

DAILY MIRROR — LADA CARS AWARDS

Introduced in the 1979-80 season, the scheme acknowledges the adjudged Team of the Month in both Division One and Two.

A panel of judges representing the Daily Mirror, Lada Cars and the Rugby League selected the two monthly winners who each received a cheque for £250 and a framed citation.

Promoted by the Daily Mirror, the awards were sponsored for the first four seasons by Shopacheck before Lada Cars took over in the 1983-84 season. Lada Cars introduced the first-ever £1,000 Team of the Year title in 1983-84, the 1986 winners Halifax receiving a bonus £1,500.

The Daily Mirror-Lada Cars Awards Roll of Honour

	1979-80 First Division	1980-81 First Division	1981-82 First Division	1982-83 First Division
Aug./ Sept.	Salford	Hull K.R.	Leigh	Leeds
Oct.	Leigh	Castleford	Widnes	Hull
Nov.	Leeds	Featherstone R.	Hull K.R.	Castleford
Dec.	Hull	Warrington	Hull★	Wigan
Jan.	Bradford N.	Halifax		Wigan
Feb.	Widnes	Wakefield T.	Leigh	Castleford
Mar.	Hull	Widnes	Bradford N.	Hull
Apr./ May	Leigh	Bradford N.	Hull	Widnes

	Second Division	Second Division	Second Division	Second Division
Aug./ Sept.	Halifax	Huddersfield	Oldham	Fulham
Oct.	Batley	Fulham	Swinton	Huyton
Nov.	Featherstone R.	Wigan	Carlisle	Wakefield T.
Dec.	Oldham	Blackpool B.	Carlisle★	Salford
Jan.	Whitehaven	Keighley		Whitehaven
Feb.	Halifax	York	Huyton	Hunslet
Mar.	Barrow	Whitehaven	Oldham	Fulham
Apr./ May	Swinton	Batley	Oldham	Cardiff C.

★A double-money award to cover both months, badly hit by adverse weather.
†Not awarded due to bad weather.

Team of the Year
1983-84: Widnes
1984-85: Hull K.R.
1985-86: Halifax

	1983-84 First Division	**1984-85** First Division	**1985-86** First Division
Aug./ Sept.	Bradford N.	Hull K.R.	Hull K.R.
Oct.	Hull K.R.	St. Helens	Wigan
Nov.	Widnes	Featherstone R.	Oldham
Dec.	Leeds	Halifax	Wigan
Jan.	Hull	Hull K.R.	Widnes
Feb.	Castleford	Wigan	†
Mar.	Wigan	Wigan	St. Helens
Apr./ May	St. Helens	St. Helens	Warrington

	Second Division	**Second Division**	**Second Division**
Aug./ Sept.	Barrow	Mansfield M.	Wakefield T.
Oct.	Halifax	Carlisle	Rochdale H.
Nov.	Swinton	Dewsbury	Leigh
Dec.	Batley	Batley	Blackpool B.
Jan.	Barrow	Batley	Doncaster
Feb.	Hunslet	Bramley	†
Mar.	Huddersfield	Dewsbury	Batley
Apr./ May	Blackpool B.	Swinton	Leigh

Daily Mirror–Lada Cars Team of the Year Halifax parade the 1986 Slalom Lager Championship Trophy through the packed streets of the town.

SLALOM LAGER-DAILY STAR STARMEN AWARDS

Introduced in 1982-83, the scheme is sponsored by Slalom Lager and promoted by the Daily Star. The Man of the Match for each team in every Slalom Lager Championship and Second Division game is awarded a rating out of 10. The top pollster in the Championship received £500 and a trophy, with £350 and a trophy being presented to the top Second Division player.

	Championship	**Second Division**
1982-83	Harry Pinner (St. Helens)	Graham Beale (Keighley)
1983-84	John Woods (Leigh)	John Wolford (Hunslet)
1984-85	Ellery Hanley (Bradford N.)	Graham Steadman (York)

1985-86 FINAL TABLES

Slalom Lager Championship

Deryck Fox (Featherstone R.) 80
Gavin Miller (Hull K.R.) 77
Gary Stephens (Halifax) 65
Graham Steadman (Featherstone R.) 61
Lee Crooks (Hull) 55
Andy Gregory (Warrington) 54
Neil Baker (Salford) 54
Paul Harkin (Hull K.R.) 48

Second Division

Dean Carroll (Carlisle) 92
Brian Garrity (Runcorn H.) 91
Phil McKenzie (Rochdale H.) 76
Steve Tickle (Barrow) 73
Peter Lister (Bramley) 69
Neil Pickerill (Batley) 62
Billy Platt (Huddersfield B.) 60
Steve Halliwell (Leigh) 57

TRAVELEADS TOP FAN AWARD

For the second time, Traveleads presented the Top Fan award to Rugby League's official Supporter of the Year. Oldham stalwart Eddie Elson received the title and a prize of a £3,000 holiday for two in Hong Kong, in association with British Airways.

At 81, Mr Elson continued his long-standing tradition of attending every home Oldham first team and A-team fixture, every first team training session and cycling to away fixtures in Lancashire.

The first-ever Traveleads Top Fan in 1985 was Mrs Joan Martin, a lifelong active supporter of Doncaster.

REFEREES

REFEREES HONOURS 1985-86

Silk Cut Challenge Cup final:
Robin Whitfield

John Player Special Trophy final:
John Holdsworth

Slalom Lager Premiership final:
Fred Lindop

Burtonwood Brewery Lancashire Cup final:
John Holdsworth

John Smiths Yorkshire Cup final:
Ron Campbell

France v New Zealand (2):
Ron Campbell

France v Great Britain Under-21s:
Fred Lindop

Rodstock War of the Roses:
Fred Lindop

REFEREES ROLL OF HONOUR

KEVIN ALLATT
Date of birth: 29.12.42
Grade Two: 1970-71
Grade One: 1972-73
Lancashire Cup 1983-84
Lancashire v Yorkshire 1975-76

MICK BEAUMONT
Date of birth: 27.6.40
Grade Two: 1973-74
Grade One: 1977-78
Lancashire v Cumbria 1979-80

GEOFF BERRY
Date of birth: 26.4.54
Grade Two: 1981-82
Grade One: 1983-84

ALEX BOWMAN
Date of birth: 20.9.56
Grade One: 1986-87

DAVE CARTER
Date of birth: 29.11.55
Grade One: 1984-85

STEVE CROSS
Date of birth: 23.3.50
Grade One: 1986-87

DEREK FOX
Date of birth: 2.1.39
Grade Two: 1977-78
Grade One: 1980-81
Lancashire v Cumbria 1981-82
Wales v England 1984-85

STEPHEN HAIGH
Date of birth: 5.4.45
Grade Two: 1980-81
Grade One: 1983-84

CLIFF HODGSON
Date of birth: 18.10.40
Grade Two: 1978-79
Grade One: 1983-84

JOHN HOLDSWORTH
Date of birth: 25.1.47
Grade Two: 1979-80
Grade One: 1980-81
John Player Trophy 1985-86
Premiership Trophy 1980-81
Lancashire Cup 1985-86
Wales v England 1980-81
Cumbria v Yorkshire 1981-82
Lancashire Cup 1982-83
France v Great Britain Under-24s 1982-83

PAUL HOUGHTON
Date of birth: 1.10.51
Grade One: 1985-86

JOHN KENDREW
Date of birth: 22.4.50
Grade Two: 1982-83
Grade One: 1983-84

GERRY KERSHAW
Date of birth: 24.10.43
Grade Two: 1969-70
Grade One: 1970-71
Challenge Cup 1980-81
Lancashire Cup 1980-81
Floodlit Trophy 1973-74
John Player Trophy 1973-74
Wales v England 1981-82
Wales v Australia 1982-83
France v Great Britain Under-24s 1981-82
Lancashire v Yorkshire 1971-72
Lancashire v Cumbria 1972-73
Cumbria v Other Nationalities 1974-75
Cumbria v Lancashire 1978-79, 1980-81

FRED LINDOP
Date of birth: 20.7.38
Grade Two: 1966-67
Grade One: 1967-68
Great Britain v New Zealand (2nd Test) 1980-81
Great Britain v Australia, 3 Tests 1967-68
France v Great Britain 1968-69
1970 World Cup:
Great Britain v Australia
Great Britain v France
Great Britain v New Zealand
Great Britain v Australia (Final)
Wales v France 1974-75
1975 World Championship:
France v Wales
New Zealand v Australia (at Auckland)
Wales v France
Wales v England 1977-78
Great Britain Under-24s v Australia 1978-79
France v Great Britain Under-24s 1979-80, 1983-84
France v Great Britain Under-21s 1985-86
Australia v New Zealand (2) 1982
Premiership Trophy 1976-77, 1982-83, 1985-86
Challenge Cup 1969-70, 1979-80, 1981-82 (+replay)
Floodlit Trophy 1967-68, 1972-73
John Player Trophy 1974-75, 1978-79, 1981-82
Lancashire Cup 1967-68, 1974-75
Yorkshire Cup 1984-85
Capt. Morgan Trophy 1973-74
Cumbria v Lancashire 1973-74
Lancashire v Other Nationalities 1974-75
Lancashire v Yorkshire 1981-82
War of the Roses 1985-86

JOHN McDONALD
Date of birth: 7.10.37
Grade Two: 1974-75
Grade One: 1975-76
Floodlit Trophy 1978-79
Yorkshire v Cumbria 1978-79, 1981-82

JOHN MEAN
Date of birth: 12.11.39
Grade Two: 1975-76
Grade One: 1983-84

BRIAN SIMPSON
Date of birth: 23.6.44
Grade One: 1985-86

JIM SMITH
Date of birth: 2.3.44
Grade Two: 1977-78
Grade One: 1983-84

KEN SPENCER
Date of birth: 29.8.47
Grade Two: 1974-75
Grade One: 1983-84

RAY TENNANT
Date of birth: 7.4.49
Grade One: 1985-86

FRANK TICKLE
Date of birth: 26.10.45
Grade One: 1984-85

PAUL VOLANTE
Date of birth: 30.6.52
Grade One: 1983-84

ROBIN WHITFIELD
Date of birth: 26.11.43
Grade Two: 1979-80
Grade One: 1980-81
Challenge Cup 1982-83, 1985-86
Yorkshire Cup 1981-82
France v Australia (2) 1982-83
New Zealand v Australia 1983
Yorkshire v Lancashire 1981-82

THE ALLIANCE

SLALOM LAGER ALLIANCE

FINAL TABLE 1985-86

	P.	W.	D.	L.	Dr.	FOR Gls.	Trs.	Pts.	Dr.	AGAINST Gls.	Trs.	Pts.	Pts.
Hull	26	22	0	4	2	112	143	798	1	56	56	337	44
Castleford	26	22	0	4	1	96	127	701	3	53	50	309	44
Widnes	26	20	0	6	2	94	125	690	5	52	55	329	40
Hull K.R.	26	19	2	5	2	103	116	672	4	49	54	318	40
Leeds	26	20	0	6	1	93	111	631	5	41	48	279	40
Wakefield T.	26	16	1	9	5	79	104	579	3	51	54	321	33
Warrington	26	15	2	9	6	105	123	708	3	72	83	479	32
Leigh	26	15	1	10	4	65	86	478	2	77	89	512	31
Barrow	26	14	2	10	3	86	102	583	0	70	99	536	30
St. Helens	26	14	1	11	2	77	108	588	4	60	72	412	29
Halifax	26	14	1	11	3	88	98	571	3	66	84	471	29
Salford	26	14	1	11	2	78	108	590	4	78	101	564	29
Wigan	26	13	2	11	2	72	100	546	5	85	93	547	28
Bradford N.	26	12	2	12	8	67	78	454	2	64	80	450	26
Swinton C.	26	11	1	14	7	69	80	465	1	75	92	519	23
Oldham	26	10	2	14	0	70	90	500	4	85	100	574	22
Dewsbury	26	9	2	15	3	57	66	381	3	64	91	495	20
Batley	26	9	0	17	2	58	63	370	6	82	103	582	18
Huddersfield P.	26	7	0	19	2	52	73	398	5	91	110	627	14
Hunslet	26	7	0	19	2	51	59	340	1	92	132	713	14
Carlisle-Penrith	26	6	2	18	2	51	70	384	4	110	136	768	14
Whitehaven	26	6	1	19	3	69	82	469	3	96	122	683	13
Featherstone R.	26	5	1	20	5	58	60	361	2	79	104	576	11
Keighley	26	0	0	26	5	34	35	213	1	136	199	1,069	0

1985-86 RESULTS

Home:	Barrow	Batley	Bradford N.	Carlisle-Penrith	Castleford	Dewsbury	Featherstone R.	Halifax	Huddersfield P.	Hull
Barrow	—	42-6	—	42-8	—	42-14	—	12-12	—	—
Batley	10-19	—	32-20	—	7-25	17-18	26-6	8-15	18-4	30-42
Bradford N.	—	18-10	—	—	23-10	14-0	18-8	—	16-10	12-14
Carlisle-Penrith	14-26	—	—	—	—	—	—	9-6	—	—
Castleford	—	32-22	20-16	—	—	28-14	20-14	—	50-22	12-2
Dewsbury	26-26	12-14	23-18	—	18-14	—	0-0	38-0	14-12	26-38
Featherstone R.	—	19-20	18-24	—	16-28	6-27	—	—	10-13	30-32
Halifax	38-12	44-10	—	26-12	—	42-0	—	—	—	—
Huddersfield P.	—	10-12	22-20	—	18-28	23-16	18-8	—	—	18-40
Hull	—	60-0	40-6	—	18-2	30-10	24-0	—	22-12	—
Hull K.R.	—	41-0	10-23	—	14-4	12-9	40-12	—	78-14	25-10
Hunslet	—	4-18	18-7	—	22-28	4-14	26-50	—	18-10	0-62
Keighley	—	5-26	14-28	4-34	6-36	6-12	16-21	—	8-28	6-32
Leeds	—	28-2	26-8	—	16-24	40-2	46-0	—	23-10	6-16
Leigh	24-16	—	—	28-11	—	—	34-0	14-10	20-12	—
Oldham	32-10	—	—	46-10	6-32	—	—	58-18	—	—
St. Helens	6-11	—	—	36-10	—	—	—	32-6	—	—
Salford	12-42	—	—	64-20	4-26	—	—	23-14	—	—
Swinton C.	18-14	—	—	30-18	—	—	—	6-18	—	—
Wakefield T.	—	36-8	14-16	62-4	1-22	28-14	18-12	—	20-18	10-12
Warrington	54-10	—	30-27	46-8	—	—	—	40-8	—	20-12
Whitehaven	18-28	—	—	16-28	—	—	—	42-16	—	—
Widnes	30-0	—	—	42-10	—	—	24-15	22-28	52-4	—
Wigan	32-20	—	40-19	52-10	—	—	—	18-2	—	24-25

Phil Windley, vice-captain of 1986 Slalom Lager Alliance Champions, Hull, receives a £1,000 prize cheque and the Alliance Trophy from Slalom Lager director Miles Eastwood, accompanied by Alliance chairman Tom Aschcroft (left) and secretary Geoff Keith.

Hull K.R.	Hunslet	Keighley	Leeds	Leigh	Oldham	St. Helens	Salford	Swinton C.	Wakefield T.	Warrington	Whitehaven	Widnes	Wigan
—	—	—	—	8-6	30-16	6-38	50-20	34-18	—	28-14	44-10	3-22	8-36
6-22	8-16	30-4	20-26	—	—	—	—	—	10-14	—	—	—	—
12-12	28-4	30-10	13-20	—	—	—	—	—	10-6	12-23	—	—	16-16
—	—	50-17	—	16-25	18-10	6-38	20-22	10-36	8-8	16-48	18-18	16-9	0-11
20-12	44-2	72-4	16-8	—	60-2	—	16-10	—	22-12	—	—	—	—
12-14	18-21	40-8	6-28	—	—	—	—	—	0-10	—	—	—	—
12-18	16-18	42-16	6-4	26-10	—	—	—	—	12-30	—	—	2-26	—
—	—	—	—	46-17	41-8	42-10	10-14	36-14	—	22-6	24-10	5-22	42-14
22-26	32-14	40-14	12-16	10-20	—	—	—	—	—	4-32	—	0-32	—
10-14	30-6	74-0	33-24	—	—	—	—	—	—	26-4	42-20	—	52-10
—	60-6	60-6	14-16	—	—	16-4	—	28-10	6-11	—	—	—	—
4-12	—	36-18	4-30	—	8-10	—	18-38	—	14-16	—	—	—	—
3-82	10-28	—	11-22	—	—	36-0	—	—	0-64	—	14-24	—	—
50-4	18-15	50-12	—	—	—	—	—	34-16	16-19	—	—	—	—
—	—	—	—	—	16-4	4-54	4-20	22-22	—	22-17	36-10	16-20	37-18
—	44-4	—	—	34-6	—	12-28	14-19	16-18	—	18-18	20-16	20-18	26-26
16-16	—	—	10-24	16-26	24-10	—	34-22	20-6	—	22-24	16-9	24-8	18-22
—	58-18	—	—	32-0	12-18	26-24	—	24-19	—	24-24	34-16	20-24	20-12
12-18	—	—	4-16	36-28	16-24	9-22	14-10	—	—	24-14	28-10	12-18	30-8
14-18	34-12	52-0	4-8	—	—	—	—	—	—	—	54-23	—	—
—	—	—	—	14-18	44-20	22-18	40-16	15-20	—	—	72-4	12-16	22-20
—	—	56-1	—	10-28	20-12	8-21	12-26	28-25	26-6	—	10-22	30-42	15-16
—	—	—	—	42-6	28-10	25-17	44-12	8-14	—	—	34-5	28-14	36-8
—	—	—	—	8-11	34-10	6-40	31-6	26-8	—	—	8-42	24-14	26-18

Swinton captain and scrum half Martin Lee receives the 1986 Slalom Lager Alliance Challenge Cup from Matthew Brown Free Trade Director Ken Moore.

SLALOM LAGER ALLIANCE CHALLENGE CUP

First Round

Batley	30	Huddersfield P.	20
Carlisle-Penrith	16	Widnes	9
Dewsbury	28	Keighley	4
Featherstone R.	19	Whitehaven	21
Hull	32	Salford	30
Hunslet	0	Swinton C.	38
(at Swinton)			
Wigan	24	Leeds	26

Byes: Barrow, Bradford N., Halifax, Hull K.R., Leigh, Oldham, St. Helens, Wakefield T., Warrington

Second Round

Bradford N.	28	Barrow	22
Carlisle-Penrith	28	Hull K.R.	4
Leeds	18	Warrington	10
Leigh	22	Halifax	12
St. Helens	26	Dewsbury	12
Swinton C.	11	Batley	0
Wakefield T.	24	Hull	23
Whitehaven	20	Oldham	12

Third Round

Carlisle-Penrith	28	Bradford N.	16
Swinton C.	22	Leigh	12
Wakefield T.	18	Leeds	22
Whitehaven	8	St. Helens	21

Semi-Finals

Leeds	28	Carlisle-Penrith	8
St. Helens	8	Swinton C.	19

Final

Leeds	16	Swinton C.	18

LANCASHIRE COUNTY CHALLENGE SHIELD 1985-86

First Round

Carlisle-Penrith	6	Barrow	12
Leigh	18	Warrington	30
Whitehaven	32	Salford	16
Widnes	39	St. Helens	10

Byes: Oldham, Rochdale H., Swinton C., Wigan

Second Round

Barrow	30	Swinton C.	10
Rochdale H.	16	Oldham	6
Whitehaven	21	Warrington	12
Widnes	30	Wigan	12

Semi-Finals

Whitehaven	21	Rochdale H.	2
Widnes	42	Barrow	14

Final

Widnes	50	Whitehaven	0

YORKSHIRE SENIOR COMPETITION CHALLENGE CUP 1985-86

First Round

Batley	48	Keighley	4
Dewsbury	22	Leeds	0
Elland (Halifax)	25	Heworth (York)	12
(at Halifax)			
Halifax	24	Castleford	20
Hull	14	Bradford N.	10
Hull K.R.	28	Huddersfield P.	18
Mysons (Hull)	6	Hunslet	20
Wakefield T.	39	Featherstone R.	12

Second Round

Batley	17	Dewsbury	8
Halifax	15	Elland	11
Hull	36	Hull K.R.	14
Wakefield T.	16	Hunslet	10

Semi-Finals

Batley	0	Wakefield T.	20
Halifax	16	Hull	24

Final

Wakefield T.	20	Hull	0

COLTS

COLTS LEAGUE

FINAL TABLES 1985-86

FIRST DIVISION

	P.	W.	D.	L.	Dr.	FOR Gls.	Trs.	Pts.	Dr.	AGAINST Gls.	Trs.	Pts.	Pts.
Wigan	20	17	0	3	2	65	102	540	3	23	24	145	34
Hull K.R.	22	14	2	6	6	62	82	458	1	23	40	207	30
Wakefield T.	22	14	0	8	3	43	59	325	3	39	41	245	28
Featherstone R.	22	13	1	8	4	54	70	392	2	48	53	310	27
Castleford	24	13	1	10	4	58	59	356	6	48	67	370	27
St. Helens	21	13	0	8	3	51	75	405	5	49	42	271	26
Hull	22	9	0	13	—	61	75	422	2	66	77	442	18
Leeds	21	4	0	17	1	40	54	297	2	68	115	598	8
Bradford N.	21	3	0	18	3	39	52	289	3	79	105	581	6
Hunslet	9	0	0	9	0	14	7	57	0	44	71	372	0

● Hunslet withdrew on 13th January 1986.

SECOND DIVISION

	P.	W.	D.	L.	Dr.	FOR Gls.	Trs.	Pts.	Dr.	AGAINST Gls.	Trs.	Pts.	Pts.
Leigh	25	20	0	5	—	81	109	598	5	46	66	361	40
Barrow	23	17	0	6	3	59	92	489	6	31	39	224	34
Halifax	21	15	0	6	4	60	75	424	4	37	40	238	30
Dewsbury	22	14	1	7	6	56	80	438	6	41	54	304	29
York	22	10	0	12	3	44	59	327	2	44	78	402	20
Huddersfield	24	9	1	14	8	43	71	378	2	55	76	416	19
Bramley	20	7	1	12	1	36	49	269	3	58	73	411	15
Doncaster	21	5	1	15	1	49	56	323	1	67	87	483	11
Swinton	22	4	0	18	6	31	39	224	3	72	101	551	8
Hunslet	8	1	0	7	1	20	24	137	1	28	40	217	2

● Hunslet joined the Second Division on 13th January 1986.

COLTS LEAGUE
1985-86 RESULTS
FIRST DIVISION

*four-pointer
Away / Home.

Home \ Away	Bradford N.	Castleford	Featherstone R.	Hull	Hull K.R.	Hunslet	Leeds	St. Helens	Wakefield T.	Wigan
Bradford N.	—	12-27 10-24	14-15		4-20		28-30	10-28	12-18	2-36
Castleford	21-6	—	30-12 6-16	6-40 24-8	12-12		34-14 32-12	6-30	6-2 0-6	25-6 2-10
Featherstone R.	22-8 56-14	15-24	—	52-2	4-4	1-38	20-0	16-14 24-10	9-8	3-26 14-10
Hull	24-20 52-16	28-8	10-18	—	22-21 0-40		26-18 40-6	8-18	*4-22	12-24
Hull K.R.	26-14	*6-7	20-2	22-12	—		42-6	*23-12	22-2	4-24
Hunslet withdrew on 13.1.86	14-30			12-34	2-54	—	4-52		10-20	2-42
Leeds	24-27	22-6	16-20	10-56	10-52 10-31		—	0-26	18-12	
St. Helens	44-22	20-8	26-16	22-8 17-10	12-11		40-29	—	10-16	13-11
Wakefield T.	20-14 0-6	22-18	34-16 9-4	26-12	14-18 12-22	26-8	20-12	22-6	—	
Wigan	34-8 46-12	42-8	24-0	40-14	26-8	76-4	*44-0	1-0	18-14	—

SECOND DIVISION

*four-pointer
Away / Home.

Home \ Away	Barrow	Bramley	Dewsbury	Doncaster	Halifax	Huddersfield	Hunslet	Leigh	Swinton	York
Barrow	—	54-4	17-15 22-15	54-0 32-14	2-26	18-8		18-0	24-0 28-0	4-8 18-4
Bramley	8-24	—		42-22	6-20	8-0		*14-44	28-7	8-12
Dewsbury	12-8	10-10	—	*38-28	9-15 0-5	29-14	50-14	23-18		32-0 28-13
Doncaster		24-16 36-4	26-28	—	22-20 18-14	8-16		22-34 28-38	10-11 6-14	
Halifax	3-14 28-8	7-10	10-33	24-8	—	28-8 40-25		8-16 22-6	34-14	34-4
Huddersfield	20-42 1-7	2-6	*16-30	12-12 20-6	8-24	—	38-26	44-20	19-8	16-8 34-20
Hunslet *joined on 13.1.86	6-22	30-36		4-13			—	11-22	34-8	
Leigh	20-18 22-2	32-24	34-24 20-4	36-8	6-8	16-8 16-6		—	60-0 46-22	38-10
Swinton	6-21	31-16 22-10	10-18 6-32		6-26	18-34 10-21		6-8	—	13-22
York	4-32	26-8 8-11	18-8	26-12	15-28	16-8	28-12	17-26 14-20	32-6 22-6	—

COLTS CHALLENGE CUP 1986

Preliminary Round

Bramley	14	Hull	18
Halifax	10	Dewsbury	18
Wakefield T.	56	Hunslet	0

First Round

Barrow	12	Wakefield T.	10
Castleford	24	Bradford N.	0
Dewsbury	10	Featherstone R.	16
Leeds	10	Hull K.R.	31
St. Helens	17	Hull	10
Swinton	10	Huddersfield	21
Wigan	32	Leigh	20
York	18	Doncaster	10

Second Round

Barrow	14	Featherstone R.	14
Castleford	12	Hull K.R.	12
St. Helens	40	Huddersfield	10
Wigan	38	York	4

Replays

Hull K.R.	21	Castleford	18
Bye: Featherstone R.			

Semi-Finals

St. Helens	24	Hull K.R.	4
Wigan	24	Featherstone R.	0

Final

St. Helens	16	Wigan	16

Replay

Wigan	18	St. Helens	9

COLTS CHALLENGE CUP ROLL OF HONOUR

1976

Wigan	24	Hull K.R.	12
at Wigan			

1977

Hull K.R.	15	St. Helens	13
at Leeds			

1978

Castleford	19	Wakefield T.	10
at Leeds			

1979

Hull	17	Widnes	17
at Bradford			
Replay			
Hull	22	Widnes	14
at Wakefield			

1980

Leeds	25	Widnes	14
at Wigan			

1981

Hull	32	Castleford	17
at Leeds			

1982

Hull	19	Hull K.R.	16
at Leeds			

1983

Hunslet	11	Hull K.R.	3
at Hull K.R.			

1984

Castleford	24	Hull	11
at Hull K.R.			

1985

Wakefield T.	23	Bradford N.	10
at Leeds			

1986

St. Helens	16	Wigan	16
at St. Helens			
Replay			
Wigan	18	St. Helens	9
at Wigan			

The Jim Challinor Memorial Trophy for the Man-of-the-Match in the Final:

1977	Steve Crooks (Hull K.R.)
1978	Paul Bastow (Castleford)
1979	Gary Peacham (Hull)
1980	Ian Mackintosh (Leeds)
1981	Lee Crooks (Hull)
1982	Tracey Lazenby (Hull K.R.)
1983	Andrew Tosney (Hunslet)
1984	Dean Mountain (Castleford)
1985	Billy Conway (Wakefield T.)
1986	Richard Russell (Wigan)

COLTS PREMIERSHIP 1986

First Round

| Hull K.R. | 20 | Wakefield T. | 12 |
| Wigan | 22 | Featherstone R. | 12 |

Final at Elland Road, Leeds

| Wigan | 21 | Hull K.R. | 6 |

COLTS PREMIERSHIP ROLL OF HONOUR

1976
| Hull K.R. | 26 | Wakefield T. | 12 |

at Swinton

1977
| Bradford N. | 29 | Hull K.R. | 15 |

at Swinton

1978
| Wakefield T. | 23 | Hull K.R. | 20 |

at Swinton

1979
| Hull | 17 | Hull K.R. | 9 |

at Huddersfield

1980
| Oldham | 21 | Leeds | 13 |

at Swinton

1981
| Hull K.R. | 27 | Hull | 21 |

at Leeds

1982
| Hull | 19 | Hull K.R. | 11 |

at Leeds

1983
| Hull | 34 | Leigh | 5 |

at Leeds

1984
| Leeds | 24 | Hull | 8 |

at Leeds

1985
| Hull K.R. | 18 | Wakefield T. | 8 |

at Elland Road, Leeds

1986
| Wigan | 21 | Hull K.R. | 6 |

at Elland Road, Leeds

The Dave Valentine Memorial Trophy for the Man-of-the-Match in the Final:

1977 Paul Harkin (Bradford N.)
1978 David Wandless (Wakefield T.)
1979 Kevin Hickman (Hull K.R.)
1980 Andrew Mackintosh (Leeds)
1981 Malcolm Beall (Hull K.R.)
1982 Shaun Patrick (Hull)
1983 Andrew Kamis (Hull)
1984 Paul Medley (Leeds)
1985 Paul Speckman (Hull K.R.)
1986 Jeff Bimpson (Wigan)

Great Britain Man of the Match Paul Medley dives in for one of a brace of tries in the return Colts international at Wigan.

COLTS INTERNATIONALS

18th December, 1985 Lezignan

GREAT BRITAIN 28 **FRANCE 6**

Gary Spencer (Wakefield T.)	1.	Mouloud Karbouch (Avignon)
Roger Simpson (Bradford N.)	2.	Philippe Chiron (Carpentras)
Richard Russell (Wigan)	3.	Philippe Bourrel (Lezignan)
Danny McLoughlin (St. Helens)	4.	Georges Belin (Le Pontet)
Eddison Riddlesden (Halifax)	5.	Christian Martinez (Pia)
Steve Hick (Hull)	6.	Jean-Pierre Gachon (Avignon)
Shaun Edwards (Wigan), Capt.	7.	Jean-Luc Albert (Villeneuve)
Ian Lucas (Wigan)	8.	Thierry Valero (Lezignan)
Martin Dermott (Wigan)	9.	Pascal Mombet (Villeneuve)
Gary Musgrave (Hull)	10.	Jean-Luc Vareilles (Villeneuve)
Paul Medley (Leeds)	11.	Daniel Divet (Limoux)
Paul Speckman (Hull K.R.)	12.	Philippe Lecina (Lezignan)
Richard Gunn (Leeds)	13.	Jacques Moliner (Lezignan)
John Rodgers (St. Helens)	14.	Bernard Llong (XIII Catalan)
Bernard Dwyer (St. Helens)	15.	Pierre Flovie (XIII Catalan)
Mark Sheals (Swinton)	16.	Jean-Pierre Boulagnon (Villeneuve)

T: Gunn, Simpson, Lucas, Spencer, Edwards
G: Hick (4)
Substitutions:
Sheals for Musgrave (49 min.)
Dwyer for Speckman (67 min.)
Rodgers for McLoughlin (70 min.)
Manager: Harry Jepson
Coach: Geoff Lyon

T: Vareilles
G: Gachon
Substitutions:
Boulagnon for Karbouch (31 min.)
Llong for Gachon (45 min.)
Flovie for Mombet (67 min.)
Half-time: 12-6
Referee: Ron Campbell (Widnes)

1st March, 1986 Wigan

GREAT BRITAIN 30 **FRANCE 12**

Michael Fletcher (Hull K.R.)	1.	Gerald Pages (XIII Catalan)
Roger Simpson (Bradford N.)	2.	Simon Campos (Carpentras)
Danny McLoughlin (St. Helens)	3.	Mohamed Amar (Avignon)
Richard Russell (Wigan)	4.	Jacques Moliner (Lezignan)
Eddison Riddlesden (Halifax)	5.	Yanic Le Pelletier (Begles)
Steve Hick (Hull)	6.	George Belin (Le Pontet)
John Rodgers (St. Helens)	7.	Jean-Pierre Boulagnon (Villefranche)
Ian Lucas (Wigan)	8.	Daniel Divet (Limoux)
Bernard Dwyer (St. Helens)	9.	Pascal Mombet (Villeneuve)
Gary Musgrave (Hull)	10.	Patrick Berdu (St. Esteve)
Paul Medley (Leeds)	11.	Bernard Llong (XIII Catalan)
Paul Speckman (Hull K.R.)	12.	Jean-Michel Fillol (Le Pontet)
Richard Gunn (Leeds), Capt.	13.	Daniel Grangeon (Avignon)
Stephen McMenamy (Wigan)	14.	Thierry Valero (Lezignan)
Gerrard Stazicker (Wigan)	15.	Alan Mazzolo (Carcassonne)
Mark Sheals (Swinton)	16.	Jean-Luc Albert (Villeneuve)

T: Medley (2), Simpson (2), Musgrave, Dwyer
G: Fletcher (3)
Substitutions:
Sheals for Speckman (55 min.)
Stazicker for McLoughlin (64 min.)
McMenamy for Richardson (64 min.)
Manager: Harry Jepson
Coach: Geoff Lyon

T: Moliner, Belin
G: Boulagnon (2)

Half-time: 10-6
Referee: Francis Desplats (Toulouse)

393

COLTS COUNTY CHAMPIONSHIP

6th November, 1985   Castleford

YORKSHIRE 44		LANCASHIRE 22
Gary Spencer (Wakefield T.)	1.	Keith Devereux (Barrow)
Roger Simpson (Bradford N.)	2.	Stephen McMenamy (Wigan)
Stuart Vass (Hull)	3.	Stephen Proctor (Barrow)
Michael Fletcher (Hull K.R.)	4.	Danny McLoughlin (St. Helens)
Eddison Riddlesden (Halifax)	5.	Shaun Barrow (St. Helens)
Steve Hick (Hull)	6.	Mark Bailey (St. Helens)
Robert Moules (Wakefield T.)	7.	John Rodgers (St. Helens)
Roger Shepherdson (Hull)	8.	Ian Lucas (Wigan)
Billy Conway (Wakefield T.)	9.	Martin Dermott (Wigan)
Dean Sampson (Castleford)	10.	Ian Connelly (St. Helens)
Paul Speckman (Hull K.R.)	11.	Mark Sheals (Swinton)
Jon Sharp (Hull)	12.	Gerrard Stazicker (Wigan)
Richard Gunn (Leeds), Capt.	13.	Bernard Dwyer (St. Helens), Capt.
Roy Southernwood (Castleford)	14.	Richard Russell (Wigan)
Chris Harrison (Hull K.R.)	15.	Steven Kellett (St. Helens)

T: Gunn (3), Speckman (2), Fletcher,
   Simpson, Riddlesden
G: Hick (4), Fletcher (2)
Substitutions:
Harrison for Sampson (22 min.)
Southernwood for Moules (54 min.)
Coach: David Redfearn (Bradford N.)
Half-time: 18-4

T: Sheals (2), Bailey

G: Dwyer (5)
Substitutions:
Russell for Devereux (5 min.)
Kellett for Connelly (60 min.)
Coach: Eric Chisnall (St. Helens)
Referee: Barry Gomersall (Queensland)

23rd April, 1986   St. Helens

LANCASHIRE 29		YORKSHIRE 12
Damien Gregory (Wigan)	1.	Chris Bibb (Featherstone R.)
Shaun Barrow (St. Helens)	2.	John Moore (Wakefield T.)
Paul Axhall (Wigan)	3.	Steve Barnett (Bradford N.)
David Shaw (Wigan)	4.	Shaun Irwin (Castleford)
Karl Buxton (Wigan)	5.	Lee Kellett (Leeds)
Allan Burrows (St. Helens)	6.	Paul Delaney (Leeds)
Mark Bailey (St. Helens)	7.	Roy Southernwood (Castleford)
Mike Stephenson (Barrow)	8.	Craig Porter (Bramley)
Mark Lee (St. Helens)	9.	George Goodyear (Hunslet)
Cliff Eccles (Leigh)	10.	Paddy Kahn (Hull)
Tim Street (Wigan)	11.	Ken Hill (Castleford)
David O'Toole (Leigh)	12.	Martin Hunter (Featherstone R.)
Paul Jones (St. Helens)	13.	Martin Wilson (Leeds)
Cyril Price (St. Helens)	14.	Darren Webb (Hunslet)
Steve Miles (Barrow)	15.	Simon Taylor (Featherstone R.)

T: Street, Buxton, Gregory, Lee,
   Bailey
G: Buxton (4, 1dg)
Substitutions:
Miles for Stephenson (59 min.)
Price for Burrows (76 min.)
Coach: Eric Chisnall (St. Helens)

T: Southernwood, Irwin

G: Goodyear (2)
Substitution:
Taylor for Porter (72 min.)
Coach: David Redfearn (Bradford N.)
Half-time: 17-6
Referee: John McDonald (Wigan)

394

POT POURRI

DIARY OF LANDMARKS

1895 August 29th... the beginning. The Northern Rugby Football Union formed at St. George's Hotel, Huddersfield, following the breakaway from the English RU by 21 clubs who wanted to pay players for taking time off work to play.
September 7th... season opens with 22 clubs.
Joseph Platt appointed Rugby League Secretary.

1897 April 24th... Batley won the first Northern Union — later Rugby League — Challenge Cup final.
Line-out abolished and replaced by punt from touch.
All goals to be worth two points.

1898 Professionalism allowed but players must be in full-time employment.

1899 Scrum if player cannot release the ball after a tackle.

1901 Punt from touch replaced by 10-yard scrum when ball is carried into touch.

1902 Two divisions introduced.
Punt from touch abolished completely.
Touch-finding rule introduced with the ball having to bounce before entering touch.

1905 Two divisions scrapped.
Lancashire and Yorkshire County Cup competitions inaugurated.

1906 Thirteen-a-side introduced, from traditional 15.

1907 Play-the-ball introduced.
First tour — New Zealand to England. The tour party were RU 'rebels'.
First Top Four play-off for championship.

1908 Australia and New Zealand launch Rugby League.
First Australian tour of England.

1910 First British tour of Australia and New Zealand.

1915 Competitive rugby suspended for duration of First World War.

1919 Competitive rugby resumed in January.

1920 John Wilson appointed Rugby League Secretary.

1922 Title of Northern Rugby Football Union changed to Rugby Football League.
Goal from a mark abolished.

1927 First radio broadcast of Challenge Cup Final — Oldham v. Swinton at Wigan.

1929 Wembley staged its first RL Challenge Cup final — Wigan v. Dewsbury.

1932 London exhibition match under floodlights at White City — Leeds v. Wigan.

1933 France staged its first Rugby League match — an exhibition between England and Australia in Paris.
London Highfield, formerly Wigan Highfield, became capital's first Rugby League team, also first to play regularly under floodlights.

1934 A French squad made a short tour of England before Rugby League was officially launched in France.

1935 European Championship introduced, contested by England, France and Wales.

1939 Second World War. Emergency war-time competitions introduced.

1945 War-time emergencies over.
Bill Fallowfield appointed Rugby League Secretary.

1946 First all-ticket match — Hull v. Hull K.R.

1948 King George VI became first reigning monarch to attend Rugby League match — Wigan v. Bradford Northern Cup final at Wembley.
First televised match — at Wembley — but shown only in London area.
Wembley's first all-ticket final.
International Board formed.

1949 Welsh League formed.
1950 Italian squad made brief tour of England.
1951 First televised match in the North — Britain v. New Zealand at Swinton.
First floodlights installation by Northern club, Bradford Northern.
1952 First nationally televised Challenge Cup final — Workington Town v. Featherstone Rovers.
1954 First World Cup competition, staged in France.
1955 London staged series of televised floodlit matches for the Independent Television Association Trophy.
Welsh League disbanded.
1956 Sunday rugby for amateurs permitted by the Rugby Football League.
1962 Two divisions reintroduced, with Eastern and Western Divisions also formed.
1964 Subsitutes allowed for injuries, but only up to half-time.
Two divisions and regional leagues scrapped. One league system with Top-16 play-off for championship.
1965 BBC-2 Floodlit Trophy competition began with regular Tuesday night series.
Substitutes allowed for any reason up to and including half-time.
English Schools Rugby League formed.
1966 Four-tackle rule introduced for Floodlit Trophy competition in October, then for all games from December.
1967 First Sunday fixtures played, two matches on December 17th.
1969 Substitutes allowed at any time.
University Rugby League Association formed.
1971 John Player Trophy competition launched.

1972 Six-tackle rule introduced.
Timekeepers with hooter system to signal end of match introduced.
Colts League formed.
1973 Two divisions re-introduced.
March 4th... British Amateur Rugby League Association formed.
1974 Drop goal value halved to one point. Had been reduced earlier in international matches.
David Oxley appointed Rugby League Secretary.
David Howes appointed first full-time Public Relations Officer to the Rugby Football League.
National Coaching Scheme launched.
1975 Premiership Trophy competition launched.
1976 Differential penalty introduced for technical scrum offences.
1977 County Championship not held for first time since 1895, excluding war years.
Anglo-Australian transfer ban agreed.
1978 Papua New Guinea admitted as full members of International Board.
1981 Rugby League Professional Players' Association formed.
1982 County Championship scrapped.
1983 January 1st... Sin bin introduced.
Try value increased to four points.
Handover after sixth tackle introduced, among several other new or amended laws following meeting of International Board.
Anglo-Australia transfer ban lifted.
1984 Alliance League introduced in reserve grade reorganisation.
1985 War of the Roses launched on Lancashire v. Yorkshire county of origin basis.
Relegation-promotion reduced to three down, three up.

DISCIPLINARY RECORDS

This sub-section is a compilation of sendings off and disciplinary verdicts for first team players.

The following information is based on the workings of the League's Disciplinary Committee which meets twice-monthly during a season.

Oldham scrum half Ray Ashton, sent off twice during the 1985-86 season.

DISMISSALS .... A review

The following is a review of the number of first team players sent off in each season since 1979-80.

— indicates where a club was not in existence.

	1985-86	1984-85	1983-84	1982-83	1981-82	1980-81	1979-80
Barrow	3	6	2	2	2	2	2
Batley	3	3	3	4	3	2	1
Blackpool B.	5	4	3	3	2	1	3
Bradford N.	4	0	3	3	11	6	3
Bramley	3	2	3	2	0	2	0
Bridgend	—	4	6	2	7	—	—
Carlisle	2	3	8	4	3	—	—
Castleford	3	1	5	4	7	4	2
Dewsbury	4	4	2	5	10	3	6
Doncaster	4	1	10	2	4	2	4
Featherstone R.	0	3	1	1	9	2	4
Fulham	5	4	6	8	3	3	—
Halifax	1	5	3	4	3	3	1
Huddersfield B.	4	4	4	2	3	3	3
Hull	5	2	3	4	3	4	4
Hull K.R.	8	2	5	4	13	5	3
Hunslet	2	4	3	1	4	0	4
Keighley	8	7	0	3	3	5	2
Leeds	2	4	0	3	5	5	4
Leigh	1	1	3	2	6	3	5
Mansfield M.	3	3	—	—	—	—	—
Oldham	6	5	5	3	8	4	3
Rochdale H.	3	4	9	1	7	1	1
Runcorn H.	12	5	5	3	3	2	4
St. Helens	0	4	3	3	2	1	0
Salford	6	5	5	6	3	1	2
Sheffield E.	6	4	—	—	—	—	—
Southend I.	—	3	3	—	—	—	—
Swinton	2	2	0	4	1	2	1
Wakefield T.	6	7	5	2	6	2	3
Warrington	6	1	6	5	10	6	7
Whitehaven	3	3	6	2	4	3	3
Widnes	5	6	7	4	3	6	5
Wigan	3	2	2	3	5	7	5
Workington T.	9	5	4	3	3	2	0
York	2	1	4	2	3	3	1
Totals	**139**	**124**	**137**	**104**	**159**	**95**	**86**

DISCIPLINARY ANALYSIS 1985-86

The following is a club-by-club disciplinary record for last season, showing the players sent off in first team matches and the findings of the League's Disciplinary Committee.

The committee's verdict is featured in the brackets after the player's name, each number indicating the match ban imposed. SOS stands for sending off sufficient and NG for not guilty. A suspension reduced or increased on appeal is shown as follows, 6 to 4.

The sin bin suspensions were imposed under the totting-up system where two points were issued for a 10-minute temporary dismissal and one point for a five-minute period off the field. A one-match ban was imposed when the running total reached six points.

SB indicates in brackets the number of one-match bans imposed under the sin bin totting-up system. It does not include a record of players' sin bin dismissals which have not reached the six-point total. The sin bin has operated only for technical offences and verbal abuse of match officials since 1984-85 season.

OC indicates in brackets the number of one-match bans imposed under the official caution totting-up system, one match for each pair of cautions in the same year or season.

* indicates where video evidence was submitted. The 1984-85 season was the first time video action other than official BBC or ITV tapes could be offered in evidence. In 1985-86 the committee considered video evidence in 25 individual cases, 10 more than during 1984-85. Four cases were considered by the committee after viewing a video, the player not having been dismissed.

Club	Total sent off	Dismissed Player	Sin Bins/ Official Cautions
Barrow	3	Kirkby (10 to 15), Richardson (*4 to 3), Turley (2)	
Batley	3	Render (4), James (4), Douglas (NG)	
Blackpool B.	5	Subritzky (2,4, SOS), Hindley (2), Nanyn (6 to SOS)	Green (1 OC)
Bradford N.	4	Sheldon (*4), Fleming (6), Mallinder (4), Jasiewicz (1)	
Bramley	3	Harrison (4), Fletcher (4), Hankin (6)	
Carlisle	2	Sutton (6), Kirkby (4)	
Castleford	3	England (*2), Horton (2), Orum (4)	
Dewsbury	4	Diskin (1), Mason (*4, 4), Moore (4)	
Doncaster	4	Pflaster (6), Gibbon (4), Green (3), Pennant (3)	
Featherstone R.	0		
Fulham	5	Duffy (2), Platt (4), Bullough (4 to 2, *4, 6)	
Halifax	1	Scott (2)	
Huddersfield B.	4	Fitzpatrick (1), Blacker (2), Johnson (2), Kenworthy (1)	
Hull	5	Crooks (SOS), Patrick (SOS), Muggleton (*2), Skerrett (2), Proctor (2)	

Hull K.R.	8	Robinson (4), Burton (2, *4), Prohm (*2), P. Johnston (*SOS, 4), Harkin (2), L. Johnston (4)	
Hunslet	2	Skerrett (3), Idle (NG)	
Keighley	8	Townend (4), Dews (3), Page (4), Goodier (4), Turner (4), Proctor (4), Butterfield (SOS), Roe (4)	Proctor (1 OC)
Leeds	2	Ward (4), Dick (4)	
Leigh	1	Pyke (SOS)	
Mansfield M.	3	Spedding (4), Dennison (6), Nicholson (2)	
Oldham	6	Ashton (2, 1), Liddiard (*NG, 2), Hobbs (*4 to 1), Jones (2)	Jones (1 OC)
Rochdale H.	3	Timson (*NG), Wood (2), Dunn (*NG)	
Runcorn H.	12	Jackson (2), Prescott (4), Daley (*NG), Fitzpatrick (*2, 4), McCabe (1, 6, 8), Blackwood (12), Tinsley (3), Woods (NG, 6)	
St. Helens	0		Haggerty (1 OC), Round (1 OC)
Salford	6	Groves (NG), Byrne (SOS), Major (NG, *4, 8), Pendlebury (2)	
Sheffield E.	6	Hooper (4), Powell (3 to 2, 4), Wright (3), Harris (6), Gamson (4)	
Swinton	2	Cassidy (*NG), Tuimavave (*4 to 1)	
Wakefield T.	6	Harkin (1), Casey (*SOS), Lyons (2,6). Thompson (4), Hopkinson (3)	
Warrington	6	Rathbone (*6, *2), A. Gregory (*NG), Kelly (6), Boyd (*NG), Gittins (4)	
Whitehaven	3	L. Gorley (SOS), Cameron (2), Banks (2)	
Widnes	5	Hulme (SOS), M. O'Neill (4), J. Myler (2), Currier (1), Sorensen (SOS)	
Wigan	3	Whitfield (*2), Kiss (*NG), West (4 to 1)	Du Toit (1 OC)
Workington T.	9	Litt (4), Maguire (4), Falcon (2), Beverley (8, 4), Frazer (4, 6), Beattie (1), W. Pattinson *for Cumbria* (2)	
York	2	Phillippo (4), Marketo (2)	

● In addition, the Disciplinary Committee carried out five 'trials by video', calling up players, who had not been dismissed, after viewing video tapes. Salford's Keiron O'Loughlin was dealt with for two separate incidents, receiving a four-match ban and a finding of not guilty. Wigan prop forward Shaun Wane was suspended for two matches, while reprimands were handed out to Oldham's Terry Flanagan and Dewsbury's Mick Collins.

SPONSORSHIP

This updated sub-section is a record of the sponsorship programme under the control of the Rugby
Football League.

Sponsorship has developed into a major subject
in the last decade and is now one of Rugby League's
biggest sources of income.

In addition to the League's sponsorship programme, the individual clubs also enter deals for
sponsorship of jerseys, kit, matches, man of the
match and match ball.

SPONSORSHIP PROGRAMME 1985-86

The following is a compendium of sponsorship activities controlled by the Rugby Football League for
the season 1985-86.

Competitions:

Silk Cut Challenge Cup	£140,000	
Slalom Lager Championship and Premiership	£ 95,000	
Whitbread Trophy Bitter Tests	£ 85,000	
John Player Special Trophy	£ 80,000	
Okells Charity Shield	£ 4,000	
Rodstock War of the Roses	£ 3,000	
		£407,000

Awards:

Greenalls Man of Steel Awards	£ 8,000	
Daily Mirror/Lada Cars Teams of the Month and Year	£ 5,000	
Greenall Whitley/Sunday People Men of the Month and Top Scorers	£ 4,000	
Daily Express/Frigidaire Men of the Month and Personality of the Year	£ 2,000	
Traveleads Top Fan	£ 3,500	
Daily Star/Slalom Lager Star Men	£ 1,000	
		£ 23,500

Miscellaneous:		£ 35,000
	GRAND TOTAL	£465,500

COMPETITION SPONSORSHIP

The following is a review of sponsorship of the game's major competitions.

SILK CUT CHALLENGE CUP

	Prel.	1st	2nd	3rd	S.F.	R.U.	Winners	Development Fund	Total
	£	£	£	£	£	£	£	£	£
1979	—	750	1,160	2,000	3,555	6,555	12,555	4,500	60,000
1980	—	750	1,160	2,000	3,555	6,555	12,555	19,500	75,000
1981	—	750	1,160	2,000	3,555	6,555	12,555	29,500	85,000
1982	1,000	1,000	1,400	2,400	4,325	8,000	14,555	30,000	100,000
1983	1,000	1,000	1,400	2,400	4,325	8,000	14,555	40,000	110,000
1984	1,000	1,000	1,400	2,400	4,325	8,000	14,555	48,000	120,000
1985	1,100	1,100	1,500	2,500	4,500	9,000	16,000	47,600	130,000
1986	1,100	1,100	1,500	2,500	4,500	9,000	16,000	57,600	140,000

● Sponsored by State Express from 1979-84.

SLALOM LAGER

	Championship winners	Second Division winners	Premiership winners	Development Fund	Total
	£	£	£	£	£
1980-81	6,000	3,000	4,000	42,000	65,000
1981-82	10,000	6,000	6,000	48,000	70,000
1982-83	12,000	7,000	7,000	54,000	80,000
1983-84	12,000	7,000	7,000	59,000	85,000
1984-85	13,000	9,000	8,000	60,000	90,000
1985-86	13,000	9,000	8,000	65,000	95,000

JOHN PLAYER SPECIAL TROPHY

	Prel.	1st	2nd	3rd	S.F.	R.U.	Winners	Development Fund	Total
	£	£	£	£	£	£	£	£	£
1971-72	—	—	—	—	1,000	2,500	5,000	—	9,500
1972-73	—	150	300	450	1,000	2,500	5,000	—	16,100
1973-74	—	150	300	450	1,000	2,500	5,000	—	16,100
1974-75	—	150	300	450	1,000	2,500	5,000	—	16,100
1975-76	—	300	450	600	1,500	3,000	6,000	—	22,800
1976-77	—	400	550	700	1,500	3,000	6,000	—	25,600
1977-78	—	450	600	750	1,750	3,500	8,000	—	30,000
1978-79	—	550	700	900	1,750	3,500	8,000	—	33,000
1979-80	—	600	800	1,000	2,000	4,000	8,500	—	36,500
1980-81	—	600	800	1,000	2,000	4,000	8,500	3,500	40,000
1981-82	700	700	900	1,175	2,500	4,500	9,000	7,000	50,000
1982-83	700	700	900	1,175	2,500	5,000	10,000	10,500	55,000
1983-84	700	700	900	1,175	2,500	5,000	10,000	15,500	60,000
1984-85	750	750	1,000	1,500	2,500	5,000	10,000	20,000	75,000
1985-86	750	750	1,000	1,500	2,750	5,500	11,000	26,000	80,000

BURTONWOOD BREWERY LANCASHIRE CUP

	Winners £	Total £
1976	1,000	4,000
1977	1,500	5,000
1978	1,800	5,500
1979	1,900	6,000
1980	2,530	10,000
1981	2,700	11,000
1982	3,000	11,500
1983	3,200	12,500
1984	3,400	13,250
1985	3,400	13,250

YORKSHIRE CUP

	Sponsor	Winners £	Total £
1972	Esso	800	4,000
1973	Esso	1,500	6,000
1974	Esso	1,400	6,000
1975	Esso	1,200	6,000
1976	Esso	1,200	6,000
1977	Esso	1,600	8,000
1978	Esso	2,000	9,000
1979	Esso	2,000	9,500
1980	Websters Brewery	2,750	13,000
1981	Websters Brewery	3,000	14,000
1982	Websters Brewery	2,500	15,000
1983	Philips Video	2,500	15,000
1984	Philips Video	2,500	15,000
1985	John Smiths	2,500	5,000

INTERNATIONAL

Great Britain v Australia Tests 1978
Forward Chemicals: £17,500

Great Britain v Australia Tests 1982
Dominion Insurance: £40,000

Great Britain v France Tests 1983
Dominion Insurance: £5,000

Great Britain v France Tests 1984
Dominion Insurance: £5,000

Great Britain Tour 1984
Modern Maintenance Products: £100,000

Great Britain 1985-86
Whitbread Trophy Bitter: £85,000

ATTENDANCES

CLUB ATTENDANCE REVIEW

The following is a review of clubs' home attendances for League matches from 1977-86.

The main figure is the individual club's average gate for League games during that season. The figure in brackets indicates an upward or downward trend compared with the previous season.

Also indicated is the division the club competed in that season, i.e.

1 — First Division, 2 — Second Division.

Club	77-78	78-79	79-80	80-81	81-82	82-83	83-84	84-85	85-86
Barrow	2 2432 (-167)	1 2988 (+556)	2 3143 (+155)	1 4065 (+922)	1 4162 (+97)	1 3852 (-310)	2 3218 (-450)	1 2728 (-490)	2 1926 (-802)
Batley	2 859 (-58)	2 915 (+56)	2 1330 (+415)	2 1329 (-1)	2 1052 (-277)	2 916 (-136)	2 864 (-52)	2 1015 (+151)	2 930 (-85)
Blackpool B.	2 658 (+265)	2 1237 (+579)	1 1576 (+339)	2 684 (-892)	2 768 (+84)	2 679 (-89)	2 625 (-54)	2 555 (-70)	2 534 (-21)
Bradford N.	1 7236 (+2567)	1 5651 (-1585)	1 6236 (+585)	1 6105 (-131)	1 5816 (-289)	1 4920 (-896)	1 5316 (+386)	1 4251 (-1065)	1 3975 (-276)
Bramley	1 2062 (+353)	2 1208 (-854)	2 1204 (-4)	2 1050 (-154)	2 928 (-122)	2 809 (-119)	2 759 (-50)	2 858 (+99)	2 831 (-27)
Bridgend	—	—	—	—	2 2008 —	2 854 (-1154)	2 581 (-273)	2 510 (-70)	—
Carlisle	—	—	— ·		2 2950 —	1 1924 (-1026)	2 752 (-1172)	2 986 (+244)	2 618 (-368)
Castleford	1 3847 (+91)	1 3672 (-175)	1 3714 (+42)	1 4612 (+898)	1 3791 (-821)	1 3548 (-243)	1 4288 (+740)	1 3217 (-1071)	1 3701 (+430)
Dewsbury	1 2160 (+200)	2 1474 (-686)	2 1552 (+78)	2 1377 (-175)	2 1048 (-329)	2 779 (-269)	2 706 (-73)	2 995 (+189)	1 1819 (+824)
Doncaster	2 811 (+323)	2 619 (-192)	2 428 (-191)	2 628 (+200)	2 556 (-72)	2 441 (-115)	2 255 (-186)	2 266 (+11)	2 689 (+423)
Featherstone R.	1 3558 (+251)	1 2661 (-897)	2 2301 (-360)	1 3007 (+706)	1 2806 (-201)	1 2647 (-159)	1 3032 (+385)	1 2541 (-491)	1 2320 (-221)
Fulham	—	—	—	2 6096 —	1 4321 (-1775)	2 2688 (-1633)	1 2238 (-450)	2 949 (-1289)	2 817 (-132)
Halifax	2 1339 (-90)	2 2314 (+975)	2 2969 (+655)	1 4090 (+1121)	2 2818 (-1272)	1 2270 (-548)	2 1254 (-1016)	1 3497 (+2243)	1 4944 (+1447)
Huddersfield B.	2 2136 (+616)	1 2533 (+397)	2 1654 (-879)	2 1769 (+115)	2 1185 (-584)	2 776 (-409)	2 699 (-77)	2 905 (+206)	2 678 (-227)
Hull	1 5112 (+1252)	2 6853 (+1741)	1 10021 (+3168)	1 11711 (+1690)	1 13190 (+1479)	1 11525 (-1665)	1 10679 (-846)	1 8525 (-2154)	1 6245 (-1280)
Hull K. R.	1 5352 (+634)	1 5945 (+593)	1 6953 (+1008)	1 8904 (+1951)	1 8723 (-181)	1 7379 (-1344)	1 6966 (-413)	1 6715 (-215)	1 4855 (-1860)
Hunslet	1 2095 (+887)	2 1469 (-626)	1 1718 (+249)	2 921 (-797)	2 744 (-177)	2 1195 (+451)	2 1338 (+143)	1 2246 (+908)	2 722 (-1524)

Club	77-78	78-79	79-80	80-81	81-82	82-83	83-84	84-85	85-86
Keighley	2 1985 (+137)	2 1594 (−391)	2 1593 (−1)	2 1612 (+19)	2 1576 (−36)	2 1085 (−491)	2 734 (−351)	2 822 (+88)	2 685 (−137)
Leeds	1 5539 (+1031)	1 5161 (−378)	1 6681 (+1520)	1 5934 (−747)	1 5599 (−335)	1 5893 (+294)	1 6542 (+649)	1 7330 (+788)	1 6928 (−402)
Leigh	2 3427 (+158)	1 3319 (−108)	1 4418 (+1099)	1 4498 (+80)	1 5939 (+1441)	1 4617 (−1322)	1 4434 (−183)	1 3822 (−612)	2 2710 (−1112)
Mansfield M.	—	—	—	—	—	—	—	2 1020 —	2 487 (−553)
Oldham	2 1785 (−266)	2 1207 (−578)	2 2367 (+1160)	1 3220 (+853)	1 2395 (−825)	1 3721 (+1326)	1 4138 (+417)	1 4562 (+424)	1 4333 (−229)
Rochdale H.	2 1976 (+128)	1 1689 (−287)	2 1210 (−479)	2 1149 (−61)	2 888 (−261)	2 619 (−269)	2 538 (−81)	2 542 (+4)	2 1267 (+725)
Runcorn H.	2 335 (+9)	2 599 (+264)	2 238 (−161)	2 270 (+32)	2 385 (+115)	2 224 (−161)	2 172 (−52)	2 509 (+337)	2 363 (−146)
St. Helens	1 5510 (+774)	1 5658 (+148)	1 5577 (−81)	1 4934 (−643)	1 4862 (−72)	1 4543 (−319)	1 4656 (+113)	1 7336 (+2680)	1 6022 (−1314)
Salford	1 4133 (−1324)	1 4100 (−33)	1 4846 (+746)	1 3458 (−1388)	2 2404 (−1054)	2 1928 (−476)	1 2399 (+471)	2 1795 (−604)	1 2520 (+725)
Sheffield E.	—	—	—	—	—	—	—	2 885 —	2 698 (−187)
Southend Invicta	—	—	—	—	—	—	2 731 —	2 216 (−515)	—
Swinton	2 1480 (+265)	2 1331 (−149)	2 1509 (+178)	2 1935 (+426)	2 1567 (−368)	2 1314 (−253)	2 1077 (−237)	2 1590 (+513)	1 2706 (+1116)
Wakefield T.	1 3808 (+877)	1 4068 (+265)	1 4559 (+491)	1 4814 (+255)	1 3716 (−1098)	2 2344 (−1372)	1 3483 (+1139)	2 1568 (−1915)	2 1714 (+146)
Warrington	1 4203 (−262)	1 5194 (+991)	1 5122 (−72)	1 4917 (−205)	1 3838 (−1079)	1 3824 (−14)	1 4059 (+235)	1 3801 (−258)	1 3618 (−183)
Whitehaven	2 889 (+274)	2 1364 (+475)	2 1761 (+397)	2 2733 (+972)	1 2710 (−23)	2 1742 (−968)	1 1639 (−103)	2 1540 (−99)	2 1878 (+333)
Widnes	1 7488 (+1359)	1 6751 (−737)	1 6143 (−608)	1 5306 (−837)	1 5485 (+179)	1 4703 (−782)	1 4687 (−16)	1 4266 (−421)	1 4019 (−247)
Wigan	1 5544 (+845)	1 4505 (−1039)	1 4665 (+160)	2 4693 (+28)	1 5497 (+804)	1 7426 (+1929)	1 7479 (+53)	1 10056 (+2577)	1 12515 (+2459)
Workington T.	1 2722 (+666)	1 2155 (−567)	1 1834 (−321)	1 2188 (+354)	2 1969 (−219)	1 1470 (−499)	2 934 (−536)	1 920 (−14)	2 702 (−218)
York	2 3188 (−287)	2 3265 (+77)	1 3934 (+669)	2 3827 (−107)	1 3677 (−150)	2 1685 (−1992)	2 1215 (−470)	2 1528 (+313)	1 2828 (+1300)

COMPETITION ATTENDANCE REVIEW

		77-78	78-79	79-80	80-81	81-82	82-83	83-84	84-85	85-86
FIRST	Total	1,051,985	990,728	1,169,956	1,226,428	1,264,520	1,113,915	1,140,548	1,137,195	1,100,329
DIVISION	Average	4,402	4,128	4,875	5,110	5,268	4,641	4,752	4,738	4,585
SECOND	Total	302,902	330,830	302,345	420,994	403,652	321,226	279,673	266,730	310,311
DIVISION	Average	1,664	1,817	1,661	2,005	1,484	1,181	914	953	1,014
LEAGUE AGGREGATE	Total	1,354,887	1,321,558	1,472,301	1,647,422	1,668,172	1,435,141	1,420,221	1,403,925	1,410,640
(1st & 2nd Div)	Average	3,218	3,123	3,489	3,661	3,258	2,803	2,601	2,700	2,584
CHALLENGE CUP	Average	9,910	9,257	10,370	9,993	11,388	8,355	8,399	8,497	8,280
JOHN PLAYER TROPHY	Average	4,704	4,427	4,314	5,362	5,590	4,219	3,893	4,881	4,232
PREMIERSHIP	Average	8,647	8,502	7,343	11,689	9,454	10,099	8,136	10,115	9,273
10,000 + ATTENDANCES (Number of)		18	12	20	36	36	37	26	27	36

20,000-plus crowds . . . . A 10-year review
All matches except the Rugby League Challenge Cup final at Wembley

20,386	Wigan v. St. Helens	RL Cup Round 2	Wigan	27 Feb. 1977
26,447	Britain v. Australia	Second Test	Bradford	5 Nov. 1978
29,627	Britain v. Australia	Third Test	Leeds	18 Nov. 1978
20,775	Bradford N. v. Hull	RL Cup Round 3	Bradford	9 Mar. 1980
29,448	Hull v. Hull K.R.	Premiership final	Leeds	16 May 1981
25,245	Hull v. Hull K.R.	John Player final	Leeds	23 Jan. 1982
21,207	Hull v. Castleford	RL Cup semi-final	Leeds	27 Mar. 1982
41,171	Hull v. Widnes	RL Cup final replay	Elland Rd, Leeds	19 May 1982
26,771	Britain v. Australia	First Test	Hull C. FC	30 Oct. 1982
23,216	Britain v. Australia	Second Test	Wigan	20 Nov. 1982
26,031	Hull v. Castleford	RL Cup semi-final	Elland Rd, Leeds	2 Apr. 1983
20,569	Hull v. Hull K.R.	Division One	Hull	8 Apr. 1983
20,077	St. Helens v. Wigan	RL Cup Round 3	St. Helens	11 Mar. 1984
25,237	Hull v. Hull K.R.	Yorks Cup final	Hull C. FC	27 Oct. 1984
26,074	St. Helens v. Wigan	Lancs Cup final	Wigan	28 Oct. 1984
25,326	Hull v. Hull K.R.	John Player final	Hull C. FC	26 Jan. 1985
20,982	Hull v. Castleford	RL Cup semi-final	Leeds	6 Apr. 1985
20,968	Hull v. Castleford	RL Cup semi-final replay	Leeds	10 Apr. 1985
22,209	Britain v. New Zealand	Third Test	Elland Rd, Leeds	9 Nov. 1985
21,813	Wigan v. St. Helens	Division One	Wigan	26 Dec. 1985
23,866	Hull K.R. v. Leeds	RL Cup semi-final	Elland Rd, Leeds	29 Mar. 1986
32,485	Hull K.R. v. Leeds	RL Cup semi-final replay	Elland Rd, Leeds	3 Apr. 1986

1985-86 ANALYSIS

FIRST DIVISION

Total attendance 1,100,329
Average 4,585

Compared with the corresponding 1983-84 figures of 1,137,195 and 4,738, there was a marginal decrease of three per cent.

Wigan topped the divisional gates chart for the second successive season, increasing their average league attendance by 2,459 per match to 12,515. Of their 15 Slalom Lager Championship fixtures at Central Park, 11 topped five-figures.

New Champions Halifax added 1,447 fans per home league encounter to move up from 11th place in the gates chart to fifth. The only other sides to record an upsurge in attendances were Challenge Cup winners Castleford and promoted quartet Swinton, Salford, York and Dewsbury.

SECOND DIVISION

Total attendance 310,311
Average 1,014

The Second Division average gate passed the four-figure mark for the first time in three seasons as the average attendence recorded a six per cent upswing compared with the 1984-85 average of 953.

Champions Leigh topped the Second Division gates chart with an average turnout of 2,710, a drop of 1,112 fans per match

compared with their relegation campaign the previous season.

Also having been relegated, Hunslet too recorded a four-figure fall in their average gate, the only annual increases being recorded by Whitehaven, Wakefield Trinity, Rochdale Hornets and Doncaster.

LEAGUE CHAMPIONSHIP

Aggregate 1,410,640
Average 2,584

The average attendance for the 34 clubs competing in the 1985-86 two-divisional set-up fell by four per cent compared with the previous season's average of 2,700. A total of 546 matches were staged during the 1985-86 campaign compared with 520 in 1984-85 when the Second Division clubs each played only 28 matches.

SILK CUT CHALLENGE CUP

A total of 314,641 spectators watched the 1986 tournament, including three replays and a four-tie preliminary round. The average gate for the 38 ties was 8,280, a decrease of three per cent compared with the 1985 average of 8,497. The traditional top attendance was the Wembley return of 82,139, the next best being a creditable 32,485 for the semi-final replay between Hull K.R. and Leeds at Elland Road, Leeds.

JOHN PLAYER SPECIAL TROPHY

The 1985-86 competition attracted a total of 148,109 fans for the 35 ties, an average of 4,232. Compared with the previous season's average of 4,881, this was an annual decrease of 13 per cent.

SLALOM LAGER PREMIERSHIP

An average of 9,273 watched the seven-tie Premiership tournament, the total turnout being 64,909. Compared with the 1985 figures of 70,807 and 10,115, this was a decrease of eight per cent.

BURTONWOOD BREWERY LANCASHIRE CUP

After last season's annual increase of a massive 77 per cent, the 1985 tournament went up a further five per cent. The 1985 figures of a total turnout of 91,007 for an average gate of 6,067 were an increase on the 1984 corresponding number of 87,036 and 5,802.

JOHN SMITHS YORKSHIRE CUP

A total of 72,886 fans viewed the 1985 Yorkshire Cup campaign which featured 16 ties including a preliminary round. The 1985 average gate of 4,555 was 16 per cent down on the previous figure of 5,418.

FIVE-FIGURE CROWDS

There were 36 gates topping the 10,000-mark during the 1985-86 season. As per tradition, the top attendance was at Wembley for the Castleford-Hull K.R. Silk Cut Challenge Cup final which attracted 82,139 spectators.

Gates of 20,000-plus were also attracted for four other games. The third Whitbread Trophy Bitter Test between Great Britain and New Zealand, the Boxing Day clash between derby rivals Wigan and St. Helens and the Silk Cut Challenge Cup drawn semi-final meeting of Hull K.R. and Leeds all topped 20,000, while the Cup semi-final replay, staged five days later, pulled in a massive gate of 32,485.

Top gate takers Wigan staged the most five-figure attendances with 19 at Central Park — including 11 in the Slalom Lager Championship — plus being involved in four others.

The five-figure gates were divided into the following categories:

League	13
Challenge Cup........................	7
Tour (incl. Tests)	4
John Player	3
Premiership	3
Lancashire Cup	3
Yorkshire Cup	3

FIRST DIVISION

	1985-86 Average	Annual Difference
Wigan	12515	(+2459)
Leeds	6928	(− 402)
Hull	6245	(−1280)
St. Helens	6022	(+1314)
Halifax	4944	(+1447)
Hull Kingston Rovers	4855	(−1860)
Oldham	4333	(− 229)
Widnes	4019	(− 247)
Bradford Northern	3975	(− 276)
Castleford	3701	(+ 430)
Warrington	3618	(− 183)
★York	2828	(+1300)
★Swinton	2706	(+1116)
★Salford	2520	(+ 725)
Featherstone Rovers	2320	(− 221)
★Dewsbury.	1819	(+ 824)

★ Promoted 1984-85

SECOND DIVISION

	1985-86 Average	Annual Difference
★Leigh	2710	(−1112)
★Barrow	1926	(− 802)
Whitehaven.	1878	(+ 338)
Wakefield Trinity	1714	(+ 146)
Rochdale Hornets	1267	(+ 725)
Batley	930	(− 85)
Bramley	831	(− 27)
Fulham	817	(− 132)
★Hunslet	722	(−1524)
★Workington Town	702	(− 218)
Sheffield Eagles	698	(− 187)
Doncaster	689	(+ 423)
Keighley	685	(− 137)
Huddersfield Barracudas	678	(− 227)
Carlisle	618	(− 368)
Blackpool Borough	534	(− 21)
Mansfield Marksman	487	(− 553)
Runcorn Highfield	363	(− 146)

★Relegated 1984-85

EXTINCT CLUBS

Rugby League's ambitious expansion programme — six new clubs in four years — was cut back at the start of the 1985-86 season with the late withdrawal of Southend Invicta and Bridgend from the announced fixture list.

A meeting of the Rugby League Council in Leeds on 28th August decided that the two outposts should be suspended from League membership, Southend Invicta because they had allegedly shown no evidence of being prepared for the new campaign and Bridgend for not securing the use of a ground.

The late decision meant that the fixture formula which had operated in 1984-85, where 20 Second Division teams each played 28 matches, had to be scrapped and the remaining 18 clubs would play each other home and away.

Neither Southend nor Bridgend applied for reinstatement by the 31st March deadline although a consortium of Lancashire businessmen made a bid to launch a new club based at Stockport County's soccer ground.

The years from 1980 to 1984 had been the most expansive for the game in this country since the early part of the century. The introduction of Fulham, Cardiff City, Carlisle, Kent Invicta, Mansfield Marksman and Sheffield Eagles brought the total of senior clubs in 1984-85 to 36 ... the largest League membership since 1902-03.

In that first ever period of two divisions, 36 clubs were split equally into two leagues. Since then the lowest number of clubs in peacetime was 25 between 1914 and 1922.

Of the 22 clubs who formed the first Northern Rugby Football League following the split with the English Rugby Union in 1895, seven are no longer in existence. Thirty more have come and gone.

In recording the number of extinct clubs, some distinction must be made between the early fatalities in the code's formative years and the many expansion attempts that followed.

Some of the early victims were clubs leaving the English Rugby Union and not strong enough to compete in the new major leagues, but continued at a lower level.

After 1895-96 the major leagues were the Lancashire and Yorkshire Senior Competitions until there was another change in 1901-02. Then there was a total of 41 senior clubs ... 14 in the NRL, 13 in the LSC and 14 in the YSC.

The following season, 1902-03, staged the first era of two divisions and it is from then that a more meaningful appraisal can be made of the clubs who have dropped out.

Clubs who departed before that eventful season were two founder members in **Tyldesley** and **Liversedge**, plus **Leeds Parish Church, Heckmondwike, Altrincham, Radcliffe, Goole** and **Sowerby Bridge.**

Wales was an immediate target for expansion and in 1908-09 there were six clubs in the Northern Rugby League ... Merthyr Tydfil, Ebbw Vale, Mid-Rhondda, Treherbert, Barry and Aberdare. By 1912 there was none.

Attention was focussed on London in the 1930s with Acton and Willesden, and Streatham and Mitcham, having brief existences. Mention must also be made of London Highfield, who began as Wigan Highfield and progressed through a change of Liverpool titles to the present day Runcorn Highfield.

Wigan Highfield entered the League in 1922 and had one season as London Highfield in 1933-34. This venture was promoted by a group of London businessmen with home games played at White City under floodlights on a Saturday night. It was a fair success to begin with, but flopped when crowds dwindled during the winter. For 'home' matches the team caught a Friday evening train from Wigan and returned on Saturday night. The following season the club became Liverpool Stanley.

THE SURVIVORS

Changes of title, or the death of one club to be immediately replaced by another, can also cause confusion. Bradford Northern and

Hunslet are two other clubs who have survived changes. CLUBS section gives details.

Castleford had a senior club between 1896 and 1906, but the present club did not enter the League until 1926-27. Other clubs who have survived since becoming members after 1901-02 are:

Featherstone Rovers (1921-22), Huyton (1922-23), Workington Town (1945-46), Whitehaven (1948-49), Doncaster (1951-52), Blackpool Borough (1954-55), Fulham (1980-81), Carlisle (1981-82), Mansfield Marksman and Sheffield Eagles, both launched in 1984-85.

FORMER CLUBS

The following is a list of clubs who have dropped out of the League since 1902-03. County references are the old boundaries.

First season	Club	Last season
1895-96	Manningham *(Yorkshire)*	1902-03
	Stockport *(Cheshire)*	1902-03
	Brighouse Rangers *(Yorkshire)*	1905-06
	Runcorn *(Cheshire)*	1914-15
	Broughton Rangers *(Lancashire)*	
	Changed to Belle Vue Rangers in 1946-1947	1954-55
1896-97	*Morecambe *(Lancashire)*	1905-06
	Holbeck *(Yorkshire)*	1903-04
1899-1900	Millom *(Cumberland)*	1905-06
1901-02	Birkenhead Wanderers *(Cheshire)*	1904-05
	Lancaster *(Lancashire)*	1904-05
	Normanton *(Yorkshire)*	1905-06
1902-03	South Shields *(Durham)*	1903-04
1903-04	Pontefract *(Yorkshire)*	1906-07
1906-07	Liverpool City *(Lancashire)*	1906-07
1907-08	Merthyr Tydfil *(Wales)*	1910-11
	Ebbw Vale *(Wales)*	1911-12
1908-09	Aberdare *(Wales)*	1908-09
	Barry *(Wales)*	1908-09
	Mid-Rhondda *(Wales)*	1908-09
	Treherbert *(Wales)*	1909-10
1910-11	Coventry *(Warwickshire)*	1912-13
1918-19	St. Helens Recreation *(Lancashire)*	1938-39
1926-27	Pontypridd *(Wales)*	1927-28
1928-29	Carlisle City *(Cumberland)*	1928-29
1935-36	Acton and Willesden *(London)*	1935-36
	Streatham and Mitcham *(London)*	1936-37
1936-37	Newcastle *(Northumberland)*	1937-38
1951-52	Cardiff *(Wales)*	1951-52
1981-82	Cardiff City *(Wales)*	
	Changed to Bridgend in 1984-85	1984-85
1983-84	Kent Invicta *(Kent)*	
	Changed to Southend Invicta *(Essex)* in 1984-85	1984-85

*Dropped out of League for two seasons 1899-1901

FIXTURES

1986   PRINCIPAL DATES

24th August	Okells Charity Shield: Castleford v. Halifax (Isle of Man)
31st August	League season commences
14th September	County Cup Competitions (First Round)
17th September	Rodstock War of the Roses, Yorkshire v. Lancashire, County of Origin (Headingley, Leeds)
24th September	County Cup Competitions (Second Round)
1st October	John Smiths Yorkshire County Cup Semi-Finals
8th October	Grunhalle Lager Lancashire County Cup Semi-Finals
11th October	John Smiths Yorkshire County Cup Final
19th October	Grunhalle Lager Lancashire County Cup Final
25th October	Whitbread Trophy Bitter First, Test Great Britain v. Australia (Old Trafford, Manchester)
8th November	Whitbread Trophy Bitter Second Test, Great Britain v. Australia (Elland Road, Leeds)
22nd November	Whitbread Trophy Bitter Third Test, Great Britain v. Australia (Central Park, Wigan)
30th November	John Player Special Trophy (First Round)
7th December	John Player Special Trophy (Second Round)
14th December	John Player Special Trophy (Quarter Finals)
20th December	John Player Special Trophy (Semi-Final 1)
27th December	John Player Special Trophy (Semi-Final 2)

1987

10th January	John Player Special Trophy Final
24th January	Whitbread Trophy Bitter Test, Great Britain v. France
1st February	Silk Cut Challenge Cup (First Round)
8th February	Whitbread Trophy Bitter Test, France v. Great Britain
15th February	Silk Cut Challenge Cup (Second Round)
1st March	Silk Cut Challenge Cup (Third Round)
8th March	France v. Great Britain, Under-21 International
14th March	Silk Cut Challenge Cup (Semi-Final 1)
22nd March	Great Britain v. France, Under-21 International
28th March	Silk Cut Challenge Cup (Semi-Final 2)
26th April	Stones Bitter Premiership (First Round)
2nd May	Silk Cut Challenge Cup Final (Wembley)
10th May	Stones Bitter Premiership (Semi-Finals)
13th May	Greenalls Man of Steel Awards
17th May	Stones Bitter Premiership Final

1986 AUSTRALIA TOUR

12th October	Wigan
15th October	Hull Kingston Rovers
19th October	Leeds
21st October	Cumbria (at Barrow)
25th October	FIRST WHITBREAD TROPHY BITTER TEST v. GREAT BRITAIN (at Old Trafford, Manchester)
29th October	Halifax
2nd November	St. Helens
4th November	Oldham
8th November	SECOND WHITBREAD TROPHY BITTER TEST v. GREAT BRITAIN (at Elland Road, Leeds)

411

12th November	Widnes
16th November	Hull
18th November	Bradford Northern
22nd November	THIRD WHITBREAD TROPHY BITTER TEST v. GREAT BRITAIN (at Central Park, Wigan) World Cup Qualifying Match

STONES BITTER CHAMPIONSHIP

SUNDAY, 31st AUGUST, 1986

Barrow	v.	Hull K.R.
Bradford N.	v.	Widnes
Featherstone R.	v.	Halifax
Hull	v.	Wakefield T.
Oldham	v.	Leeds
St. Helens	v.	Leigh
Warrington	v.	Castleford
Wigan	v.	Salford

WEDNESDAY, 3rd SEPTEMBER, 1986

Castleford	v.	Hull
Halifax	v.	Oldham
Hull K.R.	v.	Bradford N.
Leeds	v.	Featherstone R.
Salford	v.	St. Helens
Widnes	v.	Wakefield T.
Wigan	v.	Barrow

THURSDAY, 4th SEPTEMBER, 1986

Leigh	v.	Warrington

SUNDAY, 7th SEPTEMBER, 1986

Castleford	v.	Wakefield T.
Halifax	v.	Hull
Hull K.R.	v.	Featherstone R.
Leeds	v.	St. Helens
Leigh	v.	Wigan
Salford	v.	Bradford N.
Warrington	v.	Oldham
Widnes	v.	Barrow

SUNDAY, 14th SEPTEMBER, 1986
COUNTY CUP COMPETITIONS — FIRST ROUND

WEDNESDAY, 17th SEPTEMBER, 1986
RODSTOCK WAR OF THE ROSES
(at Headingley, Leeds)

SUNDAY, 21st SEPTEMBER, 1986

Barrow	v.	Castleford
Bradford N.	v.	Wigan
Featherstone R.	v.	Widnes
Hull	v.	Leigh
Oldham	v.	Hull K.R.
St. Helens	v.	Halifax
Wakefield T.	v.	Leeds
Warrington	v.	Salford

WEDNESDAY, 24th SEPTEMBER, 1986
COUNTY CUP COMPETITIONS — SECOND ROUND

SUNDAY, 28th SEPTEMBER, 1986

Castleford	v.	Featherstone R.
Halifax	v.	Warrington
Hull K.R.	v.	St. Helens
Leigh	v.	Oldham
Salford	v.	Barrow
Wakefield T.	v.	Bradford N.
Widnes	v.	Leeds
Wigan	v.	Hull

SUNDAY, 5th OCTOBER, 1986

Barrow	v.	Halifax
Bradford N.	v.	Castleford
Featherstone R.	v.	Leigh
Hull K.R.	v.	Hull

Leeds	v.	Salford
Oldham	v.	Widnes
St. Helens	v.	Wakefield T.
Warrington	v.	Wigan

SATURDAY, 11th OCTOBER, 1986
JOHN SMITHS YORKSHIRE CUP FINAL

SUNDAY, 12th OCTOBER, 1986

Barrow	v.	St. Helens
Featherstone R.	v.	Warrington
Halifax	v.	Leeds
Hull	v.	Bradford N.
Salford	v.	Hull K.R.
Wakefield T.	v.	Leigh
Widnes	v.	Castleford
Wigan	v.	AUSTRALIA

WEDNESDAY, 15th OCTOBER, 1986

Hull K.R.	v.	AUSTRALIA

SUNDAY, 19th OCTOBER, 1986
GRUNHALLE LAGER LANCASHIRE CUP FINAL

Bradford N.	v.	Barrow
Castleford	v.	Wigan
Hull	v.	Halifax
Leeds	v.	AUSTRALIA
Leigh	v.	Widnes
Oldham	v.	Featherstone R.
St. Helens	v.	Salford
Warrington	v.	Wakefield T.

TUESDAY, 21st OCTOBER, 1986

Cumbria	v.	AUSTRALIA

SATURDAY, 25th OCTOBER, 1986
GREAT BRITAIN v. AUSTRALIA
(at Old Trafford, Manchester)

SUNDAY, 26th OCTOBER, 1986

Barrow	v.	Hull
Featherstone R.	v.	Salford
Halifax	v.	Castleford
Hull K.R.	v.	Leigh
Leeds	v.	Bradford N.
Wakefield T.	v.	Oldham

WEDNESDAY, 29th OCTOBER, 1986

Halifax	v.	AUSTRALIA

SUNDAY, 2nd NOVEMBER, 1986

Bradford N.	v.	Featherstone R.
Castleford	v.	Leigh
Hull	v.	Leeds
Oldham	v.	Barrow
St. Helens	v.	AUSTRALIA
Salford	v.	Warrington
Widnes	v.	Hull K.R.
Wigan	v.	Wakefield T.

TUESDAY, 4th NOVEMBER, 1986

Oldham	v.	AUSTRALIA

SATURDAY, 8th NOVEMBER, 1986
GREAT BRITAIN v. AUSTRALIA
(at Elland Road, Leeds)

SUNDAY, 9th NOVEMBER, 1986

Barrow	v.	Widnes
Featherstone R.	v.	St. Helens

Hull K.R.	v.	Oldham
Leigh	v.	Halifax
Salford	v.	Wigan
Warrington	v.	Hull

WEDNESDAY, 12th NOVEMBER, 1986

Widnes	v.	AUSTRALIA

SUNDAY, 16th NOVEMBER, 1986

Castleford	v.	Salford
Halifax	v.	Hull K.R.
Hull	v.	AUSTRALIA
Leeds	v.	Warrington
Oldham	v.	St. Helens
Wakefield T.	v.	Barrow
Widnes	v.	Bradford N.
Wigan	v.	Leigh

TUESDAY, 18th NOVEMBER, 1986

Bradford N.	v.	AUSTRALIA

SATURDAY, 22nd NOVEMBER, 1986

GREAT BRITAIN v. AUSTRALIA
(at Central Park, Wigan)

SUNDAY, 23rd NOVEMBER, 1986

Barrow	v.	Wigan
Bradford N.	v.	Oldham
Featherstone R.	v.	Castleford
Hull K.R.	v.	Wakefield T.
Leigh	v.	Leeds
St. Helens	v.	Hull
Salford	v.	Widnes
Warrington	v.	Halifax

SATURDAY/SUNDAY, 29th/30th NOVEMBER, 1986

JOHN PLAYER SPECIAL TROPHY—FIRST ROUND

SATURDAY/SUNDAY, 6th/7th DECEMBER, 1986

JOHN PLAYER SPECIAL TROPHY—SECOND ROUND

SUNDAY, 14th DECEMBER, 1986

Castleford	v.	St. Helens
Halifax	v.	Barrow
Hull	v.	Salford
Leeds	v.	Hull K.R.
Oldham	v	Warrington
Wakefield T.	v.	Featherstone R.
Widnes	v.	Leigh
Wigan	v.	Bradford N.

SUNDAY, 21st DECEMBER, 1986

Barrow	v.	Leeds
Bradford N.	v.	Warrington
Featherstone R.	v.	Wigan
Hull K.R.	v.	Widnes
Leigh	v.	Hull
St. Helens	v.	Oldham
Wakefield T.	v.	Castleford

BOXING DAY, FRIDAY, 26th DECEMBER, 1986

Castleford	v.	Hull K.R.
Halifax	v.	Bradford N.
Hull	v.	Featherstone R.
Leeds	v.	Wakefield T.
Leigh	v.	Barrow
Oldham	v.	Salford
St. Helens	v.	Wigan
Warrington	v.	Widnes

SUNDAY, 28th DECEMBER, 1986

Bradford N.	v.	Halifax
Featherstone R.	v.	Hull

NEW YEAR'S DAY, THURSDAY, 1st JANUARY, 1987

Castleford	v.	Bradford N.
Hull K.R.	v.	Halifax
Leeds	v.	Oldham
Salford	v.	Leigh

Widnes	v.	St. Helens
Wigan	v.	Warrington

SUNDAY, 4th JANUARY, 1987

Barrow	v.	Bradford N.
Featherstone R.	v.	Hull K.R.
Halifax	v.	St. Helens
Hull	v.	Oldham
Leigh	v.	Castleford
Wakefield T.	v.	Salford
Warrington	v.	Leeds
Widnes	v.	Wigan

SUNDAY, 11th JANUARY, 1987

Bradford N.	v.	Hull
Castleford	v.	Widnes
Hull K.R.	v.	Barrow
Leeds	v.	Leigh
Oldham	v.	Wakefield T.
St. Helens	v.	Warrington
Salford	v.	Featherstone R.
Wigan	v.	Halifax

SUNDAY, 18th JANUARY, 1987

Featherstone R.	v.	Bradford N.
Halifax	v.	Salford
Hull	v.	Castleford
Leigh	v.	St. Helens
Wakefield T.	v.	Hull K.R.
Warrington	v	Barrow
Widnes	v.	Oldham
Wigan	v.	Leeds

SUNDAY, 25th JANUARY, 1987

Barrow	v.	Wakefield T.
Bradford N.	v.	Leigh
Castleford	v.	Warrington
Hull K.R.	v.	Wigan
Leeds	v.	Widnes
Oldham	v.	Halifax
Salford	v.	Hull
St. Helens	v.	Featherstone R.

SATURDAY/SUNDAY,
31st JANUARY/1st FEBRUARY, 1987

SILK CUT CHALLENGE CUP—FIRST ROUND

SUNDAY, 8th FEBRUARY, 1987

Castleford	v.	Leeds
Halifax	v.	Featherstone R.
Hull	v.	Barrow
Leigh	v.	Hull K.R.
Wakefield T.	v.	St. Helens
Warrington	v.	Bradford N.
Widnes	v.	Salford
Wigan	v.	Oldham

SATURDAY/SUNDAY, 14th/15th FEBRUARY, 1987

SILK CUT CHALLENGE CUP—SECOND ROUND

SUNDAY, 22nd FEBRUARY, 1987

Barrow	v.	Warrington
Featherstone R.	v.	Wakefield T.
Halifax	v.	Leigh
Hull K.R.	v.	Leeds
Oldham	v.	Hull
St. Helens	v.	Bradford N.
Salford	v.	Castleford
Wigan	v.	Widnes

SUNDAY, 1st MARCH, 1987

Bradford N.	v.	Hull K.R.
Castleford	v.	Oldham
Hull	v.	Widnes
Leeds	v.	Wigan
Leigh	v.	Salford
St. Helens	v.	Barrow
Wakefield T.	v.	Halifax
Warrington	v.	Featherstone R.

SUNDAY, 8th MARCH, 1987

Barrow	v.	Leigh
Featherstone R.	v.	Oldham
Hull	v.	St. Helens
Salford	v.	Leeds
Wakefield T.	v.	Warrington
Widnes	v.	Halifax
Wigan	v.	Castleford

SUNDAY, 15th MARCH, 1987

Barrow	v.	Salford
Halifax	v.	Wigan
Hull K.R.	v.	Warrington
Leeds	v.	Hull
Leigh	v.	Featherstone R.
Oldham	v.	Bradford N.
St. Helens	v.	Castleford
Wakefield T.	v.	Widnes

SUNDAY, 22nd MARCH, 1987

Bradford N.	v.	Wakefield T.
Castleford	v.	Barrow
Featherstone R.	v.	Leeds
Salford	v.	Halifax
Warrington	v.	St. Helens
Wigan	v.	Hull K.R.

SUNDAY, 29th MARCH, 1987

Hull	v.	Warrington
Leeds	v.	Barrow
Leigh	v.	Bradford N.
Oldham	v.	Castleford
St. Helens	v.	Hull K.R.
Wakefield T.	v.	Wigan
Widnes	v.	Featherstone R.

SUNDAY, 5th APRIL, 1987

Barrow	v.	Oldham
Castleford	v.	Halifax
Hull K.R.	v.	Salford
Leigh	v.	Wakefield T.
St. Helens	v.	Leeds
Widnes	v.	Hull
Wigan	v.	Featherstone R.

SUNDAY, 12th APRIL, 1987

Bradford N.	v.	St. Helens
Featherstone R.	v.	Barrow
Halifax	v.	Widnes
Hull	v.	Wigan
Leeds	v.	Castleford
Oldham	v.	Leigh
Salford	v.	Wakefield T.
Warrington	v.	Hull K.R.

GOOD FRIDAY, 17th APRIL, 1987

Bradford N.	v.	Leeds
Halifax	v.	Wakefield T.
Hull	v.	Hull K.R.
Salford	v.	Oldham
Widnes	v.	Warrington
Wigan	v.	St. Helens

EASTER MONDAY, 20th APRIL, 1987

Barrow	v.	Featherstone R.
Hull K.R.	v.	Castleford
Leeds	v.	Halifax
Oldham	v.	Wigan
St. Helens	v.	Widnes
Wakefield T.	v.	Hull
Warrington	v.	Leigh

EASTER TUESDAY, 21st APRIL, 1987

Bradford N.	v.	Salford

SECOND DIVISION

SUNDAY, 31st AUGUST, 1986

Bramley	v.	Whitehaven

Dewsbury	v.	Blackpool B.
Fulham	v.	Rochdale H.
Huddersfield B.	v.	Keighley
Runcorn H.	v.	Hunslet
Sheffield E.	v.	Mansfield M.
Swinton	v.	Batley
Workington T.	v.	Doncaster
York	v.	Carlisle

WEDNESDAY, 3rd SEPTEMBER, 1986

Bramley	v.	Mansfield M.
Carlisle	v.	Blackpool B.
Dewsbury	v.	Fulham
Huddersfield B.	v.	Swinton
Keighley	v.	Runcorn H.
Rochdale H.	v.	Whitehaven
York	v.	Batley

SUNDAY, 7th SEPTEMBER, 1986

Batley	v.	Fulham
Blackpool B.	v.	Workington T.
Carlisle	v.	Runcorn H.
Doncaster	v.	Swinton
Hunslet	v.	Dewsbury
Keighley	v.	Sheffield E.
Mansfield M.	v.	Huddersfield B.
Rochdale H.	v.	Bramley
Whitehaven	v.	York

WEDNESDAY, 10th SEPTEMBER, 1986

Workington T.	v.	Carlisle

SUNDAY, 14th SEPTEMBER, 1986
COUNTY CUP COMPETITIONS—FIRST ROUND

WEDNESDAY, 17th SEPTEMBER, 1986
RODSTOCK WAR OF THE ROSES
at Headingley

SUNDAY, 21st SEPTEMBER, 1986

Bramley	v.	Blackpool B.
Carlisle	v.	Doncaster
Dewsbury	v.	Rochdale H.
Fulham	v.	Sheffield E.
Huddersfield B.	v.	Batley
Hunslet	v.	Workington T.
Runcorn H.	v.	Mansfield M.
Swinton	v.	York
Whitehaven	v.	Keighley

WEDNESDAY, 24th SEPTEMBER, 1986
COUNTY CUP COMPETITIONS—SECOND
ROUND

SUNDAY, 28th SEPTEMBER, 1986

Batley	v.	Whitehaven
Blackpool B.	v.	Runcorn H.
Doncaster	v.	Hunslet
Keighley	v.	Carlisle
Mansfield M.	v.	Fulham
Rochdale H.	v.	Swinton
Sheffield E.	v.	Dewsbury
Workington T.	v.	Huddersfield B.
York	v.	Bramley

WEDNESDAY, 1st OCTOBER, 1986

Sheffield E.	v.	Huddersfield B.

SUNDAY, 5th OCTOBER, 1986

Blackpool B.	v.	York
Carlisle	v.	Rochdale H.
Dewsbury	v.	Bramley
Fulham	v.	Keighley
Huddersfield B.	v.	Doncaster
Hunslet	v.	Batley
Runcorn H.	v.	Workington T.
Swinton	v.	Sheffield E.
Whitehaven	v.	Mansfield M.

SATURDAY, 11th OCTOBER, 1986
JOHN SMITHS YORKSHIRE CUP FINAL

SUNDAY, 12th OCTOBER, 1986

Batley	v.	Runcorn H.
Bramley	v.	Huddersfield B.
Doncaster	v.	Whitehaven
Keighley	v.	Hunslet
Mansfield M.	v.	Blackpool B.
Rochdale H.	v.	Fulham
Sheffield E.	v.	Carlisle
Workington T.	v.	Swinton
York	v.	Dewsbury

SUNDAY, 19th OCTOBER, 1986
GRUNHALLE LAGER LANCASHIRE CUP FINAL

Blackpool B.	v.	Keighley
Carlisle	v.	Mansfield M.
Dewsbury	v.	Workington T.
Fulham	v.	Batley
Huddersfield B.	v.	Hunslet
Runcorn H.	v.	Sheffield E.
Swinton	v.	Bramley
Whitehaven	v.	Rochdale H.
York	v.	Doncaster

TUESDAY, 21st OCTOBER, 1986

Cumbria	v.	AUSTRALIA

(at Barrow)

SATURDAY, 25th OCTOBER, 1986
GREAT BRITAIN v. AUSTRALIA
(at Old Trafford, Manchester)

SUNDAY, 26th OCTOBER, 1986

Batley	v.	Huddersfield B.
Doncaster	v.	Dewsbury
Hunslet	v.	Carlisle
Keighley	v.	Whitehaven
Mansfield M.	v.	Bramley
Sheffield E.	v.	York
Workington T.	v.	Blackpool B.

SUNDAY, 2nd NOVEMBER, 1986

Blackpool B.	v.	Doncaster
Bramley	v.	Sheffield E.
Dewsbury	v.	Swinton
Fulham	v.	Hunslet
Huddersfield B.	v.	Mansfield M.
Rochdale H.	v.	Batley
Whitehaven	v.	Runcorn H.
York	v.	Workington T.

SATURDAY, 8th NOVEMBER, 1986
GREAT BRITAIN v. AUSTRALIA
(at Elland Road, Leeds)

SUNDAY, 9th NOVEMBER, 1986

Batley	v.	Keighley
Carlisle	v.	Huddersfield B.
Doncaster	v.	Rochdale H.
Runcorn H.	v.	Blackpool B.
Sheffield E.	v.	Fulham
Swinton	v.	Whitehaven
Workington T.	v.	Mansfield M.

SUNDAY, 16th NOVEMBER, 1986

Batley	v.	Bramley
Fulham	v.	Dewsbury
Huddersfield B.	v.	Sheffield E.
Hunslet	v.	Runcorn H.
Keighley	v.	Workington T.
Mansfield M.	v.	Carlisle
Swinton	v.	Doncaster
Whitehaven	v.	Blackpool B.
York	v.	Rochdale H.

SATURDAY, 22nd NOVEMBER, 1986
GREAT BRITAIN v. AUSTRALIA
(at Central Park, Wigan)

SUNDAY, 23rd NOVEMBER, 1986

Blackpool B.	v.	Mansfield M.
Bramley	v.	Fulham
Dewsbury	v.	Whitehaven
Doncaster	v.	Carlisle
Hunslet	v.	Swinton
Rochdale H.	v.	Keighley
Runcorn H.	v.	Huddersfield B.
Sheffield E.	v.	Batley
Workington T.	v.	York

SATURDAY/SUNDAY, 29th/30th NOVEMBER, 1986
JOHN PLAYER SPECIAL TROPHY—FIRST
ROUND

SATURDAY/SUNDAY, 6th/7th DECEMBER, 1986
JOHN PLAYER SPECIAL TROPHY—SECOND
ROUND

SUNDAY 14th DECEMBER, 1986

Batley	v.	Rochdale H.
Carlisle	v.	Hunslet
Fulham	v.	Blackpool B.
Huddersfield B.	v.	Workington T.
Keighley	v.	Doncaster
Mansfield M.	v.	Runcorn H.
Swinton	v.	Dewsbury
Whitehaven	v.	Bramley
York	v.	Sheffield E.

SUNDAY, 21st DECEMBER, 1986

Fulham	v.	York
Hunslet	v.	Huddersfield B.
Rochdale H.	v.	Mansfield M.
Runcorn H.	v.	Keighley
Sheffield E.	v.	Workington T.

BOXING DAY, FRIDAY 26th DECEMBER, 1986

Blackpool B.	v.	Rochdale H.
Bramley	v.	Hunslet
Carlisle	v.	Keighley
Dewsbury	v.	Batley
Mansfield M.	v.	Sheffield E.
Runcorn H.	v.	Doncaster
Swinton	v.	Fulham
Workington T.	v.	Whitehaven
York	v.	Huddersfield B.

NEW YEAR'S DAY, THURSDAY, 1st JANUARY, 1987

Batley	v.	Dewsbury
Doncaster	v.	Mansfield M.
Huddersfield B.	v.	York
Hunslet	v.	Bramley
Keighley	v.	Blackpool B.
Rochdale H.	v.	Carlisle
Whitehaven	v.	Workington T.

SUNDAY, 4th JANUARY, 1987

Blackpool B.	v.	Whitehaven
Bramley	v.	Runcorn H.
Carlisle	v.	Sheffield E.
Dewsbury	v.	York
Fulham	v.	Huddersfield B.
Mansfield M.	v.	Batley
Rochdale H.	v.	Doncaster
Workington T.	v.	Keighley

SUNDAY, 11th JANUARY, 1987

Batley	v.	Blackpool B.
Doncaster	v.	Workington T.
Huddersfield B.	v.	Carlisle
Hunslet	v.	Mansfield M.
Keighley	v.	Fulham
Runcorn H.	v.	Rochdale H.
Sheffield E.	v.	Bramley
Whitehaven	v.	Dewsbury
York	v.	Swinton

SUNDAY, 18th JANUARY, 1987

Batley	v.	Hunslet
Blackpool B.	v.	Carlisle
Bramley	v.	York
Doncaster	v.	Sheffield E.
Fulham	v.	Whitehaven
Mansfield M.	v.	Keighley
Rochdale H.	v.	Dewsbury
Swinton	v.	Huddersfield B.
Workington T.	v.	Runcorn H.

SUNDAY, 25th JANUARY, 1987

Carlisle	v.	Workington T.
Dewsbury	v.	Hunslet
Huddersfield B.	v.	Fulham
Keighley	v.	Batley
Mansfield M.	v.	Rochdale H.
Runcorn H.	v.	Bramley
Sheffield E.	v.	Swinton
Whitehaven	v.	Doncaster
York	v.	Blackpool B.

SATURDAY/SUNDAY 31st JANUARY/1st FEBRUARY 1987
SILK CUT CHALLENGE CUP—FIRST ROUND

SUNDAY, 8th FEBRUARY, 1987

Batley	v.	Mansfield M.
Blackpool B.	v.	Fulham
Bramley	v.	Dewsbury
Doncaster	v.	Runcorn H.
Hunslet	v.	Keighley
Rochdale H.	v.	York
Swinton	v.	Carlisle
Workington T.	v.	Sheffield E.

SATURDAY/SUNDAY, 14th/15th FEBRUARY, 1987
SILK CUT CHALLENGE CUP—SECOND ROUND

SUNDAY, 22nd FEBRUARY, 1987

Carlisle	v.	York
Dewsbury	v.	Doncaster
Fulham	v.	Swinton
Hunslet	v.	Sheffield E.
Keighley	v.	Huddersfield B.
Rochdale H.	v.	Workington T.
Whitehaven	v.	Batley

SUNDAY, 1st MARCH, 1987

Bramley	v.	Rochdale H.
Doncaster	v.	Blackpool B.
Runcorn H.	v.	Whitehaven
Sheffield E.	v.	Keighley
Swinton	v.	Hunslet
Workington T.	v.	Dewsbury
York	v.	Fulham

SUNDAY, 8th MARCH, 1987

Batley	v.	York
Blackpool B.	v.	Dewsbury
Fulham	v.	Runcorn H.
Huddersfield B.	v.	Bramley
Mansfield M.	v.	Hunslet
Whitehaven	v.	Swinton

SUNDAY, 15th MARCH, 1987

Bramley	v.	Batley
Dewsbury	v.	Sheffield E.
Hunslet	v.	Fulham
Keighley	v.	Mansfield M.
Runcorn H.	v.	Carlisle
Swinton	v.	Blackpool B.

SUNDAY, 22nd MARCH, 1987

Bramley	v.	Swinton
Carlisle	v.	Dewsbury
Doncaster	v.	Keighley
Rochdale H.	v.	Runcorn H.
Workington T.	v.	Hunslet
York	v.	Whitehaven

SUNDAY, 29th MARCH, 1987

Batley	v.	Swinton
Blackpool B.	v.	Bramley
Doncaster	v.	York
Huddersfield B.	v.	Runcorn H.
Keighley	v.	Rochdale H.
Sheffield E.	v.	Hunslet
Whitehaven	v.	Fulham

SUNDAY, 5th APRIL, 1987

Dewsbury	v.	Carlisle
Fulham	v.	Bramley
Hunslet	v.	Doncaster
Mansfield M.	v.	Whitehaven
Rochdale H.	v.	Blackpool B.
Runcorn H.	v.	Batley
Swinton	v.	Workington T.

SUNDAY, 12th APRIL, 1987

Carlisle	v.	Swinton
Doncaster	v.	Huddersfield B.
Fulham	v.	Mansfield M.
Sheffield E.	v.	Runcorn H.
Workington T.	v.	Rochdale H.

GOOD FRIDAY, 17th APRIL, 1987

Batley	v.	Sheffield E.
Blackpool B.	v.	Swinton
Bramley	v.	Keighley
Carlisle	v.	Whitehaven
Huddersfield B.	v.	Dewsbury
Mansfield M.	v.	Doncaster
York	v.	Hunslet

SUNDAY, 19th APRIL, 1987

Sheffield E.	v.	Doncaster

EASTER MONDAY, 20th APRIL, 1987

Blackpool B.	v.	Batley
Dewsbury	v.	Huddersfield B.
Hunslet	v.	York
Keighley	v.	Bramley
Mansfield M.	v.	Workington T.
Runcorn H.	v.	Fulham
Swinton	v.	Rochdale H.
Whitehaven	v.	Carlisle